MEN
IN
BLACK

MEN IN BLACK

R.H. Chester
& N.A.C. McMillan

Pelham Books

First published in Great Britain by
PELHAM BOOKS LTD
52 Bedford Square
London W.C.1.
1978

ISBN 0 7207 1122 3

Typeset by Monoset Trade Services Ltd, Auckland.
Designed and produced by Richard King, Waiheke Island.
Printed and bound in Hong Kong

Contents

Authors' Preface

Why this book on New Zealand International Rugby?

Firstly, because no one has attempted to cover in detail by word and picture the story of New Zealand's participation in Rugby at its highest level.

Secondly, because it is seventy-five years since that warm August afternoon in Sydney when a team representing New Zealand lined out on the Sydney Cricket Ground to do battle with a fully representative Australian side, marking our entrance into International Rugby. Until this time the highest level of football played by representative New Zealand teams had been inter-colonial fixtures. We thus became the seventh International Rugby playing nation following England (1871), Scotland (1871), Ireland (1875), Wales (1881), South Africa (1891) and Australia (1899).

Thirdly, as a tribute to the All Black players who have achieved the ultimate ambition of every Rugby player — to represent his country in an international match.

There has been some conjecture as to the definition of an "International match". In 1967 the New Zealand Rugby Football Union published the history of their first seventy-five years. Compiled by historian, Arthur Swan, this official publication listed those matches classed by the N.Z.R.F.U. as "International". We have followed this official classification, and since 1967 the Union has clearly stated which matches have been designated "Internationals".

It is interesting to note that one of the matches included is that against All America at Berkeley, California in November 1913. Press cuttings from the U.S.A. indicated that it certainly had international status even though all the American players came from California. Why a match against an American side is so recognised whilst later games against national selections from Fiji and Argentina are not, remains a mystery.

It was decided that this book would cover as far as was practical each match with equal emphasis; providing a commentary on each match, brief notes on the participating players from both sides, as well as other background aspects that we considered of interest and a statistical chart.

Our research has been extensive. Over several years we travelled throughout New Zealand to search library and newspaper files and to consult All Blacks and their families. We have written to players, Rugby writers and enthusiasts all over the Rugby world to establish or confirm facts while our publishers have also travelled overseas in search of information. As a result we unearthed facts which are at variance with published works and we have summarised these findings in an appendix.

Considerable attention has been given to the setting out of the teams in playing formation. This proved a more difficult task than envisaged. In earlier years newspapers and programmes did not always set out players, especially forwards, in their positions. However, with the combination of photographs, programmes, books, newspapers and personal interviews we are confident that the layouts finally achieved are as accurate as currently possible.

The compilation of the statistics was a meticulous but fascinating task and we hope they adequately summarise the first seventy-five years of New Zealand International Rugby.

We have received invaluable assistance and are indebted to a large number of people whom we have listed within the acknowlegements. We especially mention Fred Spurdle of the New Zealand Rugby Museum and Henry Magnussen who gave up so much of their time so willingly to assist us; Wilson Whineray, for the time and thought he put into his introduction to this book; the many All Blacks who generously made material available and newspaper illustrations editors throughout the country who gave us access to their files. To our wives and families, particular thanks for their patience over the many years of our research.

As our travels for material progressed it became obvious to us that as old players died and their families disposed of their possessions, and newspapers and photographic studios cleared their files, more of our Rugby history was becoming lost forever. It is our hope that this book has managed to record a part of this vanishing history. We trust that our book will communicate some of the pleasure and interest to the readers that we enjoyed in compiling it.

"Rugby is a great game – not ending with the blown whistle.
Years after we see again the rift in the opposing defences.
We get ready to break through with a sudden flash of speed.
Long after the event we still stretch ourselves full length,
barely to touch the heels of a flying three-quarter."

Dr. Herbert Michael Moran (captain of Australia 1908-09)

Rod Chester and Neville McMillan
January, 1978

Acknowledgements

The authors wish to acknowledge their grateful thanks to all those people and organisations listed below who loaned material or so willingly provided information.

All illustrations used have had their source, where known, acknowledged throughout the book. Every endeavour has been made to trace owners of copyright material included and if there is any breach, the authors apologise, and tender their thanks to those whose rights have been unintentionally transgressed.

Aarvold, Sir Carl
Aitken K.
Akkersdyke Studios
Alexander Turnbull Library
Allen F.R.
Auckland Grammar School
Auckland Institute & Museum
  Library
Auckland Public Library
Auckland Rugby Football
  Union (Inc)
Auckland Star
Australian Rugby Football Union
Auty T.W.J.

Badeley C.E.O.
Bell R.H.
Berghan T.
Bickley B.
Billot J.
Blackwell J.G.
Blazey C.A.
Bodis J-P.
Bonner Mrs C.L.
Bourke J.
Brennan P.
Brisbane Courier-Mail
Brisbane Public Library
Brisbane Sun
Brooke J.
Brown R.H.
Bush P.G.

Cameron D.J.
Campbell Photography Ltd.
Campion S.R.
Canterbury Public Library
Canterbury Rugby Football Union
Carroll M.
Catley Mrs. E.H.
Christ College, Brecon
Christchurch Star

Clark B.
Clarke D.B.
Clarke I.J.
Cockroft the late E.A.P.
Collins A.H.
Colorsport
Connor D.M.
Consolidated News Ltd.
Cooke R.
Crowley P.J.B.
Crown Studios

Dalley W.C.
Dalton D.
Dalziel D.G.
Davis K.
Department of Internal Affairs
Dick J.
Dick M.J.
Dominion
Dunedin Public Library
Durant B.

Elvidge R.R.
Elving R.D.
Evening Post
Evening Star

Fea W.R.
Federation Français de Rugby
Finlay J.
Fitzpatrick B.B.J.
Fogarty R.
Francis W.C.
Freebairn W.S.S.

Gallaher the late Mrs E.M.
General Assembly Library
Gilray the late C.M.
Graham D.J.
Graham M.G.
Green & Hahn Ltd.

Greyvenstein C.
Griffiths J.L.

Harding A.F.
Harman Miss A.
Heke W.R.
Hemi R.C.
Henderson P.
Hill M.J.
Hocken Library
Hore J.
Howitt R.J.

Imperial War Museum
Irish Rugby Football Union
Ivor-Smith G.
Jeffs J.M.
Jessep E.M.
Joseph C.

Kann E.W.
Kantor J.R.K.
Kelly J.W.
King B.W.
Kivell A.L.

Lensman
Lindsay D.F.
Lineen T.R.
Little P.F.
Lloyd T.
Lochore B.J.
Lochore D.W.
Lodge N.
Lucas F.R.

Macdonald "Sandy"
McHugh M.J.
McKay D.W.
McKenzie R.McC.
McKevitt G.
McLean W.M.

McLeod B.E.
McMullen R.F.
McWilliams R.G.
Magnussen H.G.
Mahoney A.
Manchester J.E.
Mataira H.
Melba Studios
Milliken H.M.
Ministry of Defence
Mirror Newspapers
Mitchell Library
Mitchell N.A.
Mitchinson F.E.
Mitchinson N.H.
Modernage B & W
  Photographics

Nathan W.J.
National Publicity Studios
Nelson College
New Plymouth Boys' High
  School
New Zealand Herald
New Zealand Listener
New Zealand Rugby Museum
New Zealand Rugby Union
New Zealand Truth
Nicholson the late G.W.

Oosthuizen W.
Otago Boys' High School
Otago Daily Times

Peter Cain Studios
Pickering E.A.R.

Powell S.W.
Press (Christchurch)
Purdue G.B.

Registrar General's & Chief
  Electoral Office
Reid A.R.
Roberts E.E.
Ross A.W.
Rubython J.
Rugby Press Ltd.

Sacred Heart College
Saunders L.
Savile J.
Saxton C.K.
Scottish Rugby Football Union
Scott R.W.H.
Scoles the late S.
Seeling C.
Shnaps T.T.
Sidney Riley Studios
Sinclair J.
Skinner K.L.
Solomon F.
Solomon H.J.
Sonntag W.T.C.
Spillane the late A.P.
Spurdle F.G.
Stanford University Library
Stansfield Mrs. E.M.
Steel A.G.
Storey the late P.W.
Strang W.A.
Sullivan J.
Sydney Morning Herald

Tanner J.M.
Thompson F.
Timaru Boys' High School
Tindill E.W.T.
Tremain K.R.
Turtill K.S.

University of California
  Library
University of Santa Clara
  Library

Vernon Clarke Studios
Vodanovich I.M.H.

Waitaki Boys' High School
Wallace J.
Wallace W.J. the family of
Walsh P.T.
Wanganui Collegiate School
Warren L.F.
Waters M.D.
Wellington College
Wellington Rugby Football
  Union
Welsh R.J.
Whineray W.J.
White R.A.
Whitmore Mrs. J.
Wiggins R.
Williams B.G.
Wilson Mrs. A.

Young D.

The Highest Honour

Old front row forwards have one foible — those who don't understand us would say we have several — but we will at least confess to one. I would like to say that it was something exotic — like fast cars or hang gliding — but, alas, this is not so! It is simply that given a chance, we will stand up in front of, or push our way into, any group willing or unwilling, to listen and talk with great authority on any subject whatsoever. The quirk probably results from years of banging heads with somebody equally odd.

Consequently, I am delighted to have the opportunity of writing an introduction to this magnificent book, as once again it affords me the chance of airing my opinions.

The matches described in detail in this volume are more than a succession of events recording successes and defeats, crises and controversy. They are a record of the participation of people and the generations from which they sprang. And just as it is people enacting the story, the words will mean different things to different readers. The historians will be provided with much to debate and discuss; the tacticians will find evidence of the triumph and tragedy of the fateful decision; many old timers will recall days long ago when the sun always shone on our Rugby — because, like all true All Black supporters, they have long since eliminated from their minds the games that don't bear remembering — and for not a few, these histories will cause the pulse to quicken and the muscles to tense as in their minds they take their place alongside Wallace or Cooke or Brownlie or Meads.

That really is the point of my contribution. We must never forget that Rugby is a very human activity, no matter how large or spectacular or publicised it becomes. The history of the game is the history of the millions of young men who, over the years, have laced up their boots and joined in the fun.

As I understand it, the origins of the game go back in time far beyond medieval Britain, to a game brought to England by Roman invaders — a game that incorporated two of the cornerstones of Rugby as we know it today — scrumming and handling the ball. The "History of London", as early as 1175, is said to record a game called "Foot-balle" a game which appears to have dwelt in the shadow of doubtful respectability over later centuries. Edward II, Edward III, Richard II and Henry VIII all spoke out against the tearaway, all-in wrestling type game, mainly on the grounds that their archers, the front line of the militia, should have something better to do than risk their arms in pursuit of "such barbarism". In time "Foot-balle" developed into what became known as the "Town Game", one town against another with 200 or more a side, playing on for hours — if not days. The BBC talk of a three day match played in 1763 between Sheffield and Norton, where it was recorded "that though many were injured, fortunately none were killed".

At the beginning of the nineteenth century the "Town Game" found its way into the Public Schools of England — at Charterhouse, Westminster and Rugby — and the reason the old Roman game of catch, carry and scrum became linked forever with Rugby School was because that school enjoyed large areas of playing fields. Obviously, with large numbers of players on each side, big playing areas were needed.

You might well ask, at this stage, where William Webb Ellis fitted in, because after all, we have always felt he started the game. His main contribution, it seems, was that he was the first to attempt, and succeed, in running forward whilst carrying the ball. After all, it took more than a little courage to hold the ball at all, let alone attempt to proceed up-field against an opposition numbering 100 or more. The gist of the game at the time was to catch the ball, claim and "mark", then kick the ball up-field until your side neared the goal line. Then the ball was held either in the hands or between the knees and the teams packed around to shove the ball carrier over the goal line. This "try" was worth nothing, other than the right to "try for a goal" in the manner of the conversion as we know it. The term "try", of course, remains in the game today. Ellis, for his part, died unknown in the South of France in 1872 — one year after the English Rugby clubs had held meetings to form The Rugby Football Union and to bring uniformity into the rules of the game. I understand that it wasn't until the late 1950's that his grave was discovered and, interestingly, it is cared for today by the French Rugby Federation.

Which brings me back to the point I started on earlier — that this game is really about people, it is for people, and its future will ebb or flow depending on the quality and quantity of people who make up its ranks. It has a long history and tradition and has a set of standards unique among today's hard physical games.

I had the good fortune to be involved with International Rugby for nine years, playing Test matches both at home and abroad. It was an exciting period for me and, in retrospect, there is little I would change today, could I do it over again. I cannot go into a changing room, even now, and smell that unique combination of embrocation and sweat, and nervousness, and anticipation, without having my pulse rate quicken. It is something a sports-person never loses.

I have often been asked what the atmosphere of a Test match is really like and to describe events from the time the team assembles until the match concludes. The occasion really starts at the time trial teams are announced and, when this happened, the instinctive action for most of us was to talk of those with whom we were playing and who we were opposing. I have often felt that if selectors could listen in to those conversations they would learn a lot about how footballers rated other footballers.

The trial system has been questioned, from time to time, as to its worth. Certainly, in my view, one good or bad trial should not erase performance at provincial level over a longer period. But they still have value in bringing into prominence relatively unknown players who can be watched closely in later provincial games, and they also give opportunity to players from smaller unions, who play consistently in losing teams, to play under better circumstances and have a chance to show their true skills. In essence, for the established player trials are a pain — for the unknown they are a passport to the stars.

I attended my first trial in 1957 as an uncertain

twenty-one year old playing in the main game. Fortunately, I had already played four seasons of provincial Rugby — the last with Canterbury in defence of the Ranfurly Shield — and, consequently, was already an experienced player. However, I still found the presence of so many great players around me unnerving, especially as many had been heroes of the great 1956 series against the Springboks. Luck was with me, and I had a game that comes to every player occasionally in his career. The ball went wherever I went, the passes all stuck and people fell over in my tackles. I could just as easily have had a bad game, which happened just as frequently.

The team is often read out at around 6 p.m. at the after-match function. Most players have a fair idea of their chances — established players playing well will be included, players playing badly, or against superior ability, will miss. They know it, expect it and accept it. I have seen scenes of great joy and utter disappointment when players on the edge of selection make or miss the big tour.

Players, by and large, show little feeling — especially those who are not selected, for they accept the system for what is is; but it is a hard system, bordering on cruel, and a revision of the method of announcing teams may well be long overdue.

The transition to All Black captain happens to some players and I think most would agree with me that it is a somewhat overrated occupation. What I found to be the least enjoyable part is that both circumstance and the position itself force you away from members of the team — many of whom are your greatest friends.

In any position of authority or leadership there must be a slight "arms length" relationship with the group. One can never again be quite "one of the boys" and it is foolish to try. A captain must always endeavour to conduct himself in a manner he expects the team to follow. Furthermore, the off-the-field demands of the U.K./France tour especially can be heavy with several speeches a week at formal dinners, on top of the normal routine of meetings with the Press, T.V. interviews, school visits, etc. Most captains, I know, would gladly give much of it away and return to the ranks.

I was fortunate to play with a group of players

who gave me enormous support — any one of six or seven could have filled the role at least as well as I did, thus discipline was no problem. In any event, in the first instance, off-the-field discipline is the role of the managers, with the captain responsible for discipline on the field.

But back to the game!

For a home series, the team would begin to assemble on the Wednesday afternoon and, providing flights were on schedule, the party was usually complete in time for the evening meal. Generally, a short team meeting would take place from, say, 7-7.30, at which time the team manager covers basic arrangements for the next few days, involving details of training sessions, social commitments, photographic arrangements etc. Then the coach would follow with a short, sharp reminder of what lay ahead and would be resolved on the turf and mud on Saturday afternoon. Players generally fill the evening in at the movies, or playing cards, but most would be asleep by 10.30 and, indeed, would sleep a lot over the coming days, endeavouring to build up a reserve of energy.

Training sessions would follow on Thursday and Friday, aimed at co-ordinating individual skills and putting some polish on tactics and patterns. Tactics are always a difficult area — and harder to change than people realise, once the game is underway. Most teams aim at having the game played in a way that they feel gives them an advantage over the opposition by playing to your own strength and against their weakness. The idea is to control enough of the ball throughout to force the other team to play the type of game you want. All of this comes unstuck, of course, if you fail to control the ball and are forced to follow your opponents.

The other problem associated with changing tactics is that there is little time for a discussion — to get the views of other experienced players — until the halftime break. I have heard it said that the difference between the levels of differing sports is the ability of top performers to operate in a shorter and shorter time zone. This, I believe, is essentially true, and certainly events move quickly in a Test match. There is an urgency, not apparent in lesser games.

However, hard as it is to change tactics sharply, we always practised that "what if" situation: "what if" we can't control the ball, "what if" our defence gets mauled, "what if" our backs are tackled out of the game, etc.? I never went on to the field in a major game without two or three options that had been discussed and agreed among the team.

Friday evening was obviously quiet — possibly a short team talk, but, generally we preferred to forego this unless it was kept to a low key. Players are getting tense and restless by this time — especially the younger ones — and too much tension inevitably leads to a restless night and fitful sleep. Cards, T.V., or possibly an early movie occupied the evening, with supper arranged for 9.30 and bed by 10.00. I found, over the years, that if I awoke during the night it was far better to turn the light on and read something light for an hour, than toss and turn for what seemed an eternity. Pre-Test, I have devoured many of the worst paperbacks ever written.

The morning of the match was, and should be, left to the individual himself. Some players prefer to rest most of the morning, others like a normal breakfast and a short stroll, and others like to kick a ball around. If the weather was of concern and the match venue not too far away, I would go over and look at the ground in order to get a feel for the elements. Of particular interest was the possibility of change in the weather and when it might occur. The wind often fades in late afternoon, and sides giving the wind away in the first half often find velocity dropping during their turn with the breeze.

Another habit I developed over the years was catching up on mail from 11 a.m. until lunch at 12.00. Lunch was never later than 12.00 for a 3 p.m. game and most players eat little. The steak devotees are few now, as that type of meal is heavy and takes hours to digest. Eggs were popular, soup perhaps, or a very small salad.

Many people believe it unwise to take liquid before strenuous exercise but I took the advice of Olympic Gold Medalist and friend, Murray Halberg, and would have a cup of tea laced with sugar up to 1½ hours before kick-off. It has been established that dehydration is a big factor in fatigue and consequential loss of performance. I found this very helpful advice.

The team would assemble for the main team talk at 1.30 p.m. in order to depart by 2 p.m. and arrive at the ground by, say, 2.30 p.m. This team talk would be demanding, positive and detailed.

Both Neil McPhail and Fred Allen were gifted in this area, blending "fire" and "detail" very cleverly. Little was said from then until kick-off with players left to their thoughts, generally going over in their minds any possibility that may evolve during the game.

Throughout the era of my involvement, "pattern" Rugby predominated, the team operating on precise patterns of attack and defence from each set piece of play. It is, of course, essential to develop skills to exploit broken play, as generally speaking, it is difficult to score points against good teams from set positions. Success followed the side that best exploited broken play opportunities.

It is interesting to recall changing rooms throughout the world, many seemingly designed to meet a "most cheerless" contest. Most are tucked in the depths of concrete grandstands and are cold, dark, smelly and depressing. Before a game they exude a spotless sterility — after they are strewn with tapes, bandages, broken laces, cans, the odd bottle and various pieces of torn gear. I once found a tooth on the floor after a game in Wales and, as it transpired that none of our people had lost it, I could only conclude that it came from an earlier boisterous encounter.

Another fascinating piece of worthless information is that most players have a deep superstition that finds its expression at changing times. Some always go to a certain part of the room, other have lucky charms, and most follow a strict pattern of changing into their playing gear. Again, many will only run on to the field at a certain place in the line and look out any newcomer who accidentally takes that position!

In the half an hour before kick-off, the coach usually touched on the key points of tactics again — but it really is too late for him to do much at this time. His work should be done on earlier days. It is hard to get concentration as players warm up and work themselves into a state of mental and physical preparedness. I preferred to have the room cleared of everyone but the team for the last ten minutes and took that time to say a few well chosen words. Once again, it is too late for anything too heavy. I would try to build confidence where appropriate — over-confidence is bad; lack of confidence is worse.

At some stage, the captains would have tossed. If I felt the elements would remain steady throughout the afternoon, and that I had the stronger side with me, I preferred to play in to the wind and/or sun initially. The basis for this was that if you take advantage of the elements, you must use them and generally our tactics were to put as much forward pressure as we could muster on the opposition for the first thirty minutes or so. Once you feel you are getting on top in the forwards — gaining more possession, going forward in all set pieces, exerting pressure in the rucks and mauls — you found your backs and loose forwards had the edge they could turn to advantage. Incidentally, you can "feel" how the forward struggle is going — only a forward can tell and probably only a tight forward.

Conversely, if I felt I was in the weaker team, especially weaker at forward, I would take the elements and chase points throughout the first half, hoping to have an advantage by the interval that could be held during the second half. It is surprising how much above themselves a side can play if they hold a slender lead against stronger opposition and time is ticking away.

The referee's whistle for the teams' appearance ends the silence and most players welcome the chance to get on with the game. Two things you notice as you leave the players' tunnel — the noise of the crowd and the sun's brightness after the gloom of the changing rooms. This is especially so in South Africa where a bright sun shines on dry, almost reflective, grass.

One never forgets the National Anthems — for my part, the two that are most moving are the Welsh and the French. I recall tears in one All Black's eyes at Cardiff as the swirl of their Anthem echoed throughout the stadium: and the crowd at Colombes in Paris — and French crowds must be the noisiest in the world — standing in total silence as the Marseillaise filled the air that wafted the Tricolour on the stand.

Once the game is underway, you are only conscious of crowd noise in a total sense as volume rises and falls and, at most of the larger grounds, one seldom hears individual voices. Crowd noise can be so intense that codes have to be visual rather than vocal, and I have known situations where the wing and forwards in the line-out couldn't hear the half-back's voice detailing where the ball was to be thrown.

As I said earlier, events move pretty quickly and I found it difficult to tread the narrow path a captain must walk — on the one hand becoming totally involved in his positional responsibilities, excluding all else and yet remaining sufficiently aloof from the game to look at it in a tactical sense. Apart from the halftime break, it really is only possible to do this at intervals throughout the game — at injury time, or any other similar delay.

The scene on returning to the changing room tends to mirror results from the field. The atmosphere ranges from gloom and depression (loss) through to an ecstatic chaos (win) and usually the number of well-wishers endeavouring to join the side reflects this, numbering zero (loss) to dozens (win). Players never care too much however — they are complete in themselves as a team, with reserves, manager and coach being the only people who really matter at that time. The other people in their lives who are important — wives, family and close friends — would never make it in to the room.

Then the after-match function and speeches, it seems to me that the speeches have remained virtually identical over the years with only the names changed to minimise confusion. Great speakers in Rugby don't seem to materialise at after-match functions but appear occasionally at formal dinners. Tom Pearce was quite outstanding in this regard and many of his speeches were superb.

The day following a home match sees the players disband, whereas a touring party would move on to prepare for the next fixture. Sunday morning there would frequently be an impromptu drink and a talk in one of the bedrooms and it was valuable to spend a little time discussing the game whilst it was still fresh in the mind. John Graham could always be relied on for helpful comment and Kelvin Tremain had an analytical mind, once he could be convinced to stop laughing. He seemed to be always enjoying himself, but, then, in less visible ways, so did the rest of the group. I have always been saddened when I hear of players who have returned from an overseas tour being quoted as not having enjoyed the experience. For my part, the opportunity to travel with good companions, and play football once or twice a week on foreign soil was an unforgettable pleasure.

Some comments on the Press. The media is harder now than in my time, especially in regard to the "Sunday" press which is geared to sensationalism. Ours, incidentally, is far more competent and consistent than those operating overseas.

I believe it is important to build up a relationship with the responsible Press and I have enjoyed, and still enjoy, the company of New Zealand Press people who have travelled with us abroad. Players must expect and accept criticism as much as they welcome praise when it comes. All we can hope is that it is fair and applies to the game as much as possible and not sensationalised off-the-field activities.

My advice to players worried about sensational, unfair or seemingly unjust Press is simple — "don't read it! Just ignore the sports section for a few days and it all goes away".

As I commented earlier, the history of Rugby is no more than a history of the people who have been involved with the game, reflecting the hopes and attitudes of their era. We of course, live in rapidly changing times and the administrators of the game must be aware of, and receptive to, new views emerging. Their task must surely be to move with these attitudinal changes yet, at the same time, preserve everything that is worthwhile in the game.

The thoughts now being expressed reflect the attitudes of many young men today and administrators would be wise to listen, heed, and work with the players whose views they respect. For their part, there are players who should realise that the wearing of the black jersey with a sliver fern is not only an honour which comes to few people, but also carries with it certain obligations and if they are unable to accept these they should not proceed further with this particular game.

I know of one great Rugby administrator, coach, manager who held every office and enjoyed every honour in New Zealand Rugby who, on the occasion of his acceptance of life membership of the Union, said that he would have given it all away just to have worn the black jersey once. In my view, there has never been a truly great All Black that hasn't felt a genuine pride in wearing the fern and known some kind of inner stirring every time he pulled the jersey over his head.

Rugby in this country seems at times to be under a state of siege. From various quarters our administrators are criticised for lack of sensitivity and poor public relations; our players are accused of over-intensity; our crowds for being partisan and boorish; and our referees for being inadequate. Overlaying all of this in recent years has been the complex question of politics and sport. Fortunately, the game and its supporters have always been big enough to meet these criticisms, strengthened in the knowledge that Rugby in this country has much of which to be proud.

No other institution has done so much to cross social, religious, racial, cultural and economic boundaries so comprehensively and with so little pretence.

What has been the contribution of the game in bringing conradeship to widely scattered and lonely rural folk in early years?

How much did the exploits of our 1905 and 1924 teams bring a sense of nationhood to a young country?

What is the measure of the game's contribution to the development of the character and physique of young people?

Where else do Pakeha and Polynesian find such a natural affinity?

What has the game meant to the pride of Maori people whose people have always played the game magnificently?

All of this lies at the heart of the game, as we know it in this country, and for these and other reasons, thousands of us continue to support and give time to the code.

Rugby as a sport has often seemed to me to be symbolised by the great grandstands at Eden Park, Athletic Park, Lancaster Park and Carisbrook. Just as the game gets buffeted by time and change, so too do these grandstands get lashed by rain, burnt by sun and, at times, nearly blown away. But they keep on standing, day after day, month after month, year after year; standing for what they represent — a basically decent and honourable game.

New Zealand's
International Rugby Matches

15 August, 1903 – 19 November, 1977

NEW ZEALAND 22

15 August, 1903

This was New Zealand's first full-scale international although thirteen inter-colonial games had been played against New South Wales between 1884 and 1901 for ten wins and three losses while Queensland had been met on seven occasions for seven wins to New Zealand. Australia had, however, played internationals against Britain in 1899.

For this match Australia wore the light blue jersey of New South Wales. Several of the home team were known to New Zealand Rugby followers, Maund, Burdon, Judd, Lutge and Wickham having toured New Zealand with the New South Wales team of 1901 while Hardcastle had played for Wellington in 1895-96-97. He also toured Australia with the 1897 New Zealand team. Sid Riley was a New Zealander whose brother, Olly, was a member of the 1894 New South Wales team in New Zealand.

Of the New Zealand team R. McGregor, Wood, Duncan and Udy had represented their country in previous seasons in matches against

New South Wales. Wallace, D. McGregor, Gallaher, Nicholson and Tyler were later to tour with the famous 1905 All Blacks to Britain, France and North America.

Dave Gallaher, who captained this great side, was born in Northern Ireland on October 30, 1873 and therefore celebrated his thirty-second birthday during the 1905 tour although the record books give his age as 29 on selection. He later became an Auckland and New Zealand selector. He had served in the Boer War with the Sixth and Tenth Contingents, rising to the rank of sergeant-major. While in South Africa he captained a Rugby team chosen from the New Zealand Contingents which played and defeated a South African side. Gallaher died from wounds received at Passchendaele on October 4, 1917.

Billy Wallace was the last survivor of the 1905 All Blacks. One of the greatest New Zealand backs of all time, he played fifty-one games for his country and scored 379 points in the All Black jersey. He later became prominent in Rugby administration and was manager of the 1932 All Blacks in Australia. Wallace died in 1972.

Duncan McGregor, who scored four tries against England in 1905 (still a record for a New Zealander in a Test) played for Canterbury and Wellington and represented both islands. In 1902 he set what was then a record in representative Rugby by scoring seventeen tries for Canterbury during the season. McGregor scored sixteen tries on the 1905 tour. He played one season after his return from Britain and then joined the Rugby League code, being a member of the "All Golds", New Zealand's pioneer League team. He died in 1947.

George Nicholson had a long career in first-class Rugby, playing thirty games for Auckland, two for the North Island and thirty-nine for New Zealand. After his retirement from the game he gave great service as an administrator and was a top-class referee and New Zealand selector. He died in 1968.

"Bubs" Tyler played thirty-eight times for New Zealand and was also Auckland's 100 yards swimming champion.

NEW ZEALAND

W.J. WALLACE
(Wellington)

A. ASHER   R.W. McGREGOR   D. McGREGOR
(Auckland)   (Auckland)   (Canterbury)

M.E. WOOD
(Canterbury)

J. DUNCAN (**Capt.**)
(Otago)

H.A.D. KIERNAN
(Auckland)

D. GALLAHER
(Auckland)

G.W. NICHOLSON   A.F. McMINN
(Auckland)   (Wairarapa)

R.J. COOKE   B.J. FANNING   A.J. LONG
(Canterbury)   (Canterbury)   (Auckland)

D.K. UDY   G.A. TYLER
(Wairarapa)   (Auckland)

F.C. NICHOLSON   E.R. LARKIN   A. BURDON
(Queensland)   (New South Wales)   (New South Wales)

J.E. JOYCE   D. LUTGE
(New South Wales)   (New South Wales)

W.R. HARDCASTLE   S.B. BOLAND   H.A. JUDD
(New South Wales)   (Queensland)   (New South Wales)

A.S. GRALTON
(Queensland)

L.J. EVANS
(Queensland)

C. WHITE   S.A. RILEY   S.M. WICKHAM (**Capt.**)   C. REDWOOD
(New South Wales) (New South Wales) (New South Wales)   (Queensland)

J.W. MAUND
(New South Wales)

AUSTRALIA

REFEREE: Dr. R. Waugh (New South Wales)
ATTENDANCE: 30,000
CONDITIONS: Weather fine, ground firm
HALFTIME: New Zealand 7, Australia 3

SCORERS

NEW ZEALAND	AUSTRALIA
Tries: Asher, Tyler, R.W. McGregor	Penalty goal: Wickham
Conversion: Wallace	
Penalty goal: Wallace	
Goals from mark (worth 4 points):	
Wallace (2)	

AUSTRALIA 3

Sydney Cricket Ground

SYDNEY MAIL

Gallaher breaks from a line-out. Duncan (10) and Asher (12) move in support while the others in camera seem remarkably lethargic.

The visitors opened the scoring when Evans was caught off-side at a ruck and Wallace kicked the goal. The Australian five-eighth soon made amends however when he broke through the New Zealand defence and kicked ahead. The blue forwards poured through and bustled the visitors, who had to carry behind to save. From the resulting scrum, Gallaher was around on Gralton too quickly and Wickham evened the score from an easy position.

Asher and White were having a tremendous battle, only the magnificent tackling of the Australian keeping his speedy opponent from scoring on several occasions. "Opae" Asher, one of the fastest men ever to play for New Zealand, was prevented from touring Britain in 1905 when he was injured in the course of his duties as a fireman but he recovered and later played Rugby League for New Zealand.

Just before halftime New Zealand went further ahead. Duncan McGregor took a mark and, under the rules then prevailing, Wallace kicked a goal to give his team a 7-3 lead at the interval.

Wickham made a brilliant run early in the second half but Wallace stopped him short of the line. New Zealand fought back and from a set scrum at half-way Kiernan sent his backs away, Asher finally managing to swerve around White to score in the corner. Wallace missed. A little later the full-back goaled again from a mark by Wood. Near the end of the game Wood made a grand run down the centre before passing to Asher who was tackled by White. The ball rolled clear for Tyler to pick up and score. Again Wallace failed to convert.

Then, almost on time, Asher was again well stopped by White and "Dick" McGregor picked up. He appeared to go into touch and the Australians held off him but there was no signal from the touch judge. McGregor galloped across the line and the referee awarded a try, which Wallace converted to end the scoring. Despite the difference in points, the game was by no means one-sided, especially in the forwards where the home players rucked and scrummed particularly well.

NEW ZEALAND 9

13 August, 1904

This match marked the entry into international football of four players who were to tour with the 1905 All Blacks. The centre, Eric Harper, had already made a name as a track athlete by winning New Zealand championships in the 440 yards hurdles and the 880 yards. He played ten times for the 1905 team, including the Test against France, and then faded out of big football. He was killed in action in Palestine in 1918.

Billy Stead, who was vice-captain on the British tour, is still regarded as one of the greatest first five-eighths in Rugby history. He toured Australia in 1903 and played 42 games in the black jersey between 1903 and 1908.

Bill Glenn won the Military Cross during World War I and later had the distinction of being the first All Black to become a Member of Parliament. He played 18 games on the 1905 tour, including the one against France.

The famous Charlie "Bronco" Seeling, the greatest of the 1905 forwards, was also playing his first game for New Zealand. He represented his country again in 1907 and 1908 before accepting an offer to play professional football for the Wigan club in England. Seeling and his wife were killed in a road accident in 1956 after they had decided to return from England to settle in Wanganui.

The New Zealand Team
Back row: W.S. Glenn, C.E. Seeling, G.W. Nicholson, D. Gallaher, B.J. Fanning, F.A. McMinn.
Second row: E.T. Harper, T. Cross, M.E. Wood, J.W. Stead (capt.), G.A. Tyler, W.J. Wallace, W. Coffey (manager).
Front row: R.W. McGregor, J.P. Gerrard (reserve), P. Harvey, D. McGregor, J. Hunter (reserve).

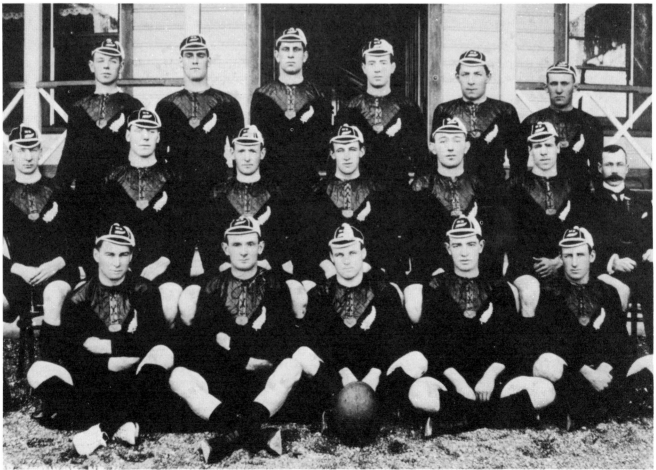

NZ RUGBY MUSEUM

GREAT BRITAIN 3

Athletic Park, Wellington

Two newcomers to New Zealand honours were Peter Harvey and "Paddy" McMinn, both of whom were playing their only game in the national colours. Harvey was considered a great prospect for the 1905 tour but he was unable to travel. Of the others, Cross had played against New South Wales in 1901 while the rest had been on the 1903 tour to Australia.

The British team took the field without its captain, the Scottish forward "Darkie" Bedell-Sivright, who was injured in the opening game of the New Zealand tour. The vice-captain, Teddy Morgan, led the side. He was later to score his team's try in the sensational defeat of the 1905 All Blacks by Wales.

The tourists had only six international players in this Test team although Bush, Vile and Bevan later played for Wales while Blair Swannell was to win a cap for Australia. He had played for Britain against Australia in 1899. He settled in Sydney and toured New Zealand with the Australian team in 1905. On April 25, 1915 he was killed in action during the Gallipoli landing. Dobson, the Oxford Blue and English International died in an unusual manner, being killed by a rhinocerous in Nyasaland during July 1916.

Arthur Harding played for Wales against the 1905 All Blacks and returned to New Zealand as captain of the 1908 Anglo-Welsh team. He later settled in New Zealand. Arthur O'Brien and Pat McEvedy were New Zealanders studying at Guy's Hospital. McEvedy toured again in 1908 before returning to his homeland to practise medicine. He became President of the New Zealand Rugby Union in 1934.

The British team had recently toured Australia where it had won all its matches, including three Tests. It played in red, white and blue hoops with black shorts.

New Zealand won the toss and almost scored in the first few minutes, Wallace just missing a penalty shot and Harper narrowly failing to kick a goal from a mark. For the first half-hour the home team was well on top and deserved to score on several occasions. At last Wallace kicked a penalty goal just before the interval but Harding kicked one for Britain right on halftime and the teams changed ends with the scores even.

Britain continued to kick into New Zealand territory during the second half but the black forwards kept working play back into their opponents' half. The home backs looked dangerous when in possession but good tackling kept them in check. Then from set play, Stead started a passing rush from which Duncan McGregor received the ball to sprint round his opposite number and score in the corner. Wallace missed from a difficult angle.

O'Brien went close with a pot at goal but New Zealand counter attacked and once more the ball went along the line to McGregor. The winger sprinted for the corner and scored his second try amid great cheering. Wallace again failed to convert but the visitors had to score twice with only a few minutes remaining. The black forwards completely dominated play for the rest of the game and there was no further scoring. At the final whistle the crowd rushed onto the field and carried McGregor off shoulder-high.

NEW ZEALAND

R.W. McGREGOR
(Auckland)

D. McGREGOR (Wellington) — E.T. HARPER (Canterbury) — W.J. WALLACE (Wellington)

M.E. WOOD (Auckland)

J.W. STEAD (**Capt.**) (Southland)

P. HARVEY (Canterbury)

D. GALLAHER (Auckland)

W.S. GLENN (Taranaki) — T. CROSS (Wellington) — B.J. FANNING (Canterbury) — C.E. SEELING (Auckland) — G.W. NICHOLSON (Auckland)

F.A. McMINN (Manawatu) — G.A. TYLER (Auckland)

D.D. DOBSON (Newton Abbott & England) — D.H. TRAILL (Guy's Hospital) — R.J. ROGERS (Bath)

T.S. BEVAN (Swansea) — R.W. EDWARDS (Malone & Ireland)

S.N. CROWTHER (Lennox) — A.F. HARDING (London Welsh & Wales) — B.I. SWANNELL (Northampton)

T.H. VILE (Newport)

P.F. BUSH (Cardiff)

E. MORGAN (**Capt.**) (Guy's Hospital & Wales) — R.T. GABE (Cardiff & Wales) — W.M. LLEWELLYN (Newport & Wales) — P.F. McEVEDY (Guy's Hospital)

A.B. O'BRIEN (Guy's Hospital)

GREAT BRITAIN

REFEREE: Mr F.T. Evans (Canterbury)
ATTENDANCE: 20,000
CONDITIONS: Weather fine, ground firm
HALFTIME: New Zealand 3, Great Britain 3

SCORERS

NEW ZEALAND	GREAT BRITAIN
Tries: D. McGregor (2)	Penalty goal: Harding
Penalty goal: Wallace	

NEW ZEALAND 14

2 September, 1905

The 1905 All Blacks had left for Britain when this match was played so the New Zealand team which opposed Australia was in the nature of a second fifteen. It contained some outstanding players however.

"Jum" Turtill, the full-back, was considered by some of the country's Rugby writers to have been unlucky not to go on tour. He later made a name for himself in professional Rugby League in Britain after touring there with the original New Zealand League team in 1907-08. He never returned to New Zealand and was killed in action in 1918 while serving with the Royal Engineers. Wrigley, Cross and Watkins were also members of New Zealand's first Rugby League team.

Colin Gilray would have toured with the 1905 All Blacks but was not available owing to university studies. He became a Rhodes Scholar and, along with Don MacPherson, later played for Scotland. MacPherson was selected for his adopted country while a student at London Hospital while Gilray was chosen from Oxford University where he won his Rugby Blue.

"Bolla" Francis, later to become Dave Gallaher's brother-in-law, was also considered unlucky to miss out on the 1905 tour. He too, later played professional football in Britain, as did Edgar Wrigley, New Zealand's youngest international. Archie McMinn, brother of the 1904 international, had already played for New Zealand as had Spencer, Cross, E. "Pat" Purdue and Dodd (killed in action in 1918). Turtill, Gilray, Bennet, MacPherson, Wrigley, Smith, Burgess, Watkins and Charlie Purdue were playing their only game for New Zealand.

Well-known Australians were the captain, Stan Wickham, McLean, Burdon, Judd and the Englishman, Swannell, who had played against New Zealand for Great Britain in 1904. McLean was the first of a famous Rugby family from Queensland. Jim Clarken, who played for the A.I.F. team after the war of 1914-18, was an outstanding surfman. He took part with fellow Wallaby Harald Baker in a famous mass rescue at Coogee in 1911.

The weather was extremely wretched for this match and postponement was seriously consi-

All Black full-back "Jum" Turtill wears a jersey typical of the era featuring the leather panel and hand stitched silver fern.

dered. The game was scheduled for the Caledonian Ground but was transferred to Tahuna Park because the original venue was unfit for play. The ground was in remarkably good order although rain fell heavily throughout the game and the 3,000 spectators received a severe soaking. As a large number of the crowd climbed through and over the fences, the official takings for the match were a mere £85 — probably an all-time low for an international.

The visitors had the advantage of a strong wind in the first spell. New Zealand immediately attacked strongly but Australia received a penalty at half-way. Wickham made a good attempt to kick a goal but the ball just fell short. The home team quickly attacked again, the New Zealand forwards taking play back to Australia's half. The ball was heeled to the home backs and from a passing rush Wrigley ran over in the corner to open the scoring. McMinn failed with the kick.

Good line kicking by Anlezark (also later prominent in English League) and Penman put the Australians on the attack soon after the kick-off and from a scrum the ball went along the visitors' back line to McLean who scored wide out. Wickham failed to convert.

AUSTRALIA 3

Tahuna Park, Dunedin

In spite of the appalling weather, play became faster, the ball travelling from end to end until the New Zealand forwards made a determined rush and Australia had to force. Then the visitors took the ball from their own 25 to the home goal line where a quick force-down by Turtill saved the situation for New Zealand. Halftime came with the score unaltered.

The second spell opened with fast play by both teams. Wickham was bowled over near the Australian line but he managed to get his kick in. Oxlade was caught offside and from the penalty kick the home pack broke away led by McMinn, who dribbled to the line where he picked up and scored. Charlie Purdue made a poor attempt to convert.

Australia forced the pace from the resumption but Clarken was ruled offside and New Zealand relieved. The forwards again invaded the visitors' half where McMinn gained possession to score his second try. This time Spencer took the conversion attempt but he failed to goal.

Soon afterwards Turtill started a movement in which nearly the whole New Zealand team handled, Cross finally scoring in a handy position for Francis to kick a goal. Good play by Australia followed and a passing rush in which Anlezark, Smith and McLean were prominent almost resulted in a try, a dropped pass at the vital moment spoiling the movement. The game ended shortly after with no further scoring.

With Australia disposed of, the New Zealand press felt confident enough to issue this challenge.

NEW ZEALAND

H.S. TURTILL
(Canterbury)
C.M. GILRAY   R. BENNET   D.G. MacPHERSON
(Otago)   (Otago)   (Otago)
E. WRIGLEY
(Wairarapa)
W.E. SMITH
(Nelson)
G.F. BURGESS
(Southland)
A.F. McMINN
(Manawatu)
A.R.H. FRANCIS   C.A. PURDUE
(Auckland)   (Southland)
T. CROSS   E. PURDUE   J.C. SPENCER (Capt.)
(Wellington)   (Southland)   (Wellington)
E.H. DODD   E.L. WATKINS
(Wellington)   (Wellington)

A. BURDON   A.M. OXLADE   J.C. CLARKEN
(New South Wales)   (Queensland)   (New South Wales)
H.J. JUDD   F.W. RICHARDS
(New South Wales)   (Queensland)
W. HIRSCHBERG   B.I. SWANNELL   B. LUCAS
(New South Wales)   (New South Wales)   (Queensland)
M.J. DORE
(Queensland)
E.A. ANLEZARK
(New South Wales)
D.J. McLEAN   L.M. SMITH   F.B. SMITH   S.M. WICKHAM (Capt.)
(Queensland)   (New South Wales)   (New South Wales)   (New South Wales)
A.P. PENMAN
(New South Wales)

AUSTRALIA

REFEREE: Mr J. Williams (Otago)
ATTENDANCE: 3,000
CONDITIONS: Weather very wet and cold, ground firm.
HALFTIME: New Zealand 3, Australia 3

SCORERS

NEW ZEALAND	AUSTRALIA
Tries: McMinn (2) Wrigley, Cross	Try: McLean
Conversion: Francis	

NEW ZEALAND 12

18 November, 1905

There were several new caps in the New Zealand side for this first international of the 1905 tour. George Gillett, who had played most of his Rugby in Auckland, had moved to Canterbury in 1905 and won South Island honours that year. He returned to Auckland after the tour and played for New Zealand in 1907 and 1908. He later joined the League code at which he was also an international. A very versatile player, he could perform well at full-back, centre, five-eighths and wing-forward.

Bob Deans, the baby of the 1905 All Blacks, was a member of a Canterbury pioneer family. A wealthy young man, he showed great generosity towards his team mates during the tour. A non-smoker and teetotaller, he was deeply religious but was no "wet blanket". The late George Nicholson told one of the authors that every member of the team had the utmost respect for Deans and took care not to offend him. His death in 1908 at the early age of 24 came as a great shock to his team-mates. The Deans Memorial Prize, for the best all-round boy at his old school Christchurch Boys' High School, is a perpetual monument to him.

Jimmy Hunter, who scored 39 tries on the British section of the tour, set a record which still stands. He had led the team during the preliminary tour of Australia (Gallaher was not available) and was All Black captain again in 1907 and 1908.

Steve Casey was a star hooker who had played for the South Island in 1905. He won All Black selection again in 1907 and 1908. Jim O'Sullivan was one of the best loose forwards in the team, playing in twenty matches including four Tests on the tour. He was an All Black again in 1907.

Alex McDonald had a long career as an international which he ended as captain of New Zealand in 1913. On his retirement he became active in Rugby administration and was honoured with life membership of the New Zealand Rugby Union. He was also a selector, coach and manager of All Black teams on several occasions.

Glasgow played for New Zealand in 1908 in one Test, thus making his total international appearances six. He died in office as an executive member of the New Zealand Rugby Union in 1939.

Both Smith and Cunningham had represented New Zealand before. George Smith, winner of fifteen New Zealand athletic titles and the British A.A.A. hurdles champion of 1902, toured New South Wales in 1897 and played against the visitors from that state at Wellington in 1901. He was born at Auckland in 1874 so was 31 when he went to Britain in 1905, although the record books show his age as 33. Smith went on tour with the "All Golds" and then returned to England to play for the Oldham club. Like his Auckland City clubmate Seeling, he never returned to New Zealand, dying in England in 1954.

The Scottish captain, "Darkie" Bedell-Sivright, had led the British on their Australasian tour of 1904. A fine forward, he won 22 caps between 1900 and 1907. While serving as a surgeon in the Royal Navy he died of blood poisoning off Gallipoli on September 5, 1915.

Also in the Scottish side was K.G. Macleod

NEW ZEALAND

G.A. GILLETT
(Canterbury)

W.J. WALLACE   R.G. DEANS   G.W. SMITH
(Wellington)   (Canterbury)   (Auckland)

J. HUNTER
(Taranaki)

J.W. STEAD
(Southland)

F. ROBERTS
(Wellington)

D. GALLAHER (Capt.)
(Auckland)

A. McDONALD   C.E. SEELING
(Otago)   (Auckland)

J.M. O'SULLIVAN   W. CUNNINGHAM   F.T. GLASGOW
(Taranaki)   (Auckland)   (Taranaki)

S.T. CASEY   G.A. TYLER
(Otago)   (Auckland)

D.R. BEDELL-SIVRIGHT (Capt.)   W.E. KYLE   J.C. MacCALLUM
(Edinburgh University)   (Hawick)   (Watsonians)

J.M. MACKENZIE   W.L. RUSSELL   W.P. SCOTT   L. WEST
(Edinburgh University) (Glasgow Academicals) (West of Scotland) (West Hartlepool)

Scrum packed 3-4 with no set positions.

P. MUNRO
(Oxford University)

E.D. SIMSON
(Edinburgh University)

L.L. GREIG
(Glasgow Academicals)

J.T. SIMSON   K.G. MACLEOD   L.M. MACLEOD   T. SLOAN
(Watsonians)   (Cambridge   (Cambridge   (Glasgow
               University)   University)   Academicals)

J.G. SCOULAR
(Cambridge University)

SCOTLAND

REFEREE: Mr W. Kennedy (Ireland)
ATTENDANCE: 21,000
CONDITIONS: Weather fine but cold, ground icy.
HALFTIME: Scotland 7, New Zealand 6

SCORERS

NEW ZEALAND	SCOTLAND
Tries: Smith (2) Glasgow, Cunningham	Try: MacCallum
	Dropped goal: E.D. Simson

SCOTLAND 7

who, at the age of 17, was making the first of his ten appearances for his country. One of the most brilliant all-rounders of his time, he won Blues at Cambridge in Rugby, athletics and cricket. His elder brother, Lewis who partnered him in the centres in this game, died following a Rugby match and at his father's request the younger Macleod gave up the game at the early age of 21. He played cricket for Lancashire as an amateur for some years. "Grunt" Macleod died in 1967 at the age of 79.

This first clash between New Zealand and Scotland took place under very difficult conditions, the surface of the ground being still frozen three hours before starting time. At one stage abandonment of the game was considered but the New Zealanders insisted on playing. The ground was very hard throughout and getting a foothold proved difficult.

New Zealand kicked off and for the first ten minutes it looked as though the All Blacks would win comfortably as their backs were going well, in spite of the difficult state of the ground. Both Wallace and Smith were recalled for forward passes when tries were on and New Zealand were given several penalty kicks in scoring positions but it proved impossible to kick goals as the ground was too hard to make a mark for the ball to stand up. Gallaher tried holding the ball for Wallace but as soon as he took his hand away the ball fell over.

After ten minutes Scotland took the lead when, from a scrum in front of the New Zealand posts, Ernest Simson received the ball and dropped a goal. Shortly after, Glasgow scored when Seeling broke away from a long throw-in. He was tackled by K.G. Macleod but as he fell he dropped the ball behind him for Glasgow to kick it over the line and score under the posts. Wallace failed to convert owing to the impossibility of placing the ball. New Zealand went ahead when Hunter made a break from which Smith went across in the corner but right on halftime MacCallum scored for the home team following a forward rush.

With the score favouring Scotland 7-6 and only four minutes left, the All Blacks were getting

Scotland gains possession in this line-out.

anxious. A scrum was formed near half-way and about fifteen yards in from touch. New Zealand heeled, Roberts "dummied" as the opposing halves swooped down on him and was away up field. He passed to Deans who drew the wing and sent on to Smith. The New Zealand flier swerved round Scoular and grounded the ball in the corner. He was carried back shoulder-high by his team-mates.

With time almost up, the All Blacks scored again when Stead kicked high to Scoular. McDonald caught the full-back in possession, the ball was dropped and Stead kicked it over the line. Both he and Casey dived but they missed the ball. However, Cunningham was right behind and he fell on the ball under the bar. He failed to convert and the whistle sounded for time.

It is interesting to note that a New Zealander, A.N. Fell, was selected for the Scottish team but he declined the invitation as he would not play against his own country. He had already won seven Scottish caps while studying medicine at Edinburgh University. Nolan Fell's replacement, Louis Greig, who was not named until the morning of the match was later equerry to the Duke of York (the future King George VI) whom he partnered in the doubles at Wimbledon in 1926.

NEW ZEALAND 15

25 November, 1905

The New Zealand captain, Dave Gallaher, was in hospital recovering from a leg injury received in the Scottish International. Progress reports of the match were telephoned to the hospital for his peace of mind. His absence led to the re-shuffling of the All Black Test team with the chosen full-back, Gillett, taking his captain's place at wing-forward.

Wallace was moved from the wing to full-back and as Smith was the only wing fit enough to play, the All Blacks were hard put to field a backline. The selection committee finally decided to play "Simon" Mynott, the Taranaki five-eighth, on the right wing. Mynott, who was the only new international in the New Zealand team, had never played on the wing before but he gave a sound display.

Harold Sugars was the only new international in the Irish team, which was considered a strong combination in view of its victories over England and Scotland during the previous season. Basil Maclear, who played four times against the 1905 All Blacks, was most impressive in the Test, troubling the New Zealand defence on several occasions with powerful individual breaks. Built like a forward and very fast, he was rated by the New Zealanders as one of the best players met on tour (George Nicholson considered him the best back in the British Isles). A regular army officer, Maclear was killed in action in 1915. Thrift, Tedford, Hamlet and Coffey were later presidents of the Irish Rugby Union. James Parke was a Davis Cup tennis player and a Wimbledon mixed doubles champion in 1914.

The game was played in excellent spirit and was well controlled by the Scottish referee. On the Thursday night before the game the teams went to the theatre together where they were sat

A British newspaper carried this enthusiastic headline of a report on the Irish match.

"ALL BLACKS" UNBEATEN

MAGNIFICENT STRUGGLE AT LANSDOWNE ROAD

BRILLIANT IRISH FORWARD PLAY

GRAND NEW ZEALAND COMBINATION

A GREAT GAME WON BY THE VISITORS

IRELAND 0

alternately in order to mix more freely. This undoubtedly did much towards the spirit in which the match was played.

Ireland won the toss and played with the wind for the first spell. New Zealand kicked off and went straight to the attack, Hunter being nearly over for a try when he slipped. Then the Irish forwards began to dominate play and for the next half-hour the All Blacks spent most of the time on defence.

It will be noted that Ireland played seven forwards with Wallace as a rover. According to George Nicholson, the British forwards did not have set places in the scrums in 1905, working on the "first up, first down" principle.

With the first half nearly over the All Black forwards worked their way down to the Irish 25 where the ball went into touch. Gillett set the backs away and Deans ended the movement with a try under the bar. Wallace converted and halftime came with the All Blacks leading 5-0.

W.J. WALLACE COLLECTION

Three members of the 1905 touring party "Mona" Thomson, Billy Wallace and Fred Roberts take their ease.

The New Zealanders attacked from the beginning of the second half and straight running by Stead and Hunter made a breach in the home defence for Deans to race over for his second try which Wallace converted. Then Smith went over but lost the ball and the Irish forced down. Play became hard and vigorous, especially in the forwards but it was as clean as it could possibly be, to the great enjoyment of players and spectators alike.

About half way through the second spell a loose scrum developed near the Irish line. The New Zealand forwards heeled quickly. McDonald detached himself from the scrum and picked up the ball to dive over near the posts. Wallace converted. There was no further scoring, New Zealand winning an exciting and by no means one-sided game.

NEW ZEALAND

W.J. WALLACE
(Wellington)

H.J. MYNOTT   R.G. DEANS   G.W. SMITH
(Taranaki)   (Canterbury)   (Auckland)

J. HUNTER
(Taranaki)

J.W. STEAD (**Capt.**)
(Southland)

F. ROBERTS
(Wellington)

G.A. GILLETT
(Canterbury)
C.E. SEELING   F.T. GLASGOW
(Auckland)   (Taranaki)
J.M. O'SULLIVAN   W. CUNNINGHAM   A. McDONALD
(Taranaki)   (Auckland)   (Otago)
G.A. TYLER   S.T. CASEY
(Auckland)   (Otago)

C.E. ALLEN (**Capt.**)   J.J. COFFEY   G.T. HAMLET
(Derry)   (Lansdowne)   (Old Wesley)
H.J. KNOX   H.S. SUGARS
(Lansdowne)   (Dublin University)
A.D. TEDFORD   H.G. WILSON
(Malone)   (Malone)

J. WALLACE
(Wanderers)

T.T.H. ROBINSON
(Dublin University)

E.D. CADDELL
(Dublin University)
C.G. ROBB   J.C. PARKE   B. MACLEAR   H. THRIFT
(Queen's Coll.   (Dublin University) (Cork County)   (Dublin University)
Belfast)

M.F. LANDERS
(Cork Constitution)

IRELAND

REFEREE: Mr J.C. Findlay (Scotland)
ATTENDANCE: 12,000
CONDITIONS: Weather drizzly, ground firm
HALFTIME: New Zealand 5, Ireland 0
SCORERS

NEW ZEALAND   **IRELAND**
Tries: Deans (2) McDonald
Conversions: Wallace (3)

27

NEW ZEALAND 15

2 December, 1905

Smith and Cunningham were unavailable for this game owing to injuries, their places being taken by McGregor and Newton respectively. The latter was playing the first of his three Tests for New Zealand. He had played for Canterbury since 1901 and was in the South Island team in 1905. A powerful lock, he was a useful second string to Cunningham.

England played a rover to counter the New Zealand wing-forward but the experiment was not successful. The All Blacks were surprised at the English selection, believing that a much stronger team could have been chosen. The stars of the English backs were Johnny Jackett and John Raphael, both of whom played very well.

Jackett, who was also a prominent amateur boxer and cyclist, toured New Zealand with the Anglo-Welsh team of 1908. Raphael, a former Oxford Blue, ran with great dash and defended gallantly in this match. He died from wounds during the First World War. The speedster

This sketch shows Braithwaite touching down behind his own line to prevent Gallaher scoring.

Alfred Hind, a former university sprint champion, looked dangerous at times while Henry Imrie was sound on defence. Dai Gent later became famous as a Rugby writer for the *Sunday Times*. He played a fair game against the All Blacks but his forwards were so badly outclassed that he had little chance to shine.

The game was played in an excellent spirit but it was not very exciting. New Zealand scored five minutes after the kick-off when Roberts worked the blind side with McGregor, who ran over in the corner. Wallace missed. Ten minutes later Stead cut through brilliantly and sent the ball along the line for McGregor to race over near the corner flag. By this time the ball was heavy from the muddy state of the ground and Wallace again missed the conversion.

The home forwards were obtaining very little possession and play seldom reached the New Zealand side of half-way. Just before halftime Roberts and Stead worked the short side again and once more McGregor was on hand to touch

NEW ZEALAND

G.A. GILLETT
(Canterbury)

D. McGREGOR   R.G. DEANS   W.J. WALLACE
(Wellington)   (Canterbury)   (Wellington)

J. HUNTER
(Taranaki)

J.W. STEAD
(Southland)

F. ROBERTS
(Wellington)

D. GALLAHER (**Capt.**)
(Auckland)

A. McDONALD   C.E. SEELING
(Otago)   (Auckland)

J.M. O'SULLIVAN   F. NEWTON   F.T. GLASGOW
(Taranaki)   (Canterbury)   (Taranaki)

S.T. CASEY   G.A. TYLER
(Otago)   (Auckland)

C.E.L. HAMMOND   V.H. CARTWRIGHT (**Capt.**)   B.A. HILL
(Harlequins)   (Nottingham)   (Blackheath)

J.L. MATHIAS   E.W. ROBERTS
(Bristol)   (Dartmouth)

R.F. RUSSELL   G.E. SUMMERSCALES
(Leicester)   (Durham City)

J.E. RAPHAEL
(Old Merchant
Taylors)

J. BRAITHWAITE
(Leicester)

D.R. GENT
(Gloucester)

A.E. HIND   H.E. SHEWRING   R.E. GODFRAY   H.M. IMRIE
(Leicester)   (Bristol)   (Richmond)   (Durham City)

E.J. JACKETT
(Falmouth)

ENGLAND

REFEREE: Mr G. Evans (Midland Counties)
ATTENDANCE: 45,000
CONDITIONS: Weather dull and cold, ground wet.
HALFTIME: New Zealand 9, England 0.

SCORERS

NEW ZEALAND   **ENGLAND**
Tries: McGregor (4), Newton

ENGLAND 0

Crystal Palace, London

down in the corner. Wallace missed his third conversion attempt.

In the second half play was more even but the English team seldom looked dangerous. However, the All Blacks did not score again until ten minutes from time, when Newton scored from loose play near the English line. Gillett missed.

Finally, Stead picked up in the open and the ball went along the chain to McGregor who ran for the corner flag and his fourth try, thus setting a record for a New Zealander in an international which still stands. Gillett missed the conversion and time was up shortly afterwards.

The official attendance was 45,000 but thousands entered the ground without paying. Some estimates place the attendance as high as 70,000.

An early example of commercial interest in Rugby.

Duncan McGregor's total of four tries in this match remains a New Zealand record for Test Rugby.

WALES 3

16 December, 1905

New Zealand played this vital game without three of its best players, viz, Smith, Stead and Cunningham. Smith's shoulder, which he had injured in the Munster match, was still too sore for him to play so McGregor retained his place. There have been various reasons given as to why Stead did not play. One version is that he was in fact in the team but withdrew when Mynott expressed disappointment at being left out. This, however, seems most unlikely. George Nicholson told one of the authors that Stead was suffering from dysentery. Another story says that he had boils. In W.J. Wallace's memoirs he states that both Stead and Cunningham were suffering from heavy colds.

The book of the 1905 tour, *The Triumphant Tour of the New Zealand Footballers*, by the team manager, G.H. Dixon, says simply that the team was weakened by the absence of Smith, Cunningham and Stead. There would seem to be no doubt that all three would have played had they been fit and their presence could have made a difference to the result. The master tactician Stead was sorely missed, especially as Mynott played so badly.

The Welsh team was very experienced, only Percy Bush being a new cap, and he had already played in Test matches with the British team in Australia and New Zealand in 1904. The team list contains some of the great names of Welsh Rugby — Teddy Morgan, Gwyn Nicholls, Bert Winfield, Willie Llewellyn, Dicky Owen, Charlie Pritchard (killed in action in 1916) and Arthur Harding.

Owen won 35 caps for Wales which remained a record until the advent of the great Ken Jones in the post World War II era. A diminutive half-back, Owen set up the movement from which Morgan scored. He came to a tragic end, taking his own life in February 1932.

Wales kicked off and McGregor returned the kick to touch. From the line-out Glasgow and Seeling broke away but they were held up and Wales made ground from a penalty kick. Every time Gallaher put the ball into the scrum he was penalised and after a while he ordered his hookers not to strike but to let Wales hook the ball.

Wales had seven forwards with C.C. Pritchard as a rover. In issuing this order Gallaher saved his team from being penalised so much but the only chance the All Blacks had to win possession was from loose play.

With so much ball the home backs were able to attack almost incessantly and Llewellyn was nearly over, only a splendid tackle by Hunter hurling him into touch. Then the Welsh forward, Joseph, got away with the ball at his toe but Gallaher and Deans stopped him. Bush narrowly missed with a drop at goal and Roberts found touch at half-way. From the line-out Nicholls drove the All Blacks back to their 25 where play continued for some time. Wales won a set scrum and Owen feinted to pass on the open side. He then slipped round on the blind side and passed to Cliff Pritchard the Welsh rover. The New Zealand backs were out of position as the ball went to Bush and on to Gabe. Finally Morgan received from his centre and flew for the corner where he grounded the ball, Gillett being just too late to stop him.

The crowd went wild with excitement and no-

NEW ZEALAND

G.A. GILLETT
(Canterbury)

D. McGREGOR   R.G. DEANS   W.J. WALLACE
(Wellington)   (Canterbury)   (Wellington)

J. HUNTER
(Taranaki)

H.J. MYNOTT
(Taranaki)

F. ROBERTS
(Wellington)

D. GALLAHER (Capt.)
(Auckland)

A. McDONALD   C.E. SEELING
(Otago)   (Auckland)
F.T. GLASGOW   F. NEWTON   J.M. O'SULLIVAN
(Taranaki)   (Canterbury)   (Taranaki)
S.T. CASEY   G.A. TYLER
(Otago)   (Auckland)

D. JONES   G. TRAVERS   C.M. PRITCHARD
(Aberdare)   (Pill Harriers)   (Newport)
J.F. WILLIAMS   J.J. HODGES   W.W. JOSEPH   A.F. HARDING
(London Welsh)   (Newport)   (Swansea)   (London Welsh)
C.C. PRITCHARD
(Newport)

R.M. OWEN
(Swansea)

P.F. BUSH
(Cardiff)

E. MORGAN   E.G. NICHOLLS (Capt.)   R.T. GABE   W.M. LLEWELLYN
(London Welsh)   (Cardiff)   (Cardiff)   (Llwynypia)
H.B. WINFIELD
(Cardiff)

WALES

REFEREE: Mr J.D. Dallas (Scotland)
ATTENDANCE: 40,000
CONDITIONS: Weather dull, ground firm
HALFTIME: Wales 3, New Zealand 0.

SCORERS
NEW ZEALAND   **WALES**
     Try: Morgan

NEW ZEALAND 0

Cardiff Arms Park

body seemed to care much when Winfield missed the conversion. The Welsh backs did not look dangerous again and halftime came with the All Blacks on attack.

Glasgow kicked off to start the second half which began with a New Zealand forward rush. Winfield's defence was too good however. Wales counter-attacked and a fine run by Gabe ended in New Zealand forcing down. Then came the most famous incident in New Zealand Test match history. Much has been written on Deans's "try" but an account of this match would not be complete without a description of this incident. According to Billy Wallace, this is what happened.

A line-out had been formed on the All Blacks' side of half-way and from a long throw in the Welsh forwards gained possession. The ball was kicked over Roberts's head and Wallace, who was on the wing on the touchline side, dashed in, scooped up the ball and cut across in front of the forwards. He then ran diagonally to the Welsh side of half-way where he side-stepped Nicholls and cut through between that player and Gabe. He now had a clear run to the Welsh full-back who was standing on the 25 mark.

As Wallace neared Winfield he was debating whether to kick over the full-back's head or to sell a dummy when he heard Deans calling "Bill! Bill!" outside him. He feinted to pass and Winfield took the dummy but recovered himself and came at Wallace again. Rather than risk any mishap, the latter threw a long pass out to Deans who took the ball perfectly and raced ahead. The centre then veered in towards the goal posts but altered course again when he saw Morgan coming across from the left wing. Had Deans not veered towards the posts he would have reached the line well ahead of Morgan but as it was he grounded the ball six inches over the line just as the Welsh wing tackled him.

The All Blacks rushed up and patted Deans on the back for they believed the score had been evened and the ensuing kick at goal was an easy one for Wallace. Then Deans made his second mistake for he got up off the ball. Had he remained lying on it the referee would have had no alternative but to award a try when he finally caught up with the play. He was dressed in street clothes and had no bars or studs on his boots so he had been left a long way behind.

According to Wallace's memoirs, Owen picked up the ball and put it down just short of the line. He then said to the referee, "He forced the ball here," and pointed to the spot where the ball was lying. The All Blacks protested strongly but the referee ordered a five yards scrum. Wallace believed that the dead silence of the crowd confirmed the fact that Deans had scored for if Morgan's tackle had prevented a try there would have been much applause.

In fact, Morgan always admitted that Deans scored. We have never seen any reference to Owen's part in the incident other than in Wallace's account and we find it incredible that Owen acted in this alleged manner. However, Wallace was on the spot and that is his version. It would seem that Deans certainly scored but the referee decided that he did not and his decision was the one that mattered.

From the five yards scrum Bush cleared but the All Blacks kept up the pressure and Mynott got across the line but was held up and could not ground the ball. Then Deans made another dash but Nicholls brought him down.

The game steadily ground to a close but in the dying minutes Roberts slipped round the blind side to send McGregor over in the corner but the referee ruled a forward pass. The final whistle sounded shortly afterwards and the original All Blacks had lost their unbeaten record.

The referee, John Dewar Dallas, had played for Scotland against England in 1903 and at 27 years of age was younger than some of the players when he controlled the New Zealand v. Wales game of 1905. He was always adamant that Deans did not ground the ball over the line and this view was shared by a number of Welsh players. The whole incident is rather confusing, since some sources state that Rhys Gabe tackled Deans. That the latter firmly believed he had scored is indicated by a telegram which he sent to the *Daily Mail* stating that he grounded the ball six inches over the line but was pulled back by Welsh players.

31

NEW ZEALAND 38

1 January, 1906

Booth, Abbott and Mackrell were new caps in the New Zealand team. "General" Booth later played for New South Wales and acquired a reputation as a coach. "Bunny" Abbott was a professional sprinter who first played serious football while serving in the Boer War. He captained Wanganui against the 1908 Anglo-Welsh team and continued playing representative Rugby until 1914. The Taranaki man worked as a farrier almost to the day he died in 1971. Wallace was the only 1905 tourist to outlive him.

Bill Mackrell was a member of the "All Golds", the first New Zealand Rugby League team. He played Test matches for New Zealand at the new code against both Britain and Australia. A kick to the head ended his football career before World War I and he died in 1917 from a stroke, probably brought on by the injury.

There were a number of interesting personalities in the French team. Crichton was an Englishman who was rated by the All Blacks as the equal of any full-back they met on tour. Gaston Lane and Lacassagne were to become First

Dave Gallaher and Billy Stead, captain and vice-captain of the 1905-06 "Originals".

World War casualties. Alan Muhr was an American, born in Chicago in 1880. He worked as an interpreter in France and was made a Commandeur de la Legion d'Honneur. He died in a German concentration camp during World War II.

The captain, Henri Amand, was a draughtsman by profession. He and Gallaher became great friends and exchanged jerseys after the game. Amand died in 1967, aged 94. Communeau was a wealthy industrialist, being a director of the French Factory of Carpets and Blankets. Georges Jerome, who later made a name as a referee, and André Verges were negroes. The last survivor of this team was Jacques Dufourcq, a doctor of medicine, who died in 1975 at the age of 95.

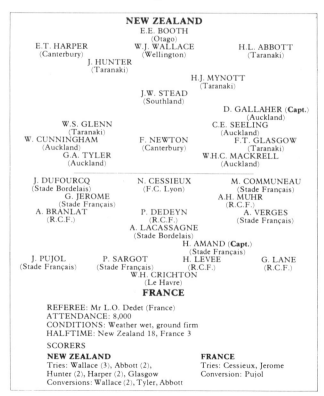

NEW ZEALAND

E.E. BOOTH
(Otago)

E.T. HARPER   W.J. WALLACE   H.L. ABBOTT
(Canterbury)   (Wellington)   (Taranaki)
              J. HUNTER
              (Taranaki)

                          H.J. MYNOTT
                          (Taranaki)
              J.W. STEAD
              (Southland)

                          D. GALLAHER (Capt.)
                          (Auckland)
    W.S. GLENN   C.E. SEELING
    (Taranaki)   (Auckland)
W. CUNNINGHAM   F. NEWTON   F.T. GLASGOW
(Auckland)   (Canterbury)   (Taranaki)
    G.A. TYLER   W.H.C. MACKRELL
    (Auckland)   (Auckland)

J. DUFOURCQ   N. CESSIEUX   M. COMMUNEAU
(Stade Bordelais) (F.C. Lyon)   (Stade Français)
    G. JEROME   A.H. MUHR
    (Stade Français)   (R.C.F.)
A. BRANLAT   P. DEDEYN   A. VERGES
(R.C.F.)   (R.C.F.)   (Stade Français)
              A. LACASSAGNE
              (Stade Bordelais)
                   H. AMAND (Capt.)
                   (Stade Français)
J. PUJOL   P. SARGOT   H. LEVEE   G. LANE
(Stade Français) (Stade Français) (R.C.F.)   (R.C.F.)
              W.H. CRICHTON
              (Le Havre)

FRANCE

REFEREE: Mr L.O. Dedet (France)
ATTENDANCE: 8,000
CONDITIONS: Weather wet, ground firm
HALFTIME: New Zealand 18, France 3
SCORERS

NEW ZEALAND	FRANCE
Tries: Wallace (3), Abbott (2),	Tries: Cessieux, Jerome
Hunter (2), Harper (2), Glasgow	Conversion: Pujol
Conversions: Wallace (2), Tyler, Abbott	

FRANCE 8

Parc Des Princes, Paris

Forward play during New Zealand's first international against France. Newton (headgear) and Tyler are joined by Mackrell and Glenn.

It is also interesting to note that the referee, Louis Dedet, never played for France but was awarded a full cap for his games against various British teams in 1893. He later became headmaster of a very select secondary school.

New Zealand kicked off and before long the first scrum was ordered. Two of the French front-row men had beards and when the scrum broke, Mackrell and Tyler had a few words to say about bearded footballers. When the next scrum was ordered they both went for the loose head and Newton was so overcome with laughing that he fell down in the scrum.

The All Blacks won a great deal of possession and before long their account was opened when Wallace scored after a passing rush and converted his own try. Next Abbott went over in the corner for an unconverted try. A rush by the home forwards took play down to the New Zealand 25 and with good control the Frenchmen dribbled to the visitors' line where Cessieux dived over for a try.

His team mates turned cartwheels, somersaults, handsprings and back flips while the spectators waved their umbrellas excitedly up and down. Pujol failed to convert. Two New Zealand tries followed in quick succession, one by Hunter and the other by Harper, both of which Wallace converted to give the All Blacks a lead of 18-3 at halftime.

Early in the second half the Frenchmen closed the gap when the visiting backs were out of position and Jerome dashed through to score for Pujol to convert. New Zealand soon struck back however and Wallace scored twice in quick succession.

Then followed tries by Hunter, Glasgow and Harper, none of which were converted. Right on time Abbott ran from his own 25 to score between the posts and convert his own try.

Despite the bad weather conditions the game was fast and open and it was played in an excellent spirit. The French had managed to score two tries against the All Blacks, which was more than any of the British international teams had managed to do.

20 July, 1907

First Test

Five of the New Zealand team were playing their first Test match. Frank Mitchinson, who had an outstanding game, went on to play ten more international games and appeared 30 times in the All Black jersey between 1907 and 1913. A fast, elusive runner, he was a prolific try scorer and ended his All Black career with 22 tries for his country. At time of writing, he was the oldest surviving ex-All Black.

Frank Fryer, the Canterbury wing, had a short international career, being an All Black in 1907 and 1908 but he was top try scorer on the 1907 tour. Jack Colman played for New Zealand again in one match in 1908. A versatile player, he represented his country at full-back, wing three-quarter and wing-forward.

"Massa" Johnston had toured with the 1905 All Blacks but did not play in a Test. He later turned to Rugby League and was a member of the famous "All Golds". He later settled in Australia where he died in 1951. "Ned" Hughes, the Southland hooker, also played against the Anglo-Welsh team of 1908 and became New Zealand's oldest international when he made a

come-back in 1921 to play against the Springboks at the age of 40. He also played Rugby League for New Zealand in 1910.

Of the Australian team, all but Watson, Rosewell and Hughes toured Britain with the Wallabies of the following year. Bede Smith had been in New Zealand with the 1905 Australians. Probably the best-known of the home side in this 1907 Test match was Chris McKivatt, a brilliant half-back and five-eighth in both Rugby codes.

The All Blacks had been soundly beaten 14-0 by New South Wales on the previous Wednesday so the home team was expected to win. The Australians played in maroon and blue, a combination of Queensland and New South Wales colours.

Two minutes after the kick-off Francis and Johnston broke from a scrum and took play into Australia's 25. From another scrum loose play developed and Seeling bustled over the line to open the scoring. Wallace failed to convert. Play

Frank Mitchinson heads for the line to score one of his three tries. Wallace is in support on his right.

AUSTRALIA 6

Sydney Cricket Ground

was mostly around centre field for some time before Mynott sent the All Black backs away from a line-out. Mitchinson made a beautiful break from inside his own half with Wallace in support. The centre sold Carmichael a "dummy" and went on to score for Wallace to convert. Mitchinson added another try before the interval when he received an in-pass from Wallace as the winger was about to go over in the corner. Wallace's conversion gave New Zealand a lead of 13-0 at halftime.

Play was even in the early stages of the second half but the All Blacks were not long in adding more points. From a line-out Johnston broke away and passed to Hughes who bullocked his way over close to the posts for Wallace to convert.

The Australians then spent some time in New Zealand territory and Carmichael opened their

Billy Wallace was successful with four conversions in this international.

scoring with a penalty goal. Shortly after he closed the gap further by kicking a goal from a mark but New Zealand's lead was increased when Hunter made a brilliant corkscrew run up the centre and passed to Francis who sent on to Mitchinson for the centre to score his third try. Wallace converted. Two minutes later the All Black forwards stormed the Australian line and Francis scored an unconverted try.

The game thus ended in an easy victory for New Zealand which rather upset the predictions of the local press.

NEW ZEALAND

E.E. BOOTH
(Otago)

W.J. WALLACE   F.E. MITCHINSON   F.C. FRYER
(Wellington)   (Wellington)   (Canterbury)

J. HUNTER (**Capt.**)
(Taranaki)

H.J. MYNOTT
(Taranaki)

F. ROBERTS
(Wellington)

J.T.H. COLMAN*
(Taranaki)

C.E. SEELING   A. McDONALD
(Auckland)   (Otago)

A.R.H. FRANCIS   W. CUNNINGHAM   W. JOHNSTON
(Auckland)   (Auckland)   (Otago)

S.T. CASEY   E. HUGHES
(Otago)   (Southland)

J. ROSEWELL††   T.S. GRIFFIN   J.T. BARNETT†
(New South Wales)   (New South Wales)   (New South Wales)

P.A. McCUE   P.H. BURGE (**Capt.**)
(New South Wales)   (New South Wales)

P. FLANAGAN   N.E. ROW   J. HUGHES
(Queensland)   (New South Wales)   (New South Wales)

F. WOOD
(New South Wales)

C.H. McKIVATT
(New South Wales)

C. RUSSELL   W. DIX   F.B. SMITH   G. WATSON
(New South Wales)   (New South Wales)   (New South Wales)   (Queensland)

P. CARMICHAEL
(Queensland)

AUSTRALIA

* Replaced by J.C. Spencer (Wellington)
† Replaced by E.W. Richards (Queensland)
†† Replaced by R. Graves (New South Wales)
REFEREE: Mr A. Brown (New South Wales)
ATTENDANCE: 50,000
CONDITIONS: Weather overcast, ground firm.
HALFTIME: New Zealand 13, Australia 0.

SCORERS

NEW ZEALAND   **AUSTRALIA**
Tries: Mitchinson (3), Seeling,   Penalty goal: Carmichael
Hughes, Francis   Goal from mark: Carmichael
Conversions: Wallace (4).

NEW ZEALAND 14

3 August, 1907

Second Test

George Nicholson returned to international Rugby in this game. He was not an original selection for the 1907 All Blacks but was on holiday in Australia when the tourists were hit by injuries and he was invited to join the team.

Australia must have fielded one of the lightest international packs of all time, for the Wallaby forwards' average weight was only 12st.3lbs. Peter Burge, the heaviest forward, weighed 14st. but the lightest forward, Vay Oxenham, was a mere 11st. In fact, four of the home vanguard were under 12st.

The 1907 season marked the first appearance in international football of the famous "Dally" Messenger. He played only two seasons of first-class Rugby Union (1906 and 1907) but he became one of the most famous Rugby League players of all time. A fast, elusive wing, he was also a magnificent goal-kicker.

The game had been in progress only a few minutes when Wallace was well tackled by Russell. Colman failed to secure the ball which was kicked over the New Zealand line and Messenger beat the All Black full-back in a race for the ball to score amid tremendous enthusiasm from the crowd. Messenger converted the try himself.

From the restart Burge and Richards led a forward rush into All Black territory where the home team received a penalty from which Messenger tried unsuccessfully to goal. The Australians had slightly the better of the game at this stage but eventually a force down by New Zealand gave the visitors a chance to get out of danger.

A splendid run by Gillett almost ended in a try but Smith tackled the All Black wing-forward in front of the posts. Just after this, Wallace failed to goal from a mark, and a little later he was wide of the posts from a penalty kick.

A New Zealand forward rush was stopped by Dix but the home full-back was penalised for not releasing the ball when tackled. Francis missed from an easy position. Australia counter attacked and brilliant play by Fihelly, Flanagan and Burge took the ball to half-way, where Smith

secured and found touch in New Zealand territory. Messenger failed to goal from a penalty and halftime came with Australia still five points in front.

Messenger kicked off to start the second half and the All Black forwards went straight to the attack. The ball came to Mynott, who dribbled to the line, where Dix failed to field the ball. Seeling scored under the bar and Wallace converted.

With a stiff breeze behind them, the visitors were beginning to look the better side and their heavier forwards were wearing down the home pack. Dix fumbled in front of his posts but Messenger relieved the situation by picking up and running across field, where he was stopped by Francis and Wallace. Loose play followed and Hunter ran through the Australian defence before passing to Wallace, who scored wide out. Francis failed to convert.

The Australian forwards, although outweighed in the scrums, were very fast in the loose and they rushed the ball past Colman. In an exciting race Wallace outpaced Parkinson and

---

NEW ZEALAND

J.T.H. COLMAN
(Taranaki)

W.J. WALLACE   F.E. MITCHINSON   F.C. FRYER
(Wellington)   (Wellington)   (Canterbury)

J. HUNTER (**Capt.**)
(Taranaki)

H.J. MYNOTT
(Taranaki)

F. ROBERTS
(Wellington)

G.A. GILLETT
(Auckland)

C.E. SEELING   G.W. NICHOLSON
(Auckland)   (Auckland)

A.R.H. FRANCIS   W. CUNNINGHAM   W. JOHNSTON
(Auckland)   (Auckland)   (Otago)

S.T. CASEY   E. HUGHES
(Otago)   (Southland)

A.M. OXLADE (**Capt.**)   V. OXENHAM   J.T. BARNETT
(Queensland)   (Queensland)   (New South Wales)

P.H. BURGE   W. CANIFFE
(New South Wales)   (Queensland)

J. FIHELLY   E.W. RICHARDS   P. FLANAGAN
(Queensland)   (Queensland)   (Queensland)

F. WOOD
(New South Wales)

E.F. MANDIBLE
(New South Wales)

H.H. MESSENGER   F.B. SMITH   C. RUSSELL   G.E. PARKINSON
(New South Wales)   (New South Wales)   (New South Wales)   (Queensland)

W. DIX
(New South Wales)

AUSTRALIA

REFEREE: Mr C.B. Cochrane (Queensland)
ATTENDANCE: 17,000
CONDITIONS: Weather fine, ground hard
HALFTIME: Australia 5, New Zealand 0

Scorers

NEW ZEALAND	AUSTRALIA
Tries: Wallace (2), Seeling, Francis	Try: Messenger
Conversion: Wallace	Conversion: Messenger

AUSTRALIA 5

Woolloongabba Ground, Brisbane

kicked the ball dead when a try seemed imminent. The All Blacks then worked their way slowly up the touch line with good line kicking until play reached the home 25. Here Dix fumbled the ball and Francis, following up fast, scored an unconverted try.

After the kick-off New Zealand set up a strong attack and from a scrum Mynott was nearly over. From another scrum Roberts ran on the blind side and fed Wallace, who scored in the corner. The winger failed to convert his own try.

The game still had 20 minutes to run but the All Blacks were in a fairly comfortable position. The crowd sat in almost complete silence as play was not very exciting in the closing stages, except for a run by Messenger which ended when he was pushed out near the corner.

New Zealand's win was due mainly to the good play of the forwards, with Seeling, Nicholson and Francis outstanding, and to the brilliance of Roberts, Mynott and Wallace in the backs.

Three Wellington members of the touring team: Wallace, Mitchinson and Roberts.

The referee keeps a close eye on play as the Australians win a scrum near touch.

NEW ZEALAND 5

10 August, 1907

Third Test

Since no Queenslanders were included in the home team, this was really the New South Wales side playing against New Zealand in Australia's colours. There were no new internationals in either team.

Australia won the toss and had the advantage of a fairly stiff breeze. The play was close and uninteresting for the first few minutes, the only feature being some good line-kicking by the All Blacks. Then the latter were driven back to their line and the game became more exciting, only good defence keeping Australia from scoring.

At last play reached half-way where Messenger could have marked and had a shot at goal but he did not claim a fair catch. A number of penalties were awarded to both sides but no score resulted. Then the visiting forwards, with Nicholson in the van, reached home quarters where they kept up a continuous attack. Wallace had an unsuccessful kick at goal from a mark and shortly after the first half ended. The Australians had the

This cartoonist boasts of New Zealand's prowess in Rugby and rowing.

better of the spell and deserved to be in front but the New Zealand defence was very sound.

From the restart, Australia made a sensational effort, showing exceptionally fine combination among the three-quarters. Russell, Mandible and Smith, by a clever succession of passes, beat tackle after tackle and carried play to the eastern corner, where a further succession of close passes wound up with a magnificent try by Wood in the corner. Messenger converted with a splendid kick.

The All Blacks attacked hard but McKivatt cleared. Fryer claimed a mark and Wallace narrowly failed to kick a goal. The Australians

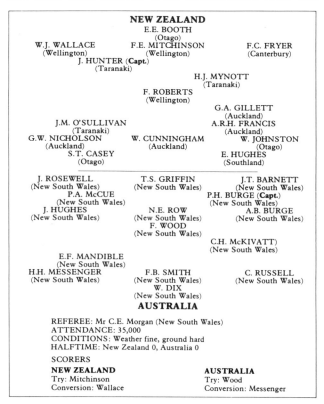

NEW ZEALAND

E.E. BOOTH
(Otago)

W.J. WALLACE   F.E. MITCHINSON   F.C. FRYER
(Wellington)   (Wellington)   (Canterbury)
J. HUNTER (**Capt.**)
(Taranaki)

H.J. MYNOTT
(Taranaki)

F. ROBERTS
(Wellington)

G.A. GILLETT
(Auckland)
J.M. O'SULLIVAN   A.R.H. FRANCIS
(Taranaki)   (Auckland)
G.W. NICHOLSON   W. CUNNINGHAM   W. JOHNSTON
(Auckland)   (Auckland)   (Otago)
S.T. CASEY   E. HUGHES
(Otago)   (Southland)

J. ROSEWELL   T.S. GRIFFIN   J.T. BARNETT
(New South Wales)   (New South Wales)   (New South Wales)
P.A. McCUE   P.H. BURGE (**Capt.**)
(New South Wales)   (New South Wales)
J. HUGHES   N.E. ROW   A.B. BURGE
(New South Wales)   (New South Wales)   (New South Wales)
F. WOOD
(New South Wales)
C.H. McKIVATT)
(New South Wales)

E.F. MANDIBLE
(New South Wales)
H.H. MESSENGER   F.B. SMITH   C. RUSSELL
(New South Wales)   (New South Wales)   (New South Wales)
W. DIX
(New South Wales)

AUSTRALIA

REFEREE: Mr C.E. Morgan (New South Wales)
ATTENDANCE: 35,000
CONDITIONS: Weather fine, ground hard
HALFTIME: New Zealand 0, Australia 0

SCORERS
NEW ZEALAND   **AUSTRALIA**
Try: Mitchinson   Try: Wood
Conversion: Wallace   Conversion: Messenger

AUSTRALIA 5

Sydney Cricket Ground

Players from the Queensland and N.S.W. Unions appear in this photograph with the All Blacks.

began a passing rush and the crowd became wildly excited as the ball swung from one player to another but a knock-on in the New Zealand 25 pulled up the movement. From the scrum the All Blacks cleared the ball to half way.

The visitors were playing well below their best form, especially in the backs, and the only passing rushes were those initiated by the home team. Fortunately for the All Blacks, Booth was playing very well at this stage and time after time he managed to run the ball into touch when his line was in danger.

With ten minutes to go the All Blacks were still struggling and the crowd could sense an Australian victory. Then the ball was kicked to Dix who, in fielding it, was bumped by "Son" Burge.

The ball fell to the ground between them and Mitchinson snapped it up to score behind the posts. Wallace kicked an easy goal to equalise the scores.

Heartened by Mitchinson's somewhat lucky try, the All Blacks began to play much better. The forwards, led by Nicholson and Francis, reached great heights but their efforts were well responded to by the Australians. From a scrum at the centre the ball went to Wood, who kicked a high one down to the New Zealand line but the visitors forced.

The New Zealand forwards worked their way back to the attack and a long punt by Cunningham went out just two yards from the corner. The All Blacks were penalised for a scrum infringement shortly after and the ball was kicked into touch to end the game.

NEW Z\[E\]ALAND 3?

6 June, 1908

First Test

The 1908 Anglo-Welsh team was the third British side to visit New Zealand. Since the Scottish and Irish Rugby Unions would not support the tour, this team consisted only of English and Welsh players. As is often the case with touring teams from the British Isles, several leading players were unavailable and although the 1908 tourists had a number of prominent backs, only four of the forwards were internationals at the time of selection.

Jackett, Gibbs, Williams, Harding, Dibble, Oldham, Kyrke and Jackson had all played against the 1905 All Blacks. Jackson was recalled to England to answer charges of professionalism on the eve of the second Test in 1908 and as he was the team's best goal-kicker, the loss was a severe one. He later returned to live in New Zealand and played Rugby League for New Zealand. He was an East Coast Rugby selector in the 1930s. His son, E.S. Jackson, was an All Black prop in 1936-37-38.

Apart from "Ranji" Wilson, who was playing the first of his 21 games for New Zealand, the home forwards had all played in Test matches. New caps in the backs were Don Cameron and "Mona" Thomson. The latter toured with the 1905 All Blacks but did not play in a Test. The inside back combination of Roberts, Stead and Hunter was the one which had been so successful in the main games of the 1905 tour. Stead had been out of international football for three seasons and his inclusion in the first Test team came as something of a surprise, especially to himself.

As the score indicates, the match was one-sided, largely because of the complete domination by the home forwards. Casey and Hughes

The New Zealand Team (Note the unusual angle of the silver ferns)
Back row: H.O. Hayward (reserve), A. McDonald, F.E. Mitchinson, A.R.H. Francis, C.E. Seeling, W. Cunningham, G.D. Gray (reserve).
Second row: A. Wilson, J.T.H. Colman, E. Hughes, J.W. Stead (capt.), S.T. Casey, G.A. Gillett, A.L. Humphries (manager).
In front: D. Cameron, H.D. Thomson, F. Roberts, J. Hunter.

WEEKLY NEWS

ANGLO-WELS 5

Carisbrook, Dunedin

hooked almost at will from the set scrums and the visitors were outclassed in the line-outs as well. Their speedy backs therefore spent most of their time on defence and only Jackett's brilliance prevented a higher score by New Zealand.

The Anglo-Welsh try was a very fine one, however. Vassall received in his own 25 and cut through the defence, leaving the experienced Hunter standing. He side-stepped Mitchinson, raced through to Colman and sent a beautiful pass out to Gibbs who swerved around the New Zealand full-back to score. Although he played only one game for England, Vassall was considered to be one of the greatest centres ever to play for Oxford University, some critics rating him with the famous R.W. Poulton.

Roberts opened the scoring with a penalty goal from in front of the posts on the 25 yard line. New Zealand kept winning possession and after several near misses Thomson, on the left wing, ran around the defence to score a brilliant try in the corner which Roberts converted. Shortly after,

WEEKLY NEWS

Roberts opens the scoring with a penalty goal.

Mitchinson cut through to score with a man over and Gillett converted. From a line-out in the Anglo-Welsh 25 Roberts sent his backs away and Mitchinson ran Cameron into position for the right wing to score after eluding "Ponty" Jones's tackle. Gillett again converted. Just before halftime, Roberts added another try following loose play on the visitors' line. Gillett failed to convert.

Roberts scored again early in the second half when Hughes, Francis and Seeling took the ball to the Anglo-Welsh line for the All Black half-back to run over on the blind side of the ruck. Gillett failed with the kick. A few minutes later, the Anglo-Welsh scored and the home side's lead was cut to nineteen points.

Following the kick-off, the visitors took play into New Zealand territory but Seeling broke away from a line-out and sent the backs away. The ball came to Hunter who dashed over the goal line for a good try. Roberts missed. Near the end of the game the ball was kicked past the visitors' backs and Mitchinson raced in to score. Francis converted with a fine kick. The game was ably controlled by the former New Zealand captain, James Duncan, the first New Zealand international player to referee a Test match.

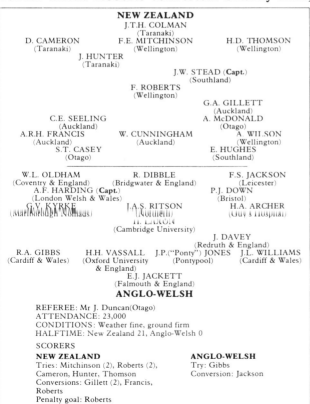

NEW ZEALAND

J.T.H. COLMAN
(Taranaki)

D. CAMERON (Taranaki)	F.E. MITCHINSON (Wellington)	H.D. THOMSON (Wellington)

J. HUNTER
(Taranaki)

J.W. STEAD (**Capt.**)
(Southland)

F. ROBERTS
(Wellington)

G.A. GILLETT
(Auckland)

C.E. SEELING (Auckland)		A. McDONALD (Otago)
A.R.H. FRANCIS (Auckland)	W. CUNNINGHAM (Auckland)	A. WILSON (Wellington)
S.T. CASEY (Otago)		E. HUGHES (Southland)

W.L. OLDHAM (Coventry & England)	R. DIBBLE (Bridgwater & England)	F.S. JACKSON (Leicester)
A.F. HARDING (**Capt.**) (London Welsh & Wales)		P.J. DOWN (Bristol)
G.V. KYRKE (Marlborough Nomads)	J.A.S. RITSON (Northern)	H.A. ARCHER (Guy's Hospital)

H. LAXON
(Cambridge University)

J. DAVEY
(Redruth & England)

R.A. GIBBS (Cardiff & Wales)	H.H. VASSALL (Oxford University & England)	J.P.("Ponty") JONES (Pontypool)	J.L. WILLIAMS (Cardiff & Wales)

E.J. JACKETT
(Falmouth & England)

ANGLO-WELSH

REFEREE: Mr J. Duncan (Otago)
ATTENDANCE: 23,000
CONDITIONS: Weather fine, ground firm
HALFTIME: New Zealand 21, Anglo-Welsh 0

SCORERS

NEW ZEALAND	**ANGLO-WELSH**
Tries: Mitchinson (2), Roberts (2), Cameron, Hunter, Thomson	Try: Gibbs
Conversions: Gillett (2), Francis, Roberts	Conversion: Jackson
Penalty goal: Roberts	

NEW ZEALAND 3

27 June, 1908

Second Test

The New Zealand selectors did something rather unusual for this match in that they made several changes in the winning first Test team. Probably confident that the home team would win the series, they blooded several young players but chose some old hands in an attempt to blend youth and experience. New All Blacks were Gray, Burns, Hamilton, Reedy, Murray and Paterson, of whom two, Don Hamilton and Peter Murray, did not play for New Zealand again. The great Billy Wallace, who had been kept out of the first Test with a knee injury, was recalled to play his last international game. Now nearly thirty years of age, he was probably getting past his best but he played very well, his line-kicking being a feature of the match. "Paddy" Burns toured Australia in 1910 and Donaldson Gray went to North America in 1913.

The result shocked Rugby followers who expected New Zealand to score another easy win. The visitors were very unlucky not to win and in fact they gained a moral victory, scoring a try to a penalty goal. The game was played in a sea of slush and although bright back play was out of the question, there was an interesting struggle between two hard-working packs. The visitors played the Welsh international three-quarter R.A. Gibbs as a rover in an attempt to combat the New Zealand formation. Jackett again gave a fine display at full-back, his handling of the muddy ball bringing rounds of applause throughout the match. The home pack was outplayed by the visitors, especially in the set scrums, where Casey and Hughes were sadly missed.

New Zealand won the toss and Harding kicked off. Right from the start the field was muddy and both packs concentrated on dribbling. Early in the game Wallace had an unsuccessful kick at goal from a penalty and Jackett found the line at half-way with a mighty punt.

"Ponty" Jones made a good run but the ball went loose in the home 25 for Seeling to relieve. New Zealand stormed into Anglo-Welsh territory and rushed play to the visitors' line, where a scrum was ordered. Jackett broke away from the scrum and ran to his 25 where he punted superbly, finding the line in the All Blacks' 25.

Rain was falling incessantly and it became almost impossible to handle or field the ball accurately. The players were unrecognisable long before halftime. However, Cameron broke away but his kick ahead was taken by "Ponty" Jones who kicked down to the New Zealand 25, where Mitchinson fielded the greasy ball beautifully before finding the line at half-way.

The game was held up while Harding received medical attention. After the resumption, Jackett kicked a high one down to Wallace, who marked and found touch in the visitors' 25. From a scrum the home forwards broke away and had Jackett under pressure but the visiting full-back managed to find the line.

Wallace had another shot at goal from a penalty but the ball fell short. Vassall cleared and the Anglo-Welsh forwards burst away in a foot rush. They reached the New Zealand 25 where the ball went into touch. With Archer, Dibble and Mor-

NEW ZEALAND

W.J. WALLACE
(Wellington)

D. CAMERON   F.E. MITCHINSON   F.C. FRYER
(Taranaki)   (Wellington)   (Canterbury)

J. HUNTER (Capt.)
(Taranaki)

G.D. GRAY
(Canterbury)

P.J. BURNS
(Canterbury)

D.C. HAMILTON
(Southland)

C.E. SEELING   A.M. PATERSON
(Auckland)   (Otago)
A.R.H. FRANCIS   W. CUNNINGHAM   A. WILSON
(Auckland)   (Auckland)   (Wellington)
W.J. REEDY   P.C. MURRAY
(Wellington)   (Wanganui)

G.R. HIND   P.J. DOWN   T.W. SMITH
(Guy's Hospital)   (Bristol)   (Leicester)
A.F. HARDING (Capt.)   E. MORGAN   H.A. ARCHER   R. DIBBLE
(London Welsh   (Swansea)   (Guy's Hospital) (Bridgwater
& Wales)   & England)
R.A. GIBBS
(Cardiff & Wales)

W.L. MORGAN
(London Welsh)
J.P. ("Tuan") JONES
(Guy's Hospital)
P.F. McEVEDY   J.P. ("Ponty") JONES   H.H. VASSALL   J.L. WILLIAMS
(Guy's Hospital)   (Pontypool)   (Oxford University   (Cardiff & Wales)
& England)
E.J. JACKETT
(Falmouth & England)

ANGLO-WELSH

REFEREE: Mr A. Campbell (Auckland)
ATTENDANCE: 10,000
CONDITIONS: Weather very wet, ground slushy
HALFTIME: New Zealand 0, Anglo-Welsh 0

SCORERS

NEW ZEALAND	ANGLO-WELSH
Penalty goal: Francis	Try: J.P. ("Ponty") Jones

ANGLO-WELSH 3

Athletic Park, Wellington

gan in the lead the visitors dribbled over the goal line but the ball was forced. The Anglo-Welsh deserved to score from this movement.

From the drop-out Mitchinson cleared and for a few minutes play see-sawed between the 25s. The Anglo-Welsh did most of the attacking and Morgan almost got across but Wallace cleared. The All Blacks were defending desperately right up to halftime, which came after Wallace had found the line from a penalty.

The early part of the second half was marked by a series of long punts between the two sets of backs. Then from a scrum in the home 25 Harding came away with the ball but Cameron picked up and dashed down field. He kicked past Jackett who had to turn and kick the ball dead. From the resulting five-yard scrum the Anglo-Welsh were offside and Francis kicked a goal from a handy position.

The Anglo-Welsh went straight to the attack from the kick-off and kept New Zealand under pressure. From a scrambling rush the visiting forwards kicked past the New Zealand backs and the ball went over the home line for "Ponty" Jones, who was following up fast, to fall on it under the bar. Things looked black for New Zealand but the ball was so greasy and heavy that Harding failed to lift it and the scores remained even.

The Anglo-Welsh forwards were playing superbly and once more Wallace had to force under pressure. Then New Zealand rallied and McEvedy had to fling himself down at the feet of the home pack to halt a dangerous rush. He was helped by Vassall and both players were injured, having to leave the field for some minutes.

Cameron made another good run before kicking high, Vassall taking a mark in front of his own posts. Jackett found touch at half-way. New Zealand fought back and a rush in which Mitchinson, Fryer, Seeling and Paterson took part ended in McEvedy forcing.

"The Battle Glorious", as seen by a cartoonist for the New Zealand Freelance.

Harding took scrums instead of line-outs, thus assuring his team of the bulk of the possession. Francis was caught offside and Jackett kicked a high one to Wallace, who was tackled as the visiting forwards stormed the home line. It was difficult to control the ball in the sea of mud however and New Zealand relieved. Then Wallace had to force down again.

McEvedy took a mark from which Gibbs narrowly failed to kick a goal. New Zealand remained pinned in the home 25 for the rest of the game, which ended without further scoring. The Anglo-Welsh had played well above themselves and were very unlucky not to score an upset win.

NEW ZEALAND 2

25 July, 1908

Third Test

The only new All Black in this team was "Circus" Hayward of Thames who played his only match for New Zealand. He later joined the League code. The inclusion of Roberts, Stead, Hunter and Deans gave the home team the back combination which had proved so successful in 1905 while another tourist of that year, Glasgow, now of Southland, was recalled to international football.

Three of the visitors' internationals, Gibbs, Davey and J.L. Williams were on the injured list and this would partly account for the inept display by the Anglo-Welsh. The team was also travel-weary after a strenuous week of sightseeing and entertainment at Rotorua while a further blow was the retirement of Harding with an injury after a few minutes of play. The All Blacks had spent a week of hard training under Dave Gallaher and they took the field in great shape.

The poor attendance was brought about by the unpleasant weather and increased charges to the ground. Also, the All Blacks were expected to win for the home side was considerably stronger than the one which had drawn the second Test.

Stead won the toss and Harding kicked off. Three minutes later, the visiting captain was injured and although he tried to play on, he was merely a passenger and left the field. McEvedy took over the captaincy. Shortly after Harding's departure New Zealand scored when Roberts worked the blind side with Mitchinson who was over the line before the crowd realised what had happened. Francis missed the conversion. A well-judged kick by Seeling after the kick-off placed his team on the attack and Stead made a good opening but a knock-on spoiled the chance of a try. New Zealand continued to press and from a scrum Roberts received to throw a long pass to Mitchinson who scored. Gillett failed to convert.

The All Blacks kept play in the Anglo-Welsh half and Seeling broke through to the 25 where his kick ahead was marked by Jackett. Following the latter's kick, Stead was stopped right on the line and the home team continued to keep up the pressure. Finally, the visitors took play back to half-way by means of a passing rush in which "Ponty" Jones, Down and Vassall took part but Francis intercepted a pass and, with the aid of Deans, carried play back to Anglo-Welsh territory. Then Seeling charged down a free kick and he and Reedy broke through to the 25 where their progress was stopped by Chapman. With so much pressure being applied by the All Blacks, the inevitable happened and Hunter scored after Hayward picked up near the posts and threw out a short pass. Cameron's attempt at goal went just outside the posts.

The final try in the first half was scored right on the interval. From a scrum near the Anglo-Welsh line the black forwards broke up quickly and took the ball over between the posts where Glasgow fell on it. Cameron missed from an easy position.

Shortly after the resumption of play, Gillett scored following a scrum on the visitors' line and although the kick at goal was not a difficult one,

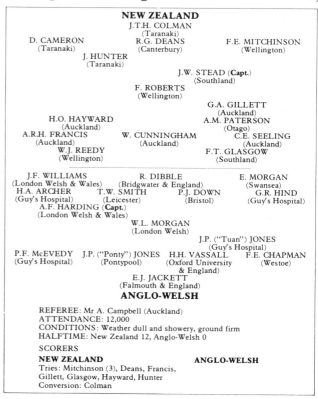

NEW ZEALAND

D. CAMERON
(Taranaki)

J.T.H. COLMAN
(Taranaki)

R.G. DEANS
(Canterbury)

F.E. MITCHINSON
(Wellington)

J. HUNTER
(Taranaki)

J.W. STEAD (**Capt.**)
(Southland)

F. ROBERTS
(Wellington)

H.O. HAYWARD
(Auckland)

G.A. GILLETT
(Auckland)

A.M. PATERSON
(Otago)

A.R.H. FRANCIS
(Auckland)

W. CUNNINGHAM
(Auckland)

C.E. SEELING
(Auckland)

W.J. REEDY
(Wellington)

F.T. GLASGOW
(Southland)

J.F. WILLIAMS
(London Welsh & Wales)

R. DIBBLE
(Bridgwater & England)

E. MORGAN
(Swansea)

H.A. ARCHER
(Guy's Hospital)

T.W. SMITH
(Leicester)

P.J. DOWN
(Bristol)

G.R. HIND
(Guy's Hospital)

A.F. HARDING (**Capt.**)
(London Welsh & Wales)

W.L. MORGAN
(London Welsh)

J.P. ("Tuan") JONES
(Guy's Hospital)

P.F. McEVEDY
(Guy's Hospital)

J.P. ("Ponty") JONES
(Pontypool)

H.H. VASSALL
(Oxford University
& England)

F.E. CHAPMAN
(Westoe)

E.J. JACKETT
(Falmouth & England)

ANGLO-WELSH

REFEREE: Mr A. Campbell (Auckland)
ATTENDANCE: 12,000
CONDITIONS: Weather dull and showery, ground firm
HALFTIME: New Zealand 12, Anglo-Welsh 0
SCORERS

NEW ZEALAND	ANGLO-WELSH
Tries: Mitchinson (3), Deans, Francis, Gillett, Glasgow, Hayward, Hunter	
Conversion: Colman	

44

ANGLO-WELS 0

Potter's Park, Auckland

Gillett scores in a tackle close by the referee's feet.

Francis missed the conversion. Cameron was almost over shortly after when he fielded a kick by Vassall and ran down the touch line but he lost the ball. Hayward was on hand however and he scored near the posts. This time Cunningham failed to convert. The visitors were now a spent force and New Zealand scored again following a passing rush in which all the backs handled before Mitchinson raced over in the corner. Colman converted with a splendid kick.

After the kick-off the visitors fared better for a brief spell but New Zealand went further ahead when Roberts whipped the ball out from a scrum and Hunter made an opening for Deans to score. Colman failed. Heavy rain then began to fall but the home team continued to handle well and Francis scored the final try when he broke through a line-out. Glasgow failed to convert. Cameron went over near the corner right on time but he was called back for an infringement.

The prediction that the All Blacks would win fairly easily was thus borne out and had the home team's goal-kicking not been so weak, the score could have been much higher. At no stage did the visitors look as though they would score.

This was the last Test played by Bob Deans. A little over two months later the young Canterbury centre died following an operation for appendicitis.

Hayward crosses for a try near the posts.

NEW ZEALAND 6

25 June, 1910

First Test

There were several new caps in the All Black team. Joe O'Leary gained a great reputation in Ranfurly Shield games for Auckland and went on to captain New Zealand in 1913. "Jack" Stohr was one of New Zealand's most prodigious goal kickers. Although he had no success on the 1910 tour he kicked very well in California and British Columbia in 1913, while as a member of the famous 1919 New Zealand Army team in South Africa, he was widely acclaimed by the local critics. He settled in South Africa after the tour and died there in 1973.

Harry Paton had played one game on the 1907 tour of Australia (against New South Wales) but did not gain All Black selection again after the 1910 tour. Fuller, McKellar, Avery, Ridland and Maguire were also having their only season as All Blacks. Avery was a regular army officer who won the D.S.O. at Gallipoli while Ridland lost his life in World War I. "Paddy" Burns, who was

the New Zealand half-back in the second Test of 1908, was chosen for the 1910 tour as a three-quarter.

Clarken, Griffin, Row and Wood had all played against New Zealand in Tests and the last-named was to do so again in 1913 and 1914, as were Dwyer and George. The latter was killed in World War I. One of Australia's greatest players, Ward Prentice, was playing his first Test against New Zealand. He played in the Tests on the 1908 British tour and went to California with the 1912 Wallabies.

Australia wore New South Wales' colours for this series. This was a hard, even Test match in which the play was of a high standard throughout. Each side did its share of attacking and if anything the home team did slightly more than

This photograph includes members of the Australian, New Zealand, American Universities and NZ Maoris teams.

NZ RUGBY MUSEUM

AUSTRALIA 0

Sydney Cricket Ground

Headline from a match report in the Sydney Sunday Times.

the winners. Bad handling ruined several scoring chances however. Also, Hodgens was too slow in sending the ball on and as a result his speedy three-quarters were handicapped. The home half-back, Fred Wood, was in his usual brilliant form but the best back on the field was the Australian full-back, Larry Dwyer. Noted for his fine all-round play, Dwyer was even better than usual in this game.

The strength of the New Zealanders was in the forwards and, with "Ranji" Wilson the best loose man on the ground, the visiting vanguard dominated their opponents for most of the match. Their handling in the open would have done credit to an international back line.

Roberts was as great as usual behind the scrum while the five-eighths and three-quarters brought off some sparkling movements. O'Leary was very sound at full-back. The strength of the All Black backs lay in resolute tackling and quick covering. Several times the home team looked like scoring but an All Black always came from somewhere and managed to do the right thing.

New Zealand won the toss and played with a slight breeze behind them. The visitors spent most of the first half on defence but early in the game they came close to scoring when Stohr narrowly failed to kick a goal from a mark near half-way. Both sides threw the ball about but

good defence kept the first half scoreless although Burns went close with a goal from a mark and Stohr had two near misses from penalties.

Well into the second half Stohr broke away but was tackled by Dwyer. As he fell, the Taranaki wing flicked the ball to Wilson who made a fine run to score in the corner. Stohr failed to convert.

The Wallabies made determined sorties into black territory but the New Zealand tackling was superb. Finally the ball was rushed into home country by the All Black forwards who kicked the ball over the line for Fuller to fall on it. Stohr again failed to convert. The curtain-raiser was between the New Zealand Maoris and the American Universities, both of whom were touring Australia. The Maoris won, 14-11, after being down 11-0 at halftime.

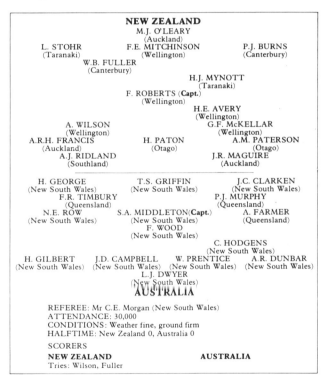

NEW ZEALAND

M.J. O'LEARY
(Auckland)

L. STOHR   F.E. MITCHINSON   P.J. BURNS
(Taranaki)   (Wellington)   (Canterbury)

W.B. FULLER
(Canterbury)

H.J. MYNOTT
(Taranaki)

F. ROBERTS (**Capt.**)
(Wellington)

H.E. AVERY
(Wellington)

G.F. McKELLAR
(Wellington)

A. WILSON
(Wellington)

A.R.H. FRANCIS   H. PATON   A.M. PATERSON
(Auckland)   (Otago)   (Otago)

A.J. RIDLAND   J.R. MAGUIRE
(Southland)   (Auckland)

H. GEORGE   T.S. GRIFFIN   J.C. CLARKEN
(New South Wales) (New South Wales)   (New South Wales)

F.R. TIMBURY   P.J. MURPHY
(Queensland)   (Queensland)

N.E. ROW   S.A. MIDDLETON(**Capt.**)   A. FARMER
(New South Wales) (New South Wales)   (Queensland)

F. WOOD
(New South Wales)

C. HODGENS
(New South Wales)

H. GILBERT   J.D. CAMPBELL   W. PRENTICE   A.R. DUNBAR
(New South Wales) (New South Wales) (New South Wales) (New South Wales)

L.J. DWYER
(New South Wales)

AUSTRALIA

REFEREE: Mr C.E. Morgan (New South Wales)
ATTENDANCE: 30,000
CONDITIONS: Weather fine, ground firm
HALFTIME: New Zealand 0, Australia 0
SCORERS

NEW ZEALAND	AUSTRALIA
Tries: Wilson, Fuller	

27 June, 1910

Second Test

Like the French Test of 1906, this match was played on a Monday. Jim Ryan was making his Test debut in the full-back position. Normally a five-eighth, he played for New Zealand in that position in 1914 and was captain of the 1919 New Zealand Army team in the King's Cup matches. He later toured South Africa with the soldiers. Mitchell and Evans were also new caps.

Undoubtedly the home team was much the better on the day. The Australians were almost incessantly on attack and were seldom called on to defend for more than a few minutes at a time. Although they had to play into the wind in the second half, they did even better than they had done during the first spell.

The home forwards were greatly improved and, just as they had been dominated in the first Test, so they dominated the visitors in this match. They were vastly superior to the All Black pack in scrums and line-outs and they won more than their share of possession in the rucks and in loose play.

With so much ball coming their way, the home backs also looked much better than they had two days before. Their handling was sure and they combined most effectively on attack. Their defence, too, left nothing to be desired. Dwyer again played an outstanding game with Prentice not far behind him.

The New Zealanders did not show their usual form, mainly because the opposition was too good. They were outplayed from start to finish but they did well to keep the score to 11 points. As they gained very little possession, the All Black backs spent nearly the whole game on defence and in this department they did their work very well.

New Zealand played into the wind for the first half and Australia soon opened the scoring when Gilbert went over from a passing rush. Row failed to convert.

The visitors then pressed and a good rush carried play to their opponents' line but the ball was kicked too hard and Australia forced. New Zea-

land attacked again and had the home team in trouble but a defensive penalty relieved the situation for Australia. The rest of the spell was fairly even and there was no further score at halftime.

From the kick-off Fuller made a good run and play became very fast with Mitchell and Roberts especially prominent. The New Zealanders were

Bert Gilbert, a fine three-quarter for Australia in both Rugby codes, scored two tries in his country's first win over New Zealand.

T.W.J. AUTY COLLECTION

NEW ZEALAND 0

Sydney Cricket Ground

slowly driven back to their own line however and they had to force. From the drop-out the Australian forwards began a dribbling rush but Fuller picked up and ran to half-way before being pulled down.

The Wallabies were soon back in the All Black 25, where a mark gave the visitors some relief. Australia came back and after a fine passing rush, Hodgens crossed the line and Norman Row converted.

Australia attacked from the kick-off but Mitchinson got possession, ran upfield and kicked. The ball crossed the home line, where it was forced down.

For a few minutes New Zealand kept Australia hemmed in but Wood obtained possession from a scrum. He broke smartly and fed back to his forwards for Murphy to make a great run. The Queenslander finally passed to Gilbert and the winger scored in the corner. Row failed to convert. The game ended soon after with the Wallabies scoring a well-deserved win, thus recording their first victory over New Zealand.

SYDNEY MAIL

New Zealand forward, Francis towers above Wood, the Australian half-back.

Two of the Australians who contributed to the New Zealand defeat were later well-known in English Rugby League. "Dinny" Campbell signed with Leeds in 1912 for £350 plus £2 a match. He played 258 games for Leeds and the club granted him a benefit game in 1920. He returned to Sydney in 1921, where he entered private business. He was later a reporter on the *Sydney Sun*. He died at Sydney in 1966, aged 77.

Campbell's fellow three-quarter, Bert Gilbert, played for Hull after touring England with the Australian League team of 1911-12. He came home in 1920 and became groundsman at the Sydney Cricket Ground.

New Zealand Maoris again beat American Universities 21-3 in the curtain raiser.

NEW ZEALAND

J. RYAN
(Wellington)

L. STOHR   P.J. BURNS   W.J. MITCHELL
(Taranaki)   (Canterbury)   (Canterbury)

F.E. MITCHINSON
(Wellington)

W.B. FULLER
(Canterbury)

F. ROBERTS (**Capt.**)
(Wellington)

H.E. AVERY
(Wellington)

A. WILSON   G.F. McKELLAR
(Wellington)   (Wellington)

A.R.H. FRANCIS   D.A. EVANS   A.M. PATERSON
(Auckland)   (Hawke's Bay)   (Otago)

A.J. RIDLAND   J.R. MAGUIRE
(Southland)   (Auckland)

H. GEORGE   T.S. GRIFFIN   J.C. CLARKEN
(New South Wales)   (New South Wales)   (New South Wales)

P.J. MURPHY   F.B. TIMBURY
(Queensland)   (Queensland)

N.E. ROW   S.A. MIDDLETON (**Capt.**)   R. STUART
(New South Wales)   (New South Wales)   (New South Wales)

F. WOOD
(New South Wales)

C. HODGENS
(New South Wales)

H. GILBERT   J.D. CAMPBELL   W. PRENTICE   A.R. DUNBAR
(New South Wales)   (New South Wales)   (New South Wales)   (New South Wales)

L.J. DWYER
(New South Wales)

AUSTRALIA

REFEREE: Mr N.B. Martin (New South Wales)
ATTENDANCE: 8,000
CONDITIONS: Weather fine, ground hard
HALFTIME: Australia 3, New Zealand 0

SCORERS

NEW ZEALAND	AUSTRALIA
	Tries: Gilbert (2), Hodgens
	Conversion: Row

NEW ZEALAND 2█

2 July, 1910

Third Test

The weather for this match was unseasonably warm and was more to the liking of the spectators than it was to the players. Once again there was a reversal of form, the final result being a decisive win to New Zealand.

The All Black forwards played splendidly to lay the foundations for their team's victory. They gave their backs plenty of possession which was used to good advantage, especially by Burns, who had a particularly good game. The return of the experienced "Simon" Mynott at first five-eighth no doubt strengthened the visitors. Mitchinson made several good openings for his three-quarters while O'Leary was again in good form at full-back. The best back on the ground however was the New Zealand captain, Fred Roberts, whose display was rated by the critics as the best seen in the history of Rugby in Sydney.

The Australians were disappointing but once more it was a case of a team playing only as well as the opposition would let it. Griffin's absence was felt, as the second Test was won to a certain

The great five-eighth, Simon Mynott, played his last Test in 1910 at the age of 34.

extent by his expert hooking. The home pack appeared to have lost its dash in the second half and was outclassed towards the end of the game.

The Australian backs spent most of their time defending and, with the exception of Hodgens, they tackled well. Dwyer again emerged as the home team's best back while Prentice and Gilbert also played well.

The All Blacks took the lead early when Burns scored from a passing rush, Stohr failing to add the extra points. Australia was soon defending again when Stohr was almost over following a break by Paton but a great line-kick by Wood put the locals on attack. Hodgens broke from a scrum and passed to Gilbert who scored near the corner and Row kicked a splendid goal to put his team into the lead.

New Zealand then pressed for a long period, Wilson being outstanding in the forwards. Mynott made several brilliant breaks and Burns scored from one of these, Stohr again failing to convert. The All Blacks had all the better of the rest of the spell but could not get over again before halftime.

NEW ZEALAND

M.J. O'LEARY
(Auckland)

L. STOHR   P.J. BURNS   W.J. MITCHELL
(Taranaki)   (Canterbury)   (Canterbury)

F.E. MITCHINSON
(Wellington)

H.J. MYNOTT
(Taranaki)

F. ROBERTS (**Capt.**)
(Wellington)

H.E. AVERY
(Wellington)

A. WILSON   G.F. McKELLAR
(Wellington)   (Wellington)

A.R.H. FRANCIS   H. PATON   A.M. PATERSON
(Auckland)   (Otago)   (Otago)

A.J. RIDLAND   J.R. MAGUIRE
(Southland)   (Auckland)

H. GEORGE   J.C. CLARKEN   S.H. SLATER
(New South Wales)   (New South Wales)   (New South Wales)

L.J. REYNOLDS   P.J. MURPHY
(New South Wales)   (Queensland)

N.E. ROW   S.A. MIDDLETON (**Capt.**)   R. STUART
(New South Wales)   (New South Wales)   (New South Wales)

F. WOOD
(New South Wales)

C. HODGENS
(New South Wales)

H. GILBERT   J.D. CAMPBELL   W. PRENTICE   A.R. DUNBAR
(New South Wales)   (New South Wales)   (New South Wales)   (New South Wales)

L.J. DWYER
(New South Wales)

AUSTRALIA

REFEREE: Mr N.B. Martin (New South Wales)
ATTENDANCE: 18,000
CONDITIONS: Weather fine, ground firm
HALFTIME: New Zealand 6, Australia 5

SCORERS

NEW ZEALAND   **AUSTRALIA**
Tries: Burns (2), Stohr (2), Paterson,   Tries: Gilbert, Row
Mitchinson, Mitchell, Paton   Conversions: Row (2)
Conversions: O'Leary (2)   Penalty goal: Row

T.W.J. AUTY COLLECTION

AUSTRALIA 13

Sydney Cricket Ground

The visitors were quickly on the attack again in the second half and Stohr scored following a line-out. Roberts missed. Then Mynott was caught off-side in front of his posts and Row kicked a goal. New Zealand struck back with a forward rush started by Francis who passed to Wilson. The Wellington man sent on to Paterson, who scored. O'Leary kicked a good goal.

Australia came back from the kick-off and short passing among the forwards ended in a try by Row behind the posts. His conversion put his team only one point behind. New Zealand worked the ball into blue territory where Wilson passed to Mynott who made an opening for a try by Mitchinson which O'Leary converted. Then Mitchell scored following a break by Roberts, this try being followed by one scored by Paton who went over from a line-out. O'Leary missed

Five Rugby Internationals from Australia and New Zealand Test matches who later played Rugby League in England. From left: J.D. Campbell, H. Gilbert, H.S. Turtill, C.E. Seeling and E.A. Anlezark.

both conversion attempts. The final points came when Stohr made a brilliant run to beat several men and score near the posts. Burns missed the conversion.

A number of the 1910 All Blacks finished their international careers at the end of the Australian tour. The most notable of these was the captain, Fred Roberts, who had played 12 Tests since 1905. Surely one of the greatest half-backs ever to play for New Zealand, Roberts, at 12st. 4lbs. was as big as some of the forwards of his time and was very dangerous near the opposition line. His brilliance was acclaimed by critics at home and overseas.

Roberts's 1905 team-mate, "Simon" Mynott, had also played his last Test. Although overshadowed by Billy Stead, Mynott was one of the great five-eighths of his time and his contribution to New Zealand Rugby was considerable. Mitchell, Fuller, Evans, Maguire, Avery, McKellar, Paton, Ridland, Francis and Paterson were also finished with Test match Rugby.

6 September, 1913

First Test

The New Zealand team was chosen from the twenty-three players who were about to leave on their tour of California and British Columbia. Three of this Test side lost their lives in World War I, viz, George Sellars, "Doolan" Downing and Henry Dewar. These three were new caps, as were the rest of the team except for McDonald and Gray.

Dick Roberts, who captained the All Blacks on their tour of Australia in 1914, was a member of the famous New Zealand Army Team which toured South Africa in 1919. Jim Wylie played for Auckland in 1910 and then moved to Sydney, where he joined the Glebe club. He played for New South Wales and was a member of the Australian team which toured California in 1912. He then returned to Auckland and won his All Black cap. He remained in California after the All Blacks' tour of 1913 and took up an appointment as Rugby coach at Stanford University. He died in 1956.

"Jock" Cuthill captained the New Zealand Universities team on its Australian tour of 1913 and played for the South Island during that year. He missed only two matches in North America. University studies made him unavailable for the All Blacks' Australian tour of 1914, however, while severe war wounds finally ended his football career.

Tom Lynch and "Dougie" McGregor were very fast wings who found the conditions in North America to their liking. Lynch toured Australia in 1914 but McGregor did not represent New Zealand at Rugby after 1913. However, he was a Rugby League international after World War I.

"Jock" McKenzie also had a very good tour in 1913 and, after moving to Auckland, he again won All Black honours in 1914. Taylor, Murray and Downing also toured Australia in 1914 but Sellars, Atkinson, Dewar and Williams were All Blacks for one year only.

Suttor and Bill Watson played for the famous A.I.F. team in the King's Cup matches in 1919, Watson being captain. Larry Wogan toured New

HEAVY DEFEAT FOR THE AUSTRALIANS.

The Umbrella Brigade.

Outclassed by the All Blacks, the Australian Rugby team cut a rather poor figure in Athletic Park in the gale and rain of Saturday afternoon. Only about 5000 people forsook the fireside or other haven of cosiness for the bleak, clay-banked paddock which we call "The Park." Many a stirring battle has been fought on that same old paddock, and there many a thousand enthusiasts have stood their little hour or two in the clay mud while the weather imps (which seem to be as predominant in Wellington as Ali Baba's commando of thieves were in the days of the Arabian Nights) did their worst. Star games are often drowned in rain, and this game did not escape. But these things by the way!

One-fifth of our enthusiastic 5000 sat in comfort in the stand; 4000 stood in clay mud, huddling together for warmth and protection from the elements, a patient and enduring umbrella and overcoat brigade. The dozen pressmen who toiled while everyone else there made holiday burn with gratitude for the thoughtful union who facilitated their work by providing them with accommodation from which they could ascertain with certainty how strong the wind was, how wet the rain was, and what an excellent shower-bath was obtainable by anyone who momentarily took one eye off the overflowing roof-gutter.

Part of match report from the Dominion.

Zealand again with the New South Wales team of 1921. He and Watson were born in New Zealand. "Doss" Wallach won the Military Cross during World War I, before dying from wounds in 1918. Other war casualties in the Australian team were George, Thompson, Tasker and Jones.

AUSTRALIA 5

Athletic Park, Wellington

Heavy rain fell throughout the game, which was played in four twenty minute spells — as far as we know, the only occasion on which a Test match has not been played in two halves. New Zealand proved far too strong for the visitors in all departments and the match was not very exciting.

The All Blacks kicked off against the wind and the tourists were on attack early but Cuthill drove them back with good line-kicking. Then the home forwards swept into Australian territory where Taylor cut in and passed to Lynch for the speedy winger to beat a man before touching down near the corner. Roberts missed the conversion. Australia struck back quickly and Carr scored following a forward rush, McMahon converting to put the visitors in front.

In the second quarter New Zealand came back strongly and Lynch scored again. Roberts missed the conversion and also failed with a penalty shot soon after but he converted the next try, scored by

NZ FREELANCE

The touring team left for California cheered by this impressive victory.

Murray, giving New Zealand a lead of 11-5 at halftime. Taylor retired at this stage, Gray going to half-back, McKenzie to first and the replacement Mitchinson to second five-eighth.

The rain fell even harder during the third quarter and there was a lot of mishandling but Lynch finally held a pass and scored. Roberts missed again. Then followed an amazing try by Gray, who side-stepped his way through almost the whole Australian team to score under the bar. Roberts converted.

The home side's sixth try was scored early in the final quarter by McKenzie, Roberts again kicking the goal and the seventh try came from Roberts who charged down a clearing kick from McMahon. Cuthill failed with the kick. Immediately after the kick-off, McKenzie intercepted a pass and scored, the final whistle going a few minutes later.

NEW ZEALAND

J.E. CUTHILL
(Otago)

A.J. McGREGOR   R.W. ROBERTS   T.W. LYNCH
(Auckland)   (Taranaki)   (South Canterbury)

R.J. McKENZIE
(Wellington)

G.D. GRAY
(Canterbury)

H.M. TAYLOR*
(Canterbury)

H.V. MURRAY
(Canterbury)

A. McDONALD (Capt.)   H. DEWAR
(Otago)   (Taranaki)

A.J. DOWNING   H. ATKINSON   J.T. WYLIE
(Auckland)   (West Coast)   (Auckland)

G.M.V. SELLARS   P. WILLIAMS
(Auckland)   (Otago)

H. GEORGE   C. O'DONNELL   W.T. WATSON
(New South Wales) (New South Wales)   (New South Wales)

E.J. FAHEY (Capt.)   C. WALLACH
(New South Wales)   (New South Wales)

E.W. CODY   F. THOMPSON   P.J. MURPHY
(New South Wales) (New South Wales)   (Queensland)

F. WOOD
(New South Wales)

W.G. TASKER
(New South Wales)

E.T. CARR   L.W. WOGAN   H.A. JONES   D.C. SUTTOR
(New South Wales) (New South Wales) (New South Wales) (New South Wales)

M.J. McMAHON
(Queensland)

AUSTRALIA

REPLACEMENT: * Replaced by F.E. Mitchinson (Wellington)
REFEREE: Mr R.L. Simpson (Wellington)
ATTENDANCE: 5,000
CONDITIONS: Weather very wet, ground muddy
HALFTIME: New Zealand 11 Australia 5
SCORERS

NEW ZEALAND	AUSTRALIA
Tries: Lynch (3), McKenzie (2), Murray, Gray, Roberts	Try: Carr
Conversions: Roberts (3)	Conversion: McMahon

13 September, 1913

Second Test

The New Zealand team to tour North America had left when the second Test of 1913 was played so that the All Black team opposing the Australian side at Dunedin was really a second fifteen. However, it contained some outstanding players such as the captain, Joe O'Leary, "Ranji" Wilson, Chas Brown, who was later to lead the 1919 Army team in South Africa and Hasell, who also played for the soldiers. O'Leary and Wilson were the only old caps. Jim Baird, Reg Taylor and Jim McNeece lost their lives in the Great War.

Australia scored first when Carr centre kicked for Wood to field and send on to Tasker. The five-eighth cut in and passed to Suttor, who went over after sixteen minutes. Simpson missed the conversion. Then O'Leary put the home team ahead when he fielded just inside his own half and potted a magnificent goal.

Australia attacked from the kick-off and Simpson narrowly missed with a penalty shot. A determined rush by the home side took New Zealand back on attack and Brown made a good break from which he passed infield to Wilson who scored behind the posts. O'Leary converted. The visitors closed the gap right on halftime when Jones won a race for the ball and dived on it over the New Zealand line. Simpson kicked a good goal.

Early in the second spell Taylor scored following a dribbling rush and O'Leary again converted. Australia hit back however when Jones

New Zealand half-back Brown, waits for the outcome of this line-out.

AU~TRALIA 1 ·

Carisbrook, Dunedin

Baird is challenged by an Australian as he clears the ball to touch. Francis (partly obscured) McNeece, Spillane and Stewart are the All Blacks coming up in support.

received from broken play and sliced through to score in a handy position for Simpson to convert. With only one point separating the teams, the All Blacks attacked relentlessly and Brown made a fine solo break from a scrum to score, O'Leary again converting. Brown made another break shortly after and in-passed to Hasell who scored. O'Leary failed. Cummings scored the final try when he beat Carr near the corner, O'Leary again missing the conversion.

The form of the New Zealand team was not impressive and the score was rather flattering. Geddes and Macky played poorly while Baird was not in international class. Despite his lack of form, the Otago centre was selected for the third Test but an injured hand forced him to withdraw. None of these three played for New Zealand again. This was also Gillespie's only appearance.

The Australian backs delighted the spectators with their nippy and fast play. Simpson, the full-back, played a fine game and all the three-quarters, especially Wogan, were very good. Tasker and Wood were brilliant at times, the latter being the best back on the ground. The best of the forwards were Watson, Horodan, Fahey and Hughes. As a whole, the Australian forwards

were inferior to the home pack but the visiting backs outplayed their opposites although O'Leary was in good form for New Zealand.

Alex Downes, the referee, had played for the South Island against the British team in 1888 and he also represented New Zealand at cricket.

NEW ZEALAND

M.J. O'LEARY (Capt.)
(Auckland)

J.V. MACKY   J.A.S. BAIRD   J.D. STEWART
(Auckland)   (Otago)   (Auckland)

A.P. SPILLANE
(South Canterbury)

W. McK. GEDDES
(Auckland)

C. BROWN
(Taranaki)

R. TAYLOR
(Taranaki)

J. BARRETT   A. WILSON
(Auckland)   (Wellington)

W. CUMMINGS   C.T. GILLESPIE   J. McNEECE
(Canterbury)   (Wellington)   (Southland)

E.W. HASELL   W.C. FRANCIS
(Canterbury)   (Wellington)

W.T. WATSON   C. O'DONNELL   A.D. HORODAN
(New South Wales) (New South Wales)   (Queensland)

E.J. FAHEY (Capt.)   P.J. MURPHY
(New South Wales)   (Queensland)

B.D. HUGHES   F. THOMPSON   E.W. CODY
(New South Wales) (New South Wales) (New South Wales)

F. WOOD
(New South Wales)

W.G. TASKER
(New South Wales)

E.T. CARR   L.W. WOGAN   H.A. JONES   D.C. SUTTOR
(New South Wales) (New South Wales) (New South Wales) (New South Wales)

R. SIMPSON
(New South Wales)

AUSTRALIA

REFEREE: Mr A.D. Downes (Otago)
ATTENDANCE: 15,000
CONDITIONS: Weather dull and cold, ground firm
HALFTIME: New Zealand 9, Australia 8

SCORERS

NEW ZEALAND	AUSTRALIA
Tries: Brown, Cummings, Hasell, Taylor, Wilson	Tries: Jones (2), Suttor
Conversions: O'Leary (3)	Conversions: Simpson (2)
Dropped goal: O'Leary	

AUSTRALIA 1

20 September, 1913

Third Test

This Test match is unique in that it is the only one played between Australia and New Zealand in which both captains were at full-back. In fact, O'Leary is the only player to lead New Zealand from this position in an international. It is also notable because the referee was a former All Black, this being one of the few occasions on which a Test has been controlled by an ex-New Zealand international.

Eric Cockroft and Fanning were new caps in the home side, the latter making his only appearance for New Zealand. His brother wore the black jersey in 1903 and 1904.

The weather was ideal for the visitors, who appreciated the hard ground. The Wallabies' running and passing were sensational but the home side was disappointing.

New Zealand scored first when Burns made a good run and kicked down to the Australian 25. Cockroft raced after the ball, picked it up and beat Dwyer but was tackled by Jones short of the line.

He threw the ball back to Fanning who, following up fast, scored near the posts for O'Leary to convert.

Australia equalised from a sensational piece of play when Wood, who gave a brilliant display throughout the game, secured at half-way and passed to Tasker, who sent on to Jones. The centre cut in and passed back to Wood, who sent on to Murphy, the ball finally going to Thompson who scored. Hughes converted with a great kick. There was no further score at halftime.

A variety of hats adorning the crowd at Lancaster Park.

NEW ZEALAND

M.J. O'LEARY (**Capt.**)
(Auckland)

E.A.P. COCKROFT   P.J. BURNS   J.D. STEWART
(South Canterbury)   (Canterbury)   (Auckland)

A.P. SPILLANE
(South Canterbury)

J.T. TILYARD
(Wellington)

C. BROWN
(Taranaki)

R. TAYLOR
(Taranaki)

J. BARRETT   A. WILSON
(Auckland)   (Wellington)

W. CUMMINGS   A.H.N. FANNING   J. McNEECE
(Canterbury)   (Canterbury)   (Southland)

E.W. HASELL   W.C. FRANCIS
(Canterbury)   (Wellington)

W.T. WATSON   H. GEORGE   D. WILLIAMS
(New South Wales)   (New South Wales)   (Queensland)

C. WALLACH   P.J. MURPHY
(New South Wales)   (Queensland)

B.D. HUGHES   F. THOMPSON   E.W. CODY
(New South Wales)   (New South Wales)   (New South Wales)

F. WOOD
(New South Wales)

W.G. TASKER
(New South Wales)

E.T. CARR   L.W. WOGAN   H.A. JONES   D.C. SUTTOR
(New South Wales)   (New South Wales)   (New South Wales)   (New South Wales)

L.J. DWYER (**Capt.**)
(New South Wales)

AUSTRALIA

REFEREE: Mr G.W. Nicholson (Auckland)
ATTENDANCE: Not recorded
CONDITIONS: Weather fine, ground hard
HALFTIME: New Zealand 5, Australia 5

SCORERS

NEW ZEALAND	**AUSTRALIA**
Try: Fanning	Tries: Suttor(2), Jones, Thompson
Conversion: O'Leary	Conversions: Hughes (2)

NEW ZEALAND 5

Lancaster Park, Christchurch

Early in the second half Australia took the lead when Wood set his backs going, Jones finally scoring a fine try which Hughes converted. Then Dudley Suttor went over following a break by Tasker and the speedy Australian wing ended the scoring when he crossed again after Wogan had thrown him a long pass from centre field. Hughes missed both conversions but the Wallabies were decisive winners.

Of the players who took part in the second and third Tests against Australia, only seven were to represent New Zealand again. Cockroft, Barrett, Francis and Wilson toured Australia in 1914 while Tilyard (as captain), Brown and Hasell

went to New South Wales in 1920.

Two notable players finished with international Rugby after this series. "Paddy" Burns began his All Black career at half-back in the second Test of 1908 and won four more caps, three at centre and one on the wing, by the end of the 1913 season. He also played six games for the South Island, being captain on four occasions. Joe O'Leary appeared in four Tests, being captain in two of them. He represented the North Island five times, three times at full-back, once at first five-eighth and once on the wing. Both Burns and O'Leary had long careers in representative football at provincial level also.

15 November, 1913

This game is classed as a Test match even though the American team consisted only of players from Californian universities and clubs. It is perhaps not generally known that Rugby was the major football code played in California between 1906 and 1919, big games often drawing up to 27,000 spectators.

This match was fast and open and was played in excellent spirit but, as the score would suggest, the home team was decisively outclassed. In fact, the All Blacks finished their tour of the Pacific Coast with a total of 610 points and had only six scored against them.

The New Zealand team, which was a very strong one, had only two new internationals, Jim Graham and Mick Cain. Both were All Blacks again in 1914 and Cain was a member of the 1919 Army team.

The American team, none of whom had toured New Zealand with the American Universities' side of 1910, contained some interesting players. Danny Carroll was an Australian who had toured Britain with the 1908-09 Wallabies. He scored two tries in the 1908 Olympic Championship in which Cornwall, chosen to represent Britain, went down to the Australians 32-3. The Wallabies played in California on their way home.

Carroll returned to California in 1912 with another Australian team (of which Wylie was also a member) and remained to study at Stanford. He served as a lieutenant in the American army in World War I, being wounded in 1918. After the war he was seconded to the Australian Army Rugby team for the King's Cup matches of 1919. He then returned to Stanford to complete a degree in geology. In 1920 Carroll was a member of the United States Rugby team which defeated France 8-0 in the final of the Olympic championship. Thus he had the unique distinction of playing Rugby for two different countries in the Olympic Games and winning a gold medal on each occasion.

According to the account of the match in *The Daily Californian,* over 10,000 persons were scattered over the three sides of the "bleachers" when Referee Hill walked on to the field at 1.45.

The spectators had paid one dollar for the best seats and fifty cents for the cheaper ones.

The field was in fair condition but it was still showing the effects of recent rain and sawdust had been sprinkled over spots which had not yet dried off. The surface was firm enough to afford the players a good footing, however, and the game was fast and open from start to finish.

The first points came after four minutes. From a scrum close to the American line, Taylor whipped the ball to Gray, who sent on to McKenzie and Roberts took a pass from the second five-eighth to swerve through a gap for a try. The centre failed to convert his own try.

After Ramage had put a couple of good kicks into touch, the New Zealand forwards broke away and McDonald picked up near the home line to force his way over. Graham missed an easy kick.

NEW ZEALAND

J.E. CUTHILL
(Otago)

A.J. McGREGOR (Auckland) R.W. ROBERTS (Taranaki) F.E. MITCHINSON (Wellington)

R.J. McKENZIE
(Wellington)

G.D. GRAY
(Canterbury)

H.M. TAYLOR
(Canterbury)

H.V. MURRAY (Canterbury)

A. McDONALD (**Capt.**) (Otago)

H. DEWAR (Taranaki)

J.T. WYLIE (Auckland) A.J. DOWNING (Auckland) J.B. GRAHAM (Otago)

G.M.V. SELLARS (Auckland) M.J. CAIN (Taranaki)

J.L. McKIM University of (California) E.B. HALL (Stanford University) G. GLASSCOCK (Barbarians)

R.R. BLASE (Stanford University) G. VOIGHT (University of Santa Clara)

W.P. DARSIE (Stanford University) W.N. KING (University of California) F.J. GARD (**Capt.**) (Stanford University)

L. CASS (Olympic Club)

M.M. MITCHELL† (Los Angeles Athletic Club)

C.A. AUSTIN (Stanford University)

J.C. URBAN (Stanford University) D.B. CARROLL (Stanford University) S.B. PEART (University of California)

J.A. RAMAGE†† (University of Santa Clara)

ALL-AMERICA

REPLACEMENTS: † Replaced by A. Knowles (University of California)
†† Replaced by H.R. Stolz (Olympic Club).
REFEREE: Mr W.W. Hill (Australia)
ATTENDANCE: 10,000
CONDITIONS: Weather fine, ground firm.
HALFTIME: New Zealand 27, All-America 3.
SCORERS

NEW ZEALAND	ALL-AMERICA
Tries: Roberts (3), McKenzie (2), Gray (2), Murray (2), McDonald (2), Wylie, McGregor	Penalty goal: Peart
Conversions: Graham (4), McDonald, Mitchinson	

ALL-AMERICA 3

Berkeley, California

The third try was quite spectacular. McKenzie kicked hard downfield and, following up fast, he dived on the ball as it rolled over the line among several defenders. McKenzie scored this try in the middle of a mud puddle and he was changing into a clean jersey as Graham kicked the goal.

The New Zealand forwards broke away from the kick-off and Dewar picked up with Downing in support. The ball was passed to McKenzie on Dewar's left and the five-eighth scored wide out. Mitchinson failed to convert.

A fine 40 yard kick to touch by Austin put the ball into All Black territory and from the line-out Gard, King and McKim broke away with Cass and Austin in support. Cuthill relieved with a long kick however and play was soon back in home territory, where Taylor dribbled the ball over the line but Ramage dived on it to save.

From the drop-out the New Zealand forwards began a passing rush which ended in a try to McDonald which Graham failed to convert. Almost immediately after the restart Taylor broke away and passed to Gray, who dropped the ball. Roberts snapped it up and ran 15 yards for a try, which Graham converted.

Then came America's only points. Louis Cass received from a scrum and fed Mow Mitchell who ran ten yards before sending on to Charlie Austin. Mitchell doubled round his second five-eighth (the Americans used the New Zealand back formation) and took the ball again. He cut through in centre field to make a brilliant break of some 35 yards, with Danny Carroll in support. Cuthill floored Mitchell with a fine tackle but the referee's whistle sounded and a penalty was awarded to the home team for interference with Carroll. Peart kicked the goal from 35 yards out and slightly to the right of the posts.

Immediately the ball was put into play again the All Black forwards romped away and Murray scored near the posts for Graham to convert. Right on halftime the All Blacks carried the ball 60 yards in a passing rush but Mitchinson was forced out and the first spell ended with the score at 27-3.

Five minutes after the kick-off Gray scored and Graham converted. Just after this try had been scored, Mitchell retired injured and Austin moved in to first five-eighth with Knowles coming on as a replacement. Mitchell, whom the All Blacks and Referee Billy Hill rated as well up to international standard, was sadly missed by the home team but Austin acquitted himself well. Incidentally, Austin was coach of the United States team which won the Olympic Rugby championship in 1924.

Taylor broke away again and passed to Gray, who found Wylie up in support and the big forward scored near the corner. Mitchinson missed. New Zealand scored again shortly after when McDonald picked up in the loose and passed to Wylie. The ball then went to Mitchinson, to Roberts and back to Mitchinson, Gray finally receiving to score. Roberts failed to convert. Then McGregor scored from a passing rush and Roberts missed the conversion.

Once more Taylor sent his backs away and McGregor came in to make the extra man. Roberts streaked away to score with Mitchinson in support. The latter took the kick and the ball dropped on the bar, bounced up and finally dropped over.

Just before the end, the All Blacks took the ball in a dribbling rush and kicked it over the American line, where Murray fell on it for the final try, which McDonald converted.

Billy Hill, the Australian referee, who also controlled the All Blacks' game against University of California on November 3, was invited by the Californian Rugby Union to referee the match between Stanford and California and to officiate in the two New Zealand games. He became President of the New South Wales Rugby Union and was a member of the International Board. He believed it was the strength of the All Black forwards which gave New Zealand its big win but he thought the whole team played very well, with Roberts and Taylor outstanding. Of the Americans, he rated Mitchell highly and paid tribute to Gard for the manner in which he captained the home team.

18 July, 1914

First Test

The referee for this game T.G. Pauling was a former New Zealand representative. He played for Wellington and was selected as a forward against the touring Queensland team in 1896 and for the Australian tour of 1897. In 1903, while refereeing the first of the two games played between New South Wales and the touring New Zealand team, he ordered the Canterbury forward, R.J. Cooke, from the field. Pauling's son played for Australia in 1936 and 1937.

The All Blacks had several players in this team who were new to international football. One of them, Jack O'Brien, made a great reputation during the 1919 Army team's tour of South Africa. He played for New Zealand again in 1920. Teddy Roberts and Bruce had toured California but neither played against All-America. Bobby Black and Irvine were other new caps. As one would expect, most of the 1914 All Blacks were later involved in World War I. Roberts, Ryan, Cain and Bruce were team-mates of O'Brien in the 1919 Army team while Black, Downing and McNeece lost their lives on active service. It is interesting to note that Taylor, who toured the Pacific Coast as a half-back, played on the wing in Australia.

This match marked the entry into international football of the famous Harald Baker, one of the most amazing all-rounders of all time. Although he tended to live in the shadow of his brother, the legendary R.L. ("Snowy") Baker, who was a top performer in no fewer than nineteen sports, the younger Baker was considered by some authorities to be the better athlete of the two. Among Harald's achievements were the winning of several Australian swimming titles, captaining the national water polo team, winning the Australian amateur heavy-weight boxing championship and, later, becoming an international boxing referee.

Baker was a keen surf lifesaver and, at Coogee in 1911, he rescued twelve bathers with the help of fellow Wallaby Jim Clarken. He served as an Australian Rugby administrator and selector and died in 1962.

Advertisement for tickets to the All Blacks' Sydney games.

Heavy rain fell the night before the Test and there were intermittent showers on the Saturday morning. The field was not muddy but it was very slippery when New Zealand kicked off into a stiff breeze. A high punt by Tasker soon had the home team on attack but Teddy Roberts found touch at half-way.

Both Wogan and Dick Roberts had unsuccessful shots from penalties, Wogan's kick being fielded by Ryan and returned to touch. From the line-out the New Zealand forwards broke away and from a ruck the ball reached Dick Roberts who made a good opening for Taylor. However, the movement was ended by Francis and Flynn, who brought the New Zealand wing to the ground.

Australia then had a turn on attack when Wood broke through a line-out. The ball went to Wogan who passed to Francis but Ryan came across and tackled the Queenslander who had Flynn unmarked outside him.

AUSTRALIA 0

Sydney Sports Ground

Baker, wearing mittens, leads an Australian attack.

A heavy squall came down just as Baker dribbled away in a grand solo effort but Ryan picked up the ball and kicked down to Dwyer. The home full-back failed to find touch and Teddy Roberts fielded the ball and kicked it out.

Australia had a chance to score when Wood broke away but instead of kicking ahead he passed and the ball went astray. The All Blacks were kept under constant pressure until a brilliant run by Black took play back into home territory.

Splendid work by Fred Thompson, Wallach and Baker had New Zealand in trouble again but the Wallaby forwards lost the ball over the line and Carr missed it when he tried to dive on it. The All Blacks forced but Australia attacked again from the drop-out and only a fine kick by O'Brien saved the visitors. Play was very even for the rest of the half and there was no score at the interval.

Wallach restarted the game and Australia attacked immediately with Baker, Watson and George taking play right to New Zealand's line where Ryan saved. Play see-sawed for a time and

both full-backs were under pressure but both showed great coolness and saved their teams with excellent line kicking.

With twenty minutes to go, Bill Francis and Bruce broke through at half-way and the former controlled the ball until he was close to the home line. The rest of the New Zealand pack was in full cry behind Francis when Tasker attempted a "speculator". McNeece snapped up the ball and hurled himself over the line near the corner flag. Graham converted with a splendid kick.

The All Blacks, encouraged by this success, went straight to the attack from the kick-off and swept into the home 25. Here Taylor was obstructed but Graham failed with the penalty attempt. This was the last occasion on which either side looked like scoring although two or three Australian movements looked promising but Downing, who played a fine game, ended them before they were properly under way.

The game throughout was strenuous, fast and closely contested and despite the bad conditions had its thrilling moments.

REFEREE: Mr T.G. Pauling (New South Wales)
ATTENDANCE: 9,000
CONDITIONS: Weather very wet, ground heavy
HALFTIME: New Zealand 0, Australia 0.

SCORERS

NEW ZEALAND	AUSTRALIA
Try: McNeece	
Conversion: Graham	

1 August, 1914

Second Test

Both teams made several changes for this Test and for some reason the home selectors changed their captain. The weather was perfect — more like summer than winter and the New Zealanders found conditions rather trying.

Australia kicked off and attacked from the start. A brilliant passing rush by the home backs threatened New Zealand's line until Francis broke away and punted ahead. The New Zealand forwards were quickly on the ball but Larry Dwyer drove them back with a long kick. An excellent rush by Wilson, Francis and Murray ended in the ball being kicked over the line and Wallaby speedster, Carr, outpacing Taylor, kicked the ball dead.

A long kick by Cockroft placed New Zealand in a good position but Dwyer relieved and the Australian forwards carried play close to the All Blacks' line. A good tackle by Taylor saved the situation and Cockroft, picking up smartly, found the line near half-way.

No illustrations of this Test could be located — the press was dominated by events in Europe. This photograph of a New Zealand attack was taken from the Queensland match played at Brisbane the week before the Test.

THE QUEENSLANDER

A brilliant passing rush by Dick Roberts, Ryan, McKenzie and Taylor led to the latter being well tackled by Dwyer close to the Wallaby line. As the ball came loose, Francis picked up and sent Taylor over unopposed after the winger had smartly regained his feet. Cockroft's kick was unsuccessful.

Australia pressed the New Zealand line from the kick-off but a kick to touch by Teddy Roberts brought relief. Bruce and Wilson took play to half-way and Taylor received on the Australian 25. Feeble tackling allowed him to score between the posts. Cockroft missed the simplest of conversions when the ball struck a post.

A period of fast, exciting play followed. Wood made a good opening but the All Blacks' tackling was excellent. Then Flynn missed a penalty from an easy position and New Zealand forced.

The visitors remained on attack and Murray made an opening for Taylor to score his third try. Cockroft failed to convert from wide out and halftime came with New Zealand leading 9-0.

Australia attacked from the restart but again

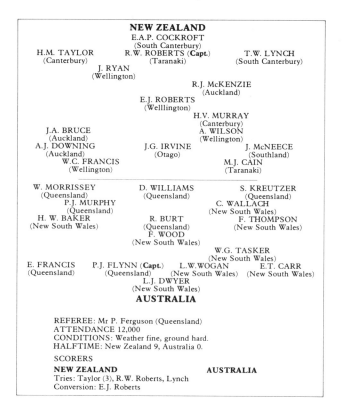

NEW ZEALAND

E.A.P. COCKROFT
(South Canterbury)

H.M. TAYLOR   R.W. ROBERTS (**Capt.**)   T.W. LYNCH
(Canterbury)   (Taranaki)   (South Canterbury)

J. RYAN
(Wellington)

R.J. McKENZIE
(Auckland)

E.J. ROBERTS
(Welllington)

H.V. MURRAY
(Canterbury)

J.A. BRUCE   A. WILSON
(Auckland)   (Wellington)

A.J. DOWNING   J.G. IRVINE   J. McNEECE
(Auckland)   (Otago)   (Southland)

W.C. FRANCIS   M.J. CAIN
(Wellington)   (Taranaki)

W. MORRISSEY   D. WILLIAMS   S. KREUTZER
(Queensland)   (Queensland)   (Queensland)

P.J. MURPHY   C. WALLACH
(Queensland)   (New South Wales)

H. W. BAKER   R. BURT   F. THOMPSON
(New South Wales)   (Queensland)   (New South Wales)

F. WOOD
(New South Wales)

W.G. TASKER
(New South Wales)

E. FRANCIS   P.J. FLYNN (**Capt.**)   L.W. WOGAN   E.T. CARR
(Queensland)   (Queensland)   (New South Wales)   (New South Wales)

L.J. DWYER
(New South Wales)

AUSTRALIA

REFEREE: Mr P. Ferguson (Queensland)
ATTENDANCE 12,000
CONDITIONS: Weather fine, ground hard.
HALFTIME: New Zealand 9, Australia 0.

SCORERS
NEW ZEALAND   **AUSTRALIA**
Tries: Taylor (3), R.W. Roberts, Lynch
Conversion: E.J. Roberts

AUSTRALIA 0

Brisbane Cricket Ground

the New Zealand defence was impregnable. Wogan broke away and punted past Cockroft but Taylor was back in support to find touch. Australia drove New Zealand back and the latter had to force. Then Wilson made a good run to get New Zealand out of trouble.

Flynn broke through the defence but his pass to Murphy was astray and the All Black forwards took the ball to their opponents' 25. Here McKenzie picked up and passed to Dick Roberts for the New Zealand captain to score between the posts. Teddy Roberts converted.

Shortly after, the ball was kicked across the field and Lynch scored an easy try. Teddy Roberts failed to convert.

Australia kept trying but the New Zealand defence held and the game ended with the visitors comfortable winners. The All Blacks showed much improvement on their first Test form and outclassed their opponents in every department.

The New Zealand Touring Team
Back row: J.G. Irvine, T.W. Lynch, A.J. Downing, J.B. Graham, J. Barrett.
Third row: W.G. Lindsay, T. Fisher, H.V. Murray, J. McNeece, J.A. Bruce, A. Wilson.
Seated: L.H. Weston, H.M. Taylor, R.W. Roberts (capt.), R.M. Issacs (manager), J. Ryan, W.C. Francis, E.A.P. Cockroft.
In front: R.S. Black, G. Loveridge, R.J. McKenzie, E.J. Roberts.
Inset: M.J. Cain **Absent:** J.G. O'Brien.

NEW ZEALAND 22

15 August, 1914

Third Test

New Zealand made only one change for this Test but there were a number of alterations to the home side, only two of the Queenslanders retaining their places. Dwyer, the former Australian captain, was moved from full-back to centre.

Australia won the toss and attacked from the kick-off. The ball was rushed to the New Zealand line where the visitors were penalised but Wogan failed at goal from an easy angle. A succession of defensive penalty kicks put New Zealand on attack but Tasker and Baker broke away from their own 25 and carried play deep into All Black territory.

Wilson started a counter-attack and from centre field Graham attempted a penalty from which Australia forced. A passing rush in which the home backs and forwards combined almost led to a try but Carr went into touch-in-goal. New Zealand gradually worked back to half-way where the forwards won a ruck and the ball went along the back line for Dick Roberts to score in the corner. Graham failed at goal.

Shortly after the restart, Lynch had an unsuccessful "pot" and Australia forced. Play was fairly even for the remainder of the half, in which the cleverness of the visitors largely nullified the disadvantage under which they were placed by the strong breeze which was blowing against them.

With the wind and sun in their favour after halftime, the All Blacks started well by scoring in the first minute. Dick Roberts cross-kicked from the corner and McKenzie caught the ball to score an easy try which Teddy Roberts failed to convert. Then the Australians opened their account with a pretty try. E. Roberts speculated on his 25 but missed the ball, which Dwyer picked up. He ran for the corner but, finding himself hemmed in, he sent a long, low pass to Wogan who ran across. Fahey failed to convert.

The pace of the game now quickened with New Zealand showing to advantage. The visiting forwards broke through the home defence and Wilson picked up near the line. He passed to Francis who dived over near the corner. Graham failed to convert.

Australia had to force down twice in quick succession but a rush by the home forwards with ball at toe had New Zealand defending desperately. At this stage Fred Wood, the home captain, was knocked out and he took no further part in the game, being removed to hospital with a lacerated ear and slight concussion.

Francis scored again from a forward rush and Dick Roberts goaled. The New Zealand captain scored his second try a few minutes later when he went over from a passing rush. The All Blacks were now playing at the top of their form but Massey-Westropp roused Australia's hopes with a great dash from the centre of the field. He ran through the visiting backs and was pulled down only inches from the line. New Zealand forced and from the drop-out Dwyer received and dropped a neat goal. The scoring ended when Taylor finished off a passing rush for Teddy Roberts to convert.

NEW ZEALAND
E.A.P. COCKROFT
(South Canterbury)

H.M. TAYLOR   R.W. ROBERTS (**Capt.**)   T.W. LYNCH
(Canterbury)   (Taranaki)   (South Canterbury)
J. RYAN
(Wellington)

R.J. McKENZIE
(Auckland)

E.J. ROBERTS
(Wellington)

H.V. MURRAY
(Canterbury)

J.B. GRAHAM   J. McNEECE
(Otago)   (Southland)
A. WILSON   J.G. IRVINE   A.J. DOWNING
(Wellington)   (Otago)   (Auckland)
W.C. FRANCIS   M.J. CAIN
(Wellington)   (Taranaki)

C.W. PRENTICE   D. WILLIAMS   H. GEORGE
(New South Wales)   (Queensland)   (New South Wales)
E.J. FAHEY   C. WALLACH
(New South Wales)   (New South Wales)
H.W. BAKER   F. THOMPSON   P.J. MURPHY
(New South Wales)   (New South Wales)   (Queensland)
F. WOOD (**Capt.**)
(New South Wales)

W.G. TASKER
(New South Wales)
M. MASSEY-WESTROPP   L.W. WOGAN   L.J. DWYER   E.T. CARR
(New South Wales)   (New South Wales) (New South Wales) (New South Wales)
B. McN. BEITH
(New South Wales)
AUSTRALIA

REFEREE: Mr C.C. Butt (New South Wales)
ATTENDANCE: 5,000
CONDITIONS: Fine and warm, ground hard
HALFTIME: New Zealand 3, Australia 0

SCORERS

NEW ZEALAND	AUSTRALIA
Tries: R.W. Roberts (2), Francis (2), McKenzie, Taylor	Try: Wogan
Conversions: R.W. Roberts, E.J. Roberts	Dropped goal: Dwyer

AUSTRALIA 7

As this match was played after the outbreak of World War I, it was given sparse coverage by the New Zealand newspapers, which were devoting almost their entire space to war news. The effect of the war on the Rugby game was profound, as it was on all sports.

After the introduction of conscription in New Zealand in 1916, participation in Rugby matches was restricted to players under 20 years of age (men between the ages of 20 and 45 were called up) so that many adult males who for one reason or another were not eligible for war service, sought other avenues of recreation. The public interest in the game also waned, especially at club level.

Rugby almost died in Australia during the war years as the New South Wales Union decided to suspend senior games for the duration. Thus the game was kept alive only by the schools. Queensland and Victorian Rugby also went into recess during the war and the road to recovery in those states was a hard one.

No international matches were played during the war but Rugby men of all nations took part in service games wherever they happened to be serving. After the war, the King's Cup competition played in Great Britain in 1919, attracted a great deal of interest. Teams from Britain, New Zealand, South Africa, Australia and Canada took part. The New Zealand side eventually won the cup with five wins and one loss (to the Australians). The New Zealanders undertook a lengthy tour of Britain and France before going to South Africa, where they played 15 games.

Thirteen All Blacks, including one non-Test player, F.R. Wilson (Auckland), lost their lives in the war. Of these the youngest was Bobby Black, who played one Test in 1914. He was killed on the Somme in 1916 at the age of 23 — the

The New Zealand manager, R. Isaacs, and the captain, Dick Roberts

youngest age at which an All Black has died. All Rugby countries, including the United States, had international players killed in the war.

NEW ZEALAND 13

13 August, 1921

First Test

The first post-war New Zealand team toured Australia in 1920 but no matches were played against fully-representative Australian teams. Thus the first true international in the postwar period was this historic first match against South Africa in 1921.

Of the New Zealand team, Storey, Belliss, Fogarty and Moffitt had toured South Africa with the Army team of 1919 while Storey, Steel, Badeley, Donald, Duncan, Moffitt and Belliss had been All Blacks in 1920.

The veteran forward, Ned Hughes reinstated from League in 1920, had represented New Zealand in 1907 and 1908. The record books give his age as 36 in 1921 while some sources put it as high as 42. His army records however show his date of birth as April 26, 1881 so he was 40 when he played in this Test series. To date he remains the oldest player to represent New Zealand.

This match marked the entry into international football of the great Mark Nicholls who, at 20 years of age, was playing the first of his 51 matches for New Zealand. Probably the greatest five-eighth ever to wear the All Black jersey, Nicholls was also an outstanding goal-kicker.

Jock Richardson, who was to be vice-captain of the famous 1924 All Blacks, was also playing his first game in the New Zealand colours. The captain, George Aitken, became a Rhodes Scholar and won a Rugby Blue at Oxford as well as playing eight games for Scotland between 1924 and 1929.

The Springboks were led in this Test by their vice-captain "Boy" Morkel, who had toured Britain in 1912. Now 35, he was still a great forward. The captain of the 1921 South African tourists, Theo Pienaar, did not play in any of the Tests and in fact he never won an international cap.

Frank Mellish had already played six times for England and was later to give long service to South African Rugby as an administrator. Gerhard Morkel, also a member of the 1912-13

Jim Moffit is prominent in this line-out. The All Blacks wore letters, rather than numbers, on their jerseys, to discourage 'pirate' programmes.

NZ FREELANCE

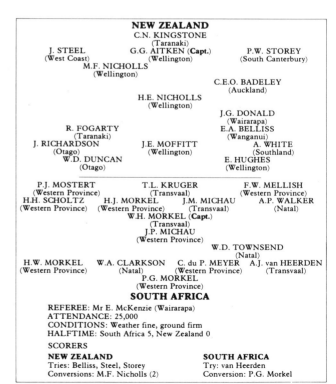

NEW ZEALAND

C.N. KINGSTONE
(Taranaki)

J. STEEL   G.G. AITKEN (**Capt.**)   P.W. STOREY
(West Coast)   (Wellington)   (South Canterbury)

M.F. NICHOLLS
(Wellington)

C.E.O. BADELEY
(Auckland)

H.E. NICHOLLS
(Wellington)

J.G. DONALD
(Wairarapa)

R. FOGARTY   E.A. BELLISS
(Taranaki)   (Wanganui)

J. RICHARDSON   J.E. MOFFITT   A. WHITE
(Otago)   (Wellington)   (Southland)

W.D. DUNCAN   E. HUGHES
(Otago)   (Wellington)

P.J. MOSTERT   T.L. KRUGER   F.W. MELLISH
(Western Province)   (Transvaal)   (Western Province)

H.H. SCHOLTZ   H.J. MORKEL   J.M. MICHAU   A.P. WALKER
(Western Province)   (Western Province)   (Transvaal)   (Natal)

W.H. MORKEL (**Capt.**)
(Transvaal)

J.P. MICHAU
(Western Province)

W.D. TOWNSEND
(Natal)

H.W. MORKEL   W.A. CLARKSON   C. du P. MEYER   A.J. van HEERDEN
(Western Province)   (Natal)   (Western Province)   (Transvaal)

P.G. MORKEL
(Western Province)

SOUTH AFRICA

REFEREE: Mr E. McKenzie (Wairarapa)
ATTENDANCE: 25,000
CONDITIONS: Weather fine, ground firm
HALFTIME: South Africa 5, New Zealand 0

SCORERS

NEW ZEALAND	SOUTH AFRICA
Tries: Belliss, Steel, Storey	Try: van Heerden
Conversions: M.F. Nicholls (2)	Conversion: P.G. Morkel

SOUTH AFRICA 5

Carisbrook, Dunedin

"Ginger" Nicholls runs from a scrum watched by the referee, Ted McKenzie. "Attie" van Heerden is the Springbok.

Springboks, considered one of the greatest of South African full-backs, had played against the 1919 Army team, as had several other members of the 1921 Springboks. Phil Mostert led his country in the Tests against the 1928 All Blacks, Theuns Kruger also appearing in two of the internationals that year. Wally Clarkson played for Natal against the 1928 team. The glamour player in the backs was the big wing, "Attie" van Heerden, who was also an Olympic Games athlete. He later played Rugby League in England.

As Aitken and Morkel led their teams out, the visitors' weight advantage was apparent. Their pack averaged 14st. 1lb. against New Zealand's 13st. 8lbs. By today's standards these forwards were very light although J.M. "Baby" Michau, at 17st and 6ft. 4ins., was a big man in anyone's language. The South African backs were also heavier, averaging 12st.4lbs. to the 11st. 8lbs. of the All Blacks.

New Zealand faced a strong sun in the first half and had trouble holding passes but Badeley and Aitken kept the home side on attack with excellent line kicking. South Africa gained most possession but Donald bustled Townsend into errors. There was no score until late in the first half when van Heerden went over in the corner following a set scrum. Gerhard Morkel converted with a fine kick.

The Springboks were almost over again early in the second half but the All Black forwards drove back into green territory. Then Aitken punted high, the bounce beat Gerhard Morkel and Belliss scored for Mark Nicholls to convert.

The second New Zealand try was one of the best ever seen in Test match Rugby. From a scrum in the centre of the field, "Ginger" Nicholls passed to Badeley who short-punted across to Steel on the right wing. The West Coaster took the ball somewhere in the vicinity of his shoulder-blade and worked it onto his shoulder as he sprinted the fifty yards to the Springboks' line. He pushed off a tackler and neither Meyer nor Gerhard Morkel, who came across fast, could reach him. Amid great enthusiasm Steel raced around behind the posts. Mark Nicholls converted. Finally, Storey scored on the blind side from a scrum to give New Zealand a rather flattering eight point win.

27 August, 1921

Second Test

Although New Zealand won the first Test of the 1921 series, Rugby writers throughout the country were not happy with the All Blacks' performance. The critics were especially concerned with the play of the inside backs. The general opinion was that "Ginger" Nicholls played very gamely and did some great work on defence but his attacking play lacked method. He took too long to clear the scrum and as a result his backline could not function properly. The New Zealand Rugby Union awarded gold medals to the best back and the best forward in each of the 1921 Tests and Nicholls received the back award for the Dunedin game. In spite of this, he was dropped for the second Test and replaced by Teddy Roberts, 1913-14-20 All Black, whom many followers and critics thought should have been New Zealand's half-back at Carisbrook. One of three brothers who played for the All Blacks (M.F. and H.G. were the others), "Ginger" Nicholls was, at 5ft 5ins and 9st 6lbs one of the smallest men to play international Rugby.

The only other change in the New Zealand backs was at half-back. Les McLean, unavailable for the first Test after selection, was fit again and he took his place in the pack at the expense of Dick Fogarty, who was relegated to the reserves. There was a third change in the team, Alf West replacing "Son" White in the forwards.

Zeller took van Heerden's place on the Springbok right wing and Meyer was moved to fly-half for the tiny Sendin to come in at centre. Only 5ft 6ins and 9st 7lbs, Sendin was an elusive runner and a courageous player. The most notable change in the South African pack was the selection of the heaviest forward, "Royal" Morkel, who weighed 17st 2lbs. The latter took the place of J.M. Michau, who received the gold medal for the best forward at Dunedin. Thus both medal winners were dropped for the second Test.

This was the first Test match played on Eden Park and the ground was packed by excited spectators. The day was like summer and the hard ground suited the visitors.

Billy Duncan and Michau vie for possession.

The All Blacks were quickly on attack, the ball going to Storey on the wing who made a good run. Then South Africa ran their backs and only a bad pass from Clarkson to Zeller spoilt a promising movement. The Springbok forwards were playing splendidly at this stage, their close passing gaining them much ground. They kept on attack and at last their efforts were rewarded when van Rooyen broke through with his backs in support. The ball went to Meyer and then to Clarkson, who had Sendin outside him with a wide overlap. The little centre took his pass and ran unopposed to the line. Gerhard Morkel kicked a splendid goal.

New Zealand attacked from the restart but were driven back by a counter-attack from which Henry Morkel almost scored, only a hard tackle by Steel stopping the Springbok on the line. Then the New Zealand forwards took the ball into Springbok territory where Roberts made a quick dash down the centre before passing to Belliss, who lost the ball in a tackle near the line. The crowd rose and roared encouragement as McLean picked up and surged over. Mark Nicholls converted to even the score.

With twelve minutes of the first half remaining, Donald passed to Badeley who kicked over

NEW ZEALAND 5

Eden Park, Auckland

The New Zealand Team on Eden Park
From left: George Aitken (capt.), Mark Nicholls, Percy Storey, Jack Steel, Ned Hughes, Ces Badeley, Teddy Roberts, Billy Duncan, Alf West, Jim Moffitt, Les McLean, "Jock" Richardson, Jim Donald, "Moke" Belliss, "Nipper" Kingstone.

the half-way line in front of Steel, but the winger knocked on. From the resulting scrum South Africa set up an attack but good defence by Nicholls and Kingstone kept the home line safe. A fumble by Badeley let Meyer through and the ball went to Sendin who passed to H. Morkel. The latter ran for the corner but was pushed out ten yards short of the line.

Meyer broke away again but was tackled by Badeley. From a scramble Gerhard Morkel found the line in his own 25 and play was still in that area when halftime sounded.

The second half began with a good run by Zeller which was stopped by Belliss. A run by the New Zealand backs broke down when Aitken dropped the ball but Steel put in a fine run shortly after. The pace of the game was very fast and the hot weather began to tell on the players, who started to slow down during the last 20 minutes. Roberts just missed with a great drop-kick from which South Africa forced. Nicholls claimed a fair catch at half-way but his attempt at goal fell short. A long kick went down to Kingstone who slipped after taking the ball. The Springboks forwards swarmed to the attack but Steel managed to kick the ball dead. From the resulting five-yard scrum Steel tried to clear but he kicked to Gerhard Morkel who dropped a fine goal.

New Zealand attacked but Michau found the line from a loose scrum. Donald and Badeley tried to open up play but a counter-attack found Meyer in All Black territory where he was tackled by Roberts. Play hovered around half-way and then Kruger led a forward rush which was stopped by Kingstone. The ball was returned to the centre of the field where it went into touch and the whistle blew for no-side.

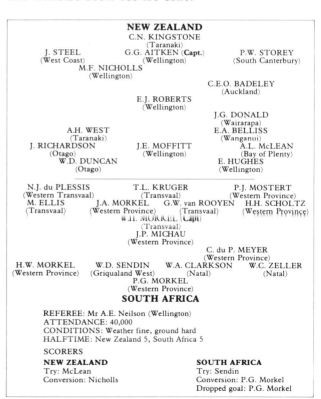

NEW ZEALAND

C.N. KINGSTONE
(Taranaki)

J. STEEL   G.G. AITKEN (**Capt.**)   P.W. STOREY
(West Coast)   (Wellington)   (South Canterbury)

M.F. NICHOLLS
(Wellington)

C.E.O. BADELEY
(Auckland)

E.J. ROBERTS
(Wellington)

J.G. DONALD
(Wairarapa)

A.H. WEST   E.A. BELLISS
(Taranaki)   (Wanganui)

J. RICHARDSON   J.E. MOFFITT   A.L. McLEAN
(Otago)   (Wellington)   (Bay of Plenty)

W.D. DUNCAN   E. HUGHES
(Otago)   (Wellington)

N.J. du PLESSIS   T.L. KRUGER   P.J. MOSTERT
(Western Transvaal)   (Transvaal)   (Western Province)

M. ELLIS   J.A. MORKEL   G.W. van ROOYEN   H.H. SCHOLTZ
(Transvaal)   (Western Province)   (Transvaal)   (Western Province)

W.H. MORKEL (Capt)
(Transvaal)

J.P. MICHAU
(Western Province)

C. du P. MEYER
(Western Province)

H.W. MORKEL   W.D. SENDIN   W.A. CLARKSON   W.C. ZELLER
(Western Province)   (Griqualand West)   (Natal)   (Natal)

P.G. MORKEL
(Western Province)

SOUTH AFRICA

REFEREE: Mr A.E. Neilson (Wellington)
ATTENDANCE: 40,000
CONDITIONS: Weather fine, ground hard
HALFTIME: New Zealand 5, South Africa 5

SCORERS

NEW ZEALAND	**SOUTH AFRICA**
Try: McLean	Try: Sendin
Conversion: Nicholls	Conversion: P.G. Morkel
	Dropped goal: P.G. Morkel

N W ZEALAND 0

17 September, 1921

Third Test

The New Zealand selectors caused a sensation by dropping the captain, George Aitken, and re-shuffling the back line. Nicholls went to centre to make room for the famous Karl Ifwersen at second five-eighth. This was Ifwersen's only game for New Zealand. He had not long been reinstated from Rugby League, at which game he also represented New Zealand.

The star backs of the New Zealand University teams of the early twenties, Keith Siddells and Billy Fea, were making their only appearance for the All Blacks. Keith Siddells normally a full-back was apparently chosen to keep the flying Springbok threequarters under control. Fea had been the youngest member of the N.Z. Army team. Charlie Fletcher had toured New South Wales in 1920 but he did not play owing to injuries. He made his first appearance for New Zealand against New South Wales on September 3, 1921 when what was virtually an All Black second fifteen were beaten by the Waratahs at Christchurch. Fogarty, normally a back row forward, returned to the side in place of Hughes.

There were also several changes in the Springbok team with van Heerden, Mellish and Walker regaining their places and new caps in Strauss and de Kock making their appearance.

Incidentally, Walker's son toured New Zealand with the 1956 Springboks.

For weeks before this match, the weather had been fine and it was anticipated that ideal conditions would prevail for the deciding Test. Shortly after six o'clock on the Friday night, however, steady rain began to fall and continued throughout the night and all day Saturday so that the game was played under appalling conditions. Nevertheless it was a good game with honours slightly in favour of the All Blacks, who played with much more purpose than they had at Auckland.

Early in the first spell the Springboks rushed play to the home line and it looked as though they would score but a force down saved the situation. A little later New Zealand had to force again but a break by Roberts put the home team on attack. However, his pass to Fea was smothered and the South Africans were put in an attacking position by Meyer, who broke through to the home line. New Zealand cleared and Zeller took a mark, from which his kick at goal was wide.

Half-back Teddy Roberts scoops up the ball as a ruck breaks up.

SOUTH AFRICA 0

Athletic Park, Wellington

As was to be expected, the game was confined mainly to the forwards but Steel made some grand runs on the wing while near the end of the first half Siddells broke away with the ball at his toe but lost control when he struck a pool of water.

The All Blacks took control early in the second half and the South African full-back was under constant pressure. He played brilliantly, finding the line time after time. Van Rooyen kept leading rushes into the New Zealand half but the home forwards, with Fletcher, West and McLean prominent, forced the visitors back. Belliss, who turned on a superb exhibition of wing-forward play, whipped the ball to Roberts who sent on to Fea but the five-eighth could not hold the pass. Steel, however, picked the ball up and was heading for the line when he slipped over in an area of surface water.

A Springbok goes back to pick up the ball on a flooded part of the ground.

Excitement ran high when Roberts made a good opening by beating four men before passing to Nicholls who had come up outside him. The centre had Steel outside him but although the right wing was unmarked Nicholls decided to cut in and was smothered by the opposing forwards. A little later, when close to their opponents' line, the home forwards kicked too hard and the ball went dead. The All Blacks kept attacking but the Springbok defence was sound and when Meyer put the ball into touch to end the game neither side had scored. With this scoreless draw the series was tied, with New Zealand ahead on points for and against. Enthusiasts in both countries now looked forward to 1928 and the All Blacks' visit to South Africa.

NEW ZEALAND

C.N. KINGSTONE
(Taranaki)

J. STEEL   M.F. NICHOLLS   S.K. SIDDELLS
(West Coast)   (Wellington)   (Wellington)

K.D. IFWERSEN
(Auckland)

W.R. FEA
(Otago)

E.J. ROBERTS (**Capt.**)
(Wellington)

E.A. BELLISS
(Wanganui)

C.J.C. FLETCHER   A.H. WEST
(North Auckland)   (Taranaki)

J. RICHARDSON   J.E. MOFFITT   A.L. McLEAN
(Otago)   (Wellington)   (Bay of Plenty)

W.D. DUNCAN   R. FOGARTY
(Otago)   (Taranaki)

F.W. MELLISH   P.J. MOSTERT   N.J. du PLESSIS
(Western Province)   (Western Province)   (Western Province)

M. ELLIS   J.A. MORKEL   G.W. van ROOYEN   A.P. WALKER
(Transvaal)   (Western Province) (Transvaal)   (Natal)

W.H. MORKEL (**Capt.**)
(Transvaal)

J.P. MICHAU
(Western Province)

J.S. de KOCK
(Western Province)

W.C. ZELLER   C. du P. MEYER   S.S.F. STRAUSS   A.J. van HEERDEN
(Natal)   (Western Province) (Griqualand West) (Transvaal)

P.G. MORKEL
(Western Province)

SOUTH AFRICA

REFEREE: Mr A.E. Neilson (Wellington)
ATTENDANCE: 18,000
CONDITIONS: Weather very wet, ground muddy,
            with large areas of surface water
HALFTIME: New Zealand 0, South Africa 0

1 November, 1924

This was the first international played by the 1924 All Blacks, perhaps the most famous of all New Zealand teams. Some of the immortals of New Zealand Rugby history made their Test debut in this game.

The 19 year old full-back, George Nepia, who played in every match of the tour, is still widely considered to be one of the greatest players of all time. Many older Rugby writers rate him the finest full-back ever. This great Maori footballer played forty-six games for New Zealand between 1924 and 1930 and made the final All Black trial for the 1935 British tour. He later turned to Rugby League and played professionally for the Streatham and Mitchum club in England. He also represented New Zealand at League but he was subsequently reinstated to Rugby and was a leading referee for some years.

"Snowy" Svenson had toured New South Wales in 1922 but he did not play on the tour owing to injury. A small, compact wing, he was a prolific try-scorer and a useful place-kicker who made thirty-four appearances for his country before he retired in 1926.

The centre, Fred Lucas, also had a long career in Test football and had played against New South Wales in 1923. Equally at home at wing or centre, Lucas played forty-one matches for New Zealand including seven Tests and was captain of Auckland for several seasons. He later became an Auckland, North Island and New Zealand selector.

Gus Hart was making his only Test appearance and his first-class career was fairly brief but in seventeen games for his country he scored 23 tries.

The second five-eighth, Bert Cooke, is one of the legendary figures of New Zealand Rugby. Those who were fortunate enough to see him play regard him as the greatest mid-field back of all time for there was something of the genius about him. Cooke also played for his country at Rugby League but like Nepia he was reinstated and became a successful coach.

Mark Nicholls had of course made his All Black debut in 1921 but Bill Dalley, the half-

Richardson leads out the All Blacks followed by Cupples and Brownlie.

back, was another newcomer to Test Rugby. Noted for his ruggedness, Dalley was a clever player who reached his peak on the 1928 tour of South Africa.

Jim Parker, the wing-forward, won selection ahead of the team captain, Cliff Porter who was injured. Parker, who scored 15 tries on the 1924 tour (he scored a further 11 points in Canada), was very fast and ideally equipped for a wing-forward. However, 1924 was his only year as an All Black.

Bill Irvine and Quentin Donald, the hookers, had both played against New South Wales in 1923. Great exponents of their craft in the two-fronted scrum they both had long careers in first-class Rugby although Donald faded from the international scene after 1924.

IRELAND 0

Lansdowne Road, Dublin

Maurice Brownlie, another of the all-time "greats" of New Zealand Rugby, was playing his first Test but he had been an All Black since 1922. He eventually played sixty-one matches in the black jersey and climaxed a brilliant career by captaining the 1928 All Blacks in South Africa. White and Richardson had both been All Blacks since 1921, Cupples since 1922 and Masters in 1923.

In the Irish team the best-known players were George Stephenson, Ernie Crawford and Jammie Clinch, who won over 100 caps among them. Also playing in this match were two brothers from the famous Hewitt family. Five of this family played for Ireland between 1925 and 1965.

Heavy rain fell for most of the game but the ground was packed when the teams ran out. Nicholls kicked off against the breeze but there was a New Zealander in front and from the resulting scrum the All Blacks were penalised. G. Stephenson found touch in the visitors' twenty-five but the black forwards won the line-out and

their backs swept into Irish territory, only to be driven back by the home captain, who took a mark. His punt was fielded by Nepia but the full-back missed touch and Clinch returned play to the New Zealand twenty-five.

Most of the action was confined to the forwards and when the backs on either side broke away they were stopped by fierce tackling. Tom Hewitt was almost over but Cooke and Nicholls brought him down. The ball went loose, Richardson and White taking it back into home territory. McDowell went down on the ball but Cooke obtained possession and ran until T. Hewitt tackled him. The ball went out to Nicholls who drew G. Stephenson before passing to Lucas. Nicholls doubled round for the return pass and on being tackled he sent on to Hart. The All Black left wing flew for the corner but Crawford flung him into touch at the corner flag amid great excitement.

Near halftime the Irish full-back again aroused the crowd when he narrowly failed to kick a penalty goal. Then an All Black passing rush, in which all the backs took part, ended with Hart again being stopped by Crawford in the left corner. Halftime came with no score on the board.

Seven minutes after the restart, Harry Stephenson picked up in front of his posts and ran across field. He was almost clear when Cooke brought him down and he lost the ball but Lucas picked it up and sent Svenson in for a try ten yards from the corner. Nepia missed the goal. Three minutes later the referee awarded New Zealand a penalty for off-side play in the middle of the Irish twenty-five and Nicholls had no difficulty in adding three points.

An injury to Frank Hewitt left Ireland a man short but the home team held the visitors very well, giving them some anxious moments when G. Stephenson sent his brother away on a determined run. The Irish wing was forced into touch however. Rain was falling in torrents and the light was very bad but few spectators left their seats as play grew very exciting towards the end. There was no further scoring however and New Zealand won an even and entertaining game.

NEW ZEALAND

G. NEPIA
(Hawke's Bay)

K.S. SVENSON   F.W. LUCAS   A.H. HART
(Wellington)   (Auckland)   (Taranaki)

A.E. COOKE
(Auckland)

M.F. NICHOLLS
(Wellington)

W.C. DALLEY
(Canterbury)

J.H. PARKER
(Canterbury)

L.F. CUPPLES   A. WHITE
(Bay of Plenty)   (Southland)
M.J. BROWNLIE   R.R. MASTERS   J. RICHARDSON (Capt.)
(Hawke's Bay)   (Canterbury)   (Southland)
Q. DONALD   W.R. IRVINE
(Wairarapa)   (Hawke's Bay)

A.W. SPAIN   R.J. COLLOPY   T.N. BRAND
(University College Dublin) (Bective Rangers) (North of Ireland)
J. McVICKER   T.A. McCLELLAND
(Collegians)   (Queen's University)
J.D. CLINCH   R.Y. CRICHTON   W.R.F. COLLIS
(Dublin University) (Dublin University) (Harlequins)

Scrum packed 3 - 2 -3 with no set positions
J.C. McDOWELL
(Instonians)

F.S. HEWITT
(Instonians)
T.R. HEWITT J.B. GARDINER G.V. STEPHENSON H.W.V. STEPHENSON
(Queen's   (North of Ireland) (Queen's University) (Capt.)
University)   (United Services)

W.E. CRAWFORD
(Lansdowne)

IRELAND

REFEREE: Mr A.E. Freethy (Wales)
ATTENDANCE: 25,000
CONDITIONS: Weather wet, ground heavy
HALFTIME: New Zealand 0, Ireland 0

SCORERS
NEW ZEALAND   **IRELAND**
Try: Svenson
Penalty goal: Nicholls

29 November, 1924

There were three new Test players in the All Black team for this match. Jimmy Mill had played against New South Wales in 1923 but this was his first full international. One of New Zealand's finest halves, Mill played thirty-three games as an All Black between 1923 and 1930. Neil McGregor and Cyril Brownlie, Maurice's brother, were new All Blacks in 1924 but both had long careers as New Zealand representatives appearing in twenty-seven and thirty-one matches respectively in the black jersey.

The Welsh captain, Jack Wetter, had first played for Wales in 1914. He won the Distinguished Conduct Medal during World War I. After the war, Wetter resumed his international Rugby career and was also capped for Wales at baseball. A versatile player, he had appeared for his country at scrum-half, fly-half and centre and was now playing as an extra half to try to combat the New Zealand wing-forward. Thus the home team had only seven forwards, as they had in 1905 against the All Blacks. Dai Parker later toured New Zealand with the British team in 1930.

This was the game which the 1924 All Blacks really wanted to win to avenge the somewhat unlucky loss to Wales by their predecessors of 1905.

The start of the game was delayed owing to a dispute over the ball but finally Wales kicked off against a slight breeze. The home forwards charged into New Zealand's half but Cooke drove them back with a fine kick. The All Blacks soon had Wales under pressure and a number of penalties were incurred by the Welsh forwards for offside play. From one of these, Nicholls steered the ball between the posts and the visitors were three points up after ten minutes.

New Zealand continued to attack and Nicholls, who played brilliantly throughout, was nearly over but he was collared on the line. Wales

The New Zealand Team
Back row: S.S.M. Dean (manager), J.L. Simpson (touch judge), J. Steel, J.H. Parker, M.J. Brownlie, C.J. Brownlie, L.F. Cupples, R.R. Masters, W. Dustin and G. Payne (visitors).
Second row: J. Brunton (referee), W.R. Irvine, Q. Donald, G. Nepia, C.G. Porter (tour capt.), J. Richardson (capt.), M.F. Nicholls, J.J. Mill, A.E. Cooke.
In front: K.S. Svenson, N.P. McGregor.

J. THOMAS

WALES 0

St. Helen's, Swansea

George Nepia makes a determined run.

relieved but the All Blacks kept up the pressure. Fifteen yards from the line, M. Brownlie gained possession and bullocked his way through a number of tackles to score a good try, which Nicholls converted.

At this stage Wetter temporarily retired after being knocked out and as he walked off the field rain began to fall. The wet ball did not deter the All Blacks however and their forwards continued to dominate the game. With ten minutes to go to halftime the visiting pack drove the ball to the Welsh line where there was a scramble from which Irvine emerged with the ball. He fell across the line for a try which Nicholls narrowly failed to convert. Thus the All Blacks had a handy 11-0 lead at the end of the first spell.

Wetter returned to the field after halftime but he was limping badly and was obviously little better than a passenger. He went into the pack but was injured again shortly after the restart.

The Welsh forwards had the New Zealand line under siege for some time but magnificent line-kicking by Nepia drove them back. Then Cooke, Steel and Parker broke away in a passing rush from which Cooke appeared to have scored, but the try was disallowed.

Both full-backs were playing brilliantly, their fielding and kicking arousing much enthusiasm among the crowd. Once more Wales pushed the visitors back and play was confined to the forwards until Steel made a powerful burst from which he almost scored. From a scrum near the corner, Mill worked the blindside with Svenson and the latter ran over for a try. Nicholls missed.

Although New Zealand now had an insuperable lead, the home team did not give up. Rowe Harding made a splendid run through the New Zealand backs but a solid tackle by Nepia ended the home team's hopes.

The light was beginning to fade in the closing stages but there was one more try to come. From a rush started by Cooke, who broke away with ball at toe, the All Blacks dribbled down field until Irvine took the ball over between the posts for a sensational try, which Nicholls converted. The 1905 defeat had surely been avenged.

NEW ZEALAND

G. NEPIA
(Hawke's Bay)

J. STEEL   A.E. COOKE   K.S. SVENSON
(West Coast)   (Auckland)   (Wellington)

M.F. NICHOLLS
(Wellington)

N.P. McGREGOR
(Canterbury)

J.J. MILL
(Hawke's Bay)

J.H. PARKER
(Canterbury)

L.F. CUPPLES   J. RICHARDSON (Capt.)
(Bay of Plenty)   (Southland)
M.J. BROWNLIE   R.R. MASTERS   C.J. BROWNLIE
(Hawke's Bay)   (Canterbury)   (Hawke's Bay)
Q. DONALD   W.R. IRVINE
(Wairarapa)   (Hawke's Bay)

D. PARKER   J. GORE   D. MARSDEN-JONES
(Swansea)   (Blaina)   (Cardiff)
C. WILLIAMS   S. MORRIS
(Llanelly)   (Cross Keys)
D.D. HIDDLESTONE   C.H. PUGH
(Neath)   (Pontypool)
                               J. WETTER (Capt.)
                               (Newport)

W.J. DELAHAY
(Cardiff)

E. WILLIAMS
(Neath)

W.R. HARDING   A. JENKINS   A.R. STOCK   E. FINCH
(Swansea)   (Llanelly)   (Newport)   (Llanelly)
T.A. JOHNSON
(Cardiff)

WALES

REFEREE: Colonel J. Brunton (England)
ATTENDANCE: 50,000
CONDITIONS: Weather fine then rain, ground firm
HALFTIME: New Zealand 11, Wales 0

SCORERS
NEW ZEALAND   **WALES**
Tries: Irvine (2), M.J. Brownlie,
Svenson
Conversions: Nicholls (2)
Penalty goal: Nicholls

NEW ZEALAND 17

3 January, 1925

The Prince of Wales was among the spectators when the teams took the field for the All Blacks' final match in Britain. With fine weather, a firm ground and very little wind, the stage was set for a great Test match as the unbeaten All Blacks faced an English team of considerable quality.

The full-back, Jim Brough, played only two games for England before turning to Rugby League, at which game he represented Great Britain against Australia and New Zealand. He was a very able footballer in both codes and later became prominent in League administration. Gibbs, on the left wing, was exceptionally fast and England had a clever pair behind the scrum.

However, it was in the forwards that the home team's strength lay. Captained by the legendary W.W. Wakefield (later Lord Wakefield of Kendal), one of the immortals of the Rugby game, this English side had a very powerful pack. It included such experienced forwards as Cove-Smith, who captained the British team in South Africa in 1924, Voyce, winner of 27 caps and later

to become President of the Rugby Union, Blakiston and Tucker, as well as Wakefield himself, who was capped 31 times.

Richardson won the toss and England kicked off. Svenson ran hard and made ground but was put down by vigorous tackling. A loose maul developed in which play became over-zealous and the referee issued a general warning to the forwards. Three minutes later the warning was repeated. Then there was a loud blast on the whistle, a scramble was broken up and Cyril Brownlie was ordered from the field. It would seem that Brownlie was unfortunate in being singled out for such drastic treatment.

The All Blacks now had to bring Parker into the pack and play with fourteen men.

About ten minutes after Brownlie's dismissal, England opened the scoring when the white pack wheeled a scrum and took the ball away at their feet. Voyce slipped the ball across Nepia and Cove-Smith dashed through to fall on it over the line. This stung the All Blacks into action and

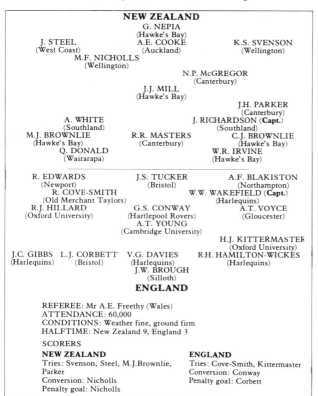

```
                    NEW ZEALAND
                      G. NEPIA
                    (Hawke's Bay)
J. STEEL            A.E. COOKE          K.S. SVENSON
(West Coast)         (Auckland)          (Wellington)
            M.F. NICHOLLS
             (Wellington)
                              N.P. McGREGOR
                               (Canterbury)
              J.J. MILL
            (Hawke's Bay)
                                       J.H. PARKER
                                       (Canterbury)
        A. WHITE         J. RICHARDSON (Capt.)
        (Southland)          (Southland)
 M.J. BROWNLIE     R.R. MASTERS        C.J. BROWNLIE
 (Hawke's Bay)     (Canterbury)        (Hawke's Bay)
        Q. DONALD              W.R. IRVINE
        (Wairarapa)            (Hawke's Bay)

 R. EDWARDS        J.S. TUCKER         A.F. BLAKISTON
  (Newport)         (Bristol)          (Northampton)
     R. COVE-SMITH           W.W. WAKEFIELD (Capt.)
  (Old Merchant Taylors)        (Harlequins)
 R.J. HILLARD      G.S. CONWAY          A.T. VOYCE
(Oxford University) (Hartlepool Rovers)  (Gloucester)
                    A.T. YOUNG
               (Cambridge University)
                                    H.J. KITTERMASTER
                                    (Oxford University)
J.C. GIBBS  L.J. CORBETT  V.G. DAVIES  R.H. HAMILTON-WICKES
(Harlequins)  (Bristol)   (Harlequins)   (Harlequins)
                    J.W. BROUGH
                     (Silloth)
                    ENGLAND
```

REFEREE: Mr A.E. Freethy (Wales)
ATTENDANCE: 60,000
CONDITIONS: Weather fine, ground firm
HALFTIME: New Zealand 9, England 3

SCORERS

NEW ZEALAND
Tries: Svenson, Steel, M.J.Brownlie, Parker
Conversion: Nicholls
Penalty goal: Nicholls

ENGLAND
Tries: Cove-Smith, Kittermaster
Conversion: Conway
Penalty goal: Corbett

Maurice Brownlie scores in the tackle of Gibbs.

NZ RUGBY MUSEUM

ENGLAND 11

Twickenham, London

Referee Albert Freethy sends Cyril Brownlie off the field in the first few minutes of the game.

Maurice Brownlie, undoubtedly furious at his brother's ordering-off, picked up a loose ball and hurtled towards the English line. He was stopped but the All Blacks switched the attack and Svenson scored in the corner.

New Zealand went into the lead when Mill passed to Steel on the blind side and the burly West Coaster broke through tackles to touch down by the corner flag. Some of the English players and a group of spectators believed Steel had put his foot into touch but when the referee questioned the touch-judge Mr Len Simpson, a well known New Zealand referee who had controlled a Test against Australia in 1913, that gentleman had no hesitation in declaring that Steel had not stepped out. Then right on halftime Hillard was caught offside in front of the posts and Nicholls kicked an easy goal.

New Zealand went further ahead when Maurice Brownlie forced his way over from a maul and Nicholls converted. A little later Parker scored from a dive in the corner although Svenson is sometimes credited with this try. The corner flag was knocked over but the try was awarded and the All Blacks were now fourteen points ahead.

The Englishmen were not done with however. Corbett drop-kicked a penalty goal and then Hamilton-Wickes made a break before passing to Kittermaster who scored the try of the match by running from half-way to score behind the posts. Conway converted.

This victory retained the All Blacks' unbeaten record and to date they remain the only team to tour the British Isles without losing or drawing a game, although they did not play Scotland, the triple crown winners in 1924-25.

77

18 January, 1925

This was the only Test played on this tour by the 1924 All Black captain, Cliff Porter, who had been stood down from two internationals in favour of Parker and had been injured after selection for the Irish Test. Porter first played for New Zealand in 1923 against New South Wales and he eventually made 41 appearances for his country. One of the most successful All Black captains, he led New Zealand teams in 1924-25-26-28-29-30. He was one of the finest exponents of the old wing-forward position and his omission from the 1928 team to South Africa came as a shock to his many admirers. He did however lead New Zealand in the home series against New South Wales that year.

Chilo, the French full-back, was a fine athlete. He was long-jump and triple-jump champion of France and earned his living as a P.T. instructor.

The fly-half, Yves du Manoir, was a regular army officer who won eight caps between 1924 and 1927. He was killed in a plane crash on January 2, 1928 the morning of the France v. Scotland match, for which he had not been selected. His statue stands at the main entrance of the Stade Yves du Manoir, in Colombes, which is named after him. Du Manoir came from a noble family in Brittany. His death at the early age of 23 was a severe blow to French Rugby.

Alex Bioussa had a reputation for rough play and was banished from the French team after the Welsh game of 1930, his eighteenth for France. Ribere won 34 caps, which was a French record until the advent of Jean Prat. Cassayet was another player who died young, being a cancer victim in 1927.

Long before the game started the ground was packed. The day was hot enough for summer and there was not a breath of wind. Both sides threw the ball around and gave a splendid exhibition of open Rugby. The game was played in the same excellent spirit that prevailed in the 1906 encounter between the two countries and the crowd, which applauded both teams with equal generosity, thoroughly enjoyed the match.

Porter opened the scoring after five minutes following a passing bout in which he twice hand-

Captain Cliff Porter, played his only international of the tour in this match scoring the first of New Zealand's eight tries.

led the ball. Nicholls missed from wide out. Three minutes later Steel scored between the posts after a thrilling passing rush and Nicholls added the extra points. The Frenchmen then launched a determined attack with du Manoir making a brilliant run but Piteu elected to kick when a pass might have resulted in a try.

Cooke cut through and passed to Lucas who outpaced the opposition to run Svenson in for a good try which Nicholls could not convert. Svenson had now completed the unique feat of scoring tries in each of the internationals on tour. A break from a line-out by Richardson was backed by Cyril Brownlie, who passed to White for the Southland forward to score after a great sprint. Jock Richardson then galloped from well

NZ RUGBY MUSEUM

FRANCE 6

Stade Des Ponts Jumeaux, Toulouse

out to score a fine individual try. Both of the latter tries were unconverted and at halftime New Zealand led 17-0.

Early in the second half du Manoir made a fine run which ended in touch but a quick throw-in gave Cassayet a try, but du Manoir failed to convert. France rallied again and a forward rush resulted in a try to Ribere. For some minutes the French held the upper hand and it was only superb defence by Cooke and Nepia which kept the home team from scoring again.

Suddenly Nicholls swung the game New Zealand's way once more. Dummying, swerving and side-stepping, he beat one opponent after another and his short punt through almost led to a try by Cooke. The All Blacks kept on attack and Irvine dived over, Nepia failing to convert. A passing

The cover of an unpublished book on the 1924-25 tour by manager, Stan Dean.

rush in which forwards and backs took part ended in a try by Cooke converted by Nicholls and towards the end of the game Svenson centre-kicked for Cooke to score again, Nicholls once more adding the extra points.

It is interesting to note that 115 journalists covered this game — 15 from the British Isles, 20 from Paris and 80 from the rest of France.

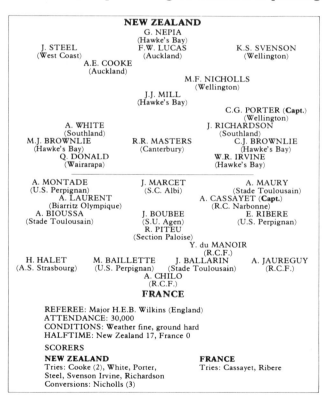

NEW ZEALAND

G. NEPIA
(Hawke's Bay)

J. STEEL   F.W. LUCAS   K.S. SVENSON
(West Coast)   (Auckland)   (Wellington)

A.E. COOKE
(Auckland)

M.F. NICHOLLS
(Wellington)

J.J. MILL
(Hawke's Bay)

C.G. PORTER (**Capt.**)
(Wellington)

A. WHITE   J. RICHARDSON
(Southland)   (Southland)

M.J. BROWNLIE   R.R. MASTERS   C.J. BROWNLIE
(Hawke's Bay)   (Canterbury)   (Hawke's Bay)

Q. DONALD   W.R. IRVINE
(Wairarapa)   (Hawke's Bay)

A. MONTADE   J. MARCET   A. MAURY
(U.S. Perpignan)   (S.C. Albi)   (Stade Toulousain)

A. LAURENT   A. CASSAYET (**Capt.**)
(Biarritz Olympique)   (R.C. Narbonne)

A. BIOUSSA   J. BOUBEE   E. RIBERE
(Stade Toulousain)   (S.U. Agen)   (U.S. Perpignan)

R. PITEU
(Section Paloise)

Y. du MANOIR
(R.C.F.)

H. HALET   M. BAILLETTE   J. BALLARIN   A. JAUREGUY
(A.S. Strasbourg)   (U.S. Perpignan)   (Stade Toulousain)   (R.C.F.)

A. CHILO
(R.C.F.)

FRANCE

REFEREE: Major H.E.B. Wilkins (England)
ATTENDANCE: 30,000
CONDITIONS: Weather fine, ground hard
HALFTIME: New Zealand 17, France 0

SCORERS

NEW ZEALAND   **FRANCE**
Tries: Cooke (2), White, Porter,   Tries: Cassayet, Ribere
Steel, Svenson Irvine, Richardson
Conversions: Nicholls (3)

NZ RUGBY MUSEUM

30 June, 1928

First Test

Apart from Dalley and Brownlie, none of the All Blacks in this first Test team of 1928 had played in a full-scale international. Dave Lindsay, a dental student from Otago University, was chosen as a three-quarter but he became the number one full-back on the tour. An injury sustained in South Africa cut short his football career although he played for Otago against the 1930 British team. Alan Robilliard had toured with the 1924 All Blacks but he played only four times in Britain owing to injuries. He played for New Zealand again in 1925 and 1926.

Syd Carleton and Bert Grenside were new All Blacks, the former gaining selection for the 1928 tour when A.E. Cooke withdrew from the team for business reasons. Archie Strang was also new to All Black honours but Lance Johnson had toured New South Wales in 1925.

The selection of George Scrimshaw ahead of Cliff Porter for the South African tour came as a shock to Rugby followers. Although a capable wing-forward with plenty of pace, Scrimshaw was not in Porter's class and he did not play for New Zealand again after the tour.

Ron Stewart first represented his country in 1923 and he toured Britain in 1924 but injuries limited his appearances. He was an All Black again in 1925 and 1926 and he played one Test against Great Britain in 1930. Altogether he appeared 39 times in the All Black jersey.

Bill Hazlett toured Australia in 1926 and later took part in all four Tests against the British team in 1930. He is now a well known racing man. Swin Hadley was another newcomer to New Zealand honours and for some inexplicable reason he did not play for his country again after the 1928 tour. "Tuna" Swain had been a reserve against New South Wales in 1923 while "Bunny" Finlayson played for New Zealand in 1925 and 1926, Geoff Alley also being a member of the 1926 team. Finlayson also played in two Tests in 1930.

Jackie Tindall, Phil Mostert and Theuns Kruger were 1921 Springboks in New Zealand while Phil Nel, as captain, and Pierre de Villiers

were to come here in 1937. The most famous of the home players in this Test however was Bennie Osler who was probably the greatest South African inside back of all time. A brilliant tactician, he controlled the game with ruthless efficiency and, together with the Springbok pack, laid the foundation for this big win. Osler's brother, Stanley, who was playing at centre, later went to Oxford as a Rhodes Scholar where he won a Rugby Blue. He played for Oxford against the 1931 Springboks, of whom his brother was captain.

The 1928 All Blacks were considered a great side on selection, yet the 17-0 defeat they suffered in the first Test, remains New Zealand's biggest defeat in an international match. With nine members of the 1924 side in their ranks, the 1928 tourists were not lacking in experience but there were certain defections which weakened the team.

Nepia and Mill were both barred from selection on racial grounds while Cooke's withdrawal

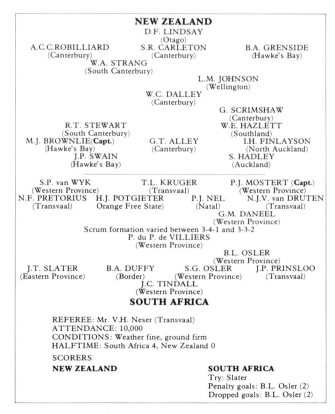

NEW ZEALAND

D.F. LINDSAY
(Otago)

A.C.C. ROBILLIARD   S.R. CARLETON   B.A. GRENSIDE
(Canterbury)   (Canterbury)   (Hawke's Bay)

W.A. STRANG
(South Canterbury)

L.M. JOHNSON
(Wellington)

W.C. DALLEY
(Canterbury)

G. SCRIMSHAW
(Canterbury)

R.T. STEWART   W.E. HAZLETT
(South Canterbury)   (Southland)

M.J. BROWNLIE (**Capt.**)   G.T. ALLEY   I.H. FINLAYSON
(Hawke's Bay)   (Canterbury)   (North Auckland)

J.P. SWAIN   S. HADLEY
(Hawke's Bay)   (Auckland)

S.P. van WYK   T.L. KRUGER   P.J. MOSTERT (**Capt.**)
(Western Province)   (Transvaal)   (Western Province)

N.F. PRETORIUS   H.J. POTGIETER   P.J. NEL   N.J.V. van DRUTEN
(Transvaal)   Orange Free State)   (Natal)   (Transvaal)

G.M. DANEEL
(Western Province)

Scrum formation varied between 3-4-1 and 3-3-2

P. du P. de VILLIERS
(Western Province)

B.L. OSLER
(Western Province)

J.T. SLATER   B.A. DUFFY   S.G. OSLER   J.P. PRINSLOO
(Eastern Province)   (Border)   (Western Province)   (Transvaal)

J.C. TINDALL
(Western Province)

SOUTH AFRICA

REFEREE: Mr. V.H. Neser (Transvaal)
ATTENDANCE: 10,000
CONDITIONS: Weather fine, ground firm
HALFTIME: South Africa 4, New Zealand 0

SCORERS

NEW ZEALAND	SOUTH AFRICA
	Try: Slater
	Penalty goals: B.L. Osler (2)
	Dropped goals: B.L. Osler (2)

N W ZEALAND 0

SPRINGBOK VERSUS KIWI —
THE GREAT STRUGGLE FOR THE WORLD'S
RUGBY SUPREMACY ——

Slater had a great chance to open the scoring when he burst away with Stanley Osler in support and only Lindsay to beat, but ten yards from the line the All Black full-back collared him in possession with Osler looking on. The Springboks kept pressing however and Bennie Osler potted a good goal from 35 yards out. At this stage both Duffy and Grenside had been laid out and neither was contributing much to the game. Robilliard was almost over but good tackling by Prinsloo stopped him. Tindall was under pressure when the halftime whistle went with the home side four points up.

South Africa resumed with only fourteen men, for Duffy had received concussion. Pretorius went to the wing, leaving the packs equal. Early in the second half South Africa heeled from a loose ruck and de Villiers passed to Bennie Osler who dropped a magnificent goal from 40 yards out. The All Blacks carried play into their opponents' half from the kick-off but a 50 yard kick by van Druten pegged the visitors back to their own 25.

A couple of minutes later Brownlie was caught offside and Bennie Osler kicked a goal. Only brilliant tackling by Lindsay saved a certain try following a Springbok back movement and the home team appeared to be well on top. South Africa went further ahead when Johnson was penalised for a late tackle on Osler after the Springbok fly-half had kicked a high one down to Lindsay. Since the kick was rightly given where the ball landed, Osler had no difficulty in kicking the goal.

From now on there was only one team in the game. Brilliant play by Stanley Osler almost had Mostert over and Prinsloo actually crossed the line but dropped the ball following a move on the blind side. A little later Stanley Osler was held up on the line after making a brilliant run. Finally, eight minutes from time, de Villiers passed to Bennie Osler from a set scrum in the All Blacks' 25. Osler ran on the blind side and passed to Slater who ran infield and wove his way through the defence to score a magnificent try. Bennie Osler failed to convert but the Springboks were handsome winners.

was a bombshell. Also the omission of Nicholls from the first three Tests was hard to understand, even though Strang and Johnson had been playing particularly well. The only survivor of the 1921 series in the 1928 All Blacks and the genius of the 1924 team, Nicholls played a vital part in the winning of the fourth Test and was rated by Bennie Osler as the best player he ever marked.

The weather was fine and the turf in excellent order when Brownlie kicked off with the sun behind him. The All Blacks were on attack early, with Brownlie obtaining plenty of line-out possession to set his backs going. The Springbok defence was very tight however and the home forwards established a superiority in the set scrums in which they varied their packing between 3-3-2 and 3-4-1. The forwards changed their scrum positions from time to time. It was permissable under the rules then prevailing to take scrums instead of line-outs and Mostert took advantage of this to wear the seven New Zealand forwards down.

21 July, 1928

Second Test

The only change in the New Zealand team from the first Test was the dropping of Scrimshaw and the moving of Stewart to his place, with McWilliams coming into the pack to play his first international game. Tall, rangy and fast, McWilliams played great football on this tour and eventually made 27 appearances as an All Black before he retired in 1930. It was in this Test that the use of the "loose head" was evolved. As soon as the All Black pack went down, Stewart, as wingforward, would get down as an extra hooker on the side that the ball was to be put in. This upset the South Africans considerably.

This Test was the first played by the famous Gerry Brand, one of the greatest South African full-backs, who was to score 100 points on the 1937 tour of New Zealand. He was a surprise selection in this game on the wing, a position he did not normally occupy, and he had not played for his province in 1928. He came in to replace the injured Slater, Prinsloo being dropped in favour of the Natal speedster Tod, who had played so well for Northern Provinces against the All Blacks, scoring two spectacular tries. Stanley Osler was on the injured list and his absence weakened the Springbok three-quarters.

The dropping of Pierre de Villiers came as a surprise for he gave a fine display in the first Test

South African fowards about to pounce upon Dalley. Robilliard is on hand to help his half-back.

SOUTH AFRICA 6

Ellis Park, Johannesburg

but the veteran, Daunce Devine, who had been the Springbok half against the 1924 British team, was in great form and he had been largely responsible for his team's win against the All Blacks in the first Transvaal game. Many Rugby followers believe that Danie Craven first introduced the dive pass but Devine was an expert at it long before Craven ever played first-class football.

New Zealand won the toss and Osler kicked off. The home team had the better of the early part of the game and twice the Springboks went close to scoring, once when Brand was tackled a yard from the line and again when the same player centre-kicked only to have Pretorius knock-on when a try was there for the taking.

The Springboks played a man short for fifteen minutes when Tod had to leave the field for attention but they kept on the attack and from an All Black drop-out, Mostert claimed a mark from which he potted a 45 yard goal to open the scoring. Brand then hit a post with a drop-kick from a penalty and the All Blacks were still defending desperately. From about half-way through the first spell however the New Zealand forwards began to get on top and, near the interval, Lindsay evened the scores with a penalty goal.

The black forwards attacked from the beginning of the second half and only good line-kicking by Osler and Brand kept the home line safe. An injury to Hadley reduced the efficiency of the All Black scrum, with Hazlett going to hooker and Hadley remaining on as an extra rover. Osler put his team ahead again with a penalty from in front of the posts and Lindsay had a chance to equalise shortly after when Devine, who had a bad game, was penalised for picking out of the scrum but the kick just missed. Then with ten minutes to go the ball came out on the open side from a scrum in the South African 25. Stewart picked up and passed to Strang who sent the ball straight between the posts with a fine drop-kick. There was no further scoring and a rather drab game ended in a sorely-needed win for the All Blacks.

Dave Lindsay closely pursued by a Springbok.

NEW ZEALAND

D.F. LINDSAY
(Otago)

A.C.C. ROBILLIARD   S.R. CARLETON   B.A. GRENSIDE
(Canterbury)   (Canterbury)   (Hawke's Bay)
W.A. STRANG
(South Canterbury)

L.M. JOHNSON
(Wellington)
W.C. DALLEY
(Canterbury)

R.T. STEWART
(South Canterbury)
W.E. HAZLETT   R.G. McWILLIAMS
(Southland)   (Auckland)
M.J. BROWNLIE (**Capt.**)   G.T. ALLEY   I.H. FINLAYSON
(Hawke's Bay)   (Canterbury)   (North Auckland)
J.P. SWAIN   S. HADLEY
(Hawke's Bay)   (Auckland)

P.J. MOSTERT (**Capt.**)   T.L. KRUGER   H.J. POTGIETER
(Western Province)   (Transvaal)   (Orange Free State)
G.M. DANEEL   P.J. NEL   S.P. van WYK
(Western Province)   (Natal)   (Western Province)
N.F. PRETORIUS   N.J.V. van DRUTEN
(Transvaal)   (Transvaal)
Scrum formation varied between 3-3-2 and 3-4-1
D. DEVINE
(Transvaal)

B.L. OSLER
(Western Province)
G.H. BRAND   J.C. van der WESTHUIZEN   J.A.R. DOBIE   N.S. TOD
(Western Province)   (Western Province)   (Transvaal)   (Natal)
J.C. TINDALL
(Western Province)

SOUTH AFRICA

REFEREE: Mr V.H. Neser (Transvaal)
ATTENDANCE: 38,000
CONDITIONS: Weather fine, ground firm
HALFTIME: New Zealand 3, South Africa 3

SCORERS

NEW ZEALAND	SOUTH AFRICA
Penalty goal: Lindsay	Penalty goal: Osler
Dropped goal: Strang	Goal from mark: Mostert

SOUTH AFRICA 11

18 August, 1928

Third Test

The Springboks discarded their usual black shorts for this game and wore white ones to avoid confusion with the New Zealand colours. As can be seen, there was a preponderance of Western Province players in the home team, the most interesting newcomer from the New Zealand point of view being the rugged forward, "Boy" Louw, who, with his brother Fanie, established a fine reputation on the 1937 tour. As usual, the Springbok scrum formation varied between 3-3-2 and 3-4-1.

On the New Zealand side the dropping of Strang hardly seemed justified, as he had played very well in the first two Tests. Johnson moved to second five-eighth with Herb Lilburne coming in at first five-eighth to play his first of ten Tests. He was the only full-back chosen in the original selection. Lindsay had been picked as a three-quarter but he was eventually recognised as the number one full-back on the tour. Lilburne played equally well at full-back or five-eighth, playing seven Tests in the latter position. He changed to Rugby League in 1935.

Brownlie kicked off under a cloudy sky, the ball going behind South Africa's goal line. Tindall forced and Osler restarted play. Within five minutes the Springboks had scored. Mostert led a rush to the New Zealand line where Carleton fielded and passed back to Lindsay. The ball bounced off the full-back's shoulder and Nel fell on it for a try which Osler converted. Brand was almost over within a few minutes but Robilliard overhauled him just in time. Johnson worked his team back on attack and from a line-out ten yards from the Springbok line, Finlayson gained possession and passed to Stewart who scored fifteen yards from the posts with three opponents hanging onto him. Lindsay's kick hit a post.

South Africa increased their lead when "Manus" de Jongh scored in the corner following a passing rush started by van Druten but the All Blacks closed the gap before halftime when Dalley put Grenside over on the blind side following a scrum. The first half ended as Lindsay failed to convert.

Bert Grenside scored one of New Zealand's tries and narrowly missed another on full-time.

The All Blacks began the second spell with a whirlwind forward rush which took play to the Springboks' line. However, the home defence was very sound and eventually the South African forwards, led by Mostert and van Druten, worked their way into New Zealand's half. Rousseau made a dash which looked dangerous but he was stopped by Lilburne and Johnson.

A scrum was ordered five yards from the New Zealand line, Mostert heeled for South Africa and the scrum wheeled for Daneel to dive across. Osler failed to convert.

New Zealand came back from the kick-off with a fine offensive, Johnson, Carleton and Grenside going away in a brilliant passing movement. A minute later Grenside intercepted a pass and raced away. With a great swerve he beat Tindall and a try looked certain but Rousseau, with an

NEW ZEALAND

Crusader Ground, Port Elizabeth

Nel crashes over for a try after an All Black error on their own line.

amazing burst of speed, caught the New Zealand left wing from behind.

South Africa then had a spell on attack but with seconds to go Lilburne burst through the home forwards. He passed to Hazlett, who sent the ball on to Swain. The hooker passed infield to Grenside and with great determination the big winger flew for the line. Tindall missed him but van der Westhuizen and Brand, who were covering desperately, caught Grenside as he dived for the corner. They threw him over the touch-line, taking the corner flag with them, and the game was saved for South Africa.

The critics praised both teams for the spirit in which the game was played and several of them described it as one of the best Test matches they had seen. The backs were more in the picture than they were in the two previous Tests but it was nevertheless a forward battle in which the slight superiority of the home pack was sufficient to turn the game South Africa's way.

NEW ZEALAND

D.F. LINDSAY
(Otago)

A.C.C. ROBILLIARD   S.R. CARLETON   B.A. GRENSIDE
(Canterbury)   (Canterbury)   (Hawke's Bay)

L.M. JOHNSON
(Wellington)

H.T. LILBURNE
(Canterbury)

W.C. DALLEY
(Canterbury)

R.T. STEWART
(South Canterbury)

W.E. HAZLETT   R.G. McWILLIAMS
(Southland)   (Auckland)

M.J. BROWNLIE **(Capt.)**   G.T. ALLEY   I.H. FINLAYSON
(Hawke's Bay)   (Canterbury)   (North Auckland)

J.P. SWAIN   S. HADLEY
(Hawke's Bay)   (Auckland)

A.F. du TOIT   P.J. MOSTERT **(Capt.)**   J.F. OLIVER
(Western Province)   (Western Province)   (Transvaal)

N.J. van DRUTEN   P.J. NEL   M.M. LOUW   N.F. PRETORIUS
(Transvaal)   (Natal)   (Western Province)   (Transvaal)

G.M. DANEEL
(Western Province)

Scrum formation varied between 3-4-1 and 3-3-2

P.du P. de VILLIERS
(Western Province)

B.L. OSLER
(Western Province)

G.H. BRAND   W.P. ROUSSEAU   J.C. van der WESTHUIZEN   H.P.K. de JONGH
(Western Province) (Western Province)   (Western Province)   (Western Province)

J.C. TINDALL
(Western Province)

SOUTH AFRICA

REFEREE: Mr V.H. Neser (Transvaal)
ATTENDANCE: 18,500
CONDITIONS: Weather cloudy, ground firm
HALFTIME: South Africa 8, New Zealand 6

SCORERS

NEW ZEALAND
Tries: Stewart, Grenside

SOUTH AFRICA
Tries: Nel, de Jongh, Daneel
Conversion: Osler

1 September, 1928

Fourth Test

As Lindsay was injured, Lilburne was played at full-back for New Zealand and Nicholls came in at second five-eighth. Carleton was also injured and Fred Lucas took his place at centre. These changes in the back line proved beneficial and, judging by Nicholls's display, his inclusion in the earlier Tests would have helped the All Blacks greatly.

The only change in the pack was the replacement of Geoff Alley by Ian Harvey who had toured Britain in 1924 although illness had limited his appearances. He had been an All Black again in Australia in 1926, when he had a very successful tour. However, illness dogged him again in South Africa and this was only his fourth game of the tour.

The only changes in the home team were in the three-quarters, where two new wings were chosen.

New Zealand won the toss and Osler kicked off into a slight breeze just as the sky cleared temporarily. Three minutes after the start a South African forward was ruled offside in the line-out and Nicholls kicked a goal. Soon after the resumption van Niekerk nearly scored but Lilburne tackled him a foot from the line. The Springboks now detached Daneel from the scrum and used him as a rover to combat the loose head play of Stewart. When the Springboks were to put the ball into the scrum de Villiers would throw it across to Daneel on the other side from which Stewart had packed down.

At last South Africa's attacking efforts were rewarded when Osler short-punted for van der Westhuizen to speculate over Lilburne's head. The Springbok centre beat Grenside in the race to the goal line and scored under the posts. Osler's conversion put the home side in front.

Nicholls broke away but Osler tackled him.

SMITH'S PHOTO SERVICE

The referee has a close look at Dalley's kick ahead.

NEW ZEALAND

H.T. LILBURNE
(Canterbury)

A.C.C. ROBILLIARD   F.W. LUCAS   B.A. GRENSIDE
(Canterbury)   (Auckland)   (Hawke's Bay)

M.F. NICHOLLS
(Wellington)

L.M. JOHNSON
(Wellington)

W.C. DALLEY
(Canterbury)

R.T. STEWART
(South Canterbury)

W.E. HAZLETT   R.G. McWILLIAMS
(Southland)   (Auckland)

M.J. BROWNLIE (**Capt.**)   I.H. HARVEY   I.H. FINLAYSON
(Hawke's Bay)   (Wairarapa)   (North Auckland)

J.P. SWAIN   S. HADLEY
(Hawke's Bay)   (Auckland)

M.M. LOUW   P.J. MOSTERT (**Capt.**)   J.F. OLIVER
(Western Province)   (Western Province)   (Transvaal)

N.J.V. van DRUTEN   P.J. NEL   A.F.du TOIT   N.F. PRETORIUS
(Transvaal)   (Natal)   (Western Province)   (Transvaal)

G.M. DANEEL
(Western Province)

P.du P. de VILLIERS
(Western Province)

B.L. OSLER
(Western Province)

J.A.van NIEKERK   W.P. ROUSSEAU   J.C. van der WESTHUIZEN   P.K. MORKEL
(Western Province)   (Western Province)   (Western Province)   (Western Province)

J.C. TINDALL
(Western Province)

SOUTH AFRICA

REFEREE: Mr V.H. Neser (Transvaal)
ATTENDANCE: 23,000
CONDITIONS: Weather wet, ground heavy
HALFTIME: New Zealand 6, South Africa 5

SCORERS

NEW ZEALAND	SOUTH AFRICA
Try: Swain	Try: van der Westhuizen
Penalty goals: Nicholls (2)	Conversion: Osler
Dropped goal: Nicholls	

SOUTH AFRICA 5

Newlands, Cape Town

Then from a line-out Dalley passed to Johnson who sent on to Nicholls. The Wellingtonian potted for goal but the ball hit a post and bounced back. Robilliard almost scored but van Niekerk held him. The All Blacks kept pounding away and finally they went into the lead again when the home team's forwards were off-side from a scrum and Nicholls kicked a goal from 35 yards. The score was still 6-5 at halftime.

Both sides had scoring chances early in the second half but good defence kept the points down. Rain began to fall heavily and the game was becoming a forward struggle. Daneel went back into the pack but the Springboks were not

hooking cleanly. From a line-out the All Black forwards broke through led by Hazlett and Swain scored in the corner. The ball was now very heavy and Nicholls's kick fell short.

The New Zealand forwards were back in Springbok territory almost at once and when a scrum went down on the home 25, Nicholls changed places with Johnson. Dalley received and passed to Nicholls, who dropped a goal. With five minutes to go this virtually gave New Zealand the game although South Africa mounted one final attack from which van Niekerk caught Lilburne in possession. From the resulting ruck the ball was passed forward and when Stewart received from the scrum he kicked out and the whistle went for full time. Once again the rubber was squared.

Morkel and Rousseau combine to tackle the All Black winger, Alan Robilliard.

AUSTRALIA 9

6 July, 1929

First Test

For the first time since 1914, a fully-representative Australian team was selected. Since World War I Rugby Union had been played only in New South Wales in most years although the 1921 Springboks played Victoria, as did the 1926 All Blacks, while the 1928 New Zealanders played Victoria on their way home. That state resumed inter-state matches in 1927, Queensland doing so in 1928.

There were some famous players in this Australian team. Alex Ross was one of the greatest full-backs to play for his country while Cyril Towers had a brilliant career extending over ten years in international football. On his day he had no superior in the world.

Tom Lawton was a Rhodes Scholar who had won Rugby Blues at Oxford in 1921-22-23. Very big and powerfully-built, he looked more like a forward than a five-eighth. He was named as a reserve for England against the 1924 All Blacks. Lawton also won an Athletics Blue in the shot-put at Oxford and represented the university at water polo and swimming. He went to Sydney after his return from Oxford and toured Britain with the 1927-28 Waratahs. He had also played

for New South Wales in 1920 and 1925 against New Zealand. After the Waratah tour Lawton settled in his native Queensland and was still playing extremely well in 1929. Inside him was Syd Malcolm, one of the finest half-backs in the world. Best-known of the Australian forwards were "Wild Bill" Cerutti, a tough prop who played for New South Wales and Australia over a ten year period, and the Queenslander, Eddie Bonis, a fine hooker.

The 1929 All Blacks set a record by becoming the first New Zealand team to lose all Tests in a series. On paper this looked quite a good side but it was not fully representative of New Zealand's Rugby strength as a number of leading players, including M.F. Nicholls, A.E. Cooke and F.W. Lucas, were not available for the tour. Also, the team suffered an incredible number of injuries.

The captain, Cliff Porter, had been injured before leaving New Zealand and did not play until the second Test while the vice-captain, Bill Dalley, who had played so well in South Africa in 1928, was injured in the second game and did not

The Australian captain, Tom Lawton, kicks high as he is tackled. Hook and Geddes follow the flight of the ball.

N W Z ALAN

play again on the tour. Thus Herb Lilburne, at the age of 21, became New Zealand's youngest Test captain, a record that still stands. Eric Leys was sent over as a replacement for Dalley but by the end of the tour the team was struggling to field fifteen fit men and several players were forced to play in unfamiliar positions.

This Test was the first for a number of the All Blacks. The two wings, Alf Waterman and Bert Geddes, were new caps, neither of whom again appeared for New Zealand after 1929. Charlie Oliver had played against New South Wales in 1928 and had appeared in 33 matches for New Zealand when he retired after the British tour of 1935, during which he was vice-captain of the All Blacks. Oliver also represented New Zealand at cricket. Jack Tuck was another who had only one season as an All Black but he played in all three of the 1929 Tests.

Lew Hook was the New Zealand centre three-quarter in all three games against the visiting New South Wales team in 1928 although he played some of his first-class matches on the wing. Because of Porter's injury, Hook was called upon to take the wing-forward position in this Test. Of the new internationals among the forwards, Eric Snow had toured South Africa in 1928 while "Beau" Cottrell went on to represent New Zealand in 22 matches between 1929 and 1932. Reside, Sonntag, Rika and Reid all failed to gain All Black selection again after the 1929 tour.

New Zealand won the toss and Lawton kicked off into a slight breeze. Early in the game Tuck made an intercept with Lilburne and Oliver in support but the ball was lost under the posts and Ross forced. The home pack worked play back to the New Zealand half and from a penalty awarded 35 yards out Tom Lawton opened the scoring with a good goal. The All Blacks came back with a great forward rush and from a back movement Waterman was pushed out at the corner.

Nepia evened the score shortly after with a long-range penalty. New Zealand kept up the pressure and following a break from mid-field Oliver dived over under the posts, Nepia convert-

ing. With halftime approaching, the All Blacks appeared be in a handy position but Lawton closed the gap with another penalty from well out.

Upon the resumption of play Stringfellow replaced Nepia, who had injured his back. The great Maori full-back took no further part in the tour. Influenza kept him out of the final Test after he had recovered from his injury.

Under an agreement between the New Zealand and Australian Unions, replacements were permitted in Tests between the two countries.

The All Blacks were soon on attack again and Geddes almost scored when Reside threw him a long pass early in the second half but he was stopped just short of the line. Play see-sawed as both sides mounted back attacks and the impartial crowd cheered the players' efforts. The Wallabies clinched the game near the end however when Malcolm sent his backs away, Gordon going over in the corner.

NEW ZEALAND

G. NEPIA*
(East Coast)

A.C. WATERMAN (North Auckland)   S.R. CARLETON (Canterbury)   J.H. GEDDES (Southland)

C.J. OLIVER (Canterbury)

H.T. LILBURNE (Capt) (Canterbury)

J.M. TUCK (Waikato)

L.S. HOOK (Auckland)

R.G. McWILLIAMS (Auckland)

E.M. SNOW (Nelson)

W.B. RESIDE (Wairarapa)   W.T.C. SONNTAG (Otago)   W.R. HEKE (RIKA) (North Auckland)

K.H. REID (Wairarapa)

A.I. COTTRELL (Canterbury)

W.H. CERUTTI (New South Wales)   E.T. BONIS (Queensland)   E. THOMPSON (Queensland)

H.A. HAMALAINEN (Queensland)   A.N. FINLAY (New South Wales)

J.A. FORD (New South Wales)   J.R.J. PALFREYMAN (New South Wales)   J.W. BRECKENRIDGE (New South Wales)

S.J. MALCOLM (New South Wales)

T.S. LAWTON (Capt.) (Queensland)

G.C. GORDON (New South Wales)   S.C. KING (New South Wales)   C.H.T. TOWERS† (New South Wales)   E.E. FORD (New South Wales)

A.W. ROSS (New South Wales)

AUSTRALIA

REPLACEMENTS: * Replaced by J.C. Stringfellow (Wairarapa)
† Replaced by A. Thorpe (New South Wales)
REFEREE: Mr A.V. Mayne (New South Wales)
ATTENDANCE: 40,000
CONDITIONS: Weather fine, ground firm
HALFTIME: New Zealand 8, Australia 6
SCORERS

NEW ZEALAND	AUSTRALIA
Try: Oliver	Try: Gordon
Conversion: Nepia	Penalty goals: Lawton (2)
Penalty goal: Nepia	

20 July, 1929

Second Test

This match is noteworthy for the fact that a player from Victoria was selected for Australia, Gordon Sturtridge thus becoming the first Wallaby from his state. He gained international honours again in 1932 and 1933 and played in England for several seasons during the 1930s. Westfield and Loudon, both of whom had played for New South Wales against New Zealand in previous seasons, were New Zealand born. Westfield had been educated at St Patrick's College, Wellington and Loudon at Christ's College.

In the New Zealand team, Carleton was playing out of position but the back line was strengthened by the return of Grenside to the left wing. Porter had also recovered and was able to lead the team for the first time during the tour. Palmer, who replaced Reid in the front row, had played against New South Wales in 1928. Alf Kivell, joining the pack in place of Reside, had only one season as an All Black, playing in five games on the 1929 tour.

The weather was like summer when Porter kicked off. Play opened with a series of line-outs, followed by a fine burst by the All Black forwards which ended in a force by Australia. From a scrum in the home 25 the ball went to Oliver, who cut in brilliantly but his pass back to Lilburne was forward when the latter had only Westfield to beat.

Sturtridge then made a similar thrilling break and from just inside half-way Lawton failed with a penalty kick. This was followed by a great move in which Westfield, King, Sturtridge and Crossman were involved but the ball was kicked too hard and Carleton relieved under pressure.

The play was fast and open at this stage, neither side being able to gain an advantage. However, a break by Porter looked promising for New Zealand and the visiting captain sent a pass to Oliver who cut through the defence to the home line where his pass went into touch. Fol-

New Zealand's 2-3-2 scrum packs down against the 3-2-3 formation used by Australia. Opposing half-backs are Tuck and Malcolm.

THE QUEENSLANDER

NEW ZEALAND

S.R. CARLETON
(Canterbury)

A.C. WATERMAN   L.S. HOOK   B.A. GRENSIDE
(North Auckland)   (Auckland)   (Hawke's Bay)
          C.J. OLIVER *
          (Canterbury)

                    H.T. LILBURNE
                    (Canterbury)

          J.M. TUCK
          (Waikato)

                              C.G. PORTER (Capt.)
                              (Wellington)
E.M. SNOW   R.G. McWILLIAMS
(Nelson)   (Auckland)
A.L. KIVELL   W.T.C. SONNTAG   W.R. HEKE (RIKA)
(Taranaki)   (Otago)   (North Auckland)
B.P. PALMER   A.I. COTTRELL
(Auckland)   (Canterbury)

W.H. CERUTTI   E.T. BONIS   E. THOMPSON
(New South Wales)   (Queensland)   (Queensland)
H.A. HAMALAINEN   A.N. FINLAY
(Queensland)   (New South Wales)
R.B. LOUDON   J.A. FORD   J.W. BRECKENRIDGE
(New South Wales) (New South Wales) (New South Wales)
          S.J. MALCOLM
          (New South Wales)

          T.S. LAWTON (Capt.)
          (Queensland)
O.C. CROSSMAN G.S. STURTRIDGE S.C. KING   G.H. McGHIE
(New South Wales) (Victoria) (New South Wales) (Queensland)
          R.E. WESTFIELD
          (New South Wales)

AUSTRALIA

REPLACEMENTS: * Replaced by R.T. Cundy (Wairarapa)
REFEREE: Mr R.C. Cooney (New South Wales)
ATTENDANCE: 18,000
CONDITIONS: Weather fine, ground hard
HALFTIME: New Zealand 3, Australia 3

SCORERS

NEW ZEALAND
Tries: Grenside, Porter
Penalty goal: Cundy

AUSTRALIA
Tries: McGhie, Crossman, Ford
Conversion: Lawton
Penalty goals: Lawton (2)

NEW ZEALAND

Exhibition Ground, Brisbane

lowing the line-out a scrum was formed and Tuck worked the blind side with Grenside who opened the scoring. Lilburne's kick was charged down by Finlay.

Play settled for some time in New Zealand territory and Lawton evened the score with a penalty goal. The All Blacks attacked from the kick-off but Australia forced them back, largely through the brilliant play of Lawton, whose running and kicking were an inspiration to his team. Just before halftime, Oliver was badly injured when he collided with Ford and he was replaced by Cundy, who went to full-back, Carleton moving to centre and Hook to second five-eighth. Oliver took no further part in the tour.

Early in the second half Grenside made a sensational break and passed to Tuck, who was stopped. Then Lilburne secured near the line and sent on to Porter, who forced his way over in the corner. Cundy could not convert. Immediately afterwards McGhie, following a kick, picked up in the loose and made a great run, beating Cundy to score under the posts. Lawton converted to put Australia in front.

The home backs were playing with great purpose and Crossman was almost over following a smart change of direction by Lawton. The All Blacks were penalised near half-way and the Australian captain put his side further ahead with a splendid kick.

Australia now had the game well under control and soon went further ahead. Malcolm broke from a scrum and passed to Lawton, who ran strongly before sending a well-judged pass to Crossman, who sprinted to the corner for a fine try. Lawton's kick narrowly missed.

The All Blacks were now eight points down and had lost most of their dash but Cundy closed the gap with a long range penalty goal. This brought New Zealand back into the game but Australia had the last word. Just on full time, Malcolm kicked from the base of the scrum and King, following up fast, took the ball and passed to Ford, who crossed in the corner. Lawton's kick hit a post and the whistle sounded to end the game. The Wallabies' convincing win gave them the Test rubber for the first time in a series against New Zealand.

AUᏚTRALIA 15

27 July, 1929

Third Test

The New Zealand back line was further disorganised because of injuries but the visitors were unlucky to lose, scoring three tries to two. However, one must not detract from the Wallabies' performance in winning all three Tests.

Australian Rugby was very strong in 1929 and eleven of the Test players had toured Britain, France and Canada with the 1927-28 New South Wales team which lost only five out of 34 games. There had been matches between New Zealand and New South Wales every year since the war except in 1927, and this had kept the standard high in Australia's principal Rugby state. With the best players from Queensland and Victoria now available, a formidable national team was able to take the field.

Clinton Stringfellow, the Wairarapa centre, had gone on in the first Test as a replacement for Nepia and he was now to play his only full game in an international. He was a player of considerable ability and it is strange that he had such a brief career as an All Black. In 1934 he captained the North Island and led the Rest of New Zealand against the All Blacks when the latter returned from their Australian tour. His form was so good that he was widely chosen by Rugby writers as a great prospect for the 1935 tour of Britain but he failed to gain selection.

Eric Leys, the New Zealand University halfback, was a new cap who also played only one season for New Zealand. He went to Australia as a replacement for the injured Dalley and played five times on the tour. An injury after his return home curtailed his career in first-class Rugby.

New Zealand opened the scoring in this Test after eight minutes when Cottrell passed infield to McWilliams for the Auckland forward to go over in a fairly handy position but Lilburne failed to convert. Four minutes later the visitors went further ahead when Stringfellow intercepted a pass and after a long run scored between the posts. Lilburne converted.

Stung by these set-backs, Australia began some strong concerted play and worked down to the New Zealand 25. Here Lawton opened his

team's scoring with a penalty, repeating the performance shortly after. New Zealand fought back and from a ruck Lilburne threw a long pass to Stringfellow who put Grenside in at the corner. Lilburne converted with a great kick. Australia narrowed the gap right on halftime when Towers drop-kicked a penalty goal.

The visitors held on to their lead for the early part of the second half but a brilliant dodging run by Towers ended in Jack Ford scoring. Lawton failed to convert but there was now only one point between the teams.

Finally, Australia made a marvellous sortie on the New Zealand line and Syd King, one of Australia's finest centres, scored a great try after starting a movement in which the ball went through eight pairs of hands before it came back to him. Lawton failed to convert but King's try had wrapped up the series for Australia.

A feature of this Test was the excellent play of the Australian forwards, with Jack Ford especially admirable. Wylie Breckenridge (who in

---

NEW ZEALAND

J.M. TUCK
(Waikato)

L.S. HOOK   J.C. STRINGFELLOW   B.A. GRENSIDE
(Auckland)   (Wairarapa)   (Hawke's Bay)
          S.R. CARLETON
          (Canterbury)
                                        H.T. LILBURNE
                                        (Canterbury)
               E.T. LEYS
               (Wellington)
                                        C.G. PORTER (Capt.)
                                        (Wellington)
     E.M. SNOW   R.G. McWILLIAMS
     (Nelson)   (Auckland)
A.L. KIVELL   W.T.C. SONNTAG   W.R. HEKE (RIKA)
(Taranaki)   (Otago)   (North Auckland)
     K.H. REID   A.I. COTTRELL
     (Wairarapa)   (Canterbury)

W.H. CERUTTI   E.T. BONIS   E. THOMPSON
(New South Wales)   (Queensland)   (Queensland)
     H.A. HAMALAINEN   A.N. FINLAY†
     (Queensland)   (New South Wales)
W.N. IVES   J.A. FORD   J.W. BRECKENRIDGE
(New South Wales)   (New South Wales)   (New South Wales)
               S.J. MALCOLM
               (New South Wales)
                                   T.S. LAWTON (Capt.)
                                   (Queensland)
G.H. McGHIE   S.C. KING   C.H.T. TOWERS   E.E. FORD
(Queensland) (New South Wales) (New South Wales) (New South Wales)
               R.E. WESTFIELD
               (New South Wales)

AUSTRALIA

REPLACEMENTS: † Replaced by G.P. Storey (New South Wales)
REFEREE: Mr A.V. Mayne (New South Wales)
ATTENDANCE: 29,000
CONDITIONS: Weather fine, ground firm
HALFTIME: New Zealand 11, Australia 9

SCORERS

NEW ZEALAND	AUSTRALIA
Tries: McWilliams, Stringfellow, Grenside	Tries: J.A. Ford, King
Conversions: Lilburne (2)	Penalty goals: Lawton (2), Towers

N[E]W Z[E]ALAND 13

Sydney Cricket Ground

"THE NEW CHAMPION"

1953 was manager of the Wallabies in South Africa) stood out for his deadly tackling.

Of the home backs, Malcolm played one of his best international games while Lawton, who led the side well, nursed his forwards and made play for the men outside him. His vast experience and his goal-kicking were invaluable. King was magnificent and Towers, especially in the second half, was well up to international standard. Both wings played well while Westfield was up to the form of his immediate famous predecessor Alex Ross.

Porter was the best player on the visitors' side. As one critic observed, "No one who saw the match will forget the New Zealand captain's heroic, inspiring effort. He was a rover, on hand in nearly every movement, back on defence as often as he was hurling himself into the attack.

His great tackling and his speed in short, sharp bursts were wonderful ... " McWilliams stood out in the All Black pack, with Sonntag and Reid giving him good support. Lilburne, Grenside and Stringfellow were the best of the visiting backs.

GREAT BRITAIN

21 June, 1930

First Test

After a series of trial matches the New Zealand selectors chose a team for the first Test against the 1930 British side which came in for criticism from the press and from Rugby followers generally. The feeling was that too many former stars had been recalled and the team was considered to be too old. Two of the "greats" of the famous Hawke's Bay Ranfurly Shield team of the 1920s, Jimmy Mill and "Bull" Irvine, who were now living in the Wairarapa, had both been out of international football for four years. They were both over 30 while Lucas, Cooke and McWilliams were 28. Cliff Porter was also on the wrong side of 30. Mill and Irvine were but shadows of the brilliant players who had toured Britain in 1924. However, the other veterans all played as well as they ever had.

An interesting newcomer to Test Rugby was George Hart, the future national 100 yards champion, who was to play 35 times for New Zealand between 1930 and 1936. One of the finest wings ever to play for his country, Hart scored 28 tries for the All Blacks. He died of wounds in Italy during 1944. The other wing, Don Oliver, had a brief career as a New Zealand player, being dropped after the second Test in 1930 and failing to find favour with the selectors again.

Walter Batty and Dick Steere had both played against New South Wales in 1928 while Steere toured Australia in 1929 but did not play in the Tests. Although slightly under 13 stone, Batty was a brilliant loose forward, especially with the ball at his toe, while Steere was a powerful lock who played 21 games for New Zealand between 1928 and 1932.

The British tour captain, F.D. Prentice, was not selected for this game and the team was led by the former Cambridge Blue C.D. Aarvold, now Sir Carl Aarvold and a judge at the Old Bailey. One of the most brilliant three-quarters to visit New Zealand, he was in peak form in 1930, as was his fellow Blue, Bowcott, then playing for Cardiff.

The brightest star in the British back line

Cooke and Nepia enjoy their half-time oranges with Mr Hollander, the referee.

however was Roger Spong, still rated by many who saw him as the greatest player in his position ever to visit New Zealand. His club mate and international partner, Wilf Sobey, was unfortunately injured in the opening match of the 1930 tour. Spong did not play in this game and as Sobey took no further part in the tour, this famous combination was never seen in action in New Zealand.

The visitors had two very fast wings in the little Welshman, Jack Morley, and the tall long-striding Englishman Jim Reeve. Morley came to New Zealand later as a British Rugby League representative. Reeve, who won eight English caps, was killed in a motor accident in 1936.

The full-back, Jack Bassett, had a distinguished career for Wales during which he captained the national side while scrum-half, Paul Murray was a versatile player who was actually chosen for the tour as a centre, a position in which he had represented Ireland.

The British pack, which averaged five pounds per man heavier than the home forwards, contained some very fine players. The heaviest, and possibly the best, of the British forwards was the 16st.3lbs. Irish airman, George Beamish. Big and powerful, he was also very fast and he excelled in both tight and loose play.

N.W Z ALAN 3

It is worthy of note that the top goal-kickers of this team were forwards, the captain Prentice, along with Black, Jones and Parker being the leading exponents. The South African Rhodes Scholar and former Oxford Blue, Brian Black, was the top scorer on the tour as well as being one of the most able forwards. Parker had played against the 1924 All Blacks for Wales while the great Llanelly player Ivor Jones was one of the finest loose forwards ever to play for his country. Both Black and Rew, the rugged English prop, lost their lives in World War II. O'Neill was a stocky, powerful prop who won six caps for Ireland while Farrell was one of the side's most experienced forwards who won 29 caps between 1926 and 1932.

The 1930 New Zealand team wore white jerseys with a silver fern on a black shield, black shorts and the usual black socks with two white bands at the top. This change to white jerseys was made to avoid confusion with the British team, who wore dark blue. British teams to tour New Zealand since World War II have worn scarlet jerseys. New Zealand again played in white in 1975 to avoid clashing with the dark blue of Scotland.

The first Test of 1930 was played under miserable conditions, snow, sleet, rain and wind prevailing before the game and during the early part of it. However, 27,000 keen spectators were at Carisbrook to see Cliff Porter lead the strangely-attired New Zealand team on to the field.

The game had been in progress for only seven minutes when the visitors scored. Spong received the ball from Murray and with a fine cross-kick he put it in front of Reeve who gathered it neatly and beat Hart to score in the corner. Black's kick missed.

Nepia had a chance to level the scores with a penalty but he failed to lift the ball, which was already very slippery. He was playing brilliantly however, saving his team time after time with his fielding, tackling and excellent line-kicking. The visitors were having the better of the scrummaging but the home forwards, with Finlayson especially prominent, were very good in the loose. Both sides had scoring chances but halftime came with Britain still in front by three points.

Finlayson and Batty led a rush at the start of the second half and Porter was nearly over. Then Mill set his backs going from a scrum and Lucas sent Hart away for the corner. The Canterbury man had his revenge on Reeve, beating the British wing beautifully before leaving Bassett behind and racing over in the corner. Nepia's goal attempt hit a post.

For the next 35 minutes neither side gained the advantage for any length of time and most of the spectators were ready to accept a draw as a fair result. With time almost up, however, their hopes rose as New Zealand stormed the British line. Then Jones came away with the ball and set off upfield. Morley ran with him and as Jones was taken by Nepia he flung the ball to Morley on half-way. The little wing galloped for the corner and scored the winning try amid great excitement as Cooke failed by a yard to get to him. Black's kick failed and the whistle sounded for full time.

NEW ZEALAND

G. NEPIA
(East Coast)

G.F. HART
(Canterbury)

F.W. LUCAS
(Auckland)

D.J. OLIVER
(Wellington)

A.E. COOKE
(Wellington)

H.T. LILBURNE
(Canterbury)

J.J. MILL
(Wairarapa)

C.G. PORTER (Capt.)
(Wellington)

W.E. HAZLETT
(Southland)

W. BATTY
(Auckland)

R.G.McWILLIAMS
(Auckland)

E.R.G. STEERE
(Hawke's Bay)

I.H. FINLAYSON
(North Auckland)

W.R. IRVINE
(Wairarapa)

A.I. COTTRELL
(Canterbury)

H. O'H. O'NEILL
(Queen's University
& Ireland)

D. PARKER
(Swansea & Wales)

H. REW
(Army & England)

J. FARRELL
(Bective Rangers & Ireland)

D.H. BLACK
(Blackheath & England)

J. McD. HODGSON
(Northern)

G.R. BEAMISH
(R.A.F. & Ireland)

I. JONES
(Llanelly & Wales)

P.F. MURRAY
(Wanderers & Ireland)

R.S. SPONG
(Old Millhillians & England)

J.S.R. REEVE
(Harlequins
& England)

H.M. BOWCOTT
(Cardiff & Wales)

C.D. AARVOLD (Capt.)
(Headingley &
England)

J.C. MORLEY
(Newport & Wales)

J. BASSETT
(Penarth & Wales)

GREAT BRITAIN

REFEREE: Mr S. Hollander (Canterbury)
ATTENDANCE: 27,000
CONDITIONS: Weather wet and extremely cold with snow showers, ground muddy
HALFTIME: Great Britain 3, New Zealand 0
SCORERS

NEW ZEALAND	GREAT BRITAIN
Try: Hart	Tries: Reeve, Morley

NEW ZEALAND 13

5 July, 1930

Second Test

Several changes were made in the New Zealand team for this Test. Merv Corner, at 5ft. 5ins. and 9st.7lbs. one of New Zealand's smallest internationals, was playing the first of his 25 games for his country. Selected in place of Mill, he gave an outstanding display in this game. Nicholls came in to replace Lilburne and played a large part in New Zealand's win. Batty was not available, his place being taken by Stewart, who was three stone heavier than the Aucklander and made a difference where weight was concerned but he had nothing over Batty in loose play. Irvine, who was suffering from injury, gave way to Hore, who had toured South Africa in 1928 without playing a Test. Hore eventually played 45 games for New Zealand, including 10 Tests.

Reeve was on the injured list and was replaced by Tony Novis, a regular army officer who had won a Blue at Oxford in 1927. Novis won seven English caps between 1929 and 1933 and captained Combined Services against the 1935 All Blacks. The British captain, Doug Prentice, came into the team in place of Hodgson.

Although the weather had been bad for some days, it was fine for the Test and a record crowd packed into Lancaster Park. The first points came after eight minutes when Nicholls claimed a fair catch just outside the British 25 and kicked a good goal.

The visitors attacked from the kick-off but Corner drove them back with good line-kicking. Then Spong made a spectacular break but the speedy Hart overhauled him. However, the brilliant British fly-half cut through again and made an opening for Morley, who sent on to Aarvold after the centre had doubled round. Aarvold raced round the defence to score near the posts, Prentice adding the extra points to put his team in front.

Twenty-four minutes had now elapsed and both packs were giving all they had to establish superiority up front. The home hookers were winning most of the ball from the set scrums but the British defence was hard to penetrate. However, the New Zealanders went ahead when Por-

Corner kicks from a scrum.

ter snapped up the ball and passed to Lucas, who sent the ball back to Porter. The home captain passed to Hart, who sprinted over the line to score in a handy position for Nicholls to convert.

NEW ZEALAND

G. NEPIA
(East Coast)

G.F. HART   F.W. LUCAS   D.J. OLIVER
(Canterbury)   (Auckland)   (Wellington)

A.E. COOKE
(Wellington)

M.F. NICHOLLS
(Wellington)

M.M.N. CORNER
(Auckland)

C.G. PORTER (**Capt.**)
(Wellington)

W.E. HAZLETT   R.T. STEWART
(Southland)   (Canterbury)

R.G. McWILLIAMS   E.R.G. STEERE   I.H. FINLAYSON
(Auckland)   (Hawke's Bay)   (North Auckland)

J. HORE   A.I. COTTRELL
(Otago)   (Canterbury)

H. O'H. O'NEILL   D. PARKER   H. REW
(Queen's University   (Swansea & Wales)   (Army & England)
& Ireland)

J.L. FARRELL   F.D. PRENTICE (**Capt.**)
(Bective Rangers & Ireland)   (Leicester & England)

B.H. BLACK   G.R. BEAMISH   I. JONES
(Blackheath & England)   (R.A.F. & Ireland)   (Llanelly & Wales)

P.F. MURRAY
(Wanderers & Ireland)

R.S. SPONG
(Old Millhillians & England)

A.L. NOVIS   H.M. BOWCOTT   C.D. AARVOLD   J.C. MORLEY
(Army & England)   (Cardiff & Wales)   (Headingley &   (Newport & Wales)
England)

J. BASSETT
(Penarth & Wales)

GREAT BRITAIN

REFEREE: Mr S. Hollander(Canterbury)
ATTENDANCE: 30,000
CONDITIONS: Weather fine, ground firm
HALFTIME: New Zealand 8, Great Britain 5

SCORERS

NEW ZEALAND	GREAT BRITAIN
Tries: Hart, Oliver	Tries: Aarvold (2)
Conversions: Nicholls (2)	Conversions: Prentice (2)
Goal from mark: Nicholls	

GREAT BRITAIN 10

Lancaster Park, Christchurch

Murray was injured soon after Hart had scored and the Irishman had to leave the field, Jones going to scrum-half. New Zealand attacked for the rest of the spell but there was no further score at the interval.

The home forwards dominated play right from the start of the second half and when the British backs did break through, Nepia's solid defence stopped them from scoring. Once, however, the visitors should have scored when Aarvold ran down to Nepia with Morley in support. The British centre tried to score himself and was flattened by the New Zealand full-back and a certain five points were lost. Then a dropped pass from Lucas to Oliver cost New Zealand a try, but Corner set up a scoring movement from a line-out when he passed to Nicholls, who ran to the right before swerving to the left to send Oliver over for a splendid try. Nicholls converted with a fine kick.

Eight minutes from time Jones dashed through the opposition and made a brilliant opening for Aarvold, who ran forty yards to score under the posts. Prentice converted and the visitors were very much back in the game. However, no-side sounded without any further scoring.

The New Zealand Team
Back row: R.G. McWilliams, R.T. Stewart, A.W. Mercer (masseur), I.H. Finlayson, W.E. Hazlett.
Second row: G.W. Nicholson (selector), J. Hore, A.I. Cottrell, N.A. McKenzie (selector), E.R.G. Steere, M.F. Nicholls, W.E. Maxwell (selector).
Third row: E. McKenzie (selector), A.E. Cooke, F.W. Lucas, C.G. Porter (capt.), A.J. Geddes (selector), G. Nepia, A. McDonald (selector).
In front: D.J. Oliver, M.M.N. Corner, G.F. Hart.

97

NEW ZEALAND 15

26 July, 1930

Third Test

New Zealand fielded a very light pack in this game, being outweighed by a stone a man. This was the first international played by Hugh McLean, who marked his Test debut by scoring two tries. He had a distinguished career as an All Black, winning international honours again in 1932-34-35. Batty returned in place of Stewart, who, along with Finlayson, was on the injured list. Oliver was dropped, Cooke went to centre, and Lucas to the wing with Strang being brought back in the five-eighth line.

The injury to Murray in the second Test necessitated the playing of an uncapped man, Howard Poole, behind the British pack. The Cardiff player, who never won a Welsh cap, gave a good account of himself, his passing being especially sound. Prentice again stood down for Hodgson to regain his place while Reeve had recovered from his injury and he returned to the left wing.

The home team kicked off into the wind and sun. Early attempts at penalty goals by both Strang and Black were unsuccessful and then Britain almost scored, a pass from Aarvold to Morley going astray. The blue forwards kept pressing and Poole received from a scrum near the New Zealand line. He passed to Spong, who cut in brilliantly before passing to Bowcott, who had a clear run to score. Jones converted. Beamish led his forwards back again into New Zealand territory after the kick-off, only fine tackling by Cooke and Nicholls keeping the home line safe.

The New Zealand forwards began to show more life, however, and won a series of scrums. From one of these set pieces Corner passed to Strang who sent on to Nicholls. The latter kicked across to Lucas who gathered the ball and ran round behind the posts for Strang to convert and even the scores. Halftime came just after Parker had narrowly missed a penalty.

Shortly after the resumption Black took a penalty shot which Prentice, acting as touch-judge, signalled as a goal but the other touch-judge, ex-All Black George Nicholson, signalled as no goal and the referee decided against the kick. New Zealand came back on attack and Bassett

Hart kicks as Reeve tackles him. Nepia and Cooke are on hand.

GREAT BRITAIN 10

Eden Park, Auckland

Lucas crosses the line to score after picking up a cross-kick from Nicholls.

cleared but McLean gathered the ball to score wide out. Strang missed the conversion.

Cooke's tackling stopped some promising British back movements and the home forwards swept back on attack. Corner received from a scrum and Nicholls, who had changed places with Strang, took Corner's pass and potted a goal. New Zealand went further ahead when McLean forced his way over from a maul near the British line. Nicholls failed to convert.

New Zealand appeared to have the game safely won but the visitors did not give up. McWilliams touched down but the try was disallowed because of a knock-on. Then Morley looked certain to score but Nepia forced him out. Rain began to fall with ten minutes left but the British backs kept throwing the ball around in spite of the change in the weather conditions. Just on time Jones picked up in the loose and ran from half-way. He passed to Aarvold who scored a runaway try between the posts. Black converted.

NEW ZEALAND

G. NEPIA
(East Coast)

G.F. HART   A.E. COOKE   F.W. LUCAS
(Canterbury)   (Wellington)   (Auckland)

M.F. NICHOLLS
(Wellington)

W.A. STRANG
(South Canterbury)

M.M.N. CORNER
(Auckland)

C.G. PORTER (**Capt.**)
(Wellington)

W. BATTY   H.F. McLEAN
(Auckland)   (Wellington)

W.E. HAZLETT   E.R.G. STEERE   R.G. McWILLIAMS
(Southland)   (Hawke's Bay)   (Auckland)

J. HORE   A.I. COTTRELL
(Otago)   (Canterbury)

H. O'H. O'NEILL   D. PARKER   H. REW
(Queen's University   (Swansea & Wales)   (Army & England)
& Ireland)

J. McD. HODGSON   J.J. FARRELL
(Northern)   (Bective Rangers & Ireland)

B.H. BLACK   G.R. BEAMISH   I. JONES
(Blackheath & England)   (R.A.F. & Ireland)   (Llanelly & Wales)

H. POOLE
(Cardiff)

R.S. SPONG
(Old Millhillians & England)

J.S.R. REEVE   H.M. BOWCOTT   C.D. AARVOLD(**Capt.**)   J.C. MORLEY
(Harlequins &   (Cardiff & Wales)   (Headingley &   (Newport & Wales)
England)   England)

J. BASSETT
(Penarth & Wales)

GREAT BRITAIN

REFEREE: Mr S. Hollander (Canterbury)
ATTENDANCE: 40,000
CONDITIONS: Weather fine rain late in game, ground slightly greasy
HALFTIME: New Zealand 5, Great Britain 5

SCORERS

NEW ZEALAND	**GREAT BRITAIN**
Tries: McLean (2), Lucas	Tries: Bowcott, Aarvold
Conversion: Strang	Conversions: Jones, Black
Dropped goal: Nicholls	

NEW ZEALAND 22

9 August, 1930

Fourth Test

Nicholls was not available for the final Test so his place was taken by Lilburne. Morley was dropped from the British team in favour of Novis, whose form towards the end of the tour was very good indeed. Welsh, the only Scot in the touring team, also gained his place in this Test at the expense of Hodgson.

New Zealand scored first when Porter went over under a pile of defenders after a forward rush, Nepia failing to convert. Parker evened the score shortly after when he kicked a penalty from near half-way in the middle of the field. The home hookers were securing a feast of the ball but good tackling by Novis and Reeve kept their opposites in check every time the ball was run to the New Zealand wings. Then from a scrum Corner sent his backs away and Lilburne cut through, only to lose the ball. Strang was on hand to pick up and score however but he failed to convert his own try. Every time Spong got the ball the British backs looked dangerous but the visitors were still trailing at halftime.

With only three points between the teams when the second half began it was anybody's game. New Zealand went quickly on to the attack and the ball went along the line to Hart, who was well tackled by Reeve, but Cooke was backing up outside his right wing and he kicked the ball through to the British line. Following with great speed, Cooke touched down fairly wide out. Strang failed to convert.

Novis then scored a fine try, using his tremendous pace to outsprint the opposition when he received at the end of a passing rush after a quick heel from a ruck. Black converted and only one point separated the teams. However, Cooke put his team further ahead when Bassett failed to

George Nepia leads this group of All Blacks off the field as police lines hold back the crowd.

WEEKLY NEWS

NEW ZEALAND

G. NEPIA
(East Coast)

G.F. HART   A.E. COOKE   F.W. LUCAS
(Canterbury)   (Wellington)   (Auckland)

H.T. LILBURNE
(Canterbury)

W.A. STRANG
(South Canterbury)

M.M.N. CORNER
(Auckland)

C.G. PORTER (**Capt.**)
(Wellington)

W. BATTY   H.F. McLEAN
(Auckland)   (Wellington)
W.E. HAZLETT   E.R.G. STEERE   R.G. McWILLIAMS
(Southland)   (Hawke's Bay)   (Auckland)
J. HORE   A.I. COTTRELL
(Otago)   (Canterbury)

H. O'H. O'NEILL   D. PARKER   H. REW
(Queens University   (Swansea & Wales)   (Army & England)
& Ireland)
W.B. WELSH   J.L. FARRELL
(Hawick & Scotland)   (Bective Rangers & Ireland)
B.H. BLACK   G.R. BEAMISH   I. JONES
(Blackheath & England)   (R.A.F. & Ireland)   (Llanelly & Wales)
P.F. MURRAY
(Wanderers & Ireland)

R.S. SPONG
(Old Millhillians & England)
J.S.R. REEVE   H.M. BOWCOTT C.D. AARVOLD(**Capt.**)   A.L. NOVIS
(Harlequins &   (Cardiff & Wales) (Headingley & England) (Army & England)
England)
J. BASSETT
(Penarth & Wales)

GREAT BRITAIN

REFEREE: Mr F.E. Sutherland (Auckland)
ATTENDANCE: 40,000
CONDITIONS: Weather fine, ground firm
HALFTIME: New Zealand 6, Great Britain 3

SCORERS

NEW ZEALAND	GREAT BRITAIN
Tries: Porter (2), Cooke (2)	Try: Novis
Strang, Batty	Conversion: Black
Conversions: Strang (2)	Penalty goal: Parker

100

GREAT BRITAIN 8

Athletic Park, Wellington

field a kick from Lucas, the New Zealand centre again kicking over the line to score in a handy position for Strang to convert.

By now the home forwards were well on top and the British were hemmed in their own half almost continually. From a scramble Corner threw a long pass to Porter and the New Zealand captain, who played one of his finest games, threw himself over the line for his second try. Strang again converted.

In the dying minutes of the game the home forwards burst through the line-out and Batty scored, Strang failing to convert. This was the most decisive of the four Tests and the victory gave New Zealand the rubber, but it had taken the home team more than half the game to establish superiority.

The 1930 season marked the end of interna-

tional Rugby for such great players as Nepia, Lucas, Cooke, Nicholls, Mill, Irvine, Stewart, Porter and Finlayson. Cooke and Nicholls both played for the North Island in 1931, Cooke then switching to Rugby League, at which code he represented New Zealand. He played much of his League at full-back. Nepia played for the North Island in 1933 and made the final All Black trial in 1935. After captaining the New Zealand Maori team on its Australian tour in 1935 he too changed to League, playing for the Streatham and Mitcham club in England.

Nepia continued playing League after his return to New Zealand but he was subsequently reinstated to Rugby. He played his last first class Rugby match in September 1950 at the age of 45. For the others in the above list however it was truly the end of the road. Lucas and Nicholls were later New Zealand selectors while Finlayson acted in a similar capacity for North Auckland.

Cartoonist, A.S. Paterson, farewells the All Black captain Cliff Porter who retired after this match.

NEW ZEALAND 20

12 September, 1931

Despite the splendid weather, a mere 15,000 came to Eden Park for the only Test played between the Wallabies of 1931 and the All Blacks. This poor attendance was undoubtedly due to the Australians' unimpressive record. Only one game had been won by the tourists before this Test was played. As is so often the case with Australian teams, the 1931 side turned on magnificent football in the international and only the kicking of the home full-back swung the match New Zealand's way.

With so many retirements of All Black stars in 1930, there were a number of new caps in the 1931 New Zealand team. Ron Bush, who played such an important part in his team's win, was an Aucklander attending Otago University for a one-year course. Although he had a long career in first-class football and seldom played a poor game, this was Bush's only appearance for New Zealand. He is unique in inter-island Rugby in that he played for the South Island at full-back in 1931 and for the North Island as a forward in 1934. In fact he was a very versatile player and

represented Auckland at full-back, centre, five-eighth and loose forward. He later became a New Zealand selector.

This game was also the first played for New Zealand by "Rusty" Page, a regular artillery officer who rose to the rank of brigadier and won decorations for outstanding gallantry and leadership in North Africa during World War II. While studying at Sandhurst, Page played for London Scottish and was a reserve for Scotland. He was normally a first five-eighth but was selected at centre when Charlie Oliver, the original choice, had to withdraw with a poisoned hand on the day before the match.

The new left wing, Nelson ("Kelly") Ball, won selection again in 1932 and 1935 and played 22 games for New Zealand, including five Tests.

Frank Solomon, making his international debut at wing-forward, has the distinction of being the last player to fill this position for New Zealand for this was the last occasion on which the traditional seven-man scrum was used. Solomon toured Australia in 1932 as a loose forward.

The other new forwards, Metcalfe, Purdue, Max and Jessep were also members of the 1932 All Blacks while Max won selection again in 1934. Purdue's father and uncle were former All Blacks. Evan Jessep settled in Melbourne and played for Australia against the 1934 All Blacks.

Archie Strang, the New Zealand captain for this Test, retired from big football at the end of the 1931 season at the early age of 24. His last game for the All Blacks was by no means his best for he did not show the fine form which he produced in 1928 and 1930.

Dave Cowper became the second Wallaby from Victoria. He represented Australia again in 1932 and 1933 before moving to Sydney and playing for New South Wales in 1934 and 1935. He was one of the best backs in the game although the outstanding player on the field was the young Queenslander, Jack Steggall, who was playing his first of nine Tests. A very versatile back, he played for Australia at full-back, wing, centre and

---

NEW ZEALAND

R.G. BUSH
(Otago)

G.F. HART   J.R. PAGE   N. BALL
(Canterbury)   (Wellington)   (Wellington)
H.T. LILBURNE
(Wellington)

W.A. STRANG (Capt.)
(South Canterbury)
M.M.N. CORNER
(Auckland)

F. SOLOMON
(Auckland)
T.C. METCALFE   W. BATTY
(Southland)   (Auckland)
G.B. PURDUE   E.R.G. STEERE   D.S. MAX
(Southland)   (Hawke's Bay)   (Nelson)
A.I. COTTRELL   E.M. JESSEP
(Canterbury)   (Wellington)

W.H. CERUTTI   E.T. BONIS   M.R. BLAIR
(New South Wales)   (Queensland)   (New South Wales)
P.B. JUDD   M.C. WHITE
(New South Wales)   (Queensland)
J.R.L. PALFREYMAN   T.D. PERRIN   J.G. CLARK
(New South Wales)   (New South Wales) (Queensland)
S.J. MALCOLM (Capt.)
(New South Wales)

J.C. STEGGALL
(Queensland)
H.A. TOLHURST   D.L. COWPER   C.H.T. TOWERS   W.H. HEMINGWAY
(New South Wales) (Victoria)   (New South Wales) (New South Wales)
A.W. ROSS
(New South Wales)

AUSTRALIA

REFEREE: Mr S. Hollander (Canterbury)
ATTENDANCE: 15,000
CONDITIONS: Weather fine, ground firm
HALFTIME: Australia 13, New Zealand 11

SCORERS

NEW ZEALAND   **AUSTRALIA**
Tries: Hart, Ball   Tries: Towers (2) Cowper
Conversion: Bush   Conversions: Ross (2)
Penalty goals: Bush (4)

AUSTRALIA 13

Eden Park, Auckland

five-eighth. Hemingway was a New Zealander by birth, being born at Auckland.

The 1931 Test became a duel between the New Zealand forwards and the Australian backs. The home inside backs were disappointing. Corner's passing was poor and Strang and Lilburne were caught flat-footed time after time.

Strang won the toss and elected to play with the sun and a slight breeze behind him. Steggall initiated an early attack when he intercepted a pass from Corner but the All Blacks retaliated and Strang cross-kicked. Ross waited for the bounce and Hart dashed up, kicked on and gathered the ball to score wide out. Bush converted with a fine kick.

Steggall was playing brilliantly and had the Wallabies constantly on attack through clever breaks but Lilburne counter-attacked to make an opening for Page, who dropped the ball. Then the home backs handled cleanly for the first time, Hart breaking away only to be caught from behind by Tolhurst.

It was then the visitors' turn. Malcolm started a movement and Steggall cut through to draw Bush. The young Queensland five-eighth fed Cowper who outpaced the opposition and scored behind the posts for Ross to even the score with a simple conversion. A few minutes later Bush put his team in front again when he kicked a magnificent penalty goal from five yards inside halfway.

Shortly after, Towers made a lovely opening and kicked past Bush. Judd gathered in and passed to Towers who scored near the posts. Ross converted to give Australia the lead for the first time.

The Wallabies were now throwing the ball about in grand style and a cut through by Steggall gave Towers another try near the posts which Ross failed to convert. Then Bush hit back with

New Zealand's last 2-3-2 Test scrum. Hookers: Cottrell and Jessep. Second row: Purdue, Steere and Max. Back row: Metcalfe and Batty.

another magnificent penalty goal but Australia led 13-11 at halftime.

The All Blacks began the second spell with great dash and the forwards took play into Wallaby territory but Ross drove them back with long line kicks. A break by Batty had New Zealand on attack again and Bush put New Zealand in front when he kicked another penalty goal. A few minutes later an Australian forward was caught off-side in his own 25 and Bush again raised the flags. Just on time Corner made a clever opening on the blind side for Solomon to draw Ross before passing to Ball, who celebrated his All Black debut by scoring wide out. Bush failed to convert.

103

AUSTRALIA 22

2 July, 1932

First Test

Five of New Zealand's backs were new to Test Rugby. Proctor, the Otago wing, was playing his only international and was not selected for New Zealand again after the 1932 tour. He scored four tries against Newcastle and this probably clinched his place in the first Test team. The other wing, Arthur Bullock-Douglas, was an All Black again in 1934 and on his day was a classy wing and a consistent try-scorer.

"Pat" Caughey, the 20 year old centre, was one of New Zealand's most brilliant backs of the 1930s. Now Sir Harcourt Caughey, he was knighted in 1972 for his outstanding services as chairman of the Auckland Hospital Board. He is the second New Zealand Rugby representative to be so honoured, the first being H.Y. Braddon of the 1884 team who settled in Australia and became Sir Henry Braddon in 1920. Caughey was a fine all-round athlete and while at King's College, Auckland, he was captain of Rugby, a member of the cricket XI, senior athletic and swimming champion and heavy-weight boxing champion. He went on to play 38 matches for New Zealand, including nine Tests.

"Bunk" Pollock won All Black honours again in 1936 and played in five Tests. He could play equally well in a variety of positions and was a very good goal-kicker. Frank Kilby, the captain, had toured South Africa in 1928 but an ankle injury limited his appearances. He was not a contender for the 1929 Australian tour but he played in the trial matches in 1930 and represented the North Island in 1931 (he played for South Island in 1927).

Opinions were divided as to who was the better half-back, Kilby or Corner. The Aucklander had been preferred to Kilby in 1930 and 1931 by the New Zealand selectors but in 1932, Kilby was honoured with the All Black captaincy, Corner being the second-string half. The latter played in only two games on the tour owing to injury but had he been fit he might have challenged Kilby for his place in the Tests. Both halves were chosen for the 1934 Australian tour with Kilby again captain of the side but Corner won selection for the British tour of 1935 and Kilby did not. There is no doubt that both were very fine half-backs. Kilby was later on the executive of the New Zealand Rugby Union and Corner became an All Black selector.

For the first time in a Test, New Zealand packed a 3-4-1 scrum. The only new cap in the

Jack Manchester gets a pass from McLean and charges into Australian territory.

NEW ZEALAND 17

Sydney Cricket Ground

forward pack was Jack Manchester who went on to play 36 games for New Zealand, including nine Tests. He captained the 1935 All Blacks and was one of the best forwards to wear the black jersey during the '30s.

The Australian team was a very experienced one in that all of the backs had played against New Zealand before, while the forwards too were all seasoned players.

Graeme Cooke, the Queensland lock, had a remarkable career in international Rugby. He remained in South Africa after touring there with the 1933 Wallabies and played for Transvaal. After the war he was selected for the 1946 Australian tour of New Zealand at the age of 34 and then went on to tour Britain with the 1947-48 Wallabies. Another Australian who was playing his first Test against New Zealand was the Victorian, Owen Bridle. English-born, he visited New Zealand with the 1931 and 1936 Australian sides, showing remarkable speed in the loose. When the 1936 team was hit by injuries, Bridle played centre in the last two games.

The All Blacks had the better of the first twenty minutes and they opened the scoring when McLean snapped up in the loose and passed to Pollock who sent Caughey racing through the gap. The centre fed Bullock-Douglas who ran round Steggall and scored near the posts for Pollock to convert. The second try was also started by McLean. He gathered the ball at half-way with three forwards in support and set off for the Wallaby goalline. Hore finally scored in a handy position but Pollock missed an easy kick.

Just on halftime the home team got on the board when Cowper made a break and passed to Bridle. The fast loose forward ran diagonally to the posts and scored, Lawton's conversion making the halftime score 8-5 to the visitors.

Lawton gave his team the lead early in the second half when he kicked two penalty goals in quick succession. The Wallabies went further ahead when Sturtridge cut past Pollock, ran fifty yards and punted past Lilburne for Cerutti to win the race to the ball and score. Lawton converted.

New Zealand now looked to be well beaten but

a dropped goal by Pollock put the visitors back in the picture. The Wallabies increased the gap however when Caughey was tackled and the ball rolled loose for Bridle to obtain possession at half-way. He passed to Cerutti who was vainly chased by Kilby for half the length of the field. Lawton failed to convert.

The All Blacks came back with a try by Purdue, who carried two forwards over the line with him. Pollock's conversion made the difference only two points and the result was still in doubt although the home team deserved to be safely ahead. Finally, Cowper put the seal on a fine game when he scored from a cross-kick by Lawton to give Australia a five-point win.

The result flattered the All Blacks who were inferior in the second half. Lawton, Malcolm and Cerutti did most to win the game for Australia and all three played outstanding football. The All Black forwards generally held their own, Cottrell with McLean and Hore being especially good, but the home backs had the edge on their opponents.

NEW ZEALAND
H.T. LILBURNE
(Wellington)
A.C. PROCTOR   T.H.C. CAUGHEY   G.A.H. BULLOCK-DOUGLAS
(Otago)   (Auckland)   (Wanganui)
H.R. POLLOCK
(Wellington)
       J.R. PAGE
       (Wellington)
F.D. KILBY (**Capt.**)
(Wellington)
T.C. METCALFE
(Southland)
J.E. MANCHESTER   E.R.G. STEERE   G.B. PURDUE   H.F. McLEAN
(Canterbury)   (Hawke's Bay)   (Southland)   (Wellington)
J. HORE   E.M. JESSEP   A.I. COTTRELL
(Otago)   (Wellington)   (Canterbury)

W.H. CERUTTI   E.T. BONIS   E.W. LOVE
(New South Wales)   (Queensland)   (New South Wales)
G.V. BLAND   G.M. COOKE
(New South Wales)   (Queensland)
J.G. BENNETT   M.M. WHITE   O.L. BRIDLE
(Queensland)   (Queensland)   (Victoria)
S.J. MALCOLM
(New South Wales)
     T.S. LAWTON (**Capt.**)
     (Queensland)
W.J. WHITE   S.C. KING   G.S. STURTRIDGE   D.L. COWPER
(New South Wales)   (New South Wales)   (Victoria)   (Victoria)
J.C. STEGGALL
(Queensland)
AUSTRALIA

REFEREE: Mr A.V. Mayne (New South Wales)
ATTENDANCE: 30,000
CONDITIONS: Weather fine, ground hard
HALFTIME: New Zealand 8, Australia 5

SCORERS
NEW ZEALAND   **AUSTRALIA**
Tries: Bullock-Douglas, Hore   Tries: Cerutti (2), Bridle, Cowper
Purdue   Conversions: Lawton (2)
Conversions: Pollock (2)   Penalty goals: Lawton (2)
Dropped goal: Pollock

NEW ZEALAND 21

16 July, 1932

Second Test

New Zealand made several changes for this game, mostly because of injuries to some first Test players. Collins, Innes and Clarke were new caps. Arthur Collins was a sound full-back and a useful goal-kicker who won selection again in 1934. Gordon Innes, who later joined the League code, was playing his only Test and Ray Clarke, who also played in the third Test, was another who had only one season as an All Black.

Bert Palmer, who had last represented New Zealand in 1929, came in as hooker. Palmer's football career ended tragically when he died following a club match shortly after his return from the 1932 tour. His memory is perpetuated by a memorial cup presented by Mr. J.M. Caughey, the All Black's father, which is awarded each season in Auckland to the junior team which displays the most outstanding sportsmanship.

Alex Ross, unavailable for the first Test, came in at full-back for the home team and Steggall was moved to the wing in place of White.

Kilby won the toss and elected to play with the sun behind him. Lawton kicked off and New Zealand received two defensive penalties in quick succession, Kilby finding the line on both occasions. The tourists made ground from a line-out and Ball burst through to be tackled near the Australian line. A ruck formed from which Cerutti was caught offside and Collins opened the scoring with a good goal after six minutes.

From the restart New Zealand worked back into Australia's half where Ross evaded a flying tackle by Ball, the home full-back earning a resounding cheer for a 50 yard punt to touch. Pollock put New Zealand back on attack however and McLean burst away from a ruck but he was offside and Lawton relieved.

The Australian backs had spent most of their time on defence so far but they counter attacked with a passing rush in which the ball reached Steggall but the Queenslander could not evade Bullock-Douglas. Lawton grazed the posts with a penalty attempt and Innes kicked into the home half following the drop-out. Ross tried to clear but Ball charged down his kick. However, Ross recovered the ball and found touch. A long kick by Lawton put Australia on attack again and from a penalty the Wallaby captain found touch five yards from the New Zealand line.

The New Zealand backs broke away and Pollock dribbled through but Ross picked up and had a drop at goal which fell short. Australia kept pressing, Cowper being caught by Ball a few feet from the line.

With play back in Australian territory, the home backs began a movement which yielded one of the finest tries seen on the Exhibition Ground. From between the Wallaby 25 and half-way, Malcolm came round the blind side of a scrum and passed to Cowper. The winger made ground before passing back to Malcolm, who returned the ball to the flying Victorian. Cowper ran across field, beating man after man, and then passed to Love who sent on to Cerutti. Sturtridge ranged up beside the big prop to take a pass, sending on to Steggall who dived over the line. Lawton's conversion attempt was poor.

NEW ZEALAND

A.H. COLLINS
(Taranaki)

G.A.H. BULLOCK-DOUGLAS   H.R. POLLOCK   N. BALL
(Wellington)   (Wanganui)   (Wellington)
G.D. INNES
(Canterbury)

J.R. PAGE
(Wellington)

F.D. KILBY (Capt.)
(Wellington)
F. SOLOMON
(Auckland)

J.E. MANCHESTER   G.B. PURDUE   R.L. CLARKE   H.F. McLEAN
(Canterbury)   (Southland)   (Taranaki)   (Wellington)
A.I. COTTRELL   B.P. PALMER   J. HORE
(Canterbury)   (Auckland)   (Otago)

W.H. CERUTTI   E.T. BONIS   E.W. LOVE
(New South Wales)   (Queensland)   (New South Wales)
G.V. BLAND   G.M. COOKE
(New South Wales)   (Queensland)
J.G. CLARK   M.C. WHITE   O.L. BRIDLE
(Queensland)   (Queensland)   (Victoria)
S.J. MALCOLM
(New South Wales)

T.S. LAWTON (Capt.)
(Queensland)

J.C. STEGGALL   G.S. STURTRIDGE   S.C. KING   D.L. COWPER
(Queensland)   (Victoria)   (New South Wales) (Victoria)
A.W. ROSS
(New South Wales)

AUSTRALIA

REFEREE: Mr F.A. Larkin (Queensland)
ATTENDANCE: 15,000
CONDITIONS: Weather fine, ground hard
HALFTIME: New Zealand 12, Australia 3

SCORERS

NEW ZEALAND   **AUSTRALIA**
Tries: Bullock-Douglas (2), Ball   Try: Steggall
Page
Conversion: Pollock
Penalty goal: Collins
Dropped goal: Pollock

106

AUSTRALIA 3

Exhibition Ground, Brisbane

Solomon has support and room to move in a mid-field break.

Shortly after this movement, Collins had a chance to put New Zealand ahead with a penalty but his kick was wide. He failed with another penalty attempt a few minutes later, but New Zealand finally regained the lead when Pollock dropped a goal from just inside half-way.

One minute later, King kicked through but Page fielded the ball. He sent Ball away and the latter in-passed to Page over the heads of three Australians for the five-eighth to race over the goal line. Pollock converted and three minutes later halftime sounded.

Australia went straight to the attack on the resumption of play but good line-kicking by Collins drove them back. Steggall fielded a kick by Pollock and centred but the ball was knocked on. Next came a run by Bullock-Douglas which was stopped just short of the line by a grand tackle on the part of Steggall.

A fine kick by Page put the All Blacks within five yards of their opponents' line where Kilby, Solomon and Bullock-Douglas worked the blind side of a ruck for the winger to cross in the corner. Collins failed.

New Zealand had the game well under control and Solomon was almost over but he went into touch. Then from a ruck Kilby and McLean broke away, the latter sending on to Bullock-Douglas, who had only five yards to run for another try in the corner. Pollock missed the conversion.

An intercept by Innes almost led to a try but Ross tackled the All Black five-eighth and secured the ball, which he put into touch. New Zealand attacked again, only a dropped pass by Bullock-Douglas preventing the Wanganui man from scoring a third try.

With eight minutes to go Manchester broke away and after a passing movement among forwards and backs, Ball finally ran over for a try which Pollock failed to convert. The game ended with Australia on attack but Sturtridge was penalised for obstructing Innes and Collins put the ball into touch to end the game.

NEW ZEALAND 21

23 July, 1932

Third Test

After the debacle of the second Test the Australian selectors made several changes. The most dramatic was the dropping of the captain, Tom Lawton. This was hard on Lawton, even though his form at Brisbane had not been up to his usual standard. He had done a great deal to win the first Test for Australia and at his best he had no superior in the world. Lindsay came in to play his only game for Australia and the versatile Steggall was moved to centre. The Victorian, "Weary" Dunlop, was given his chance in the pack and he played very well. He later became Sir Edward Dunlop, being knighted for his services to medicine.

The only change in the New Zealand team was the return of Caughey at centre, which strengthened the side considerably.

Kilby won the toss and decided to play with the wind. From the kick-off Steggall put the ball deep into New Zealand territory where Collins found the line. From the first scrum Australia received a penalty and Ross had a shot, but his kick lacked direction.

Pollock kicked through to Malcolm from the drop-out and the home captain sent his backs away. Cowper kicked and New Zealand counter attacked, Caughey's pass to Ball going astray and spoiling a good movement. Then Cooke was offside at a scrum and Kilby found the line.

A defensive penalty to Australia eased the home team's position after five minutes of play. This was followed by a glorious movement which led to the first try of the match.

Cooke picked up in his 25 and passed to Sturtridge, who sent on to his fellow Victorian outside him. Cowper cut through brilliantly and in a flash his pace had taken him clear of the opposition. He ran to half-way with Hemingway trailing him. The crowd roared as the New Zealanders converged on the flying Wallaby centre, who timed his pass to Hemingway perfectly. The All Blacks had no chance of catching the speedy Australian wing who raced over near the corner. Ross converted and the home side was five points up in as many minutes.

The All Blacks were stung into action by this early try but the Wallaby forwards were holding their own, especially in the rucks. A high kick by Sturtridge was fumbled by Bullock-Douglas and the Australians poured through on him but he recovered and managed to find the line.

There was a roar from the crowd when Steggall dropped Ball with a dive tackle right on the line but the whistle had already gone for a forward pass. Shortly after, Page cut through brilliantly. He was downed by Sturtridge but he got his pass away to Ball, who was away down the wing. Steggall dived at Ball but missed him this time and it was left to Malcolm to halt the movement.

Ross kicked down to Collins who ran hard to set his backs going. Page passed in to McLean, who was tackled in the Australian 25. From a scrum Kilby secured the ball, beat several tacklers, dummied Ross and went over for a fine try which Collins failed to convert.

Australia took play into New Zealand's 25 with a penalty and from a line-out Sturtridge was away but he held on too long. The Wallabies had another scoring chance when Cowper kicked through for Lindsay, but the winger could not get to the ball.

Collins narrowly missed a penalty from just inside half-way and Pollock failed with another attempt shortly after. Kilby sent out a poor pass from a scrum and Cowper snapped up the ball, feeding back inside to Bridle, who raced away. He kicked past Collins but Bullock-Douglas won the race to the ball and cleared.

New Zealand were almost over again when the backs ran the ball smoothly along the line to the left wing. Ball eluded Hemingway and raced ahead, swerving beautifully. As he came to Ross he had two men in support but he tried to go on his own and the great Australian full-back downed him.

The All Blacks soon took the lead, however. Kilby received from a ruck and put the ball back to his forwards. McLean bullocked his way over with two men holding on to him and Pollock kicked an easy goal.

AUSTRALIA 13

Sydney Cricket Ground

Ross failed with a penalty shortly after and play went back to centre field. Pollock had a chance to goal from a penalty after the All Blacks had worked back to the home 25, but he missed an easy kick. Steggall took the ball and passed to Cowper who made ground with a fine dash but he lost the ball and Purdue dribbled back into Wallaby territory.

Sturtridge cut through and sent on to Steggall, who fed Cowper. The latter timed his pass well to Lindsay but the Queenslander lacked the necessary speed to get clear so he passed back to Cowper. The movement broke down when Cowper elected to pass to his outside with Sturtridge unmarked inside him.

Ross narrowly missed a goal from a scrum penalty and then Sturtridge cut through again but play broke down when Hemingway failed to get clear. Halftime came with New Zealand leading 8-5.

New Zealand attacked from the beginning of the second half but good tackling by the Australian backs kept the home line safe. Twice Solomon was forced out when he looked dangerous.

Then Kilby got away and passed to Solomon who sent on to Ball. The winger was crowded so he threw the ball back to Solomon, who scored a great try. Pollock's kick hit a post.

Australia struck back with back attacks but a long pass from Steggall to Cowper was intercepted by Ball, who took play nearly to the home line, where a pass in to the forwards went astray. Ball made another dash but Bonis tackled him a few yards from the line.

New Zealand scored again when Kilby cleared a scrum quickly and shot a pass to Page. The ball went along the backline to the left wing, where Ball beat the Australian defence to race over the line. He dropped the ball however but Manchester was there to dive on it for a try which Collins converted.

For a short time, Australia began to play better but it was not long before New Zealand added more points. Kilby set his backs moving and Bullock-Douglas made a strong run down the wing. He sent the ball in to the forwards and Palmer scored for Collins to convert.

Although the result appeared to be beyond doubt, Australia did not give up. Bridle broke away from a line-out and passed to Cerutti, who returned the ball to Bridle for the Victorian to score a good try which Cowper converted. Malcolm then began a movement when he broke into the open and passed to Palfreyman who returned the ball to his half-back. Cowper was up to take a long pass and his pace took him over in the corner, too far out for Ross to convert.

That was the end of the scoring, for full time sounded shortly after. There was an unusual scene at the conclusion of the match when the 30 players joined hands in the centre of the field and sang "Auld Lang Syne" while the crowd looked joyfully on. Cheers and congratulations followed and finally the jerseys changed hands as the players left the field.

Victory in this Test gave New Zealand the rubber and with it the Bledisloe Cup, a handsome trophy presented by the Governor-General of New Zealand for competition between that country and Australia in Rugby Union.

NEW ZEALAND
A.H. COLLINS
(Taranaki)
G.A.H. BULLOCK-DOUGLAS   T.H.C. CAUGHEY   N. BALL
(Wanganui)   (Auckland)   (Wellington)
H.R. POLLOCK
(Wellington)
J.R. PAGE
(Wellington)
F.D. KILBY (Capt.)
(Wellington)
F. SOLOMON
(Auckland)
J.E. MANCHESTER   R.L. CLARKE   G.B. PURDUE   H.F. McLEAN
(Canterbury)   (Taranaki)   (Southland)   Wellington)
J. HORE   B.P. PALMER   A.I. COTTRELL
(Otago)   (Auckland)   (Canterbury)

W.H. CERUTTI   E.T. BONIS   E.W. LOVE
(New South Wales)   (Queensland)   (New South Wales)
O.V. BLAND   G.M. COOKE
(New South Wales)   (Queensland)
J.R.L. PALFREYMAN   E.E. DUNLOP   O.L. BRIDLE
(New South Wales)   (Victoria)   (Victoria)
S.J. MALCOLM (Capt.)
(New South Wales)
G.S. STURTRIDGE
(Victoria)
R. LINDSAY   J.C. STEGGALL   D.L. COWPER   W.H. HEMINGWAY
(Queensland)   (Queensland)   (Victoria)   (New South Wales)
A.W. ROSS
(New South Wales)
AUSTRALIA

REFEREE: Mr R.C. Cooney (New South Wales)
ATTENDANCE: 30,000
CONDITIONS: Weather fine, ground hard
HALFTIME: New Zealand 8, Australia 5
SCORERS
NEW ZEALAND   **AUSTRALIA**
Tries: Kilby, McLean, Solomon,   Tries: Hemingway, Bridle, Cowper
Manchester, Palmer   Conversions: Ross, Cowper
Conversions: Collins (2), Pollock

AUSTRALIA 25

11 August, 1934

First Test

This was the heaviest defeat to date inflicted on New Zealand by Australia, although New South Wales had beaten New Zealand 25-3 in 1893. It took the Wallabies thirty years to gain a bigger win over the All Blacks, their 20-5 victory in 1964 being their best so far.

Australian Rugby was very strong in the 1930s and it will be noted that the preponderance of New South Wales players was not nearly so marked as usual. In 1933, New South Wales played Victoria twice, each side winning a match, while in 1934 New South Wales had to struggle to win 17-14. Three matches were played between Queensland and New South Wales in 1934 with each state winning one game and the third drawn. Thus with the standard so even in the major Rugby states, it is not surprising that the national teams were so much more representative in this decade.

Apart from Tests against New Zealand, Australian Rugby men had played Britain in 1930 in one international for a 6-5 win while the Wallabies won two out of five Tests in South Africa in 1933.

Of the 1934 Wallabies, Alex Ross, Cyril Towers and Syd Malcolm would have had no superiors anywhere in the world in their respective positions while the wings, "Jockey" Kelaher and Doug McLean, had both established great reputations in South Africa. Both gained in stature in the next few seasons, Kelaher playing particularly well against the 1937 Springboks.

George Hart sets off with Towers chasing and Caughey in support.

WEEKLY NEWS

NEW ZEALAND 11

Sydney Cricket Ground

McLean, who was a member of a famous Queensland football family, later played for his country at Rugby League.

"Dooney" Hayes, who was to captain the 1936 Wallabies on their New Zealand tour, was a brilliant attacking back and a sound defender who could also kick goals. He was a casualty of the Second World War. In front of these classy backs was an experienced pack, in which Owen Bridle, Eddie Bonis, Aub Hodgson and ex-All Black Evan Jessep were especially effective. It is interesting to note that Wal Mackney rowed in the Australian eight at the 1936 Olympics.

The New Zealand team was also very experienced and by no means was the Australian victory won at the expense of a lot of new chums. George Hart, who had been kept out of the 1932 Tests by an injury, was back to his best form. Frank Kilby, the All Black captain, had been injured in the second match of the tour but, as we have stated elsewhere, some critics and Rugby followers considered Merv Corner a better half-back than Kilby.

All the New Zealand backs had played in previous Tests and there were only three new All Blacks in the forwards, viz, Rod McKenzie, Bill Hadley and Artie Lambourn. All three had long careers for New Zealand, playing 35, 25 and 40 matches respectively in the black jersey. Hadley, who was a younger brother of 1928 All Black Swin Hadley, was probably the best hooker to play for New Zealand in the 1930s.

The game was fast and open and the big crowd went away well satisfied. New Zealand's scrummaging was poor which made Hadley's task hard. The home team gained more possession than the visitors but the latter were first to score. The All Black forwards swept into Australian territory and Hore gathered a bouncing ball to dive over for an unconverted try after five minutes.

For the next ten minutes play went up and down the field. Then Malcolm worked the blind side and the ball was fed back on to the open side to Towers who beat Bullock-Douglas and Collins with sheer speed to score a magnificent try in the corner.

The All Blacks had a long period on defence when Caughey stood out for his solid tackling. The visiting forwards took the ball into their opponents' territory at last in a loose rush and Knight picked up to stride through the opposition for a try which Collins converted. New Zealand was on top at this stage and just before halftime, Hore broke away to slip a pass to Max who crossed wide out. Australia attacked hotly from the kick-off and from a movement in which every back handled, McLean scored. The first half ended with New Zealand leading 11-6.

A few minutes after the resumption, Ross closed the gap with a penalty and added another one when Caughey was caught offside on his own goal line. Now in front for the first time, the Wallabies came back to the attack and Ross kicked a third penalty goal. The All Blacks realised that their only hope for a win lay in throwing the ball about but, from a dropped pass, Bridle broke through for a try and Ross added the extra points. Then Lewis cut through the New Zealand backs and passed to Towers, who scored for Ross to convert.

NEW ZEALAND

A.H. COLLINS
(Taranaki)

G.F. HART
(Canterbury)

T.H.C. CAUGHEY
(Auckland)

G.A.H. BULLOCK-DOUGLAS
(Wanganui)

C.J. OLIVER
(Canterbury)

J.R. PAGE (**Capt.**)
(Wellington)

M.M.N. CORNER
(Auckland)

H.F. McLEAN
(Auckland)

J.E. MANCHESTER
(Canterbury)

A. KNIGHT
(Auckland)

R.M. McKENZIE
(Manawatu)

D.S. MAX
(Nelson)

A. LAMBOURN
(Wellington)

W.E. HADLEY
(Auckland)

J. HORE
(Otago)

E.M. JESSEP
(Victoria)

E.T. BONIS
(Queensland)

V.J. BERMINGHAM
(Queensland)

W.G. WHITE
(New South Wales)

D.B. DUNLOP
(Victoria)

O.L. BRIDLE
(Victoria)

A.J. HODGSON
(New South Wales)

W.A.R. MACKNEY
(New South Wales)

S.J. MALCOLM
(New South Wales)

L.S. LEWIS
(Queensland)

J.D. KELAHER
(New South Wales)

E.S. HAYES
(Queensland)

C.H.T. TOWERS
(New South Wales)

A.D. McLEAN
(Queensland)

A.W. ROSS (**Capt.**)
(New South Wales)

AUSTRALIA

REFEREE: Mr R.C. Cooney (New South Wales)
ATTENDANCE: 40,000
CONDITIONS: Weather fine, ground firm
HALFTIME: New Zealand 11, Australia 6

SCORERS

NEW ZEALAND	AUSTRALIA
Tries: Hore, Knight, Max	Tries: Towers(2), Bridle, McLean
Conversion: Collins	Conversions: Ross (2)
	Penalty goals: Ross (3)

NEW ZEALAND 3

25 August, 1934

Second Test

There were seven changes in the New Zealand team from the first Test. Collins was not available because of injury and Lilburne came into the side to play what was to be his last Test. After failing to gain selection for the British tour of 1935, Lilburne switched to League. Hart was also injured and Eddie Holder, a 1932 tourist, played his only international. He too joined the League code and played with Nepia for Streatham and Mitcham in England. Griffiths, the young Wellington five-eighth, was playing the first of his seven Tests. A steady, capable inside back, he was to captain New Zealand in 1936. Kilby was fit again and took his place behind the scrum.

There were three new caps in the forwards. The Hawke's Bay Maori, Hawea Mataira, did not represent New Zealand again although he played well in the 1935 trials and was unlucky to miss out on the British tour. He later played League in Auckland. Ron King eventually played 42 games for New Zealand and was the All Black captain against the 1937 Springboks. A mobile, powerful lock, he was the star forward on the 1935 tour. "Ned" Barry, who had toured Australia in 1932, was making his only Test appearance. His son, Kevin, also became an All Black.

The Australian selectors kept their back line intact but there were two changes in the pack. Ron Walden, who came to New Zealand as vice-captain of the 1936 Wallabies, took Dunlop's place in the second row. He returned to New Zealand in 1949 as manager of the only Australian team to win a Test series in this country. Walden was chief of the CIB in Sydney for some years and was in charge of the Thorne kidnapping case in 1960. The New Zealand-born player, Loudon, replaced Hodgson in the back row. Another of Australia's versatile men, Loudon had toured New Zealand as a threequarter in 1923 with the New South Wales team.

The All Blacks had improved greatly since the first Test and had recently defeated an Australian XV, which contained eleven of the 1934 Test players, by 11 points to 6. They had a slight advantage in the second Test and were probably unlucky not to win what became a hard, even game. Hadley had a great day in the set scrums but close marking prevented his backs from taking advantage of their possession. Penalties were awarded with great frequency and this marred the game as a spectacle.

Caughey turns to pass in-field as he is tackled. Lewis and Malcolm are on the left; the other All Black is Holder.

J.E. MANCHESTER COLLECTION

AUSTRALIA 3

Sydney Cricket Ground

Loudon scored for Australia late in the first half when Lilburne was overwhelmed by the green forwards, a fine tackle by Kilby just failing to prevent the try. Ross failed to convert.

Early in the second half Griffiths caught the ball and raced through the Australian forwards. When he was stopped he threw the ball to Hadley who passed to Hore. The Otago forward bullocked his way over for an unconverted try. Late in the game Lilburne had a chance to retain the Bledisloe Cup for New Zealand but his kick from a penalty grazed the upright and the trophy passed to Australia.

The New Zealand Touring Team
Back row: M. Johnson (attendant), J. Leeson, W.E. Hadley, E.C. Holder, T.H.C. Caughey, A. Lambourn, H. Mataira, J. Hore.
Third row: R.M. McKenzie, A. Knight, J.E. Manchester, E.F. Barry, D.S. Max, H.F. McLean, A. Mahoney, R.R. King.
Seated: G.A.H. Bullock-Douglas, J.L. Griffiths, H.T. Lilburne, F.D. Kilby (capt.), A.J. Geddes (manager), J.R. Page, C.J. Oliver, A.H. Collins, G.F. Hart.
In front: M.M.N. Corner, C.H. Smith.

NEW ZEALAND

H.T. LILBURNE
(Wellington)

G.A.H. BULLOCK-DOUGLAS   T.H.C. CAUGHEY   E.C. HOLDER
(Wanganui)   (Auckland)   (Buller)

J.L. GRIFFITHS
(Wellington)

J.R. PAGE
(Wellington)

F.D. KILBY (**Capt.**)
(Wellington)

H. MATAIRA
(Hawke's Bay)

J.E. MANCHESTER   R.R. KING   D.S. MAX   E.F. BARRY
(Canterbury)   (West Coast)   (Nelson)   (Wellington)

A. LAMBOURN   W.E. HADLEY   J. HORE
(Wellington)   (Auckland)   (Otago)

E.M. JESSEP   E.T. BONIS   V.J. BERMINGHAM
(Victoria)   (Queensland)   (Queensland)

R.J. WALDEN   W.G.S. WHITE
(New South Wales)   (New South Wales)

W.A.R. MACKNEY   R.B. LOUDON   O.L. BRIDLE
(New South Wales)   (New South Wales)   (Victoria)

S.J. MALCOLM
(New South Wales)

L.S. LEWIS
(Queensland)

J.D. KELAHER   E.S. HAYES   C.H.T. TOWERS   A.D. McLEAN
(New South Wales)   (Queensland)   (New South Wales)   (Queensland)

A.W. ROSS (**Capt.**)
(New South Wales)

AUSTRALIA

REFEREE: Mr A.L.C. Irving (New South Wales)
ATTENDANCE: 30,000
CONDITIONS: Weather fine, ground firm
HALFTIME: Australia 3, New Zealand 0

SCORERS

NEW ZEALAND	AUSTRALIA
Try: Hore	Try: Loudon

CROWN STUDIOS

23 November, 1935

The 1935 tour of the British Isles marked the introduction to international Rugby of several All Blacks who were to render outstanding services to New Zealand. "Brushy" Mitchell, the 21 year old Southland three-quarter, was one of the best players to represent New Zealand in his position, either at wing or centre, during the 1930s. He was to captain the All Blacks in 1938. Injuries which he suffered in 1937 had no small bearing on the result of the rubber between New Zealand and South Africa.

Another brilliant footballer playing his first Test match was "Joey" Sadler, nick-named "the pocket battleship" by the British critics. An injury sustained in 1937 cut short what could have been one of the great careers in international Rugby.

Mike Gilbert had only one season as an All Black but he played extremely well in 1935 and was one of the successes of the tour. He won selection ahead of former All Black full-backs George Nepia, Ron Bush, Arthur Collins and Herb Lilburne. A big man with a powerful boot, Gilbert was a very good goal-kicker who later did well in English Rugby League.

There were two new caps in the forwards,

Mahoney and Reid. "Tonk" Mahoney, the only All Black to come from Bush Districts, had toured Australia in 1929 and 1934 without playing a Test but he came into his own on the 1935 tour, being one of the best loose forwards in the team. Tori Reid, the big Maori from Hawke's Bay, went on to win nine caps. He continued to play first-class Rugby until he was nearly 40 and carried on at club level for some years after his retirement from big football, at one stage playing in the same team as his son.

The best-known player in the home team was the captain, Wilson Shaw, who was to win 19 caps. A shrewd tactician with good hands and an accurate boot, he had captained Glasgow and Edinburgh against the All Blacks in a game which the tourists struggled to win, 9-8. Kerr, Forrest, Murdoch, Logan and Lambie had also played in this match while Beattie had led South of Scotland against the tourists.

The score was a fair indication of the relative merits of the teams. The All Black forwards were much stronger all round. Hadley's hooking was superb while New Zealand's line-out play was far

A Scottish hand reaches to tackle the strongly running winger, Hart.

NZ RUGBY MUSEUM

SCOTLAND 8

Murrayfield, Edinburgh

Scottish half-back, Logan, makes a break, with Beattie in support. Referee Mr Gadney joins Sadler and Griffiths in the chase.

superior to that of the home side. The game was fast and thrilling throughout with the New Zealand backs making the most of their chances.

Scotland played in white instead of their usual dark blue in order to avoid confusion with the black jerseys of the New Zealanders.

After seven minutes of play the home team opened the scoring when Shaw cut through and sent on to Dick. The centre beat Caughey and passed to Fyfe, who scored in the corner. He failed to convert his own try. New Zealand soon took the lead however when Griffiths went through a gap and passed to Caughey who had a clear run to the posts. Gilbert converted. Five minutes later Hadley scored from a scramble in front of Scotland's posts and Gilbert goaled. From the kick-off the home team attacked and Forrest was stopped just short of the line. Then Fyfe went close with a long range penalty from which New Zealand counter-attacked with only a fine tackle by Murdoch keeping Hart from scoring. Right on halftime, after Oliver had almost scored, Caughey picked up in the loose and went over in the corner. Gilbert failed to convert and halftime came with New Zealand ten points up.

Scotland attacked early in the second half and a fine break by Shaw, who evaded Griffiths

neatly, led to a try by Dick which Murdoch converted. Both sides had scoring opportunities but there was no change in the points tally until three minutes from time, when Sadler made a brilliant break from the blind side of a scrum. He passed to Mitchell who threw a long pass infield to Caughey for the Aucklander to score near the corner. Gilbert converted with a good kick.

NEW ZEALAND

G.D.M. GILBERT
(West Coast)

G.F. HART	C.J. OLIVER	N.A. MITCHELL
(Canterbury)	(Canterbury)	(Southland)

T.H.C. CAUGHEY
(Auckland)

J.L. GRIFFITHS
(Wellington)

B.S. SADLER
(Wellington)
A. MAHONEY
(Bush Districts)

J.E. MANCHESTER (Capt)	S.T. REID	R.R. KING	R.M. McKENZIE
(Canterbury)	(Hawke's Bay)	(West Coast)	(Manawatu)
A. LAMBOURN	W.E. HADLEY		J. HORE
(Wellington)	(Auckland)		(Otago)

SCOTLAND

R.M. GRIEVE	G.L. GRAY	G.D. SHAW
(Kelso)	(Gala)	(Gala)

J.A. BEATTIE
(Hawick)
W.A. BURNET
(West of Scotland)

L.B. LAMBIE	J.A. WATERS	D.A. THOM
(Glasgow H.S.F.P.)	(Selkirk)	(London Scottish)

W.R. LOGAN
(Edinburgh Wanderers)

R.W. SHAW (Capt.)
(Glasgow H.S.F.P.)

K.C. FYFE	W.C.W. MURDOCH	R.C.S. DICK	J.E. FORREST
(Cambridge	(Hillhead H.S.F.P.)	(Guy's Hospital)	(Glasgow
University)			Academicals)

J.M. KERR
(Heriot's H.S.F.P.)

REFEREE: Mr C.H. Gadney (England)
ATTENDANCE: 60,000
CONDITIONS: Weather fine, ground firm
HALFTIME: New Zealand 13, Scotland 3

SCORERS

NEW ZEALAND	SCOTLAND
Tries: Caughey (3), Hadley	Tries: Fyfe, Dick
Conversions: Gilbert (3)	Conversion: Murdoch

NEW ZEALAND 17

7 December, 1935

This was the first of nine internationals played by Doug Dalton the rugged Hawke's Bay prop. He took Hore's place in the front row after the Otago man had broken a bone in his hand in the Scottish game. McKenzie was dropped, McLean coming in on the side of the scrum. "Rusty" Page, who suffered a knee injury in the second game of the tour, had played in the twenty-first match, hoping to be fit for the Irish Test. However the injury was aggravated and he did not play again on tour. His loss for almost the entire tour was a sad blow to the All Blacks for none of the other first five-eighths had quite the amount of thrust near the scrum that Page possessed.

The Irish team was strong in the forwards with Sam Walker, Deering, Ross, Bob Graves and the captain, Jack Siggins, outstanding. Walker was later captain of the 1938 Lions on their South African tour. Bob Graves was also a member of that team. Of the home backs, Morris and Morgan were well up to international standard while Boyle and Victor Hewitt, a younger brother of Frank and Tom Hewitt who had turned out for Ireland against New Zealand in 1924, were capable enough. Elsewhere however the All Black backs were superior to their opposites.

The ground was heavy and solid rain fell for most of the second half. This no doubt evened up the teams and prevented New Zealand from running up a big score.

The All Blacks scored early when McLean picked up in the loose and passed to Griffiths. The latter sent on to Caughey who cut through but Morris tackled him. The ball rolled clear and Oliver dribbled it on with Mitchell finally snapping it up to score in the corner. Gilbert missed. On two other occasions Caughey burst through gaps but the outside backs were not up quickly enough to capitalise on the Aucklander's efforts. However, New Zealand went further ahead in the twelfth minute when Dermot Morris mis-kicked in front of his posts. The ball bounced into Oliver's hands to give him a gift try under the bar. Gilbert converted.

A steady drizzle was making the ball hard to handle and the game became more even as the Irish forwards began loose foot rushes, at which they excelled. After hitting the cross-bar from a forty-yard penalty, Aidan Bailey put points on the board for the home team with a good penalty goal in the twenty-second minute. New Zealand scored again two minutes later when Mitchell came in to make the extra man to give Hart an overlap. He scored in the corner but Gilbert failed to convert. Hewitt made ground with good kicking and the home team attacked fiercely, Beamish scoring near the posts. Bailey missed the conversion and halftime came soon after.

Although Hadley was winning set scrums almost as he pleased, the wet ball prevented the All Blacks from capitalising on this advantage. The Irish forwards kept the ball at their feet in the loose and from a dribbling rush Siggins went over but a scrum was ordered for a prior infringement. Then the Irish captain kicked a penalty from right in front and only two points separated the teams. The Irish forwards mounted attack after attack but sound defence by Gilbert kept them from scoring. From a scrum infringement

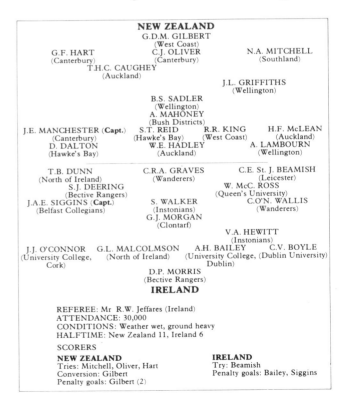

NEW ZEALAND

G.D.M. GILBERT
(West Coast)

G.F. HART   C.J. OLIVER   N.A. MITCHELL
(Canterbury)   (Canterbury)   (Southland)

T.H.C. CAUGHEY
(Auckland)

J.L. GRIFFITHS
(Wellington)

B.S. SADLER
(Wellington)

A. MAHONEY
(Bush Districts)

J.E. MANCHESTER (Capt.)   S.T. REID   R.R. KING   H.F. McLEAN
(Canterbury)   (Hawke's Bay)   (West Coast)   (Auckland)

D. DALTON   W.E. HADLEY   A. LAMBOURN
(Hawke's Bay)   (Auckland)   (Wellington)

T.B. DUNN   C.R.A. GRAVES   C.E. St. J. BEAMISH
(North of Ireland)   (Wanderers)   (Leicester)

S.J. DEERING   W. McC. ROSS
(Bective Rangers)   (Queen's University)

J.A.E. SIGGINS (Capt.)   S. WALKER   C.O'N. WALLIS
(Belfast Collegians)   (Instonians)   (Wanderers)

G.J. MORGAN
(Clontarf)

V.A. HEWITT
(Instonians)

J.J. O'CONNOR   G.L. MALCOLMSON   A.H. BAILEY   C.V. BOYLE
(University College,   (North of Ireland)   (University College,   (Dublin University)
Cork)   Dublin)

D.P. MORRIS
(Bective Rangers)

IRELAND

REFEREE: Mr R.W. Jeffares (Ireland)
ATTENDANCE: 30,000
CONDITIONS: Weather wet, ground heavy
HALFTIME: New Zealand 11, Ireland 6

SCORERS

NEW ZEALAND	IRELAND
Tries: Mitchell, Oliver, Hart	Try: Beamish
Conversion: Gilbert	Penalty goals: Bailey, Siggins
Penalty goals: Gilbert (2)	

IRELAND 9

Lansdowne Road, Dublin

near the home line the All Black full-back increased his team's lead and right on time he

Following All Black captain, Jack Manchester, onto the field are Mahoney, McLean, King, Reid and Lambourn.

added another penalty goal with a fine kick from the side-line. The Irishmen played the last thirteen minutes without their captain, Siggins, who had to retire with a shoulder injury.

WALES 13

21 December 1935

The New Zealand back line had to be rearranged for this vital game because Caughey was unavailable through injury. Oliver was moved to second five-eighth and Mitchell to centre. Ball was given his chance on the left wing and he justified his inclusion by scoring two good tries.

Players on the Welsh side well-known to New Zealanders were Vivian Jenkins, now a celebrated Rugby writer, Wilfred Wooller, another writer on the game, and the great scrum-half, Haydn Tanner who was playing his first of 25 games for Wales while still a schoolboy.

This was a thrilling game and the large crowd was kept in suspense until the final whistle. For the first fifteen minutes Wales had to defend almost without respite and only a superb tackle by Jenkins kept Hart from scoring in the corner. Then a fine break by Sadler almost led to a try by Mahoney who was dragged down only a few yards short of the Welsh line. At last Wales entered New Zealand territory and a thrilling run by Cliff Jones was stopped by the All Black forwards right on the line.

Five minutes before halftime the first score finally came when Sadler passed to Griffiths on the blind side of a scrum and the five-eighth sent on to Ball, who ran to the corner for a good try. Gilbert failed to convert. New Zealand had done much the better in the first spell and deserved to be further ahead at halftime.

Within two minutes of the restart, Wales went into the lead. Cliff Jones ran from a scrum and kicked downfield and the ball bounced perfectly for Claude Davey to gather it in and score unopposed under the posts. Jenkins converted. Four minutes later, the men in scarlet increased their lead when Wooller kicked over Gilbert's head for Rees-Jones to dash in from the wing and score beside the posts. Jenkins again converted and the game had swung away from New Zealand.

The All Blacks were clearly rattled but they rushed the ball downfield where Jones tried to kick the ball out but Gilbert fielded it and kicked

Welsh forwards, T. Rees, Williams, Lang and A. Rees, form an effective blockade. All Blacks are Reid, Mahoney, Dalton and Hadley.

SPORT & GENERAL

Cardiff Arms Park

GRAPHIC PHOTO UNION

The Welsh defence races across to cover a break by Griffiths who has Oliver and Mitchell outside him.

a fine goal from 35 yards out. This gave the tourists renewed confidence and they almost scored again but Jenkins just managed to reach the ball ahead of Hart, who had punted through.

With twenty-five minutes gone, Gilbert tried another drop at goal but the ball fell well short, landing near Rees-Jones and Davey. A misunderstanding between them resulted in the ball going to ground. Ball ran in, dribbled ahead and when the bounce was favourable picked up to score between the posts. Gilbert's conversion put New Zealand ahead again.

Wales appeared disheartened, especially when their hooker, Tarr, left the field with a serious spine injury. With six minutes to go, however, Wooller shot through the New Zealand backs and kicked ahead. The ball bounced over the New Zealand line and eluded Wooller but Rees-Jones was on hand to touch down for the winning try which Jenkins failed to convert.

NEW ZEALAND

G.D.M. GILBERT
(West Coast)

G.F. HART   N.A. MITCHELL   N. BALL
(Canterbury)   (Southland)   (Wellington)
C.J. OLIVER
(Canterbury)

J.L. GRIFFITHS
(Wellington)

B.S. SADLER
(Wellington)
A. MAHONEY
(Bush Districts)
J.E. MANCHESTER (Capt.)   S.T. REID   R.R. KING   H.F. McLEAN
(Canterbury)   (Hawke's Bay)   (West Coast)   (Auckland)
A. LAMBOURN   W.E. HADLEY   D. DALTON
(Wellington)   (Auckland)   (Hawke's Bay)

T.J. REES   D.J. TARR   H. PAYNE
(Newport)   (Swansea)   (Swansea)
E. WATKINS   T. WILLIAMS
(Cardiff)   (Cross Keys)
G. PROSSER   J. LANG   A.M. REES
(Neath)   (Llanelly)   (London Welsh)
H. TANNER
(Swansea)

C.W. JONES
(Cambridge University)
W. WOOLLER   E.C. DAVEY (Capt.)   J.I. REES   G.R. REES-JONES
(Cambridge   (Swansea)   (Swansea)   (Oxford
University)   University)
V.G.J. JENKINS
(London Welsh)

WALES

REFEREE: Mr C.H. Gadney (England)
ATTENDANCE: 50,000
CONDITIONS: Weather fine, ground firm
HALFTIME: New Zealand 3, Wales 0

SCORERS

NEW ZEALAND   **WALES**
Tries: Ball (2)   Tries: Rees-Jones (2), Davey
Conversion: Gilbert   Conversions: Jenkins (2)
Dropped goal: Gilbert

4 January, 1936

The New Zealand selection committee made several changes in the back line from the third Test team. Ball had played well against Wales and then turned in an excellent game in the second London Counties match immediately before the English Test. On the other hand, Hart had lost his usual brilliant form towards the end of the tour so Ball was given his chance, retaining his place on the left wing with Mitchell moving to Hart's place on the right. Oliver went back to centre and Caughey, who had apparently recovered from the leg injury which had kept him out of the Welsh match, regained his place at second five-eighth. However, he was not fully fit and it is doubtful whether he should have played.

The reliable Griffiths was dropped in favour of Eric Tindill, who was to play his only Test. Tindill also played cricket for New Zealand and later became an international Rugby referee and cricket umpire. Normally a half-back, he was chosen as a first five-eighth for this tour. His quick acceleration and his ability to drop goals earned him his place in the final Test.

Sadler had also lost form in recent games, largely because the opposition had become wise to his running game, whereas the experienced Corner had shown very good form in his last two games before the English match, especially in the London Counties game, in which he captained the All Blacks. Hore was fit again and returned to the front row.

The English team contained some interesting personalities. At full-back was the great all-round sportsman "Tuppy" Owen-Smith who had come to Oxford from South Africa as a Rhodes Scholar. He played for his native country at cricket and was also an outstanding boxer.

On the right wing was Alexander Obolensky, a Russian prince whose family had fled to England during the 1917 Revolution. Very fast and unorthodox, Obolensky scored two great tries in this match against the All Blacks and this game is still referred to in English Rugby circles as "Obolensky's match." Obolensky was killed in an aircraft accident while training as a fighter pilot with the R.A.F. in 1940.

Two of the forwards were well-known to New Zealanders. Kendrew had toured with the British team in 1930 but he did not play a Test. A regular army officer, he won ten English caps. He rose to the rank of brigadier during World War II, in which he had an outstanding record. He was later knighted and subsequently became Governor of

Mitchell is tackled after a strong run down the right wing.

N EW ZEALAND 0

Twickenham, London

Western Australia. Marine Webb was stationed at Auckland for some time before the war and played for Auckland in 1938. He won twelve caps for England, including one against South Africa in 1932.

England was much the better team and deserved to win by a big score. The All Blacks did well for the first twenty minutes but seldom looked like scoring thereafter. King almost scored in the twentieth minute but he was thrown out at the corner flag. England counter-attacked and from a scrum the ball went along the chain to Obolensky who beat his man and raced round Gilbert to score a good try. Dunkley hit the cross-bar with his conversion attempt.

New Zealand worked back to the home team's 25 eventually and Corner passed to Tindill from a scrum. Tindill dodged infield and linked up with Manchester who passed to McLean. The Auckland forward tried desperately hard to force his way over but was unsuccessful. Two minutes from halftime, Cranmer following a scrum and ran twenty yards before he in-passed to Candler. Obolensky dashed in-field from the right wing, took a pass from Candler and carved through a

Tom Webster, cartoonist for the Daily Mail, **commemorates "Obolensky's Match."**

gap. He ran round Gilbert, evaded Mitchell and scored on the opposite wing to his own. The kick failed but England had a handy lead at halftime.

For the first ten minutes of the second half, New Zealand showed improved form. Hadley was almost over, then Mitchell went close and both Gilbert and Tindill had drops at goal. However, a successful drop-kick by Cranmer following a set scrum gave England a ten-point lead and the game was virtually won. Finally, Candler picked up in the loose and passed in to his forwards. The ball came back to Cranmer who broke through to send Sever away on a run of 35 yards to the New Zealand line.

The simple conversion was astray and the match finished shortly after.

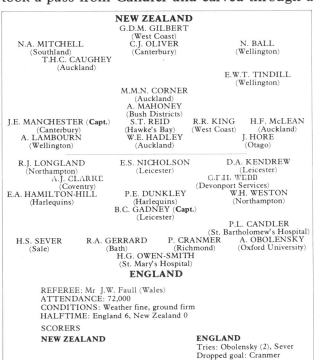

NEW ZEALAND

G.D.M. GILBERT
(West Coast)

| N.A. MITCHELL | C.J. OLIVER | N. BALL |
| (Southland) | (Canterbury) | (Wellington) |

T.H.C. CAUGHEY
(Auckland)

E.W.T. TINDILL
(Wellington)

M.M.N. CORNER
(Auckland)
A. MAHONEY
(Bush Districts)

J.E. MANCHESTER (Capt.)	S.T. REID	R.R. KING	H.F. McLEAN
(Canterbury)	(Hawke's Bay)	(West Coast)	(Auckland)
A. LAMBOURN	W.E. HADLEY		J. HORE
(Wellington)	(Auckland)		(Otago)

R.J. LONGLAND	E.S. NICHOLSON	D.A. KENDREW
(Northampton)	(Leicester)	(Leicester)
A.J. CLARKE		C.F.H. WEBB
(Coventry)		(Devonport Services)
E.A. HAMILTON-HILL	P.E. DUNKLEY	W.H. WESTON
(Harlequins)	(Harlequins)	(Northampton)

B.C. GADNEY (Capt.)
(Leicester)

P.L. CANDLER
(St. Bartholomew's Hospital)

| H.S. SEVER | R.A. GERRARD | P. CRANMER | A. OBOLENSKY |
| (Sale) | (Bath) | (Richmond) | (Oxford University) |

H.G. OWEN-SMITH
(St. Mary's Hospital)

ENGLAND

REFEREE: Mr J.W. Faull (Wales)
ATTENDANCE: 72,000
CONDITIONS: Weather fine, ground firm
HALFTIME: England 6, New Zealand 0

SCORERS

NEW ZEALAND	**ENGLAND**
	Tries: Obolensky (2), Sever
	Dropped goal: Cranmer

5 September, 1936

First Test

Five new caps appeared in the New Zealand team for the first Test against the 1936 Wallabies. Jim Watt, who played on the left wing, was very fast and ran second in the New Zealand 440 yards championship in 1937. This was his only season in international Rugby although he toured Japan with the New Zealand University team earlier in 1936 and was an All Black trialist in 1935. He was not available for the 1937 Tests because of an injury.

Brian Killeen, playing his only Test in this game, had built up a big reputation in Wellington and had played for the North Island before moving to Auckland in 1934. He captained Auckland for several seasons and, on his day, he was an extremely brilliant back.

John Wells, a robust forward from Wellington, also had only one season as an All Black but Jack Rankin, the lightweight loose forward from Canterbury, won selection again in 1937. Everard Jackson played for New Zealand again in 1937 and 1938. He was the son of F.S. Jackson, who had toured New Zealand in 1908 with the Anglo-Welsh team before settling in this country. The younger Jackson had the misfortune to lose a leg during World War II. "Bunk" Pollock, who had last represented New Zealand as a five-eighth in 1932, returned to the Test side at full-back.

The 1936 Australian team had a number of talented players yet its tour record was poor, only three games being won. The Wallabies had more than their share of bad luck however. The outstanding forward, "Wild Bill" Cerutti, was injured in the first game and did not play again until after the second Test.

The captain, E.S. "Dooney" Hayes, a brilliant centre and goal kicker who had played against the All Blacks in 1934, was also hurt in the opening game of the tour and although he played twice more he was not available for either of the Tests.

K.P. Storey, the full-back, was ill for the first Test and Ron Rankin, selected as a centre, took his place. The shortage of fit centres led to the playing of Pauling, chosen for this tour as a forward, in the three-quarter line. As mentioned earlier, Pauling's father played for New Zealand in 1897 and later became an international referee in Sydney. The younger Pauling had previously played centre and he represented New South Wales and Australia in that position against the 1937 Springboks.

Among the newcomers to Test Rugby in the Australian pack was Frank Hutchinson who, at 18, must have been one of the youngest tight forwards to play international Rugby. He was killed on air operations with the R.A.A.F. during the Second World War while Russ Kelly died in Australia as a result of war wounds in 1943.

The weather was beautiful and there was scarcely any wind as the two teams took the field. Australia scored first when Rankin kicked a penalty from ten yards inside half-way after his namesake had been caught offside at a ruck. In the early stages the visitors were on top with "Aub" Hodgson, a truly fine forward, gaining a lot of possession from the line-out. Hodgson's

NEW ZEALAND

H.R. POLLOCK
(Wellington)

G.F. HART   T.H.C. CAUGHEY   J.M. WATT
(Canterbury)   (Auckland)   (Otago)
B.A. KILLEEN
(Auckland)
                                                J.L. GRIFFITHS (**Capt.**)
                                                (Wellington)
                         B.S. SADLER
                         (Wellington)
                         J.G. RANKIN
                         (Canterbury)
J. WELLS   S.T. REID   R.R. KING   R.M. McKENZIE
(Wellington)   (Hawke's Bay)   (West Coast)   (Manawatu)
E.S. JACKSON   W.E. HADLEY   D. DALTON
(Hawke's Bay)   (Auckland)   (Hawke's Bay)

R.J. WALDEN (**Capt.**)   E.T. BONIS   J.H. MALONE
(New South Wales)   (Queensland)   (New South Wales)
A.J. HODGSON   W.G.S. WHITE   F.E. HUTCHINSON   O.L. BRIDLE
(New South Wales) (New South Wales) (New South Wales)   (Victoria)
                  R.L.F. KELLY
                  (New South Wales)
                  E. de C. GIBBONS
                  (New South Wales)
                                                V.S. RICHARDS
                                                (New South Wales)
J.D. KELAHER   T.P. PAULING   R.E.M. McLAUGHLIN   A.D. McLEAN
(New South Wales) (New South Wales) (New South Wales)   (Queensland)
                  R. RANKIN
                  (New South Wales)

AUSTRALIA

REFEREE: Mr J. Moffitt (Wellington)
ATTENDANCE: 30,000
CONDITIONS: Weather fine, ground firm
HALFTIME: Australia 6, New Zealand 5
SCORERS

NEW ZEALAND	AUSTRALIA
Tries: Hart, Hadley, Watt	Try: McLaughlin
Conversion: Pollock	Penalty goal: Rankin

AUSTRALIA 6

Athletic Park, Wellington

general play was outstanding also and his exhibition was described by the critics as one of the best seen on Athletic Park. Bridle, brilliant as ever in the loose, was almost over when he kicked over Pollock's head but Caughey beat him to the ball. Next, McLaughlin was close to scoring when he kicked the ball over the line but Pollock saved by kicking the ball dead.

Hart made a fine break, side-stepping and swerving past the opposition but he was stopped short of the line. Then followed a brilliant try by McLaughlin. Pollock took a mark from which Gibbons fielded the ball. The half-back passed to Bridle who sent on to McLaughlin. The centre beat the opposition with a beautiful swerve and side-step to score. Rankin failed to convert.

Sadler breaks from a maul as Malone (16) comes around.

Now six points down, New Zealand attacked from the kick-off. Caughey broke through from a passing rush and when tackled near the line he passed to Hart, who scored. Pollock's conversion made the score 6-5 and it was unchanged at halftime.

Caughey again started a brilliant attack shortly after the resumption and was once more stopped just short of the line. The New Zealand forwards kept hammering the Australian defence and finally Hadley went over between the posts after Reid had appeared to knock on. Pollock missed the simplest of kicks.

The game continued to be very close, the defence on both sides preventing further scoring until Watt gained an overlap to score an unconverted try in the corner after Killeen and Caughey had made ground.

12 September, 1936

Second Test

There were several changes in both teams for this Test. Mitchell, who was not available for the first Test, came in at centre to replace Caughey, who was unavailable for the Dunedin game. Killeen was rather unlucky to be dropped. Griffiths moved to second five-eighth and the Otago and New Zealand University player, Colin Gillies, made his only international appearance in the first five-eighth berth. The young Southland flanker, Ron Ward, was playing his first of three Tests.

The Wallabies were again missing some of their best players but Storey was able to take his place at full-back and Rankin moved to centre. The experienced Queenslander, Lewis, replaced Richards at five-eighth.

Australia won the toss and played with the wind and sun. The visitors were soon on attack but a wild pass by Malone spoiled a promising movement. Good line kicking by Pollock sent the Wallabies back to their own 25 but the Australians were quickly back on the attack when Gibbons broke away and in-passed to Hodgson, who ran 25 yards before sending on to Bridle. The latter passed to McLean but the winger was smothered. A kick by Bridle went past Pollock but the ball rolled into touch.

From a line-out, McLean threw a long one over the forwards and the ball rolled along the ground in front of New Zealand's posts. McLaughlin picked it up and scored for Rankin to convert.

Two minutes later, Australia incurred a scrum penalty and from the 25 Pollock raised the flags. Play was fairly even for some time with the forward encounters slightly favouring Australia. Then in the twentieth minute Ron Rankin kicked a penalty goal from near the 25 to put his team further in the lead.

From the kick-off New Zealand attacked but a knock-on by Gillies caused play to break down. Pollock's line kicking was a great asset to New Zealand and the home team spent some time on attack.

An All Black passing rush ended in Storey

stopping Watt five yards from the line but shortly after, New Zealand scored when Mitchell broke through between Rankin and McLaughlin to ground the ball near the posts. Pollock's conversion evened the score.

Bridle again kicked past Pollock and the ball rolled over the New Zealand line. Several players dived but the try was awarded to Bridle. Rankin converted. New Zealand soon closed the gap however when Hart went across at the end of a passing rush. Pollock failed to convert. Shortly before halftime, McLaughlin retired with rib injuries and Richards went on at five-eighth with Lewis moving out to centre.

Soon after the resumption, the home forwards broke away but Dalton knocked on when he had Hart unopposed outside him. Then Storey, who had played extremely well in the first half, "speculated" at the ball and missed, Hart gathering in to run behind the posts. Pollock converted to give New Zealand the lead for the first time.

NEW ZEALAND

H.R. POLLOCK
(Wellington)

G.F. HART	N.A. MITCHELL	J.M. WATT
(Canterbury)	(Southland)	(Otago)

J.L. GRIFFITHS (**Capt.**)
(Wellington)

C.C. GILLIES
(Otago)

B.S. SADLER
(Wellington)

J.G. RANKIN
(Canterbury)

R.H. WARD	S.T. REID	R.R. KING	J. WELLS
(Southland)	(Hawke's Bay)	(West Coast)	(Wellington)
E.S. JACKSON	W.E. HADLEY		D. DALTON
(Hawke's Bay)	(Auckland)		(Hawke's Bay)

R.J. WALDEN (**Capt.**)	E.T. BONIS	J.H. MALONE
(New South Wales)	(Queensland)	(New South Wales)
A.J. HODGSON	W.G.S. WHITE	F.E. HUTCHINSON	O.L. BRIDLE
(New South Wales)	(New South Wales)	(New South Wales)	(Victoria)

R.L.F. KELLY
(New South Wales)

E. de C. GIBBONS
(New South Wales)

L.S. LEWIS
(Queensland)

J.D. KELAHER	R. RANKIN	R.E. M. McLAUGHLIN†	A.D. McLEAN
(New South Wales)	(New South Wales)	(New South Wales)	(Queensland)

K.P. STOREY
(New South Wales)

AUSTRALIA

REPLACEMENT:† Replaced by V.S. Richards (New South Wales)
REFEREE: Mr H.J. McKenzie (Wairarapa)
ATTENDANCE: 25,000
CONDITIONS: Weather fine, ground firm
HALFTIME: Australia 13, New Zealand 11
SCORERS

NEW ZEALAND
Tries: Mitchell (2), Hart (2), Reid (2) Rankin (2), Watt
Conversions: Pollock (4)
Penalty goal: Pollock

AUSTRALIA
Tries: McLaughlin, Bridle
Conversions: Rankin (2)
Penalty goal: Rankin

AUSTRALIA 13

Carisbrook, Dunedin

Gibbons prepares to go down on the ball as Wells, Ward, Rankin, Dalton and Reid burst through. Bonis is at right.

Storey was in further trouble when his kick was charged down for Hart to again obtain possession. The wing started a passing burst which ended in Reid crossing wide out. Pollock missed. Another try followed almost immediately. Watt broke past McLean but was brought down in a fine dive tackle by Storey. The All Black left wing regained his feet however and dribbled the ball over the line where he fell on it near the corner. Pollock failed to convert.

An assault on the New Zealand line by the Australian forwards almost ended in a try but Hutchinson held on too long and was stopped in front of the posts. Play went back into the visitors' half and Jack Rankin took a pass from Sadler near the line to go over wide out. Again Pollock missed.

Almost immediately after the restart, Mitchell took an in-pass from Watt and raced 40 yards to score in the corner. Pollock's kick missed. Then Gillies cut in during a passing rush and sent on to Sadler, who put Rankin in for his second try. Pollock converted from a handy position. The final points came from short passing among the forwards, Reid finishing the movement with a try between the posts which Pollock converted.

By defeating Australia in the 1936 series, New Zealand recaptured the Bledisloe Cup which the Wallabies had won in 1934. The 1936 Australians sadly missed some of the 1934 stars such as Alex Ross and Syd Malcolm, who had retired, Cyril Towers, who was travelling in Europe and Africa and, of course, the 1936 skipper "Dooney" Hayes, who was still on the injured list. Towers captained New South Wales and Australia against the 1937 Springboks while Hayes, who was killed in North Africa while ferrying supplies to the troops with the R.A.A.F., played in the 1938 Tests against New Zealand.

125

NEW ZEALAND 13

14 August, 1937

First Test

After six trial games and the inter-island match, the cumbersome seven-man New Zealand panel of selectors chose a team which did not inspire much confidence in the minds of Rugby followers. None of the backs had played in a Test and several stars of recent All Black teams were discarded in favour of these new players.

The New Zealand backs had all played well in the trials, however, and most of them were very experienced at provincial level. Jack Taylor, Johnny Dick, Jack Sullivan and Jack Hooper were all to tour Australia with the 1938 All Blacks and all would probably have had long international careers had it not been for the Second World War. Sullivan became an All Black selector and was chairman of the New Zealand Rugby Union from 1969 to 1977 while Dick gave good service as selector and coach of Auckland junior teams. Donald Cobden, Dave Trevathan and Harry Simon all had only one season in international football.

"Brushy" Mitchell would undoubtedly have been the first back chosen and would almost certainly have captained the team had not an injury, suffered in the trials, made him unavailable. The loss of Mitchell was a severe blow to New Zealand but the selectors themselves were to blame for his absence. For reasons known only to themselves, they had played him in three trial matches during the week following his brilliant display in the inter-island match on July 10. He was called on to play on July 12, 14 and 17 — a ridiculous state of affairs when it was obvious that he was in a class of his own in the North-South game. The injury to "Joey" Sadler in a Wellington club match early in the season was another blow to New Zealand, especially as he did not play again.

Although the backs were all new to the international scene, the forwards were very experienced, the only new Test player being Allan Parkhill. He won selection again for the Australian tour in 1938, playing in all three Tests.

One member of this first Test team, Donald Cobden, joined the Royal Air Force on a short service commission and established a good reputation in British Rugby before losing his life in the Battle of Britain, in which he served as a fighter pilot.

There were also some shock selections in the South African team. First of all, the captain, Philip Nel, was dropped. He had playing in the 1928 Tests against New Zealand and his leadership had been outstanding on the 1937 tour. The vice-captain, the famous Danie Craven, led the side from the fly-half position, although his best place was undoubtedly behind the scrum. Pierre de Villiers, of 1928 fame, was played at scrum-half. Gerry Brand, another 1928 veteran, and now the team's first-string full-back, was injured. This meant playing Fred Turner, selected as the second full-back but generally regarded as the Springboks' best wing, in Brand's place with Pat Lyster on the left wing. The experienced prop, "Boy" Louw, was also on the injured list, Jennings thus being given his chance.

The match was won for New Zealand by the forwards and by the kicking of Trevathan. The All Black pack was outweighed and for most of

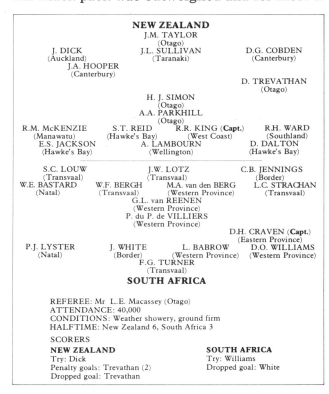

NEW ZEALAND

J.M. TAYLOR
(Otago)

J. DICK   J.L. SULLIVAN   D.G. COBDEN
(Auckland)   (Taranaki)   (Canterbury)
J.A. HOOPER
(Canterbury)

                                   D. TREVATHAN
                                   (Otago)

H. J. SIMON
(Otago)
A.A. PARKHILL
(Otago)

R.M. McKENZIE   S.T. REID   R.R. KING (**Capt.**)   R.H. WARD
(Manawatu)   (Hawke's Bay)   (West Coast)   (Southland)
E.S. JACKSON   A. LAMBOURN   D. DALTON
(Hawke's Bay)   (Wellington)   (Hawke's Bay)

S.C. LOUW   J.W. LOTZ   C.B. JENNINGS
(Transvaal)   (Transvaal)   (Border)
W.E. BASTARD   W.F. BERGH   M.A. van den BERG   L.C. STRACHAN
(Natal)   (Transvaal)   (Western Province)   (Transvaal)
                 G.L. van REENEN
                 (Western Province)
                P. du P. de VILLIERS
                 (Western Province)

                                  D.H. CRAVEN (**Capt.**)
                                 (Eastern Province)
P.J. LYSTER   J. WHITE   L. BABROW   D.O. WILLIAMS
(Natal)   (Border)   (Western Province)   (Western Province)
                 F.G. TURNER
                 (Transvaal)

SOUTH AFRICA

REFEREE: Mr L.E. Macassey (Otago)
ATTENDANCE: 40,000
CONDITIONS: Weather showery, ground firm
HALFTIME: New Zealand 6, South Africa 3
SCORERS

NEW ZEALAND	**SOUTH AFRICA**
Try: Dick	Try: Williams
Penalty goals: Trevathan (2)	Dropped goal: White
Dropped goal: Trevathan	

SOUTH A RICA 7

Athletic Park, Wellington

Sullivan, Strachan and Mr Macassey watch Dick dive over in a tackle to score.

the game was one short after Ward went out to the wing to replace Cobden, who was injured after twenty-five minutes' play. In spite of these handicaps, the home pack dominated the game and laid the foundation for an unexpected win.

New Zealand looked like scoring in the opening minutes when Dick chased a kick by Hooper but Turner saved. The home team kept up the attack and after eleven minutes, Strachan was caught offside from a scrum and Trevathan kicked an easy goal. South Africa retaliated with a fine break by de Villiers from which Lyster was nearly over while Turner had two chances from penalties in quick succession but was wide of the posts both times. Trevathan also missed an easy penalty.

Cobden left the field after being heavily dumped by Williams and Ward went on to the wing. The Springbok forwards battered their way down to All Black territory, gaining a temporary ascendancy over the depleted home pack. With four minutes to go to halftime, they heeled from a scrum and the ball finally reached Williams, who

ran round three men to dive over the corner. Turner's kick was wide. Two minutes later Lotz was penalised for lifting in the scrum and Trevathan kicked his second penalty to give New Zealand a 6-3 lead at halftime.

Two minutes after the resumption, New Zealand increased the lead when Hooper broke through with his forwards in support. The ball came back to Hooper from Dalton and the second five-eighth passed to Sullivan. He drew Lyster and made an opening for Dick to crash through a tackle and score near the corner. Trevathan missed the conversion.

The Springboks attacked after this set-back and Lyster eluded Dick to set sail for the line but Taylor grassed him with a splendid tackle. A similar fate awaited Williams after he had run round Ward and reached open country.

The All Black forwards came back to win valuable ground and from a line-out in the Springbok 25, Ward received and passed to Trevathan who dropped a brilliant goal. With only thirteen minutes left, the game was virtually decided but five minutes from the end White dropped a splendid goal to make the score look more respectable for South Africa.

SOUTH AF ICA 13

4 September, 1937

Second Test

The New Zealand selectors made only two changes in their team for the second Test even though leading critics suggested several ways in which the All Blacks could be strengthened. The powerful Maori wing, Bill Phillips, took Cobden's place and it was generally agreed that this would be an improvement. Phillips had played very well for Waikato-King Country-Thames Valley in the second game of the tour when the combined side had been unlucky to lose 6-3 to the Springboks and he was noted for his rugged qualities.

The other change was in the forwards where the 1936 All Black, Jack Rankin, who had been ill for the first Test, replaced Ward.

The Springboks had selected a much stronger team than the one that had represented them at Wellington. The great "Gerry" Brand was fit

again and was playing superbly. After making his international debut as a wing-three-quarter in 1928, Brand toured Britain as South Africa's number one full-back in 1931. He played in all five Tests against the Wallabies in 1933, three times at full-back and twice on the wing. His form in 1937 won him a reputation in both Australia and New Zealand as one of the best, if not *the* best, of full-backs to play for a touring team. Brand's 100 points scored on the 1937 tour remained a record for a tourist until the advent of Barry John of the 1971 Lions.

With Brand at full-back Turner was moved to the wing in place of Lyster and although the latter was a fine player Turner was undoubtedly better, at least in 1937.

Craven went to his best position behind the scrum in place of de Villiers, and the young Tony

Danie Craven's famous dive-pass.

NEW ZEALAND 6

Lancaster Park, Christchurch

Harris was selected to partner him. Harris, who also played cricket for South Africa, had very safe hands and was a fine runner with the ball. He would rank with Spong of the 1930 British team and Kyle of the 1950 Lions as a fly-half.

The South African pack was considerably strengthened with the inclusion of the captain, Nel, and the powerful prop, "Boy" Louw, who joined his brother "Fanie" and the tough hooker, Jan Lotz, in the front row.

It is perhaps worthy of note that S.R. Hofmeyr was originally selected at centre with de Villiers at scrum-half, White and Craven being named as reserves in case of wet weather. As there was heavy rain the night before the Test, these reserves were played.

The Springboks had rather the better of the early part of the game, their forwards dominating set play with their great weight advantage. The home forwards were still dangerous in the loose however and New Zealand scored first, about half an hour after the start. A dropped pass was pounced on by the All Black loose forwards who carried play into green territory. Then Phillips made a strong run up the left wing before passing to Rankin, who had come up in support. Rankin sent on to Simon who passed to Sullivan for the centre to race over for a try, which Trevathan failed to convert.

South Africa attacked from the kick-off and the All Blacks were defending desperately when a pass from Harris to Babrow was intercepted by Sullivan who took the ball almost out of Babrow's hands. In a flash Sullivan was in the clear but Williams turned to chase him. As the flying Springbok wing drew level with him, Sullivan kicked over the head of Brand, who had come up while his team was attacking. Running shoulder to shoulder, Sullivan and Williams chased the ball with the All Black always getting to it just a little in front and kicking it on as the crowd went wild. With inches to spare Sullivan dived on the ball to score one of the most thrilling tries in Test match history. Trevathan failed to convert and New Zealand led 6-0 at halftime.

With the chance of another win and the tying up of the rubber, the All Blacks attacked fiercely for the first five minutes of the second half. Then the South African forwards began to take control again and from the loose the ball went along the back line to White, who passed to Turner on the left wing. Dick, Simon and Taylor had Turner covered but the brilliant Springbok ran round Dick and cut infield to leave the rest of the opposition wrong-footed. He tore down the middle of the field to score a great try behind the posts. Brand's conversion reduced New Zealand's lead to a single point.

Play now became very boisterous with Rankin, "Boy" Louw and Bastard all requiring attention. The referee spoke severely to the two packs and tempers settled down. Then, well on in the second half, South Africa received a penalty. Brand took his time and with a fine kick sent the ball between the posts to give his team the lead.

The final score came from an assault on the New Zealand line in which White threw a pass to Babrow. Bastard appeared from nowhere, grabbed the ball and threw himself over the line. Brand's conversion put the result beyond doubt.

NEW ZEALAND

J.M. TAYLOR
(Otago)

J. DICK	J.L. SULLIVAN	W.J. PHILLIPS
(Auckland)	(Taranaki)	(King Country)

J.A. HOOPER
(Canterbury)

D. TREVATHAN
(Otago)

H.J. SIMON
(Otago)

A.A. PARKHILL
(Otago)

R.M. McKENZIE	S.T. REID	R.R. KING (Capt.)	J.G. RANKIN
(Manawatu)	(Hawke's Bay)	(West Coast)	(Canterbury)
E.S. JACKSON	A. LAMBOURN		D. DALTON
(Hawke's Bay)	(Wellington)		(Hawke's Bay)

S.C. LOUW	J.W. LOTZ	M.M. LOUW
(Transvaal)	(Transvaal)	(Western Province)

L.C. STRACHAN	P.J. NEL (Capt.)	M.A. van den BERG	W.E. BASTARD
(Transvaal)	(Natal)	(Western Province)	(Natal)

W.F. BERGH
(Transvaal)

D.H. CRAVEN
(Eastern Province)

T.A. HARRIS
(Transvaal)

F.G. TURNER	J. WHITE	L. BABROW	D.O. WILLIAMS
(Transvaal)	(Border)	(Western Province)	(Western Province)

G.H. BRAND
(Western Province)

SOUTH AFRICA

REFEREE: Mr J.S. King (Wellington)
ATTENDANCE: 45,000
CONDITIONS: Weather fine, ground holding
HALFTIME: New Zealand 6, South Africa 0

SCORERS

NEW ZEALAND	SOUTH AFRICA
Tries: Sullivan (2)	Tries: Turner, Bastard
	Conversions: Brand (2)
	Penalty goal: Brand

SOUTH AF RICA 17

25 September, 1937

Third Test

Seldom, if ever, has a Rugby match in New Zealand generated so much excitement as did this vital third Test of 1937. Former All Blacks Fred Lucas and Bert Cooke predicted a win for New Zealand but F.S. Murray, who played for New Zealand in 1893 and 1897, favoured the Springboks. Rugby followers and critics, as well as the officials of both teams, expected a close game whatever the result. Here their forecasts were well astray, for the Springboks completely outclassed the All Blacks and for the first time a rubber between these two teams was won rather than drawn.

Many of us who saw this great South African team in action still regard it as the best side to have visited New Zealand to date for it had no weaknesses and the football it played was superb.

The New Zealand selectors made several changes for the final Test. The second Test wings, Phillips and Dick, were dropped and Mitchell was chosen at centre with Caughey on the wing. Sullivan, who had proved to be New Zealand's most dangerous back, was shifted to the wing, where his talents were somewhat wasted. This arrangement of the three-quarter line seemed strange since of the three players chosen, Mitchell was the only one with international experience on the wing, where he had shown great form in 1935. Both Caughey and Sullivan were midfield backs although both had played the odd first-class match on the wing. In the twenty-seventh minute of the game, however, Mitchell and Caughey changed places.

Caughey had been unavailable for the earlier Tests as he had been out of the country on a business trip and Mitchell had been on the injured list. Shortly before the Test, the Southland man was brought to Auckland to play for the Auckland Second Division team against Navy in order to satisfy the selectors of his soundness.

Incidentally, Marine Webb, who had played for England against New Zealand in 1935, was in the Navy pack. Mitchell took the field heavily bandaged but he was able to run through the opposition almost at will. The outing proved very little but the selectors decided to take a chance.

Still heavily bandaged, Mitchell took his place in the third Test team and for most of the game was little better than a passenger. Caughey, on the other hand, was, along with Taylor, the best of the All Black backs, his tackling being largely responsible for keeping the South African score to 17 points.

The only change in the All Black pack was the replacement of Rankin by Ward. The South Africans kept the same pack as they had for the second Test but an injury to White gave Lochner, selected as a utility back, his cap.

The game was even more one-sided than the score suggests for the big Springbok forwards gained complete domination and Craven gave one of his finest exhibitions behind this great pack. His long dive passes provided Harris with all the time in the world to set the backs in motion and the young fly-half made the most of his opportunities. Outside him, his three-quarters ran with speed and determination while at full-back Brand was his usual reliable self, even though his goalkicking was not up to his best standard.

NEW ZEALAND

J.M. TAYLOR
(Otago)

J.L. SULLIVAN   N.A. MITCHELL   T.H.C. CAUGHEY
(Taranaki)   (Southland)   (Auckland)
J.A. HOOPER
(Canterbury)
                                                  D. TREVATHAN
                                                  (Otago)
                           H.J. SIMON
                           (Otago)
                           A.A. PARKHILL
                           (Otago)
R.M. McKENZIE   S.T. REID   R.R. KING (Capt.)   R.H. WARD
(Manawatu)   (Hawke's Bay)   (West Coast)   (Southland)
E.S. JACKSON   A. LAMBOURN   D. DALTON
(Hawke's Bay)   (Wellington)   (Hawke's Bay)

M.M. LOUW   J.W. LOTZ   S.C. LOUW
(Western Province)   (Transvaal)   (Transvaal)
L.C. STRACHAN   M.A. van den BERG   P.J. NEL (Capt.)   W.E. BASTARD
(Transvaal)   (Western Province)   (Natal)   (Natal)
                       W.F. BERGH
                       (Transvaal)
                       D.H. CRAVEN
                       (Eastern Province)
                                              T.A. HARRIS
                                              (Transvaal)
F.G. TURNER   G.P. LOCHNER   L. BABROW   D.O. WILLIAMS
(Transvaal)   (Eastern Province) (Western Province) (Western Province)
                       G.H. BRAND
                       (Western Province)

SOUTH AFRICA

REFEREE: Mr J.S. King (Wellington)
ATTENDANCE: 58,000
CONDITIONS: Weather dull, ground firm
HALFTIME: South Africa 8, New Zealand 3

SCORERS

NEW ZEALAND   **SOUTH AFRICA**
Penalty goals: Trevathan (2)   Tries: Babrow (2), Bergh, Williams,
                                   Turner
                                   Conversion: Brand

N W ZEALAND 6

Eden Park, Auckland

The crowd was a record for Eden Park and thousands came from all over the country. Many slept outside the park to ensure good places on the terraces, which were located where the present Number Four Stand is situated.

The ground was greasy following drizzling rain in the morning but the match itself was played under good conditions, there being little wind or sun.

The Springboks soon opened the scoring. Under the rules then in force, South Africa elected to take scrums instead of line-outs and it was from one of these scrums, in the home 25, that Craven sent out a long pass to Harris. The latter sent on to Lochner who made a brilliant break between Hooper and Mitchell before transferring to Babrow, who scored ten yards from the corner with a man over. Brand failed to convert.

After play had been fairly even for a short time the Springboks scored again. The ball came to Babrow in a back movement following a scrum and he put in a splendid run downfield before cross-kicking over the New Zealand line. The green forwards were on the spot and Bergh scored for Brand to convert.

The Springbok forwards were incurring frequent scrum penalties and, from one of these, Trevathan opened New Zealand's scoring when he put over a good kick from forty yards out. The home team did not look like scoring a try however and spent nearly all the first half defending desperately. Williams put in several spectacular runs down the sideline but Caughey was always across to tackle him.

Immediately after the second half opened the Springboks scored again. Much had been made of Craven's dive pass by the newspapers and it was believed that the Springbok half could send the ball much further than he actually could. A ruse had been worked out by the South Africans and it was put into effect when Taylor found touch near half-way and Nel called for a scrum. Craven waved Harris out further on the open side and the fly-half moved a few feet. Craven waved him still further until there was a wide gap between Harris and the scrum. Trevathan hesitated

WEEKLY NEWS

Harris leaves one player sprawling and wrong-foots Sullivan with this break.

and then moved out to mark Harris. Craven put the ball in and Lotz duly heeled it. Turner raced in from the blind side, took the ball from Craven and sprinted through the huge gap left by Trevathan. The winger sent on to Lochner who passed to Babrow for the latter to score in the corner. Brand missed but within five minutes the Springboks went further ahead when Williams brilliantly beat three men to score. Brand's kick hit a post.

By this time the result was well beyond doubt. The Springbok pack gained so much possession that the home team had no chance of scoring, and there was only one team running the ball. Dalton and Lambourn changed places but the Hawke's Bay man had no more success at hooking than Lambourn enjoyed and the home backs were left on the defensive.

Babrow broke through and when Taylor tackled him he released the ball. Strachan collected it and threw out a long pass to Turner, who scored near the corner after a good run. Brand again missed the conversion. Six minutes from the end, the All Blacks managed to get into Springbok territory and from a thirty-five yard penalty Trevathan steered the ball between the posts. There was no further scoring and South Africa could now rightly claim to be the world's top Rugby nation.

NEW ZEALAND 24

23 July, 1938

First Test

Although eight of the New Zealand team for this Test had played against the 1937 Springboks, the side had something of a new look about it. Mitchell was right back to his best form and Australian writers were agreed that he was one of the greatest touring three-quarters seen in their country since World War I.

The three new backs also had outstanding tours. Tom Morrison, the South Canterbury wing, was a hard, determined runner and a fierce tackler who also played a great deal of his representative football at full-back and centre. He later became Chairman of the New Zealand Rugby Union. Morrison was a capable athlete who was a place-getter in the hop, step and jump at national championships. Trevor Berghan proved a nippy and elusive five-eighth while inside him was Charlie Saxton who had, for reasons known only to the selectors, been omitted from the Test teams of 1937. He went on to captain the famous Kiwi Army team of 1945-46 and he too became an administrator at national level. It would certainly have been interesting if

Phillips closes to tackle the flying Howard.

this team could have played the Springboks, for seldom has New Zealand fielded a more capable back line.

There were four new internationals in the pack. Bowman, the snowy-headed Hawke's Bay flanker, displayed great dash around the field and was a constant source of worry to the opposing inside backs. The war cut short his international career but he represented the North Island in 1945 and was still playing representative football in 1946. Milliken, who later turned to League, was a powerful lock while Quaid and George (who later became a New Zealand selector) were rugged front rankers, although both were small by today's standards. Charlie Quaid had clinched his place in the team by out-hooking the experienced Doug Dalton in the inter-island game, in which he also gave a fine display in the loose.

Australian Rugby had received a boost following the victory of the New South Wales team over the 1937 Springboks and the 1938 Wallabies were not to be taken lightly. The full-back, Ron Rankin, had toured New Zealand in 1936 and had played for New South Wales and Australia in 1937 against South Africa. Originally a centre, he had developed into an extremely capable full-back. Max Carpenter had played for his state against the Springboks while Lewis, Richards

NEW ZEALAND

J.M. TAYLOR
(Otago)

W.J. PHILLIPS   N.A. MITCHELL (**Capt.**)   T.C. MORRISON
(King Country)   (Otago)   (South Canterbury)
J.L. SULLIVAN
(Taranaki)

T. BERGHAN
(Otago)

C.K. SAXTON
(South Canterbury)
A.A. PARKHILL
(Otago)

R.M. McKENZIE   H.M. MILLIKEN   R.R. KING   A.W. BOWMAN
(Manawatu)   (Canterbury)   (West Coast) (Hawke's Bay)
D. DALTON   C.E. QUAID   V.L. GEORGE
(Hawke's Bay)   (Otago)   (Southland)

K.M. RAMSAY   E.T. BONIS   V.W. WILSON (**Capt.**)
(New South Wales)   (Queensland)   (Queensland)
A.J. HODGSON   F.E. HUTCHINSON   R.L.F. KELLY   B.D. OXLADE
(New South Wales) (New South Wales) (New South Wales) (Queensland)
F.R. KERR
(Victoria)
C.G. STONE
(New South Wales)

V.S. RICHARDS
(New South Wales)
J. HOWARD   L.S. LEWIS   E.S. HAYES   M.G. CARPENTER
(Queensland)   (Queensland)   (Queensland)   (Victoria)
R. RANKIN
(New South Wales)

AUSTRALIA

REFEREE: Mr W.S. Chapman (New South Wales)
ATTENDANCE: 32,000
CONDITIONS: Weather fine, ground hard
HALFTIME: New Zealand 8, Australia 3

SCORERS

NEW ZEALAND   **AUSTRALIA**
Tries: Saxton (2), Sullivan, Parkhill   Penalty goals: Carpenter (3)
Conversions: Taylor (3)
Penalty goals: Taylor (2)

AUSTRALIA 9

Sydney Cricket Ground

and ex-Wallaby captain, Hayes, were seasoned internationals. Of the forwards, Hodgson, Kelly, Hutchinson, Wilson, Bonis and Ramsay had all represented Australia in Tests.

The game was a tense battle and it was not until the final stages that play began to open up. Five minutes after the kick-off Carpenter opened the scoring for Australia with a penalty goal. Taylor had three opportunities to even the score but his attempts at goal were poor, however he did succeed with his fourth effort.

Near halftime Saxton burst away from a scrum

The New Zealand Touring Team
Back row: A.H. Wright, J.L. Sullivan, A. Lambourn, W.N. Carson, E.S. Jackson, T.C. Morrison, E.W.T. Tindill.
Third row: V.L. George, H.M. Milliken, C.W. Williams, J.G. Wynyard, A.W. Bowman, R.R. King, W.J. Phillips, A.A. Parkhill.
Seated: T. Berghan, J.M. Taylor, R.M. McKenzie, G.J. Adams (manager), N.A. Mitchell (capt.), A. McDonald (manager), C.E. Quaid, A.W. Wesney, D.Dalton.
In front: J.L. Griffiths, C.K. Saxton, J.A. Hooper. **Absent:** J. Dick.

and linked up with McKenzie and the latter passed back to Saxton who scored for Taylor to convert. A few minutes after the interval Taylor kicked his second penalty goal to give New Zealand an eight point lead. A fine kick by Carpenter from near half-way resulted in another three points for the home team and the Wallabies were back in the game.

It was at this point, with the score 11-6 in their favour, that the All Blacks began to display their superiority. Sullivan centre-kicked after a great run for Parkhill to gather the ball and score between the posts, Taylor again being on target. Then Saxton scored his second try, when Stone fumbled and McKenzie kicked through. Saxton picked up and passed to Mitchell who sent the ball back to his half-back for Saxton to race over. Taylor's kick missed. The final New Zealand points came from a try by Sullivan, who scored after Lewis had mis-kicked. Taylor added the extra points. In the dying stages of the game, Carpenter kicked his third penalty goal.

MELBA STUDIOS

NEW ZEALAND 20

6 August, 1938

Second Test

There were no changes in the New Zealand team from the first Test but the Australian selectors altered their team considerably. The 19-year-old New South Welshman, Ces Ramalli, playing his first season of senior football, was brought into the side, much to the delight of the Australian critics, who hailed the youngster as the greatest half-back since Syd Malcolm. Ramalli was certainly a brilliant player but the claims made on his behalf were possibly extravagant when one recalls the splendid displays of Jan McShane, the former Rhodes Scholar and Oxford Blue, against South Africa in 1937. McShane, who played for Oxford against the 1935 All Blacks, was considered by the 1937 Springboks to be the best half-back they met on their entire tour.

Vic. Richards was unexpectedly dropped, his place being taken by Collins, who had played one Test in 1937. Winston Ide, who was later to lose his life on active service, was playing his first Test in place of the injured Lewis.

The veteran hooker, Eddie Bonis, who had been outhooked by Charlie Quaid in the first Test, was replaced by another veteran, Albie Stone. New internationals in the home pack were McDonald, Monti and Lang, all of whom had played for their states against South Africa the year before. Cliff Lang was a former member of the Bedford club in England. A surprise omission from the forwards was the tall Victorian, Kerr, who played very well in the first Test.

The famous 1927 Waratah captain and former Oxford Blue and Scottish international, "Johnnie" Wallace, who coached the Wallabies for the 1938 series, rated this game the best he had ever seen in Australia. The football played was of the highest standard and it was not until late in the game that the All Blacks established superiority. The Australian team was greatly improved and at one stage it looked like winning.

The first fifteen minutes were scoreless although New Zealand kept up a constant pressure. Then Hayes missed Sullivan, who darted through to Rankin and passed to Mitchell, who was brought down from behind. The New Zealand captain was able to get his pass away to Phillips as he fell and the winger scored an unconverted try.

A few minutes later, Milliken burst over when King passed to him and Taylor converted. At this stage, New Zealand had a slight edge and deserved to be eight points up.

Carpenter opened his team's account with a penalty goal but New Zealand went further ahead when Saxton worked the blind side with Phillips. The big winger passed infield to Bowman, who raced over, Taylor again converting. Halftime came with the All Blacks leading 13-3.

After the interval the Wallabies began to take command and with the crowd cheering them on, they moved the ball around in dazzling fashion. First Collins scored a good try when he dummied past three opponents. Then Carpenter went over for a spectacular try when he received the ball at the end of a passing rush to bring the home side within four points.

NEW ZEALAND

J.M. TAYLOR
(Otago)

W.J. PHILLIPS   N.A. MITCHELL (**Capt.**)   T.C. MORRISON
(King Country)   (Otago)   (South Canterbury)
J.L. SULLIVAN
(Taranaki)
                                                   T. BERGHAN
                                                    (Otago)
C.K. SAXTON
(South Canterbury)
A.A. PARKHILL
(Otago)

R.M. McKENZIE   H.M. MILLIKEN   R.R. KING   A.W. BOWMAN
(Manawatu)   (Canterbury)   (West Coast)   (Hawke's Bay)
D. DALTON   C.E. QUAID   V.L. GEORGE
(Hawke's Bay)   (Otago)   (Southland)

C.W.P. LANG   A.H. STONE   V.W. WILSON (**Capt.**)
(Victoria)   (New South Wales)   (Queensland)
J.C. McDONALD   A.M. MONTI   R.L.F. KELLY   B.D. OXLADE
(Queensland)   (Queensland)   (New South Wales)   (Queensland)
A.J. HODGSON
(New South Wales)
C. RAMALLI
(New South Wales)
                                                  P.K. COLLINS
                                                 (New South Wales)
J. HOWARD   E.S. HAYES   W.P.J. IDE   M.G. CARPENTER
(Queensland)   (Queensland)   (Queensland)   (Victoria)
R. RANKIN
(New South Wales)

AUSTRALIA

REFEREE: Mr P. Barnes (Queensland)
ATTENDANCE: 13,000
CONDITIONS: Weather fine, ground hard
HALFTIME: New Zealand 13, Australia 3

SCORERS

NEW ZEALAND

Tries: Phillips, Milliken, Bowman, Mitchell
Conversions: Taylor (2)
Dropped goal: Morrison

AUSTRALIA

Tries: Carpenter (2), Collins
Conversion: Carpenter
Penalty goal: Carpenter

AUSTRALIA 14

Exhibition Ground, Brisbane

Brisbane Mail cartoonist, Ian Gall, looks at the heroes of the second Test.

The Australians were unlucky not to take the lead when Hodgson knocked on with the line open in front of him. Then Collins again cut through but Hayes failed to hold his pass when he could have scored under the posts.

The New Zealand lead was increased when Mitchell finished off a back movement to score an unconverted try. The All Black skipper played a superb game which he climaxed with this good try. Shortly after, Morrison added four points with a dropped goal and it looked as though the Wallabies were finished. They had the last word, however, when Carpenter beat his man and outpaced the opposition in a brilliant run from near half-way to score by the posts. He converted his own try to cut New Zealand's margin to six points.

NEW ZEALAND 14

13 August, 1938

Third Test

Mitchell was not available for this game owing to injury and Sullivan was moved to centre with the former All Black captain, Jack Griffiths, coming in at second five-eighth.

After being selected for the 1938 All Blacks, the Auckland wing, Johnny Dick, caught measles and was unable to travel. He recovered in time to join the team for the last part of the tour, his fare to Australia being paid by local supporters. Since Dick had been replaced, he could not travel at the Rugby Union's expense. He now took his place on the All Black right wing and played a very good game.

Changes in the forwards saw the return of two former Test players, Everard Jackson and Artie Lambourn, in the front row.

The only newcomer to international Rugby in the home side was Michael Clifford, who was playing his only Test match. He was to become another World War II casualty. Max Carpenter, the brilliant Victorian wing, had to withdraw at the last minute with influenza and was replaced by O'Brien, who had played against the 1937 Springboks for New South Wales and Australia.

Johnny Dick is tackled by his opposite winger, Kelaher.

AUSTRALIA 6

Sydney Cricket Ground

The return to Test football of the classy left wing, "Jockey" Kelaher, was expected to strengthen the Australian team considerably, but he played below his normal form in this match.

It is of interest that sixteen of Australia's 1938 Test players were chosen for the 1939 Wallaby tour of the British Isles. This team arrived in Britain but returned home without playing a match because of the outbreak of World War II. The sixteen 1938 Wallabies who gained selection were Clifford, Rankin, Carpenter, Kelaher, Ide, Richards, Lewis, Collins, Ramalli, Wilson (captain), Oxlade, Hodgson, A.H. Stone, Monti, Ramsay and McDonald. Former internationals who had played against New Zealand, E. de C. Gibbons and J.H. Malone, were also in the touring party.

The third Test of 1938 was a disappointing game which at no stage reached the heights of the Brisbane match. The only highlights were an outstanding display by Berghan and the elusive running and quick acceleration of Dick. These two were the outstanding backs on the field.

The weather was uncomfortably hot and the ground was hard when Wilson and McKenzie led their teams out. New Zealand scored first when Taylor kicked a penalty after ten minutes. The visitors increased their lead with a try by Saxton, who scored by darting round the blind side from a set scrum. Taylor missed the conversion.

Play continued to be fairly even and a rather dull first half ended with New Zealand leading 6-3, the home team's points coming from a penalty goal kicked by Hayes. Thus it was still anybody's game.

Early in the second half, Dick raced along the touchline and passed infield to Bowman, who scored for Taylor to convert from a wide angle. A magnificent break by Hodgson led to a try by Ramsay wide out and Australia needed only a converted try to draw the game. However, Taylor ended the scoring with a penalty goal near the end of the match and New Zealand ran out winners by eight points.

Although the score was fairly close, the local critics were agreed that the All Blacks deserved their win. They had the edge on their opponents in the forwards while the backs made more use of their opportunities than the home rearguard did. All writers were agreed that the Tests were played in an excellent spirit, and this is confirmed for the authors by All Blacks who played in the series.

The 1938 All Blacks returned from Australia with an unbeaten record and began to prepare for the 1940 tour of South Africa. Trials were held in 1939 to select the team for this tour but it was never chosen because of the war. Three members of the 1938 team, none of whom played in the Tests, lost their lives in the world conflict. They were A.W. Wesney (Southland), W.N. Carson (Auckland), who also played cricket for New Zealand, and J.G. Wynyard (Waikato), who also toured with the 1935 All Blacks. Other war casualties among New Zealand Rugby representatives were J.H. Harris (1925), G.F. Hart (1930-31-32-34-35-36), C.S. Pepper (1935) and D.G. Cobden (1937).

NEW ZEALAND

J.M. TAYLOR
(Otago)

J. DICK   J.L. SULLIVAN   T.C. MORRISON
(Auckland)   (Taranaki)   (South Canterbury)
J.L. GRIFFITHS
(Wellington)

    T. BERGHAN
    (Otago)

C.K. SAXTON
(South Canterbury)
A.A. PARKHILL
(Otago)

R.M. McKENZIE (Capt.)   H.M. MILLIKEN   R.R. KING   A.W. BOWMAN
(Manawatu)   (Canterbury)   (West Coast)   (Hawke's Bay)
E.S. JACKSON   A. LAMBOURN   V.L. GEORGE
(Hawke's Bay)   (Wellington)   (Southland)

C.W.P. LANG   A.H. STONE   V.W. WILSON (Capt.)
(Victoria)   (New South Wales)   (Queensland)
B.D. OXLADE   F.E. HUTCHINSON   K.M. RAMSAY   J.C. McDONALD
(Queensland)   (New South Wales)   (New South Wales)   (Queensland)
A.J. HODGSON
(New South Wales)
C. RAMALLI
(New South Wales)

    P.K. COLLINS
    (New South Wales)
J.D. KELAHER   E.S. HAYES   W.P.J. IDE   F.W.H. O'BRIEN
(New South Wales)   (Queensland)   (Queensland)   (New South Wales)
M. CLIFFORD
(New South Wales)

AUSTRALIA

REFEREE: Mr W.S. Chapman (New South Wales)
ATTENDANCE: 20,000
CONDITIONS: Weather fine and hot, ground hard
HALFTIME: New Zealand 6, Australia 3

SCORERS

NEW ZEALAND	**AUSTRALIA**
Tries: Saxton, Bowman	Try: Ramsay
Conversion: Taylor	Penalty goal: Hayes
Penalty goals: Taylor (2)	

137

14 September, 1946

First Test

When New Zealand resumed international matches after World War II, a new All Black team was selected. This is not surprising, as eight years had passed since a New Zealand team had been chosen. It is also not surprising that seven members of the famous Kiwi Army team, which toured Britain and France after the war, were selected for the two Tests of 1946. Captained by 1938 All Black Charlie Saxton, the Kiwis played a superb brand of football which they showed to New Zealanders on a brief tour of their own country.

Still widely-regarded as the greatest player in his position since the war, ex-Kiwi Bob Scott was at full-back. This Test was the first of 17 which he played for his country between 1946 and 1954. A great positional player and an outstanding goal-kicker, Scott scored 242 points in 52 matches for his country.

Wally Argus, Johnny Smith and the captain, Fred Allen, were also ex-Kiwis. Argus had a short career as an All Black, playing in only four Tests but he was a big, fast wing with the ability to score tries and his withdrawal from the 1949 South African tour was a severe blow to New Zealand. Smith was the star back of the Kiwi team but his form in international matches never quite came up to his best standard. He played brilliantly in provincial games for North Auckland however, and he must rank among New Zealand's greatest midfield backs.

Allen was a great attacking player and an astute general who led New Zealand in six Tests. He made his international debut at first five-eighth but he was probably better suited to the second five-eighth position. He went on to enjoy a highly-successful career as a selector and coach of Auckland and All Black teams after his retirement from active play.

Ron Elvidge was a strong, courageous midfield back who later captained New Zealand in Tests against South Africa and the British Isles. While studying medicine at Otago University he played five times for the South Island, twice as captain. Jack Dunn, the big Auckland wing, did

not play for New Zealand again while Jimmy Haig switched to League in 1947, playing for several seasons as an international at that code.

Kiwi players in the forwards were Military Cross winner Jack Finlay, making his solitary appearance for New Zealand, and Pat Rhind, who also dropped out of Test football after 1946. Finlay, who was later an All Black selector, was a versatile player who had represented his province as a five-eighth as well as in the forwards. Ex-prisoner of war and 1938 New Zealand amateur heavy-weight boxing champion, Morrie McHugh played both Tests in 1946 and appeared in one international on the 1949 South African tour. Other forwards who played in this first post-war Test and who went to South Africa, were crack Waikato hooker, Has Catley (who had taken part in All Black trials as far back as 1935), Charlie Willocks and Harry Frazer.

There were two pre-war internationals in the touring Wallaby party. The vice-captain, Keith Windon, had played for Australia in 1936 and 1937 while Graeme Cooke was a Wallaby in 1932 and 1933. An injury in the opening game of the 1946 tour kept Windon out of the Tests however and it was left to his younger brother, Colin, to uphold the family name. The latter did this very well, being named one of the five players of the year by the New Zealand Rugby Almanack. A similar honour was accorded Charlie Eastes, a big, fast winger who must surely be one of the finest players in his position to have visited New Zealand. He later became prominent in Australian Rugby administration.

Trevor Allan, the 19 year old centre, went on to great heights and was one of Australia's most successful captains before turning to League in England. Rugby writers in Australia regarded him as the best centre since Cyril Towers. Bill McLean, the 1946 skipper, was another member of the famous Queensland family. He had been selected for the ill-fated 1939 Wallabies and could well have made his international debut that year if the war had not broken out. He was a splendid forward both in the lock and flank positions. Allan's replacement, Max Howell, later went to California, where he became a university

AUSTRALIA 8

professor. He did a lot for Pacific Coast Rugby both as player and coach.

The first Test of 1946 was not as one-sided as the score suggests, only the superior weight and rucking ability of the All Black forwards ensuring victory. The Australian backs were generally better than their opposites, this being especially true of Eastes and Allan, who outplayed Dunn and Smith respectively. After Smith's brilliance on the Kiwi tour, great things were expected of him but in fairness it should be noted that he had not properly recovered from an injury, which would account to some extent for his eclipse by the youthful Australian, who was the best back on the field.

Australia scored first when Eastes kicked over Dunn's head near half-way. The ball bounced

perfectly, the flying Wallaby gathered it in and beat Scott by sheer pace to score behind the posts. Livermore missed a simple kick.

A series of forward attacks were repulsed by spirited tackling. Then Australia counter-attacked when Allan beat Smith and only a forward pass deprived Eastes of his second try. A little later, Bernie Schulte (who had played for Queensland against the 1938 All Blacks and who had been a prisoner of war of the Japanese) lost a certain try when he tried to beat Scott with three men in support.

The New Zealand forwards took play back to Australian territory and, from a passing rush, Argus went over in the corner, uprooting the flag as he fell. Scott's kick fell just under the bar.

Three minutes later, brilliant work by Elvidge ended in a try by Haig between the posts with Scott adding the extra points. Then came a rush headed by Rhind and Elliott from which the latter scored. Scott again converted. Right on halftime, Johnson made a fine break for Allan to score under the bar, Livermore converting to make the score 13-8 at the change-over.

McRae, who had replaced Frazer at halftime, made a good run early in the second spell from which Finlay scored wide out. Scott was again on target. From a dropped pass Elvidge scooped up the ball and ran Smith into position for another try, which Scott converted.

Although now trailing by 15 points, the visitors made a determined effort to get back into the game and from a snappy passing movement in which backs and forwards combined, Windon was unlucky not to score. Then Johnson lost a try through hanging on to the ball.

The Australian forwards were well outplayed by now and New Zealand had almost unlimited possession. Argus scored again from an overlap and in the dying stages White kicked the ball out of Cremin's hands to score. Scott kicked his fifth goal and New Zealand had won by a handsome margin.

NEW ZEALAND

R.W.H. SCOTT
(Auckland)

J.M. DUNN	J.B. SMITH	W.G. ARGUS
(Auckland)	(North Auckland)	(Canterbury)

R.R. ELVIDGE
(Otago)

F.R. ALLEN (**Capt.**)
(Auckland)

J.S. HAIG
(Otago)

J. FINLAY
(Manawatu)

R.M. WHITE	K.G. ELLIOTT	C. WILLOCKS	M.J. McHUGH
(Wellington)	(Wellington)	(Otago)	(Auckland)
P.K. RHIND	E.H. CATLEY		H.F. FRAZER*
(Canterbury)	(Waikato)		(Hawke's Bay)

E. TWEEDALE†	W.L. DAWSON	R.E. McMASTER
(New South Wales)	(New South Wales)	(Queensland)

A.E. LIVERMORE W.M. McLEAN (**Capt.**) P.A. HARDCASTLE C.J. WINDON
(Queensland) (Queensland) (New South Wales) (New South Wales)

A.J. BUCHAN
(New South Wales)

B.G. SCHULTE
(Queensland)

J.F. CREMIN
(New South Wales)

C.C. EASTES	T. ALLAN††	P.A. JOHNSON	J.W.T. MacBRIDE
(New South Wales)	(New South Wales)	(New South Wales)	(New South Wales)

R.J.C. PIPER
(New South Wales)
AUSTRALIA

REPLACEMENTS: *Replaced by J.A. McRae (Southland)
† Replaced by E. Freeman (New South Wales)
†† Replaced by M.L. Howell (New South Wales)
REFEREE: Mr A.S. Fong (West Coast)
ATTENDANCE: 30,000
CONDITIONS: Weather fine, ground firm
HALFTIME: Australia 13, New Zealand 8
SCORERS

NEW ZEALAND	AUSTRALIA
Tries: Argus (2), Haig, Elliott, Finlay, Smith, White	Tries: Eastes, Allan
Conversions: Scott (5)	Conversion: Livermore

NEW ZEALAND 14

28 September, 1946

Second Test

There were several changes in the New Zealand team for this Test. Both Smith and Finlay were injured, Goddard and Budd coming into the side. Morrie Goddard had established a reputation while serving in the R.N.Z.A.F. during the war, playing for England in war-time internationals as well as for the Combined Services against the Kiwi Army team. He was later to tour Australia and South Africa. Alf Budd won a second cap against Australia in 1949.

Dunn was dropped in favour of Eric Boggs, a powerful winger who had been one of the succes-

ses during the Kiwis' tour. However, he found Eastes a handful and fared little better than had Dunn against the brilliant Australian. Boggs was an All Black again in 1949 and he later selected and coached Auckland teams for several seasons. McRae, who had gone on as a replacement at Dunedin, now filled Catley's place as hooker.

The Australian three-quarters were rearranged with Stone coming in on the right wing

Elvidge dives over to score in the tackle of Stone. Dawson and Hardcastle arrive too late to prevent the try.

AUSTRALIA 10

and MacBride moving in to Johnson's place. A significant change behind the scrum saw Cyril Burke make his Test debut. This little half-back must rate as one of the finest seen in international Rugby since World War II. During a Test career which spanned ten years, Burke played almost continuously behind beaten packs yet he always looked a class player. In the Wallaby scrum, the veteran Cooke replaced Livermore with McLean moving to the flank.

After their crushing defeat at Dunedin, the tourists were not given much chance by the 30,000 spectators who saw Fred Allen kick off in fine weather. The Wallabies had the better of the game, however, and were very unlucky to lose. Magnificently led by Bill McLean, the Australian forwards outplayed the home eight to give their brilliant backs plenty of possession.

Five minutes after the start, the Wallabies took the lead with a spectacular try. Windon broke through a ruck and the ball eventually reached the left wing where Eastes left the opposition standing to score one of the best Test match tries seen on Eden Park. Piper converted.

Two minutes later, Scott kicked a 30-yard penalty to cut the margin to two points. The visiting forwards continued to win possession and Allan slipped through but his pass to Stone went astray when a try seemed certain. A little later, Burke shot round the scrum to link up with Windon and McLean and the latter missed a try by inches as he dived for the line. The visitors had all the better of the first twenty minutes, the All Blacks appearing too casual.

At last Allen rallied his team and he made a brilliant opening from which New Zealand almost scored. The home team kept up the pressure, Argus being forced out at the corner. Right on halftime, Elvidge scored following a good movement, Stone just failing to prevent the try. Scott converted and the All Blacks led 8-5.

New Zealand dominated the early part of the second half and Argus again just failed to score after Goddard had sliced through. Then Boggs was stopped as he raced down the sideline. He threw a pass to the inside but Cremin intercepted

to break right away. The defence managed to close on him and he handed on to MacBride, who sped away to score behind the posts. Piper's conversion put his team into the lead again.

With the majority of the crowd now behind them, the Wallabies were nearly over once more when MacBride swerved his way through the defence and made an opening for Stone, who was pulled down a yard short of the line.

Midway through the spell, New Zealand took the lead when Scott kicked a penalty from a scrum infringement. The All Black full-back was playing well, his long touch finding keeping the home team out of trouble. Twelve minutes from time, Scott kicked another penalty from a difficult angle but the Wallabies still had a chance of winning. They threw everything they had into the final minutes of the game but the All Blacks held onto their lead and the better team lost. As in 1931 on the same ground, the kicking of the home full-back won the game for New Zealand.

NEW ZEALAND
R.W.H. SCOTT
(Auckland)

| E.G. BOGGS | M.P. GODDARD | W.G. ARGUS |
| (Auckland) | (South Canterbury) | (Canterbury) |

R.R. ELVIDGE
(Otago)

F.R. ALLEN (**Capt.**)
(Auckland)

J.S. HAIG
(Otago)
K.G. ELLIOTT
(Wellington)

R.M. WHITE	T.A. BUDD	C. WILLOCKS	M.J. McHUGH
(Wellington)	(Southland)	(Otago)	(Auckland)
P.K. RHIND	J.A. McRAE		H.F. FRAZER
(Canterbury)	(Southland)		(Hawke's Bay)

| E. TWEEDALE | W.L. DAWSON | R.E. McMASTER |
| (New South Wales) | (New South Wales) | (Queensland) |

| W.M. McLEAN (**Capt.**) | G.M. COOKE | P.A. HARDCASTLE | C.J. WINDON |
| (Queensland) | (Queensland) | (New South Wales) | (New South Wales) |

A.J. BUCHAN
(New South Wales)
C.T. BURKE
(New South Wales)

J.F. CREMIN
(New South Wales)

| C.C. EASTES | T. ALLAN | J.W.T. MacBRIDE | J.M. STONE |
| (New South Wales) | (New South Wales) | (New South Wales) | (New South Wales) |

B.J.C. PIPER
(New South Wales)

AUSTRALIA

REFEREE: Mr A.M. Matheson (Taranaki)
ATTENDANCE: 30,000
CONDITIONS: Weather fine, ground firm
HALFTIME: New Zealand 8, Australia 5

SCORERS

NEW ZEALAND	AUSTRALIA
Try: Elvidge	Tries: Eastes, MacBride
Conversion: Scott	Conversions: Piper (2)
Penalty goals: Scott (3)	

NEW ZEALAND 13

14 June, 1947

First Test

New All Black backs in this Test were Jack McLean, Ben Couch and Percy Tetzlaff. McLean was extremely rugged and very fast, being a noted sprinter and long-jumper. He later played League for the Bradford Northern club in England. Couch, a Maori, was a team mate of McLean's again in the 1949 Tests against Australia. He was the third All Black to become a Member of Parliament when he won the Wairarapa seat for the National Party in 1975. Tetzlaff had played for Waikato before the war but he was still a fine half-back. Small and nippy, he was a good tactician and possessed a serviceable pass.

Four ex-Kiwis were among the new caps in the forwards, viz, Neville Thornton, "Killer" Arnold, Lachie Grant and Johnny Simpson. Thornton was a big, fast number eight who began his football career as a back. He was a useful long-range goal-kicker as he showed in the second Test. Arnold, although on the light side, was a devastating flanker who harried the opposition inside backs without mercy. Although he was one of the successes of the 1947 tour, he did not play for New Zealand subsequently. Grant was an especially good line-out forward who made the tour to South Africa in 1949 while Simpson, who also played against South Africa and against the British Isles team of 1950, must surely be one of the toughest props ever to play international Rugby. Thornton, Grant and Simpson were three of the stars of the South African tour. Ray Dalton, who was also making his Test debut, had played for New Zealand Services in England. He went to South Africa as vice-captain in 1949 but did not play in a Test.

Interesting newcomers to the Wallabies selection included Alan Walker, who also played Test cricket for Australia and well-known surf lifesaver, Roger Cornforth. Prop Doug Keller was later capped for Scotland and Ken Kearney became a fine league international. Cornforth played water-polo for Australia at the Olympics in 1948.

Australian half-back, Burke, is taken in a high tackle.

BRISBANE COURIER MAIL

NEW ZEALAND

R.W.H. SCOTT
(Auckland)

J.K. McLEAN	M.P. GODDARD	W.G. ARGUS
(King Country)	(South Canterbury)	(Canterbury)

F.R. ALLEN (**Capt.**)
(Auckland)

M.B.R. COUCH
(Wairarapa)

P.L. TETZLAFF
(Auckland)

N.H. THORNTON
(Auckland)

K.D. ARNOLD	L.A. GRANT	H.F. FRAZER	R.M. WHITE
(Waikato)	(South Canterbury)	(Hawke's Bay)	(Wellington)
J.G. SIMPSON		E.H. CATLEY	R.A. DALTON
(Auckland)		(Waikato)	(Wellington)

D.H. KELLER	K.H. KEARNEY	R.E. McMASTER
(New South Wales)	(New South Wales)	(Queensland)
R.G.W. CORNFORTH	P.A. HARDCASTLE	W.M. McLEAN	C.J. WINDON
(New South Wales)	(**Capt.**)	(Queensland)	(New South Wales)
	(New South Wales)		

A.J. BUCHAN
(New South Wales)

C.T. BURKE
(New South Wales)

J.F. CREMIN
(New South Wales)

C.C. EASTES	A.K. WALKER	M.L. HOWELL	J.W.T. MacBRIDE
(New South Wales)	(New South Wales)	(New South Wales)	(New South Wales)

B.J.C. PIPER
(New South Wales)

AUSTRALIA

REFEREE: Mr T. Moore (Queensland)
ATTENDANCE: 23,000
CONDITIONS: Weather fine, ground hard
HALFTIME: New Zealand 8, Australia 0

SCORERS

NEW ZEALAND	**AUSTRALIA**
Tries: Frazer (penalty), Argus, Arnold	Try: Cornforth
Conversions: Scott (2)	Conversion: Piper

AUSTRALIA 5

Exhibition Ground, Brisbane

Most of the crowd of 23,000 considered an Australian victory likely in view of the All Blacks' defeat by New South Wales the previous week. The weather was beautifully fine and the hard ground favoured the home side.

There was no score for the first half-hour, during which play was fairly even. The visitors opened the scoring when their forwards drove the ball over the Australian line with Frazer in the lead but as the Hawke's Bay man was running for the ball he was brought down and the referee had no hesitation in awarding a penalty try, which Scott converted.

The second try followed a stab kick by God-

dard from which Dalton picked up and passed to Thornton, who threw a long pass to Argus. The winger raced in at the corner with Buchan draped round his knees. Scott failed to convert and New Zealand led 8-0 at halftime.

Within ten minutes of the restart New Zealand had scored again. Goddard intercepted a pass and linked up with White, Couch and Arnold, who broke through tackles by Walker and Piper to score. Scott converted with a fine kick.

Near the end of the game, Cornforth scored for Australia following a nice opening made by Howell, who in-passed to Windon for the latter to send on to Cornforth, who ran over between the posts. Piper converted and the game ended soon after.

The New Zealand Touring Team

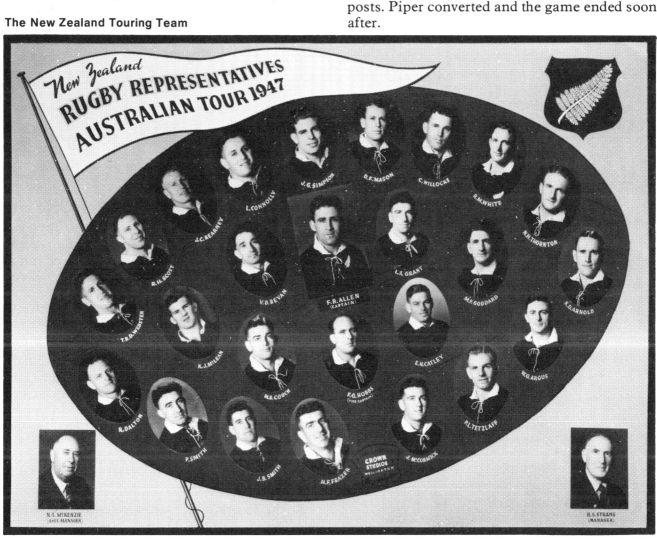

143

NEW ZEALAND 27

28 June, 1947

Second Test

There were a number of changes in the Australian team for this Test. New Wallabies were Windsor, Bourke, Emery, Shehadie and Kraefft, all of whom were selected for the tour of the British Isles, France and Canada in 1947-48. The most famous of this group was Nick Shehadie, who made several visits to New Zealand and toured South Africa in 1953. He was later knighted and is, at the time of writing, Sir Nicholas Shehadie, Lord Mayor of Sydney.

The most notable newcomer in the New Zealand team was the snowy-headed Otago five-eighth, Jim Kearney. This ex-Kiwi was possessed of very safe hands and a keen sense of anticipation which made him one of the best first five-eighths to play for New Zealand since World War II. Smith, unavailable for the first Test, came in at centre; Goddard was moved to the wing to make room for him. "Tim" Mason, who replaced Argus during the game, was a member of a well-known Wellington sporting family who moved to

Arnold breaks through with the ball at toe.

CHRISTCHURCH PRESS

South Africa soon after the 1947 tour.

Scott opened the scoring with a penalty goal after six minutes. Then followed a movement from which the home side almost scored but it broke down near the All Blacks' goal line. However, Trevor Allan put his side level with a penalty goal and then Scott kicked one from forty yards out after New Zealand had attacked from the kick-off.

The first try came when Smith fielded a rebound from Windsor and passed to Argus, who scored between the posts for Scott to convert. The second try soon followed. Allan dropped a pass in the All Black 25 but McLean was on hand to carry on and score between the posts. Allan converted to put the home team within three points of the visitors. Argus left the field at this stage to be replaced by Mason.

In the second half, Australia scored first, Allan kicking a penalty goal to even the score at 11-11.

NEW ZEALAND

R.W.H. SCOTT
(Auckland)

M.P. GODDARD — J.B. SMITH — W.G. ARGUS*
(South Canterbury) — (North Auckland) — (Canterbury)

F.R. ALLEN (Capt.)
(Auckland)

J.C. KEARNEY
(Otago)

P.L. TETZLAFF
(Auckland)

N.H. THORNTON
(Auckland)

K.D. ARNOLD — L.A. GRANT — H.F. FRAZER — R.M. WHITE
(Waikato) — (South Canterbury) — (Hawke's Bay) — (Wellington)

J.G. SIMPSON — E.H. CATLEY — R.A. DALTON
(Auckland) — (Waikato) — (Wellington)

E. TWEEDALE — K.H. KEARNEY — R.E. McMASTER
(New South Wales) — (New South Wales) — (Queensland)

W.M. McLEAN (Capt.) — D.F. KRAEFFT — N.M. SHEHADIE — A.J. BUCHAN
(Queensland) — (New South Wales) — (New South Wales) — (New South Wales)

G.M. COOKE
(Queensland)

C.T. BURKE
(New South Wales)

N.A. EMERY
(New South Wales)

C.C. EASTES — T. ALLAN — T.K. BOURKE — J.W.T. MacBRIDE
(New South Wales) — (New South Wales) — (Queensland) — (New South Wales)

C.J. WINDSOR
(Queensland)

AUSTRALIA

REPLACEMENT: * Replaced by D.F. Mason (Wellington)
REFEREE: Mr L.C. Tomalin (New South Wales)
ATTENDANCE: 30,000
CONDITIONS: Weather fine, ground hard
HALFTIME: New Zealand 11, Australia 8
SCORERS

NEW ZEALAND	AUSTRALIA
Tries: Argus, Kearney, Mason	Try: McLean
Conversions: Scott (3)	Conversion: Allan
Penalty goals: Scott (3), Thornton	Penalty goals: Allan (3)

AUSTRALIA 14

Sydney Cricket Ground

McBride fends off an attempted tackle by replacement winger, Mason. Johnny Smith has been left sprawling.

Shortly after this, the All Blacks swept into Wallaby territory and Scott joined the backline. He passed to Allen who sent on to Kearney for the Otago man to score in the corner. Scott kicked a fine goal.

A penalty by Allan brought Australia back to within two points but New Zealand increased the lead when Scott kicked his third penalty. The Australians were then penalised right on halfway and the spectators were amazed to see the big forward, Neville Thornton, prepare for a shot at goal. He sent the ball right between the posts with a splendid kick. Finally, Mason dived over between the posts for Scott to convert. The game

ended with New Zealand comfortable winners and once again the All Blacks had retained the Bledisloe Cup.

Although the 1947 tour was held early in the season, the players showed excellent form in most cases and at this stage the situation looked bright regarding the 1949 visit to South Africa. Bob Scott was a sensation in Australia, where critics rated him Nepia's equal as a full-back and the best goal-kicker since "Dally" Messenger. Others to receive high praise were Wally Argus, Jack McLean, Morrie Goddard, Fred Allen, Neville Thornton, "Killer" Arnold, Has Catley and Johnny Simpson.

Of the 1947 Test players, Tetzlaff, Arnold, White and Dalton did not appear again in an international.

SOUTH AFRICA 15

16 July, 1949

First Test

The 1949 All Blacks became the second New Zealand touring team to lose all its Test matches. Indeed, 1949 was a very black year for New Zealand Rugby, for not only did the team in South Africa lose all the internationals but the Bledisloe Cup was lost to Australia in a two Test series by a side chosen from those who were not selected to go overseas.

The tourists had lost two and drawn one of the eleven games played prior to the first Test but the odds should have favoured them against the Springboks. The South Africans had not engaged in international matches since 1938 whereas the New Zealanders had played four Tests against Australia since the war. Also, several of the 1949 All Blacks had taken part in matches with international teams during the Kiwi Army team's tour.

Cecil Moss had played for the South African 6th. Armoured Division during and after the war but all the Springboks in this first Test team were new to international Rugby. On the other hand, the only uncapped All Blacks were Henderson, Savage, McNab, Harvey and Skinner.

Peter Henderson was one of the fastest players ever to represent New Zealand at Rugby. Commonly known as "Sammy", he was the national 100 yards champion in 1949 and a member of his country's Empire Games team in 1950. He later played League in Britain.

Larry Savage did not play for New Zealand again after 1949 but he continued in first-class football for several years following his return from South Africa. He was a good running half-back but his slowness in clearing the scrum allowed the fast-breaking Springbok forwards to harass the All Black inside backs.

Lester Harvey and Jack McNab played against the Lions in 1950 and then dropped out of international Rugby. Both were rugged, hard-working Otago forwards who always produced form of the highest standard.

The other newcomer, Kevin Skinner, developed into the greatest prop forward of his time. The New Zealand amateur heavy-weight boxing

champion in 1947, Skinner was fantastically strong and very fit. An excellent scrum technique allied to such great strength made him the ideal prop. He went on to play twenty Tests and captained the All Blacks against Australia in 1952.

When the game began, before a capacity crowd, the spectators did not know what to expect from this comparatively inexperienced Springbok team and the visitors were generally expected to win.

Some of the home players were to emerge as Rugby "greats" however, especially Muller and Geffin. Hennie Muller was undoubtedly the greatest number eight forward in the world during his international career. He had the speed of a wing three-quarter, good hands, a strong boot and an abundance of energy. He was also a devastating tackler who created havoc amongst opposition backlines. The All Blacks had the utmost respect for him.

"Okey" Geffin became famous for his ability to kick goals and it was his skill in this depart-

---

NEW ZEALAND

R.W.H. SCOTT
(Auckland)

E.G. BOGGS   R.R. ELVIDGE   P. HENDERSON
(Auckland)   (Otago)   (Wanganui)
F.R. ALLEN (**Capt.**)
(Auckland

                J.C. KEARNEY
                (Otago)

L.T. SAVAGE
(Canterbury)
N.H. THORNTON
(Auckland)

J.R. McNAB   C. WILLOCKS   L.R. HARVEY   L.A. GRANT
(Otago)   (Otago)   (Otago)   (South Canterbury)
J.G. SIMPSON   E.H. CATLEY   K.L. SKINNER
(Auckland)   (Waikato)   (Otago)

A. GEFFIN   R.P. JORDAAN   C.J. van JAARSVELD
(Transvaal)   (Northern Transvaal)   (Transvaal)
L.J. STRYDOM   F. du PLESSIS (**Capt.**)   H.B. KOCH   B.S. van der MERWE
(Northern Transvaal)   (Transvaal)   (Western Province)   (Northern Transvaal)
H.S.V. MULLER
(Transvaal)
J.J. WAHL
(Western Province)

                J.D. BREWIS
                (Northern Transvaal)
C. MOSS   F.P. DUVENAGE   M.T. LATEGAN   F.P. MARAIS
(Natal)   (Griqualand West)   (Western Province)   (Boland)
J.H. van der SCHYFF
(Griqualand West)

SOUTH AFRICA

REFEREE: Mr E.W. Hofmeyr (Transvaal)
ATTENDANCE: 42,000
CONDITIONS: Weather fine, ground firm
HALFTIME: New Zealand 11, South Africa 3
SCORERS

NEW ZEALAND	**SOUTH AFRICA**
Try: Henderson	Penalty goals: Geffin (5)
Conversion: Scott	
Dropped goal: Kearney	
Penalty goal: Scott	

NEW ZEALAND 11

Newlands, Cape Town

Grant and van der Schyff see Henderson plunge through the arms of Marais to score New Zealand's try.

ment which won the first Test for his team. However, he was not brought on to kick until both Jack van der Schyff and Hannes Brewis had missed early penalty attempts. Had either of these players succeeded in kicking a goal, Geffin may not be so well-known in Rugby circles, although he was a solid prop who did his work well in the tight.

New Zealand scored first when Scott kicked a penalty goal from 35 yards after fifteen minutes. Van der Schyff had already missed with a penalty attempt and Brewis failed with his shot a few minutes after Scott had opened the scoring.

The only try of the match was scored when the All Blacks heeled from a scrum and Savage kicked through to the Springbok full-back. Van der Schyff fielded the ball but his kick was charged down by the speedster Henderson who scored for Scott to convert.

After half-an-hour the Springboks were awarded a penalty and du Plessis threw the ball to Geffin. The angle was awkward but the big prop made no mistake and the All Blacks' lead was cut to five points.

A minute before halftime, Savage whipped a quick pass to Kearney who dropped a goal and at the interval the All Blacks had a handy 11-3 lead.

Ten minutes into the second half, Geffin put over his second penalty and the home team began to play with more confidence. Brewis was keeping the ball in front of his forwards, who were starting to contain the All Black pack.

New Zealand almost increased the lead when Boggs came in from the blind side and kicked hard to Henderson's wing. The latter made ground before passing inside but the pass was fumbled when a try looked certain.

From a ruck infringement, Geffin kicked another penalty goal and only two points separated the teams. Then, from another ruck, Savage was penalised for picking the ball out and Geffin's kick gave South Africa the lead for the first time. Near the end of the game, Boggs was penalised for obstruction and Geffin landed his fifth goal to put the result beyond doubt.

13 August, 1949

Second Test

Both teams made several changes for this match. In the New Zealand side, the Otago number eight and future All Black captain, Peter Johnstone, was making his first international appearance, as was former Kiwi Bill Meates. These two talented footballers went on to play nine and seven Tests respectively. The experienced Hawke's Bay lock, Harry Frazer, replaced the injured Charlie Willocks to play what was to be his last Test.

The four changes in the South African team strengthened it considerably for there was no doubt that the better side won the match. Ryk van Schoor, the bone-shattering tackler from Rhodesia, took over from the veteran Floris Duvenage in the centres. Between the first and second Tests the All Blacks had played Rhodesia twice for a loss and a draw. Van Schoor had proved rather a handful and his contribution to Rhodesia's success was considerable. The other change in the backs was behind the scrum, where "Fonnie" du Toit replaced "Ballie" Wahl to join his Northern Transvaal team-mate, "Hannes" Brewis.

The two newcomers in the Springbok pack, "Salty" du Rand and Chris Koch, toured New Zealand with the 1956 South Africans. They both had long careers in international Rugby. Because of their mobility, they were chosen to replace two of the first Test heavyweights, van der Merwe and van Jaarsveld.

Play was tight for the first ten minutes with neither side gaining an advantage. Then South Africa was penalised on its own ten yard mark and Scott kicked a great goal from five yards in from touch. The score was soon evened however for Kearney was caught offside at a scrum in his own 25 and Geffin kicked an easy goal.

Scott had two near misses from penalty shots and then Skinner took a mark from which he initiated a good movement. He kicked high and Johnstone was up quickly to whip the ball to Simpson, who passed to Henderson. The latter flew for the corner but Marais brought him down from behind.

Bob Scott opens the scoring with a penalty goal.

A dropped pass by Koch cost South Africa a try but shortly after the home team took the lead. From a scrum wide out on the New Zealand 25 du Toit passed to Brewis, who prepared to pot at goal. Kearney quickly covered him but the scrum had wheeled and the All Black loose forwards were swung away from Brewis.

The Springbok fly-half moved to the left and headed for the goal line but he found himself covered. He stopped and feinted as though he

JOHANNESBURG STAR

NEW ZEALAND

Ellis Park, Johannesburg

meant to kick to the corner and the All Black cover defence hesitated. In a flash Brewis was off again to reach the line a yard ahead of Scott and Meates. Geffin failed to convert and the score was still 6-3 at halftime.

Eight minutes after the restart, Koch caught Savage in possession. As the ball dropped, du Rand snapped it up and passed to Muller who ran his backs into position before transferring to Brewis. The Springboks had an overlap but Lategan saw the All Black defence moving up quickly on the men outside him. When Brewis passed him the ball, Lategan sold a dummy and cut inside to run between Elvidge and Allen. He dotted down in the corner without being touched by an opponent. Van der Schyff failed to convert but the Springboks had a six point lead.

Scott failed with another penalty but, shortly after, Allen eluded van Schoor to burst through from his own 25. He passed to Elvidge who ran to half-way before sending on to Meates. The winger flew for the corner but Muller caught him three yards from the line.

Henderson also made a great run a few minutes later and Scott failed with another penalty. Brewis fielded and kicked for touch but Kearney caught the ball and dropped a magnificent goal from forty yards out. This put New Zealand in a much better position and the excitement was intense.

The Springbok pack continued to dominate however and near the end the ball came back to du Toit who passed to Brewis. The latter dropped a fine goal from forty yards to clinch the game for the home team.

RAND DAILY MAIL

The rival captains leave the field. Allen looks delighted to have lost and du Plessis seems distressed at his team's win!

NEW ZEALAND
R.W.H. SCOTT
(Auckland)

W.A. MEATES   R.R. ELVIDGE   P. HENDERSON
(Otago)   (Otago)   (Wanganui)
F.R. ALLEN (**Capt.**)
(Auckland)

J.C. KEARNEY
(Otago)

L.T. SAVAGE
(Canterbury)
P. JOHNSTONE
(Otago)

J.R. McNAB   H.F. FRAZER   L.R. HARVEY   L.A. GRANT
(Otago)   (Hawke's Bay)   (Otago)   (South Canterbury)
K.L. SKINNER   E.H. CATLEY   J.G. SIMPSON
(Otago)   (Waikato)   (Auckland)

A.C. KOCH   R.P. JORDAAN   A. GEFFIN
(Boland)   (Northern Transvaal)   (Transvaal)
L.J. STRYDOM   F. du PLESSIS (**Capt.**)   H.B. KOCH   J.A. du RAND
(Northern Transvaal)   (Transvaal)   (Western Province)   (Rhodesia)
H.S.V. MULLER
(Transvaal)
P.A. du TOIT
(Northern Transvaal)

J.D. BREWIS
(Northern Transvaal)
C. MOSS   R.A.M. van SCHOOR   M.T. LATEGAN   F.P. MARAIS
(Natal)   (Rhodesia)   (Western Province)   (Boland)
J.H. van der SCHYFF
(Griqualand West)
SOUTH AFRICA

REFEREE: Mr R.D. Burmeister (Western Province)
ATTENDANCE: 72,000
CONDITIONS: Weather fine, ground hard
HALFTIME: South Africa 6, New Zealand 3

SCORERS

NEW ZEALAND	SOUTH AFRICA
Dropped goal: Kearney	Tries: Brewis, Lategan
Penalty goal: Scott	Dropped goal: Brewis
	Penalty goal: Geffin

3 September, 1949

On the day of the vital third Test in Durban between New Zealand and South Africa, a second All Black team played the touring Australians at Wellington. Although regarded in some quarters as a third string side, since thirty players were in South Africa, this New Zealand team had a great deal of talent.

The three Maori backs, Johnny Smith, Ben Couch and Vince Bevan would almost certainly have been selected for the South African tour had they not been ineligible on racial grounds. This was Smith's third Test and Couch's second while Bevan had toured Australia in 1947 as second string half-back. Neither Smith nor Couch played international Rugby after 1949 but Bevan appeared in all four Tests against the 1950 Lions and toured Britain in 1953.

Jack Kelly's omission from the tour to South Africa had been criticised by some Rugby writers and followers of the game. An outstanding footballer and a valuable utility back, he was especially capable in the full-back position, which he preferred. An accurate goal kicker and a brilliant

"WALLABY OR NO WALLABY, I STILL DON'T THINK IT'S ETHICAL!"

"The Evening Post" SEPTEMBER 3, 1949

EVENING POST

runner with the ball, Kelly was a prolific try scorer who would undoubtedly have found South African conditions to his liking. He toured Britain in 1953 as second string to Bob Scott but he would probably have had no superior in the world with the possible exception of his fellow All Black.

Ron Dobson and Alan Blake were ex-Kiwis and were very experienced players. Dobson had played against France for the army team while Blake had taken part in all the unofficial international matches against England, Wales, Scotland and France. Both had established fine reputations by the end of the tour.

"Tiny" White, who was Poverty Bay's first All Black, went on to become one of New Zealand's most famous forwards. He played 55 games in the All Black jersey, including 23 Tests, between 1949 and 1956. A skilled line-out forward, he was also fast for a big man and his play in the loose was of high quality.

Bob Stuart was the very successful captain of the 1953 All Blacks on their British tour. An intelligent man, he was a good loose forward in his own right who gave outstanding service to university Rugby before winning his All Black jersey. He eventually played 27 matches for New Zealand, including seven Tests.

Hec Wilson won All Black honours again in a Test against the Lions in 1950 and toured Australia in 1951. He had played very well for the Otago Ranfurly Shield team in the immediate post-war years and was a South Island representative in both the prop and lock positions.

Arthur Hughes made his All Black debut in an unusual way in 1947, when he was brought in to hook for New Zealand in the match against Auckland following the Australian tour. The All Blacks had both their hookers injured so Hughes was given his chance. He played six Tests before his retirement in 1950.

Players in this team who did not represent New Zealand again after 1949 were Ron Bryers, Rex Orr, Graham Moore, the South Island forwards Bill Mumm and Bill Lunn, Smith, Dobson, Couch and Blake.

NEW ZEALAND 6

Athletic Park, Wellington

The 1947 All Black, Jack McLean, was originally selected for this Test but an injury put him out of action. The chosen full-back, Moore, was moved to the wing and Orr came into the team to play his only international match. An air force officer, Orr played for Combined Services for several years and also represented the South Island. Wally Argus was also unavailable through injury.

This Wallaby team was a very good one and fully deserved its win. The young captain, Trevor Allan, was back again after establishing a fine reputation on the British tour of 1947-48. He was even more brilliant now than he had been in 1946. The experienced Cyril Burke was again behind the scrum, which included such great forwards as the vice-captain, Colin Windon, Nick Shehadie and Rex Mossop, who, like Allan, later joined the League code, at which he also represented Australia. Another brilliant player was the flying winger, Ralph Garner.

The Australians scored all their points in the first half and led 11-0 at the interval. There was

NZ FREELANCE

Jack Kelly about to field the ball as Garner lines him up for a tackle.

no score for the first eighteen minutes but when the New Zealand forwards knocked the ball back from a line-out in their own 25, Mossop pounced and gained possession. He passed to Windon, who broke through a tackle to score.

Five minutes later Australia went further ahead when Garner went across in the corner at the end of a passing rush following good work by the Australian forwards in a line-out. Well led by Windon, the green pack was more than holding its own at this stage.

With the first half almost over, Orr came into the All Black back line but the ball was dropped by the New Zealanders and the Australians kicked it through to half way. Here it bounced right for Garner, who ran over unopposed behind the posts. Cawsey converted.

Seven minutes after the resumption, Kelly opened the scoring for New Zealand with a penalty goal. He almost landed another one shortly after but the ball hit a post.

Play was fairly even for the rest of the game and there was no further scoring until time was showing on the clock, when Moore scored an unconverted try in the corner after one of New Zealand's rare backline movements of the game.

NEW ZEALAND

R.W. ORR
(Otago)

J.W. KELLY   J.B. SMITH (**Capt.**)   G.J.T. MOORE
(Auckland)   (North Auckland)   (Otago)
R.L. DOBSON
(Auckland)

M.B.R. COUCH
(Wairarapa)

V.D. BEVAN
(Wellington)
R.C. STUART
(Canterbury)

A.W. BLAKE   R.A. WHITE   R.F. BRYERS   W.A. LUNN
(Wairarapa)   (Poverty Bay)   (King Country)   (Otago)
W.J. MUMM   A.M. HUGHES   H.W. WILSON
(Buller)   (Auckland)   (Otago)

B.J. WILSON   N.V. COTTRELL   A.J. BAXTER
(New South Wales)   (Queensland)   (New South Wales)
J.D. BROCKHOFF   R.P. MOSSOP   N.M. SHEHADIE   C.J. WINDON
(New South Wales) (New South Wales) (New South Wales) (New South Wales)
K.A. CROSS
(New South Wales)
C.T. BURKE
(New South Wales)

N.A. EMERY
(New South Wales)
R.L. GARNER   T. ALLAN (**Capt.**)   J. BLOMLEY   C.C. DAVIS
(New South Wales) (New South Wales) (New South Wales) (New South Wales)
R.M. CAWSEY
(New South Wales)

AUSTRALIA

REFEREE: Mr E.D. Hill (Auckland)
ATTENDANCE: 32,000
CONDITIONS: Weather fine, ground firm
HALFTIME: Australia 11, New Zealand 0

SCORERS

NEW ZEALAND   **AUSTRALIA**
Try: Moore   Tries: Garner (2), Windon
Penalty goal: Kelly   Conversion: Cawsey

SOUT AFRICA

3 September, 1949

Third Test

Again there were several changes in both teams. The All Black captain, Fred Allen, was dropped, thus suffering the same fate as his counterpart of 1921, George Aitken, who was also dropped from the third Test team. Morrie Goddard, who had been on the injured list, came in at centre with Ron Elvidge moving in to second five-eighth and taking over the captaincy.

Another change was the playing of Neville Black, the young Auckland five-eighth, at half-back in his only international appearance. This was a desperate move which did not come off. Black, a fine attacking five-eighth, accepted an offer to play League in England two years after the tour.

Morrie McHugh won back his Test place, this time at number eight, while the brilliant Auckland breakaway, Pat Crowley, made his Test debut. He played in all four Tests against the Lions in 1950.

The South African selectors recalled the first Test centre, Floris Duvenage, to take the place of "Buks" Marais on the right wing while the huge Orange Free Stater, "Flip" Geel, replaced "Bubbles" Koch at lock. Koch was moved out to the flank in place of Louis Strydom.

The result flattered the home team and once again the All Blacks were unlucky not to win. Scott missed an early penalty and after four minutes Geffin goaled from a scrum infringement. Three minutes later, he kicked a second penalty, awarded against Scott for allegedly using Meates as a shield when the New Zealand full-back was fielding the ball.

From this point on, the All Black pack began to dominate and the good work of the forwards was soon rewarded. A scrum was ordered following a

A panorama of Kingsmead Ground with the game in progress. The shortage of covered seating indicates Durban's dry climate.

WHYSALL'S PHOTOGRAPHIC STUDIOS

NEW ZEALAND 3

Kingsmead Ground, Durban

Peter Henderson picks up the ball as his opposite, Duvenage, closes on him.

kicked his third penalty following a scrum infringement and South Africa had the better of things for some time. Mistakes by the home team cost them tries however. When Moss cross-kicked to Lategan in front of New Zealand's posts the centre threw a bad pass which went astray and almost immediately after, a fumble by Duvenage ruined another scoring chance. Right on time Brewis intercepted a pass and elected to cross-kick with only Scott to beat. The All Blacks managed to kick the ball dead and for the second time in three Tests they had stopped the Springboks from scoring a try. Once again South Africa had won by penalty goals. There was no exultation among home pressmen at the winning of the rubber in this fashion and most of them agreed that New Zealand deserved to be 2-1 up rather than 3-0 down. They pointed out that 30 of the home team's 36 points scored in the three Tests had come from kicks — 27 of them from Geffin penalties. In fairness, however, it should be noted that each team had scored only two tries.

line-out and Catley hooked the ball. Black passed to Kearney, who kicked a high one to van der Schyff. Henderson followed up fast and bowled the full-back as he caught the ball. Elvidge picked up, fended off Moss and threw a pass infield to Goddard, who scored five yards from the corner. Scott had the same bad luck with the kick.

The All Blacks nearly scored again when Scott started a back move and Henderson was sent flying for the corner but he was stopped by Moss and Duvenage a yard short of the line.

Three minutes into the second spell, Geffin

NEW ZEALAND

R.W.H. SCOTT
(Auckland)

W.A. MEATES   M.P. GODDARD   P. HENDERSON
(Otago)   (South Canterbury)   (Wanganui)
R.R. ELVIDGE (**Capt.**)
(Otago)

J.C. KEARNEY
(Otago)

N.W. BLACK
(Auckland)
M.J. McHUGH
(Auckland)

J.R. McNAB   C. WILLOCKS   L.R. HARVEY   P.J.B. CROWLEY
(Otago)   (Otago)   (Otago)   (Auckland)
K.L. SKINNER   E.H. CATLEY   J.G. SIMPSON
(Otago)   (Waikato)   (Auckland)

A.C. KOCH   R.P. JORDAAN   A. GEFFIN
(Boland)   (Northern Transvaal)   (Transvaal)
J.A. du RAND   F. du PLESSIS (**Capt.**)   P.J. GEEL   H.B. KOCH
(Rhodesia)   (Transvaal)   (Orange Free State)   (Western Province)
H.S.V. MULLER
(Transvaal)
P.A. du TOIT
(Northern Transvaal)

J.D. BREWIS
(Northern Transvaal)
C. MOSS   M.T. LATEGAN   R.A.M. van SCHOOR   F.P. DUVENAGE
(Natal)   (Western Province)   (Rhodesia)   (Griqualand West)
J.H. van der SCHYFF
(Griqualand West)

SOUTH AFRICA

REFEREE: Mr E.W. Hofmeyr (Transvaal)
ATTENDANCE: 30,000
CONDITIONS: Weather fine and very hot, ground hard
HALFTIME: South Africa 6, New Zealand 3

SCORERS

NEW ZEALAND	**SOUTH AFRICA**
Try: Goddard	Penalty goals: Geffin (3)

17 September, 1949

Fourth Test

Although the series was already won by South Africa, there was still a lot of interest in this final Test, since one team was trying to avoid a 'white-wash' while the other was aiming at a 'grand slam'.

New Zealand fielded two new Test players in this game, neither of whom wore the black jersey again. "Red" Delamore had established something of a reputation in service Rugby during the war and had played for the North Island in 1948. Des Christian, normally a prop, took McHugh's place on the back of the scrum. He had been a North Island representative in 1947 and 1948. Savage returned to the Test side as Black was injured.

There were a number of changes in the home team for various reasons. Between the third and fourth Tests, only one match was played by the All Blacks, against Border. This team had beaten the tourists 9-0 in the New Zealanders' fifth game and the return match ended in a 6-6 draw.

Basil Kenyon, the Border captain and number eight, had played extremely well in both matches and his selection for the final Test was not unexpected, especially as du Rand was injured. The dropping of Felix du Plessis was totally unexpected however as his play and leadership in the first three Tests had been of a high standard. This was Kenyon's only Test although he captained the Springboks on their 1951-52 British tour. An eye injury sustained during the war was aggravated during the tour and this restricted Kenyon's activities in Britain so that he did not play in the internationals.

Other changes in the home team resulted in

Savage sends his backs away as Malan (left) and Geffin come through.

NEW ZEALAND 8

Crusader Ground, Port Elizabeth

Willem Barnard and Piet Malan coming into the pack while "Carrots" Geraghty replaced Duvenage on the wing.

Played in good weather with a slight breeze, this was generally regarded as the best game of the series. During the first ten minutes, Scott missed three penalties, all of which he would normally have landed. In the tenth minute, du Toit intercepted a pass and was on his way to a try but Henderson and Meates caught him a few yards from the line. Muller then raised South Africa's hopes with a magnificent run which Henderson ended with an equally magnificent tackle.

In the twenty-ninth minute, Catley won a tight head and Savage worked the blindside with Henderson. The winger kicked into the centre where Delamore took the ball at his toe to within five yards of the home line. He over-ran the ball but Johnstone picked up to dive across eleven yards from the corner. Scott failed to convert. This was the only score in the first half.

Early in the second half, Geffin kicked a penalty goal which was awarded because of obstruction on du Toit. Then, in the twentieth minute, the Springboks took the lead when they won a five-yard scrum and du Toit scored between the posts for Geffin to convert.

The South Africans continued to play the game in their opponents' half and from a line-out the ball came to Brewis, who potted a neat goal and the situation now looked grim from New Zealand's point of view.

The All Blacks, realising that they had nothing to lose, threw the ball about recklessly and eventually Delamore raced between Brewis and van Schoor to make an opening for Elvidge, who ran in under the bar. With Scott's conversion the All Blacks were back in the game but there was no further scoring and South Africa ended the series with a clean sweep.

CAPE ARGUS

NEW ZEALAND

R.W.H. SCOTT
(Auckland)

W.A. MEATES   M.P. GODDARD   P. HENDERSON
(Otago)   (South Canterbury)   (Wanganui)

R.R. ELVIDGE (**Capt.**)
(Otago)

G.W. DELAMORE
(Wellington)

L.T. SAVAGE
(Canterbury)

D.L. CHRISTIAN
(Auckland)

P.J.B. CROWLEY   C. WILLOCKS   L.R. HARVEY   P. JOHNSTONE
(Auckland)   (Otago)   (Otago)
K.L. SKINNER   E.H. CATLEY   J.G. SIMPSON
(Otago)   (Waikato)   (Auckland)

A.C. KOCH   R.P. JORDAAN   A. GEFFIN
(Boland)   (Northern Transvaal)   (Transvaal)
P. MALAN   W.H.M. BARNARD   H.B. KOCH   B.J. KENYON (**Capt.**)
(Transvaal) (Northern Transvaal) (Western Province)   (Border)
H.S.V. MULLER
(Transvaal)
P.A. du TOIT
(Northern Transvaal)

J.D. BREWIS
(Northern Transvaal)

E.M. GERAGHTY   M.T. LATEGAN   R.A.M. van SCHOOR   C. MOSS
(Border)   (Western Province)   (Rhodesia)   (Natal)
J.H. van der SCHYFF
(Griqualand West)

SOUTH AFRICA

REFEREE: Mr R.D. Burmeister (Western Province)
ATTENDANCE: 28,500
CONDITIONS: Weather fine, ground firm
HALFTIME: New Zealand 3, South Africa 0

SCORERS

NEW ZEALAND	SOUTH AFRICA
Tries: Johnstone, Elvidge	Try: du Toit
Conversion: Scott	Conversion: Geffin
	Penalty goal: Geffin
	Dropped goal: Brewis

AUSTRALIA 16

24 September, 1949

Second Test

The New Zealand selectors made a number of changes for this game. Jack McLean, recovered from his injury, returned to international Rugby to play his second and final Test. Making his debut as an All Black on the other wing was the Taranaki speedster, Roy Roper. Although on the small side, Roper was a player of top class who filled the centre berth very capably in the 1950 Tests against the Lions. The other new caps, none of whom played for New Zealand again, were Ray O'Callaghan, Harry Rowley, Des O'Donnell and the ex-Kiwi, Jack Bond.

There was only one change in the visiting team, the brilliant young John Solomon replacing Davis on the right wing. A versatile player who represented his country at wing, centre, five-eighth and full-back, Solomon went on to become one of Australia's most successful captains.

Once again, the Wallabies deserved their win. The ground and the weather suited their style of play and they treated the crowd to some good, open football.

They were by no means a great team but they had some outstanding individuals. Brockhoff played the number eight game with great intelligence and he managed to bottle up Couch all day. His spoiling and scavenging were reminiscent of Cliff Porter and Dave Gallaher at their best. Mossop was splendid in the line-outs while Cross did some fine work in cover defence. Windon did not quite reach the standard of which he was capable but he revealed great pace and determination in scoring his try.

Of the visiting backs Burke was a lively and enterprising half-back while Emery at five-eighth was sound without being spectacular. Outside him Blomley and Allan were very good indeed while Cawsey, chosen as a half-back, filled the full-back position capably. The wings, Garner and Solomon, made good use of the few chances which came their way.

The best players in the home side were White and Roper while Smith also showed good form. Lunn, O'Donnell and Hughes were impressive in the tight work and the last named had the

better of the hooking duel. Couch was too slow and his combination with O'Callaghan was not a happy one. Bevan gave away several penalties but he played a rugged game and his passing was generally good. McLean received few chances while Kelly had little to do before he had to retire. However, his tackle of Blomley, which put him out of the game, was very spectacular.

Australia scored after nineteen minutes when Bevan threw a wild pass to McLean on the blindside near his own line. The ball went astray and Solomon beat McLean to the touchdown for Cawsey to convert.

Five minutes later, the visiting forwards booted the ball through and it bounced nicely for Windon to pick up and race over. Cawsey failed to add the extra points but the Wallabies had a handy lead.

After twenty-seven minutes, Kelly retired injured; Roper went to full-back and Rowley to the wing. Although replacements had previously been allowed in games between Australia and

---

NEW ZEALAND

J.W. KELLY
(Auckland)

R.A. ROPER   J.B. SMITH (Capt.)   J.K. McLEAN
(Taranaki)   (North Auckland)   (Auckland)

T.R. O'CALLAGHAN
(Wellington)

M.B.R. COUCH
(Wairarapa)

V.D. BEVAN
(Wellington)

H.C.B. ROWLEY
(Wanganui)

R.C. STUART   T.A. BUDD   R.A. WHITE   W.A. LUNN
(Canterbury)   (Southland)   (Poverty Bay)   (Otago)

J.G. BOND   A.M. HUGHES   D.H. O'DONNELL
(Canterbury)   (Auckland)   (Wellington)

B.J. WILSON   N.V. COTTRELL   A.J. BAXTER
(New South Wales)   (Queensland)   (New South Wales)

J.D. BROCKHOFF   N.M. SHEHADIE   R.P. MOSSOP   C.J. WINDON
(New South Wales)   (New South Wales)   (New South Wales)   (New South Wales)

K.A. CROSS
(New South Wales)

C.T. BURKE
(New South Wales)

N.A. EMERY
(New South Wales)

R.L. GARNER   J. BLOMLEY   T. ALLAN (Capt.)   H.J. SOLOMON
(New South Wales)   (New South Wales)   (New South Wales)   (New South Wales)

R.M. CAWSEY
(New South Wales)

AUSTRALIA

REFEREE: Mr L. Walsh (Canterbury)
ATTENDANCE: 25,000
CONDITIONS: Weather fine, ground firm
HALFTIME: Australia 8, New Zealand 0
SCORERS

NEW ZEALAND	AUSTRALIA
Try: Roper	Tries: Solomon, Windon, Emery
Dropped goal: Smith	Conversions: Allan, Cawsey
Penalty goal: O'Callaghan	Penalty goal: Allan

NEW ZEALAND 9

Eden Park, Auckland

New Zealand, both countries had by now come into line with the no replacement rule then prevailing in international Rugby.

There was no further scoring in the first half although both sides had their chances.

Nine minutes after the interval, Smith dropped a goal from 35 yards and then O'Callaghan

kicked a penalty goal to bring New Zealand back into the game. However, obstruction on Burke from a ruck gave Allan a chance to kick a goal, which he did, but Roper, who had now gone back to the wing, scored a good try in the corner after a determined run and the game came alive again. Right on time, the All Blacks fumbled on their line and Emery scored for Allan to convert.

There was no further scoring and Australia won the series and the Bledisloe Cup. Truly, 1949 was a black year for New Zealand Rugby!

Kelly about to make a tackle on the Australian centre, Blomley. The All Black full-back was forced to leave the field with an injury received in this incident.

NEW ZEALAND 9

27 May, 1950

First Test

In many respects, the 1950 British team was the most attractive side to visit New Zealand since World War II. The average age of these Lions was higher than is usual with touring teams and many of the players had been on active service. The members of this British team established a fine reputation for their behaviour both on and off the field and they delighted the spectators with their open running Rugby.

The Lions had been soundly beaten by both Otago and Southland prior to the first Test and their chances against New Zealand were not rated highly by the critics. The All Blacks were lucky to draw the game, however.

The star British back was Jack Kyle, whom we regard as the best player seen in his position in New Zealand since the Second World War. The subsequent British teams all had very good fly-halves, but none of them possessed the Irishman's genius, especially as a runner with the ball. It should also be remembered that loose forwards had much more latitude in Kyle's day

than they now have and just how good this great Irish player would have looked under today's rules, one can only imagine.

Another back in this team who has had no superior among post-war visiting teams, was the Welsh wing three-quarter, Ken Jones. A semi-finalist in the 1948 Olympic 100 metres, Jones was an exceptionally fast runner with a brilliant swerve. He won 44 caps for Wales, a total surpassed only by Gareth Edwards.

The British forwards were on the light side and they gave away about eight pounds a man but in their captain and hooker, Karl Mullen, they had an outstanding player and leader while Peter Kininmonth and Roy John were fine line-out men.

The New Zealand Team
Back row: J.G. Simpson, L.R. Harvey, K.L. Skinner, P. Johnstone, P.J.B. Crowley, R.A. White, J.R. McNab, W.A. Meates.
Front row: V.D. Bevan, N.P. Cherrington, R.R. Elvidge (capt.), R.A. Roper, G.E. Beatty, R.W.H. Scott, A.M. Hughes.

BRITISH ISLES

Carisbrook, Dunedin

Kyle had played against the Kiwi Army team, as had Billy Cleaver, Jack Matthews and the Scottish scrum-half, Gus Black.

There were two new internationals in the New Zealand team. The big Maori wing, "Brownie" Cherrington, was given his chance when Peter Henderson was not available. The North Aucklander was a hard man to stop and he scored some great tries during a long career in first-class football. This was his only Test, however, although he toured Australia with the 1951 All Blacks. Another back who was playing his first and only Test was George Beatty, who later accepted an offer to play League in England.

The game opened in perfect weather and the visitors were soon on attack from a long kick by Kyle. Hughes was penalised for not binding and Robins kicked a penalty goal to put the Lions in front.

New Zealand attacked from the kick-off and Elvidge was stopped by Matthews, who tackled the All Black captain very heavily. Preece snapped up the ball and passed to McKay when tackled by Scott but McKay's pass to Macdonald went astray. The referee, ex-All Black "Snow" Tindill, awarded several penalties against New Zealand but Robins failed to goal from any of them. Just before halftime, John went close with a goal from a mark but the score was still 3-0 at the interval.

The All Black forwards showed improvement in the second half and began to gain more possession. However, a mis-kick by Bevan was fielded by Kyle, who cut through the defence, swerved past Scott and scored after Cherrington had failed to stop him with a shoulder-high tackle. This fine try, which Robins failed to convert, received generous applause.

New Zealand opened its account following a set scrum from which Beatty sent Roper away. The centre beat four men to score a good try, but Scott failed to convert.

The visitors were next to score following a nicely-judged punt by Kyle to the corner. Jones was right on Scott when the home full-back lost possession and the Welsh speedster touched down in the corner. Clifford's kick was outside the posts.

With nineteen minutes of play remaining, the situation looked grim for New Zealand and it looked as though the Britishers were going to repeat the victory gained by their predecessors at Carisbrook in 1930. However, Scott closed the gap with a 35 yard penalty and once more it was anybody's game.

Seven minutes from time, Scott came into the backline and kicked high towards the British goal. Clifford and John held up the rush of All Black forwards and a scrum was ordered five yards from the posts. New Zealand heeled and Elvidge ran on the blindside, where he took a pass from Bevan. The All Black captain dashed for the corner and beat three defenders to score, but it was too far out for Scott to convert. The home side had avoided defeat in the last minutes of the game.

NEW ZEALAND

R.W.H. SCOTT (Auckland)

W.A. MEATES (Otago) — R.A. ROPER (Taranaki) — N.P. CHERRINGTON (North Auckland)

R.R. ELVIDGE (Capt.) (Otago)

G.E. BEATTY (Taranaki)

V.D. BEVAN (Wellington)

P. JOHNSTONE (Otago)

J.R. McNAB (Otago) — L.R. HARVEY (Otago) — R.A. WHITE (Poverty Bay) — P.J.B. CROWLEY (Auckland)

K.L. SKINNER (Otago) — A.M. HUGHES (Auckland) — J.G. SIMPSON (Auckland)

J.D. ROBINS (Birkenhead Park & England) — K.D. MULLEN (Capt.) (Old Belvedere & Ireland) — J.T. CLIFFORD (Young Munster & Ireland)

J.W. McKAY (Queen's University & Ireland) — E.R. JOHN (Neath & Wales) — D.J. HAYWARD (Newbridge & Wales) — R.T. EVANS (Newport & Wales)

P.W. KININMONTH (Oxford University & Scotland)

A.W. BLACK (Edinburgh University & Scotland)

J.W. KYLE (N.I.F.C. & Ireland)

R. MACDONALD (Edinburgh University & Scotland) — I. PREECE (Coventry & England) — J. MATTHEWS (Cardiff & Wales) — K.J. JONES (Newport & Wales)

W.B. CLEAVER (Cardiff & Wales)

BRITISH ISLES

REFEREE: Mr E.W.T. Tindill (Wellington)
ATTENDANCE: 35,000
CONDITIONS: Weather fine, ground firm
HALFTIME: British Isles 3, New Zealand 0

SCORERS

NEW ZEALAND
Tries: Roper, Elvidge
Penalty goal: Scott

BRITISH ISLES
Tries: Kyle, Jones
Penalty goal: Robins

159

NEW ZEALAND 8

10 June, 1950

Second Test

The New Zealand selectors made two changes for this Test, both in the backs. Peter Henderson, now recovered from the injury which kept him out of the Dunedin international, took his place on the left wing. Beatty was dropped and Laurie Haig, brother of the All Black half-back of 1946, played his first Test match. Though not in Kyle's class, Haig was a reliable tradesman with good hands and an accurate boot. He was also solid on defence and gave good service in the nine Tests in which he took part.

The Lions also made two changes in the backs. Malcolm Thomas, a 20 year old naval lieutenant, replaced Ranald Macdonald on the left wing, where he played well enough to hold his place for the third Test. Thomas, who topped the points table for the 1950 tour, was a utility back who toured New Zealand again with the 1959 Lions.

The English captain, Ivor Preece, was normally a fly-half but he had played for the British team at centre in the first Test. He now gave way to the brilliant Welshman, Bleddyn Williams, who had not been available at Dunedin owing to injury. A worthy successor to the great Carl Aarvold of the 1930 British team, Williams had no superior in the world in 1950.

The game was played in bright sunshine but the ground was heavy and slippery and the crowd saw a dour, grim struggle.

There were two unfortunate features of the game. Play had been in progress only 25 minutes when McKay, the brilliant Irish loose forward, suffered concussion and a broken nose. Thus his team had to play the rest of the match a man short. Secondly, some aspects of the All Blacks' line-out play were undesirable. Obstruction of the visiting forwards was so persistent that it appeared to be part of the home team's plan for victory.

The Lions did not show their good form of the first Test, however. Their forwards were very loose while there was little attempt at combination among the backs. Nevertheless, the team deserved full marks for courage and it was only determined tackling which kept the All Blacks' score to eight points.

The best forward on the ground was Pat Crowley, who was ably supported by Jack McNab. Arthur Hughes was badly outhooked by Karl Mullen but he played well in the loose. Peter Johnstone was a lively and intelligent number eight.

Of the home backs Roy Roper was the best and Bob Scott, although he had a poor day with his goal-kicking, gave a very fine all-round display at full-back. Ron Elvidge played a stereotyped game at second five-eighth but he was sound as usual. Inside him, Laurie Haig made a useful contribution to the game while Vince Bevan gave good service behind the scrum. Neither of the wings had much to do and both were well marked by their opposites whenever they did receive the ball.

Karl Mullen led his team well and played splendidly, his hooking being especially good. He was well supported by Don Hayward, Roy

---

NEW ZEALAND

R.W.H. SCOTT
(Auckland)

W.A. MEATES   R.A. ROPER   P. HENDERSON
(Otago)   (Taranaki)   (Wanganui)
R.R. ELVIDGE (Capt.)
(Otago)

L.S. HAIG
(Otago)

V.D. BEVAN
(Wellington)
P. JOHNSTONE
(Otago)

J.R. McNAB   L.R. HARVEY   R.A. WHITE   P.J.B. CROWLEY
(Otago)   (Otago)   (Poverty Bay)   (Auckland)
K.L. SKINNER   A.M. HUGHES   J.G. SIMPSON
(Otago)   (Auckland)   (Auckland)

J.D. ROBINS   K.D. MULLEN (Capt.)   J.T. CLIFFORD
(Birkenhead Park & Wales) (Old Belvedere & Ireland) (Young Munster & Ireland)
J.W. McKAY   E.R. JOHN   D.J. HAYWARD   R.T. EVANS
(Queen's University (Neath & Wales)   (Newbridge &   (Newport & Wales)
& Ireland)   Wales)
P.W. KININMONTH
(Oxford University & Scotland)
A.W. BLACK
(Edinburgh University & Scotland

J.W. KYLE
(N.I.F.C. & Ireland)
M.C. THOMAS   B.L. WILLIAMS   J. MATTHEWS   K.J. JONES
(Devonport Services (Cardiff & Wales) (Cardiff & Wales) (Newport & Wales)
& Wales)
W.B. CLEAVER
(Cardiff & Wales)

BRITISH ISLES

REFEREE: Mr E.W.T. Tindill (Wellington)
ATTENDANCE: 43,000
CONDITIONS: Weather fine, ground heavy
HALFTIME: New Zealand 8, British Isles 0

SCORERS
NEW ZEALAND   **BRITISH ISLES**
Tries: Crowley, Roper
Conversion: Haig

BRITISH ISLES 0

Lancaster Park, Christchurch

Bevan turns to kick as the British forwards, led by Mullen, pour through.

John and Tom Clifford. Gus Black was erratic in his passing, largely because he took so much punishment from the All Black forwards, and he did not reach the form he showed in the first Test. Only three of the backs, Kyle, Jones and Cleaver were worthy of unstinted praise. Kyle was simply Kyle — quick thinking, polished and the complete footballer. Jones was impeccable on defence but he had little chance to show his attacking ability while Cleaver made gallant catches and kicks in the face of fierce All Black rushes.

The visitors lost the toss and played into a strong sun. Both Scott and Robins failed with early penalties while the home full-back also made two unsuccessful attempts to drop goals. The first score came when the Lions heeled on their own goal line and Crowley came off the scrum to dive over for a try. Scott failed to convert.

Late in the first half, New Zealand scored again when Henderson, from the blindside wing, threw a pass to Haig, who clapped on the pace. He handed on to Elvidge who passed to Roper for the centre to score a good try. Haig was entrusted with the kick and he made no mistake.

There was not much excitement in the second half until ten minutes from time, when the Lions nearly scored. Roper made a run down the touch-line and cross-kicked. A ruck was formed from which the All Blacks heeled. Roper cross-kicked again and the home forwards took the ball to their opponents' goal line where they heeled cleanly. The All Blacks switched play to the opposite wing, where Kyle tackled two men and Thomas broke away with the ball. Kyle ran up to support the Welshman, who passed to him. The Irishman ran up to Meates, beat him cleanly and raced to the All Black 25, where he kicked across for Thomas and Kininmonth. Thomas gained possession but was brought down short of the line and Bevan kicked to touch to end a very exciting two minutes of Rugby.

Neither team managed to score in the second half and the game ended with New Zealand winning 8-0 to take the lead in the series.

161

NEW ZEALAND 6

1 July, 1950

Third Test

The New Zealand team was unchanged from that which had won the second Test but the visitors were forced to make several changes through injuries. The most serious losses were Ken Jones, whose place was taken by the young Irishman, Henderson, and the captain, Karl Mullen, who was replaced by Dai Davies. Henderson won 40 caps for Ireland before his retirement in 1959 while Davies played 17 times for Wales between 1950 and 1954. Gordon Rimmer, one of three Englishmen in the touring party, took Black's place behind the scrum and an injury to Kininmonth meant a rearranging of the pack with Nelson playing his first Test match of the tour.

When Mr Fong, who had played for the South Island in 1933, signalled the kick-off the visitors had the breeze behind them. They scored first when the All Blacks were penalised in the middle of their own 25 and Robins kicked an easy penalty.

From a penalty for a late charge Scott took a shot at goal from 45 yards but the ball fell short. Matthews failed to find touch and Scott fielded the ball. He moved infield and dropped for goal but once again his kick was unsuccessful, the ball passing under the bar.

In the twentieth minute of the game, Simpson was heavily tackled and had to leave the field with a knee injury which finished his playing career. McNab moved into the front row to take his place. Shortly after, Rimmer also went to the touch-line but he returned to the field later.

While Rimmer was off, Cleaver went behind the scrum and he sent his backs away on a fine break for Williams to reach the All Black 25. McKay was not quite fast enough to get up for Williams's pass and a scoring chance was lost. Then Haig missed with a penalty kick and Peter Henderson sent Bevan over after picking up a bouncing ball but the whistle went for a forward pass.

Noel Henderson broke through with Williams and McKay in support and passed to Williams, who veered infield before sending back to Henderson, who knocked on. Seven minutes from halftime, Elvidge was badly injured in a tackle. He bumped heads with Matthews and opened up a gash which required four stitches while he also injured his collar-bone.

This injury necessitated Peter Johnstone moving to the left wing, Peter Henderson switching to the right and Bill Meates going to centre, with Roper taking Elvidge's place.

With the home team reduced to 13 men, the visitors took up the attack and for the rest of the half the All Blacks were defending desperately. Crowley and McNab relieved the situation when they dribbled 40 yards upfield and the half ended with Scott failing to kick a penalty goal.

One minute after the start of the second half, Elvidge returned to the field. One arm was hanging loose and he was obviously in great pain. He took up his position as a rover or extra back behind the backline and gave what help he could on defence.

NEW ZEALAND

R.W.H. SCOTT
(Auckland)

W.A. MEATES   R.A. ROPER   P. HENDERSON
(Otago)   (Taranaki)   (Wanganui)
R.R. ELVIDGE (**Capt.**)
(Otago)

L.S. HAIG
(Otago)

V.D. BEVAN
(Wellington)
P. JOHNSTONE
(Otago)

J.R. McNAB   L.R. HARVEY   R.A. WHITE   P.J.B. CROWLEY
(Otago)   (Otago)   (Poverty Bay)   (Auckland)
K.L. SKINNER   A.M. HUGHES   J.G. SIMPSON
(Otago)   (Auckland)   (Auckland)

J.D. ROBINS   D.M. DAVIES   J.T. CLIFFORD
(Birkenhead Park   (Somerset Police   (Young Munster
& Wales)   & Wales)   & Ireland)
J.W. McKAY   J.E. NELSON   D.J. HAYWARD   R.T. EVANS
(Queen's University   (Malone &   (Newbridge &   (Newport &
& Ireland)   Ireland)   Wales)   Wales)
E.R. JOHN
(Neath & Wales)
G. RIMMER
(Waterloo & England)

J.W. KYLE
(N.I.F.C. & Ireland)
M.C. THOMAS   B.L. WILLIAMS (**Capt.**)   J. MATTHEWS   N.J. HENDERSON
(Devonport   (Cardiff & Wales)   (Cardiff & Wales)   (Queen's University
Services & Wales)   & Ireland)
W.B. CLEAVER
(Cardiff & Wales)

BRITISH ISLES

REFEREE: Mr A.S. Fong (West Coast)
ATTENDANCE: 45,000
CONDITIONS: Weather dull, ground heavy
HALFTIME: British Isles 3, New Zealand 0

SCORERS

NEW ZEALAND	BRITISH ISLES
Try: Elvidge	Penalty goal: Robins
Penalty goal: Scott	

BRITISH ISLES 3

Athletic Park, Wellington

Bevan kicked down to British Isles territory and then sent his backs away from a ruck. Scott came up between five-eighths and centre with Johnstone outside him. The latter received the ball and as he did so Elvidge suddenly appeared on the scene. Johnstone passed to his captain, who headed for the line. With a remarkable display of courage he dived through Cleaver's tackle and scored a truly memorable try. Haig missed the conversion but things now looked much brighter for the All Blacks.

Evans made a 30 yard dash from a line-out and Kyle made a break past Haig but Williams was tackled and the movement broke down. A counter attack led by Crowley, Hughes and McNab took play back to British territory. McKay was penalised for offside play and from 30 yards Scott kicked a goal to give New Zealand the lead.

Play was very hard for the last few minutes, especially among the forwards, but there was no further scoring, although Robins just failed to draw the game with a penalty shot from the 25.

An autographed photo of Elvidge's courageous try. The All Black captain dives through Cleaver's tackle as McKay arrives on the scene.

29 July, 1950

Fourth Test

The most startling change made in the All Black team for the final Test of 1950 was the selection of John Tanner in place of the injured Ron Elvidge.

The choice of Tanner was something of a shock since he had not played for Auckland during the 1950 season prior to his selection in the Test team. He was, however, a very experienced player. After playing in the Auckland Grammar School First XV, he went to Otago University to study dentistry and during his sojourn in Dunedin, he played for Otago and for New Zealand Universities. He also won South Island honours as a wing three-quarter in 1947. Returning to Auckland after completing his dental studies, Tanner played for that union in 1949. He gave a sound display in his first international and played six times for Auckland during the rest of the 1950 season, which he ended by gaining selection in the North Island team. Tanner was vice-captain of the 1951 All Blacks and toured Britain, France and North America in 1953-54.

Simpson's place was taken by 1949 All Black Hec Wilson while McNab, who was also unavailable, was replaced by new international Graham Mexted. This was Mexted's only Test but he toured Australia in 1951.

Because of injuries to G.W. Norton (Bective Rangers and Ireland), the brilliant 19 year old Lewis Jones was flown to New Zealand as a replacement. Norton's unavailability had left the Lions with only one full-back. They also had other backs on the injured list. Jones ended the tour as second-highest points scorer in spite of his late start and his excellent all-round form won him a place in the fourth Test ahead of Billy Cleaver. He later played for Llanelly and eventually won ten Welsh caps before accepting an offer to play professional Rugby League. He also became an international at this code and was widely regarded as one of the great League players of the 1950s. In our opinion, no better full-back has toured New Zealand with a Rugby Union team since the war.

The tourists in fact made eight changes for the final Test, players from the third Test who were

Hec Wilson scores the first try of the match, at the feet of Lewis Jones.

dropped being Cleaver, Thomas, Henderson, Rimmer, Clifford, Robins, Hayward and Dai Davies, although the latter regained his place when a foot injury from the Auckland game caused Karl Mullen to withdraw from the international.

Members of this Lions' Test team who had not played against New Zealand in the earlier encounters were Lane, Willis, Budge and Cliff Davies. Graham Budge was a Canadian who won four Scottish caps in 1950. He later returned to British Columbia, where he played against the 1953-54 All Blacks. Rex Willis also played against that All Black team, appearing for Cardiff, Wales and the Barbarians.

With the exception of Matthews and Dai Davies, all the tourists' fourth Test players had been in the team which had thrashed Auckland 32-9 the week before. The Lions' backs were brilliant in that game and the All Blacks expected another hard struggle.

The fourth Test was played in glorious sunshine with no wind and it was one of the finest internationals seen on Eden Park, being by far the best of the 1950 series. Williams won the toss and elected to play with the sun behind his team.

BRITISH ISLES 8

Eden Park, Auckland

New Zealand scored first when Willis fumbled at the base of the scrum and Crowley kicked the ball away for Wilson to fall on it over the line. Scott converted after a no charge had been awarded because John moved too soon.

Lewis Jones reduced the lead when he kicked a 30 yard penalty after Haig had been caught standing offside. The All Blacks came back into British territory and John took a mark. His kick failed to find touch and Scott fielded the ball. With a glorious kick from 45 yards out, near the left-hand touch-line, the New Zealand full-back dropped a goal. There was no further scoring in the first half and the interval found the home side leading 8-3.

Within a minute of the second half, Williams tried to emulate Scott's feat but the ball fell short. Then Meates made a good run but Lewis Jones forced him into touch. Kyle and Ken Jones brought play back into New Zealand territory with a dash of 60 yards and when Pat Crowley conceded a ruck penalty, Lewis Jones missed a fairly easy shot. Then Kininmonth tried to drop a goal from a mark and Jones missed another easy penalty.

Good work by Tanner gave Meates another chance to score but Lewis Jones stopped the winger again. However, after 27 minutes Roper kicked towards touch and the ball bounced for Henderson to gather it in outstrip the defence and dive over for a spectacular try in the left corner. Scott missed.

Then came one of the greatest tries seen at Eden Park. Lewis Jones received the ball on his own goal line and shot through a gap. He ran to half-way, where Scott confronted him. Henderson had come across to cover but the young Welshman committed Scott to the tackle and lobbed the ball over Henderson's head to Ken Jones. The Olympic sprinter set off on a 50 yard run with the New Zealand backs in full cry behind him. Only Roper got anywhere near Jones, however, and he dived at the flying winger in an attempt to tap his heels. He missed and Jones ran on to score under the bar. Lewis Jones converted to bring the visitors within three points of the home side.

With three minutes to go, Scott was almost over and then the Lions nearly saved the game when Willis made a break and the ball reached Williams. The centre had a clear run to the line but a magnificent tackle by Henderson brought him down. Williams made one final effort when he dived over from a ruck but he hit the corner flag and an exciting game ended with New Zealand still three points ahead. The home forwards, among whom Crowley was outstanding, rose to the occasion and paved the way for a narrow win.

The 1950 season was the last in international Rugby for most of the New Zealand players. Henderson, Meates, Roper, Beatty, Elvidge, Bevan, Crowley, Harvey, Hughes, McNab, Simpson, Cherrington and Mexted were finished with Test matches. Bevan, Cherrington and Mexted toured with future All Black teams and although Scott announced his retirement after this Test, he came back to international Rugby for the British tour of 1953-54.

NEW ZEALAND

R.W.H. SCOTT
(Auckland)

W.A. MEATES (Otago)	R.A. ROPER (Taranaki)	P. HENDERSON (Wanganui)

J.M. TANNER
(Auckland)

L.S. HAIG
(Otago)

V.D. BEVAN
(Wellington)

G.G. MEXTED
(Wellington)

P. JOHNSTONE (Capt.) (Otago)	L.R. HARVEY (Otago)	R.A. WHITE (Poverty Bay)	P.J.B. CROWLEY (Auckland)
K.L. SKINNER (Otago)	A.M. HUGHES (Auckland)		H.W. WILSON (Otago)

C. DAVIES (Cardiff & Wales)	D.M. DAVIES (Somerset Police & Wales)	G.M. BUDGE (Edinburgh Wanderers & Scotland)
J.W. McKAY (Queen's University & Ireland)	E.R. JOHN (Neath & Wales)	J.E. NELSON (Malone & Ireland)	R.T. EVANS (Newport & Wales)

R.W. KININMONTH
(Oxford University & Scotland)

W.R. WILLIS
(Cardiff & Wales)

J.W. KYLE
(N.I.F.C. & Ireland)

M.F. LANE (University College Cork & Ireland)	B.L. WILLIAMS (Capt.) (Cardiff & Wales)	J. MATTHEWS (Cardiff & Wales)	K.J. JONES (Newport & Wales)

B.L. JONES
(Devonport Services & Wales)

BRITISH ISLES

REFEREE: Mr G. Sullivan (Taranaki)
ATTENDANCE: 58,000
CONDITIONS: Weather fine, ground firm
HALFTIME: New Zealand 8, British Isles 3

SCORERS

NEW ZEALAND	BRITISH ISLES
Tries: Wilson, Henderson	Try: K.J. Jones
Conversion: Scott	Conversion: B.L. Jones
Dropped goal: Scott	Penalty goal: B.L. Jones

23 June, 1951

First Test

The 1951 All Black side included a convincing victory over New South Wales by 24 - 3 on a saturated field at the Sydney Showgrounds, in their three match lead up to this first international. Several players were making their Test debuts for New Zealand including the 21 year old Wellington wing Ron Jarden, a former national junior 440 yard champion, who had been selected for this tour whilst in Australia with the New Zealand University team. Fast and intelligent, Jarden was also a fine goal kicker and amassed 213 points from the 37 matches he played in the All Black jersey.

Other newcomers were "Snow" Cockerill a full-back from Hawera, Percy Erceg a New Zealand Maori representative winger in 1950 and 1951, Tommy Lynch, the son of an All Black of 1913 and 1914 who had played his last match for New Zealand on this same ground; and Brian Steele, who remains the Onslow club's only All Black.

"Tiny" White charges through the mire at the Sydney Cricket Ground.

In the forwards, Bob Duff, later to lead his country to an historic victory over the Springboks in 1956, was making his debut, as was Eddie Robinson a flanker from New Zealand's most southerly club, Bluff, and Bill McCaw another flanker from Southland who later toured with the 1953-54 New Zealand team. Norman Wilson who had toured South Africa in 1949 playing ten matches, was also making his international debut.

An interesting selection in the Australian team was Keith Gudsell, an All Black of 1949 who had toured South Africa playing in only five matches and who was now studying veterinary science in Sydney. Three of the Australian team making their entry into international play, were to become familiar faces in the next few years; Eddie Stapleton the burly winger, Dick Tooth a prominent mid-field back, and Alan Cameron

NEW ZEALAND

M.S. COCKERILL
(Taranaki)

C.P. ERCEG   J.M. TANNER   R.A. JARDEN
(Auckland)   (Auckland)   (Wellington)

T.W. LYNCH
(Canterbury)

L.S. HAIG
(Otago)

L.B. STEELE
(Wellington)

P. JOHNSTONE (**Capt.**)
(Otago)

C.E. ROBINSON   R.A. WHITE   R.H. DUFF   W.A. McCAW
(Southland)   (Poverty Bay)   (Canterbury)   (Southland)

K.L. SKINNER   N.L. WILSON   H.W. WILSON
(Otago)   (Otago)   (Otago)

A.J. BAXTER   N.V. COTTRELL   N.M. SHEHADIE
(New South Wales)   (Queensland)   (New South Wales)

K.A. WINNING (**Capt.**)   C.J. PRIMMER   A.S. CAMERON   C.J. WINDON
(Queensland)   (Queensland) (New South Wales) (New South Wales)

R.P. MOSSOP
(New South Wales)

C.T. BURKE
(New South Wales)

R.M. TOOTH
(New South Wales)

C.C. DAVIS   K.E. GUDSELL   H.J. SOLOMON   E.T. STAPLETON
(New South Wales)   (New South Wales)   (New South Wales)   (New South Wales)

P.R. ROTHWELL
(New South Wales)

AUSTRALIA

REFEREE: Mr H.A. Tolhurst (New South Wales)
ATTENDANCE: 17,110
CONDITIONS: Weather fine, ground extremely heavy.
HALFTIME: New Zealand 8, Australia 0

SCORERS

NEW ZEALAND	AUSTRALIA
Try: Skinner	
Conversion: Cockerill	
Penalty goal: Cockerill	

AUSTRALIA 0

Sydney Cricket Ground

the lock forward. Arch Winning the Queensland flanker had the distinction of leading Australia in his only Test. The referee, Mr Harold Tolhurst had played on the wing for Australia against New Zealand in 1931.

Because of the extremely muddy conditions the match was largely confined to the forwards. First points came mid-way through the first half when Cockerill landed a penalty goal from near the Australian posts, and after thirty minutes, New Zealand scored the only try of the match. Jarden caught the home team napping with a quick throw-in to Skinner who plunged over the line without a hand being laid on him. Some of the Australian players disputed the try claiming that the incorrect ball had been used but the referee, after consulting the touch judge, had no

doubt as to the legality of the try. Cockerill surprised everyone by converting the try from wide out with a heavy ball.

No further scoring occurred in the match although Australia twice went close to the line during the second half. However, it was the All Black forwards who generally held control with Peter Johnstone playing a fine captain's game. Duff had received a head injury early in the game and needed stitches after the match.

As a result of their victory the New Zealand team were presented with the Commonwealth Jubilee Trophy, which had been presented to the Australian Rugby Union by the Federal Government for competition as a part of the Commonwealth's fiftieth jubilee celebrations.

7 July, 1951

Second Test

The New Zealand team took the field unchanged from the side which had won the first match of the series. Since playing that match they had recorded three wins by large scores over modest opposition. At Parkes, where the local Central West side had gone down 65-6, Ron Jarden had created a scoring record for an individual All Black, amassing 38 points from six tries and 10 conversions.

Whilst the Australian back line remained unchanged, the selectors made several changes in the forwards. Mossop had been ordered off in a club match the previous week and his subsequent suspension put him out of consideration for the final two internationals. His place was taken by Keith Cross who had played two Tests against New Zealand in 1949. The captain in the first Test, Arch Winning, was replaced on the flank by Dave Brockhoff, a fiery 23 year old University player who later became a controversial coach of Australian sides. Nick Shehadie moved from prop to take Primmer's place as lock, with Neil Betts, a 1949 tourist in New Zealand, coming in as prop to win his first international cap.

The match started sensationally when Jarden scored his maiden Test try with only 30 seconds gone in the match. From the Australian kick-off the ball came loose from the New Zealand for-

White has jumped well in this line-out but, with his eyes closed, the ball passes through his hands.

R.A. WHITE COLLECTION

AUSTRALIA 11

wards for Jarden to scoop up the ball and race down the touchline eluding Stapleton and Rothwell before touching down near the posts. Cockerill missed an easy conversion. A minute later Rothwell evened the scores with a successful penalty following a line-out infringement.

For the next ten minutes the All Blacks were defending grimly but Australia could not score. In the twenty-eighth minute Erceg crossed for New Zealand but was recalled for a forward pass. The All Blacks remained on attack however and Lynch dropped a goal after receiving from a scrum. Just on halftime Tanner was cornered and threw a long pass infield to Duff who in turn passed to Skinner, the ball finally reaching Norman Wilson who scored. Jarden missed the kick which made the halftime score 9-3 in favour of the visitors.

Early in the second half from a scrum near the All Black line, Burke fed Tooth for the five-eighth to score near the posts. Rothwell converted and after twelve minutes of the half,

SYDNEY SUN

Ron Jarden scores his second try in this Test.

Shehadie went over for a try to give Australia the lead for the first time in the series. Rothwell missed the kick and a few minutes later Gudsell failed with an attempted dropped goal. Lynch regained the lead for his team when he finished off a fine movement with a try between the posts for Cockerill to convert.

The final points of the match came when Jarden went over for his second try following a backline movement a few minutes from the end of the game. Cockerill again missed the kick and the game ended with the score 17-11. Immediately after the game Colin Windon, the Australian captain, presented the New Zealand team with the Bledisloe Cup. Jarden was picked out by the critics as being the man of the match with the all round play of Tommy Lynch also coming in for much favourable comment.

NEW ZEALAND

M.S. COCKERILL
(Taranaki)

C.P. ERCEG   J.M. TANNER   R.A. JARDEN
(Auckland)   (Auckland)   (Wellington)
T.W. LYNCH
(Canterbury)

L.S. HAIG
(Otago)

L.B. STEELE
(Wellington)
P. JOHNSTONE (**Capt.**)
(Otago)

C.E. ROBINSON   R.A. WHITE   R.H. DUFF   W.A. McCAW
(Southland)   (Poverty Bay)   (Canterbury)   (Southland)
K.L. SKINNER   N.L. WILSON   H.W. WILSON
(Otago)   (Otago)   (Otago)

A.J. BAXTER   N.V. COTTRELL   N.T. BETTS
(New South Wales)   (Queensland)   (Queensland)
J.D. BROCKHOFF   A.S. CAMERON   N.M. SHEHADIE   C.J. WINDON (**Capt.**)
(New South Wales)   (New South Wales)   (New South Wales)   (New South Wales)
R.A. CROSS
(New South Wales)
C.T. BURKE
(New South Wales)

R.M. TOOTH
(New South Wales)
C.C. DAVIS   K.E. GUDSELL   H.J. SOLOMON   E.T. STAPLETON
(New South Wales)   (New South Wales)   (New South Wales)   (New South Wales)
P.R. ROTHWELL
(New South Wales)

AUSTRALIA

REFEREE: Mr H.A. Tolhurst (New South Wales)
ATTENDANCE: 17,274
CONDITIONS: Weather fine, ground firm
HALFTIME: New Zealand 9, Australia 3

SCORERS

NEW ZEALAND	AUSTRALIA
Tries: Jarden (2), N.L. Wilson, Lynch	Tries: Tooth, Shehadie
Conversion: Cockerill	Conversion: Rothwell
Dropped goal: Lynch	Penalty goal: Rothwell

21 July, 1951

Third Test

The only change in the New Zealand side saw Ray Bell who was making his international debut, replace leading try scorer, Jarden who had injured an ankle in the match against Queensland. Following their initial choice, the Australian selectors were forced to make several changes to their side. Prop Jack Baxter withdrew with a shin injury and was replaced by Betts who had played in the second Test. Original selection Clarrie Davis was forced to withdraw for business reasons and was replaced by the centre from the first two Tests, Keith Gudsell. Davis however flew to Brisbane as a last minute replacement for Solomon when the centre had to pull out with a stomach upset on the morning of the match. Primmer came into the side to partner Cameron when Shehadie was selected for the front row. Murray Tate came into centre to win his first international cap.

A very disappointing crowd, one of the smallest ever to watch an international, saw Gudsell

Percy Erceg attempts to shrug off the grasp of Davis.

kick off for Australia. Rothwell, who had a pain killing injection in his thigh just prior to the game, had two attempts at goal from penalties in the first ten minutes but missed both.

The first points of the game came in the tenth minute when Lynch made a break before sending the ball out. Erceg inpassed to Tanner who scored in Tate's tackle. Cockerill converted. Three minutes later Rothwell missed yet another penalty attempt from a handy position. A minute later he succeeded with a further attempt from the middle of the 25 yard line.

As the spell progressed, the All Blacks began to gain the upper hand in the tight and went further ahead half-way through the spell after Bell gathered a mis-kick and raced down the touch line before inpassing to Lynch who scored. Cockerill was unable to convert. Two minutes from halftime Rothwell was caught by Lynch after he had taken a kick ahead by Haig. Lynch

NEW ZEALAND
M.S. COCKERILL
(Taranaki)

C.P. ERCEG	J.M. TANNER	R.H. BELL
(Auckland)	(Auckland)	(Otago)

T.W. LYNCH
(Canterbury)

L.S. HAIG
(Otago)

L.B. STEELE
(Wellington)

W.A. McCAW
(Southland)

C.E. ROBINSON	R.A. WHITE	R.H. DUFF	P. JOHNSTONE (Capt.)
(Southland)	(Poverty Bay)	(Canterbury)	(Otago)

K.L. SKINNER	N.L. WILSON	H.W. WILSON
(Otago)	(Otago)	(Otago)

N.T. BETTS	N.V. COTTRELL	N.M. SHEHADIE
(Queensland)	(Queensland)	(New South Wales)

J.D. BROCKHOFF	C.J. PRIMMER	A.S. CAMERON	C.J. WINDON (Capt.)
(New South Wales)	(Queensland)	(New South Wales)	(New South Wales)

K.A. CROSS
(New South Wales)

C.T. BURKE
(New South Wales)

R.M. TOOTH
(New South Wales)

C.C. DAVIS	M.J. TATE	K.E. GUDSELL	E.T. STAPLETON
(New South Wales)	(New South Wales)	(New South Wales)	(New South Wales)

P.R. ROTHWELL
(New South Wales)

AUSTRALIA

REFEREE: Mr T. Moore (Queensland)
ATTENDANCE: 4,800
CONDITIONS: Weather fine, ground hard
HALFTIME: New Zealand 11, Australia 3

SCORERS

NEW ZEALAND	**AUSTRALIA**
Tries: Tanner, Lynch, Bell, Haig	Penalty goals: Rothwell, Cottrell
Conversions: Cockerill (2)	

AUSTRALIA 6

Brisbane Cricket Ground

wrenched the ball clear and fed Bell who scored near the posts. The conversion attempt was disallowed by the referee after Cockerill had handled the ball on the ground. The halftime score was 11-3 to the visitors.

Early in the second half both Bell and Rothwell missed penalty attempts but shortly after New Zealand were penalised for an illegal tackle and Cottrell kicked an easy goal. Six minutes from time Haig, who had an outstanding match, received the ball quickly from a line-out ruck fifteen yards from the Australian line, eluded two defenders and scored. Cockerill converted to complete the scoring.

The touring team had concluded an undefeated tour and much praise was given to their

well-organised cover defence which the Australian teams had great trouble in penetrating. Rothwell's poor goal kicking form in this match drew a great deal of criticism but Cottrell, the local player who won the hooking duel by a wide margin, was compared with Eddie Bonis the noted hooker of the 1930's and current Australian selector.

On the All Blacks' return home, a match was arranged with the Auckland representative side before the team dispersed. This match was also won, by a margin of 9-3 in a dull display. Of the All Black players Cockerill, who was injured in a provincial match later in the year, Lynch who turned to League, Steele, both the Wilsons and captain Johnstone (who retired at the end of the season after playing 26 matches for New Zealand including nine internationals), did not appear in the All Black jersey again.

Tanner dummies a pass as he looks for a way round Davis and Gudsell.

AUSTRALIA 14

6 September, 1952

First Test

In the seven matches leading up to this first international of the 1952 series, the Australian tourists had enjoyed a reasonably good record, winning the first six matches before losing to a hard-rucking Southland pack on the Tuesday before the international. Despite the fact that New Zealand were fielding eight new Test players, it was expected that their forward strength would be too much for the Wallabies.

Of the new men, "Ponty" Reid the nine stone six pound half-back, had toured Australia the previous year without playing a Test but both five-eighths and the centre three-quarter were newcomers. Jim Fitzgerald and "Peg" Elsom toured with the 1953 All Blacks while John Hotop was vice-captain against Australia in 1955. In the forwards, the hooker Ian Irvine was the son of W.R. Irvine the 1923-24-25-26-30 All Black, and Kevin Meates was a brother of 1949-50 Test winger Bill Meates. Number eight Hugh McLaren and prop Eastgate were the other new men.

In the Australian side Tony Miller, who replaced Shehadie on the morning of the match, was playing the first of his 41 Tests for his country as was the diminutive half-back, Brian Cox who, at a bare nine stone became one of the lightest players to take part in an international match. The Australian captain, John Solomon,

Meates attempts to check Barker's dive following the Australian centre's brilliant run. Hotop, White, Duff, Skinner and Bell can only watch the try being scored.

NEW ZEALAND 9

Lancaster Park, Christchurch

CHRISTCHURCH PRESS

John Hotop passes as Windon launches himself into a tackle.

was making his third tour to New Zealand, although he was only 22 years old.

Bell kicked off for New Zealand into the sun and after five minutes, Fitzgerald scored following a mis-kick of a loose ball by Stapleton near his own line. Jarden was unable to convert and a few minutes later he missed a penalty attempt from near the 25. The next points came after thirty minutes when the All Black lock forward "Tiny" White picked up a loose ball 20 yards from the line and charged for the corner, scoring in a tackle. Jarden's kick narrowly failed. Australia's Johnson was off the field with a head injury at this time.

During the last ten minutes of the half Australia held the upper hand. First, Cottrell missed a penalty attempt then on the call of halftime, Cox fed Stapleton from a ruck for the fourteen stone six pound winger to cut infield and past several defenders to score under the bar. Cottrell

had no trouble converting to make the halftime score 6-5 in favour of the home team.

Eight minutes into the second half, Bell increased the lead with a penalty from wide out on the 25 yard line. Shortly after, Johnson returned to the field. Barker was the next to score after he had made a brilliantly elusive run following a scrum, dotting down ten yards from the corner. The conversion attempt failed but with Australia in control it came as no surprise when Solomon drop-kicked a goal following a scrum near the New Zealand line, thirteen minutes from the end, to take his team to an 11-9 lead.

Bell briefly raised New Zealand's hopes when he had a penalty shot from 45 yards out but the kick went outside the posts. In the final minutes veteran flanker Windon forced his way over for a try which Solomon failed to convert. The critics were unanimous that Australia's win had been well deserved with most of the praise being for the fine, well-knit performance of their forwards, particularly during the thirty minute period Johnson was off the field.

NEW ZEALAND

R.H. BELL
(Otago)

C.P. ERCEG   A.E.G. ELSOM   R.A. JARDEN
(Auckland)   (Canterbury)   (Wellington)
J.T. FITZGERALD
(Wellington)

J. HOTOP
(Canterbury)

A.R. REID
(Waikato)
H.C. McLAREN
(Waikato)

K.F. MEATES   R.H. DUFF   R.A. WHITE   C.E. ROBINSON
(Canterbury)   (Canterbury)   (Poverty Bay)   (Southland)
K.L. SKINNER (**Capt.**)   I.B. IRVINE   B.P. EASTGATE
(Otago)   (North Auckland)   (Canterbury)

A.J. BAXTER   N.V. COTTRELL   R.A.L. DAVIDSON
(New South Wales)   (Queensland)   (New South Wales)
C.J. WINDON   A.S. CAMERON   A.R. MILLER   K.A. CROSS
(New South Wales)   (New South Wales)   (New South Wales)   (New South Wales)
B.B. JOHNSON
(New South Wales)
B.P. COX
(New South Wales)
M.J. TATE
(New South Wales)
J.M. O'NEILL   H.S. BARKER   H.J. SOLOMON (**Capt.**)   E.T. STAPLETON
(Queensland)   (New South Wales)   (New South Wales)   (New South Wales)
R. COLBERT
(New South Wales)

AUSTRALIA

REFEREE: Mr A.A. Griffiths (Waikato)
ATTENDANCE: 35,000
CONDITIONS: Weather fine, ground firm
HALFTIME: New Zealand 6, Australia 5

SCORERS

NEW ZEALAND	AUSTRALIA
Tries: Fitzgerald, White	Tries: Stapleton, Barker, Windon
Penalty goal: Bell	Conversion: Cottrell
	Dropped goal: Solomon

13 September, 1952

Second Test

Predictably, the New Zealand selectors, Messrs. A.E.Marslin, T.C. Morrison and M.M.N. Corner made numerous changes to the team that had lost the international a week earlier.

Noel Bowden, who had played a good game for Taranaki against the tourists, came in at fullback, with Ray Bell moving to the right wing. "Mick" Bremner replaced Fitzgerald at second five-eighth and Keith Davis took over the halfback position. In the forwards the only change was at hooker where Ian Hammond replaced Irvine. Hammond, who had toured Australia in 1951 without playing in a Test, like Irvine was to play only one international for his country. Bowden too played only one match for New Zealand, but the other two new caps, Bremner and Davis, were called on again; Bremner in 1956 and Davis regularly until 1958.

The Australians' only change was to reinstall the now fit Shehadie in the lock position with

Miller going to number eight. Both sides made last minute changes to their teams however. McLaren withdrew from the New Zealand team with a nose injury which brought Jack Skeen in as a flanker with Meates going to the back of the scrum. The Australian change was due to Keith Cross's leg injury which brought Johnson back into the side. In the week between the Tests Australia had defeated Nelson 29-12 in a bright match.

After both teams had been introduced to the Administrator and Chief Justice, Sir Humphrey O'Leary, himself a captain of the New Zealand University team in 1909, Bell kicked off for New Zealand. With only five minutes gone, Cottrell opened the scoring with a penalty goal from near touch on the 25 yard line. Jarden equalised two minutes later from 12 yards inside the Australian half with a fine penalty attempt.

Tragedy struck the All Blacks in the tenth minute when Bell, after beating O'Neill, was tackled in mid air from behind by his opposite number as he centre kicked. He fell heavily on his right leg causing a dislocation of the knee, an injury which virtually ended his Rugby career. Bell was carried from the field and the flanker Robinson went to the vacant right wing position.

In the twenty-second minute of the half, Robinson made the opening for New Zealand's first try when he burst past O'Neill before feeding the ball infield to Bremner. He linked with his five-eighth partner Hotop who eluded the remnants of the Australian defence to score a fine try. Jarden's kick failed as did two other attempts from penalties in this spell. On the call of halftime Hotop kicked a dropped goal from the Australian 25 to make the score at the change over, 9-3 to the home team.

From the resumption, Australia went on to the attack, giving the All Blacks some anxious moments. However, it was New Zealand who scored next after their forwards had won a quick ruck near the Wallaby line. Davis fed the flying Robinson who scored a diving winger's try. Bowden, who took over the kicking, missed the conversion.

NEW ZEALAND

N.J.G. BOWDEN
(Taranaki)

R.H. BELL	A.E.G. ELSOM	R.A. JARDEN
(Otago)	(Canterbury)	(Wellington)

S.G. BREMNER
(Auckland)

J. HOTOP
(Canterbury)

K. DAVIS
(Auckland)

K.F. MEATES
(Canterbury)

J.R. SKEEN	R.H. DUFF	R.A. WHITE	C.E. ROBINSON
(Auckland)	(Canterbury)	(Poverty Bay)	(Southland)
K.L. SKINNER (Capt.)	I.A. HAMMOND		B.P. EASTGATE
(Otago)	(Marlborough)		(Canterbury)

A.J. BAXTER	N.V. COTTRELL	R.A.L. DAVIDSON
(New South Wales)	(Queensland)	(New South Wales)
C.J. WINDON	A.S. CAMERON	N.M. SHEHADIE	B.B. JOHNSON
(New South Wales)	(New South Wales)	(New South Wales)	(New South Wales)

A.R. MILLER
(New South Wales)

B.P. COX
(New South Wales)

M.J. TATE
(New South Wales)

J.M. O'NEILL	H.S. BARKER	H.J. SOLOMON (Capt.)	E.T. STAPLETON
(Queensland)	(New South Wales)	(New South Wales)	(New South Wales)

R. COLBERT
(New South Wales)

AUSTRALIA

REFEREE: Mr J. Frood (Otago)
ATTENDANCE: 27,000
CONDITIONS: Weather dull, ground firm
HALFTIME: New Zealand 9, Australia 3
SCORERS

NEW ZEALAND	AUSTRALIA
Tries: Hotop, Robinson	Try: Windon
Penalty goals: Jarden, Bowden	Conversion: Cottrell
Dropped goal: Hotop	Penalty goal: Cottrell

AUSTRALIA 8

Athletic Park, Wellington

Cox speculates the loose ball as Skinner leads an All Black forward charge.

Midway through the half, Johnson fielded a drop-out by New Zealand and put in a strong run before transferring to Windon who cleared away from the defence to score beneath the bar. Cottrell converted to make the score 12-8. Then Davis combined with Jarden to send the latter over in a fine blindside movement. But, to the chagrin of the New Zealand team and their supporters, Mr Frood had been knocked to the ground and was unsighted in the play leading up to the try and he had no option but to disallow it. With four minutes to play, Bowden was given an opportunity to goal a penalty from in front of the posts and he made no mistake to complete the scoring.

By coincidence, this international was the third in a row at this ground in which the home team had been forced to play with fourteen men for a major part of the match. All three had been won. Curiously some of the players who had played so well for New Zealand in this match were not destined to represent their country again. Foremost of these would be the flanker Eddie Robinson who had made a great success of his unaccustomed role on the wing and Bowden too had played a fine game.

WALES 13

19 December, 1953

This first international of the 1953-54 tour had been preceded by thirteen matches, one of which was lost 3-8 to the Cardiff club, and another drawn 6-6 with another Welsh club, Swansea, the week before the international.

Five of the New Zealand team for the match were appearing in their first Test. Of these, the Waikato front row pair of Ian Clarke and Ron Hemi were commencing long careers in international play which were to extend to 1963 and 1959 respectively. Flanker Bill Clark was to play a further eight Tests for his country and Nelson Dalzell, the 32 year old farmer from Culverden, was to appear in all five internationals on this, his only tour with a New Zealand side. The other newcomer was Brian Fitzpatrick who had toured Australia in 1951 without making an international appearance.

Bob Scott, John Tanner, Laurie Haig, Bill McCaw and Bob Stuart were all returning to

Fitzpatrick has two defenders, Bleddyn Williams and Gerwyn Williams, to beat as he approaches the Welsh line.

R.R.J FITZPATRICK COLLECTION

Cardiff Arms Park

international football. Stuart, who had last played for New Zealand in 1949, was something of a surprise choice as captain of the 1953 team but he did a great job both on and off the field and must be rated one of the most successful of All Black leaders. He had been out of action since the Llanelly match a month earlier but was pronounced fit for the Welsh Test.

The Welsh team contained six of the Cardiff side which had earlier defeated the tourists 8-3. Sid Judd came in as a late replacement for Glyn Davies (London Welsh) who later won his only cap against England in 1955. Bleddyn Williams, Ken Jones, Rex Willis, Roy John and Rees Stephens had toured New Zealand with the 1950 British team, all except Stephens playing in the internationals.

New Zealand was facing the bright sun as they used a switched kick-off which saw Ian Clarke kick quickly to the left. However Wales got the ball to touch and nothing came of the move.

After sixteen minutes, during which time New Zealand generally had the better of play, Willis kicked the ball away from Davis after the All Blacks had won a scrum on the Welsh 25. Judd kicked further ahead into New Zealand territory where Ken Jones gained possession. He kicked infield to the centre of New Zealand's 25 where Scott was caught by the Welsh forwards. The All Black full-back threw a pass back to Fitzpatrick but the ball went astray. Judd toed it ahead and in a desperate dive he just beat Fitzpatrick to the touchdown fifteen yards from the posts. Rowlands converted to give Wales a 5-0 lead.

Rowlands and Scott both failed with long-range attempts before Jarden opened New Zealand's score with a thirty yard penalty. Then in the twenty-ninth minute, Scott fielded a kick at half-way near touch. He beat a man, ran down the right-wing side and centre-kicked towards the posts. The Welsh defenders failed to take the ball and the New Zealand flanker Clark was first on the scene to scoop up the ball and dive over near the posts. Jarden converted to give New Zealand a lead of three points at halftime.

For twenty-five minutes in the second spell the

All Blacks attacked consistently and went close to scoring several times. On one occasion Fitzpatrick was grounded inches from the Welsh line after a determined burst on the blindside. After thirty-two minutes Rowlands kicked a penalty goal from twenty yards, when Clark was penalised at a scrum, to even the scores. Three minutes later Wales kicked the ball into the New Zealand 25 where Elsom was caught in possession by Rowlands. Clem Thomas recovered the ball looked as if he was going to pass then intuitively kicked across the field into the goal mouth. Jarden and Ken Jones converged on the bouncing ball but the bounce favoured the flying Welshman and he touched down for the try by the posts. Rowlands had no trouble in increasing the Welsh lead to five with his conversion.

The final minutes saw the All Blacks try valiantly to close the gap but to no avail. For New Zealand it had been an extremely disappointing match. Their forwards had played magnificently and the team had held a massive territorial advantage but the backs could not penetrate.

NEW ZEALAND
R.W.H. SCOTT
(Auckland)

A.E.G. ELSOM   J.M. TANNER   R.A. JARDEN
(Canterbury)   (Auckland)   (Wellington)
           B.B.J. FITZPATRICK
              (Wellington)

                                           L.S. HAIG
                                           (Otago)

              K. DAVIS
              (Auckland)
              W.A. McCAW
              (Southland)

R.C. STUART (Capt.)   R.A. WHITE   G.N. DALZELL   W.H. CLARK
(Canterbury)   (Poverty Bay) (Canterbury) (Wellington)
K.L. SKINNER   R.C. HEMI   I.J. CLARKE
(Otago)   (Waikato)   (Waikato)

C.C. MEREDITH   D.M. DAVIES   W.O.G. WILLIAMS
(Neath)   (Somerset Police)   (Swansea)
R.C.C. THOMAS   J.R.G. STEPHENS   E.R. JOHN   S. JUDD
(Swansea)   (Neath)   (Neath)   (Cardiff)
              J.A. GWILLIAM
              (Gloucester)
              W.R. WILLIS
              (Cardiff)

                        C.I. MORGAN
                        (Cardiff)
G. ROWLANDS   G.M. GRIFFITHS B.L. WILLIAMS (Capt.)   K.J. JONES
(Cardiff)   (Cardiff)   (Cardiff)   (Newport)
              G. WILLIAMS
              (London Welsh)
WALES

REFEREE: Dr. P.F. Cooper (England)
ATTENDANCE: 57,000
CONDITIONS: Weather fine, ground firm
HALFTIME: New Zealand 8, Wales 5

SCORERS
NEW ZEALAND   **WALES**
Try: Clark   Tries: Judd, Jones
Conversion: Jarden   Conversions: Rowlands (2)
Penalty goal: Jarden   Penalty goal: Rowlands

9 January, 1954

On the preceding Saturday the All Blacks had displayed disappointing form in their drawn match with Ulster and the Irish supporters were hoping that their national side could go one better and bring up Ireland's first victory over a New Zealand side.

Five changes were made in the All Black line-up from that which had lost to Wales three weeks before. The changes brought five new-comers to Test Rugby into the side. Elsom was replaced by his Canterbury team-mate Maurice Dixon, and Colin Loader came into the side in the place of Tanner at centre three-quarter. Guy Bowers, who had appeared in only three of the first fifteen matches on tour, ousted vice-captain Haig from first five-eighth, following a brilliant display in the match against the Combined Services on Boxing Day.

In the forwards, captain Stuart moved to number eight to take the place of McCaw who had broken his nose in the Ulster match. This allowed Oliver to come in on the side of the scrum and "Snow" White from the Northcote club in Auckland became Skinner's propping partner at the expense of Ian Clarke.

The Irish captain, Jack Kyle, was still showing the brilliant form which he had displayed on the Lions' tour in 1950. Two other Irish players, Noel Henderson and Jimmy McCarthy, had also been members of the 1950 Lions whilst there was widespread regret that a fourth, Jimmy Nelson, who had led the Ulster pack the week before, had been overlooked by the selectors. Lock Robin Thompson was to captain the 1955 Lions in South Africa the following year.

Kyle won the toss and rather surprisingly gave the first use of the breeze to his opponents. After two minutes Jarden was short with a 45 yard penalty and two minutes later, "Tiny" White burst through a line-out and made 35 yards in an impressive run before being brought down just short of the Irish line. In the eleventh minute, Davis kicked a high punt to the Irish line where Murphy misjudged the catch allowing the ball to bounce away from him. The fast following Clark gathered it in and scored near the corner. Scott missed the conversion.

Midway through the spell it was noticed that Jarden was limping. After half an hour, Scott landed a dropped goal from thirty yards out and almost immediately after the re-start, was awarded a penalty on the half-way which he turned into a goal with a grand kick. Jarden's injury was proving to be serious and Stuart was forced to bring Oliver out of the scrum to play on the right wing. Dixon moved to the left with

Keith Davis gets his back line away while Lawler (5) has failed to stop the All Black half-back.

IRELAND 3

Lansdowne Road, Dublin

"Tiny" White bursts from a ruck and Hemi comes around the blindside to support him.

Jarden limping around in a roving position. Halftime was reached with the score still at 9-0.

NEW ZEALAND		
	R.W.H. SCOTT	
	(Auckland)	
M.J. DIXON	C.J. LOADER	R.A. JARDEN
(Canterbury)	(Wellington)	(Wellington)
B.B.J. FITZPATRICK		
(Wellington)		
	R.G. BOWERS	
	(Wellington)	
	K. DAVIS	
	(Auckland)	
	R.C. STUART (Capt.)	
	(Canterbury)	
O.D. OLIVER	R.A. WHITE G.N. DALZELL	W.H. CLARK
(Otago)	(Poverty Bay) (Canterbury)	(Wellington)
K.L. SKINNER	R.C. HEMI	H.L. WHITE
(Otago)	(Waikato)	(Auckland)
J.H. SMITH	F.E. ANDERSON	W.A. O'NEILL
(London Irish)	(Queen's University)	(Wanderers)
J.R. KAVANAGH	P.J. LAWLER R.H. THOMPSON	J.S. McCARTHY
(Wanderers)	(Clontarf) (Instonians)	(Dolphin)
	T.E. REID	
	(Garryowen)	
	J.A. O'MEARA	
	(Dolphin)	
	J.W. KYLE (Capt.)	
	(N.I.F.C.)	
J.T. GASTON	A.C. PEDLOW N.J. HENDERSON	M. MORTELL
(Dublin University)	(Queen's University) (N.I.F.C.)	(Dolphin)
	J.G.M.W. MURPHY	
	(Lurgan)	
	IRELAND	

REFEREE: Dr. P.F. Cooper (England)
ATTENDANCE: 45,000
CONDITIONS: Weather fine but windy, ground firm
HALFTIME: New Zealand 9, Ireland 0

SCORERS

NEW ZEALAND	IRELAND
Tries: Clark, Stuart	Penalty goal: Henderson
Conversion: Scott	
Penalty goal: Scott	
Dropped goal: Scott	

Five minutes into the second half, Davis ran on the blind side from a scrum outside the Irish 25. Finding his path blocked, he threw a long pass infield to Bowers who took it on the bounce and eluded the immediate defence before unloading to Hemi who in turn fed his captain Stuart. The number eight threw himself over for a good try to the left of the posts. Scott raised the flags with his conversion to put New Zealand 14 points up.

The home forwards fought back well and went close to scoring but McCarthy failed to control the ball over the line. Murphy was wide with two penalty attempts from kicking positions. Five minutes from no-side, Bowers had to leave the field with concussion and two minutes later Henderson landed a thirty yard penalty for Ireland and this kick completed the scoring.

It had been an impressive display by the All Blacks with fine individual displays by Scott and "Tiny" White in particular, plus a sound captain's game by Stuart. Bowers, who had the unenviable job of marking Kyle in his first international, came through the match extremely well.

Dr. Peter Cooper, who had ably controlled the first two internationals of the tour, died suddenly in May 1957. He had refereed a total of nine internationals at the time of his death.

30 January, 1954

The 21 year old loose forward, Peter Jones was making his international debut in this match as was the fair-headed second five-eighth, Doug Wilson. Jones went on to play for New Zealand until 1960, but Wilson was not destined to appear in the All Black jersey again after the 1953-54 tour.

The New Zealand team had played four matches since the Irish international without defeat but England was the favoured side. In the preceding season the English had won the home unions championship and a fortnight earlier had defeated Wales 9-6. Included in their team was Gordon Rimmer, a 1950 Lion in New Zealand where he had played in the third Test at Wellington. The centre, Jeff Butterfield, was re-garded as one of the greatest centres of his time and was to establish a fine reputation in South Africa with the 1955 Lions. He toured New Zealand with the 1959 combination but injuries prevented him reaching top form and he did not appear in any of the Tests in that year. Phil Davies, another fine centre who later developed a most effective partnership with Butterfield, was rather strangely selected as a wing three-quarter.

Straw had been protecting the ground from snow and ice during the preceding week and

All Black captain, Bob Stuart, tangles with an English player. Phil Davies looks on at right.

R.C. HEMI COLLECTION

ENGLAND 0

when this was removed an hour or so before the kick-off, it revealed that the turf was in good order.

Stuart won the toss and Regan kicked off for England. Jarden missed a long range penalty attempt in the eighth minute and both sides had opportunities to score in the opening exchanges.

The only points of the match came in the nineteenth minute when White won a line-out and advanced a yard or two before being held up. A short kick ahead saw Hemi get his boot to the ball, follow up and kick again inside the English 25. Ten yards short of his goal line King threw himself on the ball but the fast-following Clark was on hand to recover the ball and feed Dalzell, the sixteen stone ten pound lock forward. Dalzell charged for the line with his head down, butting the solid English winger Woodward out of the way before scoring 10 yards in from the left hand corner. Scott's conversion was a good one. Ten minutes before the halftime whistle King was forced to leave the field but fortunately was able to return after the interval.

SPORT & GENERAL

Hemi and Jarden combine to push the big English winger, Ted Woodward, into touch.

At halftime it began to snow lightly as the teams had their oranges. The second half was closely fought between the two well matched sides with both teams giving a good exhibition of tackling which prevented any further scoring. Midway through the half Scott had a 45 yard penalty fall just short and Jarden sliced a further attempt near time.

The All Black forwards again gave a fine exhibition, with none playing better than loose head prop "Snow" White. Hemi won the hooking duel, with one report crediting him with eight tightheads. Probably the most dangerous back on the field was the fifteen stone English right winger Ted Woodward who gave Jarden many problems during the match with his powerful running. Scott too gave a magnificent display of full-back play.

The referee, Mr Ivor David, had commenced his international career when he controlled the England v. Scotland match in 1938 and was widely regarded as an outstanding exponent with the whistle. He controlled his final international in 1956.

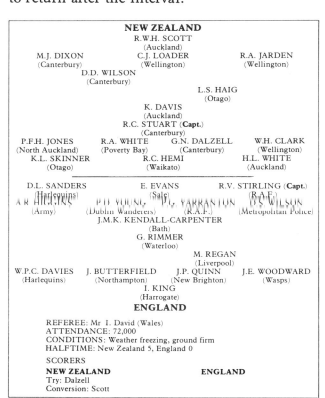

NEW ZEALAND

R.W.H. SCOTT
(Auckland)

M.J. DIXON   C.J. LOADER   R.A. JARDEN
(Canterbury)   (Wellington)   (Wellington)

D.D. WILSON
(Canterbury)

L.S. HAIG
(Otago)

K. DAVIS
(Auckland)

R.C. STUART (**Capt.**)
(Canterbury)

P.F.H. JONES   R.A. WHITE   G.N. DALZELL   W.H. CLARK
(North Auckland)   (Poverty Bay)   (Canterbury)   (Wellington)

K.L. SKINNER   R.C. HEMI   H.L. WHITE
(Otago)   (Waikato)   (Auckland)

D.L. SANDERS   E. EVANS   R.V. STIRLING (**Capt.**)
(Harlequins)   (Sale)   (R.A.F.)

A.R. HIGGINS   P.D. YOUNG   J.H. YARRANTON   D.S. WILSON
(Army)   (Dublin Wanderers)   (R.A.F.)   (Metropolitan Police)

J.M.K. KENDALL-CARPENTER
(Bath)

G. RIMMER
(Waterloo)

M. REGAN
(Liverpool)

W.P.C. DAVIES   J. BUTTERFIELD   J.P. QUINN   J.E. WOODWARD
(Harlequins)   (Northampton)   (New Brighton)   (Wasps)

I. KING
(Harrogate)

ENGLAND

REFEREE: Mr I. David (Wales)
ATTENDANCE: 72,000
CONDITIONS: Weather freezing, ground firm
HALFTIME: New Zealand 5, England 0

SCORERS

NEW ZEALAND	ENGLAND
Try: Dalzell	
Conversion: Scott	

N W ZEALAND 3

13 February, 1954

After thirteen consecutive defeats, Scotland were not expected to be strong enough to extend the New Zealand side in this international. Their selectors had re-called, to captain the team, Douglas Elliot, a loose forward who had played 25 internationals since 1947. Despite some pre-match criticism of his appointment, it proved to be a wise choice, with Elliot not only giving inspired leadership but turning in an outstanding personal performance.

Peter Kininmonth had toured New Zealand in 1950 with the Lions where he played in three of the four Tests. In 1955 both Michie and McLeod toured South Africa with the Lions and four years later Hugh McLeod came to New Zealand where he played in all four Tests.

The only change in the New Zealand team from that which had played England was in the front row where Peter Eastgate replaced White. New Zealand won the toss and Scotland kicked off. New Zealand took a long time to settle down and ten minutes had gone before the All Blacks moved into Scottish territory. Elliot was getting up on Haig quickly so that the New Zealand backs were not functioning smoothly.

After 33 minutes Marshall missed a penalty from a fairly handy position, while shortly after, Scott saved a dangerous situation when Elgie made a break and attempted to grubber kick past him. Halftime was reached with no score on the board.

New Zealand had some close calls early in the second spell before working back into Scottish territory. Then in the seventh minute of the half, from a penalty five yards outside the Scottish 25 and ten yards from the left-hand touchline, Scott managed to steer the ball between the posts and just over the cross-bar.

Inspired by this success, the All Blacks began to play their best football of the match. A break by Dalzell almost led to a try and for the next fifteen minutes the visitors kept Scotland pinned in their own half. The local side hit back however, both Weatherstone and Swan almost scoring. In the dying stages of the game Haig ran on the

An All Black arm holds back MacLachlan as he attempts to kick the ball past the covering Jarden.

SPORT & GENERAL

SCOTLAND 0

Murrayfield, Edinburgh

The New Zealand Touring Team
Back row: C.J. Loader, A.E.G. Elsom, J.W. Kelly, W.A. McCaw, K.L. Skinner, R.C. Hemi, J.M. Tanner, I.J. Clarke.
Second row: C.A. Woods, H.L. White, R.A. White, P.F.H. Jones, K.P. Bagley, R.J. O'Dea, O.D. Oliver, G.N. Dalzell, W.H. Clark.
Seated: R.A. Jarden, J.T. Fitzgerald, D.D. Wilson, R.C. Stuart (capt.), J.N. Millard (manager), A.E. Marslin (asst. manager), L.S. Haig, R.W.H. Scott, B.P. Eastgate, V.D. Bevan.
In front: B.B.J. Fitzpatrick, R.G. Bowers, K.Davis, M.J. Dixon, W.S.S. Freebairn.

blind side from a scrum on the home 25 and he appeared to score but the referee awarded a scrum. A few minutes later the game ended.

This match was vice-captain Laurie Haig's final international. Since his debut in 1950 he had played in nine Tests and had shown sound and reliable form throughout. Now thirty-one, Haig had lost a little speed but his great experience was of considerable benefit to the touring side. Both Doug Wilson, who was unable to reproduce his trials form on tour, and Peter Eastgate, also concluded their brief international careers in this match.

The Scottish loose forward "Chick" Henderson, a South African who had played for Transvaal, was later a well-known sports broadcaster in

his native land and a prominent Rugby administrator in the Wanderers and Quagga clubs and the Transvaal Union.

NEW ZEALAND		
	R.W.H. SCOTT	
	(Auckland)	
M.J. DIXON	C.J. LOADER	R.A. JARDEN
(Canterbury)	(Wellington)	(Wellington)
D.D. WILSON		
(Canterbury)		
	L.S. HAIG	
	(Otago)	
	K. DAVIS	
	(Auckland)	
	R.C. STUART (Capt.)	
	(Canterbury)	
P.F.H. JONES	R.A. WHITE G.N. DALZELL	W.H. CLARK
(North Auckland)	(Poverty Bay) (Canterbury)	(Wellington)
K.L. SKINNER	R.C. HEMI	B.P. EASTGATE
(Otago)	(Waikato)	(Canterbury)

H.F. McLEOD	R.K.G. MacEWAN	T.P.L. McGLASHAN
(Hawick)	(Cambridge University)	(Royal High School F.P.)
E.J.S. MICHIE		E.A.J. FERGUSSON
(Aberdeen University)		(Oxford University)
W.I.D. ELLIOT (Capt.)	P.W. KININMONTH	J.H. HENDERSON
(Edinburgh Academicals)	(Richmond)	(Richmond)
	L.P. MacLACHLAN	
	(London Scottish)	
	G.T. ROSS	
	(Watsonians)	
T.G. WEATHERSTONE	D. CAMERON M.K. ELGIE	J.S. SWAN
(Stewart's Coll. F.P.)	(Glasgow H.S.F.P.) (London Scottish)	(London Scottish)
	J.C. MARSHALL	
	(London Scottish)	
SCOTLAND		

REFEREE: Mr I. David (Wales)
ATTENDANCE: 50,000
CONDITIONS: Weather cold, wet and windy, ground heavy
HALFTIME: New Zealand 0, Scotland 0
SCORERS

NEW ZEALAND	SCOTLAND
Penalty goal: Scott	

FRANCE 3

27 February, 1954

This match was the thirtieth of the tour and the fifth international. Understandably the team was jaded by this time. A week earlier they had won a memorable match against the Barbarians at Cardiff 19-5 but had gone down in a mid-week game at Bordeaux 8-11.

Five changes were made to the team that had played Scotland, with the five-eighth combination that had appeared against Ireland being reintroduced, and McCaw, Oliver and "Snow" White who had appeared in earlier Tests regaining their places at the expense of Jones, Clark and Eastgate.

The French captain, Jean Prat, had appeared for France against the 2nd.N.Z.E.F. team, the Kiwis, on the same ground in March 1946. The All Black full-back, Bob Scott, had also played in this match. Prat's younger brother Maurice was at centre. Full-back Henri Claverie was making the first of his two international appearances in this match.

Stuart lost the toss and New Zealand played into the wind in the first half. Early in the game both Jarden and Boniface missed penalty attempts. Superb defence by the French prevented any breakthrough by the All Blacks who were winning the battle for possession.

The close marking tactics of the French were responsible for the only points of the match which came five minutes before halftime following a line-out on the All Black 10 yard line. The ball came back on the New Zealand side untidily and as Bowers received the pass the French loose forward, Henri Domec was on him and the ball went loose. Baulon was on hand to retrieve the ball and run to inside the New Zealand 25 where he slipped a pass inside to Jean Prat as he was tackled. The French captain plunged for the line with several pairs of hands clinging to him. Prat took the conversion himself but the kick struck the upright high up and rebounded away.

Early in the second half Scott attempted a 60 yard penalty. Although the wind was now at his back the kick was short. Jarden then went close to scoring when he chased a kick by Fitzpatrick but the bounce eluded his grasp on the goal line.

Several other All Black scoring opportunities were halted by fine defence and Scott failed with three attempted penalties, one a massive drop kick from half-way which only narrowly missed. However, no further scoring occurred and the French were jubilant at no-side to have recorded their second ever victory over a touring international team.

Jean Prat, who continued to represent his country until the 1954-55 season, by which time he had set a French record of 38 caps, was later quoted as saying that the New Zealand pack was the finest he had played against.

This match was the last of seventeen internationals played by Bob Scott, who had played in New Zealand's first post-war Test in 1946. In these matches he had scored 74 points, all from goal kicking. Widely acclaimed as one of the greatest full-backs of all time, Scott had come out of retirement to make himself available for this tour during which he had displayed that he had lost none of his considerable talent. He was three weeks past his thirty-third birthday. Other All

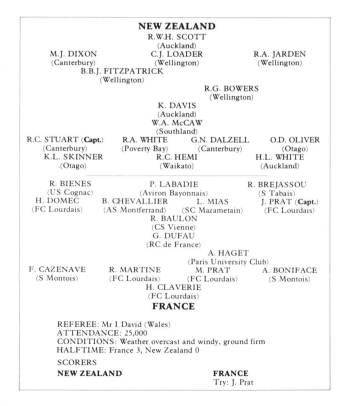

NEW ZEALAND

R.W.H. SCOTT
(Auckland)

M.J. DIXON   C.J. LOADER   R.A. JARDEN
(Canterbury)   (Wellington)   (Wellington)

B.B.J. FITZPATRICK
(Wellington)

R.G. BOWERS
(Wellington)

K. DAVIS
(Auckland)

W.A. McCAW
(Southland)

R.C. STUART (Capt.)   R.A. WHITE   G.N. DALZELL   O.D. OLIVER
(Canterbury)   (Poverty Bay) (Canterbury)   (Otago)

K.L. SKINNER   R.C. HEMI   H.L. WHITE
.(Otago)   (Waikato)   (Auckland)

R. BIENES   P. LABADIE   R. BREJASSOU
(US Cognac)   (Aviron Bayonnais)   (S Tabais)

H. DOMEC   B. CHEVALLIER   L. MIAS   J. PRAT (Capt.)
(FC Lourdais) (AS Montferrand) (SC Mazametain) (FC Lourdais)

R. BAULON
(CS Vienne)

G. DUFAU
(RC de France)

A. HAGET
(Paris University Club)

F. CAZENAVE   R. MARTINE   M. PRAT   A. BONIFACE
(S Montois)   (FC Lourdais)   (FC Lourdais) (S Montois)

H. CLAVERIE
(FC Lourdais)

FRANCE

REFEREE: Mr I. David (Wales)
ATTENDANCE: 25,000
CONDITIONS: Weather overcast and windy, ground firm
HALFTIME: France 3, New Zealand 0

SCORERS

NEW ZEALAND   **FRANCE**
                                   Try: J. Prat

NEW ZEALAND 0

Colombes Stadium, Paris

Blacks to have played in their final international were the captain Bob Stuart, also thirty-three, Nelson Dalzell, Bill McCaw and surprisingly, the youngsters Colin Loader, Brian Fitzpatrick, Des Oliver and the 21 year old Guy Bowers.

Davis breaks with Hemi in support and Andre Boniface in pursuit.

The 19 year old Andre Boniface, who played on the wing in this game, was later to tour New Zealand with the 1961 French team, and in 1964 appeared against Whineray's 1963-64 tourists. Lucien Mias was to lead the French team in South Africa in 1958 when the Tricolours were to record a win and a draw in the memorable two match series.

20 August, 1955

First Test

In their four matches leading up to this first international of the 1955 series, Australia had won three and had gone down to Hawke's Bay 11-14. John Solomon was again captain of the tourists as he had been in 1952 and other well known Wallabies playing in this match were Cyril Burke a veteran of the 1946, 1949 and 1952 tours who in this match played in the unusual position of centre, Nicholas Shehadie the rugged

prop forward who had first appeared against New Zealand in 1947, and lock Alan Cameron who had played in 1951 and 1952 as had fourteen stone six pound winger Eddie Stapleton.

Some surprises in the New Zealand team for this match included the passing over of John Hotop who had created a fine impression in the

In this wire photo, Peter Burke wins a line-out for New Zealand. Other All Blacks are White, Irwin, Vodanovich and Hemi.

AUCKLAND STAR

AUSTRALIA 8

Athletic Park, Wellington

inter-island match in July, and "Snow" White who had played in three internationals on the 1953-54 tour. Pat Walsh, just three and half months past his nineteenth birthday, was to become one of his country's youngest internationals. Among the new players in the All Black side was the durable prop Ivan Vodanovich later to become national selection panel convenor and coach of the 1970 New Zealand team in South Africa as well as a New Zealand Rugby Union executive member. Other new players were the prop Mark Irwin, a medical student from Otago University, Lindsay Townsend Otago's halfback since 1953, Robin Archer son of an old Southland representative, Canterbury's high scoring winger Ross Smith and full-back Kevin Stuart, a brother of 1953-54 All Black captain Bob Stuart.

Australia won the toss and elected to play with the southerly at their backs but it was New Zealand who went on to attack early and after ten minutes Jones burst away from a line-out and when he was checked, the ball came loose for

Clark the flanker to scoop it up and cross underneath the bar. Jarden added the two points with a simple kick. Midway through the first half, New Zealand scored a fine try after the ball was quickly moved out to Jarden from a line-out. The winger rounded Stapleton before putting in an accurate centre kick which four All Black forwards carried on to the goal line where Vodanovich scored. Jarden again converted to give New Zealand a handy 10-0 lead playing into the breeze.

Australia opened their scoring following a line-out when the ball was sent out to the speedy left winger Garth Jones, the sole Queenslander in the side, who veered infield and outsped the defence to score a try by the posts after a 50 yard run. This try was reminiscent of one scored by the same player in the second Test against South Africa in 1953, when Australia had won 18-14. Tooth converted and, on the call of halftime, Stapleton added a 35 yard penalty, following two unsuccessful attempts by Jarden, to make the score 10-8 at the interval.

The Wallabies started the second half well and Jones was almost away again but his pass went astray. It was the All Blacks who scored next when Jarden landed a penalty from near the touchline but later in the spell he missed several other attempts. The New Zealanders generally held the upper hand during the remainder of the match. In the last few minutes, an Australian passing movement inside their 25, broke down and the alert Jarden was on hand to toe the ball ahead and beat Stapleton to it as it crossed the goal line. He failed to convert his own try and the match ended with New Zealand on attack.

The All Black forwards gave a convincing performance but their backline was rarely able to mount effective attacks. Following the match the chairman of the New Zealand selection panel, Mr T.C. Morrison, made a statement in which he criticised many of the All Black players for not being as fit as they should have been. This statement was echoed by Mr J.W. Stead, one of the ten survivors of the 1905-06 All Blacks who were holding a reunion on the 50th Jubilee of their great tour to coincide with this Test.

NEW ZEALAND

K.C. STUART
(Canterbury)

R.M. SMITH   A.E.G. ELSOM   R.A. JARDEN
(Canterbury)   (Canterbury)   (Wellington)

P.T. WALSH
(Counties)

W.R. ARCHER
(Otago)

L.J. TOWNSEND
(Otago)

I.J. CLARKE (**Capt.**)
(Waikato)

P.F.H. JONES   R.A. WHITE   P.S. BURKE   W.H. CLARK
(North Auckland)   (Poverty Bay)   (Taranaki)   (Wellington)
I.M.H. VODANOVICH   R.C. HEMI   M.W. IRWIN
(Wellington)   (Waikato)   (Otago)

N.J. ADAMS   J.R. CROSS   N.M. SHEHADIE
(New South Wales)   (New South Wales)   (New South Wales)
N.M. HUGHES   A.S. CAMERON   A.R. MILLER   J.E. THORNETT
(New South Wales)   (New South Wales)   (New South Wales)   (New South Wales)
B.B. JOHNSON
(New South Wales)
B.P. COX
(New South Wales)
H.J. SOLOMON (**Capt.**)
(New South Wales)

G.G. JONES   J.A. PHIPPS   C.T. BURKE   E.T. STAPLETON
(Queensland)   (New South Wales)   (New South Wales)   (New South Wales)
R.M. TOOTH
(New South Wales)

AUSTRALIA

REFEREE: Mr F.G.M. Parkinson (Manawatu)
ATTENDANCE: 37,000
CONDITIONS: Weather fine, ground firm
HALFTIME: New Zealand 10, Australia 8
SCORERS

NEW ZEALAND	AUSTRALIA
Tries: Clark, Vodanovich, Jarden	Try: Jones
Conversions: Jarden (2)	Conversion: Tooth
Penalty goal: Jarden	Penalty goal: Stapleton

NEW ZEALAND 8

3 September, 1955

Second Test

The New Zealand selectors made several changes to the team which had won the first international. At full-back Stuart, who had played well at Wellington in what was to be his only All Black appearance, was surprisingly dropped with the 19 year old Walsh taking his place. Smith, who was nursing a leg injury, was replaced by the popular Tommy Katene. Bill Gray, who had made a good impression in the tourists' first match at Te Aroha, took over from Walsh at second five-eighth. The fourth New Zealand Maori representative in the backline was Keith Davis who came into the side at the expense of Townsend. Duff, unavailable for the first Test because of injury, took Peter Burke's place at lock.

The Australians had comfortably won all three fixtures since the previous Test but they also made numerous changes to their team. Their captain Solomon had badly dislocated his shoulder at Oamaru and was not to play again on

Rival captains, Ian Clarke and Alan Cameron, shake hands before kick-off.

tour. Half-back Cox had suffered a leg injury and was not available for this match which brought Cyril Burke back into his normal position. Tooth replaced Burke at centre, Gordon Davis came in for Solomon, Phelps went to full-back and Peter Phipps replaced his older brother Jim. The only change in the forwards was at prop where the 26 year old grazier from Orange, Don Strachan, replaced Adams.

Phipps kicked off for Australia into the bright sun and after five minutes Stapleton was given a penalty attempt from 40 yards out. This kick failed as did one from a similar distance three minutes later. There was little for the crowd to enthuse over during the first half with both teams making excessive use of the touchline. The Wallabies, looking slightly the better side, were kept from scoring only by a resolute All Black defence. At halftime there was no score.

The second half saw some improvement in the standard of play and after seventeen minutes Peter Jones gave the crowd their first real excitement when he made one of his well-known charges only to be thrown against the corner post as he dived for the line. This incident was responsible for Jones cracking two of his ribs

NEW ZEALAND
P.T. WALSH
(Counties)
T. KATENE   A.E.G. ELSOM   R.A. JARDEN
(Wellington)   (Canterbury)   (Wellington)
          W.N. GRAY
          (Bay of Plenty)
                    W.R. ARCHER
                    (Otago)
          K. DAVIS
          (Auckland)
          I.J. CLARKE (Capt.)
          (Waikato)
P.F.H. JONES   R.A. WHITE   R.H. DUFF   W.H. CLARK
(North Auckland) (Poverty Bay) (Canterbury) (Wellington)
I.M.H. VODANOVICH   R.C. HEMI   M.W. IRWIN
(Wellington)   (Waikato)   (Otago)
_____
D.J. STRACHAN   J.R. CROSS   N.M. SHEHADIE
(New South Wales) (New South Wales) (New South Wales)
J.E. THORNETT A.S. CAMERON (Capt.) A.R. MILLER N.M. HUGHES
(New South Wales) (New South Wales) (New South Wales) (New South Wales)
          B.B. JOHNSON
          (New South Wales)
          C.T. BURKE
          (New South Wales)
          G.W.G. DAVIS
          (New South Wales)
G.G. JONES   P.J. PHIPPS   R.M. TOOTH   E.T. STAPLETON
(Queensland) (New South Wales) (New South Wales) (New South Wales)
          R. PHELPS
          (New South Wales)
AUSTRALIA

REFEREE: Mr E.W.T. Tindill (Wellington)
ATTENDANCE: 25,300
CONDITIONS: Weather fine, ground heavy
HALFTIME: New Zealand 0, Australia 0

SCORERS
NEW ZEALAND   AUSTRALIA
Try: Jarden
Conversion: Jarden
Dropped goal: Elsom

188

AUSTRALIA 0

Carisbrook, Dunedin

Four three-quarters contest possession. From left: Elsom, Katene, Phipps and Jones.

which, although he played on in this match, ruled him out of consideration for the third Test at Auckland. Jarden then over ran the ball when a try was on after he had kicked ahead to the goal line.

The first points came only thirteen minutes from no-side when the ball went to Elsom just outside the Australian 25 for the centre to take aim quickly and drop kick a goal. On the call of time, Keith Davis hoisted a high kick from the base of the scrum which Stapleton, looking into the sun, could not gather. Jarden was on hand to take the loose ball and cross for a simple try near the corner. With a fine kick he converted to complete the scoring.

It had been a disappointing result for Australia whose forwards, led by captain Alan Cameron, had clearly shaded the All Black pack. Only Hemi, who had decisively outhooked his inexperienced opponent, stood out amongst the home forwards though White and Duff were gaining ascendancy in the line-outs towards the end of the game.

This victory ensured that New Zealand again retained the Bledisloe Cup. It was Katene's only appearance in the All Black jersey. He later switched to Rugby League.

189

AUSTRALIA 8

17 September, 1955

Third Test

Once again the New Zealand selectors saw fit to make several changes to their team. In the backline, Ross Brown, the 21 year old son of Handley Brown 1924-26 All Black and nephew of Henry Brown 1935 All Black, became the first of this illustrious Rugby family to play in an international, when he was chosen at centre. Elsom was shifted on to the right wing and John Hotop, who had played two Tests in 1952 came in at first five-eighth. Townsend, half-back for the first Test at Wellington, was reintroduced with Davis going into the reserves. Two newcomers, S.F. "Tiny" Hill and John Buxton, were the new side-row, and H.L. "Snow" White, who had played in three internationals during the 1953-54 tour, replaced Irwin in the front row.

The Australians had beaten Southland 11-5, Canterbury 19-8, and a combined Wanganui-King Country team 38-8 since losing the Test at Dunedin. They made only two changes with Jim Phipps taking his brother's centre berth and Keith Cross replacing Johnson as a loose forward.

Hotop kicked off with his team playing from the Dominion Road end. Twice in the first ten minutes, Stapleton missed difficult penalty attempts and mid-way through the half, K. Cross was dragged down inches short of the line. The first points came after half an hour when Stapleton intercepted a loose pass from Gray near the New Zealand 25 to scoot away and score near the corner. Tooth was unable to convert. Australia, now right on top, increased their lead five minutes later when Hughes crashed over through the defence of several All Blacks. Stapleton was successful with a difficult kick from the touchline to make the score at the interval 8-0 to the tourists.

Despite the continuing poor combination of the New Zealand inside backs, the All Blacks were playing improved football after the break and were rewarded in the fourteenth minute with a fine try. Walsh entered a backline movement to

Ian Clarke grasps at thin air as Phelps eludes his tackle. The other Wallabies are John Thornett and Garth Jones.

NEW ZEALAND 3

give an overlap to Jarden who raced away from 40 yards out to score in the corner. He was unsuccessful with the conversion which went across the face of the posts. The All Blacks, showing more enterprise, were generally in charge during the remainder of the game but a determined Wallaby cover defence prevented any further scoring. One critic was of the opinion that the New Zealand team had looked better in defeat than they had done in the earlier two matches in the series.

Brown's play was one of the highlights of the All Black team's display and he was to play a further fifteen internationals for his country. "Tiny" White was singled out for special mention by most critics for his outstanding work in the line-outs.

Strangely, neither of the prop forwards, Vodanovich or White, were invited to play for New Zealand again though both displayed good provincial form for several more years. It was the last of Alan Elsom's six internationals since 1952, and neither of the day's unhappy inside backs, Townsend and Hotop, were again called on.

Ross Brown, making his debut in this Test, is smothered by a Wallaby tackler. Bill Gray is the nearest All Black.

NEW ZEALAND

P.T. WALSH
(Counties)

A.E.G. ELSOM   R.H. BROWN   R.A. JARDEN
(Canterbury)   (Taranaki)   (Wellington)

W.N. GRAY
(Bay of Plenty)

J. HOTOP
(Canterbury)

L.J. TOWNSEND
(Otago)

I.J. CLARKE (**Capt.**)
(Waikato)

S.F. HILL   R.A. WHITE   R.H. DUFF   J.B. BUXTON
(Canterbury)   (Poverty Bay)   (Canterbury)

I.M.H. VODANOVICH   R.C. HEMI   H.L. WHITE
(Wellington)   (Waikato)   (Auckland)

D.J. STRACHAN   J.R. CROSS   N.M. SHEHADIE
(New South Wales)   (New South Wales)   (New South Wales)

J.E. THORNETT   A.S. CAMERON (Q.)   A.R. MILLER   K.A. CROSS
(New South Wales)   (New South Wales)   (New South Wales)   (New South Wales)

N.M. HUGHES
(New South Wales)

C.T. BURKE
(New South Wales)

R.M. TOOTH
(New South Wales)

G.G. JONES   J.A. PHIPPS   G.W.G. DAVIS   E.T. STAPLETON
(Queensland)   (New South Wales)   (New South Wales)   (New South Wales)

R. PHELPS
(New South Wales)

AUSTRALIA

REFEREE: Mr B.H. Wolstenholme (Poverty Bay)
ATTENDANCE: 31,000
CONDITIONS: Weather fine but humid, ground firm
HALFTIME: Australia 8, New Zealand 0

SCORERS

NEW ZEALAND	**AUSTRALIA**
Try: Jarden	Tries: Stapleton, Hughes
	Conversion: Stapleton

The veteran Australian half-back Cyril Burke who had toured New Zealand in 1946-49-52 with Australian teams and in 1954 with a N.S.W. Country side as well as playing against the All Blacks at home in 1947 and 1951, had reached the end of his international career against his old adversaries. He was to captain the Newcastle team against the 1957 New Zealand touring side and continued to play club football until injury ended his long and successful career in 1960.

14 July, 1956

First Test

There were only two new caps in the New Zealand team, the flanker Don McIntosh and half-back Pat Vincent who had been playing for Canterbury since 1945. John Buxton, who had first appeared the previous season, was not destined to play for his country again.

In the Springbok team, "Salty" du Rand, the captain, had opposed New Zealand in two Tests in 1949 and had fifteen international appearances behind him. This was du Rand's debut as a Test match captain. He was in fact the vice-captain of the touring team but the captain, S.S. Viviers, was indisposed for this game. Three Springboks were new caps, Jeremy Nel, "Peewee" Howe and Jan du Preez. Newton Walker's father had toured New Zealand in 1921, playing in the first and third Tests of that year.

The Springbok prop forward, Jaap Bekker was a member of a remarkable sporting family. His brother Dolf had been a Springbok in 1953 and another brother Martiens earned the honour in 1960 against Scotland. Yet another brother Daan was to represent his country in the 1956 Olympic Games in the boxing ring and a sister had won her Springbok colours in athletics.

After losing the first match of their New Zealand tour to Waikato, the Springboks had shown varying form and great interest centred on this match. The New Zealand public were keenly aware of the possibility of a South African defeat for the first time in a Test series which would avenge the disastrous defeats of 1937 and 1949.

Following drizzle on Friday, the weather had cleared but the ground was still soggy in patches. A large crowd of 40,000 was present as Archer kicked off. After the first minute, Dryburgh attempted a penalty from 43 yards but hit the upright and the ball bounced back into play. After eight minutes he succeeded with a 30 yard attempt to put South Africa ahead 3-0. South Africa were dominating the front row but the All Black forwards were doing better in the loose play. Neither backline was functioning well and with Ulyate kicking ahead to apparently preconceived tactics, the game developed into a close

forward struggle. A number of injuries were holding up play but after thirty-two minutes New Zealand went into the lead, following an up and under penalty kick by Jarden. The All Black forwards caught Retief in possession and drove ahead. From a maul near the Springbok line White emerged with the ball and crashed over. Jarden converted to make it 5-3.

A few minutes later South Africa mounted a backline movement with the loose forward Ackermann in to make the extra man. As he bore down on Jarden — the solitary defender — with Howe and Johnstone unmarked outside him, he hesitated before lobbing a pass which Jarden intercepted. The All Black wing raced 40 yards to score. He converted to make New Zealand 10-3 ahead at halftime.

Irwin left the field at halftime with damaged ribs. Archer had also suffered a similar injury but was able to play on. Rain and sleet fell at the break, which made the ground greasy. Early in the second spell Ackermann was carried off with a displaced cartilage in his right knee. Undaunted,

NEW ZEALAND

P.T. WALSH
(Counties)

M.J. DIXON	R.H. BROWN	R.A. JARDEN
(Canterbury)	(Taranaki)	(Wellington)

W.N. GRAY
(Bay of Plenty)

W.R. ARCHER
(Southland)

P.B. VINCENT (**Capt.**)
(Canterbury)

S.F. HILL
(Canterbury)

J.B. BUXTON	R.A. WHITE	R.H. DUFF	D.N. McINTOSH
(Canterbury)	(Poverty Bay)	(Canterbury)	(Wellington)
M.W. IRWIN	R.C. HEMI		I.J. CLARKE
(Otago)	(Waikato)		(Waikato)

H.N. WALKER	A.J. van der MERWE	H.P.J. BEKKER
(Western Transvaal)	(Boland)	(Northern Transvaal)
D.F. RETIEF	J.A. du RAND (**Capt.**) J.T. CLAASSEN	D.S.P. ACKERMANN
(Northern Transvaal)	(Northern Transvaal) (Western Transvaal)	(Western Province)

G.P. LOCHNER
(Western Province)

C.F. STRYDOM
(Orange Free State)

C.A. ULYATE
(Transvaal)

J.G.H. du PREEZ	B.F. HOWE	J.J. NEL	P.G. JOHNSTONE
(Western Province)	(Border)	(Western Province)	(Transvaal)

R.G. DRYBURGH
(Natal)

SOUTH AFRICA

REFEREE: Mr F.G.M. Parkinson (Manawatu)
ATTENDANCE: 40,000
CONDITIONS: Weather cleared after heavy showers, ground heavy
HALFTIME: New Zealand 10, South Africa 3

SCORERS

NEW ZEALAND	**SOUTH AFRICA**
Tries: White, Jarden	Try: Howe
Conversions: Jarden (2)	Penalty goal: Dryburgh

SOUTH AFRICA

Carisbrook, Dunedin

the South Africans attacked through their backs and went close to scoring on several occasions before Strydom missed out his fly-half to link with his centres. Johnstone on the wing received the ball quickly, made the break and when caught near the line in-passed to Howe who scored. Dryburgh missed the conversion. The next incident was a collision between Dixon and du Preez in which du Preez broke his left leg and was carried from the field. He was out for the rest of the tour.

The South Africans continued to attack through the backline with their six forwards gaining sufficient possession from the New Zealand seven, but were not successful in breaching the defence. Twice in the last five minutes, the Springboks had penalties awarded in kickable positions but elected to go for the up and under in an endeavour to score five points to win. However, the All Black line held and the game ended with no further score.

Springbok half-back, Strydom, fails to block Dixon's clearing kick.

4 August, 1956

Second Test

The New Zealand selectors made five changes in the All Black side for this match. "Mick" Bremner, who had last played for New Zealand on the same ground four years previously against Australia, replaced the injured Archer and Frank McAtamney replaced his injured Otago team-mate, Irwin. Nev MacEwan, Dennis Young and Bill Clark replaced Hill, Hemi and Buxton respectively. McAtamney, MacEwan and Young were new caps and some criticism was levelled at the selectors for making what appeared unnecessary changes.

The Springboks also made changes in their line up with captain "Basie" Viviers replacing Roy Dryburgh at full-back. Ian Kirkpatrick and the replacement winger for du Preez, Theunis Briers, came into the three-quarters, and Tommy Gentles took over from "Popeye" Strydom at scrum-half. Chris Koch came in for Walker as prop, and in a shuffle of positions Jan Pickard replaced Dawie Ackermann. Du Rand, playing in his nineteenth international set a new Springbok record for appearances, beating M.M. "Boy" Louw's record by one. Both Koch and du Rand had played for the Springboks against New Zealand in 1949.

A strong, cold, blustery southerly wind was blowing down the very wet ground as the team took the field, after being presented to the Governor-General, Sir Willoughby Norrie. New Zealand, with the wind behind them, kicked off. Although they spent all the first half on attack, poor tactics including high kicks which were swept by the wind over the Springboks' dead ball line, kept the New Zealand score down to 3-0.

By halftime their only points had come from a kick ahead by Walsh which was snapped up by Gray after indecision by the Springbok defence. He sent it on to Brown who scored in a handy position eight minutes after the start. Jarden's conversion attempt hit the post. Two penalty attempts by Jarden during the spell from 58 and 35 yards also failed.

Jarden, Vincent and Walsh cannot prevent Retief's try just after halftime.

NＥW ZEALAND 3

Athletic Park, Wellington

Christchurch Star **cartoonist, Paul Hanrahan, looks at the second Test selection.**

sion and South Africa had won a tremendously tough Test 8-3. Du Rand had left the field shortly before no-side with a scalp wound which required six stitches and Bekker also had retired concussed near the end of the game.

The Springboks had deserved their victory showing better tactical skill and enjoying a superiority in the forward play, particularly in the scrums where van der Merwe won the tighthead count 3-1.

This match saw the end of Pat Vincent's brief international career. The 30 year old captain and half-back had received criticism for both his tactical approach and for his own play which at times came under severe pressure from the Springbok loose forwards. It was the last international too for both the prop Frank McAtamney and first five-eighth "Mick" Bremner although both again toured with All Black teams. McAtamney went to Australia the following year and Bremner, after a further four year wait, was the vice-captain of the 1960 tourists to South Africa.

It took the Springboks only two minutes of the second half to take the lead when Gentles ran the blind from a ruck in the right hand corner and in-passed to Retief who crashed over for a try just inside the corner flag. Viviers converted right from the touchline and South Africa were ahead 5-3. They kept the pressure up and the All Blacks rarely got out of their own territory. Viviers missed penalties from 40, 35 and finally 55 yards. With only ten minutes to play the Springboks twice went close to scoring before du Rand appropriately scored a try in a similar manner to Retief's. Viviers could not manage the conver-

NEW ZEALAND

	P.T. WALSH (Counties)	
M.J. DIXON (Canterbury)	R.H. BROWN (Taranaki)	R.A. JARDEN (Wellington)
	W.N. GRAY (Bay of Plenty)	
	S.G. BREMNER (Canterbury)	
	P.B. VINCENT (**Capt.**) (Canterbury)	
	I.N. MacEWAN (Wellington)	
W.H. CLARK (Wellington)	R.A. WHITE (Poverty Bay) R.H. DUFF (Canterbury)	D.N. McINTOSH (Wellington)
I.J. CLARKE (Waikato)	D. YOUNG (Canterbury)	F.S. McATAMNEY (Otago)

A.C. KOCH (Boland)	A.J. van der MERWE (Boland)	H.P.J. BEKKER (Northern Transvaal)
G.P. LOCHNER (Western Province)	J.A. du RAND (Northern Transvaal) J.T. CLAASSEN (Western Transvaal)	D.F. RETIEF (Northern Transvaal)
	J.A.J. PICKARD (Western Province)	
	T.A. GENTLES (Western Province)	
	C.A. ULYATE (Transvaal)	
P.G. JOHNSTONE (Transvaal)	J.J. NEL A.I. KIRKPATRICK (Western Province) (Griqualand West)	T.P.D. BRIERS (Western Province)
	S.S. VIVIERS (**Capt.**) (Orange Free State)	

SOUTH AFRICA

REFEREE: Mr F.G.M. Parkinson (Manawatu)
ATTENDANCE: 50,000
CONDITIONS: Weather overcast, cold with strong southerly wind, ground heavy
HALFTIME: New Zealand 3, South Africa 0
SCORERS

NEW ZEALAND	**SOUTH AFRICA**
Try: Brown	Tries: Retief, du Rand
	Conversion: Viviers

18 August, 1956

Third Test

As expected, Jack Sullivan and his fellow selectors made several changes in their side following the defeat at Athletic Park. Some conjecture surrounded the calling of a meeting of the New Zealand Rugby Union council on the Thursday following the second Test as to whether the council attempted to influence the selectors in their third Test selection. When the team was announced after the Taranaki v. South Africa match on the preceding Saturday, it was learned that there were seven changes.

Making his debut was the sixteen stone four pound Waikato full-back, Don Clarke who had played a significant part in his province's defeat of the Springboks in their opening match in New Zealand. Don and Ian Clarke became the first set of brothers to appear in an international for New Zealand since Cyril and Maurice Brownlie played against France in 1925.

Other changes saw "Ponty" Reid, another Waikato player, who had led his province against the tourists, replace Vincent as half-back. He had previously appeared in one Test in 1952. Robin Archer reclaimed his five-eighth berth and Hemi the hooker's position. Peter Jones and "Tiny" Hill who had last appeared in the previous season also joined the forwards, but the most significant change came in the front row where Kevin Skinner, who had been out of big Rugby since the 1953/54 tour, replaced McAtamney.

The Springboks who had recorded a win and had drawn against Taranaki since the second Test, introduced Tom van Vollenhoven and the previously injured Wilfred Rosenberg to their three-quarter line and Ackermann was recalled to the flank of the scrum. Daan Retief went to number eight and Pickard was omitted.

South Africa kicked off and after three minutes Don Clarke was given his first opportunity at goal when a penalty was awarded 45 yards out and near the right-hand touch line. With a good kick he put the All Blacks into a three point lead. Early flurries among the forwards led to a further penalty six minutes later, 40 yards out in midfield, and Clarke again obliged to make it 6-0.

In his debut Test match, Don Clarke kicks the first of the 38 Test penalties he was to goal for New Zealand.

After sixteen minutes Reid kicked the ball away from Gentles following a scrum, recovered the ball and sent a long pass to Gray, moving at top speed. The five-eighth transferred the ball to Brown, who sent it out to Dixon on the wing. The right winger scampered the last 15 yards to score near the corner. After some doubt, Clarke's kick was adjudged to have gone over and New Zealand advanced to an 11-0 lead.

Although the All Blacks went close to scoring on several occasions and Viviers failed with a 35 yards penalty just on halftime, the interval was reached with the score unchanged.

SOUTH AFRICA 10

Lancaster Park, Christchurch

With the All Black forwards having the better of play for the first time in the series, there was a note of optimism around the ground. However, in the seventh minute of the second half Ackermann picked up a speculated kick ahead by Jarden and worked a scissors with Ulyate who sent van Vollenhoven away. As a lone defender loomed he gave the ball to Lochner who scored in the corner. Viviers landed a good goal. At this stage, Archer retired with a shoulder injury and Brown moved into the first five-eighth position with Bill Clark going to centre. When Archer returned to the field eleven minutes later he took up a roving position behind the backline.

Half-way through the spell South Africa scored a brilliant try, begun by Gentles breaking left from a ruck on the New Zealand 10 yard mark. He in-passed to Ackermann who sent on the ball to Bekker, who was running like a back. It was then unloaded to Claassen who threw a one-handed pass to Rosenberg who completed the try, scoring well back behind the posts. Viviers again raised the flags and the score stood at 11-10.

For the next eighteen minutes, play moved up and down the field as both sides tried to score the next vital points. With only two minutes to go, Brown scooped up a loose ball following a scrum near half-way, and kicked for the left-hand corner. Jarden took off in pursuit, finally leaping high in the air to recover the bouncing ball almost out of Briers' grasp to score in the corner. Clarke's kick was wide.

However, the All Blacks had not yet finished, and with seconds remaining, Peter Jones fastened on to a loose ball and burst to his right before linking with Dixon. The winger looked for support and it was the lock "Tiny" White who ranged up outside to take the pass and score in Viviers' tackle. Clarke again failed with the conversion but the crowd, who were in an ecstatic mood, hardly noticed as Mr Fright blew for no-side.

Much praise was lavished on Don Clarke for his goal kicking and "Ponty" Reid who controlled the play well. The revitalised forward pack all played well although none better than White who had played in his twenty-second successive Test.

Robin Archer's damaged shoulder was to rule him out of consideration for the final Test and this match was to be the last of his four internationals although he toured Australia with the 1957 New Zealand team.

The Springbok three-quarters, Wilfred Rosenberg and Tommy van Vollenhoven, appeared only in this Test during the current tour. Both later became prominent Rugby League players in England.

NEW ZEALAND

D.B. CLARKE
(Waikato)

M.J. DIXON	R.H. BROWN	R.A. JARDEN
(Canterbury)	(Taranaki)	(Wellington)

W.N. GRAY
(Bay of Plenty)

W.R. ARCHER
(Southland)

A.R. REID
(Waikato)

P.F.H. JONES
(North Auckland)

W.H. CLARK	R.A. WHITE	R.H. DUFF (Capt.)	S.F. HILL
(Wellington)	(Poverty Bay)	(Canterbury)	(Canterbury)
K.L. SKINNER	R.C. HEMI		I.J. CLARKE
(Counties)	(Waikato)		(Waikato)

A.C. KOCH	A.J. van der MERWE	H.P.J. BEKKER
(Boland)	(Boland)	(Northern Transvaal)
G.P. LOCHNER	J.T. CLAASSEN	J.A. du RAND	D.S.P. ACKERMANN
(Western Province)	(Western Transvaal)	(Northern Transvaal)	(Western Province)

D.F. RETIEF
(Northern Transvaal)

T.A. GENTLES
(Western Province)

C.A. ULYATE
(Transvaal)

K.T. van VOLLENHOVEN	W. ROSENBERG	J.J. NEL	T.P.D. BRIERS
(Northern Transvaal)	(Transvaal)	(Western Province)	(Western Province)

S.S. VIVIERS (Capt.)
(Orange Free State)

SOUTH AFRICA

REFEREE: Mr W.H. Fright (Canterbury)
ATTENDANCE: 51,000
CONDITIONS: Weather fine, ground firm
HALFTIME: New Zealand 11, South Africa 0

SCORERS

NEW ZEALAND
Tries: Dixon, Jarden, White
Conversion: D.B. Clarke
Penalty goals: D.B. Clarke (2)

SOUTH AFRICA
Tries: Lochner, Rosenberg
Conversions: Viviers (2)

NEW ZEALAND 11

1 September, 1956

Fourth Test

The only change in the New Zealand team was necessitated by the injury to Archer. Ross Brown, who had capably filled the position when Archer left the field at Christchurch, was selected at first five-eighth and Walsh, full-back in the first and second Tests, came in at centre.

In the Springbok side, Howe, who had played well in the 37-0 defeat of the New Zealand Maori side the previous week, came in to replace Ulyate at fly-half. Other changes in their side were Dryburgh and Paul Johnstone in the three-quarters for van Vollenhoven and Rosenberg, Strydom for Gentles at scrum-half and the replacement flanker Jim Starke and Walker for Ackermann and Koch. The last-named withdrew with a back injury after selection.

The ground was in perfect condition and the weather good as Nel miscued the kick off in front of the record crowd who crammed the ground. Once again the All Black forwards won control in the early stages and were playing with great fire. Viviers missed an easy penalty before Clarke missed a 62 yard effort. Clarke's kick passed only a foot or two to the left of the posts however, and gave New Zealand a great psychological advantage.

Sixteen minutes into the half it was Clarke who put the first points on the board with a 48 yard penalty. Dryburgh and Clarke both failed with penalty attempts, before halftime was reached with the score at 3-0.

Five minutes into the second spell came the only New Zealand try of the match. From a line-out on the Springbok 10 yard mark, the ball came back to Strydom who failed to clear and Hemi, coming around the front of the line-out, kicked the ball away from the half-back. Jones, coming through from his position at the end of the line-out, scooped up the loose ball and immediately headed for the goal line 35 yards away. In an amazing run he did not have a hand laid on him and on reaching the goal line he moved around to score near the posts as the large crowd erupted with joy. Clarke converted and New Zealand were up 8-0. Two minutes later Jarden left the

field with a damaged arm. He returned later to take up a position at extra full-back. Clark moved from the side of the scrum to centre with Walsh moving onto the left wing in Jarden's place.

Howe was trying to breach the New Zealand defence close to the scrum without success and during the second spell Johnstone and Howe changed places. Dryburgh missed another penalty before Clarke again struck with a 48 yard kick into the breeze after thirty minutes, to make the game safe for New Zealand.

Three minutes from time, White was injured in a flurry on the terrace touch line and had to leave the field. A minute later Dryburgh scored for South Africa after Gray, in attempting to run the ball from inside his 25, lost it in a tackle. Howe recovered the ball and inpassed to Dryburgh who scored in a handy position for Viviers to convert.

So, for the first time in sixty years, South Africa had been defeated in a Test series.

This match saw the end of the international

NEW ZEALAND

D.B. CLARKE
(Waikato)

M.J. DIXON   P.T. WALSH   R.A. JARDEN
(Canterbury)   (Counties)   (Wellington)

W.N. GRAY
(Bay of Plenty)

R.H. BROWN
(Taranaki)

A.R. REID
(Waikato)
P.F.H. JONES
(North Auckland)

W.H. CLARK   R.A. WHITE   R.H. DUFF (**Capt.**)   S.F. HILL
(Wellington)   (Poverty Bay)   (Canterbury)   (Canterbury)
K.L. SKINNER   R.C. HEMI   I.J. CLARKE
(Counties)   (Waikato)   (Waikato)

H.N. WALKER   A.J. van der MERWE   H.P.J. BEKKER
(Western Transvaal)   (Boland)   (Northern Transvaal)
D.F. RETIEF   J.T. CLAASSEN   J.A. du RAND   J.J. STARKE
(Northern Transvaal) (Western Transvaal) (Northern Transvaal) (Western Province)
G.P. LOCHNER
(Western Province)
C.F. STRYDOM
(Orange Free State)
B.F. HOWE
(Border)

R.G. DRYBURGH   J.J. NEL   P.G. JOHNSTONE   T.P.D. BRIERS
(Natal)   (Western Province)   (Transvaal)   (Western Province)
S.S. VIVIERS (**Capt.**)
(Orange Free State)

SOUTH AFRICA

REFEREE: Mr W.H. Fright (Canterbury)
ATTENDANCE: 61,240
CONDITIONS: Weather fine, ground firm
HALFTIME: New Zealand 3, South Africa 0
SCORERS

NEW ZEALAND	SOUTH AFRICA
Try: Jones	Try: Dryburgh
Conversion: D.B. Clarke	Conversion: Viviers
Penalty goals: D.B. Clarke (2)	

SOUTH AF ICA 5

Eden Park, Auckland

Peter Jones has crossed the line and heads towards the posts to score his remarkable try.

careers of several of the All Black players. Bob Duff, who later served as a New Zealand selector from 1971 to 1973, and was the assistant-manager of the All Blacks in the Northern Hemisphere in 1972-73, was retiring after eleven internationals since 1951. Kevin Skinner who had broken Maurice Brownlie's record of sixty-one appearances in all matches for New Zealand and was the new record holder at sixty-three, was also going back into retirement after his brief but notable come-back. Another record holder in Richard "Tiny" White who had completed twenty-three consecutive Test matches since 1949 was hanging up his boots. A fourth member of the pack, Bill Clark, had also played his last Test.

Of the backs, Bill Gray, the Maori five-eighth, had appeared in his final international although he accompanied the All Blacks to Australia in 1957. On a subsequent tour with the New Zealand Maori team in 1958, he had the misfortune to break a leg and although he made a wonderful recovery, he was not destined to return to international play.

Prior to the game, Ron Jarden surprised many people by announcing his retirement from all Rugby at the relatively early age of twenty-six. In his all too short All Black career since 1951, Jarden had played sixteen Tests and twenty-one other games for his country, and had been a prolific points-scorer recording forty-two in Tests including seven tries. He became a successful sharebroker, chairman of the New Zealand Broadcasting Council and owner of the New Zealand representative One Ton yacht "Barnacle Bill". In 1961 he wrote a fine book on Rugby aptly called 'Rugby on Attack'. Ron Jarden died suddenly in February, 1977 at the age of forty-seven.

25 May, 1957

First Test

After victories over New South Wales and Western New South Wales, the All Blacks faced Australia in their third match of the tour full of confidence. An original wing selection Russell Watt was prevented from playing by a torn heel tendon and was replaced by Morrie Dixon.

The Auckland mid-field backs Frank McMullen and Terry Lineen were making their international debuts as were two forwards who were to play important roles in the immediate future of New Zealand Rugby, Wilson Whineray and Colin Meads. Pat Walsh, who had previously represented New Zealand at second five-eighth, full-back and centre, was placed on the wing.

The Australian selectors experienced difficulties in the centre position when first Saxon White was unavailable through injury and then Barker, White's replacement, also had to withdraw with a muscle injury. This necessitated bringing Phelps, an original wing selection, in to centre and placing Alan Morton, a 22 year old Randwick club winger, on the right wing to make his Test debut. Another player making his debut for Australia was Terry Curley, the 18 year old full-back, who was to earn much praise for his display in this match.

Tooth kicked a penalty goal after sixteen minutes from in front of the posts to give Australia the lead for the only time in the game. Three minutes later, Don Clarke equalled the score with a penalty from a handy position. From a burst by Whineray following a line-out, a surging forward rush ended with MacEwan scoring near the corner. Clarke raised the flags with a good kick to make the score 8-3, after thirty-two minutes.

Keith Cross became the first opponent to cross the All Blacks' line on this tour when he scored following a determined run shortly after. Tooth levelled the score when he landed the conversion.

The next points came three minutes from halftime when McMullen inpassed to Walsh who had come in from the blindside wing. Hemi was there to take Walsh's pass and race the last

ten yards to score a good try. Clarke failed with the conversion and on the call of halftime Tooth once again evened the scores with his second successful penalty.

Early in the second spell Walsh again came into the backline from the blindside and gave McMullen an opening which he brilliantly made use of to score a fine try between the posts. Clarke converted and, four minutes later, was again successful with a simple penalty. The All Blacks, now firmly in control, scored another try when Reid ran on the blindside and transferred to winger Walsh who went over in the corner. Clarke missed the difficult conversion but managed a 45 yard penalty in the last minute of the game to make his contribution thirteen points for the match.

Critics were unanimous in their praise of the New Zealand forwards for their relentless display. Newcomer Whineray was picked out for his fine exhibition at prop where he was described as 'a threat in all phases'.

NEW ZEALAND

D.B. CLARKE
(Waikato)

M.J. DIXON   R.F. McMULLEN   P.T. WALSH
(Canterbury)   (Auckland)   (Counties)

T.R. LINEEN
(Auckland)

R.H. BROWN
(Taranaki)

A.R. REID (**Capt.**)
(Waikato)

P.S. BURKE
(Taranaki)

C.E. MEADS   S.F. HILL   I.N. MacEWAN   D.N. McINTOSH
(King Country)   (Canterbury)   (Wellington)   (Wellington)

I.J. CLARKE   R.C. HEMI   W.J. WHINERAY
(Waikato)   (Waikato)   (Canterbury)

F.M. ELLIOTT   J.V. BROWN   R.A.L. DAVIDSON
(New South Wales)   (New South Wales)   (New South Wales)

C.R. WILSON   A.S. CAMERON   A.R. MILLER   K.A. CROSS
(Queensland)   (New South Wales)   (New South Wales)   (New South Wales)

P.T. FENWICKE
(New South Wales)

B.P. COX
(New South Wales)

R.M. TOOTH (**Capt.**)
(New South Wales)

K.J. DONALD   J.M. POTTS   R. PHELPS   A.R. MORTON
(Queensland)   (New South Wales)   (New South Wales)   (New South Wales)

T.G.P. CURLEY
(New South Wales)

AUSTRALIA

REFEREE: Mr A.T. Tierney (New South Wales)
ATTENDANCE: 28,125
CONDITIONS: Weather fine, ground firm
HALFTIME: New Zealand 11, Australia 11

SCORERS

NEW ZEALAND   **AUSTRALIA**
Tries: MacEwan, Hemi, McMullen,   Try: Cross
Walsh   Conversion: Tooth
Conversions: D.B. Clarke (2)   Penalty goals: Tooth (2)
Penalty goals: D.B. Clarke (3)

AUSTRALIA 11

Sydney Cricket Ground

With only two internationals arranged on the tour, this victory was sufficient to retain the

Terry Lineen lines up his tackle on the Wallaby winger Alan Morton.

Bledisloe Cup for New Zealand. History was also made when this match became the first Rugby international in Australia to be covered by television.

SYDNEY MORNING HERALD

201

NEW ZEALAND 2?

1 June, 1957

Second Test

After a mid-week victory over Queensland under floodlights, the All Black side faced this second and final international of 1957 as firm favourites. Their team was unaltered from that which played the match at Sydney. Watt had suffered a further injury in the Queensland match and was again unavailable for the Test.

There were five changes in the Australian line-up. Ken Donald, with a wrist injury, and vice-captain Alan Cameron were not available, their places being taken by Brian Ford, another 18 year old making his debut in the side, and Neil Latimer respectively. Other changes saw Emanuel replace "Chilla" Wilson on the side of the scrum and Bill Gunther, who had captained Western New South Wales at Warren, come in for Fenwicke at the back of the scrum.

The veteran Nick Shehadie took over at prop to play what was his last Test against New Zealand. Since his first game in 1947, he had played eleven internationals against the All Blacks.

Australian captain Dick Tooth kicked off and his team went on to early attack. Curley missed a penalty attempt from 30 yards in the third minute but, two minutes later, Tooth was successful with his attempt to put Australia into an early lead. After nine minutes Brown placed a crosskick into the Australian in-goal area which gave Dixon a try. Don Clarke converted. Tooth and Curley both missed penalty attempts in the next ten minutes before the Wallabies registered an increase to their score.

This came when Walsh was caught in possession following a high kick by Phelps. The ball came back to Cox from the resulting maul and he fed Morton on the blind side for the speedy winger to race over in the corner. Curley failed to add to the total with his conversion attempt.

Six minutes from halftime McMullen scored for New Zealand after Reid had broken from a

Whineray and Ian Clarke lead this All Black rush past the diminutive Australian half-back, Cox.

BRISBANE TELEGRAPH

AUSTRALIA 9

Exhibition Ground, Brisbane

scrum and made a long accurate pass to his centre who touched down ten yards from the corner. Don Clarke missed the conversion. In the final minute of the spell, McMullen pierced the defence before passing to Dixon who centre-kicked where Brown gathered a good bounce and beat the Australian defence to score near the posts. Clarke converted this try to make the score 13-6 to the tourists at halftime.

The first points after the interval came when Colin Meads, deputising on the wing after McMullen had received a bump, got the ball on the end of a backline movement to hurl himself over for the first of his seven tries in international matches. Clarke missed the kick from wide out, and, with twenty minutes to play, the All Blacks held a ten point margin.

Shortly after, Don Clarke took a fair catch near the Australian 25 yard line. He moved the mark back to 45 yards from the posts, where his brother Ian held the ball, and Clarke kicked the first goal

EVENING POST

The All Blacks return with the Bledisloe Cup.

from a mark for New Zealand since Mark Nicholls successfully landed one at Lancaster Park in 1930 against the British team.

By this time the Australian forwards were visibly wilting and New Zealand held a firm grip on the game. Reid then whipped the ball to Brown from a ruck on the Australian 25 for the five-eighth to calmly drop a goal. With thirty seconds to play Tooth kicked a penalty from right in front of the New Zealand posts following a scrum infringement.

Poor goalkicking by Tooth and Curley was seen by some critics as a big handicap to Australia's chances of winning the match. Between them, the Wallaby kickers missed six relatively easy opportunities.

The All Black captain "Ponty" Reid, Taranaki captain Peter Burke, Don McIntosh and ebullient winger Morrie Dixon had played their last Test for New Zealand. As well as Nick Shehadie, captain Dick Tooth, Brian Cox and Keith Cross, all well known opponents during the 1950's, had played their final international match against New Zealand.

NEW ZEALAND

D.B. CLARKE
(Waikato)

M.J. DIXON   R.F. McMULLEN   P.T. WALSH
(Canterbury)   (Auckland)   (Counties)

T.R. LINEEN
(Auckland)

R.H. BROWN
(Taranaki)

A.R. REID (Capt.)
(Waikato)

P.S. BURKE
(Taranaki)

C.E. MEADS   S.F. HILL   I.N. MacEWAN   D.N. McINTOSH
(King Country)   (Canterbury)   (Wellington)   (Wellington)

I.J. CLARKE   R.C. HEMI   W.J. WHINERAY
(Waikato)   (Waikato)   (Canterbury)

N.M. SHEHADIE   J.V. BROWN   R.A.L. DAVIDSON
(New South Wales)   (New South Wales)   (New South Wales)

D.M. EMANUEL   A.R. MILLER   N. LATIMER   K.A. CROSS
(New South Wales)   (New South Wales)   (New South Wales)   (New South Wales)

W.J. GUNTHER
(New South Wales)

B.P. COX
(New South Wales)

R.M. TOOTH (Capt.)
(New South Wales)

B. FORD   J.M. POTTS   R. PHELPS   A.R. MORTON
(Queensland)   (New South Wales)   (New South Wales)   (New South Wales)

T.G.P. CURLEY
(New South Wales)

AUSTRALIA

REFEREE: Mr N. Haydon (Queensland)
ATTENDANCE: 13,372
CONDITIONS: Weather fine, ground firm
HALFTIME: New Zealand 13, Australia 6

SCORERS

NEW ZEALAND	AUSTRALIA
Tries: Dixon, McMullen, Brown, Meads	Try: Morton
Conversions: D.B. Clarke (2)	Penalty goals: Tooth (2)
Dropped goal: Brown	
Goal from mark: D.B. Clarke	

NEW ZEALAND 25

23 August, 1958

First Test

Following a narrow defeat in their opening match against Hawke's Bay, Australia had won the three other provincial matches leading up to this first international including a 12-0 victory over Ranfurly Shield holders, Taranaki.

Despite this win, it was felt that the All Blacks would be too strong all round for the visitors. The New Zealand team contained three new internationals, "Mick" Cossey, Tom Coughlan and John Graham. The first two played only one match for their country but Graham, a loose forward listed as being two pounds over thirteen stone, went on to play in twenty-two internationals. Keith Davis was making his first Test appearance since 1955.

Interesting personalities in the Wallaby side included Des Connor who was considered unlucky to miss selection for Australia the previous year against New Zealand. He had proved a great success on the Wallaby tour of

Europe during the summer months. Three years later he was to play for New Zealand. Eddie Stapleton had toured in 1952 and 1955 and Rod Phelps in 1955. Kevin Ryan was amateur heavy-weight boxing champion of Queensland and later played League for Australia. Arthur Summons was Australia's captain at League for several years.

After both teams had been introduced to the Governor-General, Lord Cobham, it was seen that Australia who had won the toss had elected to play into the breeze in the first half. New Zealand went on to early attack and in the fifteenth minute the new captain, Whineray, went over for a try following a backline movement and a centring kick by Brown. Clarke missed the conversion. Whineray was over again eight minutes later. He was first to the ball when it had been kicked through by Coughlan after coming loose from a tackle. Don Clarke again failed with the conversion and then missed a simple penalty attempt a few minutes later.

In the thirty-first minute of the spell, Brown

Playing in only his third Test, Wilson Whineray was chosen as captain at the age of 23, and celebrated by scoring two tries. Keith Davis acclaims the first of Whineray's tries above.

EVENING POST

NEW ZEALAND

D.B. CLARKE
(Waikato)

R.R. COSSEY   P.T. WALSH   R.F. McMULLEN
(Counties)   (Counties)   (Auckland)

T.R. LINEEN
(Auckland)

R.H. BROWN
(Taranaki)

K. DAVIS
(Auckland)

D.J. GRAHAM
(Canterbury)

T.D. COUGHLAN   C.E. MEADS   I.N. MacEWAN   P.F.H. JONES
(South Canterbury)   (King Country)   (Wellington)   (North Auckland)

I.J. CLARKE   D. YOUNG   W.J. WHINERAY (**Capt.**)
(Waikato)   (Canterbury)   (Waikato)

K.J. ELLIS   R.W. MEADOWS   P.K. DUNN
(New South Wales)   (New South Wales)   (New South Wales)

C.R. WILSON (**Capt.**)   J.K. CARROLL   J.P.L. WHITE   D.R. LOWTH
(Queensland)   (New South Wales)   (New South Wales)   (New South Wales)

K.J. RYAN
(Queensland)

D.M. CONNOR
(Queensland)

A.J. SUMMONS
(New South Wales)

A.R. MORTON   R. PHELPS   B.J. ELLWOOD   E.T. STAPLETON
(New South Wales)   (New South Wales)   (New South Wales)   (New South Wales)

T.G.P. CURLEY
(New South Wales)

AUSTRALIA

REFEREE: Mr C.R. Gillies (Waikato)
ATTENDANCE: 32,000
CONDITIONS: Weather showery with moderate wind, ground greasy
HALFTIME: New Zealand 9, Australia 0

SCORERS

NEW ZEALAND   **AUSTRALIA**
Tries: Whineray (2), Walsh (2),   Try: Ellwood
     Graham, McMullen, Jones
Conversions: D.B. Clarke (2)

AUSTRALIA 3

Athletic Park, Wellington

Frank McMullen challenges Summons who passes on to his winger, Eddie Stapleton.

made a good break before the ball was moved out to McMullen on the left wing. As he was taken into touch by Curley and Connor the ball bounced loose for Walsh to pick up and cross unopposed. Again Clarke was unable to convert and halftime was reached with the score at New Zealand 9, Australia 0.

It was Australia's turn to go on to attack in the opening minutes of the second half with the wind at their backs. But, after thirteen minutes, it was newcomer Graham who scored next when he broke from a line-out near the Australian 25, kicked over Curley's head, regained the ball on his finger tips and dived over. Clarke was cheered when he raised the flags with his conversion. Four minutes later, Walsh scored his second try after Cossey had been overhauled by Morton after getting an overlap, and the alert centre was on hand to take the ball and dive over. The conversion was missed by Clarke who was having a poor day with his boot.

The next points came with nine minutes to play when quick passing by the All Black backs got the ball out to McMullen who sped across for a good try. Clarke's conversion skimmed inside the posts and New Zealand were 22 points ahead. Their last points came when Peter Jones crashed over in "Chilla" Wilson's tackle following a short passing burst by the All Black forwards. Yet again the conversion was missed.

The Australian try came in the last minutes of the game when Stapleton made a break before in-passing to Wilson who in turn handed on to Ellwood to finish the movement off by scoring near the corner flag. Curley was unable to convert and the game ended, New Zealand 25, Australia 3.

New Zealand was so clearly superior it was only the relatively poor kicking that prevented them winning by over forty points. Wilson Whineray, who at only twenty-three had been a great success as captain was destined to lead his country in a further twenty-nine Tests.

AUSTRALIA 6

6 September, 1958

Second Test

In the match following the first international, the Wallabies went down heavily to Southland 8-26, but then defeated both Otago and South Canterbury.

Both the Clarke brothers were unavailable through injury and the selectors made two further changes to the New Zealand team. Cossey, who was thought to lack pace, and Coughlan, who had had a reasonably good game at Wellington, were replaced by Russell Watt and Rex Pickering respectively. Both had toured Australia the previous year without playing in a Test match. Lloyd Ashby who had scored fourteen points in Southland's match against the tourists, came in at full-back to play his only match in the national jersey whilst Mark Irwin replaced Ian Clarke in the front row.

Stapleton had aggravated a thigh injury in the Wellington match which subsequently led to his withdrawal from the rest of the tour. He had opposed the All Blacks in nine internationals since 1951 and was on his third tour to New Zealand. Morton switched wings, with Rod Phelps moving from centre to the left wing. Robert Kay came into the team in the vacant centre position and became the first Victorian to win a Test berth against the All Blacks since 1938. The only other change in the Wallaby line-up saw John Thornett replace Lowth on the side of the scrum.

It was generally felt that the New Zealand team would repeat their first Test victory without too much trouble.

Australia kicked off from the northern end and after four minutes Ashby missed a 40 yard penalty. However it was soon apparent that the Wallabies' play, especially in the forwards, was far superior to that seen in the Wellington international. Kay narrowly missed a try when he lost the ball over the goal line in the thirtieth minute after a fine opening by Morton, and it was left to Curley to open the scoring on the stroke of halftime with a well-kicked penalty goal from thirty yards out.

On the resumption, Peter Jones made his pre-

NZ HERALD

Ross Brown scored New Zealand's only points in this match with his second half try.

sence felt with a typical crashing run of nearly fifty yards. The All Blacks held the advantage early in the spell and in the eighth minute, when Brown made a break on the blindside from a scrum on the Australian 25 he found Watt in support inside him. Watt was held up five yards from the line but found Brown still outside him to take the pass and cross right in the corner to equal the score. Ashby was unable to convert.

The Australians were quickly on to attack from the re-start and two minutes later Curley

NEW ZEALAND 3

Lancaster Park, Christchurch

Above: **Ryan wrestles the ball free from a line-out to feed his half-back Connor who** (right) **clears as John Graham appears.**

missed a penalty from forty yards. Midway through the half Australia regained the lead when Morton scored a brilliant individual try. Receiving the ball from loose play forty yards out from the All Black line and near touch, he combined pace, swerve, and side-step to elude several defenders before scoring in the right hand corner. Curley's kick was to the left of the posts.

It was Curley, playing an outstanding game at full-back, who turned back many of the New Zealand attacks in the last twenty minutes of the game. The All Blacks tried desperately to save the game without success in the final minutes but the sound of Roy Gillies' whistle for no-side saw Australia still ahead by three points.

The Wallaby forwards had shaded the New Zealand eight at the line-outs in the first half although MacEwan had evened things up in the second and for once, Dennis Young failed to win a tight head heel in the scrums. A disturbing feature of the match, as far as the New Zealanders were concerned, was the penalty count

which was reported as being nineteen to six in the Wallabies' favour.

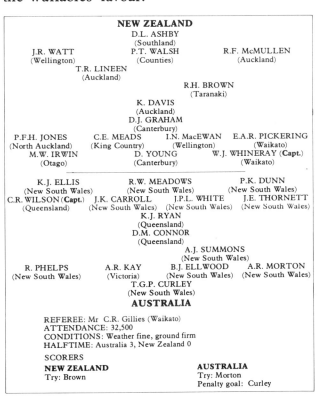

NEW ZEALAND

D.L. ASHBY
(Southland)

J.R. WATT   P.T. WALSH   R.F. McMULLEN
(Wellington)   (Counties)   (Auckland)

T.R. LINEEN
(Auckland)

R.H. BROWN
(Taranaki)

K. DAVIS
(Auckland)

D.J. GRAHAM
(Canterbury)

P.F.H. JONES   C.E. MEADS   I.N. MacEWAN   E.A.R. PICKERING
(North Auckland)   (King Country)   (Wellington)   (Waikato)

M.W. IRWIN   D. YOUNG   W.J. WHINERAY (Capt.)
(Otago)   (Canterbury)   (Waikato)

K.J. ELLIS   R.W. MEADOWS   P.K. DUNN
(New South Wales)   (New South Wales)   (New South Wales)

C.R. WILSON (Capt.)   J.K. CARROLL   J.P.L. WHITE   J.E. THORNETT
(Queensland)   (New South Wales)   (New South Wales)   (New South Wales)

K.J. RYAN
(Queensland)

D.M. CONNOR
(Queensland)

A.J. SUMMONS
(New South Wales)

R. PHELPS   A.R. KAY   B.J. ELLWOOD   A.R. MORTON
(New South Wales)   (Victoria)   (New South Wales)   (New South Wales)

T.G.P. CURLEY
(New South Wales)

AUSTRALIA

REFEREE: Mr C.R. Gillies (Waikato)
ATTENDANCE: 32,500
CONDITIONS: Weather fine, ground firm
HALFTIME: Australia 3, New Zealand 0

SCORERS

NEW ZEALAND	**AUSTRALIA**
Try: Brown	Try: Morton
	Penalty goal: Curley

NEW ZEALAND 17

20 September, 1958

Third Test

Following their victory in the second international, the Australians had displayed disappointing form losing to both Manawatu and North Auckland and drawing with Waikato 14-14. They predictably named the same side as had won the Christchurch Test but brought Tom Baxter into the side when Kay was forced to withdraw with an injured ankle. Baxter, who on his return home was to proceed to Oxford University as Queensland Rhodes Scholar, later won Rugby Blues as a wing and as a loose forward. This match was his only international.

The Clarke brothers, restored to fitness, returned to the New Zealand team and the selectors brought in "Tiny" Hill as a lock with Meads going to the side of the scrum and Peter Jones taking over from Graham at number eight. On the other side of the scrum, the selectors introduced Dave Gillespie who had toured Australia the previous year without gaining a Test cap. Although Gillespie again toured with the All Blacks in South Africa in 1960, this match was to remain his only international. Another new cap was Adrian Clarke, a 20 year old Auckland first five-eighth from the Waitemata club, who had recorded some impressive performances for his province during the season. His selection saw the existing backline move out one place with Watt dropping out.

The match was played at the Epsom Showgrounds, as construction of the new Number One grandstand at Eden Park was in progress.

The All Blacks kicked off and went on to early attack. The first points came after quarter of an hour when Don Clarke landed his second penalty attempt following a line-out infringement. He succeeded with a forty yard kick six minutes later and, although Australia mounted several promising movements, no further scoring occurred during the half.

Early in the second half, both full-backs missed attempts at goal before the first try of the match was recorded. This came in the sixteenth minute when Brown angled a punt into the left hand corner. Meads was on hand to drag the ball

down and crash over. Clarke kicked a fine conversion from wide out and two minutes later landed a thirty yard penalty from the opposite touchline to take New Zealand to a 14-0 lead with twenty minutes to play.

Australia opened their scoring when Curley kicked a forty yard penalty shortly after. The Wallabies then tested the New Zealand defence with an all out attack. Phelps was pushed out in the corner after one promising move, but it was Clarke once again who scored the next points when he slammed over his fourth penalty from forty yards. The big middle row forward, John Carroll, finally managed to go over near the posts for Australia following a movement that covered over half of the field in the last minute of the match. Curley converted to complete the scoring.

Although New Zealand had won by a comfortable margin their victory was dependent to a large extent on the excellent goal kicking of Don Clarke.

This match brought to an end the promising

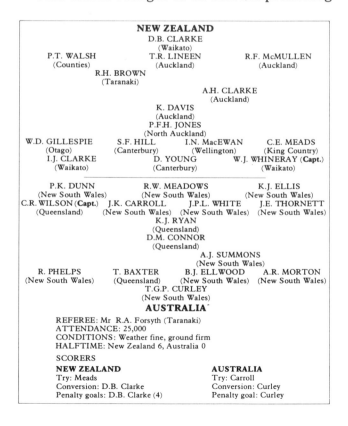

NEW ZEALAND

D.B. CLARKE
(Waikato)

P.T. WALSH　　　　T.R. LINEEN　　　　R.F. McMULLEN
(Counties)　　　　(Auckland)　　　　(Auckland)

R.H. BROWN
(Taranaki)

A.H. CLARKE
(Auckland)

K. DAVIS
(Auckland)

P.F.H. JONES
(North Auckland)

W.D. GILLESPIE　　S.F. HILL　　I.N. MacEWAN　　C.E. MEADS
(Otago)　　(Canterbury)　　(Wellington)　　(King Country)

I.J. CLARKE　　　D. YOUNG　　　W.J. WHINERAY (**Capt.**)
(Waikato)　　　(Canterbury)　　　(Waikato)

P.K. DUNN　　　　R.W. MEADOWS　　　　K.J. ELLIS
(New South Wales)　　(New South Wales)　　(New South Wales)

C.R. WILSON (**Capt.**)　J.K. CARROLL　　J.P.L. WHITE　　J.E. THORNETT
(Queensland)　(New South Wales)　(New South Wales)　(New South Wales)

K.J. RYAN
(Queensland)

D.M. CONNOR
(Queensland)

A.J. SUMMONS
(New South Wales)

R. PHELPS　　　T. BAXTER　　　B.J. ELLWOOD　　A.R. MORTON
(New South Wales)　(Queensland)　(New South Wales)　(New South Wales)

T.G.P. CURLEY
(New South Wales)

AUSTRALIA

REFEREE: Mr R.A. Forsyth (Taranaki)
ATTENDANCE: 25,000
CONDITIONS: Weather fine, ground firm
HALFTIME: New Zealand 6, Australia 0

SCORERS

NEW ZEALAND	**AUSTRALIA**
Try: Meads	Try: Carroll
Conversion: D.B. Clarke	Conversion: Curley
Penalty goals: D.B. Clarke (4)	Penalty goal: Curley

AUSTRALIA 8

Epsom Showgrounds, Auckland

The New Zealand Team
Back row: K. Davis, R.W. Caulton (reserve), A.H. Clarke, K.C. Briscoe (reserve).
Third row: E.T. Walsh, J.J. Clarke, M.W. Irwin (reserve), T.R. Lineen, R.F. McMullen,
Second row: W.D. Gillespie, P.F.H. Jones, C.E. Meads, I.N. MacEwan, S.F. Hill, D.B. Clarke.
Seated: T.D. Coughlan (reserve), R.R. King (selector), W.J. Whineray (capt.), J.L. Sullivan (selector), R.H. Brown, R.A. Everest (selector), D. Young.

career of Terry Curley who announced his retirement to enter the Marist Brothers at the end of the season. He had played ten Tests for Australia during his short career and his loss was a severe one for Australian Rugby. Like Clarke, he had played an outstanding game for his country in this match.

It was also the last international for the All Blacks' fine running half-back Keith Davis. Since 1952 he had played ten Tests for his country.

18 July, 1959

First Test

The 1959 Lions side contained several interesting personalities. O'Reilly and Jackson, the two wing three-quarters, were to prove two of the most prolific try scorers to tour New Zealand. Tony O'Reilly had toured South Africa in 1955 with the Lions of that year as a 19 year old and had played in all four Tests on tour. The 28 year old Peter Jackson had come into the English team in 1956 and was renowned for his elusive, jinking runs.

The centre David Hewitt was the son of Tom Hewitt who had represented Ireland against the 1924 All Blacks, a nephew of Frank Hewitt who had also represented his country against the All Blacks of 1924, and Victor Hewitt who was Ireland's fly-half in the 1935 encounter with New Zealand. Noel Murphy was another whose father had been capped for Ireland.

Beverley Risman, the fly-half, was a son of A.J. (Gus) Risman the noted British Rugby League captain who had toured New Zealand on several occasions. The younger Risman also turned to League in 1961 with considerable success.

Half-back Dickie Jeeps, like O'Reilly, had toured South Africa in 1955, where he played in all four Tests before being capped by his native England. In 1962 he became the first player to be selected for three Lions tours when he again toured South Africa.

Captain Ronnie Dawson, a quietly spoken Irishman, went on to win twenty-seven caps for his country and later acted as assistant-manager to the 1968 Lions tour of South Africa.

The team had won both internationals on their six match tour of Australia before coming to New Zealand, although they had gone down 14-18 to New South Wales in the second match of the tour. In New Zealand, they had opened their tour with a brilliant 52-12 win over Hawke's Bay. They continued their impressive form until they met Otago with an injury-ridden side and went down 8-26. It was expected however that they would provide stiff opposition for the All Blacks at Carisbrook with a far stronger side.

The New Zealand selectors included three new 'caps' in the All Black team. "Tuppy" Diack had been impressive in both the Otago match and in the tourists' match against New Zealand Universities aggregating twenty-seven points in the two matches. He was selected on the wing, but was forced to withdraw with a leg injury and was replaced by another newcomer, Bruce McPhail, from the Christchurch club. At half-back, Roger Urbahn, who had made a name for himself behind the Ranfurly Shield holders' pack, was making his debut. In the forwards, Brian Finlay was to win his first and only 'cap' at the advanced age of thirty-one. Originally a five-eighth he had moved to the side of the scrum where his pace was an obvious advantage. He had made his debut for Manawatu in 1950.

Scotland kicked off in front of a record Carisbrook attendance. The All Blacks went on to attack early and after three minutes' play, Don Clarke attempted a 30 yard penalty but the kick was astray. In the tenth minute Finlay was in-

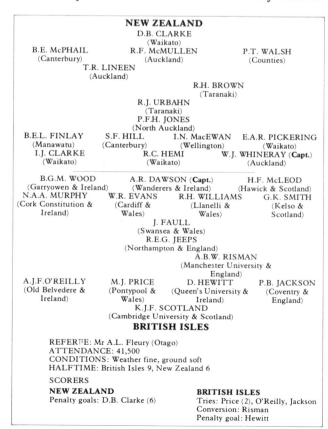

NEW ZEALAND

D.B. CLARKE
(Waikato)

B.E. McPHAIL (Canterbury) — R.F. McMULLEN (Auckland) — P.T. WALSH (Counties)

T.R. LINEEN (Auckland)

R.H. BROWN (Taranaki)

R.J. URBAHN (Taranaki)

P.F.H. JONES (North Auckland)

B.E.L. FINLAY (Manawatu) — S.F. HILL (Canterbury) — I.N. MacEWAN (Wellington) — E.A.R. PICKERING (Waikato)

I.J. CLARKE (Waikato) — R.C. HEMI (Waikato) — W.J. WHINERAY (Capt.) (Auckland)

B.G.M. WOOD (Garryowen & Ireland) — A.R. DAWSON (Capt.) (Wanderers & Ireland) — H.F. McLEOD (Hawick & Scotland)

N.A.A. MURPHY (Cork Constitution & Ireland) — W.R. EVANS (Cardiff & Wales) — R.H. WILLIAMS (Llanelli & Wales) — G.K. SMITH (Kelso & Scotland)

J. FAULL (Swansea & Wales)

R.E.G. JEEPS (Northampton & England)

A.B.W. RISMAN (Manchester University & England)

A.J.F. O'REILLY (Old Belvedere & Ireland) — M.J. PRICE (Pontypool & Wales) — D. HEWITT (Queen's University & Ireland) — P.B. JACKSON (Coventry & England)

K.J.F. SCOTLAND (Cambridge University & Scotland)

BRITISH ISLES

REFEREE: Mr A.L. Fleury (Otago)
ATTENDANCE: 41,500
CONDITIONS: Weather fine, ground soft
HALFTIME: British Isles 9, New Zealand 6

SCORERS

NEW ZEALAND
Penalty goals: D.B. Clarke (6)

BRITISH ISLES
Tries: Price (2), O'Reilly, Jackson
Conversion: Risman
Penalty goal: Hewitt

Carisbrook, Dunedin

Don Clarke, seen here eluding the flying Peter Jackson, kicked six penalty goals to frustrate a Lions' win.

went close to scoring for New Zealand following a quick ruck near the Lions' goal line. Five minutes from halftime O'Reilly scored a try in the left corner, after a break by Risman from a scrum on the New Zealand 25, and the score stood at six all after Scotland failed to convert. Just before the interval, Price scored again for the Lions after both Jackson and Don Clarke had over-run a cross kick by Risman over the goal line. Hewitt failed with the conversion, but at halftime the Lions were ahead by 9-6.

Early in the second half, Clarke missed a 30 yard penalty. Shortly after, Evans intercepted a pass from Urbahn and sent the ball to Smith who in turn gave it to the winger Jackson who scored in the corner. Risman this time missed the conversion. Twice in close succession, Clarke missed long range penalty attempts but then kicked a simple goal from near to the posts to reduce the lead to three points.

Twenty seven minutes into the second half, the Lions went further ahead with a try started by Risman who picked up a loose ball, following a knock-on by McMullen, and kicked ahead. McPhail, in attempting to fly-kick to touch, missed the ball and Price again kicked on and infield. Scotland gathered the ball near the New Zealand line, eluded Walsh and passed to Price, who scored. Risman converted to give the Lions a 17-9 lead. Don Clarke reduced the leeway with a 50 yard penalty following a line-out infringement and with seven minutes to go, Clarke again kicked a penalty, this time from 45 yards.

In a tense atmosphere, Clarke kicked the last of his six successful penalties two minutes from time to gain victory for New Zealand by a single point. The Lions mounted a last tremendous attack in the remaining two minutes and went close to scoring before a defensive penalty was awarded to New Zealand.

With his six penalty goals, Don Clarke set a record for a New Zealander in an international. Some controversy raged after the game about the number of penalties awarded and some of the referee's decisions were disputed.

jured in tackling Jeeps. After treatment he played on but was limping quite noticeably. Jones was also injured in the first quarter of an hour and was little better than a passenger for the rest of the game.

The first points of the match came after twenty minutes when Clarke kicked a 40-yard penalty following a scrum infringement. Two minutes later, he kicked another penalty when Faull was caught offside 35 yards from his posts. Hewitt opened the Lions' score when he landed a simple 30 yard penalty after thirty minutes. Brown then

15 August, 1959

Second Test

Following their controversial defeat in the first international at Dunedin, the Lions had gone down to a strong Canterbury team on the succeeding Saturday 14-20, but had recorded some impressive performances since, defeating Wellington and Taranaki in their Saturday matches. Injury was dogging the tourists and four of the first Test team, Risman, Hewitt, Jackson and Scotland, were unavailable through various injuries. This forced the management to play Malcolm Price, a three-quarter, at fly-half and bring the uncapped replacement player Bill Patterson into the centres. Patterson was capped twice for England in 1961. His partner in this match was Malcolm Thomas who had the distinction of becoming the first player to tour twice with Lions' teams to New Zealand. On his earlier visit in 1950, he had appeared in two internationals.

John Young, who replaced Jackson on the right wing, had been the AAA 100 yards champ-

ion in 1956, and had recorded a best time over the distance of 9.6. Terry Davies, who had sixteen caps for Wales, had recovered from a leg muscle injury received in the match against the West Coast-Buller side at Greymouth, and took over from the injured Scotland. In the forwards Syd. Millar, later to tour with both the 1962 and 1968 Lions to South Africa and win thirty-seven caps for his native Ireland, came into the team replacing Wood. Alan Ashcroft on the side of the scrum and David Marques at number eight completed the changes to the team.

The All Blacks also underwent numerous changes for this match. "Tuppy" Diack, who had been forced to withdraw from the first Test team owing to injury, took over from his replacement McPhail. On the other wing, Walsh gave way to Ralph Caulton, the 22 year old left winger from the Poneke club, giving the club their nineteenth All Black.

One inside back combination from Taranaki gave way to another pairing from the same province when Kevin Briscoe and John McCullough, both from the Tukapa club and making their debuts, replaced Urbahn and Brown. Neither Peter Jones nor Finlay were considered through injury and they were replaced by the newcomer Dick Conway and Colin Meads respectively. On the other side of the scrum, Pickering gave way to an energetic young flanker who was to establish himself as one of the finest players in the world over the next decade, Kelvin Tremain. The only other change in the team saw Des Webb, making his only appearance in the All Black jersey, replace Hemi as hooker.

Davies kicked off in front of the large crowd, which included members of the International Board who had been meeting at Wairakei the previous week, and members of the 1935-36 New Zealand team who had had a reunion the night before the match.

Both Davies and Clarke missed penalty attempts early in the game. After fourteen minutes Lineen cross-kicked towards the left-hand corner. The bounce beat Young and Davies, and Caulton picked up to score in the corner. Clarke missed the conversion.

NEW ZEALAND

D.B. CLARKE
(Waikato)

E.S. DIACK   R.F. McMULLEN   R.W. CAULTON
(Otago)   (Auckland)   (Wellington)

T.R. LINEEN
(Auckland)

J.F. McCULLOUGH
(Taranaki)

K.C. BRISCOE
(Taranaki)

R.J. CONWAY
(Otago)

C.E. MEADS   S.F. HILL   I.N. MacEWAN   K.R. TREMAIN
(King Country) (Canterbury) (Wellington) (Canterbury)

I.J. CLARKE   D.S. WEBB   W.J. WHINERAY (Capt.)
(Waikato)   (North Auckland)   (Auckland)

S. MILLAR   A.R. DAWSON (Capt.)   H.F. McLEOD
(Ballymena & Ireland)   (Wanderers & Ireland)   (Hawick & Scotland)

N.A.A. MURPHY   W.R. EVANS   R.H. WILLIAMS   A. ASHCROFT
(Cork Constitution   (Cardiff &   (Llanelli &   (Waterloo &
& Ireland)   Wales)   Wales)   England)

R.W.D. MARQUES
(Harlequins & England)

R.E.G. JEEPS
(Northampton & England)

M.J. PRICE
(Pontypool & Wales)

A.J.F. O'REILLY M.C. THOMAS W.M. PATTERSON J.R.C. YOUNG
(Old Belvedere & (Newport & Wales) (Sale) (Oxford University &
Ireland)   England)

T.J. DAVIES
(Llanelli & Wales)

BRITISH ISLES

REFEREE: Mr C.R. Gillies (Waikato)
ATTENDANCE: 53,000
CONDITIONS: Weather fine, ground firm
HALFTIME: New Zealand 6, British Isles 0

SCORERS

NEW ZEALAND	BRITISH ISLES
Tries: Caulton (2), D.B. Clarke	Try: Young
Conversion: D.B. Clarke	Conversion: Davies
	Penalty goal: Davies

BRITISH ISLES 8

Athletic Park, Wellington

Four minutes later, after Lineen had beaten Patterson with a beautiful run and subsequent play had forced a five-yard scrum, Caulton scored again after McCullough had run the blindside. Clarke again missed the conversion. There was no further scoring before halftime.

With ten minutes gone in the second half, Davies kicked a penalty following a blatant piece of obstruction by Don Clarke. The Lions went into the lead after twenty minutes with a try by Young after a brilliant run by Price, following a scrum near the All Black line, which Davies converted. Only a minute of play remained when

New Zealand scored their winning try. From a ruck near the Lions' goal line McCullough again ran the blindside and passed to Don Clarke who was up in the line. The unopposed Clarke ran the ten yards to the line and, with a massive dive, scored midway between the posts and corner flag. He converted his own try and New Zealand had again narrowly defeated the Lions on the call of time.

Considering the number of changes and players new to international play, this had been a satisfactory performance by New Zealand despite their last minute scoring to win the match.

Caulton's performance, in scoring two tries in his maiden international, had not been achieved since Wally Argus had done so against Australia at Dunedin in 1946.

Having kicked New Zealand to victory in the first Test, Don Clarke saved his team at Wellington with a last minute try and conversion.

EW ZEALA D 22

29 August, 1959

Third Test

In an endeavour to add weight to the New Zealand forwards, the selectors recalled Hemi and Mark Irwin to the front row of the scrum, the latter for the first time in the series. In the backline, Ross Brown returned to the centre three-quarter position in which he had first played for New Zealand and Frank McMullen shifted out to the wing in place of Diack whose lack of pace was his only short-coming. Briscoe injured an ankle in training prior to the game and

was replaced by the first Test half-back, Roger Urbahn.

The Lions' side had several key players again available and looked a stronger combination than the team that had lost the second Test so narrowly. The versatile Scotland returned to the full-back berth and Peter Jackson to the right

This photo shows a variety of reactions to Caulton's second try. Jeeps and Jackson (3) are the nearest Lions.

CHRISTCHURCH PRESS

BRITISH ISL S 8

Lancaster Park, Christchurch

wing. Hewitt and Price re-joined forces in the centres. Phil Horrocks-Taylor was given the difficult task of playing in the demanding fly-half position after a preparation of one game on the Tuesday before the match. He had arrived to join the tour party as a replacement for the injured Mick English who had returned home. A new trio of loose forwards was selected with Smith and John Faull regaining their places of the Dunedin Test and Haydn Morgan winning his first Test place on tour. Gordon Wood came in for Millar at prop, claiming back the place he lost for the second Test.

After both teams had been introduced to the Governor General, Lord Cobham, Ken Scotland kicked off for the Lions following New Zealand's winning of the toss. Both sides missed early penalty attempts before New Zealand opened the scoring with a try in the left hand corner in the fourteenth minute after winning a tighthead ten yards from the Lions' goal line. Urbahn ran on the blind from the scrum, drawing Jackson before unloading to Caulton who dotted down. Clarke missed the conversion.

Four minutes later the British team evened the score when John Faull kicked a 25 yard penalty. The game took a definite swing towards New Zealand in the twenty-fourth minute when Don Clarke landed a 50 yard penalty and two minutes later he kicked a remarkable dropped goal after fielding a 'speculator' 35 yards from the posts. Eluding the fast-following Lions he snapped over a left-footed drop kick as he was moving towards the touch line.

With four minutes to the interval, Hewitt scored a magnificent try after the Lions had won a scrum inside the New Zealand 25. Horrocks-Taylor made a half-break before passing to David Hewitt. The brilliant young centre took the outside gap between Lineen and Brown with blinding speed and continued on to the goal line, side-stepping the defence in a memorable solo run. Faull brought the scores to within a point with a successful conversion.

On the call of halftime the ball went loose on the Lions' side of a line-out inside their 25 and the All Black forwards swept through to regain

possession and carry on for Meads to cross for a try in the corner. Clarke struck the ball truly and the conversion carried to the posts to give his side a 14-8 lead at the break.

No further scoring occurred until the second half had been going for thirty minutes although the All Black forwards steadily gained control of the game during this period. Caulton made a strong burst up the left wing after gathering a wild kick ahead by the Lions, before inpassing to Conway and Tremain. They were stopped close to the line but as the ball came loose, Urbahn dived over in the corner. Clarke's kick failed. In the concluding minutes Caulton again gathered a kick ahead and burst down the touch line. Jeeps partially stopped him but the winger's momentum was sufficient to carry him to the line. Clarke converted from a handy position to complete the scoring in the match and leave New Zealand with a most convincing victory of twenty-two points to eight.

NEW ZEALAND

D.B. CLARKE
(Waikato)

R.F. McMULLEN   R.H. BROWN   R.W. CAULTON
(Auckland)   (Taranaki)   (Wellington)

T.R. LINEEN
(Auckland)

J.F. McCULLOUGH
(Taranaki)

R.J. URBAHN
(Taranaki)

R.J. CONWAY
(Otago)

C.E. MEADS   S.F. HILL   I.N. MacEWAN   K.R. TREMAIN
(King Country) (Canterbury)   (Wellington)   (Canterbury)
M.W. IRWIN   R.C. HEMI   W.J. WHINERAY (Capt.)
(Otago)   (Waikato)   (Auckland)

B.G.M. WOOD   A.R. DAWSON (Capt.)   H.F. McLEOD
(Garryowen & Ireland) (Wanderers & Ireland)   (Hawick & Scotland)
G.K. SMITH   W.R. EVANS   R.H. WILLIAMS   H.J. MORGAN
(Kelso & Scotland) (Cardiff & Wales) (Llanelli & Wales) (Abertillery & Wales)

J. FAULL
(Swansea & Wales)
R.E.G. JEEPS
(Northampton & England)
J.P. HORROCKS-TAYLOR
(Leicester & England)

A.J.F. O'REILLY   D. HEWITT   M.J. PRICE   P.B. JACKSON
(Old Belvedere & (Queen's University & (Pontypool &   (Coventry &
Ireland)   Ireland)   Wales)   England)

K.J.F. SCOTLAND
(Cambridge University &
Scotland)

BRITISH ISLES

REFEREE: Mr C.R. Gillies (Waikato)
ATTENDANCE: 57,000
CONDITIONS: Weather fine, ground firm
HALFTIME: New Zealand 14, British Isles 8

SCORERS

NEW ZEALAND	BRITISH ISLES
Tries: Caulton (2), Meads, Urbahn	Try: Hewitt
Conversions: D.B. Clarke (2)	Conversion: Faull
Penalty goal: D.B. Clarke	Penalty goal: Faull
Dropped goal: D.B. Clarke	

215

19 September, 1959

Fourth Test

The New Zealand team for this final Test of the series included only one change. Adrian Clarke, who was unable to command a regular place in his provincial team, was chosen by the All Black selectors as second five-eighth instead of in his usual position of first five-eighth. Lineen and McMullen were each moved one place out but a chipped bone in his right shoulder suffered at training during the week before the match, prevented McMullen from playing. He was replaced by the first Test winger McPhail who, three weeks earlier, had scored a record seven tries for his province against the N.Z. Combined Services. Another defection from the New Zealand team occurred when the lock forward MacEwan withdrew suffering from a dose of measles and was replaced by Pickering from the reserves, who went on to the side of the scrum with Colin Meads taking MacEwan's locking position.

Four victories in the matches since the third Test saw the Lions approach the match in an optimistic mood. A convincing win over North Auckland by 35-13 on the previous Saturday encouraged the team's selectors to retain the backline that had performed so well in that match.

Jeeps had been suffering from a hip injury since the third Test and was not considered and the replacement halfback for the injured Scot, Stan Coughtrie, Irishman Andy Mulligan, took over behind the scrum.

Scotland, who had appeared in every backline position on tour with the exception of wing, was one of the centres for this match with the Welshman Davies taking the full-back berth.

In the forwards, a surprise omission was Gordon Wood who had been in excellent form in recent games. His replacement was the bulldozer driver from Pontypool, Ray Prosser. Roddy Evans had been forced to return home with a knee injury and his place was taken by Bill Mulcahy playing his only international on tour, whilst Murphy came in for Smith on the side of the scrum.

After a long, dry period in Auckland, the ground staff at Eden Park decided to water the concrete-like cricket pitch area on the afternoon before the match. However, on the morning of the match, heavy rain fell which left the field in a greasy state.

The Whangarei accountant, Mr Pat Murphy, officiating in the first of the thirteen internationals he was destined to control, set the game in motion at 2.30 with Ken Scotland kicking off. After missing two early attempts, Don Clarke put the first points on the board when he landed a 28 yard penalty in the ninth minute. Both Davies and Clarke missed further penalty attempts before the next points were registered.

In the thirtieth minute, O'Reilly came from the blindside into a backline movement following a line-out. Taking the ball outside Risman, he made a break up the middle of the field before unloading to Scotland with a long pass. The centre got the ball to Jackson about 35 yards from the All Black line and with a weaving, side-

NEW ZEALAND

D.B. CLARKE
(Waikato)

B.E. McPHAIL   T.R. LINEEN   R.W. CAULTON
(Canterbury)   (Auckland)   (Wellington)

A.H. CLARKE
(Auckland)

J.F. McCULLOUGH
(Taranaki)

R.J. URBAHN
(Taranaki)

R.J. CONWAY
(Otago)

E.A.R. PICKERING   S.F. HILL   C.E. MEADS   K.R. TREMAIN
(Waikato)   (Canterbury)   (King Country)   (Canterbury)

M.W. IRWIN   R.C. HEMI   W.J. WHINERAY (Capt.)
(Otago)   (Waikato)   (Auckland)

T.R. PROSSER   A.R. DAWSON (Capt.)   H.F. McLEOD
(Pontypool & Wales)   (Wanderers & Ireland)   (Hawick & Scotland)

N.A.A. MURPHY   W.A. MULCAHY   R.H. WILLIAMS   H.J. MORGAN
(Cork Constitution & Ireland)   (University College Dublin & Ireland)   (Llanelli & Wales)   (Abertillery & Wales)

J. FAULL
(Swansea & Wales)

A.A. MULLIGAN
(Wanderers & Ireland)

A.B.W. RISMAN
(Manchester University & England)

A.J.F.O'REILLY   D. HEWITT   K.J.F. SCOTLAND   P.B. JACKSON
(Old Belvedere & Ireland)   (Queen's University & Ireland)   (Cambridge University & Scotland)   (Coventry & England)

T.J. DAVIES
(Llanelli & Wales)

BRITISH ISLES

REFEREE: Mr J.P. Murphy (North Auckland)
ATTENDANCE: 60,000
CONDITIONS: Weather overcast after rain, ground slippery
HALFTIME: New Zealand 3, British Isles 3

SCORERS

NEW ZEALAND	BRITISH ISLES
Penalty goals: D.B. Clarke (2)	Tries: O'Reilly, Jackson, Risman

NEW ZEALAND

Eden Park, Auckland

stepping run he confounded the defence, finally diving over in the attempted tackle of Caulton right in the corner. Davies failed with the conversion. There was no further scoring in the half and the teams were tied at three all when the halftime whistle sounded.

The second half was only four minutes old when the Lions increased their score. Mulligan passed to O'Reilly on the blindside following a line-out maul near the New Zealand line. The winger had sufficient room to beat McPhail and score in the corner. This was his seventeenth try of the tour, a record for any tourist to New Zealand, beating the previous highest total of sixteen scored by Ken Jones in 1950. Davies had the misfortune to have the ball topple over as he ran in to convert and the kick went wide.

Five minutes later Mulcahy was adjudged off-side in front of his posts and Don Clarke had little trouble in equalling the scores from 24 yards out.

Davies was having a poor day with his kicking and missed two further penalty attempts before the final Lions' try came midway through the spell. From a scrum on the All Black 25, Mulligan and blindside wing O'Reilly made to run on the open side but the half-back passed to Bev Risman moving back towards him. The fly-half shot around the blindside of the scrum, beating McPhail with a side-step and eluding the All Black defence to dive over in the corner. Scotland, who introduced the 'round the corner' style of kicking to New Zealand at an international level, was given the kick but his attempt was no better than that of Davies, and the score remained at 9-6.

Over the last fifteen minutes the All Blacks threw everything into attack but the Lions' defence held. With five minutes remaining on the clock, Morgan fell off-side on the 25 and 15 yards in from touch. The crowd were hushed as Clarke lined up the kick, but the full-back who had already scored thirty-nine points in the series, hooked the ball badly across the face of the posts. The Lions held out for the remainder of the match to score the first Test victory by a British

Bev Risman dives to score a fine, solo try to put the Lions into the lead.

NZ RUGBY MUSEUM

team on tour in New Zealand since the first international of the 1930 tour.

It was a popular victory, for the Lions had been an unlucky side suffering many injuries and last minute losses in both the Dunedin and Wellington internationals.

Of the All Black team, Stan "Tiny" Hill announced his retirement following this game after eleven internationals since 1955. During the 1959 series he had drawn comment for wearing shoulder pads from the Lions' manager, Mr Alf Wilson. Subsequently these types of pads were outlawed from the game.

McCullough after three and Bruce McPhail after two internationals in this year were not called on again to represent their country. Urbahn, Pickering and Ron Hemi were all selected to tour with the 1960 All Black team but were not chosen to participate in the international series. Hemi had appeared in fifteen Tests since breaking into Test Rugby as a 20 year old in 1953.

SOUTH AFRICA 13

25 June, 1960

First Test

The New Zealanders went into this first international of the 1960 series with a record of six provincial victories and a draw with Natal behind them. A decisive 27-3 win over Northern Transvaal on the Saturday before the Test had established them as pre-match favourites.

Terry O'Sullivan was the only newcomer to international Rugby in the chosen side. Apart from Young and Watt, the remainder of the players had all appeared against the Lions the previous year.

Ron Hemi had severely damaged his rib ligaments in the Boland match, an injury that had made it necessary for a replacement to be flown from New Zealand. Although Hemi appeared in three minor fixtures towards the end of the tour he was not considered for any of the Tests in the series.

Six new caps were included in the Springbok side — the wings Hennie van Zyl and Michael Antelme, the halves Keith Oxlee and Dick Lockyear, number eight "Lofty" Nel and the lock, Avril Malan. Chris Koch, who had represented South Africa against New Zealand in 1949 and

Peter Jones bursts away with Nel and van Zyl covering. Conway and Briscoe follow the number eight.

NZ HERALD

NEW ZEALAND 0

Ellis Park, Johannesburg

1956, equalled the South African record of "Salty" du Rand in winning his twenty-first cap. Other survivors of the 1956 Test series in New Zealand were the captain Roy Dryburgh, centre Ian Kirkpatrick and lock Johan Claassen.

Don Clarke put the kick-off over the dead ball line on the first bounce, but from the 25 drop-out, the Springbok forwards stormed into the attack and carried play into All Black territory. Dryburgh missed a penalty from 30 yards out in the fourth minute. After ten minutes, Don Clarke claimed a fair catch 50 yards out from the posts and when the Springbok forwards charged too early the referee ruled 'no-charge'. But, in placing the ball, the kicker had overlooked the requirement of the law that this should be done by another member of the team, and the kick was declared void. However, from the resulting scrum a penalty to New Zealand was awarded but the big full-back could not land the goal.

The first points came in the twentieth minute from a scrum inside the All Black half. Lockyear

set his backline moving and Antelme was in from the blindside wing to take the pass from Oxlee and carve through the gap. Timing his pass to Kirkpatrick well, Antelme enabled the centre to draw Don Clarke before giving Hennie van Zyl a clear run-in to score behind the posts. Dryburgh had no trouble in converting and South Africa led 5-0. Although no further scoring occurred before halftime, it was obvious that South Africa were holding the initiative.

Dryburgh missed a 40 yard penalty early in the second half, from a scrum infringement. The All Blacks were giving the impression they were rattled when they committed a series of errors during the early part of the spell. The second try of the match came again in the twentieth minute of the half and was executed in a similar fashion to the previous one. Antelme again came in from the blindside wing following a scrum and drew the defence. The ball reached Hennie van Zyl with only Don Clarke in a position to impede his progress. The six foot three and a half inch left wing beat Clarke on the outside as he headed towards the line and the cover defence was unable to get across to prevent him scoring near the corner. Lockyear took the kick and raised the flags, to score the first of his eighteen points in the series.

Then, for the first time in the match, the All Blacks, led by their forwards, looked like wresting control from their opponents. However, desperate defence by South Africa kept their line intact. From a line-out penalty 35 yards out, Lockyear goaled his second kick of the match to complete the scoring fifteen minutes from no-side. Even if the defeat by thirteen points was the largest loss by a New Zealand team in an international since England had scored an identical win in 1936, there was some hope for the following Tests based on the All Black performance in the final twenty minutes.

This match had been the final international for both Peter Jones and Adrian Clarke. The North Auckland fisherman, Peter Jones, had played in eleven internationals since his debut in 1954, and had gained undying fame with his great try against South Africa at Auckland in 1956.

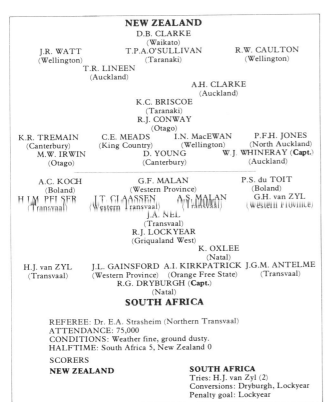

NEW ZEALAND

D.B. CLARKE
(Waikato)

J.R. WATT   T.P.A.O'SULLIVAN   R.W. CAULTON
(Wellington)   (Taranaki)   (Wellington)

T.R. LINEEN
(Auckland)

A.H. CLARKE
(Auckland)

K.C. BRISCOE
(Taranaki)

R.J. CONWAY
(Otago)

K.R. TREMAIN   C.E. MEADS   I.N. MacEWAN   P.F.H. JONES
(Canterbury)   (King Country)   (Wellington)   (North Auckland)

M.W. IRWIN   D. YOUNG   W.J. WHINERAY (Capt.)
(Otago)   (Canterbury)   (Auckland)

A.C. KOCH   G.F. MALAN   P.S. du TOIT
(Boland)   (Western Province)   (Boland)

H.J.M. PELSER   J.T. CLAASSEN   A.S. MALAN   G.H. van ZYL
(Transvaal)   (Western Transvaal)   (Transvaal)   (Western Province)

J.A. NEL
(Transvaal)

R.J. LOCKYEAR
(Griqualand West)

K. OXLEE
(Natal)

H.J. van ZYL   J.L. GAINSFORD   A.I. KIRKPATRICK   J.G.M. ANTELME
(Transvaal)   (Western Province)   (Orange Free State)   (Transvaal)

R.G. DRYBURGH (Capt.)
(Natal)

SOUTH AFRICA

REFEREE: Dr. E.A. Strasheim (Northern Transvaal)
ATTENDANCE: 75,000
CONDITIONS: Weather fine, ground dusty.
HALFTIME: South Africa 5, New Zealand 0

SCORERS
NEW ZEALAND

SOUTH AFRICA
Tries: H.J. van Zyl (2)
Conversions: Dryburgh, Lockyear
Penalty goal: Lockyear

23 July, 1960

Second Test

In the seven matches played between the first and second Tests, the All Blacks had won six and had gone down to Orange Free State by one point after scoring two tries to the Free State's three penalty goals. It was felt by many enthusiasts that the All Blacks would have their best opportunity of defeating the Springboks in this game, which was played at sea level.

New Zealand had made several changes to the side that had lost the Ellis Park Test. Peter Jones had pulled a groin muscle in the match against the Junior Springboks and Terry O'Sullivan was nursing a broken wrist. Neither could be considered for selection. Kevin Laidlaw came into the side in O'Sullivan's place and McMullen took over the left wing berth. Adrian Clarke, who was suffering from a shoulder injury, was replaced by Steve Nesbit, making his Test debut. In the forwards, Ian Clarke, John Graham and Ron Horsley supplanted the incumbents Irwin, Jones and Conway with Colin Meads taking the number eight position and Horsley partnering his team-mate from Wellington, MacEwan, as lock.

The Springboks made only one change to their team. The 1956 Test hooker, Bertus van der Merwe, won a place at the expense of Abe Malan to make it an all Boland front row.

Whineray won the toss for New Zealand and Oxlee put the ball into play. An early penalty to the tourists had Don Clarke putting the All Blacks on to attack. Watt was forced into touch inches from the corner as New Zealand mounted a movement through their backline. In the fourth minute, a further penalty was awarded to New Zealand only 32 yards from the Springbok posts when Koch appeared to be off-side at a ruck. To the unrestrained joy of the coloured section of the crowd, Don Clarke had no trouble in putting the All Blacks three points up.

Play see-sawed up and down the field, with both sides failing to capitalise on scoring chances, before the Springboks managed to equalise after twenty-six minutes. From a five-yard scrum, Lockyear ran wide before reverse-passing to Oxlee who was cutting in-field. The defence was caught napping and the fly-half dived over for a try amidst the grasping arms of the All Blacks. Dryburgh hooked the conversion badly.

Throughout the half the referee had considerable trouble with the packing of the front rows where du Toit was attempting to unsettle the New Zealanders. Mr Slabber also had to ask Meads and Hugo van Zyl to shake hands after feelings had run high following one incident. Just before halftime Gainsford crossed for South Africa only to be recalled for an earlier infringement. The teams changed around with the score still at three all.

In the second half, the All Black forwards played magnificently and gradually gained control but they were unable to add to their score until seven minutes from time. Earlier, Don Clarke had missed a comparatively easy penalty after van Zyl had come around a scrum too fast but this had been only a temporary lapse as the

NEW ZEALAND

D.B. CLARKE
(Waikato)

J.R. WATT   K.F. LAIDLAW   R.F. McMULLEN
(Wellington)   (Southland)   (Auckland)

T.R. LINEEN
(Auckland)

S.R. NESBIT
(Auckland)

K.C. BRISCOE
(Taranaki)

C.E. MEADS
(King Country)

D.J. GRAHAM   I.N. MacEWAN   R.H. HORSLEY   K.R. TREMAIN
(Canterbury)   (Wellington)   (Wellington)   (Canterbury)

I.J. CLARKE   D. YOUNG   W.J. WHINERAY (**Capt.**)
(Waikato)   (Canterbury)   (Auckland)

A.C. KOCH   A.J. van der MERWE   P.S. du TOIT
(Boland)   (Boland)   (Boland)

H.J.M. PELSER   J.T. CLAASSEN   A.S. MALAN   G.H. van ZYL
(Transvaal)   (Western Transvaal)   (Transvaal)   (Western Province)

J.A. NEL
(Transvaal)

R.J. LOCKYEAR
(Griqualand West)

K. OXLEE
(Natal)

H.J. van ZYL   J.L. GAINSFORD   A.I. KIRKPATRICK   J.G.M. ANTELME
(Transvaal)   (Western Province)   (Orange Free State)   (Transvaal)

R.G. DRYBURGH (**Capt.**)
(Natal)

SOUTH AFRICA

REFEREE: Mr M.J. Slabber (Transvaal)
ATTENDANCE: 45,250
CONDITIONS: Weather fine, ground firm
HALFTIME: New Zealand 3, South Africa 3

SCORERS

NEW ZEALAND	**SOUTH AFRICA**
Try: Meads	Try: Oxlee
Conversion: D.B. Clarke	
Penalty goal: D.B. Clarke	
Dropped goal: D.B. Clarke	

SOUTH AF ICA 3

Newlands, Cape Town

Briscoe gets his pass away despite the attentions of Pelser. Tremain, Nel and Whineray are the onlookers.

full-back was playing well and earned applause for some of his prodigious touch finding.

In the thirty-third minute, Nesbit kicked across towards the left hand corner where Antelme was taken by McMullen as he gathered the catch. As the ball spilled clear Laidlaw was on hand to gather and transfer to Lineen. When confronted by Dryburgh the five-eighth in-passed to Meads who had a clear run to the line to dot the ball down. Don Clarke converted with a good kick, to bring up his 100 points on tour. Four minutes later, the big full-back was on target again after he received the ball direct from Briscoe following a scrum 40 yards from the South African line and sent a left-footed drop kick goalwards. This successful kick raised another milestone for Clarke with his century of points in internationals, scored in only twelve appearances.

In the last few minutes Dryburgh failed with a

long range drop kick attempt then forewent a shot at goal from a penalty 38 yards from the posts in favour of an 'up and under'. This was to no avail and the All Blacks remained in front by 11-3 when the final whistle blew. This victory was New Zealand's first Test win on South African soil since 1928, and the All Blacks were acclaimed as being definitely the better side on the day.

It was the end of the international careers of three of the Springboks, all of whom had been tourists to New Zealand in 1956. Chris Koch, who had created a South African record of twenty-two caps, and his front row partner and Boland team-mate, hooker, van der Merwe, who had twelve international appearances, were considered too slow and both lost their places for the remaining Tests. Captain, Roy Dryburgh, who had been strongly criticised for monopolising the place-kicking despite his poor form, was another to incur the selectors' displeasure for the final two internationals.

NEW ZEALAND 11

13 August, 1960

Third Test

The only change in the New Zealand team for this Test was the replacement of Ian Clarke by MacEwan, with Meads moving from number eight to lock and Dick Conway returning to the side on the back of the scrum. Despite a surprise loss to the Combined Services, the All Blacks had continued to show good form and had recorded impressive victories over both Transvaal and Western Transvaal.

The Springbok selectors made four changes in their team. A major surprise was the selection of 27 year old Lionel Wilson at full-back in place of Dryburgh. Although not regarded as international material and having the disadvantage of not being a goal kicker, Wilson was nevertheless a sound and reliable full-back who was to fully justify the selectors' faith in him, going on to play twenty-seven internationals for his country. Abe Malan regained the hooker's berth, and Fanie Kuhn took over from Koch at prop. The only other change was at number eight where Doug Hopwood, who had appeared earlier in the year against the touring Scottish team, replaced Nel. Avril Malan became South Africa's youngest Test captain when he was appointed in Dryburgh's place. Born in April 1937, Malan was just four months past his twenty-third birthday.

This match was only the second Test to have been played at Bloemfontein; the previous one was the fifth test between Australia and South Africa in 1933. Whineray won the toss and Oxlee kicked off into a slight breeze. Early in the game the All Blacks tested the new 'Bok full-back with high kicks but Wilson proved to be a very sound player.

Both sides missed penalty attempts in the first sixteen minutes but Clarke had given a demonstration of his powerful kicking when he gained a full 80 yards with a line kick early in the game.

Briscoe turns to help his team-mate Watt who is held by Hennie van Zyl. Abe Malan and Pelser approach at right.

RAND DAILY MAIL

SOUTH AFRICA 11

Free State Stadium, Bloemfontein

The only points of the first half came in the twentieth minute when Lockyear landed a penalty from 38 yards after Tremain had been caught off-side at a scrum.

Within a minute of the restart, Clarke had equalled the scores after Lockyear had been penalised putting the ball into a scrum 48 yards out. The full-back's kick was on target from the time it left his boot. Only two minutes later, Lockyear regained the lead with a further penalty from 40 yards.

The first try came in the sixteenth minute of the spell. Briscoe had passed directly back to Clarke from a defensive scrum but the clearing kick was charged down by the Springbok flanker, Martin Pelser, and the ball had gone loose. Kirkpatrick gathered the rolling ball and eluded Lineen, then cut back in-field before linking on his right with Oxlee who went over between the posts. Lockyear's conversion gave the home side an 11-3 lead. Clarke sliced a penalty minutes later from 40 yards then Lineen was on to a kick

ahead by Briscoe which had bounced away from Wilson. A promising move was spoiled by the five-eighth not being able to link up with his supports. Lockyear missed two long range penalties and things were looking bad for New Zealand.

Six minutes from time, Clarke managed to put his side within striking distance of the Springbok score when he was successful with a penalty from five yards inside his own half. Throwing everything into attack, the All Blacks took play into the South African half where Whineray opted for a tap-kick from a penalty in an endeavour to gain the five points needed to save the match. With only ninety seconds remaining, the All Blacks won a ruck fifteen yards inside the Springbok half and Briscoe threw a desperate, hurried pass along the ground past Nesbit where it was picked up by Lineen who quickly fed Laidlaw. The centre ran through a gap before putting a kick towards the left hand corner where McMullen, sprinting past Antelme, gathered a favourable bounce and scored five yards in from the corner. As he lay still, ambulancemen ran to him but he soon recovered and Don Clarke placed the ball straight up and down for the vital conversion. His kick flew straight and true. Appropriately, his brother Ian, the touch judge for this match, signalled his success before the ball reached the posts.

Although the play had been cautious and dour, the sensational finish had elevated this match to one of the most memorable played between the two sides. It had perhaps been Don Clarke's greatest match and his two fine kicks in the last six minutes under extreme pressure, were well worthy of the most accomplished kicker the game had known.

Because of injury prior to the final Test, this had been Terry Lineen's last international. This incisive mid-field back had appeared in twelve internationals since 1957, though strangely had not scored a try in any of them. Steve Nesbit, who later went to the United States for some time was not destined to play any further Tests. Both Lineen and Nesbit were from the Marist club in Auckland.

NEW ZEALAND
D.B. CLARKE
(Waikato)

J.R. WATT	K.F. LAIDLAW	R.F. McMULLEN
(Wellington)	(Southland)	(Auckland)

T.R. LINEEN
(Auckland)

S.R. NESBIT
(Auckland)

K.C. BRISCOE
(Taranaki)

R.J. CONWAY
(Otago)

D.J. GRAHAM	C.E. MEADS	R.H. HORSLEY	K.R. TREMAIN
(Canterbury)	(King Country)	(Wellington)	(Canterbury)
I.N. MacEWAN	D. YOUNG		W.J. WHINERAY (**Capt.**)
(Wellington)	(Canterbury)		(Auckland)

S.P. KUHN	G.F. MALAN	P.S. du TOIT
(Transvaal)	(Western Province)	(Boland)
H.J.M. PELSER	J.T. CLAASSEN A.S. MALAN (**Capt.**)	G.H. van ZYL
(Transvaal)	(Western Transvaal) (Transvaal)	(Western Province)

D.J. HOPWOOD
(Western Province)

R.J. LOCKYEAR
(Griqualand West)

K. OXLEE
(Natal)

H.J. van ZYL	J.L. GAINSFORD	A.I. KIRKPATRICK	J.G.M. ANTELME
(Transvaal)	(Western Province)	(Orange Free State)	(Transvaal)

L.G. WILSON
(Western Province)

SOUTH AFRICA

REFEREE: Mr R.D. Burmeister (Western Province)
ATTENDANCE: 56,000
CONDITIONS: Weather fine and hot, ground hard
HALFTIME: South Africa 3, New Zealand 0

SCORERS

NEW ZEALAND	SOUTH AFRICA
Try: McMullen	Try: Oxlee
Conversion: Clarke	Conversion: Lockyear
Penalty goals: Clarke (2)	Penalty goals: Lockyear (2)

27 August, 1960

Fourth Test

An unconvincing display at Aliwal North, where North-Eastern Districts were beaten by 15-6 followed by a rather more satisfying performance against Border where a 30-3 victory resulted, was the All Blacks' record leading up to the crucial final Test.

A dislocated shoulder in the Border match had robbed New Zealand of the services of Terry Lineen. The selectors moved the existing back line in one place with Caulton, who had been out of favour since the first Test, coming in on the left wing. The selectors made two other changes, both of which were rather surprising. The young Aucklander, Tony Davies, who had featured in only four games on tour as a five-eighth, was preferred to Nesbit in the vital first five-eighth position. In a scrum reshuffle, Ian Clarke returned to the front row and the flanker, John Graham, whom many critics considered the All Blacks' most effective loose forward, was omitted.

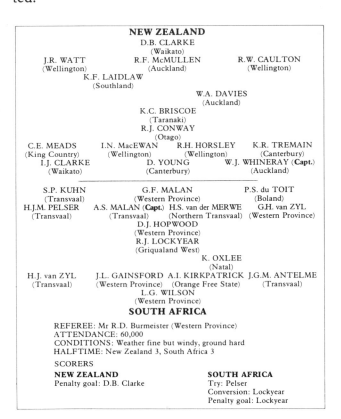

NEW ZEALAND
D.B. CLARKE (Waikato)
J.R. WATT (Wellington) — R.F. McMULLEN (Auckland) — R.W. CAULTON (Wellington)
K.F. LAIDLAW (Southland)
W.A. DAVIES (Auckland)
K.C. BRISCOE (Taranaki)
R.J. CONWAY (Otago)
C.E. MEADS (King Country) — I.N. MacEWAN (Wellington) — R.H. HORSLEY (Wellington) — K.R. TREMAIN (Canterbury)
I.J. CLARKE (Waikato) — D. YOUNG (Canterbury) — W.J. WHINERAY (Capt.) (Auckland)

S.P. KUHN (Transvaal) — G.F. MALAN (Western Province) — P.S. du TOIT (Boland)
H.J.M. PELSER (Transvaal) — A.S. MALAN (Capt.) (Transvaal) — H.S. van der MERWE (Northern Transvaal) — G.H. van ZYL (Western Province)
D.J. HOPWOOD (Western Province)
R.J. LOCKYEAR (Griqualand West)
K. OXLEE (Natal)
H.J. van ZYL (Transvaal) — J.L. GAINSFORD (Western Province) — A.I. KIRKPATRICK (Orange Free State) — J.G.M. ANTELME (Transvaal)
L.G. WILSON (Western Province)
SOUTH AFRICA

REFEREE: Mr R.D. Burmeister (Western Province)
ATTENDANCE: 60,000
CONDITIONS: Weather fine but windy, ground hard
HALFTIME: New Zealand 3, South Africa 3

SCORERS
NEW ZEALAND — Penalty goal: D.B. Clarke
SOUTH AFRICA — Try: Pelser — Conversion: Lockyear — Penalty goal: Lockyear

Only one change in the Springbok side was made when Engelbrecht, first capped against Scotland earlier in the year, replaced Antelme. However tonsilitis forced him to withdraw and Antelme was recalled. Claassen suffered a bad bruising of the left thigh in training and he withdrew on the morning of the match allowing "Stompie" van der Merwe, who had been flown down as a standby, to take his place and make the first of his five appearances for South Africa.

Malan won the toss and elected to play into the strong wind in the first half. It was obvious that New Zealand would have to hold a reasonable lead at halftime to stand a chance of taking the Test series. Davies missed an early dropped goal attempt, then McMullen set off on an elusive run down the left hand side and looked set to score when Oxlee managed to dive and hand trip him two yards short of the line. McMullen was on his feet instantly and went over to score what he thought was a try but Mr Burmeister, strangely, was of the opinion that it had been a tackled ball and awarded a penalty to South Africa.

Further dropped goal attempts by both Davies and Don Clarke went wide before New Zealand were awarded a penalty in the thirteenth minute,

NEW ZEALAND 3

Boet Erasmus Stadium, Port Elizabeth

30 yards out and 15 yards from touch. Clarke was successful with the kick and New Zealand went three points up. Six minutes later, the Springboks equalised when Lockyear goaled a 35 yard penalty with a well judged kick. No further scoring occurred in this spell and things looked ominous for New Zealand.

With the sun as well as the wind in their faces, the All Blacks were soon defending desperately. With seven minutes of the half gone, New Zealand had to concede a five yard scrum when Briscoe fired a wild pass from the base of the scrum near his own line. From the Springbok heel, the scrum was half wheeled and Pelser gathered the ball as it emerged and he plunged over unopposed. Lockyear's conversion from midway between the posts and the corner flag was successful. This was the final score of the match and the

series, although both Lockyear and Clarke missed further penalty attempts.

In the last few minutes, the All Blacks tried hard to come from behind as they had done at Bloemfontein and McMullen featured in several promising moves, all to no avail and the series belonged to South Africa who had shown themselves to be the better all-round team.

This tour saw the finish of several international careers in the All Black side. Among these were Frank McMullen, later to turn his attention to refereeing, who had played in eleven Tests and scored four tries, Kevin Laidlaw who had proved himself a most reliable centre and a fine tackler, and Ron Horsley who, although he again toured with the All Black team to Europe and America in 1963-64, did not gain Test selection. He had improved greatly on this tour and his three Tests were well deserved. Although he appeared in the All Black jersey on thirty-one occasions he did not play a single match for New Zealand in his own country.

In the middle of this confused gathering on the New Zealand line, Pelser has scored a try to clinch the series for the Springboks.

CENTRAL PRESS

NEW ZEALAND 13

22 July, 1961

First Test

This tour by the French team was not only the first to New Zealand by a French side but the first by an individual European country.

Andre Boniface was the sole survivor of the team which had defeated New Zealand in Paris in 1954. Since that time he had been in and out of the French team and had won fifteen caps. Also in the team was his brother Guy who partnered him in the centres.

Since defeating South Africa in a two match series in 1958, France had won the European International championship in 1959, shared it with England in 1960 and won it again in 1961. Despite winning only two of their four matches in New Zealand leading up to the first Test, it was expected that the French would severely extend the home side.

There were five new players in the New Zealand team. Des Connor had already played ten internationals for his native Australia, including all three against New Zealand in 1958. Since

shifting to Auckland early in 1960, he had quickly established himself as a vital part of the Ranfurly Shield holders' team.

Other newcomers were Victor Yates, an energetic and controversial number eight forward; Neil Wolfe, a brilliant 19 year old five-eighth; Don McKay, the first All Black from the North Shore club in its eighty-eight year history and Stan Meads, younger brother of Colin. The latter two replaced original selections Caulton and Tremain who withdrew with injuries.

A unique feature of this match was the appearance of two sets of brothers in the All Black team — the Meads and the Clarkes plus a further set in the French side.

Mr Allan Farquhar, who was refereeing the first of his six internationals, signalled the start of play and Don Clarke kicked deep to the left hand corner where the ball went dead. From the drop-out, a man was ruled in front and it was New Zealand's ball to the scrum. Connor ran on the blind after Young had hooked. He passed to

The two sets of brothers who appeared for New Zealand in this Test: Stan and Colin Meads, Don and Ian Clarke.

CROWN STUDIOS

NEW ZEALAND

D.B. CLARKE
(Waikato)

D.W. McKAY   T.P.A. O'SULLIVAN   J.R. WATT
(Auckland)   (Taranaki)   (Wellington)

R.H. BROWN
(Taranaki)

T.N. WOLFE
(Wellington)

D.M. CONNOR
(Auckland)

V.M. YATES
(North Auckland)

S.T. MEADS   C.E. MEADS   I.N. MacEWAN   D.J. GRAHAM
(King Country)   (King Country)   (Wellington)   (Canterbury)

I.J. CLARKE   D. YOUNG   W.J. WHINERAY (**Capt.**)
(Waikato)   (Canterbury)   (Auckland)

A. DOMENECH   J. LAUDOUAR   P. CAZALS
(C.A. Brive)   (A.S. Soustons)   (Stade Montois)

M. CRAUSTE   G. BOUGUYON   J.P. SAUX   F. MONCLA (**Capt.**)
(F.C. Lourdais)   (F.C. Grenoble)   (Section Paloise)   (Section Paloise)

M. CELAYA
(Stade Bordelais)

P. LACROIX
(S.U. Agen)

P. ALBALADEJO
(U.S. Dax)

G. CALVO   A. BONIFACE   G. BONIFACE   H. RANCOULE
(F.C. Lourdais)   (Stade Montois)   (Stade Montois)   (F.C. Lourdais)

M. VANNIER
(R.C. Chalon)

FRANCE

REFEREE: Mr A.B. Farquhar (Auckland)
ATTENDANCE: 60,000
CONDITIONS: Weather fine, ground firm
HALFTIME: France 6, New Zealand 5

SCORERS

NEW ZEALAND	FRANCE
Tries: McKay, O'Sullivan	Dropped goals: Albaladejo (2)
Conversions: D.B. Clarke (2)	
Dropped goal: D.B. Clarke	

226

FRANCE 6

Eden Park, Auckland

Whineray reaches for the ball with Young, MacEwan and Ian Clarke close at hand. The Frenchmen are Lacroix and Cazals.

Wolfe who drew Calvo before sending McKay away in the clear. The winger crossed for the try in the corner after shrugging off Vannier's tackle. It was a coincidence that the three new caps in the All Black back line, all handling the ball for the first time, engineered the try. Don Clarke converted from right by the touch-line with a fine kick to make it 5-0 to New Zealand after barely two minutes' play.

France went on to attack from the re-start and, after four minutes they won a line-out 10 yards from the All Black line and Albaladejo landed the first of his dropped goals. Ten minutes later he received the ball again from a line-out and repeated his earlier successful dropped goal to give France a one point lead. Although no

further scoring occurred in this half, both sides missed numerous penalty opportunities.

The start of the second half was almost as sensational as the first. From a scrum on the French 25 two minutes after the resumption, Young won a tighthead and Connor threw a long pass back to Don Clarke who slammed over a 40 yard dropped goal to regain the lead for New Zealand. The final scoring of the match came in the twenty-third minute after Guy Boniface dropped the ball in a passing rush inside his own half and O'Sullivan toed it ahead. He was favoured with a kind bounce to scamper away for a try 10 yards to the left of the posts. Clarke, who had not kicked well, managed to convert this try to complete the scoring. The French went close to scoring on several occasions but when the final whistle blew, the score remained unchanged.

227

5 August, 1961

Second Test

There were three changes in the New Zealand team for this match. The now fit Tremain regained his place on the side of the scrum and Caulton replaced Watt who was under suspension after being ordered off in a club match on the previous Saturday. When O'Sullivan was forced to withdraw with a sprained ankle, Paul Little came into the side to make his international debut. An incisive runner, Little also had the useful ability to run his wings into scoring positions.

The Frenchmen had beaten both Bay of Plenty and Manawatu since the first Test but had gone down 3-5 to the New Zealand Maori team at Napier in a rough match. Their selectors had made three changes in the backline and reshuffled the pack with one new man, Roland Lefevre, coming in to play at number eight.

During the night before the game, a southerly gale had developed and by morning the wind was raging with gusts up to 80 mph preventing the ship 'Canberra', on its maiden voyage, from berthing at Wellington. Consideration was given to postponing the match but finally the New Zealand Rugby Union decided that it should go ahead as scheduled.

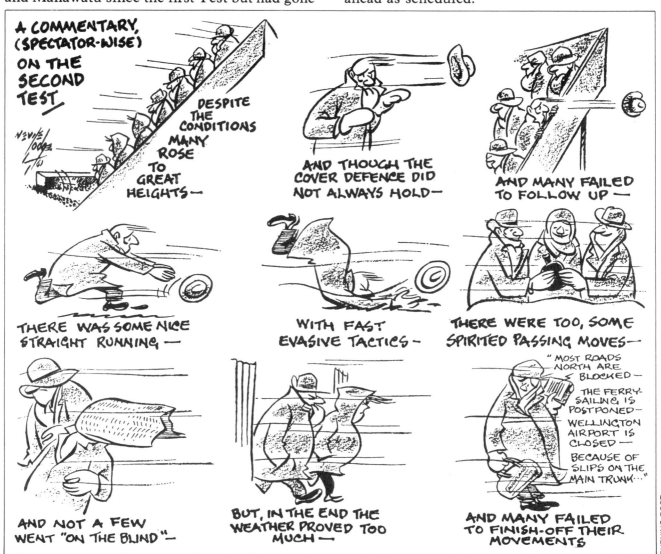

A COMMENTARY, (SPECTATOR-WISE) ON THE SECOND TEST

DESPITE THE CONDITIONS MANY ROSE TO GREAT HEIGHTS —

AND THOUGH THE COVER DEFENCE DID NOT ALWAYS HOLD—

AND MANY FAILED TO FOLLOW UP —

THERE WAS SOME NICE STRAIGHT RUNNING —

WITH FAST EVASIVE TACTICS –

THERE WERE TOO, SOME SPIRITED PASSING MOVES—

AND NOT A FEW WENT "ON THE BLIND"—

BUT, IN THE END THE WEATHER PROVED TOO MUCH —

"MOST ROADS NORTH ARE BLOCKED — THE FERRY SAILING IS POSTPONED— WELLINGTON AIRPORT IS CLOSED — BECAUSE OF SLIPS ON THE MAIN TRUNK…"

AND MANY FAILED TO FINISH-OFF THEIR MOVEMENTS

EVENING POST

FRANCE 3

Athletic Park, Wellington

Few hardy spectators braved the upper deck of the recently-finished Millard Stand as Brown kicked off for New Zealand after Moncla had won the toss and elected to play with the gale at his back. Although France, as expected, were soon camped inside All Black territory, some magnificent play by the All Black forwards, with MacEwan dominating the line-outs, kept them from scoring. Such was the dominance of the pack that Whineray was able to drop Graham back to a position of second full-back to strengthen the defence. Moncla, in an endeavour to put points on the board, neglected to take shots at goal from penalties near the New Zealand line, opting for tap kicks but the points did not come and at halftime there was no score.

After such a dominating first half, it was ex-

pected that the All Blacks would win the match comfortably but this was not to be the case. Early in the spell, Meads crossed for what appeared to be a try but the referee was unsighted, then Don Clarke attempted a penalty from inside his own half with brother Ian holding the ball to prevent it toppling but the kick was wide. A little later he missed what looked like a simple chance from only 20 yards but in the prevailing weather conditions, no kick was simple and the ball again went wide.

With fifteen minutes to play, a try finally came, not to New Zealand but to France. A pass from Connor had missed Wolfe 30 yards from the French line and before Wolfe could recover the loose ball, Pique had grabbed it and was making up-field. Bearing left, he drew McKay in-field before tossing a pass to the now unmarked Dupuy who bolted the last 40 yards to the line, scoring eight yards in from the left corner. Albaladejo failed with the almost impossible task of converting into the teeth of the gale.

From the restart McKay narrowly missed scoring but, from a scrum on the French line, Lacroix passed back to Lacaze to clear. The full-back's kick was charged down by Tremain who fell on the ball to score 10 yards in from the corner. Don Clarke took the conversion attempt back to the 25 and kicked almost parallel to the goal line for the wind to catch the ball and miraculously carry it over the bar to give New Zealand the lead and cruelly dash the French hopes.

For the last twelve minutes both sides attacked and counter-attacked. Clarke had an abortive shot at goal from well out but no further scoring occurred and a quite remarkable Test match ended with New Zealand perhaps fortunate to have carried the day.

Like the All Blacks in the first half, the French had defended magnificently in the second half.

NEW ZEALAND
D.B. CLARKE
(Waikato)
D.W. McKAY   P.F. LITTLE   R.W. CAULTON
(Auckland)   (Auckland)   (Wellington)
R.H. BROWN
(Taranaki)
T.N. WOLFE
(Wellington)
D.M. CONNOR
(Auckland)
V.M. YATES
(North Auckland)
D.J. GRAHAM   I.N. MacEWAN   C.E. MEADS   K.R. TREMAIN
(Canterbury)   (Wellington) (King Country) (Canterbury)
I.J. CLARKE   D. YOUNG   W.J. WHINERAY (Capt.)
(Waikato)   (Canterbury)   (Auckland)

A. DOMENECH   J. LAUDOUAR   G. BOUGUYON
(C.A. Brive)   (A.S. Soustons)   (F.C. Grenoble)
M. CRAUSTE   M. CELAYA   J.P. SAUX   F. MONCLA (Capt.)
(F.C. Lourdais) (Stade Bordelais) (Selection Paloise) (Selection Paloise)
R. LEFEVRE
(C.A. Brive)
P. LACROIX
(S.U. Agen)
P. ALBALADEJO
(U.S. Dax)
J. DUPUY   G. BONIFACE   J. PIQUE   H. RANCOULE
(Stade Tarbais) (Stade Montois) (Selection Paloise) (F.C. Lourdais)
C. LACAZE
(F.C. Lourdais)
FRANCE

REFEREE: Mr A.B. Farquhar (Auckland)
ATTENDANCE: 35,000
CONDITIONS: Weather 80mph gale, ground heavy
HALFTIME: New Zealand 0, France 0

SCORERS
NEW ZEALAND   **FRANCE**
Try: Tremain   Try: Dupuy
Conversion: D.B. Clarke

19 August, 1961

Third Test

It was surprising, in view of their performance in the second Test at Wellington, that the French team found it necessary to make five alterations to the team to contest this final international. Wins over both Southland and Otago had been followed by a surprise loss to South Canterbury, despite the tourists scoring four tries to the home side's two. In the matches since the Athletic Park Test, Albaladejo had been forced to withdraw with a throat infection whilst Dupuy was troubled with a thigh injury.

The only change in the All Black side saw Watt come back into the team after his period of suspension.

Mr Farquhar had the distinction of being chosen again to control the match — the first time a referee had been honoured in New Zealand by refereeing all internationals in a series.

Whineray won the toss and chose to play into the bright sun. Two minutes after the start, New Zealand won a line-out ruck on their own 25. Wolfe made a half-break before passing to Brown who beat Guy Boniface with a dummy and cut back infield linking with Yates on the French 10 yard line. Young was there to take Yates's pass and transfer to Connor who took play into the French 25 before Graham received the ball and covered the remaining few yards to the line where he scored five yards in from the corner flag. Clarke struck the ball well to raise the flags and put New Zealand up by five points.

Two minutes later, Guy Boniface received the ball following a line-out inside the New Zealand 25 and ran back into the forwards dodging and weaving. He was finally caught in the corner but slipped the ball to Crauste to score. Camberabero's kick failed.

Half of the spell had gone when Connor broke from a scrum where Young had won a tighthead. As the defence closed around him, Connor threw a long over-hand pass to Little who ran hard to score 10 yards in from the corner. Clarke, in fine form with his boot, converted from the wide angle.

Both sides were opening up play whenever they had the opportunity and provided the spectators with some thrilling Rugby. Just before halftime, Clarke landed a 50 yard penalty to make the score 13-3 at the break.

Five minutes after the resumption, Little was dangerously tackled and Don Clarke's kick from 50 yards hit the cross-bar and bounced over. Three minutes later, New Zealand were awarded a scrum penalty right on the French line and, when a quick tap kick was taken, Tremain dived over through a mass of players. Clarke was again on target with his conversion. The All Blacks were firmly in control although the French were still showing flashes of brilliance.

The next points came in the twelfth minute, from a further Clarke penalty, this time from a range of only 15 yards.

After half an hour, Tremain burst from a line-out inside the French 25 before transferring to Meads who scored in the corner. Clarke again converted to make the score 27-3.

NEW ZEALAND
D.B. CLARKE
(Waikato)

D.W. McKAY   P.F. LITTLE   J.R. WATT
(Auckland)   (Auckland)   (Wellington)
R.H. BROWN
(Taranaki)

T.N. WOLFE
(Wellington)
D.M. CONNOR
(Auckland)
V.M. YATES
(North Auckland)

D.J. GRAHAM   I.N. MacEWAN   C.E. MEADS   K.R. TREMAIN
(Canterbury)   (Wellington)   (King Country)   (Canterbury)
I.J. CLARKE   D. YOUNG   W.J. WHINERAY (**Capt.**)
(Waikato)   (Canterbury)   (Auckland)

A. DOMENECH   J. ROLLET   G. BOUGUYON
(C.A. Brive)   (Aviron Bayonnais)   (F.C. Grenoble)
M. CRAUSTE   M. CASSIEDE   J.P. SAUX   F. MONCLA (**Capt.**)
(F.C. Lourdais)   (U.S. Dax)   (Selection Paloise)   (Selection Paloise)
M. CELAYA
(Stade Bordelais)
P. LACROIX
(S.U. Agen)
G. CAMBERABERO
(La Voulte)
G. CALVO   A. BONIFACE   G. BONIFACE   J. PIQUE
(F.C. Lourdais)   (Stade Montois)   (Stade Montois)   (Selection Paloise)
C. LACAZE
(F.C. Lourdais)
FRANCE

REFEREE: Mr A.B. Farquhar (Auckland)
ATTENDANCE: 57,000
CONDITIONS: Weather fine, ground firm
HALFTIME: New Zealand 13, France 3
SCORERS

NEW ZEALAND	**FRANCE**
Tries: Graham, Little, Tremain,	Try: Crauste
Meads, Yates	
Conversions: D.B. Clarke (4)	
Penalty goals: D.B. Clarke (3)	

FRANCE 3

Lancaster Park, Christchurch

Calvo brings down Little in a tackle which was ruled illegal. From the penalty, Clarke's kick hit the cross bar and bounced over for a goal.

In the dying minutes of the game, New Zealand won a scrum five yards from the French line and Connor threw a long pass across the field to Yates standing off the scrum. The number eight cut through at an angle to score between the posts and Clarke had no trouble in converting to complete the scoring.

Don Clarke, who had shown outstanding goal-kicking form in this match, scored seventeen points — only one short of his own record scored against the Lions in 1959.

The French team, whilst showing brilliant form at times, were far too inconsistent throughout their tour to do themselves justice. Poor goal-kicking had been a source of worry to the team and, in the thirteen tour matches, only nine of the thirty-two tries had been converted. The total of successful penalty goals was only four, half the number of dropped goals scored. By comparison, Don Clarke had kicked a total of forty-two points in his four matches against the tourists.

This match was the last international played by Victor Yates. He toured Australia the following year with the All Blacks and later turned to League.

231

26 May, 1962

First Test

In 1962, for the first time, a home and away series of internationals between Australia and New Zealand was arranged. The All Blacks toured in May and June with the Wallabies returning the visit towards the end of the season.

On the Saturday preceding the first Test, New South Wales had defeated the tourists 12-11, and although the All Blacks had scored the only two tries in the match, there were high hopes that Australia would inflict their first defeat on an All Black team at home since 1934.

The All Black team contained three new caps — winger Rod Heeps, the national 100 yards sprint champion; Bruce Watt, a first five-eighth from the Christchurch club and Waka Nathan, who had played impressively on the side of the scrum for the Ranfurly Shield holders, Auckland. Nathan's international career was to extend until 1967.

It was unfortunate that the Wallaby captain,

Nathan, with a typically probing run, is pursued by Wallaby flanker Heinrich.

Jim Lenehan, who had inspired New South Wales' victory the previous week, was forced to withdraw with a knee injury. This necessitated a reshuffle in the Australian back line with Rod Phelps going to the vacant full-back position and local winger Lloyd McDermott taking Phelps's place on the wing. In the forwards another original selection, Heming, withdrew and was replaced by the 22 year old Queenslander Paul Perrin. Perrin, who was a son of Tom Perrin, a 1931 Australian international against New Zealand, was playing his only Test.

Another interesting feature of the match was the appearance of former Wallaby half-back Des Connor behind the All Black scrum. Connor had played all three Tests for Australia against New Zealand in 1958, and a total of ten altogether.

The Australian team took the field in gold jerseys for the first time, instead of their traditional green. The new colour had been adopted because of the clash with both South Africa and Ireland.

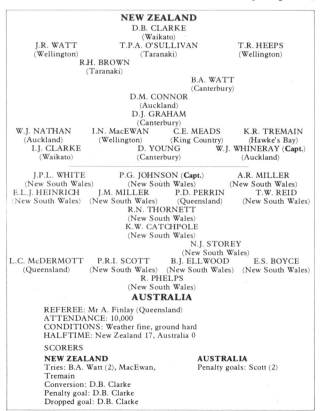

NEW ZEALAND
D.B. CLARKE
(Waikato)

| J.R. WATT (Wellington) | T.P.A. O'SULLIVAN (Taranaki) | T.R. HEEPS (Wellington) |

R.H. BROWN
(Taranaki)

B.A. WATT
(Canterbury)

D.M. CONNOR
(Auckland)

D.J. GRAHAM
(Canterbury)

| W.J. NATHAN (Auckland) | I.N. MacEWAN (Wellington) | C.E. MEADS (King Country) | K.R. TREMAIN (Hawke's Bay) |

| I.J. CLARKE (Waikato) | D. YOUNG (Canterbury) | W.J. WHINERAY (**Capt.**) (Auckland) |

| J.P.L. WHITE (New South Wales) | P.G. JOHNSON (**Capt.**) (New South Wales) | A.R. MILLER (New South Wales) |

| E.L.J. HEINRICH (New South Wales) | J.M. MILLER (New South Wales) | P.D. PERRIN (Queensland) | T.W. REID (New South Wales) |

R.N. THORNETT
(New South Wales)

K.W. CATCHPOLE
(New South Wales)

N.J. STOREY
(New South Wales)

| L.C. McDERMOTT (Queensland) | P.R.I. SCOTT (New South Wales) | B.J. ELLWOOD (New South Wales) | E.S. BOYCE (New South Wales) |

R. PHELPS
(New South Wales)
AUSTRALIA

REFEREE: Mr A. Finlay (Queensland)
ATTENDANCE: 10,000
CONDITIONS: Weather fine, ground hard
HALFTIME: New Zealand 17, Australia 0
SCORERS

NEW ZEALAND	**AUSTRALIA**
Tries: B.A. Watt (2), MacEwan, Tremain	Penalty goals: Scott (2)
Conversion: D.B. Clarke	
Penalty goal: D.B. Clarke	
Dropped goal: D.B. Clarke	

AUSTRALIA 6

Exhibition Ground, Brisbane

After eighteen minutes, Connor passed back to D.B. Clarke from a scrum and the full-back drop-kicked a left-footed goal. A minute later, McDermott mulled a high kick near his own goal line and Bruce Watt was on hand to secure and run over for a try in the corner. Clarke was unable to convert but shortly after he landed a 28 yard penalty.

Another defensive lapse by Australia in the thirty-fifth minute let new-comer Watt in for his second try when Phelps allowed a kick through by New Zealand to bounce unfavourably away from him. Clarke converted this try but missed a further attempt when MacEwan scored on the stroke of halftime following a maul in the Australian goalmouth.

Connor dive passes watched by Graham, Reid, Heinrich, Tremain and J. Miller. Graham appears to be blocking Reid's progress.

With a 17-0 lead at halftime, the All Blacks appeared to be heading for a large win. However, in the second half play became indecisive and the Australian centre Peter Scott kicked penalty goals from 20 and 40 yards early in the spell to reduce the leeway. Both back lines were using the kick to touch excessively and, as a spectacle, the game became rather dull.

With ten minutes to play, Tremain charged down a clearing kick and Meads and he took the ball ahead at toe for Tremain to score wide out. Clarke again was unable to land the conversion.

There was never much doubt about New Zealand's superiority in this match with the forwards especially completely dominating their opponents. It was Ross Brown's last international. Since his debut in 1955 he had played in sixteen Tests and had scored three tries and a dropped goal.

NEW Z ALAND 1²

4 June, 1962

Second Test

Since the first Test, the All Blacks had run up a record 103-0 victory over a Northern New South Wales side at Quirindi. This match saw the New Zealanders scoring twenty-two tries, including eight by left winger Rod Heeps — an individual try scoring record for an All Black. On the Saturday before the Test (which was played on the Queen's Birthday holiday), Newcastle went down to the tourists 29-6.

Ross Brown had torn a leg muscle during the match at Newcastle and was replaced by the first Test centre, Terry O'Sullivan. Paul Little, following an impressive match at Quirindi, was brought into the side as was first five-eighth Neil Wolfe.

The Australian team underwent several

Meads gets up to gather the ball in this line-out. Other All Blacks are Nathan, MacEwan, Ian Clarke, Whineray and Young.

AUSTRALIA 5

changes from that which lined up in the Test at Brisbane. Lenehan and Heming, restored to fitness, were brought in to the side at full-back and back row respectively. Ellwood moved from the centres to five-eighth in place of Storey with Dick Marks being selected for the vacant centre berth. John Thornett was joined by his younger brother Dick in the middle of the scrum and O'Gorman replaced Reid on the side of the scrum. On the morning of the match, Marks was forced to withdraw with gastric trouble and was replaced by Rod Phelps.

Australia kicked off and went on to attack early in the half. However, it was Don Clarke who put the first points on the board with a successful penalty in the seventh minute. Within minutes, the Wallabies had taken the lead when Dick Thornett threw his sixteen stone frame over for a try from a line-out near the New Zealand goal line and Scott converted.

In the twenty-eighth minute came a turning point of the game when Clarke placed the ball for an attempted penalty seven yards inside the All

McDermott cannot prevent Watt's try in the corner.

(vertical caption: SYDNEY MORNING HERALD)

Black half. The jeers from the 'Hill' turned to unrestrained cheering as the ball comfortably cleared the bar. It was estimated that the ball carried, from kick to the pitch, some 72 yards.

Though the Australians continued to attack and went close on two or three occasions, halftime was reached with no further addition to the score.

Early in the second half, the All Blacks strengthened their hold on the match with two quick tries. From the kick off, the ball was taken by Tremain who in-passed to Ian Clarke for the prop to make 15 yards before centre-kicking to the Wallaby goal mouth. Lenehan was unable to gather the ball cleanly and Nathan was on hand to take the ball and score. Clarke converted to give New Zealand an 11-5 lead.

Eight minutes later, Connor made a blindside break before unloading to Wolfe who timed his pass to the flying Watt well, and the winger went over in the corner. Clarke failed with the attempted conversion. New Zealand were taking a firm grip on the game as their forwards started to dominate the Wallaby pack but for the remaining half hour no further scoring was recorded.

NEW ZEALAND

D.B. CLARKE
(Waikato)

J.R. WATT   P.F. LITTLE   T.R. HEEPS
(Wellington)   (Auckland)   (Wellington)

T.P.A. O'SULLIVAN
(Taranaki)

T.N. WOLFE
(Wellington)

D.M. CONNOR
(Auckland)

D.J. GRAHAM
(Canterbury)

W.J. NATHAN   I.N. MacEWAN   C.E. MEADS   K.R. TREMAIN
(Auckland)   (Wellington)   (King Country)   (Hawke's Bay)

I.J. CLARKE   D. YOUNG   W.J. WHINERAY (**Capt.**)
(Waikato)   (Canterbury)   (Auckland)

J.P.L. WHITE   P.G. JOHNSON   A.R. MILLER
(New South Wales)   (New South Wales)   (New South Wales)

E.L.J. HEINRICH   R.N. THORNETT   J.E. THORNETT   J.F. O'GORMAN
(New South Wales)   (New South Wales)   (New South Wales)   (New South Wales)

R.J. HEMING
(New South Wales)

K.W. CATCHPOLE
(New South Wales)

B.J. ELLWOOD
(New South Wales)

L.C. McDERMOTT   P.R.I. SCOTT   R. PHELPS   E.S. BOYCE
(Queensland)   (New South Wales)   (New South Wales)   (New South Wales)

J.K.M. LENEHAN (**Capt.**)
(New South Wales)

AUSTRALIA

REFEREE: Dr. I.R. Vanderfield (New South Wales)
ATTENDANCE: 28,206
CONDITIONS: Weather overcast, ground firm
HALFTIME: New Zealand 6, Australia 5

SCORERS

NEW ZEALAND	AUSTRALIA
Tries: Nathan, Watt	Try: R.N. Thornett
Conversion: D.B. Clarke	Conversion: Scott
Penalty goals: D.B. Clarke (2)	

NEW ZEALAND 9

25 August, 1962

First Test

The twenty-five man Australian touring team was led by John Thornett whose international career had commenced in 1955. All four matches preceding the first international of the tour were won by the tourists, and although the All Blacks were firm favourites, some hope was held for a bold showing being made by the Wallabies.

The Australian selectors chose seven new caps in the original selection but one of these, centre Bruce Harland later withdrew and was replaced by Victorian Jim Douglas, also winning his first cap, who went on to the wing, with Boyce taking a centre berth. The surprises of the selection were the inclusion of Ken McMullen ahead of established half-back Catchpole and the omission of the big, fast forward Peter Crittle.

In the New Zealand team the selectors had chosen two new caps, winger John Morrissey and second five-eighth Ray Moreton who had come in to the team undoubtedly because Russell Watt, Don McKay and Ross Brown, were all on the injured list at selection time.

Don Clarke attempts to burst through the tackle of the Australian winger, Walsham.

After both teams had been introduced to the Prime Minister, Mr Keith Holyoake, the ball was put into play by Don Clarke. The first half was one of missed opportunities by both sides, with Lenehan and Clarke being unable to land any of the penalty attempts, and poor handling spoiling several promising movements.

Three minutes before halftime, a clearing kick by Lenehan was charged down, and right winger Morrissey won the race to the ball, touching down for the try deep in the Australian in-goal and inches from touch-in-goal. Clarke's conversion attempt was to the left of the posts. On the call of halftime Chapman missed a 28 yard penalty and the score was 3-0 in favour of the All Blacks at the break.

Despite the All Blacks being on attack for the opening ten minutes of the second half, it was Australia who scored next when Chapman raised the flags with a 35 yard penalty, to even the score

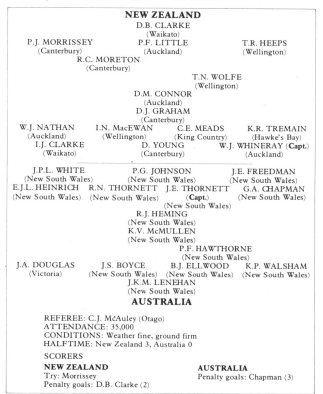

NEW ZEALAND

D.B. CLARKE
(Waikato)

P.J. MORRISSEY   P.F. LITTLE   T.R. HEEPS
(Canterbury)   (Auckland)   (Wellington)

R.C. MORETON
(Canterbury)

T.N. WOLFE
(Wellington)

D.M. CONNOR
(Auckland)

D.J. GRAHAM
(Canterbury)

W.J. NATHAN   I.N. MacEWAN   C.E. MEADS   K.R. TREMAIN
(Auckland)   (Wellington)   (King Country)   (Hawke's Bay)

I.J. CLARKE   D. YOUNG   W.J. WHINERAY (Capt.)
(Waikato)   (Canterbury)   (Auckland)

J.P.L. WHITE   P.G. JOHNSON   J.E. FREEDMAN
(New South Wales)   (New South Wales)   (New South Wales)

E.J.L. HEINRICH   R.N. THORNETT   J.E. THORNETT   G.A. CHAPMAN
(New South Wales) (New South Wales) (Capt.)   (New South Wales)
                                 (New South Wales)

R.J. HEMING
(New South Wales)

K.V. McMULLEN
(New South Wales)

P.F. HAWTHORNE
(New South Wales)

J.A. DOUGLAS   J.S. BOYCE   B.J. ELLWOOD   K.P. WALSHAM
(Victoria)   (New South Wales) (New South Wales) (New South Wales)

J.K.M. LENEHAN
(New South Wales)

AUSTRALIA

REFEREE: C.J. McAuley (Otago)
ATTENDANCE: 35,000
CONDITIONS: Weather fine, ground firm
HALFTIME: New Zealand 3, Australia 0

SCORERS

NEW ZEALAND   **AUSTRALIA**
Try: Morrissey   Penalty goals: Chapman (3)
Penalty goals: D.B. Clarke (2)

AUSTRALIA 9

Athletic Park, Wellington

in the eleventh minute of the half. Clarke missed a further penalty before Chapman again goaled from 33 yards to give Australia the lead with nineteen minutes to play.

Five minutes later, Clarke recorded his first successful kick of the day from a line-out penalty 40 yards out.

A good attacking move by the Wallabies saw Heeps unable to field a kick through by McMullen. From the resultant desperate defence by New Zealand, Clarke was forced to concede a five yard scrum. New Zealand were penalised in the scrum and Chapman, taking the ball back to just outside the 25, again put Australia into the lead with a good goal.

Morrissey's progress is halted by Lenehan's head-on tackle.

In the last five minutes New Zealand attacked desperately. Moreton toed the ball to the Wallaby line only to see the ball booted away as he was diving to score, then Little made a break but the pass to Morrissey with the line wide open was put down. With a minute to no-side, Clarke placed the goal to even the scores. Mr McAuley's whistle for full time sounded immediately after and the All Blacks left the field fortunate that they had forced a draw at the last moment.

Probably the best player on the field was the Australian full-back Jim Lenehan who had impressed with some prodigious line kicking. He had made his international debut as a 19 year old on the 1957-58 tour of the Northern hemisphere and had developed into one of Australia's finest players.

NEW ZEALAND 3

8 September, 1962

Second Test

The New Zealand selectors made sweeping changes in their team for this match. Seasoned internationals Ian Clarke, Dennis Young, Kelvin Tremain and Colin Meads were dropped from the forwards and a new pair of five-eighths in Bruce Watt and Tony Davies was introduced to the team. The replacement forwards were Keith Nelson, a dentistry student at Otago University, at number eight, making his international debut; Stan Meads, replacing his brother at lock, and the Canterbury pair, hooker John Creighton and prop Jules LeLievre who had toured Australia earlier in the year and who were making their only Test appearances. Paul Little

withdrew from the team with an injury prior to the match and was replaced by first Test second five-eighth Ray Moreton.

The Australian team had lost two of their three matches since the first Test, but these losses were by narrow margins and the side was confident they could carry the day. Surprise first Test omissions, Catchpole and Crittle were brought into the team, and Dick Marks was included in the centres with Jim Boyce moving to the left wing.

New Zealand won the toss and chose to play

Morrissey watches Bruce Watt kick to touch from one of the sawdust areas on the field.

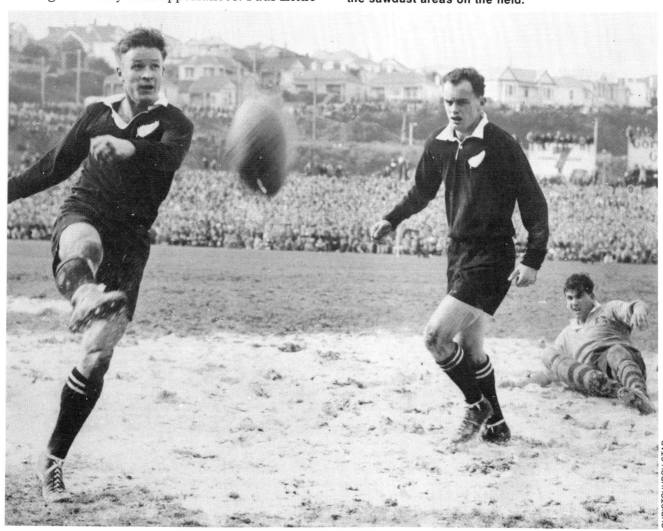

238

AUSTRALIA 0

Carisbrook, Dunedin

with the sun at their backs. Ellwood kicked off for Australia but the kick failed to reach the ten yard mark. The early part of the match was dominated by a series of line-outs and penalty kicks. From one of these penalties, Lenehan attempted a drop kick from a mark nine yards inside the All Black half but the kick was wide of the posts. Two minutes later, Chapman missed a further penalty from near touch on the New Zealand 25. As the spell progressed it became apparent that the All Black forwards were finding it difficult to match their opponents.

Lenehan attempted a further shot from a penalty 48 yards out after quarter of an hour but this kick was also wide of the mark. Midway through the half the All Black forwards made a bold bid to score with Meads being brought down two yards from the goal line. Clarke, who had earlier missed an attempt at goal from a penalty, missed a further kick from 35 yards out in the twenty-second minute.

Immediately following this it was Australia's turn to mount a strong attack. It started with a determined burst by Dick Thornett from inside his 25. When confronted at half-way he kicked ahead and had the New Zealand defence well stretched. Morrissey got to the ball first and was wrapped up in a maul but the ball came back to the Wallabies and only over-eagerness prevented a certain try when Catchpole was penalised for playing a tackled ball. As the spell came to an end, the All Blacks got the ball back to Clarke from a line-out but the full-back's left footed dropped goal attempt was just wide of the posts. Lenehan added to his list of missed penalties in the fortieth minute when his left footed drop kick from 40 yards was wide.

On the resumption of play the match went through a quiet period until the twelfth minute when Clarke, with a fine kick from a line-out penalty 40 yards out, landed the goal to record the only points of the match. He missed a further shot five minutes later and then Chapman missed two attempts from handy positions. Fifteen minutes from the end, Clarke placed the ball for a shot at goal on his own 10 yard mark. The crowd gave him a tremendous cheer as the ball passed a

yard outside the upright. The Australians, in a desperate bid to snatch victory, bombarded the All Blacks with a series of high kicks as the sun came out from behind a cloud. One of the game's brightest moments came two minutes from time when Heeps made a brilliant 65 yard run from near his own goal line using his great pace combined with tricky footwork, before the movement was snuffed out. The game came to an end with the All Blacks on attack.

Once again the All Blacks had depended on the powerful boot of Don Clarke to win this rather dull match. In this second international he had played on Carisbrook, he again contributed all his side's points as he had done in 1959 against the Lions. The Wallaby pack had outplayed the rather makeshift New Zealand eight and it was obvious some of the experienced forwards dropped for this match would have to be recalled. This match brought together for the first time in international play the Australian inside back combination of Catchpole and Phil Hawthorne who later played many fine games for their country.

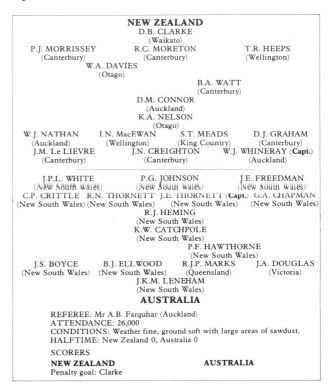

NEW ZEALAND
D.B. CLARKE
(Waikato)

P.J. MORRISSEY   R.C. MORETON   T.R. HEEPS
(Canterbury)   (Canterbury)   (Wellington)
W.A. DAVIES
(Otago)

B.A. WATT
(Canterbury)
D.M. CONNOR
(Auckland)
K.A. NELSON
(Otago)

W.J. NATHAN   I.N. MacEWAN   S.T. MEADS   D.J. GRAHAM
(Auckland)   (Wellington)   (King Country)   (Canterbury)
J.M. Le LIEVRE   J.N. CREIGHTON   W.J. WHINERAY (Capt.)
(Canterbury)   (Canterbury)   (Auckland)

J.P.L. WHITE   P.G. JOHNSON   J.E. FREEDMAN
(New South Wales)   (New South Wales)   (New South Wales)
C.P. CRITTLE   R.N. THORNETT   J.E. THORNETT (Capt.)   G.A. CHAPMAN
(New South Wales) (New South Wales)   (New South Wales)   (New South Wales)
R.J. HEMING
(New South Wales)
K.W. CATCHPOLE
(New South Wales)
P.F. HAWTHORNE
(New South Wales)

J.S. BOYCE   B.J. ELLWOOD   R.J.P. MARKS   J.A. DOUGLAS
(New South Wales)   (New South Wales)   (Queensland)   (Victoria)
J.K.M. LENEHAM
(New South Wales)
AUSTRALIA

REFEREE: Mr A.B. Farquhar (Auckland)
ATTENDANCE: 26,000
CONDITIONS: Weather fine, ground soft with large areas of sawdust.
HALFTIME: New Zealand 0, Australia 0
SCORERS
NEW ZEALAND   **AUSTRALIA**
Penalty goal: Clarke

NEW ZEALAND 16

22 September, 1962

Third Test

Following the second international, the Wallabies had gone down to both Southland and Thames Valley but had recorded a clear cut victory over Wanganui on the preceding Saturday. The only change in their side was brought about by an injury to Catchpole, who was replaced by the red-headed half-back from Wagga, Ken McMullen.

The New Zealand selectors, N.J. McPhail, J. Finlay and R.G. Bush, continued to ring the changes in the All Black team. A major surprise was the dropping of lock forward, Nev MacEwan, a veteran of twenty internationals, who made way for the return of Colin Meads to partner his brother Stan. Other changes in the forwards saw the return of Dennis Young as hooker and the introduction of a new front row prop from the Manukau club in Auckland, Barry Thomas.

Another new cap was "Mac" Herewini at first five-eighth. He had been displaying outstanding form for the Ranfurly Shield holders and his selection came as no surprise. A now fit Little returned to the centre berth.

New Zealand's kick-off saw Davies kicking deep after Clarke had feinted to kick the opposite way. In the second minute of the match, Clarke gathered an unsuccessful touch finder from Lenehan two yards on his own side of half-way and let fly with a tremendous dropped goal attempt which thudded into the cross-bar before rebounding into the field of play.

The All Black forwards were dominating the match and Connor was keeping the ball in front of them with high kicks. Sustained pressure by the All Blacks led to the first points in the match when Morrissey went over for a try following good work by Nathan, Whineray and Graham before the ball was moved briskly through the backline. Clarke was unable to convert from the touchline, and the home side was ahead 3-0 after twenty-four minutes.

Five minutes later the All Blacks were in again after Nelson made a break from a ruck before passing to the backline. Davies beat Douglas before passing to Little who put Heeps in for a try

in the left hand corner. With an excellent kick Clarke turned the try into a goal.

Chapman missed a penalty goal attempt two minutes later from 40 yards which was his side's first real opportunity to open their scoring. At this stage of the match, Davies left the field with Graham moving into the backline. Five minutes before halftime, Herewini landed a left footed dropped goal from a five yard scrum in front of the posts. Halftime saw New Zealand ahead by 11-0.

Davies returned to the field five minutes into the second spell with his thigh bandaged. Australia lifted their game in the early part of this half but they were denied points as several penalty attempts were astray. Midway through the half, Chapman finally landed a penalty from 35 yards.

The Wallabies' brightest moment came with ten minutes to play when McMullen broke down

Douglas and Meads appear to be playing "blind-man's bluff" in this incident.

AUSTRALIA 8

Eden Park, Auckland

While all the attention is focussed upon Nelson touching down by the Australian post, referee Farquhar brings play back for an infringement.

the blindside before passing to the flying Lenehan. He offloaded to Boyce and was there to take the in-pass and score the Wallabies' first try of the series. Chapman, who had become Australia's highest pointscorer on a New Zealand tour, landed the conversion from wide out to bring his side within three points of the New Zealand total. Lenehan missed a long range dropped goal in the thirty-fourth minute and another, two minutes later.

It was Herewini who finally made the game safe for New Zealand with a try after a typical jinking run following a ruck near the Wallaby line. Clarke converted from almost in front as the final whistle sounded.

There was general agreement following the match that this had been the best of the five internationals played between the two sides during the season. An interesting feature of the game had been the appearance of the two sets of brothers locking the two scrums.

Dick Thornett was to accept an offer to play League before the start of the next season and this was his final Rugby international. In 1960 he had represented Australia at water polo at the Rome Olympics and he was destined to again represent his country at Rugby League. The loss of this sixteen stone, mobile forward was a severe one for the code.

NEW ZEALAND		
	D.B. CLARKE	
	(Waikato)	
P.J. MORRISSEY	P.F. LITTLE	T.R. HEEPS
(Canterbury)	(Auckland)	(Wellington)
W.A. DAVIES		
(Otago)		
	M.A. HEREWINI	
	(Auckland)	
	D.M. CONNOR	
	(Auckland)	
	K.A. NELSON	
	(Otago)	
D.J. GRAHAM	S.T. MEADS	C.E. MEADS	W.J. NATHAN
(Canterbury)	(King Country)	(King Country)	(Auckland)
B.T. THOMAS	D. YOUNG	W.J. WHINERAY (Capt.)
(Auckland)	(Canterbury)	(Auckland)

J.P.L. WHITE	P.G. JOHNSON	J.E. FREEDMAN
(New South Wales)	(New South Wales)	(New South Wales)
C.P. CRITTLE	R.N. THORNETT	J.E. THORNETT	G.A. CHAPMAN
(New South Wales)	(New South Wales)	(Capt.)	(New South Wales)
		(New South Wales)	
	R.J. HEMING	
	(New South Wales)	
	K.V. McMULLEN	
	(New South Wales)	
	P.F. HAWTHORNE	
	(New South Wales)	
J.S. BOYCE	B.J. ELLWOOD	R.J.P. MARKS	J.A. DOUGLAS
(New South Wales)	(New South Wales)	(Queensland)	(Victoria)
	J.K.M. LENEHAN	
	(New South Wales)	
	AUSTRALIA	

REFEREE: Mr A.B. Farquhar (Auckland)
ATTENDANCE: 48,000
CONDITIONS: Weather fine, ground firm
HALFTIME: New Zealand 11, Australia 0

SCORERS

NEW ZEALAND	AUSTRALIA
Tries: Morrissey, Heeps, Herewini	Try: Lenehan
Conversions: Clarke (2)	Conversion: Chapman
Dropped goal: Herewini	Penalty goal: Chapman

NEW ZEALAND 21

25 May, 1963

First Test

For the first time, New Zealand were hosts to a side from the Home Unions, when England, who had won the five-nation championship during the 1962-63 season, arranged to make a five match, two Test tour during the early part of the 1963 season. After defeating Wellington in their initial match, the tourists had gone down to Otago 9-14 in their second game.

The only player known to New Zealanders was Phil Horrocks-Taylor who had come to New Zealand as a replacement for the 1959 Lions, playing in four matches including the third Test. The captain, Mike Weston, had won sixteen caps for his country and had toured South Africa with the 1962 Lions. After selection, the lock forward John Owen, who had been carried from the field in the final minutes of the game against Otago, withdrew from the Test team and was replaced by Tom Pargetter a 30 year old, six foot four inch baker, who was winning his third and final cap.

The New Zealand team included two players making their Test debuts in Ian Uttley, the 21 year old Victoria University centre whose father had represented Otago and N.Z. Universities, and the 22 year old lock Allan Stewart who had impressed with his play during the previous season. An injury to Paul Little gave Uttley his chance. After selection Rod Heeps was forced to withdraw with a shoulder injury and was replaced by Ralph Caulton who arrived in Auckland on the morning of the match. The brothers Don and Ian Clarke were both playing their twenty-third Test equalling R.A. White's record of international appearances for New Zealand.

Conditions were perfect as England kicked off and almost immediately they were awarded a penalty from a line-out 10 yards outside the All Black 25. Roger Hosen, making the first of his ten international appearances at the age of 29, was successful with the kick to open the scoring. He landed a further penalty after eight minutes when Meads was adjudged off-side 30 yards from his posts. Don Clarke had missed an early penalty and midway through the spell failed with a dropped goal attempt and two long range penalties.

Halftime was reached with England still ahead by six points but, in the first minute of the second half, Don Clarke landed his first successful kick of the match when a 43 yard attempt went over.

In the fifth minute England won a ruck on the All Black 25 and Simon Clarke broke away on the blindside, with Rogers, Phillips and Ranson in support. As Connor tackled Clarke the pass went to Rogers who transferred to Ranson. Don Clarke tried to spoil the pass but the winger eluded the big full-back and sprinted around Wolfe to score a well-engineered try fifteen yards to the right of the posts. Hosen converted to lengthen the English lead to 11-3.

New Zealand struck back five minutes later when Watt kicked for the corner following a ruck on the English 25 and the five-eighth had run on the blind. Don Clarke was up to gather the ball and force down with one hand as Phillips attempted to tackle him. The full-back converted with a fine kick after a no-charge had been ruled by the referee whilst an abortive first attempt was being taken.

NEW ZEALAND

D.B. CLARKE
(Waikato)

| D.W. McKAY | I.N. UTTLEY | R.W. CAULTON |
| (Auckland) | (Wellington) | (Wellington) |

T.N. WOLFE
(Taranaki)

B.A. WATT
(Canterbury)

D.M. CONNOR
(Auckland)

D.J. GRAHAM
(Canterbury)

K.R. TREMAIN	C.E. MEADS	A.J. STEWART	W.J. NATHAN
(Hawke's Bay)	(King Country)	(Canterbury)	(Auckland)
I.J. CLARKE		D. YOUNG	W.J. WHINERAY (Capt.)
(Waikato)		(Canterbury)	(Auckland)

P.E. JUDD	H.O. GODWIN	C.R. JACOBS
(Coventry)	(Coventry)	(Northampton)
D.P. ROGERS	T.A. PARGETTER	A.M. DAVIS	V.R. MARRIOTT
(Bedford)	(Coventry)	(Torquay Athletic)	(Harlequins)

D.G. PERRY
(Bedford)

S.J.S. CLARKE
(Cambridge University)

J.P. HORROCKS-TAYLOR
(Leicester)

| J.M. DEE | M.S. PHILLIPS | M.P. WESTON (Capt.) | J.M. RANSON |
| (Hartlepool) | (Fylde) | (Durham City) | (Rosslyn Park) |

R.W. HOSEN
(Northampton)

ENGLAND

REFEREE: Mr C.F. Robson (Waikato)
ATTENDANCE: 53,000
CONDITIONS: Weather fine, ground firm
HALFTIME: England 6, New Zealand 0

SCORERS

NEW ZEALAND	ENGLAND
Tries: Caulton (2), D.B. Clarke	Try: Ranson
Conversions: D.B. Clarke (3)	Conversion: Hosen
Penalty goal: D.B. Clarke	Penalty goals: Hosen (2)
Dropped goal: D.B. Clarke	

ENGLAND 11

Eden Park, Auckland

Colin Meads decides to barge through Judd rather than seek a way round him. English half-back, Simon Clarke, and All Black prop, Ian Clarke, close in.

It was in the twentieth minute of the half when New Zealand took the lead for the first time in the match. From a scrum near the English 25, Wolfe nudged a kick ahead that was taken by Uttley who ran a few yards before sending Caulton away. The winger shrugged off a tackle before running around behind the posts to score. Clarke goaled to make the score 13-11. Although the game looked as if it was equally poised at this stage the English forwards were tiring and it was the All Blacks who were doing most of the attacking.

With five minutes to go, Caulton scored his second try from a blindside move following an attacking ruck. Watt made a short burst before handing on to Caulton who went around to score deep in in-goal close to the line of the posts. Clarke again converted to make the game safe for New Zealand.

To complete the unique feat of scoring in all four ways in a Test, Clarke fielded a long pass back from Connor and with only seconds remaining, coolly dropkicked a goal from 37 yards out.

Right from the restart England were awarded a penalty but Hosen could not kick the goal and the game ended immediately after.

N W ZEALAND 9

1 June, 1963

Second Test

In the only match played since the first Test the previous Saturday, the English team had been beaten by the surprisingly wide margin of 20-5 by Hawke's Bay. In this game, future All Black Ian MacRae had distinguished himself by scoring three fine tries.

For the international, the English selectors brought in the 35 year old Frank Sykes to play on the right wing with Ranson switching to the left in place of Dee. Sykes, who had last played an international in 1955, had been one of England's better players at Napier. Perry was moved from the back row to partner Davis at lock with Brian Wightman taking over at number eight. A schoolmaster, Wightman emigrated to Canada the following year and, in 1967, represented British Colombia against New Zealand.

The New Zealand selectors made only one change to the All Black side, replacing Wolfe with Pat Walsh, a versatile back who had played internationals in four backline positions. Walsh

English captain, Mike Weston, looks on in dismay as Pat Walsh scores ahead of Davis.

had not played for New Zealand since the first Test of the 1959 series against the Lions.

England won the toss and decided to take first use of the fresh southerly wind. Clarke was wide with a penalty attempt from 50 yards in the fifth minute, as was Hosen from a yard inside his own half in the fourteenth. Clarke missed a further shot from a wide angle three minutes later. At this stage, the big English lock forward Mike Davis was forced to leave the field with a dislocated shoulder.

The first points in the match came after twenty-five minutes when Connor broke from mid-field. He linked with Meads and Tremain who fed the flying McKay 25 yards out. The winger sprinted the distance to score near the corner. Clarke was unable to convert from the wide angle. Davis, after having his shoulder

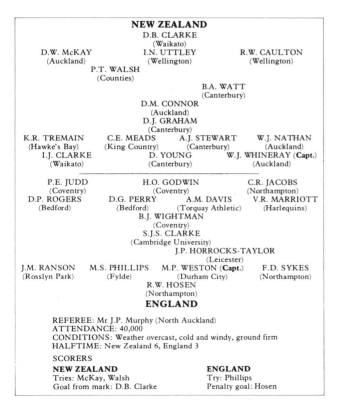

NEW ZEALAND

D.B. CLARKE
(Waikato)

D.W. McKAY	I.N. UTTLEY	R.W. CAULTON
(Auckland)	(Wellington)	(Wellington)

P.T. WALSH
(Counties)

B.A. WATT
(Canterbury)

D.M. CONNOR
(Auckland)

D.J. GRAHAM
(Canterbury)

K.R. TREMAIN	C.E. MEADS	A.J. STEWART	W.J. NATHAN
(Hawke's Bay)	(King Country)	(Canterbury)	(Auckland)
I.J. CLARKE		D. YOUNG	W.J. WHINERAY (**Capt.**)
(Waikato)		(Canterbury)	(Auckland)

P.E. JUDD	H.O. GODWIN	C.R. JACOBS
(Coventry)	(Coventry)	(Northampton)
D.P. ROGERS	D.G. PERRY	A.M. DAVIS	V.R. MARRIOTT
(Bedford)	(Bedford)	(Torquay Athletic)	(Harlequins)

B.J. WIGHTMAN
(Coventry)

S.J.S. CLARKE
(Cambridge University)

J.P. HORROCKS-TAYLOR
(Leicester)

J.M. RANSON	M.S. PHILLIPS	M.P. WESTON (**Capt.**)	F.D. SYKES
(Rosslyn Park)	(Fylde)	(Durham City)	(Northampton)

R.W. HOSEN
(Northampton)

ENGLAND

REFEREE: Mr J.P. Murphy (North Auckland)
ATTENDANCE: 40,000
CONDITIONS: Weather overcast, cold and windy, ground firm
HALFTIME: New Zealand 6, England 3
SCORERS

NEW ZEALAND	**ENGLAND**
Tries: McKay, Walsh	Try: Phillips
Goal from mark: D.B. Clarke	Penalty goal: Hosen

NGLAND 6

Lancaster Park, Christchurch

Don Clarke Saves N.Z. with The Daddy of All Kicks

Headline from a match report in the Christchurch Star.

strapped, returned to the field to complete the game with only one useful arm.

Hosen evened the score after thirty-one minutes with a 35 yard penalty from almost in front. Two minutes before halftime, New Zealand scored again following a movement that saw a Caulton centre-kick taken by Meads and a maul formed. The ball emerged and moved along the backline to McKay who dropped the ball in a tackle. Walsh was on hand however to toe the ball to the line and beat a gallant Davis to the touch in a desperate dive. Clarke was again astray with the conversion, and the halftime score was 6-3 in favour of the home side.

Five minutes after the resumption, Ranson made the opening for England's try when he beat McKay inside his own half and moved up to the 10 yard mark before in-passing to Rogers as he was tackled from behind. The flanker put a long raking punt towards the All Black line where Phillips was up quickly to gather and score in the corner. Hosen's kick missed and the teams were locked at 6-6, a score that was to stand until five minutes from no-side when Don Clarke claimed a fair catch in the face of the charging English forwards just on half-way towards the left hand touch line. He retired about a further eight yards, where his brother held the ball, and prepared to kick this vital goal. A preliminary movement induced the anxious English players on the mark to charge prematurely and the referee ruled that the charge be forfeited. After Ian had placed the ball, Don magnificently goaled the 65 yard kick to win the match. In the remaining minutes Hosen had a chance to save the game for England with a 38 yard penalty, but the attempt was astray.

It was a match that New Zealand had been fortunate to win. Despite their poor tour record and the serious injury of Davis, England had risen to the challenge valiantly and were desperately unlucky not to have drawn the match. Their intensive tour, which had seen them play two tough Test matches and three of the country's strongest provinces in eighteen days, was considered by many critics to be too hard. On the Tuesday following this match they went down to Australia at Sydney 9-18 to complete their tour.

Of the New Zealand team, three-quarters McKay and Uttley, Pat Walsh and veteran prop Ian Clarke had played in their final international.

"AND DON'T FORGET TO TELL 'EM OVER THERE WHAT THEY'VE GOT COMING TO 'EM"

EVENING POST

NEW ZEALAND 6

7 December, 1963

The 1963-64 All Blacks had played thirteen matches on tour leading up to this first international, winning twelve and losing only the third match, to Newport by 0-3. Impressive victories over South-Western Counties 38-6, and Midland Counties 37-9, immediately preceding the Test made the New Zealanders firm favourites.

Making their Test debuts for New Zealand were Malcolm Dick the 22 year old son of 1937-38 All Black winger Johnny Dick; Derek Arnold a red-headed five-eighth who had greatly impressed in the trial matches with his elusive running, and Ken Gray, embarking on his international career that was to last until 1969. During that time he established himself as one of the world's finest prop forwards.

Familiar players in the Irish team were captain of the 1959 Lions, Ronnie Dawson, and other

players of that combination in Bill Mulcahy and Noel Murphy who had played in the Tests in 1959. A fourth member of the team appearing in this match was Mick English who had returned home injured in 1959. Other Irish forwards who were to become familiar names to New Zealanders in the years to come were "Willie-John" McBride and Ray McLoughlin.

After the two captains had met Eamon de Valera, President of the Irish Republic, himself a keen Rugby man and a Munster trialist at full-back in 1904, Herewini kicked off for New Zealand.

Although the All Black pack soon established themselves, winning a good supply of ball, the half-back combination of Briscoe and Herewini was under severe pressure from the Irish loose forwards and was not functioning well. After seventeen minutes, Duggan entered an Irish

IRELAND 5

backline movement from the blindside wing to take English's pass which he had trouble in controlling. However, he got the ball to Jerry Walsh (whose return home from Australia, when his father was seriously ill, deprived the 1966 Lions of one of their best backs). Walsh threw a long pass to Fortune and the tall winger ran the last ten yards to score. Kiernan goaled the conversion to the crowd's delight and Ireland were five points up.

The All Blacks were soon back on attack and were unlucky not to score when Stewart was dragged down inches short of the Irish line after an All Black surge had covered more than half of the field then, two minutes later, Herewini hit the post with a dropped goal attempt. Six minutes before halftime, Stan Meads broke from a scrum

The All Black forwards watch Briscoe spin out his pass as the Irish defence sets off.

AUCKLAND STAR

near the Irish line before feeding the ball in to Tremain who crashed over through Kiernan's tackle for a typically determined try. Clarke rather surprisingly sliced the conversion from a comfortable angle, and Ireland was left with a 5-3 lead at the change around.

Early in the second half, the New Zealanders were again dominating play but were finding it difficult to increase their score as several chances went begging. Midway through the half, New Zealand received a scrum penalty 35 yards out and Clarke made no mistake to give the All Blacks the lead for the first time in the match. Apart from one attack which ended with a scramble over the New Zealand goal line it was the All Blacks who kept the Irish on defence for the remainder of the game. Although the score had been close it was generally conceded that the All Blacks had been the better team on the day and, but for some aimless kicking and mistakes under pressure, could have won by a comfortable margin.

NEW ZEALAND

D.B. CLARKE
(Waikato)

M.J. DICK (Auckland)   P.F. LITTLE (Auckland)   R.W. CAULTON (Wellington)

D.A. ARNOLD
(Canterbury)

M.A. HEREWINI
(Auckland)

K.C. BRISCOE
(Taranaki)

S.T. MEADS
(King Country)

D.J. GRAHAM (Canterbury)   A.J. STEWART (Canterbury)   C.E. MEADS (King Country)   K.R. TREMAIN (Hawke's Bay)

K.F. GRAY (Wellington)   D. YOUNG (Canterbury)   W.J. WHINERAY (**Capt.**) (Auckland)

R.J. McLOUGHLIN (Gosforth)   A.R. DAWSON (Wanderers)   P.J. DWYER (University College, Dublin)

N.A.A. MURPHY (Cork Constitution)   W.A. MULCAHY (Bective Rangers)   W.J. McBRIDE (Ballymena)   E.P. McGUIRE (University College, ...)

P.J.A. O'SULLIVAN
(Galwegians)

J.C. KELLY (**Capt.**)
(University College, Dublin)

M.A.F. ENGLISH
(Lansdowne)

A.T.A. DUGGAN (Lansdowne)   J.C. WALSH (University College Cork)   P.J. CASEY (University College, Dublin)   J.J. FORTUNE (Clontarf)

T.J. KIERNAN
(Cork Constitution)

IRELAND

REFEREE: Mr H. Keenan (England)
ATTENDANCE: 32,000
CONDITIONS: Weather fine but cold, ground firm
HALFTIME: Ireland 5, New Zealand 3

SCORERS

NEW ZEALAND	IRELAND
Try: Tremain	Try: Fortune
Penalty goal: Clarke	Conversion: Kiernan

21 December, 1963

Although in the games since the Irish international the All Blacks had struggled manfully to defeat Munster, Swansea and Western Counties, the critics tended to favour their chances over a side that had finished last in the previous year's championship. But no New Zealand team had won an international at Cardiff Arms Park so there was some speculation as to whether this team would break the hoodoo.

The only changes in the side were at first five-eighth where Bruce Watt came in for Herewini, who had been criticised for his excessive kicking in the Irish Test, and on the side of the scrum where Waka Nathan, restored to fitness after suffering a broken finger in the Cardiff game earlier in the tour, replaced Stan Meads.

The Welsh team included two new caps. John Uzzell, who had landed the dropped goal for Newport to register the tourists' only defeat, was at left centre. Alan Thomas, a constructive forward whose selection had kept 1959 and 1962 Lion, Haydn Morgan, out of the team, was at flanker. An original selection, Denzil Williams, was forced to withdraw from the team with strained chest muscles and was replaced by the 1962 Lion, Kingsley Jones.

Hodgson kicked off for Wales and, from the second line-out of the game, New Zealand was awarded a penalty. Clarke lined up the ball for a shot at goal 58 yards from the posts and his long kick struck the upright above the cross-bar and bounced away. Three minutes later, Clarke was given a further opportunity when Hayward fell off-side at a scrum and this time he landed the goal from 20 yards out to open the scoring. In the sixth minute Clarke again attempted a long range goal from 54 yards and again he struck the post to give the All Blacks a psychological advantage.

The tourists' pack was playing with great fire and most of the play for the next half hour was played in the Welsh half, though one dangerous break by Uzzell was only halted when Price dropped the ball with the line open. On another occasion, Tremain went within an ace of scoring only to see his pass knocked on.

Ralph Caulton is upended by his Welsh opposite, Morgan.

At halftime the score still stood at 3-0. Straight after the resumption, the New Zealand pack marched the Welsh forwards back for twenty yards in a display of scrummaging power. In the thirteenth minute, Young took a tighthead from Gale and Watt propped inside Hayward to drop-kick a goal from just outside the 25. Four minutes earlier Clarke, now suffering a groin injury in his right leg, was unable to do himself justice from a penalty 40 yards out. Little distinguished himself with two good tackles which halted Welsh attacks then Hodgson had his first shot at goal from 35 yards in the thirty-second minute but it was a weak attempt as was an attempted drop-kick a minute later.

In the final minutes Welsh captain, Clive Rowlands, was charged by Meads as he claimed a fair catch. He was unable to continue and as he was carried from the field, an outbreak of booing broke out which persisted until the final whistle blew.

WALES 0

Cardiff Arms Park

CROWN STUDIOS

The New Zealand Touring Team
Back Row: C.R. Laidlaw, W.L. Davis, D.J. Graham, R.W. Caulton, P.F. Little, J.M. Le Lievre, W.J. Nathan, I.S.T Smith, P.T. Walsh.
Second row: I.R. MacRae, K.E. Barry, K.A. Nelson, S.T. Meads, C.E. Meads, A.J. Stewart, R.H. Horsley, B.J. Lochore, K.F. Gray, K.R. Tremain.
Seated: D.A. Arnold, I.J. Clarke, D.B. Clarke, K.C. Briscoe, F.D. Kilby (manager), W.J. Whineray (captain), N.J. McPhail (asst. manager), D. Young, E.W. Kirton, J. Major, M.J. Dick.
In front: B.A. Watt, M.A. Herewini.

Apart from some slight disappointment about their inability to include a try in the final tally, the New Zealand team were delighted at their comprehensive victory over their old adversaries at Cardiff. As in the Irish Test, the score was not an accurate indication of the extent to which New Zealand had dominated the game. Mr Ewart Davies, President of the Welsh Rugby Union, was reported as saying that the New Zealand team was the best touring party to visit Wales from any country yet and made the accurate prediction that they would not be beaten again on tour.

Bebb, Ken Jones, David Watkins, Alan Pask and Brian Price were all to tour New Zealand with the 1966 Lions.

NEW ZEALAND		
	D.B. CLARKE	
	(Waikato)	
M.J. DICK	P.F. LITTLE	R.W. CAULTON
(Auckland)	(Auckland)	(Wellington)
D.A. ARNOLD		
(Canterbury)		
		B.A. WATT
		(Canterbury)
	K.C. BRISCOE	
	(Taranaki)	
	K.R. TREMAIN	
	(Hawke's Bay)	
D.J. GRAHAM	C.E. MEADS	A.J. STEWART	W.J. NATHAN
(Canterbury)	(King Country)	(Canterbury)	(Auckland)
K.F. GRAY	D. YOUNG	W.J. WHINERAY (**Capt.**)
(Wellington)	(Canterbury)	(Auckland)
K.D. JONES	N.R. GALE	L.J. CUNNINGHAM
(Cardiff)	(Llanelli)	(Aberavon)
A. THOMAS	B. PRICE	B.E. THOMAS	D.J. HAYWARD
(Newport)	(Newport)	(Neath)	(Cardiff)
	A.E.I. PASK	
	(Abertillery)	
	D.C.T. ROWLANDS (**Capt.**)	
	(Pontypool)	
	D. WATKINS	
	(Newport)	
D.I.E. BEBB	J. UZZELL	D.K. JONES	D.R.R. MORGAN
(Swansea)	(Newport)	(Oxford University)	(Llanelli)
	G.T.R. HODGSON	
	(Neath)	
	WALES	

REFEREE: Mr R.C. Williams (Ireland)
ATTENDANCE: 58,000
CONDITIONS: Weather fine, ground firm
HALFTIME: New Zealand 3, Wales 0

SCORERS
NEW ZEALAND   **WALES**
Penalty goal: Clarke
Dropped goal: Watt

NEW ZEALAND 14

4 January, 1964

The only change in the New Zealand team's line-up was necessitated by a jaw injury suffered by Nathan in the team's previous match against Llanelli. The choice of his replacement appeared to lie between Nelson and Lochore and finally it was decided that the Wairarapa farmer, Brian Lochore, would play. It was his international debut and the start of a Test career which lasted until 1971.

In the English side, Horrocks-Taylor was a survivor of the 1959 Lions' Test teams in New Zealand and was one of the ten players who had appeared in the two internationals for his country in New Zealand early in the 1963 season.

After five minutes New Zealand was awarded a penalty 46 yards out and Clarke nonchalantly kicked the goal. With the All Black pack dominating the play and half-back Briscoe in his finest form, England was being kept on the defensive, and after twenty-two minutes, a further penalty was awarded to New Zealand only 24 yards from the English posts. Clarke had no trouble in goaling and New Zealand were ahead by six points.

After half an hour following a line-out maul, Tremain burst away with the ball before feeding his captain Whineray who crashed into the English full-back John Willcox as he slipped a pass back to Tremain. Infield went the flanker, draw-

Meads crashes over between the posts after a movement begun by Caulton's interception of an English pass.

AUCKLAND STAR

ENGLAND 0

After exchanging jerseys at the end of the match, Meads and Gray solemnly reflect on the All Black win.

Twickenham, London

The defeat suffered by England was the biggest in points margin the home team had incurred since Twickenham opened fifty-four years earlier.

The All Black pack had all played exceptionally well with perhaps Tremain standing out as the man of the match and newcomer Lochore also playing a grand all-round game.

English full-back and captain, John Willcox, earned much praise for his fearless tackling but the other backs had looked unimaginative. Simon Clarke, behind the beaten pack, had a torrid day with the All Black loose forwards continually putting him under pressure. The much vaunted English loose forwards were unable to make much impact on the game and it was the tight core of Davis, Judd and hooker Godwin who were England's best forwards.

Don Clarke, although not completely fit and favouring his right leg, was still a dominant player and his early goals were the basis for the New Zealand victory.

ing the defence before passing to Caulton on the left wing who ran in the try wide out past the clutching hands of Phillips. Clarke could not manage to convert.

Halftime was reached with the score still at 9-0. Two minutes after the restart, an English attack broke down when a long, high pass from Horrocks-Taylor towards his wing Phillips was intercepted by Caulton who shot away upfield. The winger found Graham in support and he took play inside the English 25 before getting the ball to Meads who crashed through Willcox's tackle to score between the posts. Clarke's conversion was little more than a formality.

Despite the frustration of conceding five points from one of their own attacks, the English team hit back with a determined rally. They were unable to open their account, though two penalty attempts from Willcox went close. Surprisingly, the All Blacks did not score again and some criticism was later made of their safety-first tactics. Indeed in some of the line-outs it appeared the backline was an extension of the line of forwards. At a subsequent meeting of the International Board, a ten yard gap from the line of touch was made mandatory for backs.

NEW ZEALAND		
	D.B. CLARKE	
	(Waikato)	
M.J. DICK	P.F. LITTLE	R.W. CAULTON
(Auckland)	(Auckland)	(Wellington)
D.A. ARNOLD		
(Canterbury)		
	B.A. WATT	
	(Canterbury)	
	K.C. BRISCOE	
	(Taranaki)	
	B.J. LOCHORE	
	(Wairarapa)	
D.J. GRAHAM	A.J. STEWART C.E. MEADS	K.R. TREMAIN
(Canterbury)	(Canterbury) (King Country)	(Hawke's Bay)
K.F. GRAY	D. YOUNG	W.J. WHINERAY (Capt.)
(Wellington)	(Canterbury)	(Auckland)
N.J. DRAKE-LEE	H.O. GODWIN	P.E. JUDD
(Cambridge University)	(Coventry)	(Coventry)
V.R. MARRIOTT A.M. DAVIS J.E. OWEN		D.P. ROGERS
(Harlequins) (Torquay Athletic) (Coventry)		(Bedford)
	D.G. PERRY	
	(Bedford)	
	S.J.S. CLARKE	
	(Cambridge University)	
	J.P. HORROCKS-TAYLOR	
	(Middlesbrough)	
J. ROBERTS	R.D. SANGWIN M.P. WESTON	M.S. PHILLIPS
(Sale)	(Hull & East Riding) (Durham City)	(Fylde)
	J.G. WILLCOX (Capt.)	
	(Harlequins)	
ENGLAND		

REFEREE: Mr D.C.J. McMahon (Scotland)
ATTENDANCE: 65,000
CONDITIONS: Weather misty and cold, ground firm
HALFTIME: New Zealand 9, England 0
SCORERS

NEW ZEALAND	ENGLAND
Tries: Caulton, Meads	
Conversion: Clarke	
Penalty goals: Clarke (2)	

18 January, 1964

The only change in the New Zealand team saw Mac Herewini, normally a first five-eighth, come in at second five-eighth to replace Arnold, who had his right leg in plaster. Nathan was still out of action with his jaw injury.

The Scottish selectors had chosen the same team that had defeated France 10-0 a fortnight earlier. Two days before the match, the powerfully-built centre, Brian Henderson, was forced to withdraw and he was replaced by Jim Shackleton. With Ken Scotland not available, the captaincy had reverted to Brian Neill, a prop forward who had made his debut the previous year.

Although a hard frost had covered the area on the morning of the game, the field was in perfect order for the match because of the use of the electric blanket under the turf which had been funded by an anonymous Scottish supporter.

It was the All Blacks who did the early attacking but both sides were having difficulty in handling the ball which was made greasy by a film of dew on the turf. Clarke failed with a 45 yard penalty and Scotland managed to clear the ball.

After seventeen minutes, Scotland mounted their first dangerous attack when scrum-half Tremayne Rodd broke on the blindside from a scrum inside his own half. He burst up-field past

Young bursts away with the ball towards Rodd, the Scottish half-back. Whineray keeps an eye on play from the middle of the maul.

CENTRAL PRESS

SCOTLAND 0

Murrayfield, Edinburgh

a surprised defence before linking with Elliot. Stewart Wilson, playing his second international, was on hand to take the in-pass and Grant finally put in a kick ahead that Little ran into touch-in-goal. Fortunately Young, who was in fine form, won a tighthead at the five yard scrum and the position was relieved.

From this point on however, the Scottish team started to assert themselves and the game ebbed and flowed on even terms. Midway through the spell, Meads was called out by the referee for some over-vigorous play and a penalty was awarded to Scotland. Wilson made a good attempt at goal but the distance was a little beyond him.

Clarke, whose kicking form had slipped a little in recent matches, missed a penalty attempt from a wide angle. Then Graham was quickly on to a dropped pass by Sharp on the Scottish ten yard mark and fed Tremain who shrugged off one tackle in a determined run only to be dragged down with a fine smothering tackle by Iain Laughland a few yards from the line. Halftime was reached with no score having been recorded and the crowd simmering with excitement.

At the start of the second half, once again the All Black forwards were straight on to attack but the inside back combination of Briscoe, Watt and Herewini was unable to achieve very much cohesion and chances went begging. Although Stewart, playing his finest game of the tour, was dominating the line-outs and Young was outclassing Bruce in the hooking duel, the All Black pack were not being allowed to dominate the game as they had in the previous internationals on the tour. During a period of Scottish pressure both Sharp and Laughland were wide with dropped goal attempts, and a well organised cover defence halted several promising backline movements.

As time moved on, a hint of desperation crept into the play on both sides. Clarke attempted a further long range penalty from nearly 60 yards and well out but the kick passed just wide of the posts. A few minutes later he was short with another shot from well out. From this latter attempt, Rodd's clearing kick had gone back to

Clarke whose massive drop kick also was just wide.

In the final minutes it was again Clarke who endeavoured to save the match when he entered a backline movement and burst 50 yards up the middle of the field. Losing support, he lofted a kick to the Scottish line where Wilson, who had been the man of the match for his side, calmly gathered and cleared. This was the last scoring chance and when the game ended shortly after the crowd spilled on the field in an ecstatic mood to mob their heroes who had denied the tourists the chance of being the first All Black team to defeat all four home unions on tour.

This match marked the end of vice-captain Kevin Briscoe's Test career. Since 1959 this rugged half-back had appeared in nine Test matches, eight of which had been on tour. Throughout his career he had had severe competition not only at national level, where Urbahn, Connor and finally Laidlaw had unseated him from the international berth at various times, but also at provincial level where Urbahn had earlier been preferred behind the Taranaki scrum.

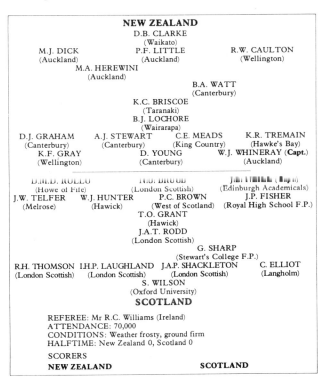

NEW ZEALAND

D.B. CLARKE
(Waikato)

M.J. DICK   P.F. LITTLE   R.W. CAULTON
(Auckland)   (Auckland)   (Wellington)

M.A. HEREWINI
(Auckland)

B.A. WATT
(Canterbury)

K.C. BRISCOE
(Taranaki)

B.J. LOCHORE
(Wairarapa)

D.J. GRAHAM   A.J. STEWART   C.E. MEADS   K.R. TREMAIN
(Canterbury)   (Canterbury)   (King Country)   (Hawke's Bay)

K.F. GRAY   D. YOUNG   W.J. WHINERAY (**Capt.**)
(Wellington)   (Canterbury)   (Auckland)

D.M.D. ROLLO   H.O. BRUCE   J.B. NEILL (**Capt.**)
(Howe of Fife)   (London Scottish) (Edinburgh Academicals)

J.W. TELFER   W.J. HUNTER   P.C. BROWN   J.P. FISHER
(Melrose)   (Hawick)   (West of Scotland) (Royal High School F.P.)

T.O. GRANT
(Hawick)

J.A.T. RODD
(London Scottish)

G. SHARP
(Stewart's College F.P.)

R.H. THOMSON I.H.P. LAUGHLAND J.A.P. SHACKLETON   C. ELLIOT
(London Scottish) (London Scottish) (London Scottish)   (Langholm)

S. WILSON
(Oxford University)

SCOTLAND

REFEREE: Mr R.C. Williams (Ireland)
ATTENDANCE: 70,000
CONDITIONS: Weather frosty, ground firm
HALFTIME: New Zealand 0, Scotland 0

SCORERS
NEW ZEALAND   **SCOTLAND**

253

NEW ZEALAND 12

8 February, 1964

Both Arnold and Nathan, restored to fitness, in time for this match were included in place of Watt and Lochore with Herewini moving in to his usual position of first five-eighth. Taking his place in the Test team for the first time was Chris Laidlaw, who had been in outstanding form behind the scrum in recent matches. The well-built half-back, who had turned twenty earlier on the tour, possessed a long and accurate pass and was seen as a player of great potential.

The French team included a familiar face in Andre Boniface who had played against Bob Stuart's team ten years earlier as well as touring New Zealand in 1961. Injury forced his brother Guy to drop out of the chosen side after selection. Other 1961 tourists in the team were Lacaze, Pique, Albaladejo and Michel Crauste.

The referee for this fifth international of the tour was again Ray Williams from Ulster. He had already controlled the Welsh and Scottish internationals. Mr Williams's international career had commenced in 1957 and, by the time he reached retirement from the international panel, he had controlled a total of twenty internationals.

After only three minutes France received a line-out penalty and, from 40 yards out, Pierre Albaladejo landed the goal. A few minutes later, Clarke was given the opportunity to reply from a handy position but with this and a further chance just after, also from close in, he failed rather dismally. When the next opportunity arose, in the fifteenth minute, Whineray handed the ball to Herewini who evened the score from 30 yards.

The All Blacks took the lead soon after when Herewini, after receiving the ball from a line-out, kicked high for the corner where the diminutive winger Gachassin gathered but had the mortification of seeing his clearing kick charged down by Caulton who recovered the ball and rolled over to score an opportunist's try. Herewini was unable to raise the flags with his conversion attempt.

When the French backs were given the opportunity to run, they proved that they could breach the All Black line and it was surprising that Fabre insisted on tactics that saw them en-

deavour to fight it out in the forwards rather than open play up. Halftime was reached with New Zealand still holding their 6-3 lead and controlling the game well.

The second half started with the French team opening play up at every chance and during the first ten minutes they were continually dangerous. Only fine cover defence saved the New Zealand line on several occasions. Albaladejo missed a penalty from 40 yards and, a short time later, Herewini was also unsuccessful with a 30 yard shot.

Gradually the All Black forwards regained control of the match and, from a scrum 30 yards from the French line, Herewini, going left, was blocked and managed to get the ball back to Laidlaw who was backing up. The half-back quickly sighted the posts and drop-kicked a goal to make the game secure with ten minutes to play.

Clarke was entrusted with the next goal kicking chance but from 28 yards he was no more successful than Herewini had been. Five min-

NEW ZEALAND
D.B. CLARKE
(Waikato)

M.J. DICK
(Auckland)

P.F. LITTLE
(Auckland)

R.W. CAULTON
(Wellington)

D.A. ARNOLD
(Canterbury)

M.A. HEREWINI
(Auckland)

C.R. LAIDLAW
(Otago)

K.R. TREMAIN
(Hawke's Bay)

D.J. GRAHAM
(Canterbury)

A.J. STEWART
(Canterbury)

C.E. MEADS
(King Country)

W.J. NATHAN
(Auckland)

K.F. GRAY
(Wellington)

D. YOUNG
(Canterbury)

W.J. WHINERAY (**Capt.**)
(Auckland)

J. BAYARDON
(R.C. Chalon)

J. De GREGORIO
(F.C. Grenoble)

J.B. AMESTOY
(S. Montois)

M. CRAUSTE
(F.C. Lourdais)

J. Le DROFF
(F.C. Auch)

B. DAUGA
(S. Montois)

A. HERRERO
(R.C. Toulonnais)

J. FABRE (**Capt.**)
(S. Toulousain)

J.C. LASSERRE
(U.S. Dax)

P. ALBALADEJO
(U.S. Dax)

C. DARROUY
(S. Montois)

A. BONIFACE
(S. Montois)

J. PIQUE
(S. Paloise)

J. GACHASSIN
(F.C. Lourdais)

C. LACAZE
(S.C. Angouleme)

FRANCE

REFEREE: Mr R.C. Williams (Ireland)
ATTENDANCE: 42,000
CONDITIONS: Weather overcast, ground firm
HALFTIME: New Zealand 6, France 3

SCORERS

NEW ZEALAND
Tries: Caulton, Gray
Penalty goal: Herewini
Dropped goal: Laidlaw

FRANCE
Penalty goal: Albaladejo

FRANCE 3

Colombes Stadium, Paris

Playing in his first international, Laidlaw shows the smooth passing style which earned him a place behind the All Black scrum. The French flanker, Herrero, dives in vain to block the pass.

utes from time, Dick came into a backline movement from the blindside. He was tackled but Ken Gray was there to pick up the loose ball just short of the line and stretch out a long arm to score. To complete a pretty dismal day's kicking, Herewini was unable to land a simple conversion.

However the team had completed the five internationals of the tour with a record of four wins and a draw which was the best performance from an All Black side on tour in Europe since the 1924-25 tour though Scotland had been omitted from that side's itinerary.

Three of the New Zealand team had played their last internationals in this match. Derek Arnold, the brilliant and unpredictable five-eighth, although just twenty-three did not don the All Black jersey again although he represented his province until 1969 and appeared in the South

Island side for the next three years. Paul Little, one of the finest centres to have played for his country, was retiring after appearing in ten internationals and twenty-nine matches for New Zealand. A superb passer of the ball and an expert at setting up his wings, Little was a key player in the great Auckland Ranfurly Shield teams of the early sixties. Since his retirement he has given fine service as a coach and selector of junior teams in Auckland.

Also retiring was Dennis Young, only a few weeks short of his thirty-fourth birthday. Since 1956 he had hooked in twenty-two Tests and had missed only one international since 1960. Young, who made his first appearance for Canterbury in 1950 and for the South Island in 1951, had outhooked every opponent he had met during his international career and he justly deserved the rating of the world's best hooker.

Following one more match in France the All Blacks returned to Cardiff Arms Park where they played a memorable match against the Barbarians which they won 36-3.

N W ZEALAND 14

15 August, 1964

First Test

The twenty-three man Australian team of 1964 included eighteen who had toured South Africa the previous year where the four match Test series had been squared, and fourteen from the 1962 tour of New Zealand. John Thornett, the captain, was on his fourth tour with an Australian team to New Zealand, having toured with the 1955, 1958 and 1962 teams.

A loss to Auckland, and victories over Wanganui and East Coast was the record of the tourists leading up to the first international.

Several changes to the New Zealand team that had played in the internationals on the 1963-64 tour of Europe were necessary. Young and Little had retired whilst Whineray had restricted his

play to club level for the season. Don Clarke was forced to withdraw after selection with a knee ailment, breaking a run of twenty-four consecutive internationals.

New players in the All Black team were Mick Williment, a 25 year old teacher from the Evans Bay Intermediate School who replaced Clarke; John Collins, a Maori second five-eighth from the Marist club in Gisborne; Ian Smith (who had scored eight tries in his fifteen matches for New Zealand on the 1963-64 tour without appearing in an international) on the right wing; Don Clark a flanker from Cromwell and Bruce McLeod, playing the first of his twenty-four Tests as Dennis Young's successor at hooker. John Graham was leading New Zealand for the first time in an international.

Hawthorne kicked off for Australia but New Zealand went on to early attack. Twice in the first ten minutes, Williment failed with penalty attempts before the first points in the game were scored. From a scrum inside the Australian half,

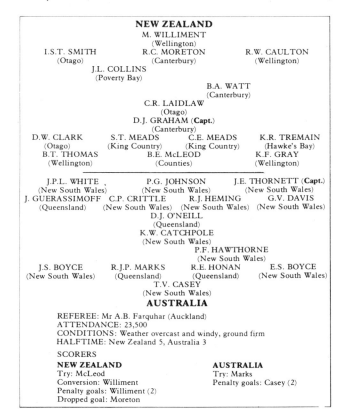

Mick Williment had a good debut, landing a conversion and two penalty goals.

K. & D. LLOYD

NEW ZEALAND

		M. WILLIMENT (Wellington)		
I.S.T. SMITH (Otago)		R.C. MORETON (Canterbury)		R.W. CAULTON (Wellington)
	J.L. COLLINS (Poverty Bay)			
			B.A. WATT (Canterbury)	
		C.R. LAIDLAW (Otago)		
		D.J. GRAHAM (**Capt.**) (Canterbury)		
D.W. CLARK (Otago)	S.T. MEADS (King Country)	C.E. MEADS (King Country)		K.R. TREMAIN (Hawke's Bay)
B.T. THOMAS (Wellington)		B.E. McLEOD (Counties)		K.F. GRAY (Wellington)

J.P.L. WHITE (New South Wales)		P.G. JOHNSON (New South Wales)		J.E. THORNETT (**Capt.**) (New South Wales)
J. GUERASSIMOFF (Queensland)	C.P. CRITTLE (New South Wales)	R.J. HEMING (New South Wales)		G.V. DAVIS (New South Wales)
		D.J. O'NEILL (Queensland)		
		K.W. CATCHPOLE (New South Wales)		
			P.F. HAWTHORNE (New South Wales)	
J.S. BOYCE (New South Wales)	R.J.P. MARKS (Queensland)	R.E. HONAN (Queensland)		E.S. BOYCE (New South Wales)
		T.V. CASEY (New South Wales)		

AUSTRALIA

REFEREE: Mr A.B. Farquhar (Auckland)
ATTENDANCE: 23,500
CONDITIONS: Weather overcast and windy, ground firm
HALFTIME: New Zealand 5, Australia 3

SCORERS

NEW ZEALAND	**AUSTRALIA**
Try: McLeod	Try: Marks
Conversion: Williment	Penalty goals: Casey (2)
Penalty goals: Williment (2)	
Dropped goal: Moreton	

AUSTRALIA 9

Carisbrook, Dunedin

Gray has his hand on the ball but Bruce McLeod scored the try after following up a centre kick. He has slid over the ball and appears on the ground at right.

Watt ran on the blindside before hoisting a centre kick. McLeod won the race to the loose ball and scored near the posts. Williment had no trouble with the conversion.

The only other scoring in the half came in the twenty-seventh minute following a counter attack started by Casey from well inside his own territory. The move ended with Gray dragging down O'Neill just short of the New Zealand line. From the ensuing scrum Laidlaw was unable to find touch and Stewart Boyce, a twin brother of left winger Jim, put in a high kick to the goal line where Marks outjumped Williment to take the ball and crash over. Casey was unable to convert.

Halftime was reached with the score still at 5-3

to the home team. In the fourth minute of the second spell Williment goaled a 45 yard penalty and six minutes later repeated his success with a further penalty from a line-out infringement on the 25. Casey kicked a simple penalty from in front of the posts in the thirteenth minute of the half to bring the score to 11-6 to the All Blacks. He narrowed the gap again, seven minutes later, with another penalty following an off-side decision against an All Black forward 35 yards out.

The final scoring in the match came five minutes before no-side when the Matamata-born Wallaby flanker, Greg Davis, who had represented both Thames Valley and Bay of Plenty before settling in Sydney, kicked the ball clear from a desperate situation near his own line into the arms of Moreton who promptly drop kicked a good goal.

257

22 August, 1964

Second Test

As expected the All Black selectors made several changes to the side that had played at Dunedin. A fit Don Clarke was restored to the fullback berth, and former Wallaby half-back Des Connor replaced Laidlaw. A newcomer, Peter Murdoch, earned selection at first five-eighth following impressive play for the New Zealand Colts in Australia earlier in the season. A badly bruised back forced Collins to withdraw after selection, and Moreton was brought in to second five-eighth with another newcomer from Auckland, Ron Rangi, taking the centre position. The thirteen stone Rangi had acquired a reputation as an enterprising attacker and a devastating tackler.

In their only match since the first Test, the Wallabies had suffered a surprise 10-16 defeat at the hands of Mid-Canterbury. Their selectors made only one change to their Test line up with 20 year old Dave Grimmond, playing his sole international, replacing Jim Boyce.

Once they had settled down, the All Blacks

Caulton has Rangi and Smith outside him as he begins an All Black attack.

showed a completely different approach from that of the previous week. Both Clarke and Casey narrowly missed early penalties before the first points came in the fifteenth minute. Smith swooped on to a loose ball following a heavy tackle by Rangi on Honan, and ran 50 yards before throwing a pass to Murdoch who crossed over for a try under the bar. In converting the try, Clarke raised his 201st point in international play.

Seven minutes before halftime, the All Black backs featured in a classic movement started from a line-out outside the Australian 25. Smith came in from the blindside wing outside Murdoch to put Moreton into the gap. Rangi finished off the attack by touching down between the posts. Clarke had no difficulty in converting and halftime was reached with the All Blacks ahead by 10-0. It was interesting to note that all the tries scored by New Zealand this far in the series had been by players making their debut.

Although Australia had the better of the opening minutes of the second spell, it was another

NEW ZEALAND
D.B. CLARKE
(Waikato)

I.S.T. SMITH	R.E. RANGI	R.W. CAULTON
(Otago)	(Auckland)	(Wellington)

R.C. MORETON
(Canterbury)

P.H. MURDOCH
(Auckland)

D.M. CONNOR
(Auckland)

D.J. GRAHAM (**Capt.**)
(Canterbury)

D.W. CLARK	S.T. MEADS	C.E. MEADS	K.R. TREMAIN
(Otago)	(King Country)	(King Country)	(Hawke's Bay)

B.T. THOMAS   B.E. McLEOD   K.F. GRAY
(Wellington)   (Counties)   (Wellington)

J.P.L. WHITE	P.G. JOHNSON	J.E. THORNETT (**Capt.**)
(New South Wales)	(New South Wales)	(New South Wales)

J. GUERASSIMOFF	C.P. CRITTLE	R.J. HEMING	G.V. DAVIS
(Queensland)	(New South Wales)	(New South Wales)	(New South Wales)

D.J. O'NEILL
(Queensland)

K.W. CATCHPOLE
(New South Wales)

P.F. HAWTHORNE
(New South Wales)

D.N. GRIMMOND	R.J.P. MARKS	R.E. HONAN	E.S. BOYCE
(New South Wales)	(Queensland)	(Queensland)	(New South Wales)

T.V. CASEY
(New South Wales)

AUSTRALIA

REFEREE: Mr J.P. Murphy (North Auckland)
ATTENDANCE: 35,000
CONDITIONS: Weather fine, ground firm
HALFTIME: New Zealand 10, Australia 0

SCORERS

NEW ZEALAND	AUSTRALIA
Tries: Murdoch, Rangi, Moreton, Gray	Try: Marks
Conversions: Clarke (3)	

AUSTRALIA 3

Lancaster Park, Christchurch

well-engineered try by the New Zealand backs that led to the next addition to the score. McLeod won a tight head inside the Wallaby 25 and again Smith came in from the blindside but Murdoch's pass missed him out to leave Moreton in the gap. The second five-eighth cut through on the angle to score near the posts without a hand being laid on him. Clarke again had no trouble with the conversion.

During the next period of play, Australia again looked dangerous but poor handling and over-eagerness cost them the opportunity to open their account. Gray scored New Zealand's final try twelve minutes from time following a blindside movement started by Tremain and carried on by Caulton. An in-pass found the big prop in support ten yards from the line and he scored wide out. Clarke's kick was wide.

Australia had to wait until the last minute of the game to open their account. Thornett made a determined run in midfield before unloading to Guerassimoff who sped into the open before passing to Marks. The centre scored a good try but Casey failed with the conversion. New Zealand were on attack as the final whistle blew.

Below: **Moreton beats Casey and Boyce to score with referee Pat Murphy on the spot to award the try.**

CHRISTCHURCH STAR

AUSTRALIA 20

29 August, 1964

Third Test

For the third Saturday in a row the two teams lined up to do battle. The only change in the All Black side saw the recall of Allan Stewart, who had played in all five internationals on the 1963-64 tour as Colin Meads's locking partner as well as in two Tests against England early in 1963. On this occasion he was locking with Stan Meads with Colin moving to the number eight position. Captain John Graham moved to the flank and Otago's Don Clark dropped into the reserves.

After again showing only mediocre form in their mid-week match, this time against Bush who had come with a powerful second half surge to go down by only 13-19, the Wallabies did not appear to have sufficient form to hold what was considered a strong All Black team. Jim Boyce regained his place on the left wing, and Beris Ellwood, the experienced centre, came into the side to play his only Test on the tour. In the forwards, the English-born Victorian, David Shepherd, was making his international debut at number eight.

Thornett won the toss and gave the All Blacks the first use of the light northerly breeze. It was soon obvious that the Wallaby team, playing with great resolution, were going to be difficult to beat. The only scoring in the first half came in the twentieth minute when Johnson won a tight head on the All Black 25 and Catchpole ran on

Blatant obstruction by Johnson as he holds Ken Gray off the Australian half-back, Catchpole.

NEW ZEALAND 5

the blindside eluding the loose forwards and drawing Caulton before passing to the unmarked Stewart Boyce. Boyce sprinted to the corner to score a try which Casey was unable to convert. Clarke, who had earlier missed two penalty attempts, narrowly failed with a long dropped goal after half an hour.

Midway through the second spell, Australia increased their lead when Casey landed a penalty from 35 yards following a scrum infringement. Four minutes later, New Zealand scored their only try when Connor fed Murdoch on the blindside for the five-eighth to hoist a high kick to the Wallaby line. With a spectacular leap Murdoch took the ball above the heads of the defenders and scored. Clarke landed the conversion and recorded what were to be his final points in international play.

The Australians hit back almost immediately when Hawthorne kicked a 40 yard dropped goal. Now rampant, the Australians went further ahead with another Casey penalty, this time from 40 yards, in the thirtieth minute. Casey landed his third penalty five minutes from time, after Clarke failed to release the ball following a tackle near his own goal line. The final points in the match came on the call of no-side when Caulton was caught in a ruck on his 25 yard line. Australia won the ruck and quickly moved the ball out to the unmarked blindside wing, Stewart Boyce who kicked ahead and was favoured by the bounce to score his second try. Casey converted to complete the totally unexpected but well deserved victory by Australia.

The Australian win was the biggest loss incurred by the All Blacks since the 0-17 defeat by South Africa in the first international of the 1928 series. A lethargic All Black pack, in which only Stan Meads emerged with any credit, was blamed for the loss. The back line which had sparkled at Christchurch was unable to operate with any fluency. This match saw the end of the international careers of several well-known All Blacks.

Don Clarke, the seventeen stone full-back, who had become a household name in the years since his first Test in 1956, was forced into retirement prior to the 1965 season by a recurring

knee injury. In his thirty-one Tests he had scored a total of 207 points, the highest total recorded by an individual in international play. His prodigious kicking feats would remain a legend in New Zealand Rugby folklore.

Captain, John Graham, was another All Black retiring after a long international career which had seen him appear in twenty-two Tests since 1958. A lightweight loose forward, he combined speed and intelligence to maximum effect.

The outstanding half-back, Des Connor, had played twelve internationals for New Zealand and ten for his native Australia, but he did not receive the national selectors' nod again. He returned to Brisbane later where he became an Australian national coach.

Others to have played their last Tests were winger Ralph Caulton, with eight tries from his sixteen appearances, and forwards Allan Stewart and Barry Thomas. Thomas had collapsed in the dressing room after the match with severe concussion.

NEW ZEALAND

D.B. CLARKE
(Waikato)

I.S.T. SMITH   R.E. RANGI   R.W. CAULTON
(Otago)   (Auckland)   (Wellington)
              R.C. MORETON
              (Canterbury)

                                  P.H. MURDOCH
                                  (Auckland)
                    D.M. CONNOR
                    (Auckland)
                    C.E. MEADS
                    (King Country)
D.J. GRAHAM (Capt.)   A.J. STEWART   S.T. MEADS   K.R. TREMAIN
(Canterbury)   (South Canterbury) (King Country)   (Hawke's Bay)
B.T. THOMAS   B.E. McLEOD   K.F. GRAY
(Wellington)   (Counties)   (Wellington)

J.P.L. WHITE   P.G. JOHNSON   J.E. THORNETT (Capt.)
(New South Wales)   (New South Wales)   (New South Wales)
J. GUERASSIMOFF   C.P. CRITTLE   R.J. HEMING   G.V. DAVIS
(Queensland)   (New South Wales) (New South Wales) (New South Wales)
                    D.J. SHEPHERD
                    (Victoria)
              K.W. CATCHPOLE
              (New South Wales)
                    P.F. HAWTHORNE
                    (New South Wales)
J.S. BOYCE   R.J.P. MARKS   B.J. ELLWOOD   E.S. BOYCE
(New South Wales) (Queensland) (New South Wales) (New South Wales)
              T.V. CASEY
              (New South Wales)

AUSTRALIA

REFEREE: Mr J.P. Murphy (North Auckland)
ATTENDANCE: 33,000
CONDITIONS: Weather fine, ground firm
HALFTIME: Australia 3, New Zealand 0

SCORERS

NEW ZEALAND	AUSTRALIA
Try: Murdoch	Tries: E.S. Boyce (2)
Conversion: Clarke	Conversion: Casey
	Penalty goals: Casey (3)
	Dropped goal: Hawthorne

31 July, 1965

First Test

The Springboks came to this first Test of the 1965 series with a record of eight wins and a loss. In the second match of the tour the Springboks had gone down to Wellington by the wide margin of 6-23. Six of the tourists had participated in the previous Test series in 1960, five of whom, Lionel Wilson, John Gainsford, Keith Oxlee, "Lofty" Nel and Abe Malan, were playing in this match.

Injuries to two of the chosen All Black side, Dick and Nathan, saw the tall, lean, Christchurch club winger Bill Birtwistle making his first All Black appearance, and Dick Conway, who had been off the international scene since the final Test of the 1960 series, come into the team.

Heavy rain on the two days preceding the match left the ground in slippery condition and as the teams took the field, a fifty mile an hour southerly wind was chilling the spectators.

NEW ZEALAND

M. WILLIMENT
(Wellington)

W.M. BIRTWISTLE   R.E. RANGI   I.S.T. SMITH
(Canterbury)   (Auckland)   (North Otago)

J.L. COLLINS
(Poverty Bay)

P.H. MURDOCH
(Auckland)

C.R. LAIDLAW
(Otago)

B.J. LOCHORE
(Wairarapa)

R.J. CONWAY   S.T. MEADS   C.E. MEADS   K.R. TREMAIN
(Bay of Plenty)   (King Country)   (King Country)   (Hawke's Bay)

K.F. GRAY   B.E. McLEOD   W.J. WHINERAY (Capt.)
(Wellington)   (Counties)   (Auckland)

C.G.P. van ZYL   G.F. MALAN   A.W. MACDONALD
(Orange Free State)   (Transvaal)   (Rhodesia)

J. SCHOEMAN   F.C.H. du PREEZ   J. NAUDE   J.H. ELLIS
(Western   (Northern   (Western   (South West
Province)   Transvaal)   Province)   Africa)

J.A. NEL
(Western Transvaal)

D.J. de VILLIERS (Capt.)
(Western Province)

K. OXLEE
(Natal)

G.S. BRYNARD   F. du T. ROUX   J.L. GAINSFORD   J.P. ENGELBRECHT
(Western   (Griqualand   (Western   (Western
Province)   West)   Province)   Province)

L.G. WILSON
(Western Province)

SOUTH AFRICA

REFEREE: Mr J.P. Murphy (North Auckland)
ATTENDANCE: 46,250
CONDITIONS: Weather overcast and windy, ground slippery
HALFTIME: New Zealand 6, South Africa 0

SCORERS

NEW ZEALAND	SOUTH AFRICA
Tries: Birtwistle, Tremain	Dropped goal: Oxlee

De Villiers won the toss and elected to play into the wind in the first half. Williment put the ball into play and New Zealand were soon attacking strongly. From a five yard scrum in the fifth minute, Laidlaw passed to the blindside where Williment was up to take the ball from the half-back, draw the winger and give Birtwistle the overlap for a try right in the corner. Williment was unable to succeed with a difficult conversion. At this stage of the match the Springbok centres were getting up on to their opposite numbers quickly and taking them with hard tackles which prevented any All Black backline movements gaining momentum.

In the tenth minute, Williment attempted a long dropped goal that only just failed and shortly after he missed a penalty from a handy position. Although the All Blacks were dominating the battle for possession, the side was unable to add to its score until just on halftime.

Following another unsuccessful drop kick at goal by Williment, the All Blacks mounted an attack which saw them win a heel close to the South African line. Again Laidlaw passed to the blind where Williment was up to try to repeat the move which had brought the earlier try. This time he was tackled by de Villiers and the ball went loose. The ever-alert Tremain was first to gather the ball and plunge over near the right hand corner. Some controversy surrounded the awarding of this try, some critics claiming that Williment had knocked the ball forward and that Tremain was in an off-side position when he played the ball. However Mr Murphy had no doubts and, despite Williment's kick again going astray, the All Blacks were to turn around with a lead, if only by six points.

The slender lead was whittled away in the seventh minute of the second half when Oxlee landed a drop kick following a five yard scrum in front of the New Zealand posts. The fly-half missed a further attempt from well out after sixteen minutes and six minutes later, Naude was astray with a penalty from well out.

Throughout this spell, playing into the gale, the All Black pack was in magnificent form, limiting the Springbok opportunities. A further

SOUTH AFRICA 3

Athletic Park, Wellington

Tremain clutches the ball over the goal line while referee Pat Murphy confirms the try. Brynard, McLeod and Malan look on.

long range penalty from Naude was short and Oxlee was wide with another dropped goal.

Conway was despatched back to a second full-back berth to strengthen the defence and was responsible for halting the most promising Springbok movement of the day when he dragged down Brynard just short of the goal line after Gainsford had made a good break.

Close to no-side, Gray and Whineray com-bined in a burst upfield from a line-out, gaining 50 yards which brought sustained applause from the crowd. No further scoring opportunities arose and the game ended shortly after.

In spite of the controversy connected with Tremain's try, it was generally agreed that the New Zealand team had shown superior form in this match and had deserved their victory.

On the weekend that this match was played, the four survivors of the 1905-06 All Black team, George Nicholson, Billy Wallace "Bunny" Abbott and Alex McDonald celebrated the 60th jubilee of their famous tour.

NEW ZEALAND 13

21 August, 1965

Second Test

The only change in the New Zealand line-up saw Ray Moreton replace the luckless Collins, whose failure to impress in the first Test could partly be blamed on the men inside him.

The South Africans made two changes to their team with "Nelie" Smith taking over at half-back from captain de Villiers who had suffered a cut eye in a clash with Auckland full-back Tony Davies on the previous Saturday. Piet Goosen replaced Naude at lock to win his first Test cap.

The heavy going, caused by rain over the twenty-four hours before the match, diminished the Springbok chances and enhanced the home team's prospects.

McLeod dives on the ball which he had kicked over the Springbok line. Meads watches with satisfaction; Ellis and Schoeman are the South Africans.

Williment kicked off for New Zealand and the All Blacks were soon on attack. Only five minutes had gone when the Springboks won a scrum just short of their line and Smith, bustled by Laidlaw, was unable to gather. As the ball went loose Tremain, from the side of the scrum, dived across to score the try. Williment kicked a good conversion from near the touchline.

Owing to the state of the ground, there was little constructive football and, as in the previous Test, the All Black forwards were clearly the better pack. Oxlee was short with a penalty from the 25 after ten minutes and Williment suffered the same fate in the nineteenth minute.

The next points came in the thirty-second minute of the half following a rush by the All Blacks. From a ruck ten yards out from the Springbok line, McLeod booted the ball ahead and won the race to slither over for an opportunist's try. This time Williment was unable to convert with a ball that was by now very heavy and greasy.

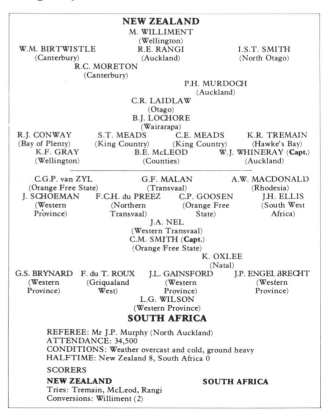

NEW ZEALAND

M. WILLIMENT
(Wellington)

W.M. BIRTWISTLE   R.E. RANGI   I.S.T. SMITH
(Canterbury)   (Auckland)   (North Otago)

R.C. MORETON
(Canterbury)

P.H. MURDOCH
(Auckland)

C.R. LAIDLAW
(Otago)

B.J. LOCHORE
(Wairarapa)

R.J. CONWAY   S.T. MEADS   C.E. MEADS   K.R. TREMAIN
(Bay of Plenty)   (King Country)   (King Country)   (Hawke's Bay)

K.F. GRAY   B.E. McLEOD   W.J. WHINERAY (**Capt.**)
(Wellington)   (Counties)   (Auckland)

C.G.P. van ZYL   G.F. MALAN   A.W. MACDONALD
(Orange Free State)   (Transvaal)   (Rhodesia)

J. SCHOEMAN   F.C.H. du PREEZ   C.P. GOOSEN   J.H. ELLIS
(Western   (Northern   (Orange Free   (South West
Province)   Transvaal)   State)   Africa)

J.A. NEL
(Western Transvaal)

C.M. SMITH (**Capt.**)
(Orange Free State)

K. OXLEE
(Natal)

G.S. BRYNARD   F. du T. ROUX   J.L. GAINSFORD   J.P. ENGELBRECHT
(Western   (Griqualand   (Western   (Western
Province)   West)   Province)   Province)

L.G. WILSON
(Western Province)

SOUTH AFRICA

REFEREE: Mr J.P. Murphy (North Auckland)
ATTENDANCE: 34,500
CONDITIONS: Weather overcast and cold, ground heavy
HALFTIME: New Zealand 8, South Africa 0

SCORERS

NEW ZEALAND	SOUTH AFRICA
Tries: Tremain, McLeod, Rangi	
Conversions: Williment (2)	

SOUTH AFRICA 0

Carisbrook, Dunedin

There was no further score before halftime and the teams turned around with the All Blacks ahead by 8-0.

The second half continued with the All Blacks applying the pressure and only an outstanding match by Lionel Wilson at full-back for South Africa, prevented them from piling on the points. Oxlee was unable to turn a penalty from just outside the New Zealand 25 into points in the sixteenth minute. Then Engelbrecht just beat Smith to the touch down over his own line after a desperate chase following a kick ahead.

Mr Murphy pulled a leg muscle midway through the half but after treatment was able to continue, though with a noticeable limp.

In the thirtieth minute, New Zealand won a ruck in front of the posts and Laidlaw passed to

Murdoch has Smith outside him as he breaks on the blindside.

Murdoch on his right who fed Rangi cutting through on the angle and the latter scored wide out. Williment landed a magnificent goal to complete the scoring.

It had been a clear cut victory by New Zealand and despite the fact that conditions had not been conducive to the open play that they preferred, the South Africans did not appear to have much chance of beating New Zealand in the final two internationals on the tour.

Milestones in this match were reached by Colin Meads, who equalled Don Clarke's record of thirty-one Test appearances for New Zealand, and John Gainsford who equalled Johan Claassen's Springbok record of twenty-eight caps.

This match saw the first victory for the home side in the second international of a South African tour of New Zealand, and it was the biggest margin New Zealand had ever achieved over their illustrious opponents.

4 September, 1965

Third Test

Only one change was made in the New Zealand side with Malcolm Dick, who had been unavailable through injury for the first two Tests of the series, coming in for Ian Smith.

As expected after their team's mediocre showing in the Dunedin Test, the South African selectors made several changes. In an endeavour to add some more attacking ability to the backline, the 20 year old Jannie Barnard came in for Oxlee who had not been playing up to the standard expected of him on the tour. As his partner, de Villiers, again match fit, replaced Smith.

In the forwards, the experienced Doug Hopwood, who had been hampered by a back injury early in the tour, came in to play his twenty-first Test. "Lofty" Nel was shifted to the side of the scrum in the place of Schoeman, and Naude, possibly because of his goal kicking ability with Oxlee not playing, was selected to partner du Preez at lock. Walton, regarded as a better all round forward than Malan, was named as the hooker.

Although the chances for a dry field were dashed when heavy rain started to fall on the previous day, the sun broke through before the match started and the game was played in bright sunshine.

Dr. Danie Craven, President of the South African Rugby Board, had arrived from South Africa on the Wednesday before the game, and was among the spectators as Williment kicked off for the All Blacks with the strongish breeze behind him. From the first line-out, five yards inside the Springbok 25, Dick threw in deep over the line-out where Roux failed to get to the ball but Colin Meads, playing a record thirty-second Test, gathered and passed to Tremain who ran through with ridiculous ease to score his third try in as many Tests in this series. Williment's kick missed.

Almost from the kick off to restart play, Williment was unable to control a kick through by South Africa and conceded a five yard scrum. From this scrum the ball went through de Vil-

Gainsford scores one of his two tries in this Test. Stan Meads is too late with his attempted tackle.

WEEKLY NEWS

liers and Barnard to Gainsford who chopped inside and cut through the defence to score 10 yards to the right of the posts. "Tiny" Naude converted to give the Springboks the lead for the first time in the series.

Barnard missed a drop kick shortly after and it was the Springboks who were having slightly the better of the play at this stage. The next points came after twenty minutes' play from a scrum inside South African territory when Dick came into the backline from the blindside. As he was tackled the ball came loose to Moreton who punted ahead over the Springbok line. Wilson, who appeared to have ample time to get to the ball, was beaten by the bounce and a fast-following Rangi threw himself on the ball to gain the try. Williment goaled from a handy position.

A minute or two later, Mr Murphy, who had been experiencing trouble with the leg he had injured at Dunedin, left the field and was replaced by Mr Alan Taylor who had been a touch judge. He had previously controlled the tourists' match against Southland.

From a line-out penalty, Williment again raised the flags with a 50 yarder, a few minutes later. Over the final fifteen minutes of this half the All Blacks applied a great deal of pressure and were rewarded when de Villiers was caught in possession following a line-out. From the maul Laidlaw fed Murdoch on the blindside. He drew the defence and passed to Moreton who scored in the right hand corner. Williment again converted and the All Blacks had what appeared to be an unassailable lead of 16-5 after thirty-three minutes, the score remaining the same till halftime.

Five minutes after the resumption, South Africa started their revival. From a scrum inside the All Black 25, de Villiers ran on the open side before setting his backs in motion. Gainsford cut through the gap between Moreton and Rangi before passing to Roux who sent Brynard away to score a fine try. Naude was unable to add the extra points but the movement had given confidence to the Springboks. Williment was short with a penalty into the wind, but this was one of New Zealand's few scoring opportunities in this spell.

From a scrum de Villiers ran on the blind then switched play to the open side, after Gainsford had been held. Barnard ran across field through a gap before sending a high overhand pass to Brynard who cut back in-field and completed the movement with a spectacular leap over Williment's tackle to score a fine try. Naude converted to put his team within three points of the New Zealanders after 14 minutes of the second half.

By now the Springbok forwards were playing well and shading the All Blacks. Naude missed a long range penalty, then Gainsford, who was showing outstanding form in this, his record making twenty-ninth Test, scored his second try.

In the twenty-third minute a scrum went down in the middle of the 25 when Williment's drop-out went out on the full. Roux made a half break for Gainsford to cut through and beat Williment on the way to score in the corner.

Naude was unable to put his side into the lead with the conversion but with no points coming during the next thirteen minutes, his next chance came with two minutes to play when South Africa were awarded a penalty just outside the All Black 25. He appeared to top the kick but the ball just carried over the bar and the Springboks were jubilant to have retrieved the game from an almost impossible position.

This match was to be the final international appearance of the New Zealand five-eighth pair of Peter Murdoch and Ray Moreton. Murdoch had played five Tests in a row since his debut the previous year and Moreton had played in seven since 1962.

NEW ZEALAND

M. WILLIMENT
(Wellington)

W.M. BIRTWISTLE R.E. RANGI M.J. DICK
(Canterbury) (Auckland) (Auckland)
R.C. MORETON
(Canterbury)

P.H. MURDOCH
(Auckland)
C.R. LAIDLAW
(Otago)
B.J. LOCHORE
(Wairarapa)

R.J. CONWAY S.T. MEADS C.E. MEADS K.R. TREMAIN
(Bay of Plenty) (King Country) (King Country) (Hawke's Bay)
K.F. GRAY B.E. McLEOD W.J. WHINERAY (Capt.)
(Wellington) (Counties) (Auckland)

C.G.P. van ZYL D.C. WALTON A.W. MACDONALD
(Orange Free State) (Natal) (Rhodesia)
J.A. NEL F.C.H. du PREEZ J. NAUDE J.H. ELLIS
(Western (Northern (Western (South West
Transvaal) Transvaal) Province) Africa)
D.J. HOPWOOD
(Western Province)
H.J. van der MERWE
(Western Province)
J.H. BARNARD
(Transvaal)
G.S. BRYNARD F. du T. ROUX J.L. GAINSFORD J.P. ENGELBRECHT
(Western (Griqualand (Western (Western
Province) West) Province) Province)
L.G. WILSON
(Western Province)

SOUTH AFRICA

REFEREE: Mr J.P. Murphy (North Auckland)
   replaced during first half because of injury by
   Mr A.R. Taylor (Canterbury)
ATTENDANCE: 52,650
CONDITIONS: Weather fine, ground wet and greasy
HALFTIME: New Zealand 16, South Africa 5
SCORERS

NEW ZEALAND	SOUTH AFRICA
Tries: Tremain, Rangi, Moreton	Tries: Gainsford (2), Brynard (2)
Conversions: Williment (2)	Conversions: Naude (2)
Penalty goal: Williment	Penalty goal: Naude

NEW ZEALAND 20

18 September, 1965

Fourth Test

The question being posed before this match was, "Can the Springboks who have shown good form in their three matches since the last Test, and who have, for the first time struck a firm ground for an international, tie the series"?

Opinions varied of course but most critics thought that the New Zealand forwards would carry the day. Understandably the Springboks retained their winning third Test combination, hoping that their forwards would again hold the All Black pack, giving their brilliant backs the chance to win the game for them as they had done at Lancaster Park.

On the other hand, the New Zealand selectors made four backline changes. Both Williment, who had suffered concussion in the tourists' match against the N.Z. Universities, and Dick, who had a leg injury, were unavailable. They were replaced by Fergie McCormick, playing his first international, and Ian Smith, North Otago's first All Black (having shifted to Oamaru from Gimmerburn prior to the season) who had played in the first two Tests of the series.

Also reintroduced to the team were John Collins, replacing Moreton, who had been repeatedly beaten by Gainsford at Christchurch, and "Mac" Herewini, who had last appeared for New Zealand on the 1963-64 tour. Herewini's inclusion seemed to indicate that the All Blacks were going to revert to the kicking five-eighth style of play.

An interesting feature of the New Zealand team was that the forwards, all from the North Island, had been kept intact for the entire series.

After being introduced to the Governor-General, Sir Bernard Fergusson, the two sides prepared to commence this vital match. Whineray had won the toss and elected to play into the lightest of breezes and the sun. Naude kicked off with a long kick which resulted in the All Blacks dropping out from the 25.

Five minutes after the start, McCormick was given a shot at goal from a penalty 45 yards out but the kick was short. Barnard however mulled the catch and a scrum was called for the knock-on. A perfect attacking position was wasted when Herewini mis-kicked a cross kick with two men outside him and the ball went into touch on the full. The large crowd groaned. A scrum was called from the resultant line-out and Tremain picked up the ball as it emerged. He endeavoured to make progress on the blind before passing to Conway who crashed over five yards from the left hand corner through the tackles of Hopwood and Engelbrecht. McCormick's kick was unsuccessful. Both sides missed penalty attempts during the remainder of the half, and neither team looked like scoring a try.

South Africa equalled the score in the tenth minute of the second half when Naude goaled a 45 yard scrum penalty. A minute later, de Villiers fed Brynard on the blind from a scrum just inside the Springbok half. The winger was unable to take a poor pass and his opposite number Birtwistle was quickly on to the loose ball and sprinted down the right hand touchline. As Barnard and

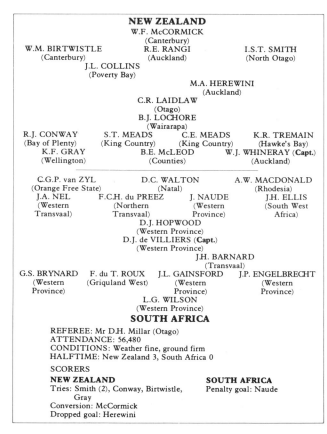

NEW ZEALAND

W.F. McCORMICK
(Canterbury)

W.M. BIRTWISTLE	R.E. RANGI	I.S.T. SMITH
(Canterbury)	(Auckland)	(North Otago)

J.L. COLLINS
(Poverty Bay)

M.A. HEREWINI
(Auckland)

C.R. LAIDLAW
(Otago)

B.J. LOCHORE
(Wairarapa)

R.J. CONWAY	S.T. MEADS	C.E. MEADS	K.R. TREMAIN
(Bay of Plenty)	(King Country)	(King Country)	(Hawke's Bay)
K.F. GRAY	B.E. McLEOD	W.J. WHINERAY (Capt.)
(Wellington)	(Counties)	(Auckland)

C.G.P. van ZYL	D.C. WALTON	A.W. MACDONALD
(Orange Free State)	(Natal)	(Rhodesia)
J.A. NEL	F.C.H. du PREEZ	J. NAUDE	J.H. ELLIS
(Western Transvaal)	(Northern Transvaal)	(Western Province)	(South West Africa)

D.J. HOPWOOD
(Western Province)

D.J. de VILLIERS (Capt.)
(Western Province)

J.H. BARNARD
(Transvaal)

G.S. BRYNARD	F. du T. ROUX	J.L. GAINSFORD	J.P. ENGELBRECHT
(Western Province)	(Griqualand West)	(Western Province)	(Western Province)

L.G. WILSON
(Western Province)

SOUTH AFRICA

REFEREE: Mr D.H. Millar (Otago)
ATTENDANCE: 56,480
CONDITIONS: Weather fine, ground firm
HALFTIME: New Zealand 3, South Africa 0

SCORERS

NEW ZEALAND	SOUTH AFRICA
Tries: Smith (2), Conway, Birtwistle, Gray	Penalty goal: Naude
Conversion: McCormick	
Dropped goal: Herewini	

SOUTH AFRICA 3

Eden Park, Auckland

Engelbrecht comes over from the opposite wing to see Birtwistle score after a clever run.

Wilson converged on him he reached the goal line. Birtwistle braked, allowing Barnard to hurtle harmlessly by. He then side-stepped inside to elude Wilson and score close to the corner. Herewini was no more successful with his kick than McCormick had been.

Within three minutes the All Blacks were over again after the Springboks had endeavoured to open up play from a tap penalty inside their own 25. Barnard covered about 20 yards before throwing a pass behind Roux as he was confronted by the regrouped defence. Smith gathered the ball on the bounce and raced the 20 or 30 yards to score in the left hand corner. Herewini was again unable to convert.

Smith made it a double only two minutes later when Barnard, again from inside his 25, tried a short tactical kick as he attempted to start an attack but the kick was pulled down by Lochore. He ran through two or three ineffectual tackles before linking with Rangi who sent Smith away with an overlap. The winger again sprinted the few remaining yards to the corner where he touched down for his second try. Herewini was

astray again with his conversion but made amends four minutes later when he landed a neat dropped goal following a scrum on the left hand side of the field inside the South African 25. These twelve points in eleven minutes made the game safe for New Zealand but with three tries coming as a direct result of breakdowns in Springbok attacks inside their own half, the South Africans had virtually given the game to New Zealand on a plate.

The All Blacks now took control of the game but were unable to score again until right on the call of time when Herewini endeavoured to make a break on the blindside following a scrum on the Springbok 25. As he was caught he managed to get a pass infield to Gray who burst away to run around and score by the posts. McCormick, whose father Arch had played one match for New Zealand as a hooker in the 2-3-2 scrum in 1925, was called up to take the simple conversion which he duly goaled to complete the scoring in this match.

The victory by twenty points to three was the largest score totalled by New Zealand in a match against South Africa, and was the most comprehensive defeat the Springboks had suffered in an international.

Prior to the match the New Zealand captain, Wilson Whineray, had announced that this would be his final international appearance. Since 1957 he had made thirty-two Test appearances, thirty of which had been as captain, easily a record for an All Black. The previous highest was seven by Cliff Porter. A tremendously popular leader, he was a mobile, constructive and intelligent forward, and certainly one of New Zealand's Rugby 'greats'. Whineray was also a good schoolboy cricketer, a successful back-stroke swimmer and heavy-weight boxing champion of the New Zealand Universities.

Other All Blacks to reach the end of their Test careers in this match were the lively flanker, Dick Conway, whose play had probably shown more maturity in this series than in his previous six internationals in 1959-60, and the Maori five-eighth, John Collins who had appeared in three Tests.

NEW ZEALAND 20

16 July, 1966

First Test

After an unbeaten eight match tour of Australia, culminating in a 31-0 defeat of the Wallabies at Brisbane, the 1966 Lions team had made heavy weather of the early part of the New Zealand section of the tour. In the opening fixture they had gone down to Southland and on successive Saturdays following this match, Otago and Wellington had also taken the honours. By the time the first Test was reached, the tourists had won five of their nine matches (having drawn with Bay of Plenty).

Of the Test team, Jones, Bebb, Watkins, Pask and Price for Wales and Wilson and Telfer for Scotland had opposed New Zealand in the internationals on the 1963-64 tour.

New faces in the All Black side were Ian Mac-Rae, the solid centre from the Marist club in Napier; Tony Steel the national sprint champion and relative of the famous winger of the 1920's, Jack Steel; and Jack Hazlett who had claimed

EVENING POST

Both McLeod and Tremain appear to reflect upon the situation after a try scored by the All Black hooker.

Whineray's place in the front row following a sterling display as captain of Southland against the tourists. MacRae had played seventeen matches on the 1963-64 All Black tour as a 20 year old without winning a Test position.

Mr John Pring was controlling his first international after refereeing touring teams since 1956.

The Lions kicked off with the wind at their backs, but were soon defending desperately. Herewini was prevented from scoring only through touching one of his own men in front of him as he prepared to dive over, but after eight minutes Herewini was again instrumental in initiating an attacking move after he had received the ball following a line-out. When he was caught after jinking past Watkins, he slipped the ball to Nathan who transferred to McLeod who scored the try. Williment converted from a wide angle.

NEW ZEALAND
M. WILLIMENT
(Wellington)

I.S.T. SMITH   R.E. RANGI   A.G. STEEL
(North Otago)   (Auckland)   (Canterbury)

I.R. MacRAE
(Hawke's Bay)

M.A. HEREWINI
(Auckland)

C.R. LAIDLAW
(Otago)

B.J. LOCHORE (**Capt.**)
(Wairarapa)

K.R. TREMAIN   S.T. MEADS   C.E. MEADS   W.J. NATHAN
(Hawke's Bay)   (King Country)   (King Country)   (Auckland)
K.F. GRAY   B.E. McLEOD   E.J. HAZLETT
(Wellington)   (Counties)   (Southland)

C.H. NORRIS   K.W. KENNEDY   D. WILLIAMS
(Cardiff & Wales)   (C.I.Y.M.S. & Ireland)   (Ebbw Vale & Wales)
R.A. LAMONT   M.J. CAMPBELL-LAMERTON   B. PRICE   J.W. TELFER
(Instonians &   (London Scottish &   (Newport &   (Melrose &
Ireland)   Scotland) (**Capt.**)   Wales)   Scotland)
A.E.I. PASK
(Abertillery & Wales)
R.M. YOUNG
(Queens University & Ireland)
D. WATKINS
(Newport & Wales)
D.I.E. BEBB   C.M.H. GIBSON   D.K. JONES   C.W. McFADYEAN
(Swansea & Wales)   (Cambridge University   (Cardiff & Wales)   (Moseley & England)
& Ireland)
S. WILSON
(London Scottish & Scotland)
BRITISH ISLES

REFEREE: Mr J.P.G. Pring (Auckland)
ATTENDANCE: 43,000
CONDITIONS: Weather overcast and cold, ground slightly soft
HALFTIME: New Zealand 8, British Isles 3

SCORERS

NEW ZEALAND	BRITISH ISLES
Tries: McLeod, Williment, Lochore	Penalty goal: Wilson
Conversion: Williment	
Penalty goals: Williment (2)	
Dropped goal: Herewini	

270

Carisbrook, Dunedin

Two minutes later Wilson kicked the Lions' only points in this match when he landed a 37 yard penalty to make the score 5-3. Both full-backs missed penalty attempts before New Zealand won a scrum on the Lions' 25 in the thirty-second minute, and Laidlaw sent the ball to Herewini who successfully kicked a dropped goal. This was the extent of the scoring in the first half and the teams changed ends with the score standing at 8-3.

Four minutes after the interval, New Zealand went further ahead after the forwards won a maul

inside the Lions' 25 and the ball went from Laidlaw to Herewini on the blind. He sent on to Smith who found Williment up outside him to take the pass and score in Gibson's tackle in the corner. Williment was unable to convert his own try.

Halfway through the spell, Nathan was on hand to gather the ball that had gone loose in a tackle and make a strong run before handing on to his captain Lochore who crossed two yards in from the corner. Williment was again unable to add the extra points, but at 14-3 the game looked safe for the All Blacks. Two minutes later, following an impressive 40 yard run by Colin Meads with the ball held in one hand, Kennedy was spotted by the referee entering the All Black side of a maul in front of his own posts, and Williment kicked the easiest of goals. With ten minutes to play, Williment was provided with another straight-forward penalty from nearly in front on the tourists' 25 and he had no trouble in landing his second penalty of the match.

The New Zealand Team
Back row: M.A. Herewini, G.F. Kember (reserve), I.R. MacRae, M. Williment, E.J. Hazlett, P.E. Scott (reserve), R.E. Rangi, J. Major (reserve).
Second row: V.L. George (selector), B.E. McLeod, K.F. Gray, C.E. Meads, S.T. Meads, K.R. Tremain, W.J. Nathan, D.L. Christian (selector).
Front row: R.L. Burk (manager), A.G. Steel, C.R. Laidlaw, B.J. Lochore (capt.), I.S.T. Smith, L.J. Davis (reserve), F.R. Allen (selector).

CAMPBELL PHOTOGRAPHY

NEW ZEALAND 16

6 August, 1966

Second Test

Only one change was made in the All Black line up for this match, with Bill Birtwistle being selected for the right wing berth in place of Smith. However, owing to an injury suffered in training, Birtwistle was forced to withdraw and Smith came back into the side, making the team unchanged from that which had won the first Test.

On the other hand, the Lions made seven changes to their side — reduced to six when newcomer McLoughlin was forced to pull out, suffering from a high temperature on the morning of the match. The captain, Campbell-Lamerton, was dropped in favour of the uncapped Llanelli lock Delme Thomas, with the captaincy going to David Watkins. Noel Murphy, who had played in three of the internationals on the 1959 Lions' tour as well as appearing for Ireland against New Zealand in 1963 in Dublin, earned selection on the side of the scrum, with Telfer taking Pask's place in the back row. "Willie John" McBride, who had also appeared for Ireland in 1963, came in to partner Thomas in the middle row, and Frank Laidlaw replaced Kennedy as hooker. The new scrum-half was Allan Lewis and Hinshelwood went on to the wing to replace McFadyean who took Jones's centre position.

Watkins kicked off with the wind at his back and after five minutes Wilson was given an opportunity from a penalty wide out on the All Black 25. A well judged kick put the first points on the board. He missed a further chance from the same position a few minutes later when the ball deflected away off the posts, and then Williment was short with a fifty yard attempt into the wind.

New Zealand took the lead after they had won a line-out three yards inside the Lions' half. A long pass from Laidlaw missed Herewini and was taken by MacRae who burst through the tackle of his opposite number and ran strongly up the middle of the field before linking up with Laidlaw. The half-back passed to McLeod and finally Tremain, with the line open, scored the try midway between the posts and the corner flag. Williment did well to convert into the strong wind,

giving New Zealand the lead after quarter of an hour.

Almost immediately the Lions regained the lead when Watkins dropped a goal from a Lions' tighthead inside the All Black 25. Wilson put his side further ahead with another wide angled penalty in the twenty-eighth minute. A minute later Williment goaled a fine 45 yard penalty to reduce the leeway to one point.

The Lions' forwards were playing much better than they had done at Dunedin and their backline was operating with more freedom, one glorious movement during the first half being recalled for a forward pass as Gibson dotted down in the corner.

The Lions held their narrow one point lead as the teams changed around at halftime. Three minutes into the second half, Watkins was caught in possession inside his own half and Nathan gathered the ball and started a rush up

---

NEW ZEALAND

M. WILLIMENT
(Wellington)

I.S.T. SMITH (North Otago) — R.E. RANGI (Auckland) — A.G. STEEL (Canterbury)

I.R. MacRAE (Hawke's Bay)

M.A. HEREWINI (Auckland)

C.R. LAIDLAW (Otago)

B.J. LOCHORE (Capt.) (Wairarapa)

K.R. TREMAIN (Hawke's Bay) — S.T. MEADS (King Country) — C.E. MEADS (King Country) — W.J. NATHAN (Auckland)

K.F. GRAY (Wellington) — B.E. McLEOD (Counties) — E.J. HAZLETT (Southland)

C.H. NORRIS (Cardiff & Wales) — F.A.L. LAIDLAW (Melrose & Scotland) — D. WILLIAMS (Ebbw Vale & Wales)

R.A. LAMONT (Instonians & Ireland) — W.J. McBRIDE (Ballymena & Ireland) — W.D. THOMAS (Llanelli) — N.A.A. MURPHY (Cork Constitution & Ireland)

J.W. TELFER (Melrose & Scotland)

A.R. LEWIS (Abertillery & Wales)

D. WATKINS (Capt.) (Newport & Wales)

D.I.E. BEBB (Swansea & Wales) — C.M.H. GIBSON (Cambridge University & Ireland) — C.W. McFADYEAN (Moseley & England) — A.J.W. HINSHELWOOD (London Scottish & Scotland)

S. WILSON (London Scottish & Scotland)

BRITISH ISLES

REFEREE: Mr J.P. Murphy (North Auckland)
ATTENDANCE: 44,425
CONDITIONS: Weather overcast and windy, ground muddy
HALFTIME: British Isles 9, New Zealand 8
SCORERS

NEW ZEALAND	BRITISH ISLES
Tries: Tremain, C.E. Meads, Steel	Penalty goals: Wilson (3)
Conversions: Williment (2)	Dropped goal: Watkins
Penalty goal: Williment	

BRITISH ISLES 12

Athletic Park, Wellington

Laidlaw is well protected as he kicks from a line-out. The All Black forwards are McLeod, Gray, Colin Meads, Stan Meads, Tremain and Lochore.

field before passing to Smith, who turned the ball back inside to Tremain. The flanker fed a rampaging Colin Meads who scored ten yards from the posts. Williment converted to put the All Blacks 13-9 up.

With the wind now at their backs, the All Blacks attacked strongly and were unlucky not to increase their lead. Williment failed narrowly with two penalty attempts and Steel was pushed out in the corner after Colin Meads had figured prominently in a movement.

No further scoring occurred until only eight minutes were left on the clock. After the Lions

had won a line-out, Watkins had his kick charged down by Stan Meads and the All Blacks obtained possession. Rangi was held as he headed off down field but Colin Meads gained possession and linked with Lochore who put the speedy Steel away for the corner where he scored the try. This time Williment was unable to convert.

The final points in the match came with three minutes to play when Wilson landed his third penalty from a line-out infringement on the All Black 25.

Despite the muddy conditions the two teams had entertained the crowd to a fine exhibition of running Rugby and the improvement in the Lions' play augured well for the two remaining matches of the series.

27 August, 1966

Third Test

For the third international in a row the New Zealand side took the field unchanged. This was the first occasion on which this had occurred.

On the other hand, the Lions' team featured three alterations, with Stuart Watkins replacing Hinshelwood on the right wing, Pask taking Telfer's place in the back of the scrum, and the major surprise of placing Thomas, who had come through his Test baptism well at Wellington, in the front row. Presumably this was to allow team captain Campbell-Lamerton to come back into the side partnering McBride at lock. This appeared to be a strange decision, especially as the Lions had props available of the calibre of McLoughlin, Williams and Powell.

Williment kicked off and New Zealand were soon on attack. The Lions were showing flashes of brilliance but were unable to put points on the board. Sixteen minutes had gone when Willi-

ment kicked a fine penalty from wide out on the Lions' 25 to open the scoring. He was again successful with a further penalty six minutes later when the Lions were penalised at a ruck inside their 25.

In the twenty-ninth minute of the half the Lions scored their first try of the series following a scrum 10 yards outside the All Black 25. Lewis got the ball to Watkins who tried to find an opening before sending on to Gibson who brilliantly burst into the open. The centre found Stuart Watkins inside him but the Newport winger was caught by Rangi right on the goal line. From the ensuing scramble Lamont threw himself on the ball to score 10 yards in from the corner. Wilson missed the kick.

Three minutes before the interval, Stuart Watkins kicked a loose ball away after Rangi had been tackled on the Lions' 25 and, showing clever control, kept the ball at toe until he was inside the All Blacks' 25. Here Steel went down on the ball but Stuart Watkins recovered possession and threw a long overhand pass to Pask who had been intelligently following up. Pask found Gibson and David Watkins in support and it was the little fly-half who scooted away to score a brilliant try 10 yards in from the left corner. Wilson again failed with the conversion and the halftime score was level at 6-6.

During the first ten minutes of the second half, with a freshening wind at their backs, the Lions looked as if they could take control of the match. Gibson made another fine break which failed only narrowly to yield a try and David Watkins just missed a drop kick at goal.

When the All Blacks came back on to attack after twelve minutes, Herewini was held up on the goal line from a five yard scrum. As the ball came clear, Laidlaw was able to send Steel away unmarked and the winger dotted down fifteen yards in from the corner. Williment's conversion was astray.

Midway through the half MacRae punted ahead from the half-way line and the ball bounced back in-field, wrong footing the defenders. Before the Lions' backs could get the ball

---

NEW ZEALAND

M. WILLIMENT
(Wellington)

I.S.T. SMITH   R.E. RANGI   A.G. STEEL
(North Otago)   (Auckland)   (Canterbury)

I.R. MacRAE
(Hawke's Bay)

M.A. HEREWINI
(Auckland)

C.R. LAIDLAW
(Otago)

B.J. LOCHORE (Capt.)
(Wairarapa)

K.R. TREMAIN   S.T. MEADS   C.E. MEADS   W.J. NATHAN
(Hawke's Bay)   (King Country)   (King Country)   (Auckland)

K.F. GRAY   B.E. McLEOD   E.J. HAZLETT
(Wellington)   (Counties)   (Southland)

C.H. NORRIS   F.A.L. LAIDLAW   W.D. THOMAS
(Cardiff & Wales)   (Melrose & Scotland)   (Llanelli)

R.A. LAMONT   W.J. McBRIDE   M.J. CAMPBELL-LAMERTON   N.A.A. MURPHY
(Instonians &   (Ballymena &   (London Scottish   (Cork Constitution &
Ireland)   Ireland)   & Scotland) (Capt.)   Ireland)

A.E.I. PASK
(Abertillery & Wales)

A.R. LEWIS
(Abertillery & Wales)

D. WATKINS
(Newport & Wales)

D.I.E. BEBB   C.M.H. GIBSON   C.W. McFADYEAN   S.J. WATKINS
(Swansea & Wales)   (Cambridge University)   (Moseley & England)   (Newport & Wales)
     & Ireland)

S. WILSON
(London Scottish & Scotland)

BRITISH ISLES

REFEREE: Mr J.P. Murphy (North Auckland)
ATTENDANCE: 52,000
CONDITIONS: Weather overcast and cold, ground greasy
HALFTIME: New Zealand 6, British Isles 6

SCORERS

NEW ZEALAND	BRITISH ISLES
Tries: Nathan (2), Steel	Tries: Lamont, D. Watkins
Conversions: Williment (2)	
Penalty goals: Williment (2)	

BRITISH ISLES

Lancaster Park, Christchurch

under control, Nathan was through with the All Black forwards to gather and race away to score in the corner. This time Williment raised the flags with a good kick to take the score to New Zealand 14, British Isles 6.

With seven minutes to play, New Zealand scored their final points of the match when Mac-Rae made a burst following a scrum. He linked the ball to Gray who transferred it to Tremain. He returned it to Gray who was tackled on the

line. Nathan was on hand to pick up and score behind the posts. Williment chipped the ball over to complete the scoring.

This had been a game in which the Lions had done themselves less than justice with poor finishing. Their midfield backs, and Mike Gibson in particular, had made some brilliant breaks but needless infringements prevented points being scored.

It had been Ian Smith's last international. In the three seasons since 1964 this reliable three-quarter had played nine Tests.

Tremain blocks this kick by Pask. Lochore and Murphy (7) seem confused by the whereabouts of the ball.

NEW ZEALAND 24

10 September, 1966

Fourth Test

The only change in the team which represented New Zealand during this series took place for this match when Dick replaced Smith on the right wing.

Once again the Lions' side featured several changes with Hinshelwood replacing Stuart Watkins who had received a leg injury; Pask going on to the side of the scrum in the injured Murphy's place with Telfer regaining his place at number eight; and the experienced Brian Price taking Campbell-Lamerton's place at lock. The experiment of playing Delme Thomas at prop came to an end when he tore a ligament in his back during the match against Counties on the previous Tuesday, and he was replaced by Denzil Williams. Ray McLoughlin, whose eighteen caps for his country had included an international against New Zealand in 1963 came in for Norris. To complete a new front row, Ken Kennedy took over as hooker.

The large crowd that had paid a record sum of £43,000 to see the match, watched Williment kick off and the All Blacks go on to early attack. Williment missed a penalty in the first minute but generally it was a quiet start until the thirteenth minute when Bebb hurriedly scrambled the ball to touch a yard short of his goal line when Herewini prevented him from taking a short kick. Colin Meads was speedily to the ball and took a quick throw in to Nathan who crossed for his third Test try in succession six yards from the right hand corner. The speed of the movement caught the Lions napping. Williment converted with a fine kick.

New Zealand went further ahead nine minutes later following an attempted dropped goal by Herewini from a line-out inside the Lions' 25. When the ball rebounded off McFadyean, Dick was in to pick up the spinning ball brilliantly, evade three defenders and score by the posts. The conversion was little more than a formality for Williment, and the All Blacks were up by ten points.

Shortly after this try the Lions suffered another setback when Pask was upended at the back of a line-out. He fell heavily on the point of his shoulder and was forced to retire. Subsequent examination confirmed that his collar bone had been fractured. His loss was a severe one for the Lions, but they fought back well and in the fourteen minutes to halftime had scored two tries and brought themselves to within two points of the New Zealand total.

Hinshelwood leaves Herewini sprawling as he dives to score.

NZ HERALD

276

Eden Park, Auckland

Their first try came in the thirty-fifth minute of the half after Wilson had come into a back line movement following a line-out on the New Zealand 25 and given Hinshelwood the overlap. The winger raced past Steel, stepped inside Williment, eluded the tackle of Herewini, and scored with a dive at the line five yards from the corner. Wilson was wide with his conversion but within two minutes the Lions were over again. This time Lewis made a break when Laidlaw was unable to gather a tighthead, on half-way, and he sent away Gibson who brilliantly wrong-footed the defence before unloading to the flying McFadyean on the 25. No one had a chance of stopping the centre and he scored between the posts for Wilson to kick the conversion.

With the score at New Zealand 10, British Isles 8 at the interval, the game was again wide open. By now the sun had come out and the All Blacks were to play into it in the second half. The Lions attacked strongly in the opening minutes of the second half and were unlucky not to score on at least one occasion when Gibson was recalled with the line wide open after the ball had rebounded off his knee.

However the All Black eight gradually wore the depleted Lions' pack down and in the twenty-fourth minute the vital points came to New Zealand. After Gibson had mishandled in a passing movement Nathan and then Tremain toed the ball ahead to be joined by MacRae and between them the ball was taken down to the Lions' line where MacRae won a desperate race to score by the posts. Williment landed his third successive conversion to bring the score to 15-8.

Two minutes later Herewini was successful with a drop kick from 35 yards. The final try of the match came with nine minutes to play, following a drop out by the Lions. Laidlaw opened play up before getting the ball to McLeod who found Tremain in support. The powerful flanker was tackled just short of the line but Hazlett got a long pass to Steel who scored two yards in from the corner. Williment missed the conversion. In the final three minutes, first Wilson from 35 yards then Williment from 28 yards in front of the posts, kicked penalties to complete the scoring in the match and the series.

Potentially a fine side, the Lions had made too many errors under pressure during the series to warrant victory, but their determined efforts and mid-field brilliance had deserved a better fate than a 0-4 drubbing. Whilst less spectacular than their opponents the All Blacks had played sound football backed up by reliable goalkicking. They enjoyed the good fortune to be able to play the series using only sixteen men.

Players to reach the end of their Test careers in this match were Ron Rangi the thickset centre, who was to face a disciplinary suspension for a time, and Stan Meads. Rangi in his ten internationals had scored three tries, and Stan Meads, whose early withdrawal from serious Rugby robbed New Zealand of one of their finest forwards, had appeared in fifteen Tests since his debut in 1961.

NEW ZEALAND

M. WILLIMENT
(Wellington)

M.J. DICK	R.E. RANGI	A.G. STEEL
(Auckland)	(Auckland)	(Canterbury)

I.R. MacRAE
(Hawke's Bay)

M.A. HEREWINI
(Auckland)

C.R. LAIDLAW
(Otago)

B.J. LOCHORE (**Capt.**)
(Wairarapa)

K.R. TREMAIN	S.T. MEADS	C.E. MEADS	W.J. NATHAN
(Hawke's Bay)	(King Country)	(King Country)	(Auckland)
K.F. GRAY	B.E. McLEOD		E.J. HAZLETT
(Wellington)	(Counties)		(Southland)

R.J. McLOUGHLIN	K.W. KENNEDY	D. WILLIAMS
(Gosforth & Ireland)	(C.I.Y.M.S. & Ireland)	(Ebbw Vale & Wales)
A.E.I. PASK	B. PRICE	W.J. McBRIDE	R.A. LAMONT
(Abertillery & Wales)	(Newport & Wales)	(Ballymena & Ireland)	(Instonians & Ireland)

J.W. TELFER
(Melrose & Scotland)

A.R. LEWIS
(Abertillery & Wales)

D. WATKINS (Capt.)
(Newport & Wales)

D.I.E. BEBB	C.M.H. GIBSON	C.W. McFADYEAN	A.J.W. HINSHELWOOD
(Swansea & Wales)	(Cambridge University & Ireland)	(Moseley & England)	(London Scottish & Scotland)

S. WILSON
(London Scottish & Scotland)

BRITISH ISLES

REFEREE: Mr J.P. Murphy (North Auckland)
ATTENDANCE: 58,000
CONDITIONS: Weather fine, ground firm
HALFTIME: New Zealand 10, British Isles 8

SCORERS

NEW ZEALAND	**BRITISH ISLES**
Tries: Nathan, Dick, MacRae, Steel	Tries: Hinshelwood, McFadyean
Conversions: Williment (3)	Conversion: Wilson
Penalty goal: Williment	Penalty goal: Wilson
Dropped goal: Herewini	

NEW ZEALAND 2

19 August, 1967

As part of the New Zealand Rugby Union's Seventy-fifth Jubilee celebrations in Wellington, a match was arranged between New Zealand and her oldest rival on the Rugby field, Australia. Several hundred past All Blacks, Test referees and prominent administrators were present at Athletic Park to view this match. Before the match a parade of nearly 300 ex-All Blacks was held. Two survivors of the first international played by New Zealand in 1903 against Australia, W.J. Wallace and G.W. Nicholson, together with a 1905 team mate, H.L. Abbott, led the parade.

This Test marked the entry to international Rugby of Sid Going, the famous North Auckland half-back. Although inferior to such players as Connor and Laidlaw as a passing half-back, Going has had no equal as a runner from behind the pack. As a match-winner he has been in a class of his own. Other newcomers to Test Rugby were Sam Strahan, John Major, Bill Davis and Brian Muller.

Only a slight southerly breeze marred an otherwise pleasantly fine day as Brass kicked off for Australia in front of an estimated crowd of 50,000. After five minutes Herewini dropped a goal from a wide angle and ten minutes later Williment landed a fine 50 yard penalty.

Midway through the spell, nineteen year old Rod Batterham scored the first of his tries, following a cross kick by Hawthorne. Batterham failed with the conversion. A few minutes later the Wallaby centre Phil Smith had to retire with an injured shoulder. He returned to the field near halftime with his arm heavily strapped to his side.

Five minutes before halftime, Bill Davis made a brilliant run from well inside his half to the Australian 25, where a forward pass halted a promising move. From the ensuing scrum Australia were penalised and Williment kicked a simple goal to make it 9-3 to New Zealand at the interval.

Early in the second half Batterham kicked a 35 yard penalty to close the gap to three points. However, only three minutes later, Bill Davis gathered in a kick ahead by MacRae and ran 20 yards to score a try which Williment converted. Four minutes after this, Herewini made a break on the blindside before unloading to Steel, who ran 50 yards to score behind the posts for Williment to again convert.

Only two minutes later New Zealand were in again when Going, playing extremely well in his first international, broke from a ruck. Meads was on hand to carry on the movement and finally pass to Tremain who scored and again Williment found the posts with his conversion. In nine minutes, New Zealand had gone from 9-6 to a comfortable 24-6. Australia scored next when they spun the ball along their backline following an All Black drop-out, and Batterham ran 20 yards to score a try which he could not convert.

Five minutes from the end came perhaps the best try of the match. From a scrum on half-way, Herewini threw an overhead pass to Bill Davis who beat his man with a dummy and drew the defence, before passing to Steel who showed his

---

NEW ZEALAND

M. WILLIMENT
(Wellington)

M.J. DICK   W.L. DAVIS   A.G. STEEL
(Auckland)   (Hawke's Bay)   (Canterbury)

I.R. MacRAE
(Hawke's Bay)

M.A. HEREWINI
(Auckland)

S.M. GOING
(North Auckland)

B.J. LOCHORE (**Capt.**)
(Wairarapa)

K.R. TREMAIN   S.C. STRAHAN   C.E. MEADS   W.J. NATHAN
(Hawke's Bay)   (Manawatu)   (King Country)   (Auckland)

B.L. MULLER   J. MAJOR   E.J. HAZLETT
(Taranaki)   (Taranaki)   (Southland)

A.R. MILLER   P.G. JOHNSON   R.B. PROSSER
(New South Wales)   (New South Wales)   (New South Wales)

G.V. DAVIS   R.G. TEITZEL   A.M.F. ABRAHAMS   J.L. SAYLE
(New South Wales)   (Queensland)   (New South Wales)   (New South Wales)

H.A. ROSE
(New South Wales)

K.W. CATCHPOLE (**Capt.**)
(New South Wales)

P.F. HAWTHORNE
(New South Wales)

R.P. BATTERHAM   P.V. SMITH   J.E. BRASS   I.J. PROCTOR
(New South Wales)   (New South Wales)   (New South Wales)   (New South Wales)

R.C.S. MANNING
(Queensland)

AUSTRALIA

REFEREE: Mr J.P.G. Pring (Auckland)
ATTENDANCE: 50,000
CONDITIONS: Weather fine, ground firm
HALFTIME: New Zealand 9, Australia 3

SCORERS

NEW ZEALAND   **AUSTRALIA**
Tries: Steel (2), Davis, Tremain   Tries: Batterham (2)
Conversions: Williment (4)   Penalty goal: Batterham
Penalty goals: Williment (2)
Dropped goal: Herewini

278

AUSTRALIA 9

Athletic Park, Wellington

With a look of satisfaction, Bill Davis scores ahead of Phil Smith and Greg Davis.

great speed to outstrip everyone in a thrilling sideline run before going round to score behind the posts. Williment's kick was a formality.

Less than a month later, the selectors surprisingly omitted Williment from the thirty-strong New Zealand side which was to tour in Europe and he was not destined to play for his country again. In his nine internationals Williment had scored seventy points, all but three from his boot.

It was also Waka Nathan's last international.

Though he was chosen for the European tour, injuries restricted his appearances. Nathan had the distinction of never playing in a losing New Zealand team in his fourteen internationals since 1962. He had scored four tries.

It was also the end of the international career of the Australian stalwart, Tony Miller. Now thirty-eight, Miller had first appeared for his country in 1952 against New Zealand and had played forty-one Tests, an Australian record. John Major played his only Test after having been a reserve for the previous seventeen.

NEW ZEALAND 23

4 November, 1967

Following the postponement of a proposed tour of South Africa in 1967, an eighteen match tour of the four Home Unions, Canada and France was arranged for a New Zealand team. With three fairly comfortable wins over English regional sides, New Zealand went into this international as favourites.

Both Earle Kirton, who had toured in 1963-64 without making a Test selection, and Graham Williams, who was the Wellington club's thirteenth All Black, were playing their first internationals.

Bill Gittings and Bob Lloyd were new caps in the English side, Lloyd in particular being impressive in the tourists' match at Leicester on the previous Saturday.

After the Queen and the Duke of Edinburgh had been introduced to the two teams on the field, the referee, Mr McMahon, who had controlled the previous fixture between the teams in January 1964, blew his whistle to start play. England kicked off switching direction out to the right where Birtwistle dropped the ball.

New Zealand soon set their stamp on the game and in the sixth minute scored their first try following a wild pass by Gittings that went astray. The All Black forwards led by Meads were immediately on to the ball and started a movement to the left where Davis made an incisive run. He unloaded the ball to Kirton as he was tackled, and the five-eighth went over near the posts.

The All Blacks complete their haka at Twickenham before the Queen and Duke of Edinburgh.

SPORT & GENERAL

ENGLAND 11

McCormick had no trouble with the conversion and New Zealand were five points up.

The full-back was unable to goal a long-range penalty soon after, and New Zealand were unable to gain points from several promising forays until the twenty-fifth minute when Williams made a break from loose play, before kicking ahead. In the scramble near the English line it was Birtwistle who gathered to score in the left hand corner. A fine kick from McCormick saw the score go to 10-0.

Sustained pressure by New Zealand saw a further try in the thirty-second minute when England heeled from a scrum on their goal line only to see the alert Laidlaw and Williams dive among the forwards as the ball reached the line. Laidlaw was awarded the try. McCormick was unable to convert.

Play had only just restarted when Lochore made a powerful burst after detaching from a scrum. As he was halted inside the English 25, a maul formed and the ball came back to Laidlaw who passed to Kirton on his left. The five-eighth,

sensing a gap in the defence, made a brilliant solo break going on the diagonal to score right in the left hand corner. A fine kick by McCormick saw the flags go up again for New Zealand to lead by the large margin of eighteen points after thirty-three minutes.

England hit back in the few remaining minutes before halftime and, after Rutherford had missed a simple penalty, they scored a well executed try from a scrum near half-way. Savage entered the back line movement from the blindside, piercing the defence before sending on to McFadyean who put Lloyd over for the try right on the call of halftime. Rutherford, who had been a Lion in New Zealand the previous year, but returned home with a broken arm midway through the tour, converted to make the score 18-5.

New Zealand were back on to attack in the early minutes of the second spell, and in the third minute, Davis broke past a high tackle, drew Rutherford before sending out to Dick who scored in the tackle of Sherriff wide out. McCormick's conversion struck the upright but fortunately bounced the right way for him and New Zealand led by the formidable margin of 23-5.

Again England fought back well, but both sides squandered chances before the next scoring occurred. With ten minutes remaining, Larter, who had taken over as the English goalkicker, managed to land a 30 yard penalty, and in the final moments of play Gittings kicked a long kick across the field towards Dick who was unable to gather cleanly. Lloyd was quickly on the scene to gather and scoot away from McCormick and score his second try. Larter could not convert and the score stayed at 23-11.

England had shown a remarkable recovery in the second half but had been too far behind to have much chance of saving the match. This had been the highest total recorded by New Zealand in a match against England. It had been Jack Hazlett's sixth and last Test. The Southland prop was forced to give way in later internationals to Ken Gray, who had been unavailable for this match.

NEW ZEALAND

W.F. McCORMICK
(Canterbury)

M.J. DICK   W.L. DAVIS   W.M. BIRTWISTLE
(Auckland)   (Hawke's Bay)   (Waikato)

I.R. MacRAE
(Hawke's Bay)

E.W. KIRTON
(Otago)

C.R. LAIDLAW
(Otago)

B.J. LOCHORE (Capt.)
(Wairarapa)

G.C. WILLIAMS   S.C. STRAHAN   C.E. MEADS   K.R. TREMAIN
(Wellington)   (Manawatu)   (King Country)   (Hawke's Bay)
B.L. MULLER   B.E. McLEOD   E.J. HAZLETT
(Taranaki)   (Counties)   (Southland)

P.E. JUDD (Capt.)   H.O. GODWIN   A.L. HORTON
(Coventry)   (Coventry)   (Blackheath)
R.B. TAYLOR   P.J. LARTER   J.E. OWEN   D.P. ROGERS
(Northampton)   (Northampton)   (Coventry)   (Bedford)
G.A. SHERRIFF
(Saracens)
W.J. GITTINGS
(Coventry)
J.F. FINLAN
(Moseley)
R.E. WEBB   R.H. LLOYD   C.W. McFADYEAN   K.F. SAVAGE
(Coventry)   (Harlequins)   (Moseley)   (Northampton)
D. RUTHERFORD
(Gloucester)

ENGLAND

REFEREE: Mr D.C.J. McMahon (Scotland)
ATTENDANCE: 74,000
CONDITIONS: Weather showery, ground greasy
HALFTIME: New Zealand 18, England 5

SCORERS

NEW ZEALAND	ENGLAND
Tries: Kirton (2), Birtwistle, Laidlaw, Dick	Tries: Lloyd (2)
	Conversion: Rutherford
Conversions: McCormick (4)	Penalty goal: Larter

NEW ZEALAND 13

11 November, 1967

On the Saturday after the English match, New Zealand lined up for their second international of the tour on a miserable day in Cardiff. During the week they had had a hard but entertaining match against West Wales at Swansea, before coming out on top by 21-14.

The only change in the side saw the return of Ken Gray who had been out of action until the Swansea game after breaking a bone in his hand four weeks earlier.

The Welsh team featured six new men — Wheeler, Hall, Keri Jones, the Australian-born Wiltshire, Hughes and John Jeffery. Their selectors were unable to consider the ace goal kicker Keith Jarrett and Gerald Davies who were injured, and David Watkins who had turned to League with Salford a month earlier. Denzil Williams and Stuart Watkins had both played for the Lions in the Test series the previous year.

Norman Gale won the toss for Wales and gave the All Blacks first use of the strong wind which was driving the rain in from the River Taff end of the ground. After Wheeler had made a poor attempt from a penalty in the early stages of the game, it was the All Blacks who made their presence felt. When Raybould was caught off-side at a scrummage on his own 25 in the tenth minute, McCormick took a successful shot at goal to open the scoring.

In the eighteenth minute, a scrum went down inside the Welsh 25 and Wales hooked, then as they tried to wheel the scrum, they lost control of the ball and it came to Laidlaw who fed his backline, who had already shown that, despite the conditions, they were prepared to attack. When Davis received the ball he was able to beat Hall and set up Birtwistle for a try right in the corner. McCormick landed a brilliant conversion with the sodden ball to give New Zealand an eight point advantage.

No further scoring occurred in this half although McCormick had two unsuccessful penalty attempts and Williams only narrowly missed a try in a scramble over the Welsh line.

It was doubted by many that an eight point lead in these conditions was enough to withstand the Welsh assault in the second half. This view was strengthened on the resumption of play when Wales quickly went on to attack, using the boot of Edwards or John to keep the ball well inside All Black territory.

Following a series of scrummages on the New Zealand line, Barry John, partnering Gareth Edwards for the first time in an international, received from a scrum and dropped a neat goal from the left of the posts to reduce the leeway to five points with thirty-two minutes to play.

With the game so poised it was evident that the side to score next would be in a strong position. It was in the thirteenth minute of the spell that the score came, following one of the All Blacks' rare attacks to this stage in the half. New Zealand were awarded a penalty on the Welsh 10 yard line and there was some surprise when McCormick was brought forward to attempt a goal into the teeth of the wind. A good kick by the full-back was only just short but as the speedy Davis followed up, the Welsh number eight John Jeffery, who had taken the ball flung it wildly back over

---

NEW ZEALAND

W.F. McCORMICK
(Canterbury)

M.J. DICK   W.L. DAVIS   W.M. BIRTWISTLE
(Auckland)   (Hawke's Bay)   (Waikato)

I.R. MacRAE
(Hawke's Bay)

E.W. KIRTON
(Otago)

C.R. LAIDLAW
(Otago)

B.J. LOCHORE (**Capt.**)
(Wairarapa)

G.C. WILLIAMS   S.C. STRAHAN   C.E. MEADS   K.R. TREMAIN
(Wellington)   (Manawatu)   (King Country)   (Hawke's Bay)
B.L. MULLER   B.E. McLEOD   K.F. GRAY
(Taranaki)   (Counties)   (Wellington)

D. WILLIAMS   N.R. GALE (**Capt.**)   B.E. THOMAS
(Ebbw Vale)   (Llanelli)   (Neath)
J. TAYLOR   M.L. WILTSHIRE   W.T. MAINWARING   D. HUGHES
(London Welsh) (Aberavon)   (Aberavon)   (Newbridge)
J.J. JEFFERY
(Newport)
G.O. EDWARDS
(Cardiff)

B. JOHN
(Cardiff)

W.K. JONES   I.J. HALL   W.H. RAYBOULD   S.J. WATKINS
(Cardiff)   (Aberavon)   (London Welsh)   (Newport)
P.J. WHEELER
(Aberavon)

WALES

REFEREE: Mr M.H. Titcomb (England)
ATTENDANCE: 58,500
CONDITIONS: Weather wet and windy, ground soft turning to mud
HALFTIME: New Zealand 8, Wales 0

SCORERS

NEW ZEALAND
Tries: Birtwistle, Davis
Conversions: McCormick (2)
Penalty goal: McCormick

WALES
Penalty goal: Gale
Dropped goal: John

WALES 6

Cardiff Arms Park

his shoulder. Several defenders attempted to get to the ball but it was Davis who beat everyone to the touch-down by the posts. McCormick's comparatively simple conversion put the margin between the teams to ten and changed the whole complexion of the game.

Over the next ten minutes, Wales had three unsuccessful kicks at goal, two by Wheeler and one by Edwards, but were unable to register any points. Stuart Watkins also got over the line but was held up and unable to ground the ball.

Two great half-backs in action as Gareth Edwards is about to wrap up Chris Laidlaw.

Ten minutes from the end saw another penalty to Wales and this time it was skipper Gale who took the kick, successfully placing the goal from 35 yards.

This proved to be the final scoring in the match, which had been won and lost by chances taken and opportunities missed. Once again it had been the All Black pack that had dominated the play and several times in the concluding minutes of the match they had marched the Welsh pack back. Jeffery, whose wild pass had led to Davis's try, was not selected again for his country.

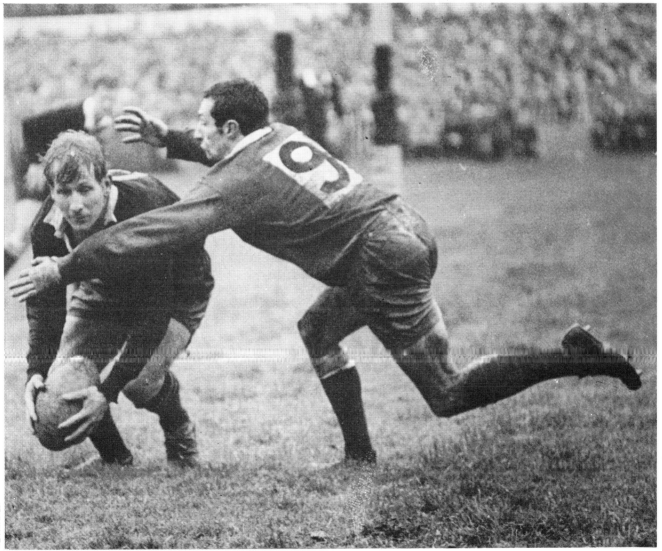

NZ HERALD

NEW ZEALAND 21

25 November, 1967

There were three changes to the New Zealand team for this international, with Steel, a surprise selection, replacing Birtwistle; the fast-improving Sid Going who had played an excellent game against France "B" coming in for Laidlaw; and 21 year old Ian Kirkpatrick continuing his meteoric rise in the game by ousting Tremain from the side of the scrum. Tremain had played in the previous twenty-one internationals in a row, which emphasised the standard that Kirkpatrick had attained.

Gachassin, who had played as a wing three-quarter, and Dauga, were the only French survivors from the 1964 clash on the same ground.

Going watches Lochore with a critical eye as the All Black captain performs the half-back's role.

FRANCE 15

Colombes Stadium, Paris

After the crowd had sung the Marsellaise, France kicked off. Four minutes after the start Carrere was penalised at a ruck 45 yards from his posts and McCormick duly goaled. Three minutes later, the diminutive Gachassin evened the score when he landed a dropped goal following a ruck just outside the New Zealand 25. A promising All Black back movement just failed to register a try when the ball was knocked out of Davis's grasp as he crossed the goal line shortly after.

The first try of the game came after twenty-four minutes from a scrum in which the French lost control of the ball. Meads was able to gather and pass to Kirkpatrick who fed Going and the half-back scored the try wide out. McCormick was unable to convert. A minute later Villepreux kicked the first of his penalties from 32 yards to equalise the score at 6-6.

Before the half ended both sides had missed penalties and Gachassin had been wide with another dropped goal attempt.

Near halftime New Zealand took the lead with a well engineered try from a ruck. Davis was held as he tried to burst through but managed to get a pass to MacRae who had come around outside him and the five-eighth sent Steel away to score his sixth Test try from his six internationals. McCormick's kick from near the left touch line was a good one and New Zealand led by 11-6.

In injury time Villepreux added his second penalty after Muller late-tackled Puget to make it 11-9 at the interval. It had been a hard and often brutal forty minutes, with both sides suffering injuries of various types, the worst being a deep cut above Meads's left ear which later required several stitches.

The second half had run ten minutes when a further penalty by Villepreux put France into the lead for the first time in the match.

Fifteen minutes of the match remained when New Zealand regained the lead following a break from a scrum by Going on the French 25. Meads carried on the movement, finally giving the ball to Kirkpatrick who ran the final 10 yards to the line and crashed over for a try which McCormick converted.

The All Blacks were now applying the pressure with well organised back attacks and these paid off four minutes later when McCormick entered a back movement only to be held up. As the ball came loose it was kicked over the French line and both Dick and Williams dived at the ball. The former was awarded the try right by the posts. McCormick again added the two points to put New Zealand in the strong position of being 21-12 up with ten minutes to play.

In the final minutes of play, the French mounted their best attack of the match when Puget ran from a tapped penalty before transferring the ball inside to flanker Quilis who sent Gachassin away on a brilliantly elusive run to the New Zealand 25. He threw a long pass to his left which was taken by Campaes who scored near the left hand corner. Villepreux missed the conversion to make the final score 21-15.

It had been a match in which the All Blacks had displayed one of their finest exhibitions of fifteen man Rugby in a hard, vigorous and exciting encounter.

NEW ZEALAND

W.F. McCORMICK
(Canterbury)

M.J. DICK (Auckland)   W.L. DAVIS (Hawke's Bay)   A.G. STEEL (Canterbury)

I.R. MacRAE
(Hawke's Bay)

E.W. KIRTON
(Otago)

S.M. GOING
(North Auckland)

B.J. LOCHORE (Capt.)
(Wairarapa)

G.C. WILLIAMS (Wellington)   S.C. STRAHAN (Manawatu)   C.E. MEADS (King Country)   I.A. KIRKPATRICK (Canterbury)

B.L. MULLER (Taranaki)   B.E. McLEOD (Counties)   K.F. GRAY (Wellington)

A. ABADIE (SC Graulhet)   J.M. CABANIER (A.S. Montauban)   A. GRUARIN (R.C. Toulonnais)

C. CARRERE (Capt.)   B. DAUGA   A. PLANTEFOL   A. QUILIS

W. SPANGHERO
(R.C. Narbonne)

M. PUGET
(C.A. Brive)

J. GACHASSIN
(F.C. Lourdais)

A. CAMPAES (F.C. Lourdais)   J. TRILLO (C.A. Beglais)   C. DOURTHE (U.S. Dax)   J.M. CAPENDEGUY (C.A. Beglais)

P. VILLEPREUX
(S. Toulousain)

FRANCE

REFEREE: Mr R.P. Burrell (Scotland)
ATTENDANCE: 35,000
CONDITIONS: Weather overcast and cold, ground firm
HALFTIME: New Zealand 11, France 9

SCORERS

NEW ZEALAND
Tries: Going, Steel, Kirkpatrick, Dick
Conversions: McCormick (3)
Penalty goal: McCormick

FRANCE
Try: Campaes
Penalty goals: Villepreux (3)
Dropped goal: Gachassin

NEW ZEALAND 14

2 December, 1967

Following great games in the All Blacks' only match between the French and Scottish internationals, against a Scottish Districts team at Melrose, Laidlaw and Tremain played their way back into the Test team. Tremain's return to the team was possibly assisted by the broken nose suffered by Kirkpatrick at Paris but on his display at Melrose he deserved to be back in the side. Birtwistle, who had scored three tries against Scottish Districts returned to the side in place of Dick and Alister Hopkinson won his first international jersey at the expense of Muller.

The Scottish team included Stewart Wilson, Laidlaw and Hinshelwood who had appeared for the Lions in the Test series against New Zealand the previous year, whilst Derrick Grant had also been a member of the 1966 Lions. Wilson had also appeared against New Zealand for Scotland in the scoreless draw in 1964 as had Rollo and the captain, Pringle Fisher.

An interesting player in the Scottish line up was the tall lock, Peter Stagg, who stood six feet ten inches — undoubtedly the tallest player to take the field in an international match. Between 1965 and 1970 Stagg played twenty-eight internationals.

After ten minutes Chisholm opened the scoring with a left-footed dropped goal following a scrum, and midway through the spell McCormick evened the scores with a straightforward penalty goal from only 22 yards, to bring up his 100 points for the tour. The first try of the match came from a 'willie away' movement from a line-out inside the Scottish half started by Meads, (playing with a conspicuous bandage protecting his scalp injury) and carried powerfully on by Gray who threw a pass to MacRae. The five-eighth ran strongly for 20 yards to score New Zealand's first try against Scotland since 1935. McCormick was unable to add the extra points from wide out, but five minutes later he landed a 39 yard penalty to make the score 9-3, a score which was unaltered when the halftime whistle blew.

For the first thirty-five minutes of the second half neither side was able to add to the score though both teams had their opportunities. Finally from a line-out on the Scottish 25, the ball went from Laidlaw to Kirton to MacRae then to Kirton, who had doubled around outside his partner. He made a short break before sending Davis away to sprint the last 15 yards to score a well-engineered try near the left hand corner. McCormick's conversion was straight and true.

Although this was the end of the scoring in this match, sadly it was not the end of the controversy. From Scotland's kick-off a ruck was soon formed and as the ball emerged on the Scottish side, Meads, who had also emerged on the Scottish side, and Chisholm pursued it. As Chisholm reached to pick the ball up, Meads aimed a kick at it and the two players went to ground. Mr Kelleher then blew his whistle and Meads was ordered from the field.

It later became known that during the first half Mr Kelleher had formally cautioned Meads at a collapsed maul for dangerous play when the lock forward had been endeavouring to get to the ball which appeared to be in among players on the ground. To some critics, this maul had been al-

---

NEW ZEALAND

W.F. McCORMICK
(Canterbury)

W.M. BIRTWISTLE   W.L. DAVIS   A.G. STEEL
(Waikato)   (Hawke's Bay)   (Canterbury)

I.R. MacRAE
(Hawke's Bay)

E.W. KIRTON
(Otago)

C.R. LAIDLAW
(Otago)

B.J. LOCHORE (Capt.)
(Wairarapa)

G.C. WILLIAMS   S.C. STRAHAN   C.E. MEADS   K.R. TREMAIN
(Wellington)   (Manawatu)   (King Country)   (Hawke's Bay)

A.E. HOPKINSON   B.E. McLEOD   K.F. GRAY
(Canterbury)   (Counties)   (Wellington)

A.B. CARMICHAEL   F.A.L. LAIDLAW   D.M.D. ROLLO
(West of Scotland)   (Melrose)   (Howe of Fife)

J.P. FISHER (Capt.)   P.K. STAGG   G.W.E. MITCHELL   D. GRANT
(London Scottish)   (Sale)   (Edinburgh Wanderers)   (Hawick)

A.H.W. BOYLE
(London Scottish)

A.J. HASTIE
(Melrose)

D.H. CHISHOLM
(Melrose)

R.R. KEDDIE   J.N.M. FRAME   J.W.C. TURNER   A.J.W. HINSHELWOOD
(Watsonians)   (Edinburgh University)   (Gala)   (London Scottish)

S. WILSON
(London Scottish)

SCOTLAND

REFEREE: Mr K.D. Kelleher, (Ireland)
ATTENDANCE: 60,000
CONDITIONS: Weather fine, ground firm
HALFTIME: New Zealand 9, Scotland 3

SCORERS

NEW ZEALAND	SCOTLAND
Tries: MacRae, Davis	Dropped goal: Chisholm
Conversion: McCormick	
Penalty goals: McCormick (2)	

SCOTLAND 3

Murrayfield, Edinburgh

ASSOCIATED PRESS

The All Blacks stand in disbelief as Meads leaves the field, sent off by referee Kevin Kelleher for dangerous play.

lowed to continue after the ball had become unplayable. Meads thus joined Cyril Brownlie as being the only players to have been ordered off in an international match to this time.

Lochore moved into lock and the remaining few minutes were played without further incident. Although clear-cut victors in this tense, and for the most part dull, match and having become the first All Black side to win all internationals on a European tour since the 'invincible' 1924-25 team, the New Zealand team trooped off Murrayfield a sad and dejected side.

On the following Tuesday, the adjudicating committee of the International Board suspended Meads for two tour games.

This match marked the end of Bill Birtwistle's international career. The slim winger had scored four tries in his seven international appearances and had always been a source of danger with a fluid and prodigious sidestep.

The international against Ireland set down for December 16th, had been cancelled at the request of the Irish Department of Agriculture because of the outbreak of foot and mouth disease that was sweeping England. The Test was replaced by a match against the Barbarians at Twickenham.

287

NEW ZEALAND 27

15 June, 1968

First Test

A twenty-five man team to tour Australia was announced following two trial matches at Wellington on 4th. May. The eleven match tour included two internationals the first of which was played at Sydney. Up until this match the All Blacks had comfortably accounted for each team they had met, including New South Wales who had gone down by 5-30 on the previous Saturday, and were regarded as firm favourites to win well.

Newcomers to Test Rugby in the All Black side included Grahame Thorne, usually regarded as a centre but selected on the wing in this match, and Wayne Cottrell, both of whom toured Europe and Canada the previous year with the New Zealand side. Another to make his debut in this match was Tom Lister, a brother of golf professional John Lister, who was considered unlucky to miss out on the 1967 All Blacks.

Well-known opponents in the Australian team

included captain Ken Catchpole and Peter Johnson who had played Tests against New Zealand in 1962, 1964 and 1967. The Australian coach, Des Connor, was a former Australian and New Zealand international.

From the kick-off the Australian forwards, playing with great fire, had New Zealand on the defensive and after five minutes the first opportunity to score was given to McGill when he was brought up to attempt a straightforward penalty from only 25 yards out, but the kick was wide.

Within a couple of minutes Lochore was to leave the field with a thumb injury, returning five minutes later. However, a hamstring injury in the twenty-second minute necessitated his leaving the field for good and subsequent examination revealed that his left thumb had been fractured. This injury was to keep him out of New Zealand's next two internationals.

A recent International Board law change now allowed injured players in Test matches to be replaced, and Ian Kirkpatrick took the field to be the first player to act as a substitute for a New Zealand Test team since Tim Mason replaced Wally Argus at Sydney in 1947.

McCormick opened the scoring after thirty-five minutes with a simple penalty as New Zealand started to gain control in the forward battle. The Wallabies had been playing a spoiling game, packing six man scrums and playing five man line-outs in an endeavour to upset the All Black pattern and negate any constructive back play.

Just before halftime Kirton received the ball from a ruck close to the Australian line and was held as he tried to go across, but Kirkpatrick was on hand and he took the ball and plunged over ten yards to the left of the posts. McCormick goaled the conversion to make the score 8-0 at halftime.

The All Blacks were quickly into stride in the second half and four minutes after the resumption, Brian Muller made a short break before passing to Steel for the winger to make ground down the left hand side of the field then send a pass inside to Kirton who scored a good try by the posts which, surprisingly, McCormick was unable to convert.

NEW ZEALAND

W.F. McCORMICK
(Canterbury)

G.S. THORNE   W.L. DAVIS   A.G. STEEL
(Auckland)   (Hawke's Bay)   (Canterbury)

W.D. COTTRELL
(Canterbury)

E.W. KIRTON
(Otago)

C.R. LAIDLAW
(Canterbury)

B.J. LOCHORE (Capt.)*
(Wairarapa)

T.N. LISTER   S.C. STRAHAN   C.E. MEADS   K.R. TREMAIN
(South Canterbury) (Manawatu)   (King Country)   (Hawke's Bay)

B.L. MULLER   B.E. McLEOD   K.F. GRAY
(Taranaki)   (Counties)   (Wellington)

J.P. ROXBURGH   P.G. JOHNSON   R.B. PROSSER
(New South Wales)   (New South Wales)   (New South Wales)

H.A. ROSE   A.M.F. ABRAHAMS   P.N. REILLY   G.V. DAVIS
(New South Wales) (New South Wales) (Queensland) (New South Wales)

D.A. TAYLOR
(Queensland)

K.W. CATCHPOLE (Capt.)††
(New South Wales)

J.P. BALLESTY
(New South Wales)

A.M. CARDY   P.V. SMITH   J.E. BRASS †   J.W. COLE
(New South Wales) (New South Wales) (New South Wales) (New South Wales)

A.N. McGILL
(New South Wales)

AUSTRALIA

REPLACEMENTS: * replaced by I.A. Kirkpatrick (Canterbury)
† replaced by B.D. Honan (Queensland)
†† replaced by J.N.B. Hipwell (New South Wales)
REFEREE: Dr. I.R. Vanderfield (New South Wales)
ATTENDANCE: 24,800
CONDITIONS: Weather fine, ground firm
HALFTIME: New Zealand 8, Australia 0

SCORERS

NEW ZEALAND   **AUSTRALIA**
Tries: Kirkpatrick (3), Kirton, Steel,   Try: Cardy
  Laidlaw   Conversion: McGill
Conversions: McCormick (3)   Penalty goals: McGill (2)
Penalty goal: McCormick

AUSTRALIA 11

Sydney Cricket Ground

It was Steel himself who scored the next try when McLeod won a tight head near the Wallaby line and Laidlaw sent Steel away on the blindside. Again McCormick was astray with his conversion from wide out.

The first Australian points came in the eighteenth minute of the half when McGill kicked a 40 yard penalty making the score 14-3 in favour of the tourists. Almost immediately New Zealand scored a further try when Tremain made a powerful burst from a maul. As the defence gathered he threw a pass to Kirkpatrick who went across for a try close to the posts. McCormick's conversion increased the lead to 19-3.

At this stage John Brass was forced to leave the field with a shoulder injury and he was replaced by Barry Honan playing his first Test. Honan's brother Bob had represented Australia in New Zealand in 1964.

Six minutes later another substitute was required in the Australian side when Catchpole was roughly dragged from a ruck by Meads causing a severe groin injury which necessitated his

retiring on a stretcher. This injury was to end the brilliant half-back's international career. His replacement was the 20 year old John Hipwell who, like Honan, was making his Test debut. Shortly after this incident Laidlaw shot around a ruck on the Australian line to score a try which McCormick was unable to convert.

With five minutes to play McGill kicked his second penalty from 29 yards to make the score 22-6.

Kirkpatrick scored his third try from loose play two minutes before no-side and McCormick converted. Considering he had been on the field for only fifty-eight minutes of the game, Kirkpatrick's contribution was an outstanding one. The last occasion that an All Black had scored three tries in an international was in 1935 when "Pat" Caughey had scored a similar number against Scotland.

In the last movement of the match, Ballesty kicked a nicely judged grubber to recover the ball himself and send Alan Cardy away to beat McCormick and score Australia's only try. McGill converted to make the final score 27-11.

Fergie McCormick is just inches short of the line in his attempt to score.

SYDNEY MORNING HERALD

289

22 June, 1968

Second Test

Broken left thumbs were to keep both Lochore and Ken Gray out of this match, whilst Kelvin Tremain was forced to withdraw, after selection, with a damaged knee. Tremain and Gray had incurred their injuries in the mid-week match against Queensland which was won by New Zealand 34-3. These injuries saw Kirkpatrick remain in the side at number eight, Graham Williams come in to take Tremain's place and Tony Kreft, who was flown to Australia earlier in the tour when injuries to Gray and Hopkinson left the team short of props, took the tighthead in what was to be his only international appearance. Hopkinson, who was injured at first Test time, came in to the loose head prop position.

First Test replacements, Honan and Hipwell, retained their places in the Wallaby team whilst Abrahams, who was still suffering from rib cartilage trouble, withdrew and was replaced by the tall Queenslander, Stuart Gregory.

It soon became obvious that the Wallaby tactics for this match would be little different from those they had employed in the Sydney Test.

After six minutes McGill missed a penalty but two minutes later, he was successful with a further attempt from 28 yards to open the scoring. In the eleventh minute McCormick equalised when he chipped a penalty from close range after the Wallaby backs had moved up off-side at a line-out. With quarter of an hour gone an untidy knock back from a three man line-out had New Zealand in trouble, and from a resultant ruck Australia had the ball quickly back to Hipwell who dived to score a try near the corner. McGill was unable to place the conversion.

The lead swung back to New Zealand eight minutes later when McCormick converted a try scored by Lister following a scrum ten yards from the Australian line. Kirkpatrick had detached and fed Lister who had crashed through the attempted tackles of Smith and McGill.

Four minutes later McCormick was on target again when Australia were caught off-side 35 yards out. In the closing three minutes of the half McGill was successful with two penalties from

close range to give Australia a 12-11 lead at halftime.

Seven minutes after the re-start McGill was again on target with a penalty from 33 yards out. Half the spell had gone before there was any further scoring and this time it was New Zealand who mounted one of the rare attacks of the match. A forward rush had the All Blacks heeling from a ruck and with Steel in the movement from the blind, Davis was able to send Thorne away to score in the corner. McCormick's missed conversion left Australia holding a one point lead which was increased to four when McGill kicked his fifth penalty of the match from under the posts eight minutes later.

As the last ten minutes of the match ticked away it began to look as if Australia were going to end the All Blacks' winning sequence of thirty-three matches and eleven internationals since the third Test of the 1965 series against South Africa. However with two minutes to play, sensation was to enter into the game as New Zealand

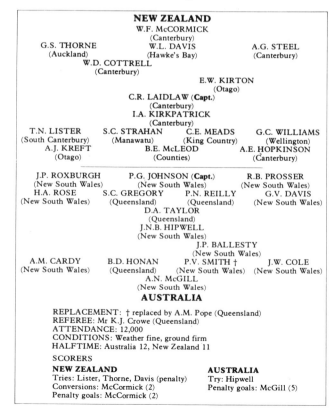

NEW ZEALAND

W.F. McCORMICK
(Canterbury)

G.S. THORNE (Auckland)   W.L. DAVIS (Hawke's Bay)   A.G. STEEL (Canterbury)

W.D. COTTRELL
(Canterbury)

E.W. KIRTON
(Otago)

C.R. LAIDLAW (**Capt.**)
(Canterbury)

I.A. KIRKPATRICK
(Canterbury)

T.N. LISTER (South Canterbury)   S.C. STRAHAN (Manawatu)   C.E. MEADS (King Country)   G.C. WILLIAMS (Wellington)

A.J. KREFT (Otago)   B.E. McLEOD (Counties)   A.E. HOPKINSON (Canterbury)

J.P. ROXBURGH (New South Wales)   P.G. JOHNSON (**Capt.**) (New South Wales)   R.B. PROSSER (New South Wales)

H.A. ROSE (New South Wales)   S.C. GREGORY (Queensland)   P.N. REILLY (Queensland)   G.V. DAVIS (New South Wales)

D.A. TAYLOR
(Queensland)

J.N.B. HIPWELL
(New South Wales)

J.P. BALLESTY
(New South Wales)

A.M. CARDY (New South Wales)   B.D. HONAN (Queensland)   P.V. SMITH † (New South Wales)   J.W. COLE (New South Wales)

A.N. McGILL
(New South Wales)

AUSTRALIA

REPLACEMENT: † replaced by A.M. Pope (Queensland)
REFEREE: Mr K.J. Crowe (Queensland)
ATTENDANCE: 12,000
CONDITIONS: Weather fine, ground firm
HALFTIME: Australia 12, New Zealand 11

SCORERS

NEW ZEALAND
Tries: Lister, Thorne, Davis (penalty)
Conversions: McCormick (2)
Penalty goals: McCormick (2)

AUSTRALIA
Try: Hipwell
Penalty goals: McGill (5)

AUSTRALIA 1

Ballymore Oval, Brisbane

CROWN STUDIOS

The New Zealand Touring Team
Back row: W.D. Cottrell, B.E. McLeod, G.C. Williams, B.L. Muller, M.O. Knight, P.A. Johns, A.G. Steel.
Second row: K.F. Gray, I.A. Kirkpatrick, C.E. Meads, S.C. Strahan, A.R. Sutherland, T.N. Lister, A.E. Hopkinson, K.R. Tremain.
Seated: W.D.R. Currey, G.S. Thorne, C.R. Laidlaw, D.K. Ross (manager), B.J. Lochore (capt.), F.R. Allen (asst. manager), T.N. Wolfe, W.L. Davis, T.M. McCashin.
In front: W.F. McCormick, S.M. Going, E.W. Kirton.
Inset: A.J. Kreft (replacement).

mounted a backline attack on the Australian 25. As Davis received the ball he headed into the outside gap before punting ahead, but as he went to follow up the ball Honan, who had been lining him up, took him with a copybook tackle. As the ball bounced into in-goal, referee Mr Kevin Crowe had no hesitation in awarding a penalty try between the posts, a decision with which many of the local supporters did not agree. Some

doubt surrounded the decision, as to which illegality led to the award (Thorne having been obstructed by his opposite number in the same movement) but Mr Crowe subsequently made it clear that the late tackle by Honan was the infringement for which the penalty try decision was made. McCormick was able to convert from in front to win the game for New Zealand.

Governed by the tactics employed by Australia, it had again been a largely dull and uninteresting match which had been scattered with abrasive clashes between the two forward packs.

This was the last Test match for the lightweight loose forward Graham Williams, who continued to give his Union good service for many seasons, and for the speedy winger, Tony Steel, whose seven tries in nine internationals had been surpassed by only five All Blacks. An achilles heel injury brought this fine winger's career to an untimely end.

NEW ZEALAND 12

13 July, 1968

First Test

Three weeks after the international at Brisbane, the All Blacks lined out on a wet, slippery field at Christchurch to meet France, in New Zealand for a three Test, twelve match tour.

The only new player in the New Zealand team was the wing, Mike O'Callaghan, a 22 year old veterinary student from Massey University who replaced the original selection, Steel, who had withdrawn with an achilles heel injury. In the absence of Lochore, still unavailable with his thumb injury, the captaincy of the team went to Kelvin Tremain who became the first All Black leader from Hawke's Bay since Maurice Brownlie in 1928.

The captain of the touring French side, Christian Carrere, twisted his ankle in training for this match and was forced to withdraw. His place on the side of the scrum went to Michel Greffe, and the leader's job to the veteran of the 1961 tour, Claude Lacaze, who had also appeared against New Zealand in 1964.

After losing the opening game of their tour to Marlborough, 19-24, the French team had beaten both Otago and Southland before this international.

France won the toss and elected to play with the sun behind them. McCormick kicked off for New Zealand and in the second minute he attempted a 50 yard penalty but the ball was well short. From a good attacking position, Lacaze missed a dropped goal from straight in front, but, three minutes later, landed a more difficult shot with his left foot.

Within four minutes McCormick had two

Andre Piazza kicks high ahead of O'Callaghan's challenge. Greffe and Lister follow the ball's flight.

FRANCE 9

Lancaster Park, Christchurch

Both Tremain and Lacaze take the business of captaincy very seriously.

further penalty attempts from handy positions but although the first just missed, the second was well wide. He was astray again after twenty minutes with a 40 yard attempt. Finally, with half an hour showing on the clock, he goaled his fifth attempt from wide out on the 25.

France spent the remainder of the half on attack, and although Davis was forced to drop back quickly to save a dangerous situation on one occasion, there was no further score registered before the interval.

It was New Zealand who applied the pressure early in the second half and one blindside movement saw McCormick bundled out just short of the corner. The All Black full-back was given a further penalty, a decision that was greeted by the French with a display of argument and gesticulation, but McCormick was unable to register any points. It was not until the French worked their way back on attack that Pierre Villepreux goaled a line-out penalty from 30 yards out.

Four minutes later, McCormick was given the easiest of opportunities when France were penalised only 15 yards from their posts and he was able to level the scores with a kick that just

slithered over. Ten minutes remained when McCormick put New Zealand into the lead for the first time in the match with his tenth shot at goal, from the French 25.

Villepreux appeared to have saved the match for his side when he kicked a magnificent penalty with the heavy ball from 45 yards out two minutes from time.On the call of no-side, however, France won a defensive scrum and as Puget went to pass back to Villepreux, Laidlaw was around to harass him and the ball slithered along the ground to the full-back who just had time to fly kick quickly for touch. The ball hit blindside winger Thorne on the shoulder and rebounded high into in-goal, where several desperate hands endeavoured to gain control of it. The ball then hit Tremain on the head and rebounded further into in-goal where Kirton, flashing up on the scene, threw himself on it in a sliding dive to score the winning try. McCormick's kick from five yards in from touch failed to go over and the game ended with New Zealand being rather lucky winners.

NEW ZEALAND

W.F. McCORMICK
(Canterbury)

G.S. THORNE (Auckland) — W.L. DAVIS (Hawke's Bay) — * M.W. O'CALLAGHAN (Manawatu)

I.R. MacRAE (Hawke's Bay)

E.W. KIRTON (Otago)

C.R. LAIDLAW (Canterbury)

I.A. KIRKPATRICK (Canterbury)

T.N. LISTER (South Canterbury) — S.C. STRAHAN (Manawatu) — C.E. MEADS (King Country) — K.R. TREMAIN (**Capt.**) (Hawke's Bay)

B.L. MULLER (Taranaki) — B.E. McLEOD (Counties) — A.E. HOPKINSON (Canterbury)

J.M. ESPONDA — J.P. BAUX — J. IRACABAL

J.P. SALUT (Toulouse OEC) — B. DAUGA (S. Montois) — E. CESTER (Toulouse OEC) — M. GREFFE (F.C. Grenoble)

W. SPANGHERO (R.C. Narbonne)

M. PUGET (C.A. Brive)

C. LACAZE (**Capt.**) (Scd'Angouleme)

A. CAMPAES (F.C. Lourdais) — J. TRILLO (C.A. Beglais) — J. MASO (U.S. Perpignan) — A. PIAZZA (U.S. Montauban)

P. VILLEPREUX (S. Toulousain)

FRANCE

REFEREE: Mr D.H. Millar (Otago)
ATTENDANCE: 55,749
CONDITIONS: Weather fine, ground wet and muddy
HALFTIME: New Zealand 3, France 3

SCORERS

NEW ZEALAND	FRANCE
Try: Kirton	Penalty goals: Villepreux (2)
Penalty goals: McCormick (3)	Dropped goal: Lacaze

NEW ZEALAND 9

27 July, 1968

Second Test

The return to the New Zealand team, after injuries, of Brian Lochore and Ken Gray strengthened the pack for this international but the centre Bill Davis was forced to withdraw with a leg muscle injury after selection. This necessitated MacRae moving out a place and the introduction of Wayne Cottrell from the reserves to take over at second five-eighth.

France, who had won each of their three provincial matches since the first Test, made four changes to their side. The elusive Christian Boujet was brought in to replace Claude Lacaze, Bonal for Piazza on the right wing, Plantefol for the injured Cester and Bernard Dutin added more weight to the scrum in place of the lightweight flanker Salut.

Both teams were introduced to the Governor-General, Sir Arthur Porritt before Villepreux kicked off with the cold, northerly wind at his back. The kick-off carried the ball between the posts, and New Zealand were forced to drop out. With the wind advantage, France did most of

the early attacking and after five minutes Villepreux was given a penalty attempt from two yards inside the New Zealand half but the kick was short.

The All Blacks' first attack was mounted following a tap-penalty taken by Laidlaw, which saw the forwards maintain a hand to hand rush to the French 25.

The first hint of trouble in the forwards came in the seventeenth minute when tempers boiled over and Mr Pring brought the two captains together to help cool the situation. Five minutes after this incident McCormick had a shot at goal from 34 yards but was unable to raise the flags.

In the twenty-eighth minute of the half, Villepreux was called up to have an attempt at goal from a penalty awarded eight yards inside his own half and 15 yards in from the right hand touch line. Some laughter around the crowd soon turned to cheering when it was seen that the ball would carry over the cross bar comfortably and register the game's first points. This kick rated as one of the longest in the history of international Rugby was variously estimated at between 65 and 70 yards.

In the remaining minutes of the spell, McCormick failed with a long range penalty and Puget was astray with a drop kick at goal. So halftime arrived with France holding on to a three point margin.

In the opening minute of the second half, McCormick equalled the score when he goaled a penalty from in front of the posts after a French back had been caught off-side at a ruck. France had despatched the flanker, Dutin, to an extra full-back position and the remaining seven forwards were finding the All Black pack difficult to contain. Although several strong All Black attacks had been repulsed, it was becoming evident that the French would be hard pressed to hold the New Zealanders.

In the thirteenth minute McCormick put his side into the lead when he kicked a straightforward penalty from 30 yards. From this point on the forward play, which had been simmering for some time, became very willing and only the firm

---

NEW ZEALAND

W.F. McCORMICK
(Canterbury)

G.S. THORNE   I.R. MacRAE   M.W. O'CALLAGHAN
(Auckland)   (Hawke's Bay)   (Manawatu)

W.D. COTTRELL
(Canterbury)

E.W. KIRTON
(Otago)

C.R. LAIDLAW
(Canterbury)

B.J. LOCHORE (Capt.)
(Wairarapa)

I.A. KIRKPATRICK   S.C. STRAHAN   C.E. MEADS   K.R. TREMAIN
(Canterbury)   (Manawatu)   (King Country)   (Hawke's Bay)

K.F. GRAY   B.E. McLEOD   A.E. HOPKINSON
(Wellington)   (Counties)   (Canterbury)

J. IRACABAL   J.P. BAUX   J.M. ESPONDA
(A. Bayonnais)   (A.C. Lannemezan)   (U.S. Perpignan)

M. GREFFE   A. PLANTEFOL   B. DAUGA   B. DUTIN
(F.C. Grenoble)   (S.U. Agen)   (S. Montois)   (S. Montois)

W. SPANGHERO
(R.C. Narbonne)

M. PUGET (Capt.)
(C.A. Brive)

C. BOUJET
(F.C. Grenoble)

A. CAMPAES   J. TRILLO   J. MASO   J.M. BONAL
(F.C. Lourdais)   (C.A. Beglais)   (U.S. Perpignan)   (S. Toulousain)

P. VILLEPREUX
(S. Toulousain)

FRANCE

REFEREE: Mr J.P.G. Pring (Auckland)
ATTENDANCE: 49,978
CONDITIONS: Weather fine but windy, ground soft
HALFTIME: France 3, New Zealand 0

SCORERS

NEW ZEALAND   **FRANCE**
Penalty goals: McCormick (3)   Penalty goal: Villepreux

FRANCE 3

Athletic Park, Wellington

The New Zealand team absorb coach Fred Allen's team talk prior to match.

control of referee, John Pring, prevented the match from getting completely out of hand. New Zealand were attacking throughout this half but magnificent French defence was still preventing the All Blacks from scoring any tries. McCormick landed his third penalty of the match from a wide angle on the 25 with quarter of an hour to play.

From the few opportunities they received, the French backs looked to be the more dangerous but they too were unable to finish off promising movements. In the last ten minutes McCormick was given further penalty attempts from 30 and 35 yards but neither kick was good enough to score points and this disappointing, and often sour Test came to a close with no further addition to the score.

This match saw Colin Meads equal Jack Kyle's world record of forty-six internationals for his country. Marcel Puget, the French captain in this match, fractured his thumb during the game and returned home the following week.

295

NEW ZEALAND 19

10 August, 1968

Third Test

Injury beset the New Zealand selection for this match with Laidlaw who had suffered a broken thumb at Wellington, Davis still troubled with a hamstring injury, and MacRae having aggravated a back injury, not being available.

The selectors retained Cottrell at second five-eighth, moved Thorne in from the wing to play at centre, and introduced a newcomer, Owen Stephens, on the right wing. Sid Going came out of the reserves to replace Laidlaw behind the scrum.

France made eight changes to their side, with Lux and Dourthe coming into the three-quarters; Berot replacing the repatriated Puget; a now fit Carrere taking one of the side row positions; and Billiere, playing his only international the other. Cester, also restored to fitness, returned to lock the scrum with Dauga. A new front row completed the changes. Maso, who had played the earlier Tests in the centres, was shifted into fly-half in what turned out to be an inspired move.

Mr Pat Murphy, the Whangarei public accountant, was refereeing his eleventh international as he blew the whistle to commence the match in ideal conditions. For the first time in New Zealand's Rugby history, the ground had been pre-sold and the gates did not open until 12.15 p.m.

McCormick kicked off and New Zealand spent the early minutes on attack, with Thorne standing out on two occasions when he made promising breaks. After twelve minutes France were penalised at a scrum and McCormick opened the scoring from 27 yards. Five minutes later the New Zealand pack, storming on to attack, won a ruck inside the French 25 and as Going got the ball, he found that several retiring French players were between him and his backs, so he quickly shot around the blindside to catch the French defence napping, and scored 20 yards in from the right hand corner. McCormick converted to bring the score to 8-0 but missed a penalty three minutes later from just outside the 25.

The next points came following a line-out which the All Blacks had won, and despite the

Pat Murphy signals the first of Going's two brilliant tries at Eden Park.

speed of the French coming through, Cottrell was able to drop-kick a goal on the run from around 35 yards.

Just three minutes later Going was over for his second brilliant try. New Zealand won a deep line-out right on the French goal line, and the elusive half-back again scuttled away on the blindside before moving back towards the posts to score in almost the same place that he had scored his earlier try. McCormick again converted to give New Zealand the commanding lead of 16-0 with eight minutes to go to halftime. Going narrowly failed to bring up his third try right on the interval when he lost the ball on the line.

France opened their scoring four minutes after the resumption when they won a line-out five yards from the New Zealand line. Carrere broke across field with the ball linking with Maso who found Spanghero in support. The ball went from Dourthe to Trillo and the centre scored France's first try in the series with a spectacular dive through McCormick's tackle. Villepreux missed the conversion as he had a penalty two minutes earlier.

Stephens was bundled out in the corner after a blindside run by Kirton but it was France who stormed back to register a fine try in the twelfth minute of the spell. Brilliant inter-passing bet-

FRANCE 12

ween Maso and Lux made the opening before the ball went to Carrere. He passed to Spanghero and was on hand to take the return and crash over in Cottrell's attempted tackle. Villepreux missed the conversion from a wide angle.

Midway through the half Trillo landed a dropped goal and France were only seven points behind.

McCormick goaled a 30 yard penalty in the twenty-third minute with a well-judged kick into the breeze to make it 19-9 to the All Blacks. This kick gave McCormick a tally of twenty-eight out of the forty points scored by the All Blacks in the series.

Over the remaining minutes of the half, the tempo of this already quick-moving game increased even further. Stephens came into a movement from the blind to send O'Callaghan away but the French defence held. Then Lochore started a promising move which ended on the French 25. Three minutes from time Gray was held up on the line after being sent away by Cottrell.

In the final moments of this great game the most spectacular try of the afternoon was scored. France won a maul just inside their own half and Villepreux was up on the blindside to link with Lux on the left wing. Stephens was outflanked, and as Lux in-passed back to Villepreux, McCormick was wrong-footed but valiantly moved back to clip the full-back's heels as the ball was again spun out to Lux. He ran the last 20 yards to score near the corner as Kirkpatrick and finally O'Callaghan from the far wing tried to get to him. Understandably, the weary Villepreux was unable to convert and the match was all over.

The game had produced much memorable Rugby and, after the spirit that had prevailed in the earlier two internationals, had done much to end the tour on a high note.

This match, rather surprisingly, proved to be the last international played by the great All Black flanker, Kelvin Tremain. Since 1959 he had played thirty-eight Tests for his country, a figure exceeded only by Colin Meads who had played a world record-breaking forty-seven in

this match. Tremain had scored nine tries in internationals. His try total was the highest recorded by a forward and only one fewer than Frank Mitchinson's New Zealand record that had stood since 1913.

Other All Blacks who had played their final internationals for New Zealand were wingers Mick O'Callaghan, later to play for the Stade Toulousain club in France and subsequently win a Rugby Blue for Cambridge University whilst continuing his veterinary studies, and Owen Stephens who joined the ranks of those who played internationals for both Australia and New Zealand, before transferring to the League code.

Another who was severing his direct connections with international Rugby was the convenor of the national selectors, and coach of the All Blacks over the past three years, Fred Allen. He had built up an outstanding unbeaten Test record and developed a fifteen man involvement style of play that had been universally approved.

NEW ZEALAND
W.F. McCORMICK
(Canterbury)
O.G. STEPHENS   G.S. THORNE   M.W. O'CALLAGHAN
(Wellington)   (Auckland)   (Manawatu)
W.D. COTTRELL
(Canterbury)
E.W. KIRTON
(Otago)
S.M. GOING
(North Auckland)
B.J. LOCHORE (**Capt.**)
(Wairarapa)
I.A. KIRKPATRICK   S.C. STRAHAN   C.E. MEADS   K.R. TREMAIN
(Canterbury)   (Manawatu)   (King Country)   (Hawke's Bay)
K.F. GRAY   B.E. McLEOD   A.E. HOPKINSON
(Wellington)   (Counties)   (Canterbury)

M. LASSERRE   M. YACHVILI   J.C. NOBLE
(S.U. Agen)   (S.C. Tulle)   (La Voulte S.)
C. CARRERE (**Capt.**)   E. CESTER   B. DAUGA   M. BILLIERE
(R.C. Toulonnais)   (Toulouse OEC)   (S. Montois)   (S. Toulousain)
W. SPANGHERO
(R.C. Narbonne)
J.L. BEROT
(S. Toulousain)
J. MASO
(U.S. Perpignan)
J.P. LUX   C. DOURTHE   J. TRILLO   J.M. BONAL
(U.S. Tyrosse)   (U.S. Dax)   (C.A. Beglais)   (S. Toulousain)
P. VILLEPREUX
(S. Toulousain)
FRANCE

REFEREE: Mr J.P. Murphy (North Auckland)
ATTENDANCE: 55,000
CONDITIONS: Weather fine ground firm
HALFTIME: New Zealand 16, France 0

SCORERS

NEW ZEALAND	FRANCE
Tries: Going (2)	Tries: Trillo, Carrere, Lux
Conversions: McCormick (2)	Dropped goal: Dourthe
Penalty goals: McCormick (2)	
Dropped goal: Cottrell	

31 May, 1969

First Test

The five match tour, which included two internationals, made by Wales in the early part of the 1969 season was the first made by a Welsh national team to New Zealand and was keenly looked forward to by Rugby supporters. Led by Brian Price, a veteran of the 1963 Test at Cardiff, and of the 1966 Lions, the Welsh had the extremely meagre preparation of one match prior to this international, a 9-all draw with Taranaki. Many doubted that this was sufficient for what was bound to be such a hard game.

Only one new cap was chosen for the All Black side, Alan Smith from Stratford, who had toured with the 1967 New Zealand team, being chosen to partner Colin Meads at lock.

The Welsh team featured the half-back combination of Gareth Edwards and Barry John who had first combined in the Welsh team against New Zealand in 1967 and had built up a big reputation in the interim.

Barry John is pursued by Thorne with Bill Davis and MacRae also in the chase.

CHRISTCHURCH PRESS

WALES 0

The British Leader of the Opposition, Mr Edward Heath, was amongst the spectators as McCormick kicked off for New Zealand into the breeze. With the forwards dominating possession, New Zealand quickly took the upper hand in the match.

Quarter of an hour after the start, the All Blacks won a line-out near half-way and after Kirton had doubled around MacRae to create an opening, the ball had gone out to Thorne on the wing. He cut back inside before linking up with the forwards. Lochore and Meads carried on the movement, then McLeod handed to Kirton and the five-eighth tossed a high pass to Dick who juggled for a moment before getting control and crossing for a fine try in the tackle of Gerald Davies. McCormick was unable to convert from the wide angle.

The next points came after half an hour when Watkins was unable to take a high kick from McCormick, and the seventeen stone Muller gathered the loose ball. Showing a surprising turn of speed he ran to inside the Welsh 25 where he found McLeod in support on his right, and it was the hooker who scampered the final twenty yards to dot down between the posts and give McCormick a simple conversion.

The same two front row forwards were prominent in a blindside movement three minutes later which ended with captain Lochore crossing for a try which McCormick also converted to bring the score to 13-0.

No further scoring occurred before the interval and it was not until thirty minutes had passed in the second half that any further points were posted. Again, it was the elusive Thorne who created an opening after taking a high kick before linking up with his forwards and this time Gray surged at the line in a determined rush which yielded a try. McCormick was wide with the conversion.

Just before this try, Welsh hooker Jeff Young had been felled at a line-out and was off the field with an injury that was diagnosed as a broken jaw. He was replaced by veteran international Norman Gale whose career had commenced in 1960 when he was in the Welsh side against Ireland.

Five minutes from the final whistle McCormick was on target with a 35 yard penalty to complete the scoring.

The Triple Crown winners and Five Nation champions were well outclassed in this match, in which the All Black pack had displayed awesome power and control whilst the backs handled the greasy ball well. Keith Jarrett, the Welsh goal kicker, who had scored nineteen points in his first international against England in April 1967 as an eighteen year old, failed with five attempts at goal, two of which were from long range.

The injury to Young ruled him out of consideration for the remainder of the tour, and a replacement hooker, Vic Perrins, was flown out.

NEW ZEALAND

W.F. McCORMICK
(Canterbury)

M.J. DICK	W.L. DAVIS	G.S. THORNE
(Auckland)	(Hawke's Bay)	(Auckland)

I.R. MacRAE
(Hawke's Bay)

E.W. KIRTON
(Otago)

S.M. GOING
(North Auckland)

B.J. LOCHORE (Capt.)
(Wairarapa)

I.A. KIRKPATRICK	A.E. SMITH	C.E. MEADS	T.N. LISTER
(Poverty Bay)	(Taranaki)	(King Country)	(South Canterbury)
B.L. MULLER	B.E. McLEOD		K.F. GRAY
(Taranaki)	(Counties)		(Wellington)

D.J. LLOYD	J. YOUNG †	D. WILLIAMS
(Bridgend)	(Harrogate)	(Ebbw Vale)
W.D. MORRIS	B.E. THOMAS B. PRICE (Capt.)	J. TAYLOR
(Neath)	(Neath) (Newport)	(London Welsh)

T.M. DAVIES
(London Welsh)

G.O. EDWARDS
(Cardiff)

B. JOHN
(Cardiff)

M.C.R. RICHARDS	T.G.R. DAVIES	K.S. JARRETT	S.J. WATKINS
(Cardiff)	(Cambridge University)	(Newport)	(Newport)

J.P.R. WILLIAMS
(London Welsh)

WALES

REPLACEMENT: † replaced by N.R. Gale (Llanelli)
REFEREE: Mr J.P. Murphy (North Auckland)
ATTENDANCE: 55,000
CONDITIONS: Weather showery, ground muddy
HALFTIME: New Zealand 13, Wales 0

SCORERS

NEW ZEALAND	WALES

Tries: Dick, McLeod, Lochore, Gray
Conversions: McCormick (2)
Penalty goal: McCormick

---

14 June, 1969

Second Test

The Welsh team recorded wins over Otago by 27-9, and Wellington by 14-6, following the Christchurch international, and although the New Zealand team remained firm favourites, it was expected that the visitors would make a bold showing in this match.

Several changes were made to their Test team with Gerald Davies moving out to the right wing to replace Watkins and John Dawes, the senior back in the side, coming in to play in the centres. In the forwards Brian Thomas replaced Lloyd at prop, his place in the second row going to 1966 Lion Delme Thomas, and Dennis Hughes came in for the bearded Taylor on the side of the scrum.

Although the team originally announced by the New Zealand selectors contained no changes, subsequent knee injuries to Muller and Thorne saw Alister Hopkinson and Waikato winger George Skudder make the side as replacements. Skudder was the first international from the great nursery of Maori Rugby, Te Aute College.

Wales kicked off in fine, warm and windless conditions towards the scoreboard end. After missing a simple penalty in the opening minutes, Jarrett landed an even more simple kick from just fifteen yards to commence the scoring in the ninth minute. McCormick replied with a fine 30 yard effort from the touchline to even the score in the fourteenth minute.

Twenty-two minutes were gone when John Williams came into the backline and created an overlap for Maurice Richards on the left wing near the All Black 25. The Cardiff winger appeared to be well covered by Kirton and McCormick but, with a hesitation followed by a tremendous surge of acceleration, he cleanly beat both of these defenders to race away and score a brilliant individual try in the corner. Jarrett, who had six minutes earlier missed a penalty, also failed with the conversion attempt.

From the resumption the All Blacks roared on to attack and within two minutes had also scored. The try came from a scrum inside the Welsh 25

which New Zealand won near the left touch. Lochore detached and passed to Going who ran on the blindside until confronted by Davies. He whipped a pass to Skudder who eluded a flying tackle from full-back Williams and made a spectacular dive to score in the corner. McCormick, showing the form which was to bring him nineteen more points in this match, converted with a great kick to give New Zealand the lead for the first time in the match.

Further penalties in the twenty-eighth minute, from 30 yards, and in the thirty-ninth minute, from 40 yards, brought the score to 14-6 at the interval.

From the restart New Zealand went back on to attack and in the third minute McCormick raised his personal tally in the match to fourteen with another penalty, this time from 25 yards out. Jarrett, who was having a less successful day with his boot, missing a number of kickable goals, was finally rewarded when he raised the flags from close-in, ten minutes into the half.

NEW ZEALAND

W.F. McCORMICK
(Canterbury)

M.J. DICK   W.L. DAVIS   G.R. SKUDDER
(Auckland)   (Hawke's Bay)   (Waikato)

I.R. MacRAE
(Hawke's Bay)

E.W. KIRTON
(Otago)

S.M. GOING
(North Auckland)

B.J. LOCHORE (**Capt.**)
(Wairarapa)

I.A. KIRKPATRICK   A.E. SMITH   C.E. MEADS   T.N. LISTER
(Poverty Bay)   (Taranaki)   (King Country)   (South Canterbury)
K.F. GRAY   B.E. McLEOD   A.E. HOPKINSON
(Wellington)   (Counties)   (Canterbury)

D. WILLIAMS   N.R. GALE   B.E. THOMAS
(Ebbw Vale)   (Llanelli)   (Neath)
W.D. MORRIS   B. PRICE (**Capt**)   W.D. THOMAS   D. HUGHES
(Neath)   (Newport)   (Llanelli)   (Newbridge)
T.M. DAVIES
(London Welsh)
G.O. EDWARDS
(Cardiff)

B. JOHN
(Cardiff)

M.C.R. RICHARDS   K.S. JARRETT   S.J. DAWES   T.G.R. DAVIES
(Cardiff)   (Newport)   (London Welsh)   (Cambridge University)
J.P.R. WILLIAMS
(London Welsh)
WALES

REFEREE: Mr J.P. Murphy (North Auckland)
ATTENDANCE: 55,000
CONDITIONS: Weather fine, ground firm
HALFTIME: New Zealand 14, Wales 6

SCORERS

NEW ZEALAND	**WALES**
Tries: Skudder, MacRae, Kirkpatrick	Tries: Richards, Jarrett
Conversions: McCormick (3)	Penalty goals: Jarrett (2)
Penalty goals: McCormick (5)	
Dropped goal: McCormick	

WALES 12

Fergie McCormick created a world record for individual scoring in an international. He kicked three conversions, a dropped goal and five penalty goals for a total of 24 points.

Midway through the half Going made a break before getting a pass to McLeod 10 yards inside the Welsh 25. As the hooker was tackled by John Williams, the loose ball was gathered by Lister, who ran through an attempted tackle by John before being halted by Dawes. He managed to get the ball out to MacRae who ran the last five yards to score by the right hand upright. The conversion presented the in-form McCormick with no problems and New Zealand led 22-9.

Three minutes later, McCormick fielded a clearing kick by John and from 55 yards rammed home a fine dropped goal from near touch. A fifth penalty two minutes after the dropped goal, saw McCormick equal the long standing individual point scoring record in international play, held by the English three-quarter, Daniel Lambert when he scored two tries, five conversions and two penalty goals against France in January 1911.

A try six minutes from time by Kirkpatrick from the back of a line-out, five yards from the Welsh line, gave McCormick the chance to create a new record. His conversion from 15 yards in from touch was a good one and brought the score to 33-9.

In the final minute of play, the Welsh mounted a backline attack which ended with Keith Jarrett going over for a try in the corner which he was unable to improve on with the conversion attempt.

It had been an unbelievably large win by New Zealand, their widest margin ever against Wales. The highlight was undoubtedly McCormick's wonderful kicking form which had contributed much to the large score. It was the final international for the All Black prop forward, Ken Gray, who had played in twenty-four Tests since his debut in 1963. During this time he had been recognised as one of the finest front row forwards in the world. Immensely strong and intelligent, he was also extremely mobile and his loss to the New Zealand team was to be a severe one.

This match was George Skudder's only appearance in a Test, and another figure who was not to grace the international field again was referee Pat Murphy, who had controlled thirteen Tests since 1959, a record for a New Zealand referee.

25 July, 1970

First Test

Following an unbeaten record in their ten matches on tour leading up to this first Test of the 1970 series, the All Blacks were generally expected to win. The Springboks had had a disappointing tour of the United Kingdom during the 1969-70 season, losing two of the internationals and drawing the other two.

Despite the loss of Colin Meads, who had suffered a broken bone in his left forearm during the match against Eastern Transvaal, the All Blacks took the field with a fairly experienced side, only the 19 year old Bryan Williams being new to Test Rugby.

Of the Springboks, Frik du Preez, Sid Nomis, Mannetjies Roux, Jan Ellis, Hannes Marais and captain Dawie de Villiers had toured New Zealand in 1965 with all but Nomis and Marais playing in the internationals. The kick-off for South Africa was taken by Piet Visagie looking into the sun, and the Springboks went immediately on to attack, putting severe pressure on the New Zealand defence.

Only three minutes had elapsed when the All Blacks won a scrum inside their 25 but, as Laidlaw went back to gather the ball, he was bustled and the ball went loose. Greyling, coming through quickly, got his foot to the ball and kicked it through to the All Black line. In the chase for the ball, de Villiers narrowly beat Wayne Cottrell to the touchdown and scored South Africa's first points, near the left hand corner. The new Springbok full-back, Ian McCallum, hooked the conversion. However, with only a further four minutes gone, Visagie slammed over a fine left-footed dropped goal, following a line-out. He thus became the first Springbok to register a hundred points in international play.

Just prior to this successful kick, Cottrell had been heavily tackled by Jansen and although he slowly got to his feet and continued to play, he was obviously badly shaken.

After twelve minutes' play the referee, Mr Piet Robbertse, detected several New Zealand backs up in an off-side position at a line-out just outside

their 25, and McCallum was able to put South Africa further ahead with a 27 yard penalty. The All Black woes were further increased when Laidlaw received a bump on the head a minute or so later, which appeared to affect his play quite markedly.

Before the half was over McCallum had increased the Springbok lead to 12-0 when he was on target from 45 yards out after Laidlaw was adjudged off-side at a scrum. Earlier, Visagie missed a further drop goal attempt and on the call of halftime, McCormick was just short with a 43 yard penalty in one of New Zealand's few scoring opportunities during the fateful first half.

Straight after the resumption, McCormick was astray with a 40 yard penalty and in the third minute Laidlaw left the field with slight concussion, a result of the blow he had taken in the first half. Following a medical examination of Laidlaw which lasted several minutes, Going was permitted to take the field as his substitute and

---

NEW ZEALAND

W.F. McCORMICK
(Canterbury)

M.J. DICK (Auckland)	G.S. THORNE (Auckland)	B.G. WILLIAMS (Auckland)

I.R. MacRAE
(Hawke's Bay)

W.D. COTTRELL
(Canterbury)

C.R. LAIDLAW *
(Otago)

B.J. LOCHORE (**Capt.**)
(Wairarapa)

I.A. KIRKPATRICK (Poverty Bay)	S.C. STRAHAN (Manawatu)	A.E. SMITH (Taranaki)	T.N. LISTER (South Canterbury)
B.L. MULLER (Taranaki)	B.E. McLEOD (Counties)		A.E. HOPKINSON (Canterbury)

J.B. NEETHLING (Western Province)	J.F.P. van WYK (Northern Transvaal)	J.F.K. MARAIS (Eastern Province)
J.H. ELLIS (South West Africa)	F.C.H. du PREEZ (Northern Transvaal) J.J. SPIES (Northern Transvaal)	P.J.F. GREYLING (Transvaal)

A.J. BATES
(Western Transvaal)

D.J. de VILLIERS (**Capt.**)
(Transvaal)

P.J. VISAGIE
(Griqualand West)

G.H. MULLER (Western Province)	J.S. JANSEN (Orange Free State)	F. du T. ROUX (Griqualand West)	S.H. NOMIS (Transvaal)

I.D. McCALLUM
(Western Province)

SOUTH AFRICA

REPLACEMENT: *replaced by S.M. Going (North Auckland)
REFEREE: Mr P. Robbertse (Eastern Transvaal)
ATTENDANCE: 55,000
CONDITIONS: Weather fine, ground hard
HALFTIME: South Africa 12, New Zealand 0

SCORERS

NEW ZEALAND	**SOUTH AFRICA**
Try: Williams	Tries: de Villiers, Nomis
Penalty goal: McCormick	Conversion: McCallum
	Penalty goals: McCallum (2)
	Dropped goal: Visagie

NEW ZEALAND

Loftus Versfeld Stadium, Pretoria

W. OOSTHUIZEN

Laidlaw suffers the combined onslaught of du Preez and Malan.

quickly made himself conspicuous with two devastating breaks.

Twelve minutes into the half McCormick opened the All Blacks' scoring when he landed a simple penalty from in front of the posts.

Midway through the spell, Going made a blindside break from a scrum before passing to the brilliant young winger, Bryan Williams, and with a surge to take himself clear of the immediate defence and a massive side-step inside McCallum, the teenager scored his maiden Test try from 40 yards out. McCormick, who did not kick well in this match, missed a comparatively simple conversion.

Now within six points, it looked as if New

Zealand had a slim chance to win the game, but the Springboks were still able to apply pressure and were enjoying a territorial advantage. Both sides had attempts at goal from drop kicks and penalties but no further scoring occurred until New Zealand took one of a series of tap-penalties in the second half, on their own 10 yard mark. Captain Brian Lochore threw an ill directed lobbed pass to his right which was accepted by the Springbok wing, Sid Nomis and with the defence out of position he sprinted up the middle of the field to score between the posts. McCallum converted to bring the score to 17-6 and place the game beyond the grasp of the All Blacks.

Thus ended a winning run of seventeen internationals by New Zealand since South Africa had won the third Test in 1965.

303

NEW ZEALAND 9

8 August, 1970

Second Test

In the two provincial matches since the first Test, the All Blacks had scored convincing victories, downing Eastern Province 49-8 and Boland 35-9.

Five changes were made to the Test side which had lost at Pretoria, but of these, Neil Thimbleby was unable to take the field because of an infected thumb, which allowed Muller to retain his place. Grahame Thorne moved on to the left wing, with Williams replacing Dick on the right and Bill Davis coming in to the centre position. Earle Kirton resumed his partnership with Laidlaw at the expense of Cottrell, and Wyllie and Sutherland, both making their Test debuts, took over from the injured Lister and Smith in the forwards. Not surprisingly there was no change in the Springbok side.

A few seconds after three o'clock, Fergie McCormick kicked off for New Zealand from the Wynberg end of the field with the breeze at his back. Two minutes after the start the All Black full-back was short with a 48 yard penalty attempt and the tense feeling surrounding the game was soon evident as fighting broke out among the forwards.

Sutherland made a poor attempt at a penalty from the middle of the half-way line in the sixth minute, but early All Black pressure soon paid off when Laidlaw secured the ball following an untidy tap by South Africa from a short throw-in on the Springbok goal line. Hunched up, he broke around the short end of the line-out to dive through Nomis's tackle and score by the corner flag. McCormick's kick was short and New Zealand led by 3-0 after eleven minutes.

Both Visagie and McCallum missed penalties in the next five minutes but generally it was the All Blacks who held control throughout this half. Two minutes before halftime, New Zealand won a scrum just inside the Springbok 25 and after some indecisive play, the ball was passed to Kirkpatrick who set off on a brilliant run, evading tackle after tackle until he scored a good try to the right of the posts. McCormick's attempted conversion was a poor effort and the teams went to the halftime break with the score at 6-0.

A Springbok foot clearly hits the corner post as Bryan Williams dives to force the ball. But right, the All Black winger looks up to find the touch judge indicating that Williams had hit the post. The try was disallowed.

Bryan Williams made a brilliant burst down the right hand touch line only narrowly failing to score, thirteen minutes after halftime. A minute later one of the worst incidents of the match occurred when Nomis suffered a severe mouth injury after a clash with McCormick's elbow while he was following up a kick. From the resultant penalty Visagie was short with his kick at goal.

South Africa's first points came nineteen minutes into the second half when they won a scrum close to the All Black line and Visagie fed the 22 year old Free State University student, Joggie Jansen, with a short pass and the centre ran powerfully at the All Black defence to force his way over the line in the combined tackles of Lochore and Thorne. Ian McCallum, from close to the posts, converted to bring his side to within a point of the New Zealand total. McCormick was given an opportunity to kick a penalty from only 27 yards out when Laidlaw was late tackled by Ellis, but the kick failed.

SOUTH AFRICA 8

Newlands, Cape Town

Four minutes later another brilliant run by Williams down the right wing appeared to have secured New Zealand further points, but as the referee raised his hand to award the try the touch-judge, international referee Mr Max Baise, signalled that the ball had been touch-in-goal as Williams apparently had grazed the corner post in his dive at the line.

A vigorous ruck, a minute or two later, broke up to reveal the Springbok hooker, Piston van Wyk, lying on the ground. After treatment he was led from the field with blood pouring from a facial injury. His replacement was Robbie Barnard, the balding Transvaal hooker.

Nine minutes from time the All Black forwards were penalised for being off-side and McCallum put South Africa into the lead with a well-struck goal from 35 yards. The All Blacks attacked desperately. McCallum brought Thorne down as the winger looked dangerous in one movement, and then as another All Black attack was being mounted on the Springbok 25, Bill Davis was tackled by a blatantly off-side Roux. Only three minutes remained on the clock as McCormick came forward to take the crucial kick, from just to the left of the posts. Although he had been in poor kicking form in this match, McCormick brought joy to the All Black followers when he landed the goal. From the restart the Springboks made a last desperate attack which

ended with the ball being scrambled into touch near the All Black corner flag.

It had been a bitter, tense and often brutal match and the list of injuries suffered ran to six players, most with cuts that required stitching.

Two long serving New Zealand internationals completed their Test careers in this match. Bill Davis had played in eleven internationals since 1967 and had scored four tries. It was unfortunate that a knee injury prevented him from reaching the fine form he had shown on the 1967 tour. A sharp incisive runner he also had the ability to run his wings into scoring positions. A versatile sportsman he also represented New Zealand at softball.

The rapid development of Ron Urlich on this tour, coupled with an eye injury affecting his play, saw the end of Bruce McLeod's Test career after twenty-four matches. Since his debut in 1964 he had seldom been beaten by any hooker he had opposed, and his tireless play in the loose had brought four tries.

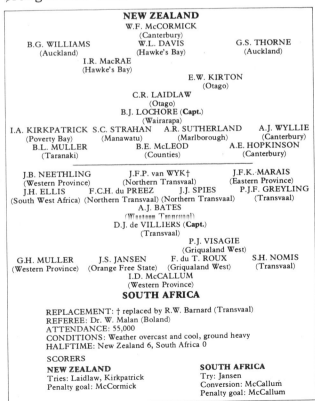

NEW ZEALAND

W.F. McCORMICK
(Canterbury)

B.G. WILLIAMS   W.L. DAVIS   G.S. THORNE
(Auckland)   (Hawke's Bay)   (Auckland)
I.R. MacRAE
(Hawke's Bay)

E.W. KIRTON
(Otago)
C.R. LAIDLAW
(Otago)
B.J. LOCHORE (**Capt.**)
(Wairarapa)

I.A. KIRKPATRICK   S.C. STRAHAN   A.R. SUTHERLAND   A.J. WYLLIE
(Poverty Bay)   (Manawatu)   (Marlborough)   (Canterbury)
B.L. MULLER   B.E. McLEOD   A.E. HOPKINSON
(Taranaki)   (Counties)   (Canterbury)

J.B. NEETHLING   J.F.P. van WYK†   J.F.K. MARAIS
(Western Province)   (Northern Transvaal)   (Eastern Province)
J.H. ELLIS   F.C.H. du PREEZ   J.J. SPIES   P.J.F. GREYLING
(South West Africa) (Northern Transvaal) (Northern Transvaal)   (Transvaal)
A.J. BATES
(Western Transvaal)
D.J. de VILLIERS (**Capt.**)
(Transvaal)

P.J. VISAGIE
(Griqualand West)
G.H. MULLER   J.S. JANSEN   F. du T. ROUX   S.H. NOMIS
(Western Province) (Orange Free State) (Griqualand West)   (Transvaal)
I.D. McCALLUM
(Western Province)

SOUTH AFRICA

REPLACEMENT: † replaced by R.W. Barnard (Transvaal)
REFEREE: Dr. W. Malan (Boland)
ATTENDANCE: 55,000
CONDITIONS: Weather overcast and cool, ground heavy
HALFTIME: New Zealand 6, South Africa 0

SCORERS

NEW ZEALAND   **SOUTH AFRICA**
Tries: Laidlaw, Kirkpatrick   Try: Jansen
Penalty goal: McCormick   Conversion: McCallum
                   Penalty goal: McCallum

29 August, 1970

Third Test

Colin Meads, who had resumed playing in the match following the Newlands Test and had featured in each match since, was included in the line-up for this game. Other changes in the side included Thimbleby and Ron Urlich, both making their first Test appearances, at the expense of Muller and McLeod in the front row. Bryan Williams, after an impressive match in the position against Western Province during which he scored two tries, was brought into the centre berth with Thorne exchanging wings and "Buff" Milner, a surprise selection, coming in on the left wing.

The Springbok selectors made two changes to their team, bringing in the veteran 270 pound prop "Mof" Myburgh, who had a reputation as a strong scrummager, and the number eight "Lofty" Nel, who had made his debut against New Zealand in 1960 and who at thirty-six was the oldest man to have represented South Africa.

Lochore won the toss and elected to play into the wind with the bright sun at his back. McCallum kicked off and the Springboks started with plenty of fire. In the opening minutes Nomis hoisted a high kick to McCormick standing on his own goal line. As the full-back took the ball, he was hit with a crunching tackle by Greyling, which left him prostrate for some time before he was able to continue.

Ten minutes had gone when McCallum attempted a penalty from 60 yards out. An excellent kick, it just passed under the bar. During the next ten minutes the All Blacks made sporadic attacks, one of which saw Laidlaw narrowly miss scoring a try as he chased a kick over the Springbok goal line.

In the twentieth minute, New Zealand were awarded a penalty 10 yards outside the South Africa 25 and near the touch line, following a late tackle by Jansen. Williams, deputising for the shaken McCormick, calmly landed the goal. Two minutes later McCallum missed a simple penalty attempt from 24 yards, but a few minutes

Kirkpatrick sets off on a determined run with Meads and Laidlaw in support. Dawie de Villiers leads the chasing South Africans.

NZ HERALD

NEW ZEALAND 3
Boet Erasmus Stadium, Port Elizabeth

after made no mistake with a further penalty from a wide angle on the 25 to even the scoring.

Some magnificent cover defence by the All Blacks led by Alex Wyllie prevented any further addition to the score throughout the remainder of the spell.

Six minutes after the resumption, Williams had a further penalty attempt from half-way but his direction was astray. The game had developed into a grim, tense struggle with both sides trying to achieve forward control. Williams had to have his left ankle strapped eleven minutes into the second half after falling awkwardly in a tackle.

Halfway through the spell, Hopkinson foolishly obstructed McCallum as he punted into the All Black 25 and McCallum neatly kicked the goal from the resultant penalty to give his side the lead at a most critical period of the game. Four minutes later, de Villiers ran on the blind from a ruck on his own 25, drawing the defence before unloading to left winger Gert Muller who showed his great pace as he raced 70 yards down the touch line to score an impressive try in the corner. McCallum could not convert and the score remained at 9-3 to the home side.

The Springboks now held control, and Visagie looked dangerous as he made a break, then narrowly missed an attempted dropped goal. Six minutes from time, the final nail in the New Zealand coffin was driven home when Williams was unable to cleanly field a pass from Wyllie as the flanker was held after making a determined dash. Roux was quickly on to the ball and headed off up-field. As the All Black defence regrouped, Roux flung a pass to his left where Muller gathered and again sprinted to the corner. McCormick's dive knocked him to the ground a few yards from the line but the momentum of his run was sufficient to carry him to the goal line where the referee awarded a try a yard in from the corner post. On this occasion McCallum landed the conversion with a good kick, to put the final result beyond doubt.

There was no further scoring and the unbroken run of success in international play enjoyed by South Africa at Port Elizabeth since 1910 continued. The All Blacks' play, particularly in the second half, had been disappointing with fundamental errors creeping in.

Apart from Milner and Thimbleby, who had made their only Test appearances in this match, it was the final international for the Otago University clubmates, Earle Kirton and Chris Laidlaw, who had paired for New Zealand nine times in Test matches. Kirton had played in thirteen internationals, scoring four tries, and Laidlaw had appeared in twenty since 1963, returning from studies at Oxford University, after having won a Rhodes Scholarship in 1968, to play in the trials for the 1970 side. A powerfully-built half-back, he had achieved a fine reputation for his long, spiralling passes from the base of the scrum.

It had been Colin Meads's fiftieth Test match, but sadly this fine player had been unable to recapture the brilliant form he had displayed in the matches on tour prior to the breaking of his forearm.

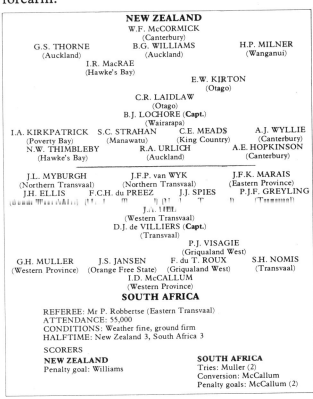

NEW ZEALAND
W.F. McCORMICK
(Canterbury)
G.S. THORNE   B.G. WILLIAMS   H.P. MILNER
(Auckland)   (Auckland)   (Wanganui)
I.R. MacRAE
(Hawke's Bay)
E.W. KIRTON
(Otago)
C.R. LAIDLAW
(Otago)
B.J. LOCHORE (Capt.)
(Wairarapa)
I.A. KIRKPATRICK   S.C. STRAHAN   C.E. MEADS   A.J. WYLLIE
(Poverty Bay)   (Manawatu)   (King Country)   (Canterbury)
N.W. THIMBLEBY   R.A. URLICH   A.E. HOPKINSON
(Hawke's Bay)   (Auckland)   (Canterbury)

J.L. MYBURGH   J.F.P. van WYK   J.F.K. MARAIS
(Northern Transvaal)   (Northern Transvaal)   (Eastern Province)
J.H. ELLIS   F.C.H. du PREEZ   J.J. SPIES   P.J.F. GREYLING
J.L. FREY
(Western Transvaal)
D.J. de VILLIERS (Capt.)
(Transvaal)
P.J. VISAGIE
(Griqualand West)
G.H. MULLER   J.S. JANSEN   F. du T. ROUX   S.H. NOMIS
(Western Province)   (Orange Free State)   (Griqualand West)   (Transvaal)
I.D. McCALLUM
(Western Province)
SOUTH AFRICA

REFEREE: Mr P. Robbertse (Eastern Transvaal)
ATTENDANCE: 55,000
CONDITIONS: Weather fine, ground firm
HALFTIME: New Zealand 3, South Africa 3
SCORERS
NEW ZEALAND   SOUTH AFRICA
Penalty goal: Williams   Tries: Muller (2)
                               Conversion: McCallum
                               Penalty goals: McCallum (2)

SOUTH AFRICA 20

12 September, 1970

Fourth Test

The New Zealand team entered this game undefeated in twenty non-international tour matches and it was hoped that the form displayed in these matches would be sufficient to draw the Test series. No fewer than eight changes were made to the side for this vital game, bringing the number of players used by New Zealand during the series to twenty-seven.

Laidlaw, who had to have his appendix removed shortly after the third Test, was unavailable and was replaced by Sid Going. His partner at first five-eighth was Blair Furlong making his Test debut probably in the place of Wayne Cottrell who was unavailable owing to a hamstring injury. After a disappointing start to the tour, Furlong had improved his form to a level comparable to that which he had reached during Hawke's Bay's tenure of the Ranfurly Shield in the late 1960's and a good match against Northern Transvaal had secured his Test place.

Another to find form in the latter stages of the tour was Victoria University utility back, Gerald Kember, who had kicked a total of thirty-four points in the match against North East Cape at Aliwal North. He won selection for his first international at full-back in place of McCormick who had not played since the Port Elizabeth Test. Williams reverted to the left wing with Grahame Thorne coming in to the centre berth and Malcolm Dick winning his place back on the right wing.

In the forwards, Alan Sutherland partnered Meads at lock whilst Tom Lister came in for Wyllie on the side of the scrum. A new pair of props Keith Murdoch, also winning his first Test place, and Brian Muller, were introduced. The South Africans fielded their third Test side. On the Thursday before the match, some concern was evident in the New Zealand camp when Going was unable to run freely owing to a knee injury, and McCormick was brought in to practise as a half-back with the Test side. However, Going was able to take his place after treatment.

With the wind behind them, the Springboks were soon attacking strongly and their early efforts were rewarded in the seventh minute when Visagie cut past Furlong and fought his way through an ineffectual cover defence to score to the right of the posts, a try which McCallum converted. Three minutes later it was McCallum who again raised the flags when he goaled a penalty from near the half-way line to put South Africa eight points up.

Kember was able to reduce the leeway in the twenty-first minute, with a good kick into the wind from just inside the 10 yard mark, which narrowly scraped over the bar. McCallum replied three minutes later with a further penalty from the New Zealand 10 yard line and, with a magnificent kick five yards inside his own half, he extended the lead to 14-3 two minutes before the interval.

Two minutes after the resumption, Kember landed his second goal from a line-out penalty 52 yards out, to which McCallum answered with his fourth penalty of the match from close in, three minutes later.

```
                    NEW ZEALAND
                    G.F. KEMBER
                    (Wellington)
M.J. DICK           G.S. THORNE            B.G. WILLIAMS
(Auckland)          (Auckland)             (Auckland)
            I.R. MacRAE
            (Hawke's Bay)
                            B.D.M. FURLONG
                            (Hawke's Bay)
                    S.M. GOING
                    (North Auckland)
                    B.J. LOCHORE (Capt.)
                    (Wairarapa)
I.A. KIRKPATRICK    A.R. SUTHERLAND   C.E. MEADS      T.N. LISTER
(Poverty Bay)       (Marlborough)     (King Country)  (South Canterbury)
B.L. MULLER         R.A. URLICH       K. MURDOCH
(Taranaki)          (Auckland)        (Otago)

J.L. MYBURGH        J.F.P. van WYK         J.F.K. MARAIS
(Northern Transvaal)(Northern Transvaal)   (Eastern Province)
J.H. ELLIS     F.C.H. du PREEZ   J.J. SPIES       P.J.F. GREYLING
(South West    (Northern         (Northern        (Transvaal)
Africa)        Transvaal)        Transvaal)
                    J.A. NEL
                    (Western Transvaal)
                    D.J. de VILLIERS (Capt.)
                    (Transvaal)
                            P.J. VISAGIE
                            (Griqualand West)
G.H. MULLER     J.S. JANSEN        F. du T. ROUX    S.H. NOMIS
(Western Province)(Orange Free State)(Griqualand West)(Transvaal)
                    I.D. McCALLUM
                    (Western Province)
                    SOUTH AFRICA
```

REFEREE: Mr A. Woolley (Eastern Transvaal)
ATTENDANCE: 67,000
CONDITIONS: Weather fine but windy, ground firm
HALFTIME: South Africa 14, New Zealand 3

SCORERS

NEW ZEALAND	SOUTH AFRICA
Try: Williams	Tries: Visagie, Muller
Conversion: Kember	Conversion: McCallum
Penalty goals: Kember (4)	Penalty goals: McCallum (4)

NEW ZEALAND 17

Ellis Park, Johannesburg

WEEKLY NEWS

Playing in his only Test, Gerald Kember kicked 14 points. Referee Woolley watches this attempt.

In the twelfth minute came a memorable try by Bryan Williams, following a tighthead by Urlich. Going spurted away on the blindside, drawing the defence before timing his pass to the brilliant winger to perfection. Williams beat Nomis with surprising ease and crossed the goal line near the corner, before turning in-field where he side-stepped his way past Jansen and Muller and touched down by the posts. Kember converted to reduce the Springbok lead to 17-11.

A further penalty by Kember four minutes later brought the All Blacks to within striking distance with twenty-four minutes of the game remaining.

For the next sixteen minutes it was anyone's match. The vital points came as Kember joined a backline movement 40 yards out from the New Zealand line. As he received the ball he was hit by a crunching tackle from Jansen and the ball spilled to the ground. In a movement reminiscent of his second try at Port Elizabeth, Muller received from Roux who had recovered the loose ball, and the 22 year old student sprinted the 40

yards to the corner, eluding both Dick and Furlong before grounding the ball eight yards from the corner post. McCallum was unable to convert but with the score standing at 20-14 the All Blacks were faced with scoring twice in the last few minutes to save the game. Kember managed to land another penalty to make his contribution to the match fourteen points and the game ended shortly after.

As in the third Test, errors at crucial times had prevented New Zealand winning this match. It had been a disappointing Test series for the All Blacks, who had played consistently well during the tour without being able to reproduce their best form in the internationals.

Apart from Furlong and Kember, who appeared in only this one international, it was the end of the Test careers of several leading All Black players. Malcolm Dick, always a winger of true class, had appeared in fifteen Tests since 1963 and had scored four tries. Grahame Thorne, who for the next few years returned to settle in South Africa and went close to representing the Springboks, had played in ten Tests since his debut in 1968. Ian MacRae was another who had played a leading part in his country's Rugby since winning his first Test cap in 1966. He had scored three tries in his seventeen internationals.

Of the forwards, only hooker Ron Urlich, after a brief career of two Tests, was not destined to play another international but he later won selection for the 1972-73 Northern Hemisphere tour.

Another player who had reached the end of his international career was the Springbok captain Dawie de Villiers, who had led South Africa in two Test series against New Zealand and had captained South Africa a record number of twenty-two times. His partnership with Piet Visagie had extended for seventeen internationals since 1967.

Although destined to appear in one further international, Brian Lochore had led New Zealand for the last time. Since the first Test of the 1966 series against the Lions he had been captain of the New Zealand international team on eighteen occasions.

26 June, 1971

First Test

The 1971 Lions were one of the best teams ever to tour New Zealand. With an outstanding coach in former Welsh international, Carwyn James, an equally outstanding captain in John Dawes and a diplomatic manager in 1950 Lion, Doug Smith, the tourists were very popular both on and off the field. Their backs were brilliant and, unlike Lions' teams which had preceded them, they had forwards to match the New Zealand packs, especially in scrummaging, where the British held a slight edge over the All Blacks.

There were seven newcomers to Test Rugby in the New Zealand team. Bruce Hunter, the national 800 metres champion in 1970 and 1971, had toured South Africa in 1970 but injuries restricted his appearances. At no stage had he been considered a Test prospect in South Africa, however.

Ken Carrington, on the other wing, was not chosen by the New Zealand selectors after 1971. He was always prepared to "have a go" but he lacked pace compared with the British speedsters.

Bob Burgess, the new first five-eighth, played for the All Blacks again in 1972 and 1973. He had good hands and ran well with the ball but his defence was weak and his kicking was not always accurate.

The new forwards were Allan McNaughton, Peter Whiting, Tane Norton and Ritchie Guy. Whiting developed as a very talented line-out forward while he was also a fast man around the field for a player of his size. He was to become a key man in future All Black teams.

Neither McNaughton nor Guy played in Tests after 1971 although both gave good service against the Lions. Guy made the team when Keith Murdoch was unavailable and while the North Aucklander's scrummaging was not of top class, he was an excellent forward in the loose. Norton went on to become New Zealand's most-capped hooker.

The selection of Bryan Williams at centre was something of a surprise. While he was regarded by Rugby critics all over the world as a top class

Norton, Guy and Meads show the physical strain of Test Rugby as they await the throw-in at this line-out.

wing, Williams was not rated highly as a centre.

The Lions had not lost a game in New Zealand prior to the first Test and some of their wins over major unions had been most impressive. Included in their team for this international were Gibson, McBride and Thomas of the 1966 British team. Thomas, together with Williams, both Davies, John, Edwards, Dawes and Taylor had toured with the 1969 Welsh team.

Meads lost the toss and Dawes elected to take the kick-off. John prepared to kick but Taylor ran in and booted the ball in the direction of Davies' wing. The ruse did not succeed, for it was the home side that went on to the attack.

The All Blacks made several assaults on the British line and went close to scoring several times. Thus it was against the run of play when the visitors opened the scoring with a try in the sixteenth minute. They bustled the All Black

Carisbrook, Dunedin

defence and took the ball into their opponents' territory for the first time in the game. Sutherland tried to clear on his own line but McLauchlan charged the kick down to score. John missed the conversion.

No further scoring took place until almost halftime when Dawes was judged offside at a maul. McCormick, who had failed with two penalty attempts so far, made no mistake with this one and the interval came with the scores level.

Early in the second half, John failed when he dropped for goal and Gerald Davies, chasing hard on the right wing, missed a try by inches as the ball rolled away from him to touch-in-goal. Then in the sixteenth minute the All Blacks gave away a penalty for offside play and John put the Lions into the lead with a good kick from 30 yards out.

Then New Zealand made a superb effort to close the gap and only John's line kicking kept the home side out of the Lions' half. The crack

P.G. BUSH

Lions' manager Doug Smith and veteran centre Mike Gibson hug each other in the joy of victory.

Welsh fly-half was receiving fine service from "Chico" Hopkins, who had replaced Edwards in the seventh minute of the game, and John was able to stand clear of the marauding All Black loose forwards.

With four minutes to go, McNaughton late-tackled John and from 30 yards the latter kicked the goal to make the game safe for his team. For the second time in Rugby history, the Lions had won a Test at Carisbrook.

This match ended the international career of Fergie McCormick. John's tactical kicking had kept him under pressure throughout the match and both his general play and goal kicking had been below his normal standard.

A gritty and popular player he had played in sixteen Tests and had scored 121 points, a total surpassed only by Don Clarke.

NEW ZEALAND

W.F. McCORMICK
(Canterbury)

B.A. HUNTER	B.G. WILLIAMS	K.R. CARRINGTON
(Otago)	(Auckland)	(Auckland)

W.D. COTTRELL
(Canterbury)

R.E. BURGESS
(Manawatu)

S.M. GOING
(North Auckland)

A.R. SUTHERLAND
(Marlborough)

I.A. KIRKPATRICK	P.J. WHITING	C.E. MEADS (Capt.)	A.M. McNAUGHTON
(Poverty Bay)	(Auckland)	(King Country)	(Bay of Plenty)
B.L. MULLER		R.W. NORTON	R.A. GUY
(Taranaki)		(Canterbury)	(North Auckland)

J. McLAUCHLAN	J.V. PULLIN	J.F. LYNCH
(Jordanhill College & Scotland)	(Bristol & England)	(St. Mary's College & Ireland)
J. TAYLOR	W.D. THOMAS	W.J. McBRIDE	P.J. DIXON
(London Welsh & Wales)	(Llanelli & Wales)	(Ballymena & Ireland)	(Harlequins & England)

T.M. DAVIES
(London Welsh & Wales)

G.O. EDWARDS †
(Cardiff & Wales)

B. JOHN
(Cardiff & Wales)

J.C. BEVAN	C.M.H. GIBSON	S.J. DAWES (Capt.)	T.G.R. DAVIES
(Cardiff College of Ed. & Wales)	(N.I.F.C. & Ireland)	(London Welsh & Wales)	(Cambridge University & Wales)

J.P.R. WILLIAMS
(London Welsh & Wales)

BRITISH ISLES

REPLACEMENT: † replaced by R. Hopkins (Maesteg & Wales)
REFEREE: Mr J.P.G. Pring (Auckland)
ATTENDANCE: 45,000
CONDITIONS: Weather fine, ground greasy
HALFTIME: New Zealand 3, British Isles 3

SCORERS

NEW ZEALAND	BRITISH ISLES
Penalty goal: McCormick	Try: McLauchlan
	Penalty goals: John (2)

NEW ZEALAND 22

10 July, 1971

Second Test

Following their first Test victory, the Lions had scored good wins over Southland, Taranaki and New Zealand Universities and they were generally favoured to win the Christchurch international. They made only one change to their team, David Duckham replacing the brilliant but erratic John Bevan on the left wing. Built like a loose forward, Duckham was an outstanding footballer and was equally capable at wing or centre. Bevan later switched to League and returned to New Zealand as a British representative at that code.

There were three changes in the New Zealand team. Laurie Mains was playing his first Test in

Gerald Davies tackles Bryan Williams before the All Black winger receives the ball. Referee John Pring awarded New Zealand a penalty try for this infringement.

BRITISH ISLES 12

place of McCormick while another new cap, Howard Joseph, was brought in at centre with Williams moving to the wing in place of Carrington. Sutherland, who had had the misfortune to break a leg in a charity match, was replaced by Alex Wyllie. Mains gained All Black selection again in 1976 but Joseph did not wear the New Zealand jersey after 1971.

The Lions kicked off and right from the start, the All Blacks applied the pressure in the forwards. Within five minutes their efforts were rewarded when Going fed Burgess on his left from a scrum in front of the Lions' posts and the first five-eighth ran through a gap to score 10 yards from the corner. Mains failed to convert, and he had no better luck with a long-range penalty shortly after.

In the twenty-first minute, John Williams fielded a misdirected punt on his 25 yard line. He made ground upfield before passing to Gibson, who drew Mains to send Gerald Davies away on a 50 yard run to the line for an excellent try. Surprisingly, John missed the simple conversion.

Three minutes later, after a series of scrums on the Lions' line, Going snapped up the ball as it came out of a ruck to dive over for Mains to convert, John reduced the leeway with a 50 yard penalty and New Zealand led 8-6 at halftime.

Ten minutes after the start of the second half, New Zealand had a penalty try awarded after an early tackle on Bryan Williams by Gerald Davies when the All Black wing was waiting for a pass from Going. Mains had no trouble with the conversion and New Zealand went to a seven-point lead.

Ten minutes later, the lead was further increased when Going worked the blindside with Burgess from a scrum and the latter ran over for his second try, which Mains failed to convert from wide out.

The Lions were now badly rattled and their anxiety was not helped when John missed a penalty from 30 yards. In the thirtieth minute

McBride late-tackled Joseph and from an easy position Mains added another three points.

With six minutes to go, a maul formed just inside the All Blacks' half. Suddenly, Kirkpatrick came away with the ball and set off into British territory. He stumbled slightly as he fended off John Williams but he ran on to score a remarkable try in the corner. Mains missed the conversion but with the score at 22-6 the result of the game was beyond doubt.

The Lions did not give up, however, and they had the last word, for Gerald Davies scored a try from an overlap created by Williams and, right on time, Barry John dropped a fine goal from nearly 40 yards out. The New Zealanders' win was decisive and on the day they were the better team.

This was to be the only loss suffered by the Lions on their New Zealand tour.

NEW ZEALAND

L.W. MAINS
(Otago)

B.A. HUNTER   H.T. JOSEPH   B.G. WILLIAMS
(Otago)   (Canterbury)   (Auckland)

W.D. COTTRELL
(Canterbury)

R.E. BURGESS
(Manawatu)

S.M. GOING
(North Auckland)

A.J. WYLLIE
(Canterbury)

I.A. KIRKPATRICK   P.J. WHITING   C.E. MEADS (Capt.)   A.M. McNAUGHTON
(Poverty Bay)   (Auckland)   (King Country)   (Bay of Plenty)

B.L. MULLER   R.W. NORTON   R.A. GUY
(Taranaki)   (Canterbury)   (North Auckland)

J. McLAUGHLAN   J.V. PULLIN   J.F. LYNCH
(Jordanhill College &   (Bristol & England)   (St. Mary's College &
Scotland)   Ireland)

J. TAYLOR   W.D. THOMAS   W.J. McBRIDE   P.J. DIXON
(London Welsh &   (Llanelli & Wales)   (Ballymena &   (Harlequins
Wales)   Ireland)   & England)

T.M. DAVIES
(London Welsh & Wales)

G.O. EDWARDS
(Cardiff & Wales)

B. JOHN
(Cardiff & Wales)

D.J. DUCKHAM   C.M.H. GIBSON   S.J. DAWES (Capt.)   T.G.R. DAVIES
(Coventry &   (NIFC &   (London Welsh &   (Cambridge University
England)   Ireland)   Wales)   & Wales)

J.P.R. WILLIAMS
(London Welsh & Wales)

BRITISH ISLES

REFEREE: Mr J.P.G. Pring (Auckland)
ATTENDANCE: 57,500
CONDITIONS: Weather fine, ground muddy
HALFTIME: New Zealand 8 British Isles 6

SCORERS

NEW ZEALAND	BRITISH ISLES
Tries: Burgess (2), Going, Kirkpatrick, Williams (penalty)	Tries: T.G.R. Davies (2)
Conversions: Mains (2)	Penalty goal: John
Penalty goal: Mains	Dropped goal: John

31 July, 1971

Third Test

The day before the third Test, the New Zealand selectors caused a sensation when they brought the semi-retired ex-All Black captain, Brian Lochore, into their team to replace Peter Whiting who had been injured at training. The only other change in the home side was the withdrawal of Bryan Williams with a groin injury, and the selection of Ken Carrington in his place.

There were also two changes in the visiting team, both in the forwards. The only uncapped player in the Lions' party, Derek Quinnell, took Dixon's place on the flank and the big Scottish lock, Gordon Brown, replaced Thomas.

The Lions won the toss and Dawes elected to play with the fresh breeze behind him. After four minutes it became obvious that the intensive rucking drills practised by the visitors were going to pay off. Gerald Davies broke through and kicked ahead for Hunter to gather the ball. Instead of kicking, the New Zealander speedster tried to counter attack by running but he was pulled down and the British forwards drove into the ruck which formed. They heeled quickly for Edwards to throw a long pass to John who calmly opened the scoring by dropping a goal from 28 yards out.

John's accurate kicking kept the ball in front of his forwards and the Lions kept the pressure on. In the eighth minute however Hunter caused the tourists some concern when he kicked over Williams's head and sped after the ball. Just as it seemed his great pace would prevail, Gibson came back on the angle and managed to reach the ball first. After forcing down he picked up quickly and ran back to the 25, where he threw the ball to John for a quick drop-out which gained some 55 yards. Edwards ran from a ruck to put Gerald Davies over on the blindside and John converted after the ball had hit a post. With the Lions' forwards dominating the line-outs their backs had a lot of possession and the All Blacks spent most of the first half on defence. The little possession which did come New Zealand's way was untidy, especially from the line-outs, where the British forwards poured through the gaps to make Going's life miserable. Burgess did some

ineffective kicking and the home midfield backs were an unhappy combination. The wings saw little of the ball for most of the half and when it did reach them they could do nothing with it.

In the eighteenth minute John kicked deep into New Zealand territory where the ball went into touch. From the line-out the Lions won possession and Edwards ran strongly. He pushed Burgess off before passing to John who ran across for a try which he converted himself. There was no further scoring in the first half but the Lions turned round with an impressive thirteen point lead and the situation looked bad for the home team.

Two minutes after the restart Cottrell found a gap but instead of sending the ball on he tried to barge through Williams and a possible scoring chance was lost. Then Duckham put the All Blacks on the defensive when he beat Hunter and made a long run down the left touch before being forced out.

NEW ZEALAND
L.W. MAINS
(Otago)
B.A. HUNTER   H.T. JOSEPH   K.R. CARRINGTON
(Otago)   (Canterbury)   (Auckland)
W.D. COTTRELL
(Canterbury)
R.E. BURGESS*
(Manawatu)
S.M. GOING
(North Auckland)
A.J. WYLLIE
(Canterbury)
A.M. McNAUGHTON B.J. LOCHORE C.E. MEADS (Capt.) I.A. KIRKPATRICK
(Bay of Plenty) (Wairarapa-Bush) (King Country) (Poverty Bay)
B.L. MULLER   R.W. NORTON   R.A. GUY
(Taranaki)   (Canterbury)   (North Auckland)

J. McLAUCHLAN   J.V. PULLIN   J.F. LYNCH
(Jordanhill College &   (Bristol & England)   (St. Mary's College &
Ireland)   Ireland)
D.L. QUINNELL   G.L. BROWN   W.J. McBRIDE   J. TAYLOR
(Llanelli)   (West of Scotland (Ballymena &   (London Welsh
& Scotland)   Ireland)   & Wales)
T.M. DAVIES
(London Welsh & Wales)
G.O. EDWARDS
(Cardiff & Wales)
B. JOHN
(Cardiff & Wales)
D.J. DUCKHAM   C.M.H. GIBSON   S.J. DAWES (Capt.) T.G.R. DAVIES
(Coventry &   (N.I.F.C. &   (London Welsh & (Cambridge University
England)   Ireland)   Wales)   & Wales)
J.P.R. WILLIAMS
(London Welsh & Wales)
BRITISH ISLES

REPLACEMENT: *replaced by M.G. Duncan (Hawke's Bay)
REFEREE: Mr J.P.G. Pring (Auckland)
ATTENDANCE: 50,000
CONDITIONS: Weather fine, ground soft
HALFTIME: British Isles 13, New Zealand 0

SCORERS
NEW ZEALAND   **BRITISH ISLES**
Try: Mains   Tries: T.G.R. Davies, John
                                Conversions: John (2)
                                Dropped goal: John

NEW ZEALAND 3

Athletic Park, Wellington

Dawes, Duckham and Hunter watch Laurie Mains score New Zealand's only points. Hunter had taken part in the blindside movement leading to this try.

The All Blacks had a brief period on attack when Meads rallied his forwards and led them in some determined rushes. Both Kirkpatrick and Wyllie tried to crash over and the latter did in fact score what seemed to be a fair try but the referee had already blown his whistle for a scrum.

Meads made a crashing run from which he passed to Hunter but the winger, who had a very bad day, knocked on. A tighthead to New Zealand gave Burgess a chance to run on the blindside and this time Hunter managed to hold his pass. He tossed the ball to Mains outside him and the full-back dived over. He missed an easy conversion.

After twenty-five minutes Burgess was heavily tackled by Taylor and as he fell he collided with Muller's hip. As he lay on the ground it was obvious he had been badly hurt but fortunately John Williams, who was a fourth-year medical student, was quickly on the spot. He could see that Burgess was in danger of choking so he prised the All Black's mouth open and managed to stop him from swallowing his tongue. Burgess was taken to the Wellington Hospital with concussion.

Duncan went on at second five-eighth and Cottrell moved in to first. Thus Duncan made his Test debut as a replacement.

New Zealand spent the latter part of the game on attack but the British defence was too good. There was no more scoring and for the first time ever a Lions team was approaching the final Test with a 2-1 lead over New Zealand.

NEW ZEALAND 14

14 August, 1971

Fourth Test

New Zealand Rugby supporters looked towards this Test with concern, hoping that the All Blacks could tie the series with a win. On the other hand, British followers saw the prospect of victory over New Zealand in a series for the first time. Thus, with so much at stake, a hard game was expected and hard it most certainly was.

With Burgess unavailable because of his third Test injury, the selectors moved Cottrell to the vital first five-eighth position and brought in newcomer Phil Gard to partner him. Gard had played well at Timaru against the Lions and he was a strong player of good provincial standard. He did not play for New Zealand again. Other changes in the backs saw Williams return to the wing with Duncan playing his first and only full Test at centre.

In the forwards, Whiting returned to lock the

scrum with Meads and McNaughton was dropped for Tom Lister to again take his place on the side of the All Black scrum.

The Lions made one last-minute change, when Quinnell was unfit to play and Dixon took his place.

Mr John Pring was selected to control the match, thus becoming the first referee to have charge of all Test matches of a four match series in New Zealand.

Meads won the toss and the Lions kicked off just as a light shower began to fall. In the second line-out, Whiting punched Brown and was spoken to severely by the referee and not long after this incident there was a flare-up in front of the number four stand. However, Mr Pring, aided by Meads, restored order and the players settled down to play football.

In the fourth minute the All Blacks opened the scoring with an excellent try. A scrum was formed ten yards from the British line with Going to put the ball in. Wyllie stood off the scrum, which was duly won by New Zealand. Going passed to his number eight, who dummied to the inside before passing to Gard. Dawes tackled the North Otago man but the latter got his pass away to Cottrell, who had doubled around behind him, and the All Black first five-eighth sprinted for the line to score. Mains converted.

Six minutes later, Edwards was penalised for putting the ball under his hooker's feet in a set scrum and Mains kicked a good goal from 34 yards out.

Both sides were tense and the football was below Test match level for most of the first half. There was little venturesome play, especially from the Lions, who resorted to kicking in spite of being eight points down.

John had an unsuccessful penalty attempt in the twenty-fourth minute and was again astray some ten minutes later when Lister was caught offside 45 yards from his line. However, three minutes from halftime, Guy was penalised at a ruck and this time John made no mistake.

With the interval about to come up, Duckham

NEW ZEALAND

L.W. MAINS
(Otago)

K.R. CARRINGTON (Auckland) — M.G. DUNCAN (Hawke's Bay) — B.G. WILLIAMS (Auckland)

P.C. GARD
(North Otago)

W.D. COTTRELL
(Canterbury)

S.M. GOING
(North Auckland)

A.J. WYLLIE
(Canterbury)

T.N. LISTER (South Canterbury) — P.J. WHITING (Auckland) — C.E. MEADS (Capt.) (King Country) — I.A. KIRKPATRICK (Poverty Bay)

B.L. MULLER (Taranaki) — R.W. NORTON (Canterbury) — R.A. GUY (North Auckland)

J. McLAUCHLAN (Jordanhill College & Scotland) — J.V. PULLIN (Bristol & England) — J.F. LYNCH (St. Mary's College & Ireland)

J. TAYLOR (London Welsh & Wales) — G.L. BROWN† (West of Scotland & Scotland) — W.J. McBRIDE (Ballymena & Ireland) — P.J. DIXON (Harlequins & England)

T.M. DAVIES
(London Welsh & Wales)

G.O. EDWARDS
(Cardiff & Wales)

B. JOHN
(Cardiff & Wales)

D.J. DUCKHAM (Coventry & England) — C.M.H. GIBSON (N.I.F.C. & Ireland) — S.J. DAWES (Capt.) (London Welsh & Wales) — T.G.R. DAVIES (Cambridge University & Wales)

J.P.R. WILLIAMS
(London Welsh & Wales)

BRITISH ISLES

REPLACEMENT: † replaced by W.D. Thomas, (Llanelli & Wales)
REFEREE: Mr J.P.G. Pring (Auckland)
ATTENDANCE: 56,000
CONDITIONS: Weather cloudy, ground firm
HALFTIME: British Isles 8, New Zealand 8
SCORERS

NEW ZEALAND	BRITISH ISLES
Tries: Cottrell, Lister	Try: Dixon
Conversion: Mains	Conversion: John
Penalty goals: Mains (2)	Penalty goals: John (2)
	Dropped goal: Williams

BRITISH ISLES 14

Eden Park, Auckland

"Willie John" McBride consoles Colin Meads after the series defeat. This was the great All Black lock's fifty-fifth and last Test. His international career stretched from 1957 to 1971.

chased a kick from Edwards and, after robbing Mains of the ball, was pushed out at the corner flag. Carrington broke an elementary rule by throwing to the end of the line-out when his team was desperately defending and from the ruck which formed after the Lions had won the ball, Edwards broke towards the New Zealand line. Dixon was on hand to carry on when the Welshman was stopped and the flanker dived over in a handy position for John to convert.

The Lions took the lead three minutes after halftime when Muller stamped on Dixon and John kicked a good goal from 40 yards. Seven minutes later, the All Blacks equalised after Bryan Williams made a splendid break which ended at the corner flag. From the line-out, Lister caught the ball and fell over for a try, which Mains failed to convert from a relatively easy position.

Four minutes later, the visitors were back in the lead when the ball came to John Williams 44 yards from the All Blacks' posts. The full-back quickly sighted his target and dropped a magnificent goal, sending the ball soaring between the uprights. Just after this goal, Brown left the field with a bad gash on his knee and was replaced by Thomas.

Eight minutes from time, Dixon was offside at a scrum and Mains evened the score with a 25 yard penalty. Both Bryan Williams and Duckham made determined runs after this, Duncan was caught just short of the line and John went close with a drop at goal but the game ended with no further scoring.

This draw, which was predicted by Lions' manager, Doug Smith, was enough to give the British team the series. For the first time since 1949 and for only the third time ever, New Zealand had lost a Test rubber at home.

The fourth Test of 1971 marked the end of Colin Meads's international career. Considered by Rugby writers of all nationalities to be one of the greatest forwards ever to play the game, Meads played in fifty-five Tests between 1957 and 1971 to set a record for a New Zealander. He was thirty-five years of age when he took over the All Black captaincy and still a great player even though he was past his best.

Other long-serving All Blacks to end their Test careers after this match were Wayne Cottrell, "Jazz" Muller and Tom Lister, with nine, fourteen and eight internationals respectively.

NEW ZEALAND 29

19 August, 1972

First Test

In the four matches leading up to this first international, the Australian team had recorded a sole victory over Taranaki by 20-15, a draw with Bay of Plenty, and losses to both Otago and Buller. The captain, Greg Davis, was an old adversary, having appeared in internationals against the All Blacks in 1964-67-68. Now thirty-three, he had lost a little of his former pace but his experience was invaluable to this Australian team. Three of the visitors' forward pack, Tony Gelling, Bruce Brown and hooker Mick Freney, were newcomers to international play as was half-back Gary Grey.

The New Zealand selectors, Messrs. I.M.H. Vodanovich, R.H. Duff and J. Gleeson, chose a side which contained seven new caps. Of these, full-back Trevor Morris, Duncan Hales, Bruce Robertson and Graham Whiting, had toured with a New Zealand team on a nine match internal tour of the country earlier in the season. Alistair Scown, a flanker from the Patea club, prop Jeff Matheson and Mike Parkinson (a son-in-law of J.B. Smith the noted centre of the 1940's), were appearing in the All Black jersey for the first time. Bob Burgess withdrew with flu

after selection allowing John Dougan to come into the team from the reserves to give the side its eighth new cap.

Peter McDavitt became the first Wellington referee to control an international since Mr E.W.T. Tindill, seventeen years earlier.

McGill kicked off for Australia into the strong northerly wind but it was not long before New Zealand were on attack forcing play to the Wallaby goal line. From a five yard scrum in the fifth minute, Going moved on the blind side to put Dougan in for the first four point try registered by New Zealand in international play. This try was scored 10 yards in from the right hand corner, a position from which Morris converted with a well-judged kick.

The All Blacks kept up the pressure on the Australian line and were further rewarded in the eighteenth minute when Going ran from a ruck near the line to score unopposed midway between the posts and the corner flag to make it 10-0. Morris was unable to convert and eight

Going chips a kick over the Australian forwards. Whiting, Matheson, Norton and Strahan are at left.

P.G. BUSH

AUSTRALIA 6

minutes later he missed a penalty attempt from 40 yards out.

New Zealand's third try came in the twenty-seventh minute from a scrum on the Wallaby line. Sutherland picked up the ball after it had been hooked by Norton, and crashed over between the posts. Morris had no trouble converting. Peter Sullivan limped from the field with a leg injury two minutes later and was replaced by Barry Stumbles making his Test debut.

Seven minutes before halftime, Morris gathered a clearing kick from McGill on the touch line and kicked a fine 45 yard dropped goal. Jeff McLean, whose grandfather and three uncles had played Rugby for Australia, attempted a long range penalty on the call of halftime but the kick went wide. With the score standing at 19-0 to the home side and the All Black forwards dominating possession, there appeared little chance that the Australians could bridge the gap in the second half.

John Dougan opens the scoring for New Zealand, crossing in the tackle of McGill. Sutherland backs up the tryscorer.

Only two minutes had elapsed from the restart when New Zealand went further ahead. Going was caught near the Wallaby line, but the ball came clear to Dougan who linked up with Robertson and Williams. The latter eluded Gelling and scored 10 yards in from the right hand corner. Morris was unable to convert.

Australia's first points came in the seventh minute of the half when McLean raised the flags with an angled penalty from the 25 yard line. Three minutes later Fairfax was late tackled which gave McLean a further chance from 40 yards out and again he found the posts with a good kick.

During the remainder of the match, New Zealand went close to scoring on several occasions but it was not until the final minute that they added to their score. Following a break by Going down the touch line, the ball was passed in-field through several pairs of hands before Peter Whiting threw himself over the goal line near the posts. Morris again converted to complete the scoring.

NEW ZEALAND

T.J. MORRIS
(Nelson-Bays)

B.G. WILLIAMS   B.J. ROBERTSON   D.A. HALES
(Auckland)   (Counties)   (Canterbury)

R.M. PARKINSON
(Poverty Bay)

J.P. DOUGAN
(Wellington)

S.M. GOING
(North Auckland)

A.R. SUTHERLAND
(Marlborough)

I.A. KIRKPATRICK (Capt.)   P.J. WHITING   S.C. STRAHAN   A.I. SCOWN
(Poverty Bay)   (Auckland)   (Manawatu)   (Taranaki)

G.J. WHITING   R.W. NORTON   J.D. MATHESON
(King Country)   (Canterbury)   (Otago)

B.R. BROWN   M.E. FRENEY   R.B. PROSSER
(Queensland)   (Queensland)   (New South Wales)

P.D. SULLIVAN†   R.A. SMITH   G. FAY   G.V. DAVIS (Capt.)
(New South Wales)   (New South Wales)   (New South Wales)   (New South Wales)

A.M. GELLING
(New South Wales)

G.O. GREY
(New South Wales)

R.L. FAIRFAX
(New South Wales)

J.J. McLEAN   R.D. L'ESTRANGE   D.R. BURNET   J.W. COLE
(Queensland)   (Queensland)   (New South Wales)   (New South Wales)

A.N. McGILL
(New South Wales)

AUSTRALIA

REPLACEMENT: † replaced by B.D. Stumbles (New South Wales)
REFEREE: Mr P.A. McDavitt (Wellington)
ATTENDANCE: 35,000
CONDITIONS: Weather fine but windy, ground firm
HALFTIME: New Zealand 19, Australia 0

SCORERS

NEW ZEALAND	**AUSTRALIA**
Tries: Dougan, Going, Sutherland, Williams, P.J. Whiting	Penalty goals: McLean (2)
Conversions: Morris (3)	
Dropped goal: Morris	

NEW ZEALAND 30

2 September, 1972

Second Test

Victories over King Country and Nelson Bays and a one point loss to Hawke's Bay, was the Australian team's record leading up to this second Test. Four changes were made in their side from that which had lost the first Test. John Howard replaced Brown at prop, Stumbles, the first Test replacement, won his place at the expense of Reg Smith and Cocks came in to the side as the number eight. The fourth change became necessary when Fairfax withdrew with a groin injury and was replaced by Geoff Richardson who had appeared in all three internationals against South Africa the previous year.

No changes were made by the selectors to the All Black side it being announced that Burgess was still unavailable through illness. However injuries to Bruce Robertson and John Dougan brought two new men, Graham Sims and Lyn Jaffray, into the side to make their Test debuts.

Morris kicked off for New Zealand into the sun

NEW ZEALAND

T.J. MORRIS
(Nelson-Bays)

B.G. WILLIAMS   G.S. SIMS   D.A. HALES
(Auckland)   (Otago)   (Canterbury)

R.M. PARKINSON
(Poverty Bay)

J.L. JAFFRAY
(Otago)

S.M. GOING
(North Auckland)

A.R. SUTHERLAND
(Marlborough)

I.A. KIRKPATRICK (Capt.)   P.J. WHITING   S.C. STRAHAN   A.I. SCOWN
(Poverty Bay)   (Auckland)   (Manawatu)   (Taranaki)

G.J. WHITING   R.W. NORTON   J.D. MATHESON
(King Country)   (Canterbury)   (Otago)

J.L. HOWARD   M.E. FRENEY   R.B. PROSSER
(New South Wales)   (Queensland)   (New South Wales)

P.D. SULLIVAN   B.D. STUMBLES   G. FAY   G.V. DAVIS (Capt.)†
(New South Wales)   (New South Wales)   (New South Wales)   (New South Wales)

M.R. COCKS
(New South Wales)

G.O. GREY
(New South Wales)

G.C. RICHARDSON
(Queensland)

J.J. McLEAN   R.D. L'ESTRANGE   D.R. BURNET   J.W. COLE
(Queensland)   (Queensland)   (New South Wales)   (New South Wales)

A.N. McGILL
(New South Wales)

AUSTRALIA

REPLACEMENT: † replaced by R.A. Smith (New South Wales)
REFEREE: Mr J.P.G. Pring (Auckland)
ATTENDANCE: 35,400
CONDITIONS: Weather fine, ground firm
HALFTIME: New Zealand 24, Australia 4

SCORERS

NEW ZEALAND	AUSTRALIA
Tries: Kirkpatrick (2), Sutherland, P.J. Whiting, Williams	Tries: McLean (2), Cole
Conversions: Morris (2)	Conversion: McLean
Penalty goals: Morris (2)	Dropped goal: Richardson

---

and a light breeze. The All Blacks went on to early attack and after four minutes scored a try when Sutherland gathered the ball, following a fumble by the Australian half-back Grey, and scored eight yards in from the left hand corner. Morris landed the conversion to put the All Blacks into a six point lead. McLean was short with a penalty attempt from near half-way a few minutes later. The New Zealand forwards were again showing their superiority over the Australians.

Midway through the half Going made a typical blindside run making nearly 40 yards before a high tackle by McGill brought him down. The tackle was adjudged by the referee to be dangerous and Morris had a successful penalty attempt from 40 yards.

Two minutes later the Australians opened their scoring with a well-executed try. Cole came into the backline from the blind side to make a break before unloading to L'Estrange who fed the flying McLean. The 25 year old left winger outpaced the defence to score in the corner. McGill was unable to convert. McLean missed a penalty from 35 yards three minutes later but Morris landed an attempt from a similar distance in the twenty-seventh minute to put his side into a 12-4 lead.

In the last five minutes of the spell the All Blacks increased their lead with three unconverted tries. First, Kirkpatrick crashed over following a maul close to the Australian goal line. The next try came from a backline movement on the short side. Williams received the ball hemmed in by defenders but with a strong sidestepping run he out-manoeuvred them and then scored a brilliant try midway between goal posts and corner flag. Finally, a short passing rush by the All Black forwards ended with Peter Whiting crossing for a try to give the All Blacks an unassailable 24-4 lead at halftime.

Davis left the field after two minutes of the second half with a knee injury and was replaced by Reg Smith. In the tenth minute of the spell, following a period on attack, Australia won a ruck for Burnet to find a gap before putting Cole

AUSTRALIA 17

Lancaster Park, Christchurch

GREEN & HAHN

The New Zealand Team
Back row: A.J. Wyllie (reserve), G.J. Whiting, P.J. Whiting, S.C. Strahan, A.R. Sutherland, A.I. Scown, K. Murdoch (reserve).
Middle row: B.G. Williams, R.W. Norton, R.M. Parkinson, G.N. Kane (reserve), R.A. Urlich (reserve), J.D. Matheson, G.S. Sims, T.J. Morris.
Front row: P.C. Gard (reserve), R.H. Duff (selector), I.A. Kirkpatrick (capt.), J.M.H. Vodanovich (selector), S.M. Going, J. Gleeson (selector), G.L. Colling (reserve).
In front: D.A. Hales, J.L. Jaffray.

in for a try in the corner which McLean was unable to convert.

Kirkpatrick scored his second try between the posts after Graham Whiting made ground with a "willie away" peeling off movement from a line-out. The movement was carried on by Scown who took the ball to the goal mouth before feeding Kirkpatrick who went over with McGill

hanging on to his collar. Morris had no trouble in raising the flags to make the score 30-8, midway through the half.

Twelve minutes from the end, the Wallabies won a line-out on the All Black 25 and mounted a back line attack. McGill was in to make the overlap and McLean, showing his pace, was over for his second try which he converted himself. The final scoring in the match came four minutes later when Richardson landed a dropped goal from nearly 40 yards out.

Although New Zealand had the game well in hand at halftime, there was much admiration for the Wallaby side who had come back into the game so well in the second half. Left winger Jeff McLean was probably the outstanding player of the match scoring two good winger's tries as well as kicking a conversion from the sideline.

NEW Z ALAND 3

16 September, 1972

Third Test

Since the second Test, Australia had scored two wins in mid-week fixtures over North Otago and Poverty Bay-East Coast combined. However, despite a contribution of twenty points from Jeff McLean, Australia had gone down to Waikato 24-26 in their match the previous Saturday.

Sullivan, who had been injured in the match at Oamaru was unavailable and his place was filled by Cocks. Stumbles moved from lock to number eight and second Test replacement Smith partnered Fay as lock. Bruce Brown replaced Howard in the front row.

Both Burgess and Robertson were again available to take their places in the All Black back line whilst Keith Murdoch, after a series of ailments during this and the previous season, was able to gain selection at the expense of Graham Whiting in the front row. Mr Alan Taylor became the first Canterbury referee, since Bill Fright in 1956, to gain an international appointment although he had controlled part of a Test in 1965 when Mr Murphy was forced to retire with a leg injury at Christchurch and Mr Taylor, one of the touch judges, took over for the final fifty-five minutes.

This match was the first international to be covered by live television in New Zealand. The television fee was reported as being $8,750. Officials were pleased with the attendance at the game but the effects were felt in other parts of the country. A small crowd of only 1,750 attended the Canterbury versus West Coast Ranfurly Shield match at Christchurch.

Again the Wallabies failed to reach international standard in this match and in the first half managed to get play into the All Black territory on rare occasions.

Going cannot reach Grey as the raised leg of Stumbles protects the Australian half-back.

EVENING POST

AUSTRALIA 3

Eden Park, Auckland

Morris kicked off for New Zealand, putting the ball over the dead ball line. From McGill's drop-out, the New Zealand full-back took the ball at half-way and attempted a long range dropped goal which passed just to the left of the posts. In the sixth minute Morris opened the scoring with a 38 yard penalty.

After sustained pressure, Kirkpatrick scored a try in the twelfth minute following a break by Going. When the half-back was tackled, Kirkpatrick was on hand to recover the ball, brush two tacklers aside and score close to the posts. Morris converted to make the score 9-0.

The All Blacks' next try came from a five yard scrum when Sutherland managed to get his hand to the ball first after the scrummage collapsed on the goal line. Morris missed a reasonably easy conversion. Three minutes before the interval New Zealand were awarded a penalty 45 yards out and Morris raised the flags with a good kick to give New Zealand a 16-0 lead at halftime.

The Wallabies went on to attack early in the second spell but the stronger All Black pack soon forced them back on to defence. From a line-out near the Australian line, Sutherland gained possession and passed to Scown who scored midway between the corner flag and the posts. Morris again goaled to put New Zealand twenty-two points up with thirty-three minutes to play.

Six minutes later, Going ran on the blindside from a line-out maul 15 yards from the Australian line and as he was tackled, he managed to stretch out to score wide out. Morris was unable to convert.

Over the next twenty minutes the Australians mounted several attacks and came close to scoring. Finally in the thirty-fourth minute of the half, McLean succeeded with a penalty from the touchline two yards outside the 25 yard line.

With two minutes to play, Robertson centrekicked to the Wallaby line where the ball was allowed to bounce and as it descended, the seventeen stone four pound Whiting gathered the ball going at full speed, giving the defenders no chance of stopping the try. Morris converted.

Right on time, Going took a tap penalty near his own 25 and the forwards carried on the movement into the Wallaby half before the ball was sent along the back line to Robertson, who made a scintillating break. As he was tackled a few yards from the Australian line, he got a pass to Williams who scored the best try of the match. Morris brought his match tally to fourteen with a good kick from the side line.

Despite the margin of the All Black victory, the critics were not entirely satisfied with the performance, alleging that the ball had rarely reached the three-quarters and that the home team had won by playing ten-man Rugby.

The following Saturday, All Black trials were played in Wellington after which the team to tour Europe was announced. With the exception of Strahan who was not available, all members of this third Test side were selected for this tour, but Jaffray, Sims and Dougan, who had appeared in the earlier Tests, failed to be included in the final selection.

NEW ZEALAND

T.J. MORRIS
(Nelson-Bays)

B.G. WILLIAMS   B.J. ROBERTSON   D.A. HALES
(Auckland)   (Counties)   (Canterbury)

R.M. PARKINSON
(Poverty Bay)

R.E. BURGESS
(Manawatu)

S.M. GOING
(North Auckland)

A.R. SUTHERLAND
(Marlborough)

I.A. KIRKPATRICK (**Capt.**)   P.J. WHITING   S.C. STRAHAN   A.I. SCOWN
(Poverty Bay)   (Auckland)   (Manawatu)   (Taranaki)

K. MURDOCH   R.W. NORTON   J.D. MATHESON
(Otago)   (Canterbury)   (Otago)

B.R. BROWN   M.E. FRENEY   R.B. PROSSER
(Queensland)   (Queensland)   (New South Wales)

M.R. COCKS   R.A. SMITH   G. FAY   G.V. DAVIS (**Capt.**)
(New South Wales) (New South Wales) (New South Wales) (New South Wales)

D.D. STUMBLES
(New South Wales)

G.O. GREY
(New South Wales)

G.C. RICHARDSON
(Queensland)

J.J. McLEAN   R.D. L'ESTRANGE   D.R. BURNET   J.W. COLE
(Queensland)   (Queensland)   (New South Wales)   (New South Wales)

A.N. McGILL
(New South Wales)

AUSTRALIA

REFEREE: Mr A.R. Taylor, (Canterbury)
ATTENDANCE: 43,000
CONDITIONS: Weather fine apart from one heavy shower, ground firm
HALFTIME: New Zealand 16, Australia 0

SCORERS

NEW ZEALAND	AUSTRALIA
Tries: Kirkpatrick, Sutherland, Scown, Going, Whiting, Williams	Penalty goal: McLean
Conversions: Morris (4)	
Penalty goals: Morris (2)	

2 December, 1972

This first international of the 1972-73 All Black tour was the eleventh match of the European part of the itinerary. Two losses had been incurred already, the side going down 3-9 to the Llanelli club celebrating their centenary in the third match, and 14-16 to a North-Western Counties team at Workington, who became the first English side other than the national selection to defeat a New Zealand team in seven tours since 1905. Serious deficiencies in the All Black scrummaging were evident and it was expected that Wales would be too strong in this match.

Joe Karam, who had shown considerable ability whilst playing in the first XV at St.Patrick's College, Silverstream, had assumed the first string full-back berth owing to a leg injury suffered by Trevor Morris in the match against New York Metropolitan and was appearing in his first international. Other new caps were the 21 year old winger, Grant Batty, whose early promise had earned him an All Black trial as an 18 year old in 1970, and Hamish Macdonald who had been a consistently good player for his province at lock.

The experienced Welsh team featured only one new cap, Neath's Glyn Shaw, whilst John Williams, Gerald Davies, John Bevan, Gareth Edwards, Mervyn Davies, John Taylor, Delme Thomas and Derek Quinnell had all toured New Zealand with the successful 1971 Lions side. Jeff Young, Phil Bennett, Barry Llewelyn and David Morris had also had experience of playing against New Zealand sides when they accompanied the 1969 Welsh team on their short tour. Arthur Lewis, who had been appointed captain of the Welsh team, was forced to withdraw with a recurring hamstring injury and was replaced by Jim Shanklin, the leadership transferring to Thomas.

Bennett kicked off but it was New Zealand who attacked from the outset, and only two minutes after the start, Karam goaled the first of his penalties from the Welsh 25 when Morris was caught off-side at a scrum. Six minutes later he repeated the effort from 30 yards when a scrum penalty went against the home team.

After eighteen minutes, Whiting won a line-out for New Zealand inside the Welsh half, and Going hoisted a kick up the right wing side. As Bevan got under the ball he was tackled by the All Black half who had followed up quickly, and the ball went loose. Once again Going, scrambling on his knees, was first to the ball and he flipped a pass up into the arms of Keith Murdoch pounding up the touchline. The massive prop was caught as he neared the line but his momentum and the slippery surface enabled him to slide over to score a try. Karam was unable to convert from wide out.

Bennett opened the Welsh scoring with a penalty four minutes later after New Zealand had been penalised at a ruck, and Karam landed his third successful attempt, when hooker Young was penalised on his own 25 in front of the posts, with fifteen minutes of the half remaining. New Zealand kept the pressure on Wales until halftime but no further scoring occurred and the All Blacks crossed over in front with the surprisingly wide margin of 10 points.

NEW ZEALAND

J.F. KARAM
(Wellington)

B.G. WILLIAMS   D.A. HALES   G.B. BATTY
(Auckland)   (Canterbury)   (Wellington)

R.M. PARKINSON
(Poverty Bay)

R.E. BURGESS
(Manawatu)

S.M. GOING
(North Auckland)

A.R. SUTHERLAND
(Marlborough)

I.A. KIRKPATRICK (**Capt.**)   P.J. WHITING   H.H. MACDONALD   A.J. WYLLIE*
(Poverty Bay)   (Auckland)   (Canterbury)   (Canterbury)

K. MURDOCH   R.W. NORTON   J.D. MATHESON
(Otago)   (Canterbury)   (Otago)

D.B. LLEWELYN   J. YOUNG   G. SHAW
(Llanelli)   (R.A.F.& London Welsh)   (Neath)

W.D. MORRIS   D.L. QUINNELL   W.D. THOMAS (**Capt.**)   J. TAYLOR
(Neath)   (Llanelli)   (Llanelli)   (London Welsh)

T.M. DAVIES
(Swansea)

G.O. EDWARDS
(Cardiff)

P. BENNETT
(Llanelli)

J.C. BEVAN   J.L. SHANKLIN   R.T.E. BERGIERS   T.G.R. DAVIES
(Cardiff)   (London Welsh)   (Llanelli)   (London Welsh)

J.P.R. WILLIAMS
(London Welsh)

WALES

REPLACEMENT: *replaced by A.I. Scown (Taranaki)
REFEREE: Mr R.J.F. Johnson (England)
ATTENDANCE: 52,000
CONDITIONS: Weather showery, ground sodden
HALFTIME: New Zealand 13, Wales 3

SCORERS

NEW ZEALAND	**WALES**
Try: Murdoch	Try: Bevan
Penalty goals: Karam (5)	Penalty goals: Bennett (4)

WALES 16

Cardiff Arms Park

Five minutes of the second half had gone when Going, after running on the open side from a scrum, was tackled by Edwards and the ball spilled loose. It was toed ahead and recovered by Bennett who passed to Bevan on his left. The strong six foot winger bolted away on a forty yard run to the corner, having too much pace for the All Black defence. Hales appeared to have him covered but was unable to muster sufficient pace to complete the tackle. Bennett was wide with his conversion but the try had stirred the previously sedate crowd into a high state of excitement.

Wales now attacked feverishly and Karam and Sutherland were forced to take fair catches under extreme pressure. The home side were awarded a line-out penalty, and Bennett was on target from 40 yards to reduce the All Black lead to three points. Next the Welsh fly-half had a 55 yard attempt which went close.

Quarter of an hour into the second spell, Karam was given an opportunity from a ruck penalty 40 yards out and the young full-back, showing admirable temperament against a noisy background, kicked straight and true. A minute later Bevan was foolishly obstructed and Bennett landed his third penalty to bring the score to New Zealand 16, Wales 13.

In the battle of the penalty kicks, Bennett missed a further shot at goal before Karam was given a chance from 45 yards when Young was caught infringing at the put-in. This kick went over and New Zealand were back to a six point advantage. The Welsh were exerting great pressure at this stage and only desperate defence was keeping them from scoring. Wyllie, who had been looking uncomfortable with a rib injury, was finally persuaded to leave the field, and was replaced by Alistair Scown.

One Welsh attack saw a wall of players go over the New Zealand line, but as they appealed for a try, the referee was seen penalising John Williams for apparently playing a tackled ball.

Some All Blacks now looked a little rattled and they conceded foolish penalties. From one of these in the last few minutes, when Gerald Davies was late tackled, Bennett closed the gap to three points. Wales now attacked constantly but with a hint of desperation and in the final seconds were awarded yet another penalty for a late charge. There was confusion as Bennett wanted to take a tap kick but Thomas over-ruled him and Bennett took a shot at goal from 30 yards. It passed just outside the upright and New Zealand were left with a fortuitous victory over their old foes, who had staged a strong recovery in the second half.

There was little doubt that the All Blacks owed a great deal to the superb goal kicking of Karam in this match. Bennett, on the other hand, had missed several goal attempts which had in the final summing up meant the difference between victory and defeat.

An unfortunate incident in the Angel Hotel during the victory celebration led to Keith Murdoch, who had played a leading part in the win by scoring a try and assisting his hooker to take three tightheads, being returned home. Always a controversial player, he had played in three Tests.

The centre, Duncan Hales, was another who completed his international career in this match. He had received some criticism for allowing Bevan through to score his try in this match, but, if lacking the pace of a true international three-quarter, he was a competent all-round player and gave good service to Manawatu in later years as a five-eighth. He had appeared in four Tests.

This match was the first international to be transmitted live by satellite to New Zealand where an estimated 200,000 viewers saw the match in the early hours of Sunday morning.

N W ZEALAND 14

16 December, 1972

The New Zealanders' form since the Welsh international had not been convincing. Following Murdoch's dismissal from the touring party, a demoralised side had gone down 8-16 to Midland Counties (West) at Moseley, and had struggled to defeat both North Eastern Counties and the combined Edinburgh and Glasgow teams.

Two late replacements were necessary in the international team selected when Sutherland (with 'flu) and Burgess (suffering a leg injury), withdrew from the selected side and were replaced by Alistair Scown, going on to the side of the scrum with Wyllie dropping back to number eight, and Ian Stevens. For Stevens, normally a half-back but selected for this tour as a five-eighth, it was his first Test. Bruce Robertson, having made an appearance in the previous match, was declared fit. He had broken his thumb in the Cardiff encounter, but was now able to replace Hales. Murdoch's place went to Graham Whiting, a seventeen stone seven pound prop who had played two Tests against the Australians earlier in the year.

The Scottish captain, Peter Brown, was a survivor of the 1964 scoreless draw on the same ground, and the props "Sandy" Carmichael and "Ian" McLauchlan, as well as Rodger Arneil and Gordon Brown, younger brother of Peter, had all been members of the 1971 Lions side. Carmichael had returned home after being injured in the Canterbury match. Four of the side, Andy Irvine, Ian Forsyth, Dave Shedden and Ian McGeechan, were appearing in their first international.

Georges Domercq was the first French referee to be appointed to control an international fixture in the United Kingdom involving a touring overseas side.

It was a tense opening and after five minutes the All Blacks suffered a setback when tighthead prop Jeff Matheson was escorted from the field in pain with rib injuries serious enough to end his

Alex Wyllie surges from this collapsed scrum to score. Going had run wide and in-passed to the charging number eight.

PRESS ASSOCIATION

SCOTLAND 9

active participation on the tour, and his international career. His replacement was the 21 year old Kent Lambert, coming on to play in his Test debut. He was given the unenviable task of propping against the experienced McLauchlan.

No scoring occurred in the half until five minutes of injury time had elapsed. From a scrum near the Scottish line, Going ran wide before in-passing to a charging Wyllie who crashed through to ground the ball. Karam placed the goal to put New Zealand up by six points to nil at the interval.

Five minutes of the second half had passed when Peter Brown landed a penalty goal for Scotland from 35 yards out.

New Zealand increased their lead quarter of an hour after the resumption when Robertson received the ball just outside the Scottish 25. Despite an injured hamstring muscle in his right leg, he burst back in-field, side-stepping his way past several defenders before veering out again. As the cover defence closed on him Robertson

AUCKLAND STAR

Grant Batty attempts to smother the Scottish loose forward, Nairn MacEwan.

nudged a kick towards the left corner where the alert Batty was quickly on to the ball to score a well-engineered try. Karam was unable to convert.

New cap Ian McGeechan dropped a fine goal from 35 yards out in the twenty-seventh minute and two minutes later Irvine was on target with a magnificent penalty from 55 yards.

Over the last eleven minutes the Scots made valiant efforts to grab the lead, but in the final minute Going fastened on to an in-pass from McHarg near the half-way line, as the Scots were mounting another attack, and the half-back scooted away to outpace everyone and dive for the try in the quickly gathering gloom. Karam was again unable to convert from a wide angle and that was the end of the match.

Special mention must be made of the fine game played by Lambert. He had started the tour as the most inexperienced prop but because of Murdoch's absence and Matheson's injury, had been forced into an international against formidable opponents. Apart from Matheson, it was also the final Test appearance of Patea's Alistair Scown who had played a total of five internationals.

NEW ZEALAND

J.F. KARAM
(Wellington)

B.G. WILLIAMS   B.J. ROBERTSON   G.B. BATTY
(Auckland)   (Counties)   (Wellington)

R.M. PARKINSON
(Poverty Bay)

I.N. STEVENS
(Wellington)

S.M. GOING
(North Auckland)

A.J. WYLLIE
(Canterbury)

I.A. KIRKPATRICK (Capt.)   H.H. MACDONALD   P.J. WHITING   A.I. SCOWN
(Poverty Bay)   (Canterbury)   (Auckland)   (Taranaki)

J.D. MATHESON*   R.W. NORTON   G.J. WHITING
(Otago)   (Canterbury)   (King Country)

J. McLAUCHLAN   R.L. CLARK   A.B. CARMICHAEL
(Jordanhill)   (Edinburgh Wanderers)   (West of Scotland)

R.J. ARNEIL   G.L. BROWN   A.F. McHARG   N.A. MacEWAN
(Northampton)   (West of Scotland)   (West of Scotland)   (Gala)

P.C. BROWN (Capt.)
(Gala)

I.G. McCRAE
(Gordonians)

I.R. McGEECHAN
(Headingley)

D. SHEDDEN   J.M. RENWICK   I.W. FORSYTH   W.C.C. STEELE
(West of Scotland)   (Hawick)   (Stewart's College F.P.)   (Bedford)

A.R. IRVINE
(Heriots F.P.)

SCOTLAND

REPLACEMENT: *replaced by K.K. Lambert (Manawatu)
REFEREE: Mr G. Domercq (France)
ATTENDANCE: 50,000
CONDITIONS: Weather overcast, ground firm
HALFTIME: New Zealand 6, Scotland 0

SCORERS

NEW ZEALAND	SCOTLAND
Tries: Wyllie, Batty, Going	Penalty goals: P.C. Brown, Irvine
Conversion: Karam	Dropped goal: McGeechan

NEW ZEALAND 9

6 January, 1973

Since the international at Murrayfield, the All Blacks had displayed improved form and had won each of their four matches comfortably, including a game played in thick fog at Cardiff against an East Glamorgan side.

With Lambert retaining his place, the New Zealand side was the same as that which had appeared against Scotland.

The English team selected for the match saw two changes owing to injury with John Finlan replacing Old, and Frank Anderson winning his cap and becoming the first member of his club to be so honoured. He took Cotton's place at tight-head prop after the nominated substitute, Mike Burton, had broken his leg. Centre Peter War-

Ian Kirkpatrick crosses between the posts to score his eleventh Test try breaking a long-standing record held by Frank Mitchinson.

NGLAND u

field was the other new cap in the English side. His co-centre was Peter Preece, a son of Ivor Preece, an English international in 1948-49-50-51, and a member of the 1950 Lions side in New Zealand. Both Dave Duckham and captain John Pullin had toured with the 1971 Lions and had played in the Test series.

The British Prime Minister, Mr Edward Heath, was among the capacity crowd on this grey day as England kicked off. No doubt the home team hoped to repeat the form that had carried them to a surprise victory over South Africa during the previous June at Johannesburg.

After eight minutes, Batty heaved a long throw-in over the end of the line-out, just outside the English 25 where Going was on hand to pick up and break through some weak tackling. Ten yards inside the 25 he unloaded to Wyllie who made a few yards before passing back to Sutherland. Sutherland created a maul in the shadow of the posts and as the ball emerged, Kirkpatrick gathered, threw a dummy pass and dived over between the posts to score his eleventh Test try. This total exceeded the All Black record of ten, formerly held by the great centre of the pre-World War One era, Frank Mitchinson. Karam had no trouble in kicking the conversion.

No further points were forthcoming during this half though Sam Doble, the English fullback, who had scored an incredible 581 points in all matches the previous season, missed penalty chances in the eighteenth, twenty-sixth and thirtieth minutes.

Karam also missed with a long range shot five minutes before halftime. Finlan was pushed into touch 10 yards from the New Zealand line, and a high overhead pass by Batty which went astray following a brilliant run by the little winger, prevented further tries being scored from promising movements during a rather lifeless first half.

Doble missed a further penalty opportunity twelve minutes after the resumption from 45 yards, before New Zealand increased their lead six minutes later. This occurred when Finlan

failed to find touch with a clearing kick from in front of his posts. Bryan Williams fielded the ball near the right touch line, moved infield and slammed over a fine drop kick from 38 yards. Just prior to this goal, England had won a ruck near the All Black 25 and Warfield had sent Preece away for what looked to be a probable try only to hear the referee's whistle blow for a forward pass.

As the spell wore on it became evident that New Zealand had a firm grip on the match. Kirkpatrick was denied a second try when he lost the ball forward in-goal after a surging run of nearly 25 yards, late in the game.

The game ended with no addition to the scoreboard and it was generally agreed that New Zealand had been the stronger side on the day, although had Doble produced some of the goal kicking form of which he was capable, the final score would have been closer. Sid Going, who had been a constant thorn in the English side with his swift, powerful breaks had earned much favourable comment.

NEW ZEALAND

J.F. KARAM
(Wellington)

B.G. WILLIAMS   B.J. ROBERTSON   G.B. BATTY
(Auckland)   (Counties)   (Wellington)

R.M. PARKINSON
(Poverty Bay)

I.N. STEVENS
(Wellington)

S.M. GOING
(North Auckland)

A.R. SUTHERLAND
(Marlborough)

I.A. KIRKPATRICK (Capt.)   P.J. WHITING   H.H. MACDONALD   A.J. WYLLIE
(Poverty Bay)   (Auckland)   (Canterbury)   (Canterbury)

K.K. LAMBERT   R.W. NORTON   G.J. WHITING
(Manawatu)   (Canterbury)   (King Country)

C.B. STEVENS   J.V. PULLIN (Capt.)   W.F. ANDERSON
(Penzance & Newlyn)   (Bristol)   (Orrell)

J.A. WATKINS   P.J. LARTER   C.W. RALSTON   A. NEARY
(Gloucester)   (Northampton)   (Richmond)   (Broughton Park)

A.G. RIPLEY
(Moseley)

J.G. WEBSTER
(Moseley)

J.F. FINLAN
(Moseley)

D.J. DUCKHAM   P.S. PREECE   P.J. WARFIELD   A.J. MORLEY
(Coventry)   (Coventry)   (Rosslyn Park)   (Bristol)

S.A. DOBLE
(Moseley)

ENGLAND

REFEREE: Mr J. Young (Scotland)
ATTENDANCE: 72,000
CONDITIONS: Weather overcast and cold, ground soft
HALFTIME: New Zealand 6, England 0

SCORERS

NEW ZEALAND	ENGLAND
Try: Kirkpatrick	
Conversion: Karam	
Dropped goal: Williams	

NEW ZEALAND 10

20 January, 1973

New Zealand made two changes to the team that had beaten England. Burgess and Hurst, who had combined impressively at five-eighths against Midland Counties (East), replaced Stevens and Parkinson. For Ian Hurst, whose Rugby career had made a meteoric advance during the 1972 season, it was his first international.

Since the Twickenham international the All Blacks had struggled to defeat Newport 20-15 in an ill-tempered match. They had scored a convincing victory at Leicester over Midland Counties (East) by 43-12, and managed to scramble out of the match against Munster with a late penalty to draw 3-3.

Ireland fielded a very experienced team. The 34 year old captain, Tom Kiernan, had won fifty-one caps since 1960 including one against New Zealand in 1963. Two other survivors of the 1963 match were the forwards "Willie John" McBride and Ray McLoughlin, both of whom had toured New Zealand with the 1966 and 1971 Lions. Others who had toured New Zealand with Lions sides included the hooker Ken Kennedy (1966), the brilliant midfield back, Mike Gibson (1966 and 1971), and forwards Fergus Slattery and "Sean" Lynch, both of whom had been in the 1971 party. The only new cap in the side was the six foot five and half inch lock forward, Kevin Mays.

New Zealand kicked off into the breeze, and after seven minutes during which time Ireland had been on attack, and had seen McGann miss a 45 yard penalty, the home side grabbed an early lead when the fly-half was successful with a second kick from 50 yards.

Gradually the All Black pack began to obtain control in a hard-fought contest, and in the twenty-seventh minute, Going was round quickly on an Irish heel inside their 25, to rob Moloney of the ball. In a typically strong burst, he wrestled over the line for a well-taken try. Karam converted with a good kick from wide out.

There was no further scoring in this half, and it was not until the seventeenth minute of the second spell that the All Blacks went further ahead, when Lambert peeled off a maul with ball in

hand, before passing to Burgess moving on the blindside. The first five-eighth made ground towards the Irish left hand corner before turning the ball in to Wyllie, and the determined flanker crashed through Kiernan's tackle to give his side their second try of the match. Karam was wide with the conversion.

As the minutes ticked by, Ireland, now playing into the strong breeze, appeared to have an almost impossible task to save the match. Then with ten minutes remaining McGann goaled a second penalty when Going, who had trouble satisfying the referee as to the fairness of his feeding of the scrum throughout this game, was penalised just outside the 25.

Karam's kick-off was deep but carried into touch on the full and from the resultant scrum, McGann put in a short kick that had the All Blacks at full stretch. The Irish forwards poured into the maul to win the ball and Moloney broke on the blindside. He drew Batty before unloading to winger Tom Grace who, when confronted by Karam, kicked a flat punt ahead which rolled

---

NEW ZEALAND

J.F. KARAM
(Wellington)

B.G. WILLIAMS   B.J. ROBERTSON   G.B. BATTY
(Auckland)   (Counties)   (Wellington)

I.A. HURST
(Canterbury)

R.E. BURGESS
(Manawatu)

S.M. GOING
(North Auckland)

A.R. SUTHERLAND
(Marlborough)

I.A. KIRKPATRICK (Capt.)   H.H. MACDONALD   P.J. WHITING   A.J. WYLLIE
(Poverty Bay)   (Canterbury)   (Auckland)   (Canterbury)

K.K. LAMBERT   R.W. NORTON   G.J. WHITING
(Manawatu)   (Canterbury)   (King Country)

R.J. McLOUGHLIN   K.W. KENNEDY   J.F. LYNCH
(Blackrock College)   (London Irish)   (St. Mary's College)

J.F. SLATTERY   W.J. McBRIDE   K.M.A. MAYS   J.C. DAVIDSON
(Blackrock College)   (Ballymena)   (U.C. Dublin)   (Dungannon)

T.A.P. MOORE
(Highfield)

J.J. MOLONEY
(St. Mary's College)

B.J. McGANN
(Cork Constitution)

A.W. McMASTER   C.M.H. GIBSON   M.K. FLYNN   T.O. GRACE
(Ballymena)   (N.I.F.C.)   (Wanderers)   (St. Mary's College)

T.J. KIERNAN (Capt.)
(Cork Constitution)

IRELAND

REFEREE: Mr M. Joseph (Wales)
ATTENDANCE: 50,000
CONDITIONS: Weather overcast, ground slightly soft
HALFTIME: New Zealand 6, Ireland 3

SCORERS

NEW ZEALAND	IRELAND
Tries: Going, Wyllie	Try: Grace
Conversion: Karam	Penalty goals: McGann (2)

IRELAND 10

Lansdowne Road, Dublin

The crowd regards Wyllie's try with apparent disbelief. The Irish full-back, Kiernan, lies in Wyllie's wake while Kent Lambert raises his arms in jubilation.

deep into in goal. In a thrilling race, Grace and Burgess converged on the ball as it approached the dead ball line, and a desperate dive saw the Irishman win by a split second, to the immense delight of the spectators.

Barry McGann's conversion from the touchline would have given Ireland an historic victory but it faded away past the far post at the last moment.

So the New Zealanders who had never defeated all four home unions on one tour, were denied this honour by an inspired finish from the Irish team.

FRANCE 13

10 February, 1973

This match was the thirty-second and final match of the 1972-73 New Zealand team's tour. In the matches since the Irish international, the All Blacks had gone down to a powerful Barbarian side at Cardiff, 11-23, in what had been described as "the finest exhibition of Rugby in recent years". Since that match the New Zealanders had defeated their three French opponents, but had shown signs of obvious weariness in doing so.

The team selected for this match was unchanged from that which had played in the drawn Test at Lansdowne Road.

Several of the French team had played in previous internationals against New Zealand. Claude Dourthe, Andre Campaes (who had been a late replacement for this match) and captain Walter Spanghero had all played in Paris in 1967. These three, together with Jean-Pierre Lux, Elie Cester and Jean Iracabal had appeared during the series in New Zealand in 1968.

Played at the new Parc des Princes which had

Batty looks on from the left wing as the bearded French lock, Esteve, peels off a maul.

been opened in the previous June, the game did not reach the heights expected. The ultra-modern stadium which was able to seat in comfort the 55,000 spectators, had been erected on the site of the first ever encounter between these sides in 1906.

The early pressure came from France and they lost a certain try seven minutes after the start when Lux tried to go alone with unmarked men outside him. France eventually opened the scoring in the twenty-third minute when the ball was thrown over the end of a four man line-out. Spanghero recovered and combined with Barrau who ran in to midfield before unloading to Dourthe, and the centre had a 20 yard run to score.

This try was not converted but almost immediately Karam had a penalty attempt from 40 yards out which was successful.

The second try of the match came just before halftime after Spanghero detached from a scrum in centre field and fed half-back Max Barrau who broke brilliantly. Spanghero was up to take the return pass and feed Dourthe who put Roland

NEW ZEALAND

J.F. KARAM
(Wellington)
B.G. WILLIAMS   B.J. ROBERTSON   G.B. BATTY
(Auckland)   (Counties)   (Wellington)
          I.A. HURST
          (Canterbury)
                    R.E. BURGESS
                    (Manawatu)
          S.M. GOING
          (North Auckland)
          A.R. SUTHERLAND
          (Marlborough)
I.A. KIRKPATRICK (Capt.) H.H. MACDONALD   P.J. WHITING A.J. WYLLIE
(Poverty Bay)   (Canterbury)   (Auckland)   (Canterbury)
K.K. LAMBERT   R.W. NORTON   G.J. WHITING
(Manawatu)   (Canterbury)   (King Country)

J. IRACABAL   R. BENESIS   J.L. AZARETE
(A Bayonne)   (S.U. Agen)   (St. Jean de Luz)
O. SAISSET   A. ESTEVE   E. CESTER   P. BIEMOURET
(A.S. Beziers)   (A.S. Beziers) (Valence)   (S.U. Agen)
          W. SPANGHERO (Capt.)
          (R.C. Narbonne)
          M. BARRAU
          (Stade Toulousain)
                    J.P. ROMEU
                    (A.S. Montferrand)
A. CAMPAES   J.P. LUX   C. DOURTHE   R. BERTRANNE
(F.C. Lourdais) (U.S. Dax) (U.S. Dax)   (R.C. Toulon)
          J. CANTONI†
          (A.S. Beziers)
          FRANCE

REPLACEMENT: † replaced by M. Droitecourt (A.S. Montferrand)
REFEREE: Mr D.P. D'Arcy (Ireland)
ATTENDANCE: 55,000
CONDITIONS: Weather overcast then rain, ground heavy
HALFTIME: France 10, New Zealand 3

SCORERS
NEW ZEALAND   FRANCE
Penalty goals: Karam (2)   Tries: Dourthe, Bertranne
                               Conversion: Romeu
                               Penalty goal: Romeu

N EW Z ALAND

Bertranne away on a 30 yard sprint to the corner. Romeu converted with a fine kick to take the halftime score to 10-3 in favour of the home team.

In the thirtieth minute of the first half, full-back Jack Cantoni was forced to leave the field with a heavily bruised thigh and was replaced by Michel Droitecourt.

As the second half got under way the threatening overhead skies opened up and rain fell for the rest of the match. In the seventh minute Karam was on target with his second penalty from in front of the posts and eleven minutes later Romeu replied with an angled penalty for France.

As the match wore on it became apparent that the All Blacks were unable to muster sufficient fire to retrieve the situation and the French halves kept the All Blacks under constant pressure. Some observers were of the opinion that had the ground remained firm the French could have won by twenty points.

Graham Whiting, who subsequently turned to League in Auckland, had played the last of his five Tests. Alan Sutherland continued to show good form at provincial level in subsequent years but was ignored by the national selectors until he won a place in the 1976 All Black side that toured South Africa. However he was unable to gain a Test place on this tour. Sutherland had appeared in ten internationals.

Bob Burgess was another who had appeared in his last Test for New Zealand. Since he had burst on the international scene in 1971 he had played in seven Tests. On this tour he had been unable to reproduce the form that he had shown in the second Test of 1971 when he had scored two brilliant tries. In later seasons Burgess returned to France to study and whilst there played in club Rugby.

Barrau, the French half-back, heads for the gap between Ian Hurst and Bruce Robertson.

COLORSPORT

ENGLAND 1

15 September, 1973

Following the cancellation of a tour to the Argentine, The Rugby Union agreed to undertake a short tour of Fiji and New Zealand. After a narrow 13-12 win over Fiji, the Englishmen were beaten in all three of their provincial matches in New Zealand and they were very much the underdogs for the international.

The home side had three new Test players in Bob Lendrum, Ken Stewart and Murray Jones, all of whom had taken part in an All Black internal tour the previous month. Stewart had also been a member of the 1972-73 team on its visit to the Northern Hemisphere. Terry Morrison, later a national 200 metre sprint champion, who came on when Parkinson was injured, was also making his Test debut.

Nine players from each team had taken part in the New Zealand versus England match of the previous January.

The referee, Mr Frank McMullen, had played eleven Tests for the All Blacks between 1957 and 1960. He was the fourth New Zealand representative to control an international match.

There was a brisk westerly breeze blowing from behind the home team when Old kicked off. New Zealand attacked immediately and for eight minutes England had to defend continuously. The All Blacks won a scrum near the English line, Wyllie picked up and fed Going on the blindside and the latter drew the opposition before transferring to Batty, who had a short sprint to score. Lendrum's kick missed.

Three minutes later, England took the lead when Webster made a break following a scrum on the New Zealand 25 to send Squires across in the corner. Rossborough's conversion from the sideline was a fine one.

In the twenty-seventh minute, Williams cross-kicked and his forwards won a ruck in front of the English posts. Going threw a long pass to Hurst, who eluded the opposition to score handy to the uprights. Lendrum converted to make the score 10-6, which was unaltered at halftime.

Two mistakes by New Zealand in the second half led to English tries and gave the visitors a well-deserved but unexpected victory. After eight

minutes, Lendrum failed to find touch from inside his 25 and Webster caught the ball. He ran before feeding back to his forwards who carried on the movement, Stevens eventually crossing for a try.

Five minutes from time, Lendrum failed to take a high kick and once again Webster came away with the ball. He passed to Old who in turn sent on to Neary for the flanker to score midway between the posts and the corner flag. Rossborough converted and New Zealand had to score twice to win.

The home team attacked desperately in the dying stages but the Englishmen were playing with great spirit and were determined not to relinquish their lead. They were still six points ahead at full time, thus recording a truly historic victory.

While not wishing to detract from the merit of England's win, we feel that this must have been one of the most inept displays ever by an All

---

NEW ZEALAND
R.N. LENDRUM
(Counties)
B.G. WILLIAMS   I.A. HURST   G.B. BATTY
(Auckland)   (Canterbury)   (Wellington)
R.M. PARKINSON*
(Poverty Bay)
J.P. DOUGAN
(Wellington)
S.M. GOING
(North Auckland)
A.J. WYLLIE
(Canterbury)
I.A. KIRKPATRICK (Capt.) S.C. STRAHAN H.H. MACDONALD K.W. STEWART
(Poverty Bay) (Manawatu) (Canterbury) (Southland)
K.K. LAMBERT R.W. NORTON M.G. JONES
(Manawatu) (Canterbury) (North Auckland)

C.B. STEVENS J.V. PULLIN (Capt.) F.E. COTTON
(Penzance & Newlyn) (Bristol) (Coventry)
J.A. WATKINS R.M. UTTLEY C.W. RALSTON A. NEARY
(Gloucester) (Gosforth) (Richmond) (Broughton Park)
A.G. RIPLEY
(Rosslyn Park)
J.G. WEBSTER
(Moseley)
A.G.B. OLD
(Leicester)
D.J. DUCKHAM P.S. PREECE G.W. EVANS† P.J. SQUIRES
(Coventry) (Coventry) (Coventry) (Harrogate)
P.A. ROSSBOROUGH
(Coventry)
ENGLAND

REPLACEMENTS: * Replaced by T.G. Morrison (Otago)
† Replaced by M.J. Cooper (Moseley)
REFEREE: Mr R.F. McMullen (Auckland)
ATTENDANCE: 56,000
CONDITIONS: Weather overcast, ground firm
HALFTIME: New Zealand 10, England 6
SCORERS
NEW ZEALAND　　　　　　**ENGLAND**
Tries: Batty, Hurst　　　　Tries: Squires, Stevens, Neary
Conversion: Lendrum　　　Conversions: Rossborough (2)

334

NEW ZEALAND 10

Eden Park, Auckland

Black team. The home side, especially the forwards, played most of the game with an almost complete lack of purpose and very few wearers of the black jersey looked like internationals. There also seemed to be an alarming absence of leadership.

This was Wyllie's last Test appearance. He had appeared in eleven internationals. It was also Murray Jones's only Test: He lost his life in tragic circumstances, when he and his young son were victims of a boating mishap in 1975.

John Dougan about to swing a pass to Batty. All Blacks in the background are Macdonald, Strahan, Stewart, Wyllie and Norton.

N EW ZEALAND 11

25 May, 1974

First Test

Messrs J.J. Stewart, J. Gleeson and E.A. Watson, the national selectors, had included no fewer than fifteen new All Blacks in their twenty-five man side to tour Australia, following trials in mid-April. Six of these newcomers, Andy Leslie the captain whose father had represented New Zealand at soccer, John Callesen a six foot five inch lock forward, both the props Bill Bush and Kerry Tanner, and the half-back combination of Bruce Gemmell and Duncan Robertson, won selection for this match.

An interesting player making his debut for Australia was Paul McLean, the 20 year old brother of winger Jeff, who was the latest of the great Queensland Rugby family to represent his country. Mark Loane selected at number eight had played for Australia against the touring Tongans the previous season at the age of eighteen.

The All Blacks had amassed a total of 318 points in their seven unbeaten matches leading up to this first international of the 1974 series, which included a record breaking score of 117-6

against South Australia in the opening match of the tour, and a 20-0 victory over New South Wales.

Large areas of the ground were covered with water as Hipwell and Leslie led their teams out on to the field. With the cold wind gusting to 50 m.p.h., playing conditions were the worst that had been encountered for some years by an All Black Test team.

The Wallabies started the game strongly despite the fact that they were playing into the wind in the first half. Eight minutes after the start Australia were given a penalty attempt in a handy position. Paul McLean's kick was pushed across the face of the goal posts by the wind where the All Black defenders failed to make the ball dead and fast-following Australian flanker, Ray Price, threw himself on it to score the opening points of the match. The young McLean made no mistake with the conversion from close range.

Peter Whiting, at left, peers through the murk to see Kirkpatrick going to ground in a tackle.

RUGBY PRESS

AUSTRALIA 6

Sydney Cricket Ground

RUGBY PRESS

Duncan Robertson speculates at the ball lying in a pool of water.

No further scoring occurred until a few minutes before halftime when New Zealand were awarded a penalty after the Australians were adjudged off-side around a maul just inside their 25. After Leslie had gone down on his knees to sweep away the surface slush and Norton had steadied the ball Karam managed to land the goal with the sodden ball to reduce the leeway to three points at the interval.

The All Blacks surprisingly showed improved form playing into the wind in the second half with Ian Kirkpatrick in particular displaying outstanding form. Quarter of an hour had passed before they were able to gain the lead. Then from a line-out Gemmell threw a pass to Duncan Robertson who threw a dummy towards his outside backs then cut back towards the touch line beating player after player on the treacherous

surface in a brilliant 40 yard run to score 10 yards in from the corner in Fay's tackle. Karam's attempted conversion held up in the wind and dropped just under the bar.

Eight minutes from no-side the final points in the match came when a scrum went down close to the Wallaby goal line. Australia got the ball back to Hipwell but the scrum had screwed and the half-back was quickly wrapped up by the New Zealand loose forwards. As the ball was wrenched free, Kirkpatrick was able to gather and crash over for a try. Karam again was unable to convert the try in almost impossible conditions.

The Zingari-Richmond first five-eighth, Duncan Robertson had widely impressed in his Test debut. After playing for the first six years of his first class career with Otago mostly as a second five-eighth he moved into the inner berth at the start of the 1972 season. The following year his career made spectacular progress and he thoroughly earned his All Black selection at the start of this season.

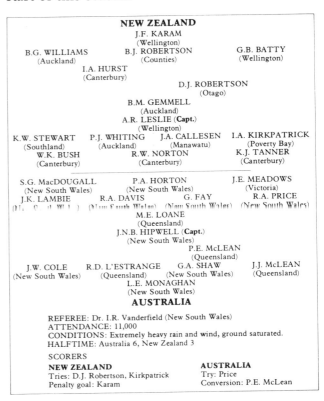

NEW ZEALAND

J.F. KARAM
(Wellington)

B.G. WILLIAMS (Auckland) B.J. ROBERTSON (Counties) G.B. BATTY (Wellington)

I.A. HURST (Canterbury)

D.J. ROBERTSON (Otago)

B.M. GEMMELL (Auckland)

A.R. LESLIE (**Capt.**) (Wellington)

K.W. STEWART (Southland) P.J. WHITING (Auckland) J.A. CALLESEN (Manawatu) I.A. KIRKPATRICK (Poverty Bay)

W.K. BUSH (Canterbury) R.W. NORTON (Canterbury) K.J. TANNER (Canterbury)

S.G. MacDOUGALL (New South Wales) P.A. HORTON (New South Wales) J.E. MEADOWS (Victoria)

J.K. LAMBIE (Queensland) R.A. DAVIS (New South Wales) G. FAY (New South Wales) R.A. PRICE (New South Wales)

M.E. LOANE (Queensland)

J.N.B. HIPWELL (**Capt.**) (New South Wales)

P.E. McLEAN (Queensland)

J.W. COLE (New South Wales) R.D. L'ESTRANGE (Queensland) G.A. SHAW (New South Wales) J.J. McLEAN (Queensland)

L.E. MONAGHAN (New South Wales)

AUSTRALIA

REFEREE: Dr. I.R. Vanderfield (New South Wales)
ATTENDANCE: 11,000
CONDITIONS: Extremely heavy rain and wind, ground saturated.
HALFTIME: Australia 6, New Zealand 3

SCORERS

NEW ZEALAND	AUSTRALIA
Tries: D.J. Robertson, Kirkpatrick	Try: Price
Penalty goal: Karam	Conversion: P.E. McLean

337

1 June, 1974

Second Test

Owing to an injured left hand, Grant Batty was a last minute withdrawal from the New Zealand side. His replacement Jon McLachlan who was making his international debut was the first Test player from the College Rifles club. This was the only change to the All Black team which had won the first Test at Sydney.

One of the three changes made by the Australian selectors saw Owen Stephens, who played one Test for New Zealand in 1968 against France, replace Jeff McLean on the left wing. Stephens, now an insurance agent in Sydney, became only the second New Zealand international to subsequently represent another country against New Zealand. The other changes were in the forwards where first Test reserve Greg Cornelson replaced the injured Mark Loane and Ron Graham came in for the Victorian prop John Meadows.

The only match played since the Test in Sydney was against Queensland where New Zealand romped away in the second half to an easy 42-6 victory.

Australia had the best of the early exchanges in the match and they took the lead when Paul McLean landed a penalty goal.

Midway through the spell, Williams when blocked on the right wing lofted a high centring kick which was caught by the fresh breeze and blown back. However after some confusion the All Blacks recovered the ball and Robertson, Leslie and Karam moved the ball quickly out to the left wing side where Ian Hurst outstripped the Wallaby defence and scored in the corner. Karam's attempted conversion carried across the face of the posts.

McLean regained the lead for Australia when he landed a further penalty from close in. In the last minute of the half Karam grabbed the lead back for the All Blacks when he landed a fine 45 yard penalty after Stewart had been obstructed.

New Zealand went further ahead early in the second half after Duncan Robertson charged down a clearing kick by Mongahan and Leslie was able to recover and run over for a try. Karam

converted this try with a good kick from wide out. The New Zealand full-back increased the lead even further in the twentieth minute of the half when he raised the flags with a 50 yard penalty. It seemed with the 16-6 lead and a decreasing wind behind them the All Blacks were coasting to a comfortable win.

This did not prove the case however and in the last sixteen minutes the Australians hit back strongly, scoring two particularly fine tries.

The first of these started from a determined run down the left wing by Owen Stephens. When the movement was checked, Australia won a quick ruck and sent the ball right through their backline. When the move looked to be in danger of losing momentum, captain John Hipwell was up outside Cole to take the pass and elude the last remnants of the All Black defence and score wide out. McLean converted with a fine kick to make the score 16-12 to New Zealand.

With five minutes to go Australia scored again after a backline movement following a ruck.

NEW ZEALAND
J.F. KARAM
(Wellington)

| B.G. WILLIAMS | B.J. ROBERTSON | J.S. McLACHLAN |
| (Auckland) | (Counties) | (Auckland) |

I.A. HURST
(Canterbury)

D.J. ROBERTSON
(Otago)

B.M. GEMMELL
(Auckland)
A.R. LESLIE (Capt.)
(Wellington)

K.W. STEWART	J.A. CALLESEN	P.J. WHITING	I.A. KIRKPATRICK
(Southland)	(Manawatu)	(Auckland)	(Poverty Bay)
W.K. BUSH		R.W. NORTON	K.J. TANNER
(Canterbury)		(Canterbury)	(Canterbury)

S.G. MacDOUGALL	P.A. HORTON	R. GRAHAM
(New South Wales)	(New South Wales)	(New South Wales)
G. CORNELSON	G. FAY	R.A. DAVIS	R.A. PRICE
(New South Wales)	(New South Wales)	(New South Wales)	(New South Wales)

J.K. LAMBIE
(New South Wales)
J.N.B. HIPWELL (Capt.)
(New South Wales)
P.E. McLEAN
(Queensland)

| O.G. STEPHENS | R.D. L'ESTRANGE | G.A. SHAW | J.W. COLE |
| (New South Wales) | (Queensland) | (New South Wales) | (New South Wales) |

L.E. MONAGHAN
(New South Wales)
AUSTRALIA

REFEREE: Mr R. Burnett (Queensland)
ATTENDANCE: 13,000
CONDITIONS: Weather fine, ground firm
HALFTIME: New Zealand 7, Australia 6

SCORERS

NEW ZEALAND	AUSTRALIA
Tries: Hurst, Leslie	Tries: Hipwell, Monaghan
Conversion: Karam	Conversion: McLean
Penalty goals: Karam (2)	Penalty goals: McLean (2)

AUSTRALIA 1

Ballymore Oval, Brisbane

MacDougall leaps over his team-mate Fay who has been tackled by Hurst. Graham and Bruce Robertson are at right.

Monaghan was up from full-back to recover a short kick ahead and score ten yards in from the corner. McLean was offered the chance to give Australia its first home win over New Zealand since 1934 when he took the conversion but he was unable to repeat his earlier fine effort.

The Australian team had fought back brilliantly and much praise was lavished on the forwards who had dominated the line-outs particularly in the second half. During the last fifteen minutes the Wallaby pack had won six out of seven line-outs and had provided the base from which the Australian revival had come.

8 June, 1974

Third Test

Following Australia's sterling performance in the second Test at Brisbane, a greatly increased local interest in this match was assured. The Australian team took the field unchanged but the New Zealand team saw four alterations.

Grant Batty, now fit regained his place and the durable North Aucklander, Joe Morgan came in at second five-eighth to make his international debut.

The all round ability and improving form of Ian Stevens won him the nod over Gemmell behind the scrum whilst the only forward change saw Ash Gardiner, the Tukapa club's twelfth All Black, make his international debut at the expense of Bush, at tighthead prop.

Dr. Roger Vanderfield, the General Medical Superintendent of the Royal North Shore Hospital in Sydney, who had controlled the first international of the series, was again to officiate. His international refereeing career had commenced in 1956 when he had refereed the Test in Sydney between Australia and South Africa.

Once again the Australians started the match well and dominated the early battle for possession. Gradually the All Blacks fought their way back into the game and after half an hour's play managed to score the first points of the match. Following sustained pressure on the Wallaby line a five yard scrum was awarded and from this Duncan Robertson ran strongly on the blindside. As he was held up Ian Kirkpatrick was there to wrench the ball away and force his way

After a blindside run by Duncan Robertson, Kirkpatrick was on hand to continue the move and score, catching the Australians unaware.

AUSTRALIA 6

Sydney Cricket Ground

over in the corner. Karam converted from wide out.

No further scoring was registered in this half but after seven minutes' play in the second spell Duncan Robertson hoisted a kick that was mulled by Hipwell near his own line. The All Blacks won the ensuing maul and with Cole caught up in the forwards Stevens ran on the blindside and passed to the unmarked Batty who scored in the corner. Karam's conversion was wide.

Three minutes later McLean opened the Wallaby scoring with a 45 yard scrum penalty. After quarter of an hour's play the All Blacks won a ruck inside their opponents' 25 and Stevens again ran on the blindside unopposed and was able to dot the ball down a yard in from the corner post. Karam goaled the conversion to put New Zealand into the lead by 16-3.

The final points of the match came thirteen minutes from the end when McLean added a close range penalty.

At no stage had Australia looked like repeating their performance in Brisbane and once again New Zealand had retained the Bledisloe Cup.

Ian Stevens, who had played his first Test at half-back, after two previous appearances at first five-eighth, was one of New Zealand's best players, whilst Kirkpatrick again had played an outstanding game. This was Gardiner's only Test appearance. He was forced to retire from the game on medical grounds at the end of the following season.

The outstanding Australian player throughout the series was probably flanker Ray Price, a 21 year old carpenter, who later turned to League.

Others from the Wallaby side to change codes included wingers, Owen Stephens who signed with Parramatta at the end of the season and subsequently with the English club, Wakefield Trinity, and John Cole.

AUCKLAND STAR

NEW ZEALAND

J.F. KARAM
(Wellington)

B.G. WILLIAMS   B.J. ROBERTSON   G.B. BATTY
(Auckland)   (Counties)   (Wellington)

J.E. MORGAN
(North Auckland)

D.J. ROBERTSON
(Otago)

I.N. STEVENS
(Wellington)

A.R. LESLIE (**Capt.**)
(Wellington)

I.A. KIRKPATRICK   J.A. CALLESEN   P.J. WHITING   K.W. STEWART
(Poverty Bay)   (Manawatu)   (Auckland)   (Southland)

A.J. GARDINER   R.W. NORTON   K.J. TANNER
(Taranaki)   (Canterbury)   (Auckland)

S.G. MacDOUGALL   P.A. HORTON   R. GRAHAM
(New South Wales)   (New South Wales)   (New South Wales)

G. CORNELSON   R.A. DAVID   O. FAY   R.A. PRICE
(New South Wales) (New South Wales) (New South Wales) (New South Wales)

J.K. LAMBIE
(New South Wales)

J.N.B. HIPWELL (**Capt.**)
(New South Wales)

P.E. McLEAN
(Queensland)

O.G. STEPHENS   R.D. L'ESTRANGE   G.A. SHAW   J.W. COLE
(New South Wales) (New South Wales) (New South Wales) (New South Wales)

L.E. MONAGHAN
(New South Wales)

AUSTRALIA

REFEREE: Dr. I.R. Vanderfield (New South Wales)
ATTENDANCE: 37,225
CONDITIONS: Weather fine, ground soft
HALFTIME: New Zealand 6, Australia 0

SCORERS

NEW ZEALAND	AUSTRALIA
Tries: Kirkpatrick, Batty, Stevens	Penalty goals: McLean (2)
Conversions: Karam (2)	

NEW ZEALAND 15

23 November, 1974

As part of the Irish Rugby Union's centenary celebrations, a New Zealand team was invited to make a six match tour of Ireland culminating in an international match against their hosts. A twenty-seven player team was chosen for the tour following trials in Auckland in mid-September. Matches against a Welsh XV and the Barbarians were played following the Irish section of the tour.

After an uncertain start against a Combined Irish Universities side at Cork, the tourists improved match by match until they reached Dublin for the international.

The Irish side contained two new caps — James Crowe whose father, Morgan, had been capped for Ireland thirteen times between 1929 and 1934, and Pat Parfrey a 24 year old wing three-quarter noted for his defensive ability. The side was led by "Willie John" McBride who earlier in 1974 had captained the unbeaten British Lions side in South Africa. It was the 34 year old Ulsterman's fifty-ninth international for Ireland.

Joe Karam seeks a way round Irish back-row forward, Terry Moore. All Black captain, Andy Leslie, is at left.

Another very experienced player was prop Ray McLoughlin also a survivor of the 1963 match with New Zealand who was earning his thirty-sixth cap. A notable absentee was the outstanding mid-field back Michael Gibson who was injured.

Following twelve hours' rain, the ground was heavy as Quinn kicked off for Ireland. In the ninth minute Karam missed a straight forward penalty attempt but shortly afterwards, following sustained forward pressure, Going passed to his right from a ruck near the Irish line. Karam was up to take the ball and elude the cover defence and score the only try of the match to the right of the posts. The full-back converted to give New Zealand a 6-0 lead.

In the seventeenth minute Ensor kicked the first of his two penalty goals from 35 yards following a late tackle by Stewart. Three minutes before halftime Karam kicked the first of his penalties following a line-out infringement on the Irish 25 to give New Zealand a 9-3 lead at halftime.

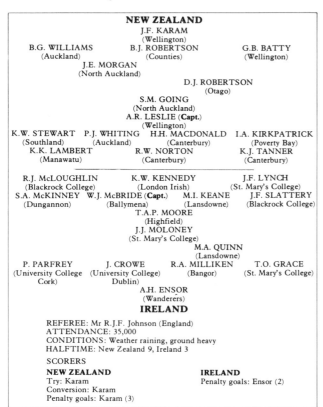

NEW ZEALAND

J.F. KARAM
(Wellington)

B.G. WILLIAMS   B.J. ROBERTSON   G.B. BATTY
(Auckland)   (Counties)   (Wellington)

J.E. MORGAN
(North Auckland)

D.J. ROBERTSON
(Otago)

S.M. GOING
(North Auckland)

A.R. LESLIE (**Capt.**)
(Wellington)

K.W. STEWART   P.J. WHITING   H.H. MACDONALD   I.A. KIRKPATRICK
(Southland)   (Auckland)   (Canterbury)   (Poverty Bay)

K.K. LAMBERT   R.W. NORTON   K.J. TANNER
(Manawatu)   (Canterbury)   (Canterbury)

R.J. McLOUGHLIN   K.W. KENNEDY   J.F. LYNCH
(Blackrock College)   (London Irish)   (St. Mary's College)

S.A. McKINNEY   W.J. McBRIDE (**Capt.**)   M.I. KEANE   J.F. SLATTERY
(Dungannon)   (Ballymena)   (Lansdowne)   (Blackrock College)

T.A.P. MOORE
(Highfield)

J.J. MOLONEY
(St. Mary's College)

M.A. QUINN
(Lansdowne)

P. PARFREY   J. CROWE   R.A. MILLIKEN   T.O. GRACE
(University College   (University College   (Bangor)   (St. Mary's College)
Cork)   Dublin)

A.H. ENSOR
(Wanderers)

IRELAND

REFEREE: Mr R.J.F. Johnson (England)
ATTENDANCE: 35,000
CONDITIONS: Weather raining, ground heavy
HALFTIME: New Zealand 9, Ireland 3

SCORERS

NEW ZEALAND	**IRELAND**
Try: Karam	Penalty goals: Ensor (2)
Conversion: Karam	
Penalty goals: Karam (3)	

IRELAND 6

Lansdowne Road, Dublin

The New Zealand Touring Team
Back row: D.J. Robertson, T.W. Mitchell, J.E. Morgan, B.G. Williams, O.D. Bruce, J.F. Karam.
Third row: A.J. Gardiner, K.A. Eveleigh, W.K. Bush, R.W. Norton, G.N. Kane, K.K. Lambert, K.T. Going.
Second row: K.W. Stewart, I.A. Kirkpatrick, L.G. Knight, J.A. Callesen, P.J. Whiting, H.H. Macdonald, K.J. Tanner, B.J. Robertson.
Front row: N.H. Stanley (manager), G.M. Crossman, S.M. Going, A.R. Leslie (capt.), G.B. Batty, I.N. Stevens, I.A. Hurst, J.J. Stewart (asst. manager).

Early in the second half, Ensor landed his second goal and the 35,000 hardy spectators hoping for an Irish resurgence, gave voice to their feelings. Their hopes were soon dashed as Karam kicked his second penalty in the seventh minute of the spell from 25 yards out after Moore was caught offside at a ruck. The New Zealand forwards were holding a decided advantage during this half and the chances of an Irish victory were diminishing. Karam kicked the final points of

the match in the twenty-second minute from 30 yards.

The very experienced Irish pack was well outplayed on the day and the backs were strangely unenterprising. Ireland's coach Syd Millar had no complaints after the game and thought the All Black pack far better than the eight who played in 1973. Sid Going who made himself available to tour at a late stage played a fine game apart from some handling lapses. His tactics and the weather conditions did not allow the other New Zealand backs many opportunities.

The Irish hope of having their maiden victory over a New Zealand side, never looked like becoming a reality.

In the week following this match New Zealand defeated a Welsh XV 12-3 and drew 13-13 with a powerful Barbarian team that included the complete 1974 Lions pack.

343

NEW ZEALAND 24

14 June, 1975

During May and June 1975 Scotland made their first Rugby tour of New Zealand. A seven match itinerary was arranged culminating in an international at Auckland.

Following losses to Otago and Canterbury, Scotland were not favoured to win this match. The selection of their international team included a few surprises. Irvine, the British Lions' full-back was selected as a wing three-quarter to allow Bruce Hay to win his first cap in the full-back position. Graham Birkett and the hooker Colin Fisher, whose father had won two Scottish caps in 1947, were also making their international debuts.

The New Zealand team featured one new international, 20 year old Bill Osborne at centre three-quarter. Bruce Robertson, who was recovering from a broken arm, was not available.

New Zealand played in white jerseys to avoid confusion with Scotland's dark blue.

An original Scottish selection, George Mackie the number eight forward, had to withdraw with an injured leg and was replaced by Bill Watson. Extremely heavy rain started to fall in Auckland during the early hours of the day of the match and by 2.30p.m., areas of the ground, particularly in-

The All Blacks, wearing white jerseys, complete their haka in front of the crowd sheltering under umbrellas. A large pool of water lies in front of the grandstand.

R. COOKE

SCOTLAND 0

Eden Park, Auckland

goal and in the corners, were covered with surface water. Although the ground had been pre-sold only an estimated 45,000 brave spectators were present to see Scotland kick off towards the Dominion Road end.

After thirteen minutes Osborne appeared to cross for a try in the middle of a lake in the left-hand corner but was recalled for an infringement. Two minutes later Going broke to his right from a ruck in front of the posts. Held up five yards from the goal line, he had the ball wrenched free by Kirkpatrick who fed Macdonald who was moving at full pace. The lock crashed over in a shower of spray 10 yards to the right of the posts. After Hay, who had broken his right arm in this movement had left the field, Karam added the conversion. Steele, who replaced Hay, went to the right wing and Irvine moved to full-back.

No further scoring occurred during this half, but after four minutes in the second half, Karam gathered a kick near half-way and linked with Williams on his right. The latter beat several defenders before hoisting a high kick to the Scottish goal line where Steele gathered the ball but as he started to run the greasy ball slid from his grasp and the fast following Williams dived on it to score. Karam converted to make the score 12-0.

Another lapse by the Scottish defence after eighteen minutes led to a similar try, this time by Robertson after he had placed an 'up and under' to the Scottish goal line where two defenders collided. Before they could recover, Robertson was through to score wide out. Karam converted with a fine kick.

With seven minutes to play, a further defensive error by the visitors led to New Zealand's final try. A cross kick placed behind the Scottish left wing, Dick, was fly kicked to touch but in the saturated conditions the ball failed to reach the line. Williams scooped up the ball inches from touch and veering in-field, beat numerous opponents before forcing his way over the Scottish line just to the right of the posts. Karam completed a fine day's kicking in trying conditions by converting to make the final score 24-0.

An interesting feature of the game was that of the thirteen penalty kicks awarded (eleven to Scotland) not one kick at goal was attempted.

In the twenty-four hours of this very wet Saturday, a total of 3.89 inches of rain was recorded, almost three inches having fallen between 6 a.m. and 4 p.m.

With his shift into the Horowhenua Union's area Joe Karam gave that Union its first Rugby international and only its second All Black, with his selection for this match. It was Karam's last international for early in the following year he announced that he had accepted an offer to play Rugby League in Auckland. He had appeared in ten internationals and had scored sixty-five points. His loss was to prove a serious one for New Zealand.

Bill Osborne became Wanganui's first international since Peter Henderson twenty-five years earlier.

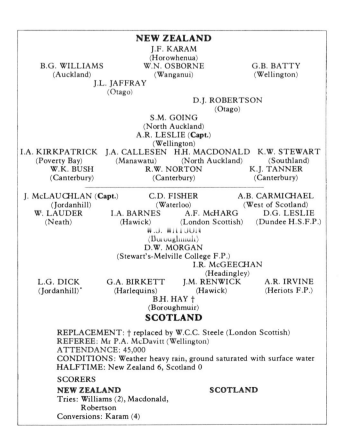

NEW ZEALAND

J.F. KARAM
(Horowhenua)

B.G. WILLIAMS   W.N. OSBORNE   G.B. BATTY
(Auckland)   (Wanganui)   (Wellington)

J.L. JAFFRAY
(Otago)

D.J. ROBERTSON
(Otago)

S.M. GOING
(North Auckland)

A.R. LESLIE (**Capt.**)
(Wellington)

I.A. KIRKPATRICK   J.A. CALLESEN   H.H. MACDONALD   K.W. STEWART
(Poverty Bay)   (Manawatu)   (North Auckland) (Southland)

W.K. BUSH   R.W. NORTON   K.J. TANNER
(Canterbury)   (Canterbury)   (Canterbury)

J. McLAUCHLAN (**Capt.**)   C.D. FISHER   A.B. CARMICHAEL
(Jordanhill)   (Waterloo)   (West of Scotland)

W. LAUDER   I.A. BARNES   A.F. McHARG   D.G. LESLIE
(Neath)   (Hawick)   (London Scottish) (Dundee H.S.F.P.)

W.S. WATSON
(Boroughmuir)

D.W. MORGAN
(Stewart's-Melville College F.P.)

I.R. McGEECHAN
(Headingley)

L.G. DICK   G.A. BIRKETT   J.M. RENWICK   A.R. IRVINE
(Jordanhill)*   (Harlequins)   (Hawick)   (Heriots F.P.)

B.H. HAY †
(Boroughmuir)

SCOTLAND

REPLACEMENT: † replaced by W.C.C. Steele (London Scottish)
REFEREE: Mr P.A. McDavitt (Wellington)
ATTENDANCE: 45,000
CONDITIONS: Weather heavy rain, ground saturated with surface water
HALFTIME: New Zealand 6, Scotland 0

SCORERS

NEW ZEALAND	SCOTLAND
Tries: Williams (2), Macdonald, Robertson	
Conversions: Karam (4)	

5 June, 1976

At the beginning of the 1976 season the Irish Rugby Union sent a twenty-five man side, later reinforced by two replacement players, to play a seven match tour of New Zealand. The international was the final match of the tour and had been preceded by a record of four victories and two losses to provincial sides.

Following rather moderate results in the home internationals in the early months of 1976, which featured a sole victory over England, Ireland were not expected to be strong enough to extend the All Black side but only in their match against Canterbury were they clearly outplayed.

The captain was Tom Grace, a 27 year old accountant who had won nineteen caps on the right wing, including matches against the All Blacks in 1973 (when he scored a thrilling try to even the scores late in the game) and 1974. At centre was Mike Gibson who had already won fifty-seven caps for his country and a further dozen on tours with the Lions in 1966-68-71. Now thirty-three, he had lost little of the considerable ability he had displayed on his two Lions' tours to New Zealand.

The New Zealand team contained two new internationals in Otago's Neil Purvis on the left wing, and Lyn Davis, regular Canterbury half-back since 1964, behind the scrum. Purvis, who had commenced his representative career as a five-eighth for Wairarapa-Bush in 1971 at the age of eighteen, had developed as a sound, all-round three-quarter. Davis, who was making his Test debut at the age of thirty-two, had served sixteen times as an All Black reserve, and on five occasions had played for the South Island. Laurie Mains at full-back had last represented his country in 1971 when he made three appearances against the Lions. Batty was not available for selection owing to an injured knee.

Mains put the ball into play and two minutes later attempted a long range dropped goal from a penalty that passed under the bar. He was more successful with a kick from just outside the 22 metre line in the fifteenth minute to open the scoring.

Midway through the half, New Zealand were fortunate when a wild pass from Duncan Robertson which passed in front of both Jaffray and Bruce Robertson, was picked up on the bounce by Mains coming up into the backline. Mains made a short break before transferring to Bruce Robertson who had ranged up outside him. The slim centre sprinted on the diagonal to the right hand corner where he scored a good try. Mains was unable to convert.

Three minutes before the break Davis swooped on a loose ball at the back of the Irish scrum 20 metres from their goal line to feed Kirkpatrick coming off the side of the scrum. The six foot three inch flanker ran powerfully for the line before leaping high and crashing down through McGann's tackle to score by the posts. The simple conversion by Mains was wide.

On the call of halftime Davis, who had suffered a recurrence of a calf muscle injury, limped off the field and was replaced by Going who was making his twenty-third Test appearance.

NEW ZEALAND

L.W. MAINS
(Otago)

B.G. WILLIAMS   B.J. ROBERTSON   N.A. PURVIS
(Auckland)   (Counties)   (Otago)

J.L. JAFFRAY
(Otago)

D.J. ROBERTSON
(Otago)

L.J. DAVIS *
(Canterbury)

A.R. LESLIE (Capt.)
(Wellington)

I.A. KIRKPATRICK P.J. WHITING H.H. MACDONALD K.W. STEWART
(Poverty Bay) (Auckland) (North Auckland) (Southland)

W.K. BUSH   R.W. NORTON   K.J. TANNER
(Canterbury)   (Canterbury)   (Canterbury)

P.A. ORR   P.C. WHELAN   P. O'CALLAGHAN
(Old Wesley)   (Garryowen)   (Dolphin)

S.A. McKINNEY R.F. HAKIN M.I. KEANE J.C. DAVIDSON
(Dungannon) (C.I.Y.M.S.) (Lansdowne) (Dungannon)

W.P. DUGGAN
(Blackrock College)

J. ROBBIE
(Trinity College, Dublin)

B.J. McGANN
(Cork Constitution)

A.W. McMASTER J.A. McILRAITH C.M.H. GIBSON T.O. GRACE (Capt.)
(Ballymena) (Ballymena) (N.I.F.C.) (St. Mary's College)

A.H. ENSOR
(Lansdowne)

IRELAND

REPLACEMENT: * replaced by S.M. Going (North Auckland)
REFEREE: Mr T.F. Doocey (Canterbury)
ATTENDANCE: 37,000
CONDITIONS: Weather overcast, ground firm
HALFTIME: New Zealand 11, Ireland 0

SCORERS

NEW ZEALAND	**IRELAND**
Tries: B.J. Robertson, Kirkpatrick	Penalty goal: McGann
Penalty goal: Mains	

IRELAND 3

Athletic Park, Wellington

After the interval, with the breeze at their backs, the Irish became a more effective side and started to dominate the play. Although they managed only a straightforward penalty goal by McGann in the sixteenth minute following a scrum infringement, their scoring could have been much greater had McGann, and latterly

Grace, managed to land any of the several opportunities they had to kick goals during the spell.

As an overture to the All Blacks' forthcoming tour to South Africa, this match was a disappointment to most followers of the game. On the morning after this match the team for South Africa was announced with all the players who participated gaining selection. This had been the eighth meeting of the two countries but the first in New Zealand. Except for a drawn match in 1973 New Zealand had won all of the encounters.

Bruce Robertson scores in the corner after a break by Mains. Irish captain, Tom Grace, Bryan Williams and Mike Gibson appear at right.

SOUTH AFRICA 16

24 July, 1976

First Test

In the seven matches leading up to the first Test at Durban the All Black side had failed to display really convincing form and the team's goalkickers had not been consistent. On the Saturday before this Test they had gone down to the strong Western Province team 11-12 when the home side had scored a late converted try. The team's selectors showed their concern over the full-back position when they took a gamble on playing five-eighth Duncan Robertson there ahead of the two specialist full-backs in the side.

Doug Bruce, a school teacher from Canterbury, was the only newcomer to Test Rugby in the New Zealand side. He had first represented his province in 1970 and since that time had built up a reputation for sound reliable play.

The Springbok selectors too introduced one new cap, 21 year old right winger Edrich Krantz, who had captained a South African under twenty-one side in South America the previous year. After selection the Western Province full-back Dawie Snyman was forced to withdraw with hamstring trouble and his place was taken by Ian Robertson originally in the team as a centre.

Another Western Province player, Peter Whipp, came into the side to take the vacant centre position.

Interesting personalities in the Springbok team were veteran flanker Jan Ellis who had made his Test debut against New Zealand in 1965, now playing his thirty-eighth international, and captain Morne du Plessis who completed a unique double when he emulated his father Felix in leading a Springbok side against New Zealand. Another son of a Springbok was Derek van den Berg whose father Mauritz had locked the Springbok scrum in all three internationals in 1937.

South Africa kicked-off and within a couple of minutes their ace kicker Gerald Bosch was having an attempt at goal from near the half-way line. The kick failed and it was New Zealand who had the next scoring opportunity when Leslie chased a kick over the South African line only to see the ball bounce tantalisingly on the opposite side of the upright to allow the Springbok

Krantz has beaten Duncan Robertson and Batty to score. John Williams congratulates the Springbok winger and Bayvel raises his arms in triumph.

N EW ZEALAND 7

defence to hastily touch down. After twelve minutes Bryan Williams, who although a powerful kicker was not always an accurate one, was given an opportunity at goal from 37 metres after a line-out infringement and he put the first points on the board. Bosch almost immediately missed a further long range penalty and then the All Blacks spent a long period on attack but were unable to add to their total.

South Africa evened the score after thirty minutes when Bosch landed a 30 metre penalty. Bruce then failed with an attempted drop goal and shortly after Williams missed a 27 metre penalty. In the final minutes before halftime Bosch missed a dropped goal attempt from close in.

The second half opened quite sensationally when the All Blacks switched the kick-off and Leslie kicked a short one to his left. Du Plessis took the ball but as he was tackled, Batty inter-

cepted his pass and headed off for the goal line. He was caught 10 metres from his objective but managed to get a pass away to Stewart who fed a flying Lyn Jaffray and the five-eighth scored in the corner. Williams's kick was a poor one and the score remained at 7-3.

Nine minutes later the Springboks replied with a good try after Ian Robertson entered a backline movement near the half-way line and drew the defence before sending Germishuys away. The winger ran around Duncan Robertson coming across and eluded the cover defence to score well out. Bosch was on target with his conversion to give his team the lead for the first time in the match. Shortly after the fly-half was astray with both a penalty and a dropped goal attempt. New Zealand spent most of the next twenty minutes on attack but no further scoring occurred.

With seven minutes to play the Springboks won a ruck outside the All Black 22 metre line and Bayvel broke down the blindside. Going's desperate dive was sufficient to put the Springbok off balance but he managed to flick a pass in-field which was accepted by Krantz and the winger scored right in the corner. Bosch's conversion attempt struck an upright and bounced away. The fly-half, who it was later reported was running a high temperature, left the field at this stage and was replaced by the 22 year old De Wet Ras, who had impressed the All Blacks in both the games he had played against them. Within a couple of minutes he had a penalty attempt from 47 metres which was not good enough to register points. In the final minute of the game Duncan Robertson failed to find touch from inside his own 22 and his Rhodesian name-sake Ian gathered the ball and moving in-field slammed home a drop goal from 45 metres.

It had been a disappointing match for New Zealand with errors creeping into their play at vital moments. Captain Andy Leslie, who had probably played his finest match for his country, was unlucky not to score on two occasions. This was the first match that had ended in defeat for New Zealand since Leslie had taken over the captaincy.

NEW ZEALAND
D.J. ROBERTSON (Otago)
B.G. WILLIAMS (Auckland) — B.J. ROBERTSON (Counties) — G.B. BATTY (Bay of Plenty)
J.L. JAFFRAY (Otago)
O.D. BRUCE (Canterbury)
S.M. GOING (North Auckland)
A.R. LESLIE (**Capt.**) (Wellington)
I.A. KIRKPATRICK (Poverty Bay) — P.J. WHITING (Auckland) — H.H. MACDONALD (North Auckland) — K.W. STEWART (Southland)
K.K. LAMBERT (Manawatu) — R.W. NORTON (Canterbury) — K.J. TANNER (Canterbury)

J.C.J. STANDER (Orange Free State) — R.J. COCKRELL (Western Province) — D.S. van den BERG (Western Province)
J.H.H. COETZEE (Western Province) — J.G. WILLIAMS (Northern Transvaal) — J.L. van HEERDEN (Northern Transvaal) — J.H. ELLIS (Transvaal)
M. du PLESSIS (**Capt.**) (Western Province)
P.C.R. BAYVEL (Transvaal)
G.R. BOSCH † (Transvaal)
J.S. GERMISHUYS (Orange Free State) — P.J.M. WHIPP (Western Province) — J.J. OOSTHUIZEN (Western Province) — E.F.W. KRANTZ (Orange Free State)
I.W. ROBERTSON (Rhodesia)
SOUTH AFRICA

REPLACEMENT:† Replaced by W.J. De Wet Ras (Orange Free State)
REFEREE: Mr I. Gourlay (Natal)
ATTENDANCE: 45,000
CONDITIONS: Weather hot and sunny, ground hard.
HALFTIME: New Zealand 3 South Africa 3

SCORERS
NEW ZEALAND
Try: Jaffray
Penalty goal: Williams

SOUTH AFRICA
Tries: Germishuys, Krantz
Conversion: Bosch
Penalty goal: Bosch
Dropped goal: Robertson

NEW ZEALAND 15

14 August, 1976

Second Test

New Zealand had shown better form in the five matches since the first Test of the series, all of which had been won. Their team for this match showed five changes from that which contested the Durban Test. "Kit" Fawcett, who had given an improved performance against Transvaal, came into the side in place of Duncan Robertson who was not a success at full-back at Durban. This was Fawcett's international debut and he was the fourth full-back tried by New Zealand in the past four Tests.

Joe Morgan replaced Jaffray at second five-eighth, and two new caps, Kevin Eveleigh and Brad Johnstone came into the forwards. Johnstone was a son of Ron Johnstone a member of the 1945-46 Kiwi Army team and later an Auckland and North Island representative. A back injury suffered by Stewart in the match against South African Universities allowed Eveleigh to gain his place. In the Springbok side

a now fit Dawie Snyman regained the full-back berth with Ian Robertson returning to the centre position. Western Province's Chris Pope took over from first Test try scorer Krantz on the wing, whilst in the forwards a 21 year old giant seventeen stone two pound, six foot four and threequarter inch, Thuens Stofberg replaced the 33 year old Jan Ellis who was denied the opportunity of breaking the South African record of thirty-eight internationals he shared with Frik du Preez. Ellis's play in both the Durban Test and the tourists' match with Transvaal had been less than impressive.

Bosch kicked off for South Africa toward the southern end of the ground and after five minutes' play, Going, who had taken over the All Black goal-kicking had his first attempt at goal after a line-out obstruction three metres inside the Springbok 22 metre line. He duly goaled to open the scoring.

The next points came in the eighteenth minute when Bosch evened the score with a well struck penalty from 40 metres out. Three minutes later he missed a further opportunity from half-way. It was at this stage that the tall Springbok lock, John Williams, was forced to retire with a broken and badly cut nose and he was replaced by Kevin de Klerk. Some over-vigorous rucking in the twenty-seventh minute gave Sid Going, who had been on the ground during the ruck, a chance to put his side ahead from 30 metres out with the resultant penalty. He was successful and New Zealand led 6-3. Shortly after, Bruce was wide with a drop kick, but with half an hour gone the only try in the game was scored. From a scrum on the Springbok 22, Going moved right then threw a reverse pass to the left where his Mid-Northern club-mate Joe Morgan gathered and bolted through a wide gap left by the momentarily nonplussed defence. He completed his brilliant solo run by scoring to the left of the posts without a hand being laid on him. Going converted. Three minutes before the interval, the Springboks were awarded a line-out penalty inside the All Black 22 which Bosch took back to the 22 from where he goaled without difficulty. He missed a further attempt before the

---

NEW ZEALAND

C.L. FAWCETT
(Auckland)

B.G. WILLIAMS   B.J. ROBERTSON   G.B. BATTY *
(Auckland)   (Counties)   (Bay of Plenty)

J.E. MORGAN
(North Auckland)

O.D. BRUCE
(Canterbury)

S.M. GOING
(North Auckland)

A.R. LESLIE (**Capt.**)
(Wellington)

K.A. EVELEIGH   P.J. WHITING   H.H. MACDONALD   I.A. KIRKPATRICK
(Manawatu)   (Auckland)   (North Auckland) (Poverty Bay)

W.K. BUSH   R.W. NORTON   B.R. JOHNSTONE
(Canterbury)   (Canterbury)   (Auckland)

J.C.J. STANDER   R.J. COCKRELL   D.S. van den BERG
(Orange Free State) (Western Province) (Western Province)

J.H.H. COETZEE   J.G. WILLIAMS†   J.L. van HEERDEN   M.T.N. STOFBERG
(Western Province) (Northern Transvaal) (Northern Transvaal) (Orange Free State)

M. du PLESSIS (**Capt.**)
(Western Province)

P.C.R. BAYVEL
(Transvaal)

G.R. BOSCH
(Transvaal)

J.S. GERMISHUYS I.W. ROBERTSON J.J. OOSTHUIZEN   C.F. POPE
(Orange Free State) (Rhodesia)   (Western Province) (Western Province)

D.S.L. SNYMAN
(Western Province)

SOUTH AFRICA

REPLACEMENTS: * Replaced by W.M. Osborne (Wanganui)
              † Replaced by K.B.H. de Klerk (Transvaal)
REFEREE: Mr G. Bezuidenhout (Transvaal)
ATTENDANCE: 71,000
CONDITIONS: Weather fine, ground hard and dusty.
HALFTIME: New Zealand 12 South Africa 6

SCORERS
NEW ZEALAND   **SOUTH AFRICA**
Try: Morgan   Penalty goals: Bosch (3)
Conversion: Going
Penalty goals: Going (2)
Dropped goal: Bruce

SOUTH AFRICA

Free State Stadium, Bloemfontein

Joe Morgan leaves du Plessis sprawling and heads for the goal line to score his fine try. Fawcett is the other All Black in the picture.

break after Bryan Williams had been penalised for playing a tackled ball.

Batty, who had taken the field with a bandage covering a cumbersome-looking brace on his right knee, did not take his place until a couple of minutes had passed in the second spell and played only a further twelve minutes before leaving the field to be replaced by Bill Osborne who went to centre with Bruce Robertson going to the vacant left wing. In the meantime Going had missed a penalty after five minutes but three minutes later Bosch had struck again for South Africa, from 50 metres after the All Blacks had been marched back ten metres following a penalty at a short line-out. The score stood at 12-9 for the next eighteen minutes until the All Black forwards drove to within five metres of the

Springbok goal line where a scrum was awarded. New Zealand won the scrum and held the ball before letting it out to Going who threw a pass between his legs to Bruce standing behind him. The five-eighth calmly kicked a left-footed dropped goal to complete the scoring. South Africa then mounted attack after attack on the All Black line but great defence, by Morgan and Whiting in particular, thwarted these offensives. A tackle of a rampaging Coetzee in the corner by Whiting brought applause from the South African crowd.

Eight minutes from time Going had another shot at goal following a late charge on Fawcett by Pope but the kick from 10 metres outside the 22 was sliced wide. The game ended with New Zealand on attack and one promising move started by Eveleigh and carried on by Kirkpatrick was unlucky not to increase the New Zealand total.

It had been a hard-fought and dramatic match which New Zealand had well deserved to win.

4 September, 1976

Third Test

Both sides made changes for this vital Test. In the New Zealand team, a now fit Ken Stewart regained his place at the expense of Eveleigh despite the latter's fine performance in the second Test, whilst in the front row two changes were forced on the selectors. Johnstone, who like Eveleigh had created a favourable impression in the Bloemfontein Test, had aggravated a chest cartilage injury in the Northern Transvaal match and on medical advice was invalided out of the tour. His replacement was little-known Sanson farmer Perry Harris who had made his debut for Manawatu in 1970. After a rush trip from New Zealand where he had just assisted his province to lift the Ranfurly Shield from Auckland, he arrived in time to watch the tourists' match against Natal and play against the Leopards at East London. With Bush not considered because of an ankle injury, and Kerry Tanner still very much below top fitness, the choice of props was forced on the selectors as Harris and Lambert. The only change in the backs saw Duncan Robertson replace Bruce, who could be considered unfortunate to lose his place after his competent display at Bloemfontein.

The Springboks also made two changes to their front row with the Transvaal strong man, Johan Strauss replacing van den Berg at tight-head prop, and controversial hooker "Piston" van Wyk coming in for Cockrell. Van Wyk had played in all four internationals against New Zealand in 1970. As expected Kevin de Klerk held his place, but the dropping of Ian Robertson to the reserves to allow Peter Whipp to regain his place and the retention of Snyman at full-back were rather surprising.

Since the previous Test the All Blacks had achieved a remarkable last minute win over a Quagga-Barbarian side 32-31 after fighting back from a 9-31 deficit, a last minute loss to Northern Transvaal 27-29, and comfortable victories over a Transvaal Country XV, Natal and the Bantu 'Leopard' side.

A fresh northerly breeze favoured the All Blacks as Williams kicked off. Both Bosch and Williams missed long distance penalty attempts in the opening minutes before New Zealand notched the first points. A long kick into Springbok territory saw Germishuys under pressure as he tried to clear. A pass in-field went loose and Bruce Robertson got to the scene in time to toe the ball ahead, gather it and score in the right hand corner. Going's attempted conversion was wide.

Quarter of an hour had elapsed before Bosch opened the Springbok scoring with a penalty from 30 metres. Midway through the half Going missed a simple penalty from inside the 22, but five minutes later Bryan Williams landed a fine goal from five metres inside his own half to make it 7-3 to the tourists. The Springboks then spent the next ten minutes on attack during which time Bosch landed a further penalty after the All Blacks had been marched up-field 10 metres for disputing a referee's decision. The Springbok fly-half missed two other penalty attempts in this period.

NEW ZEALAND
C.L. FAWCETT
(Auckland)
B.G. WILLIAMS B.J. ROBERTSON G.B. BATTY
(Auckland) (Counties) (Bay of Plenty)
J.E. MORGAN
(North Auckland)
D.J. ROBERTSON
(Otago)
S.M. GOING
(North Auckland)
A.R. LESLIE (Capt.)
(Wellington)
I.A. KIRKPATRICK P.J. WHITING H.H. MACDONALD K.W. STEWART
(Poverty Bay) (Auckland) (North Auckland) (Southland)
K.K. LAMBERT R.W. NORTON P.C. HARRIS
(Manawatu) (Canterbury) (Manawatu)

J.C.J. STANDER J.F.B. van WYK J.H.P. STRAUSS
(Orange Free State) (Northern Transvaal) (Transvaal)
J.H.H. COETZEE K.B.H. de KLERK J.L. van HEERDEN M.T.N. STOFBERG
(Western (Transvaal) (Northern (Orange Free
Province) Transvaal) State)
M. du PLESSIS (Capt.)
(Western Province)
P.C.R. BAYVEL
(Transvaal)
G.R. BOSCH
(Transvaal)
J.S. GERMISHUYS P.J.M. WHIPP J.J. OOSTHUIZEN C.F. POPE
(Orange Free (Western (Western (Western
State) Province) Province) Province)
D.S.L. SNYMAN
(Western Province)
SOUTH AFRICA

REFEREE: Mr G. Bezuidenhout (Transvaal)
ATTENDANCE: 47,000
CONDITIONS: Weather fine with fresh breeze, ground firm.
HALFTIME: New Zealand 7 South Africa 6

SCORERS
NEW ZEALAND
Try: B.J. Robertson
Penalty goals: Williams (2)

SOUTH AFRICA
Try: Oosthuizen
Conversion: Bosch
Penalty goals: Bosch (2)
Dropped goal: Snyman

N W Z ALAND 10

Newlands, Cape Town

Just before the interval a strange ruling by the referee deprived New Zealand of a further penalty attempt when he disallowed a shot at goal from 28 metres after Going had the placed ball topple over twice as he prepared to kick. A slim lead of only one point and the prospect of playing into the stiff breeze in the second half ensured that the All Blacks would have to struggle to gain a victory.

From the restart they went on to attack and after eight minutes Going failed with another penalty attempt, this time from 30 metres. Bosch rather surprisingly missed a close range penalty five minutes later as the South Africans commenced their sustained pressure on the All Black line. In the eighteenth minute of the spell an error by the All Black backline saw the Springboks gratefully accept an opportunity to swing the match irretrievably in their favour.

From a line-out inside their half the All Black backs moved the ball quickly to their right where Morgan threw a long pass across Bruce Robertson to Fawcett who had come up into the movement. The full-back was unable to take the high pass and the ball rebounded from his shoulder into the air where Johan Oosthuizen gathered it and set off down field through the unguarded territory. His 45 metre run ended when he scored by the posts to give Bosch an easy conversion.

Eight minutes later Bosch hit the posts with a penalty from the 22 and the ball rebounded away. From one of the All Blacks' rare incursions into Springbok territory during the second half Williams was given a chance at goal from the right hand touchline 12 metres outside the 22. He successfully goaled the kick to put New Zealand within two points of the South African total with ten minutes to play. However the Springbok front row had been exerting tremendous pressure, with the tighthead prop Strauss in particular appearing to adopt questionable tactics, which were seriously disrupting the All Black pattern. In addition Fawcett who had had a good first half was proving vulnerable under the high kicks that the Springboks were hoisting.

In fact it was the home team that did the attacking in the final ten minutes of the match. Bosch

AUCKLAND STAR

De Klerk secures possession in this lineout with help from his team mates. Going gets a "worm's-eye view" of the incident.

missed a wide angle penalty before Going, in attempting to clear from a defensive scrum, missed the touch line and Snyman gathered to move in and hammer home a left-footed drop goal from 35 metres, to complete the scoring.

It had been a match that had been lost by New Zealand through errors at vital times and inconsistent goalkicking.

SOUTH AFRICA 15

18 September, 1976

Fourth Test

Since the third Test the All Blacks had won two mid-week matches but had gone down to a strong Orange Free State side 10-15 in their Saturday match. This loss gave rise to serious doubts that the All Blacks could square the series at Ellis Park for their form at Bloemfontein in this match had been below standard.

The Test selection saw several changes to the line-up. A major surprise was the inclusion of Duncan Robertson again at full-back, a position he had occupied without distinction in the first Test and had not played in since. Doug Bruce replaced him at first five-eighth. In the forwards Kevin Eveleigh came in for Stewart on the side of the scrum, and Frank Oliver, after some sterling performances throughout the tour, took over from Macdonald. In the front row Kent Lambert switched to the loose head to allow Bush to regain his place at tighthead prop.

The Springbok selectors made two changes to their side reintroducing Ian Robertson at full-back in place of Snyman, and bringing in the eighteen stone Free State lock, "Klippies" Kritzinger who had won six caps for South Africa, on the side of the scrum in place of Stofberg.

New Zealand were first to score in the match after five minutes when Going ran on the blindside from a ruck near the Springbok 22 before passing to Norton who quickly got the ball to Kirkpatrick and the flanker crossed in the left hand corner. Going's attempted conversion was well astray. Two minutes later Bosch received the ball from a scrum and from nearly 40 metres out landed a well-judged dropped goal. For the next twenty-five minutes the hard, tense struggle continued to ebb and flow up and down the field with neither side being able to assert domination over the other. After thirty-five minutes a maul formed in the Springbok left hand corner and as the ball emerged on the All Black side Going slipped around the open side and burrowed his way through Kritzinger's tackle to score eight metres in from the corner. Again Going's attempted conversion was well wide.

Near the end of the first half the Springboks

Kevin Eveleigh prepares to pass as Oosthuizen closes in on him.

won a five metre scrum and Kritzinger, who had swopped places with du Plessis for this scrum picked up the ball and surged at the New Zealand goal line around the open side. Eveleigh failed to halt the movement and the giant loose forward crossed in Bruce's tackle. Bosch, showing again his goal kicking ability, comfortably landed the conversion. Williams was given a 50 metre shot at goal which fell short and was knocked on near the call of halftime. The resulting scrum saw a desperate attack by New Zealand in the

N W ZEALAND 14

Ellis Park, Johannesburg

Springbok goal mouth but further points did not come and the interval was reached with South Africa holding a one point lead.

Doug Bruce was able to put the All Blacks into the lead six minutes into the second spell after he had taken Going's clearing pass from a ruck with his back to the goal posts. He spun quickly, sighted the posts and kicked a neat left-footed dropped goal.

The lead was short lived however and two minutes later Bush was penalised at a line-out 30 metres from the New Zealand line and Bosch again landed the goal. Quarter of an hour had passed when the the most controversial moment of the match occurred. From an attacking movement by the All Blacks, Bruce Robertson received the ball from Eveleigh inside the South African 22 and being covered, chipped a kick ahead into the Springbok in-goal. As he accelerated to follow the ball his Springbok name-sake Ian blatantly obstructed him and the chance to score a try was lost. Mr Bezuidenhout awarded a penalty for the obstruction which Bryan Williams duly landed from a metre outside the 22 and eight metres in from the left hand touch line. However, many in the All Black camp, and critics, including the well known Rugby writer from London's *Daily Telegraph,* John Reason, were of the opinion that a penalty try should have been awarded. This opinion was also expressed by the president of the South African Rugby Board, Dr. Danie Craven at the reception after the match.

For the second time in the series Grant Batty was forced to retire with his troublesome knee twenty-eight minutes into the half and was replaced by Terry Mitchell playing in his first international. A minute later a line-out penalty was awarded to South Africa five metres outside the All Black 22 and Gerald Bosch came forward to kick the goal, taking South Africa back into a one point lead. A slightly concussed Joe Morgan left the field two minutes later and was replaced by Osborne. The final eight minutes of this desperately fought match were played in a very tense atmosphere but the All Blacks were unable to snatch the lead back. They were extremely unlucky not to have won this match and square the series.

Although the New Zealanders were incensed at the referees' rulings throughout the series, shortcomings in the All Blacks' play, notably, goalkicking and at full-back, were also responsible for their loss in the Test series.

This was the last international played by captain Andy Leslie and lock Peter Whiting, both announcing their retirement at the start of the 1977 season.

Leslie had captained for his country in all ten Tests he had played since his debut in 1974 and the three internationals lost in the 1976 series were the only reverses suffered during this period. Since his debut in 1971 "Pole" Whiting, the six foot six inch lock had appeared in twenty Tests and had been referred to by some critics as the best line-out player in the world. His form during the 1976 series had, despite nagging injuries, been the best of his career.

NEW ZEALAND

D.J. ROBERTSON
(Otago)

B.G. WILLIAMS   B.J. ROBERTSON   G.B. BATTY *
(Auckland)   (Counties)   (Bay of Plenty)

J.E. MORGAN **
(North Auckland)

O.D. BRUCE
(Canterbury)

S.M. GOING
(North Auckland)

A.R. LESLIE (**Capt.**)
(Wellington)

I.A. KIRKPATRICK   F.J. OLIVER   P.J. WHITING   K.A. EVELEIGH
(Poverty Bay)   (Southland)   (Auckland)   (Manawatu)

W.K. BUSH   R.W. NORTON   K.K. LAMBERT
(Canterbury)   (Canterbury)   (Manawatu)

J.C.J. STANDER   J.F.B. van WYK   J.H.P. STRAUSS
(Orange Free State)   (Northern Transvaal)   (Transvaal)

J.H.H. COETZEE   K.B.H. de KLERK   J.L. van HEERDEN   J.L. KRITZINGER
(Western Province)   (Transvaal)   (Northern Transvaal)   (Orange Free State)

M. du PLESSIS (**Capt.**)
(Western Province)

P.O.R. BAYVEL
(Transvaal)

G.R. BOSCH
(Transvaal)

J.S. GERMISHUYS   P.J.M. WHIPP   J.J. OOSTHUIZEN   C.F. POPE
(Orange Free State)   (Western Province)   (Western Province)   (Western Province)

I.W. ROBERTSON
(Rhodesia)

SOUTH AFRICA

REPLACEMENTS: *Replaced by T.W. Mitchell (Canterbury)
     ** Replaced by W.M. Osborne (Wanganui)
REFEREE: Mr G. Bezuidenhout (Transvaal)
ATTENDANCE: 75,000
CONDITIONS: Weather sunny and hot, ground hard
HALFTIME: South Africa 9, New Zealand 8

SCORERS

NEW ZEALAND	SOUTH AFRICA
Tries: Kirkpatrick, Going	Try: Kritzinger
Penalty goal: Williams	Conversion: Bosch
Dropped goal: Bruce	Penalty goals: Bosch (2)
	Dropped goal: Bosch

18 June, 1977

First Test

There were only three new caps in the New Zealand team for the first Test of 1977. They were 21 year old Colin Farrell, who had represented Auckland at full-back since 1974, lock Andy Haden and the big loose forward from Gisborne, Lawrie Knight. Farrell's selection came as a great surprise to most Rugby followers as he had not been given a run in the trials. Knight, however, had been an All Black since 1974 and his selection in this, his first Test team, was generally predicted. A former Aucklander, he is the son of 1925 All Black Lawrie Knight and the nephew of "Bubs" Knight, who played for New Zealand in 1926-28-34. Unfortunately, Lawrie senior died a few months before his son became an All Black. Haden had toured Britain in 1972-73 and went to Argentina in 1976.

The 1977 Lions had lost only one game prior to the first Test, going down 21-9 to New Zealand Universities four days before the interna-tional. They were a very good side but they lacked the real class of the 1971 team, who also enjoyed better public relations than did the 1977 tourists.

A number of the touring party had been to New Zealand before. The manager, George Burrell, a former international referee who had been capped for Scotland, was the manager of the 1975 Scottish team while coach John Dawes was a member of the 1969 Welsh team and captain of the 1971 Lions. The captain, Phil Bennett, had also visited New Zealand with Wales in 1969 as understudy to Barry John. Other 1977 Lions who were veterans of former tours were Mike Gibson the great Irish back who surprisingly was not played in any of the Tests, Bruce Hay, Andy Irvine, Ian McGeechan, Peter Squires, Douglas

Batty scores a brilliant solo try after his interception and 60 metre run. The Lions are Price and Irvine.

DOMINION

Athletic Park, Wellington

Morgan, Derek Quinnell, Willie Duggan, Tony Neary, Gordon Brown, Moss Keane, Phil Orr and Fran Cotton.

The game had been in progress only two minutes when the Lions took the lead. From a line-out the New Zealand forwards were ruled offside and Irvine kicked a splendid goal from just inside his own half with the aid of the southerly wind.

New Zealand attacked from the re-start and the home forwards were gaining the ascendancy. With five minutes of the game gone, they won a line-out and the ball went along the backline to Osborne, who burst through before sending on to Robertson. The ball reached Batty, who went as far as he could before setting up a ruck. Going received and was about to pass to Duncan Robertson when he decided to break in the opposite direction. The way was blocked however so he changed direction again to run through the Lions' pack and dive over for a fine solo try. Williams failed to convert.

The All Black forwards continued to dominate but the backs made little use of the ball. Good kicking by Bennett and Irvine saved the Lions repeatedly and eventually the visitors worked their way into home territory. Duncan Robertson was caught offside at a scrum and Bennett goaled from 45 metres. A few minutes later Robertson gave away another penalty, this time for obstruction, and once again Bennett made no mistake.

With only five minutes of the first half left, Bryan Williams took a penalty shot. The ball was held up in the strong wind before dropping just in front of the posts where it bounced off Bennett. Johnstone, who had been following up, gathered the ball to score. Williams converted and New Zealand took the lead again.

A minute later, Going was penalised for not putting the ball into a scrum correctly and Bennett kicked an easy goal. Once more the Lions had taken the lead.

In the closing stages of the first half, the Lions won a scrum in their own half. Brynmor Williams received and broke. He then threw a pass in-field to Fenwick who linked up with his

flanker, Evans. The latter was heavily tackled by Bruce Robertson as he got his pass away to Bennett. However, the visiting captain did not receive the pass, for Batty intercepted it and set sail for the line with Irvine, who had come up into the backline, and Price after him. The flying winger ran some 60 metres, with Irvine closing on him rapidly, to score beside the posts as the crowd went wild. Williams converted and the All Blacks went into the second spell with a four point lead.

The second half proved to be one of the dullest seen in a Test match in New Zealand. The home forwards won a great deal of possession but the ball was not put to good use. Going threw some very bad passes to Duncan Robertson who further hindered his backs by poor kicking and by being caught in possession. As a result the speedy All Black three-quarters hardly saw the ball. Starved of possession, the Lions could only defend, which they did well enough to prevent any further scoring and there was no improvement on the halftime score.

NEW ZEALAND

C.P. FARRELL
(Auckland)

| B.G. WILLIAMS (Auckland) | B.J. ROBERTSON (Counties) | G.B. BATTY (Bay of Plenty) |

W.M. OSBORNE
(Wanganui)

D.J. ROBERTSON
(Otago)

S.M. GOING
(North Auckland)

L.G. KNIGHT
(Poverty Bay)

| K.A. EVELEIGH (Manawatu) | F.J. OLIVER (Southland) | A.M. HADEN (Auckland) | I.A. KIRKPATRICK (Poverty Bay) |
| K.K. LAMBERT (Manawatu) | R.W. NORTON (Capt.) (Canterbury) | | B.R. JOHNSTONE (Auckland) |

| P.A. ORR (Old Wesley & Ireland) | R.W. WINDSOR (Pontypool & Wales) | | G. PRICE (Pontypool & Wales) |
| T.J. COBNER (Pontypool & Wales) | A.J. MARTIN (Aberavon & Wales) | M.I. KEANE (Lansdowne & Ireland) | T.P. EVANS (Swansea & Wales) |

W.P. DUGGAN
(Blackrock College & Ireland)

D.B. WILLIAMS
(Cardiff)

P. BENNETT (Capt.)
(Llanelli & Wales)

| J.J. WILLIAMS (Llanelli & Wales) | I.R. McGEECHAN (Headingley & Scotland) | S.P. FENWICK (Bridgend & Wales) | P.J. SQUIRES (Harrogate & England) |

A.R. IRVINE
(Heriot's F.P. & Scotland)

BRITISH ISLES

REFEREE: Mr P.A. McDavitt (Wellington)
ATTENDANCE: 43,000
CONDITIONS: Overcast and cold with light rain, ground soft
HALFTIME: New Zealand 16, British Isles 12

SCORERS

NEW ZEALAND	BRITISH ISLES
Tries: Going, Johnstone, Batty	Penalty goals: Bennett (3),
Conversions: Williams (2)	Irvine

9 July, 1977

Second Test

New Zealand's original selection for the second Test contained only two changes. Duncan Robertson was dropped for Doug Bruce to return to Test football and Lambert, who was ill was replaced by Bill Bush, who had played his first international in 1974. Thus there were no new caps until Batty, after a training session at Lincoln College, found that his knee, which had been troubling him since before the South African tour, was by no means right. He dropped a bombshell by not only withdrawing from the team but also by announcing his retirement from Rugby. His place was taken by Mark Taylor who had toured Argentina in 1976 and was now to play his first Test. Then Bruce Robertson also withdrew with concussion received in the

Counties-Auckland match and Bill Osborne was moved to centre with Lyn Jaffray coming in at second five-eighth to play his fifth Test.

The Lions made six changes, all based on current form, for the whole touring party was fit at this stage. The changes in the pack were predictable for Brown and Beaumont were undoubtedly a better pair of locks than Keane and Martin while Quinnell strengthened the loose forwards considerably. Cotton and Wheeler also had a slight edge on Orr and Windsor. However, the dropping of Squires for Gareth Evans hardly seemed justified.

As a spectacle this was a poor game. There was very little excitement and it was not played in the best of spirits, an all-out brawl which followed a late tackle by Eveleigh on Bennett being particularly nasty.

The Lions began well and soon had the All Blacks back on their heels. Within seven minutes Bennett had opened the scoring with a 30 metre

Bryan Williams kicks one of his three successful penalty goals in this Test.

CHRISTCHURCH STAR

NEW ZEALAND

C.P. FARRELL
(Auckland)

B.G. WILLIAMS   W.M. OSBORNE   N.M. TAYLOR
(Auckland)   (Wanganui)   (Bay of Plenty)

J.L. JAFFRAY
(Otago)

O.D. BRUCE
(Canterbury)

S.M. GOING
(North Auckland)

L.G. KNIGHT
(Poverty Bay)

K.A. EVELEIGH   F.J. OLIVER   A.M. HADEN   I.A. KIRKPATRICK
(Manawatu)   (Southland)   (Auckland)   (Poverty Bay)

W.K. BUSH   R.W. NORTON (**Capt.**)   B.R. JOHNSTONE
(Canterbury)   (Canterbury)   (Auckland)

F.E. COTTON   P.J. WHEELER   G. PRICE
(Sale & England)   (Leicester & England)   (Pontypool & Wales)

T.J. COBNER   W.B. BEAUMONT   G.L. BROWN   D.L. QUINNELL
(Pontypool   (Fylde &   (West of Scotland   (Llanelli &
& Wales)   England)   & Scotland)   Wales)

W.P. DUGGAN
(Blackrock College & Ireland)

D.B. WILLIAMS
(Cardiff)

P. BENNETT (**Capt.**)
(Llanelli & Wales)

G.L. EVANS   I.R. McGEECHAN   S.P. FENWICK   J.J. WILLIAMS
(Newport &   (Headingley &   (Bridgend &   (Llanelli &
Wales)   Scotland)   Wales)   Wales)

A.R. IRVINE
(Heriot's F.P. & Scotland)

BRITISH ISLES

REFEREE: Mr B.W. Duffy (Taranaki)
ATTENDANCE: 50,000
CONDITIONS: Cold and clear, ground very heavy
HALFTIME: British Isles 13, New Zealand 6

SCORERS

NEW ZEALAND	**BRITISH ISLES**
Penalty goals: Williams (3)	Try: J.J. Williams
	Penalty goals: Bennett (3)

NEW ZEALAND

Lancaster Park, Christchurch

penalty goal after Going had been caught offside. Eight minutes later the visiting captain put a short kick into the centre of the field following a line-out then speculated the ball further forward where Farrell failed to gather. Brown gained possession from a maul and sent on to Quinnell, who passed to McGeechan. Finally, the ball went to the Lions' right wing, Williams, who sold Taylor a dummy and went on to score in the corner. Bennett's conversion hit the upright and bounced away.

The tourists had by now established a marked superiority, especially in the mauls, where Brown, Duggan and Quinnell were outstanding. Play was taking place mostly in New Zealand's half and in the twentieth minute Bennett increased his team's lead when he put over another penalty goal from a handy position.

Four minutes later the Lions were caught offside and Bryan Williams, who had missed several shots at goal, at last opened the All Blacks' account with a kick from in front of the posts. The Lions were still looking the better side however and twenty-eight minutes into the half Bennett kicked his third penalty when Going fed the scrum illegally.

With ten minutes of the first spell remaining, Bryan Williams kicked a simple penalty after offside play by the Lions at a ruck to take the score to 13-6. Both Williams and Irvine were short with penalty attempts and there was no further scoring before halftime.

The second half was a rather drab affair, marred by the brawl mentioned above after eleven minutes. Williams failed with two relatively easy penalty kicks early in the half and he failed again in the twenty-fifth minute. After thirty minutes however he kicked one from 35 metres and New Zealand needed only a converted try to win.

The All Blacks certainly tried hard to score in the closing stages of the game. Going, Kirkpatrick and Haden all went close to tries and in the last moment Osborne broke through after working a scissors with Going. The New Zealand centre drew Fenwick and McGeechan before tossing a high pass to Jaffray who had burst up outside him. Jaffray juggled the ball but finally

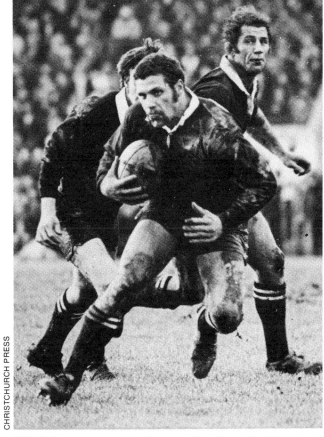

CHRISTCHURCH PRESS

Bill Osborne props to change direction. Eveleigh is in close support.

lost it across the line, where Evans forced down. Had Jaffray managed to hold the pass he could have scored under the bar and the Lions would very likely have been robbed of a win which they deserved.

The retirement of Batty before this Test was a serious blow to New Zealand Rugby. Rated by a number of writers as currently one of the best left wings in the world, Batty was without question a most talented All Black. He scored forty-five tries in fifty-six matches for New Zealand, a very good average even for a wing three-quarter. Rather on the small side as modern players go, Batty was nevertheless exceptionally strong and he could hold his own against much bigger opponents. Kevin Eveleigh announced his retirement from international play at the end of this season and this was the last of his four Tests.

30 July, 1977

Third Test

The New Zealand selectors made six changes to the team which had been beaten by the Lions at Christchurch. The young Otago full-back, Bevan Wilson, replaced Farrell to make his Test debut and Bruce Robertson, restored to fitness, came back to the centre berth for Osborne to move in to second five-eighth in place of Jaffray. Taylor gave way to another new cap, Brian Ford from Kaikoura.

Once again Going was replaced by Lyn Davis. The dropping of the great North Auckland half-back caused much argument among followers of the game, especially after his outstanding display for New Zealand Maoris against the tourists. However, his passing in the first two Tests had been below par and the very fine All Black backline had not been able to function to the best of its ability. New Zealand's most capped half-back, Going made a tremendous contribution to Rugby at all levels. Very strong and tough, he proved a match-winner over and over again with his devastating running close to the goal line. It is interesting to note that Davis had acted as an All Black reserve in both the 1966 and 1971 series against the British tourists. Kevin Eveleigh was dropped in favour of Graham Mourie, who had been the All Black captain in Argentina and who was now to play his first official Test. Another Argentinian tourist, John McEldowney, took Johnstone's place at loose-head prop.

The Lions made only one change from their second Test team, David Burcher taking Ian McGeechan's place at centre. No doubt the visitors thought the home selectors were in a state of panic and the Lions were confident of another win.

This match had a most spectacular beginning. From the kick-off by Bryan Williams, Bennett fielded the ball and found touch near his own 10 metre line. New Zealand won the line-out and the ball went along the chain to Robertson, who chipped a kick through. The Lions' defence were unable to control the ball and as it rolled over the line Kirkpatrick was there to score a try after fifty-four seconds. While the Lions were still re-

covering from the shock Wilson was lining up the ball to kick at goal. From wide out he added the extra points and the All Blacks were six points up in the first minute.

Irvine had a chance to close the gap when Knight was caught offside at a ruck 46 metres out but he hooked to the left of the posts. From the drop out the home pack drove forward. A set scrum was ordered and from this Bennett found touch near the All Blacks' line. Another scrum followed the line-out and once more the Lions heeled. Their scrum-half, Brynmor Williams, broke around the blindside and sent the ball infield to Duggan. The latter forced his way over in the corner but Bennett missed the conversion to leave the All Blacks in front by two points after seven minutes.

Bryan Williams had a shot at goal from 55 metres when his namesake Brynmor was caught

---

NEW ZEALAND

B.W. WILSON
(Otago)

B.G. WILLIAMS	B.J. ROBERTSON	B.R. FORD
(Auckland)	(Counties)	(Marlborough)

W.M. OSBORNE
(Wanganui)

O.D. BRUCE
(Canterbury)

L.J. DAVIS
(Canterbury)

L.G. KNIGHT
(Poverty Bay)

I.A. KIRKPATRICK	F.J. OLIVER	A.M. HADEN	G.N.K. MOURIE
(Poverty Bay)	(Southland)	(Auckland)	(Taranaki)
W.K. BUSH	R.W. NORTON (**Capt.**)		J.T. McELDOWNEY
(Canterbury)	(Canterbury)		(Taranaki)

F.E. COTTON	P.J. WHEELER	G. PRICE
(Sale & England)	(Leicester & England)	(Pontypool & Wales)
T.J. COBNER	W.B. BEAUMONT	G.L. BROWN	D.L. QUINNELL
(Pontypool &	(Fylde &	(West of Scotland	(Llanelli &
Wales)	England)	& Scotland)	Wales)

W.P. DUGGAN
(Blackrock College & Ireland)

D.B. WILLIAMS †
(Cardiff)

P. BENNETT (**Capt.**)
(Llanelli & Wales)

G.L. EVANS	D.H. BURCHER	S.P. FENWICK	J.J. WILLIAMS ††
(Newport & Wales)	(Newport & Wales)	(Bridgend & Wales)	(Llanelli & Wales)

A.R. IRVINE
(Heriot's F.P. & Scotland)

BRITISH ISLES

REPLACEMENTS: † Replaced by D.W. Morgan (Stewart's Melville F.P. & Scotland)
†† Replaced by I.R. McGeechan (Headingley & Scotland)
REFEREE: Mr D.H. Millar (Otago)
ATTENDANCE: 43,000
CONDITIONS: Fine and cold, ground soft
HALFTIME: New Zealand 10, British Isles 4

SCORERS

NEW ZEALAND	BRITISH ISLES
Tries: Kirkpatrick, Haden	Try: Duggan
Conversion: Wilson	Penalty goal: Irvine
Penalty goals: Wilson (2)	
Dropped goal: Robertson	

offside at a scrum but the ball fell short. Bennett kicked back into New Zealand territory but good line-kicking by Wilson drove the Lions back. Then from a drop-out by the visitors a scrum was ordered for a man in front. Norton hooked cleanly and the ball came to Bruce, who changed direction before linking up with Ford on the blindside. A ruck formed on the British goal line, the ball came loose and Haden got a hand to it five metres in from the corner to put New Zealand six points ahead. Wilson failed to convert.

The Lions' backs hoisted a few high kicks up to Wilson but the youngster never faltered. Playing in front of his home crowd, he gave a splendid exhibition of fielding and touch finding. He had a chance to put his team further ahead when Duggan was offside in a line-out but the ball was wide of the posts.

The All Black forwards kept bustling the Lions and Mourie just missed scoring when he dived from a line-out. However, the Lions managed to work their way upfield where Bennett missed a penalty shot from 35 metres. Shortly after, McGeechan replaced J.J. Williams who had suffered a leg injury. McGeechan went to the left wing for Evans to change to the right.

New Zealand spent most of the rest of the half on attack but could not score again and the halftime whistle sounded with the score at 10-4.

Irvine re-started the game and Wilson picked up the ball on the bounce to kick to touch. The Lions won two line-outs in quick succession to give their backs a run but the New Zealand tackling was good and the visitors failed to make ground. The Lions kept the pressure on however and for a time it looked as though New Zealand would not win back the initiative.

The Lions' scrum-half, Williams, came off for medical attention in the tenth minute of the half and Cobner moved in behind the scrum until Morgan came on. Davis was caught offside at a scrum in an easy position for Bennett to goal but the British captain missed. However, Irvine succeeded from in front of the New Zealand posts shortly after and made the score 10-7.

Now very much in the game, the Lions kept up a determined attack but an interception by Bruce, who kicked down to the British line, almost led to a try, Fenwick just beating Williams to the touch-down. The All Blacks kept the pressure on and when they were awarded a penalty from a ruck, Wilson landed a good goal from 30 metres.

Irvine had a chance to shorten New Zealand's lead again when he was late-tackled by Bush but he failed from a handy position. Then the All Blacks looked dangerous again when Mourie broke away with the whole team in support but the Lions counter-attacked. The ball eventually came to Bruce, who relieved with a kick.

Both teams did their share of attacking but it was the home side that managed to score the points. The Lions conceded a penalty for offside in centre field and from 38 metres Wilson made no mistake.

A brilliant break by Haden was supported by backs and forwards and Ford dived over among a mass of defenders but a five metre scrum was ordered. From this scrum the All Blacks were penalised and the Lions relieved.

Following a series of line-outs a penalty gave the Lions a chance to run the ball from a tap kick but nothing came of the movement. Another penalty followed in centre field but Irvine missed the goal.

In the closing moments of the game, the All Blacks threw everything into the attack. Kirkpatrick kicked through and from a maul the ball came back to Davis, who sent a long pass out to Robertson. The centre calmly dropped a goal from right in front and the whistle sounded for full time.

N W ZEALAND 10

13 August, 1977

Fourth Test

The only changes in the New Zealand team for this deciding match of the series were in the front row, where Bush and McEldowney gave way to Johnstone and Lambert. The latter, widely regarded as the best prop in the country, had now recovered from the appendectomy which had kept him out of the second and third Tests and his return was welcomed. However, Johnstone pulled a hamstring at training and McEldowney was restored to the team with Bush going into the reserves.

Cobner and Quinnell were injured and their places were taken by Squire and Neary. McGeechan regained his Test place ahead of Burcher on merit but the uncapped winger, Elgan Rees, was a late replacement for John Williams, who had injured himself at training on the Thursday before the game.

There was intense interest in this game, for which Eden Park was a complete sell-out. Trafficking in tickets was rife and a number changed hands at greatly inflated prices.

Bennett kicked off and Williams returned the ball to touch. The Lions won the first line-out and Ford fumbled a kick through. From the resulting scrum the visitors gained possession again and their backs moved the ball but New Zealand cleared.

The first exciting move in the game came from a scrum following a line-out. The ball came to Robertson who made a brilliant break but Bennett managed to clip his heels and bring him down. A good kick by Davis was chased by Ford but the ball beat him into touch. A scrum followed the line-out and the Lions' backs were caught offside for Wilson to open the scoring from a handy position.

The Lions were quickly on attack from the kick off. They won a line-out in the All Blacks' half but Morgan was well wrapped up by Mourie. However, the visiting forwards had established dominance at this stage and they were giving their backs a great deal of possession. New Zealand conceded a line-out penalty and Morgan equalised the scores after twenty-five minutes.

The Lions kept New Zealand under pressure and only good kicking by Wilson kept the home line safe. Irvine came into a back movement but he was stopped by sound tackling. Then it was New Zealand's turn to attack when Williams chopped through but Bennett was back to pass to Irvine, who found touch.

With the first half ticking away the British forwards broke from a line-out. They were stopped on the home 22 metre line but Fenwick picked up. He was tackled but Morgan gained possession from the ruck and ran wide to break through Wilson's tackle for a good try, which he converted himself.

The British forwards kept attacking for the rest of the half, Price being especially prominent, but there was no more scoring in the first spell.

Early in the second half Bruce put New Zealand on attack with a fine kick. The All Black backs made a good break from a scrum with Wilson in the line but he lost the ball when a try looked imminent.

Ford gashed his knee and retired for Taylor to take his place. Just after Ford had left the field, the home backs had two runs and Irvine had to move quickly to clear as Williams charged through after a kick. Shortly after McEldowney injured his shoulder and was replaced by Bush. Before Bush arrived on the field the All Blacks packed a three man scrum on one occasion but the referee blew for an infringement and the controversial experiment was not tried again.

The Lions' forwards were so superior that New Zealand gained very little clean possession and it was only the good defence of the All Blacks that kept the visitors from scoring. From a tap kick the home team gained little ground but Norton won a tighthead from a set scrum and his backs attacked hotly. Then the British forwards gave away a scrum penalty near their own posts and Wilson kicked an easy goal.

Knight and Mourie broke from a scrum shortly after the kick-off but they were held up and from a penalty awarded to the Lions Irvine place-kicked to touch. The ball was worked back into New Zealand territory where the All Blacks counter-

Eden Park, Auckland

attacked from their own line. When Bennett failed to find touch Osborne kicked ahead from half-way and when Fenwick fielded the ball Osborne was there to bowl him over as he flung a pass to Wheeler. Mourie knocked the Lions' hooker over and the ball spilled loose. Knight picked it up and stormed to the corner 10 metres away as the crowd went mad. Wilson missed the conversion.

With four minutes to play the Lions were desperate. They kicked into the New Zealand half but Taylor made a good run to over half-way, where a defensive penalty was awarded to the visitors. They ran the ball but the New Zealand forwards held them up.

From a ruck the British backs ran the ball again and Rees kicked ahead but it went out in the corner when Robertson narrowly beat the kicker to the ball. From the resulting line-out a scrum was awarded and the Lions tried for a push-over try but another scrum was ordered and

NZ HERALD

Lions captain, Phil Bennett, is obviously distressed by his team's loss of the series. Tane Norton joins in the crowd's farewell song to the tourists.

this time Duggan detached himself and picked up the ball. As he plunged forward he was held up inches from the line and yet another scrum was given. The Lions' backs tried to find an opening but Irvine knocked on a low pass and Mr Millar blew his whistle to end the game.

That the All Blacks were lucky to win most people would agree, but any team which gained as much possession as the visitors did at Eden Park should have won handsomely yet the Lions could manage only one try.

The All Black captain Tane Norton announced his retirement before the season ended. He had hooked for New Zealand in every Test match since the first international of the 1971 series against the Lions and had given sterling service.

This was also the final Test for tough prop Kent Lambert who signed with the Sydney League Club, Penrith during the summer months. Since his Test debut as a replacement against Scotland in 1972 he had played in eleven internationals.

NEW ZEALAND

B.W. WILSON
(Otago)

B.G. WILLIAMS	B.J. ROBERTSON	B.R. FORD *
(Auckland)	(Counties)	(Marlborough)

W.M. OSBORNE
(Wanganui)

O.D. BRUCE
(Canterbury)

L.J. DAVIS
(Canterbury)

L.G. KNIGHT
(Poverty Bay)

I.A. KIRKPATRICK	F.J. OLIVER	A.M. HADEN	G.N.K. MOURIE
(Poverty Bay)	(Southland)	(Auckland)	(Taranaki)
K.K. LAMBERT	R.W. NORTON (**Capt.**)		J.T. McELDOWNEY**
(Manawatu)	(Canterbury)		(Taranaki)

F.E. COTTON	P.J. WHEELER	G. PRICE
(Sale & England)	(Leicester & England)	(Pontypool & Wales)
A. NEARY	W.B. BEAUMONT G.L. BROWN	J. SQUIRE
(Broughton Park	(Fylde & (West of Scotland	(Newport &
& England)	England) & Scotland)	Wales)

W.P. DUGGAN
(Blackrock Coll. & Ireland)

D.W. MORGAN
(Stewart's Melville F.P. & Scotland)

P. BENNETT (**Capt.**)
(Llanelli & Wales)

G.L. EVANS	S.P. FENWICK	I.R. McGEECHAN	H.E. REES
(Newport & Wales)	(Bridgend & Wales)	(Headingley & Scotland)	(Neath)

A.R. IRVINE
(Heriot's F.P. & Scotland)

BRITISH ISLES

REPLACEMENTS: * Replaced by N.M. Taylor (Bay of Plenty)
** Replaced by W.K. Bush (Canterbury)

REFEREE: Mr D.H. Millar (Otago)
ATTENDANCE: 58,000
CONDITIONS: Weather sunny, ground firm
HALFTIME: British Isles 9, New Zealand 3

SCORERS

NEW ZEALAND	BRITISH ISLES
Try: Knight	Try: Morgan
Penalty goals: Wilson (2)	Conversion: Morgan
	Penalty goal: Morgan

11 November, 1977

First Test

The New Zealand team which left for a short tour of Italy and France in October 1977 had something of a new look about it. Tane Norton announced his retirement before the season ended. He had hooked for New Zealand in every Test match since the first international of the 1971 series against the Lions and had given sterling service.

Kent Lambert was unavailable for the tour and in December signed with the Sydney League club, Penrith. Since his Test debut as a replacement against Scotland in 1972 he had played in eleven internationals.

Neither of the half-backs who played in the Tests against the Lions won selection and for the first time since he came on as a replacement against Australia in 1968 the great loose forward, Ian Kirkpatrick, was dropped from the All Blacks. With thirty-nine Test appearances to his credit Kirkpatrick ranks second to Colin Meads in the list of New Zealand internationals for appearances. He does however hold two records. His sixteen tries in Test matches and his thirty-eight consecutive internationals have not been matched by any other N.Z. player. Like Sid Going, Grant Batty and Tane Norton, Kirkpatrick made a memorable contribution to New Zealand Rugby and there is no doubt that his presence on the tour would have been welcomed by the other team members for his experience alone.

The loss of these four players in one season left gaps which were difficult to fill but the All Blacks had won all of their six tour games when they faced France in the first Test. The manager, Ron Don, coach Jack Gleeson and new captain Graham Mourie were the leaders on the All Black tour to Argentina in 1976 so they had overseas touring experience.

The first Test team contained six new caps. At full-back was Brian McKechnie, who had also played for New Zealand at cricket. Normally a five-eighth, he found himself called on to fill the full-back position because of a leg injury to Bevan Wilson. He had no first class football experience in this position prior to this Test. Other newcomers were Stuart Wilson, Mark

Donaldson, Gary Seear, John Black and Gary Knight. The latter had also represented New Zealand at wrestling in the 1974 Commonwealth Games.

The French team had won the Five Nations Championship during the previous European season without having its line crossed and it was a very experienced side. The front row was especially strong while the fly-half, Romeu, who had played in the last Test between the two countries in 1973, enjoyed a great reputation for his goal-kicking ability and for his general play. Another survivor of that match was centre Roland Bertranne.

This game was played on Armistice Day, a public holiday in France, which in this year fell on a Friday.

McKechnie kicked off and the New Zealand forwards, led by Haden, swarmed into French territory. From a ruck Romeu and Sangalli were adjudged offside and within one minute

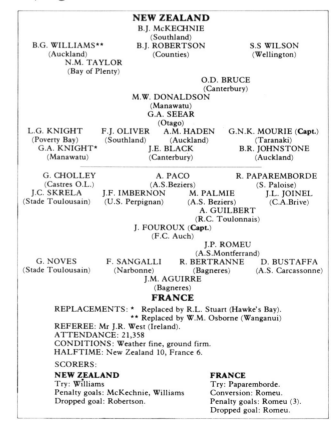

NEW ZEALAND

B.J. McKECHNIE
(Southland)

B.G. WILLIAMS**   B.J. ROBERTSON   S.S WILSON
(Auckland)   (Counties)   (Wellington)
N.M. TAYLOR
(Bay of Plenty)

O.D. BRUCE
(Canterbury)
M.W. DONALDSON
(Manawatu)
G.A. SEEAR
(Otago)

L.G. KNIGHT   F.J. OLIVER   A.M. HADEN   G.N.K. MOURIE (Capt.)
(Poverty Bay)   (Southland)   (Auckland)   (Taranaki)
G.A. KNIGHT*   J.E. BLACK   B.R. JOHNSTONE
(Manawatu)   (Canterbury)   (Auckland)

G. CHOLLEY   A. PACO   R. PAPAREMBORDE
(Castres O.L.)   (A.S.Beziers)   (S. Paloise)
J.C. SKRELA   J.F. IMBERNON   M. PALMIE   J.L. JOINEL
(Stade Toulousain)   (U.S. Perpignan)   (A.S. Beziers)   (C.A.Brive)
A. GUILBERT
(R.C. Toulonnais)
J. FOUROUX (Capt.)
(F.C. Auch)
J.P. ROMEU
(A.S.Montferrand)
G. NOVES   F. SANGALLI   R. BERTRANNE   D. BUSTAFFA
(Stade Toulousain)   (Narbonne)   (Bagneres)   (A.S. Carcassonne)
J.M. AGUIRRE
(Bagneres)

FRANCE

REPLACEMENTS: * Replaced by R.L. Stuart (Hawke's Bay).
               ** Replaced by W.M. Osborne (Wanganui).
REFEREE: Mr J.R. West (Ireland).
ATTENDANCE: 21,358
CONDITIONS: Weather fine, ground firm.
HALFTIME: New Zealand 10, France 6.

SCORERS:

NEW ZEALAND   **FRANCE**
Try: Williams   Try: Paparemborde.
Penalty goals: McKechnie, Williams   Conversion: Romeu.
Dropped goal: Robertson.   Penalty goals: Romeu (3).
                                      Dropped goal: Romeu.

N W Z ALAND 1᠎

Stadium de Toulouse, Toulouse

McKechnie had opened the scoring with a good goal from just inside the 22.

Play was even for the next few minutes but France gave away a number of penalties for offside and for obstruction.

After twelve minutes a ruck formed from which the French were offside in front of their posts but McKechnie missed the simplest of goals.

Romeu was close with a kick from 42 metres when New Zealand conceded a penalty from a maul and he failed again when Seear infringed in a line-out three minutes later. Then the French fly-half received from a line-out and booted a high one down the centre which his forwards charged after. The All Black defence failed to take the ball and Bertranne recovered and made ground to inside the All Black 22 where he passed to Skrela. The loose forward was stopped near the line but Paparemborde picked up and used his strength to crash over near the posts. Romeu converted, giving France a 6-3 lead after eighteen minutes.

In the twenty-fourth minute Williams had a shot from 45 metres but his kick went to the right of the posts. He was given another chance shortly after when Robertson was deliberately kicked but he missed again.

New Zealand kept attacking and won two rucks in succession. From the second of these Robertson dropped a goal to even the score. A 50 metre penalty by Williams just failed to clear the bar then McKechnie missed a simple kick a minute later, when France gave away a penalty for using hands in a ruck. With only two minutes of the first half remaining New Zealand managed to take the lead. A pass from Fouroux was intercepted by Taylor who ran up the centre until he was confronted by the defence. He kicked ahead on the angle and Robertson dribbled to inside the 22 where he gathered the ball. The centre threw a pass along the ground to his right as he was tackled and Williams was able to retrieve the ball and score right in the corner. McKechnie failed to convert and the All Blacks were four points ahead at halftime.

All Black captain, Graham Mourie, lunges to catch Romeu as the French fly half is about to kick.

Romeu missed a penalty early in the second half but Williams made no mistake from 45 metres after six minutes when the French were penalised in a line-out. Romeu redeemed himself by dropping a goal from a fairly wide angle following a line-out. He then kicked a penalty goal when New Zealand were offside at a maul to bring the score to 13-12, after quarter of an hour's play in the second half.

Half way through the spell, Gary Knight left the field with an eye injury and was replaced by Robbie Stuart playing his first Test. Two minutes later France were awarded a penalty for an obstruction on Fouroux and Romeu's kick from 42 metres went over after the ball had struck the right upright.

With six minutes to go, Bruce made an unsuccessful attempt to drop a goal. Then Robertson made a break and passed to Williams, who ran strongly before being heavily tackled. In the tackle he dislocated his hip and was taken off on a stretcher, his place being taken by Osborne.

With time showing on the clock Romeu kicked a high one in front of the New Zealand posts. A scramble took place and Johnstone was penalised for trampling on an opponent. Romeu kicked a simple goal and the match was over.

NEW ZEALAND 15

19 November, 1977

Second Test

There was only one change in the French team for this match, Jacques Gasc replacing the injured original selection Joinel on the side of the scrum. There were several changes in the New Zealand side however. Williams, along with Bevan Wilson, had returned home injured. Taylor was moved to the right wing, Osborne came in at second five-eighth and there was a change in the forwards with Andy Dalton replacing Black as hooker. The son of 1947-49 All Black Ray Dalton, the Counties captain was making his first appearance in a Test.

France kicked off and attacked early in the half. They had a chance to open the scoring with a penalty from 40 metres after three minutes but Romeu failed to goal. In the ninth minute inside his 22 Bertranne picked up and passed to Aguirre, who kicked for touch. McKechnie fielded the ball skilfully as he skidded towards the left touchline quickly regained his feet and, from about 35 metres out, potted a fine goal to open the scoring.

The New Zealand Touring Team

Back row: N.M. Taylor, K.A. Eveleigh, O.D. Bruce, B.J. McKechnie.
Third Row: S.S. Wilson, G.A. Knight, J.C. Ashworth, R.G. Myers, B.R. Johnstone, J.E. Black, B.J. Robertson.
Second row: R.M. Don (manager), R.L. Stuart, V.E. Stewart (injured — did not tour), A.M. Haden, G.A. Seear, F.J. Oliver, L.G. Knight, J. Gleeson (assistant-manager).
Seated: B.W. Wilson, M.W. Donaldson, W.M. Osborne, G.N.K. Mourie (captain), A.G. Dalton, K.M. Greene, B.R. Ford.
In front: B.G. Williams. **Inset:** J.T. McEldowney.

VERNON CLARKE STUDIOS

FRANCE 3

After sixteen minutes Palmie was penalised for obstruction at a ruck and McKechnie goaled from 32 metres.

In the eighteenth minute France won a tight-head and Guilbert dropped off the back of the scrum to pick up the ball, which he sent straight to Romeu. The fly-half immediately let fly with a drop kick from inside the New Zealand 22 but he failed to goal.

For the next six minutes, the All Blacks were confined to their own half but Mourie put his team on attack when he made a break into French territory.

Lawrie Knight won a line-out and from a high kick the New Zealand forwards poured through but the ball was knocked on. Then came an exciting move when Robertson picked up the ball on the bounce and passed to Osborne. The latter burst inside the French 22 and when blocked by Aguirre and Noves, sent the ball back to Robertson and the centre raced over the line but

the final pass was well forward. Then Bruce made a good break but his pass to Wilson was also ruled forward.

With thirty-one minutes gone, the French were penalised for dangerous play at a ruck and Seear kicked a good goal from 45 metres. Three minutes later, the All Blacks won a line-out but lost control of the ball and a ruck formed. France received a penalty for offside at the ruck and Romeu kicked a fairly easy goal from 20 metres out and to the left of the posts. Halftime came with the score favouring New Zealand by 9-3.

The All Blacks developed some effective shortened line-out ploys involving Dalton, Haden and Lawrie Knight, successfully counteracting the French dominance in this phase of the game and reducing the frequency of mauls.

Within the first two minutes of the second half the All Blacks won the ball from a quick throw-in by Mourie outside the French 22. Donaldson sent the backs away and Robertson cut between Romeu and Bertranne before sending a long pass to Wilson over the head of Osborne. The left wing coming back infield beat Bustaffa and wrong-footed Aguirre to score a fine try by the posts. McKechnie had no trouble with the conversion.

Romeu had a chance to close the gap in the twelfth minute when New Zealand was penalised at a ruck but the French fly-half missed again from 20 metres out.

In the twenty-seventh minute Fouroux was offside at a scrum but McKechnie was short with a kick at goal from 40 metres to the right of the posts. Four minutes later, he was again to the right from a line-out penalty.

In the closing stages of the game Taylor made a good run and Haden led the New Zealand forwards in a promising rush but there was no further scoring. That the better team won there is no doubt and the result was a triumph for Jack Gleeson and his relatively inexperienced players.

So the first seventy-five years of New Zealand's international Rugby history finished, as it started, on a winning note.

NEW ZEALAND

B.J. McKECHNIE
(Southland)

N.M. TAYLOR	B.J. ROBERTSON	S.S. WILSON
(Bay of Plenty)	(Counties)	(Wellington)

W.M. OSBORNE
(Wanganui)

O.D. BRUCE
(Canterbury)

M.W. DONALDSON
(Manawatu)

G.A. SEEAR
(Otago)

L.G. KNIGHT	F.J. OLIVER	A.M. HADEN	G.N.K. MOURIE (Capt.)
(Poverty Bay)	(Southland)	(Auckland)	(Taranaki)
G.A. KNIGHT		A.G. DALTON	B.R. JOHNSTONE
(Manawatu)		(Counties)	(Auckland)

G. CHOLLEY	A. PACO	R. PAPAREMBORDE
(Castres O.L.)	(A.S. Beziers)	(S. Paloise)
J.C. SKRELA	J.F. IMBERNON	M. PALMIE	J. GASC
(Stade Toulousain)	(U.S. Perpignan)	(A.S. Beziers)	(S.C. Graulhetois)

A. GUILBERT
(R.C. Toulonnais)

J. FOUROUX (Capt.)
(F.C. Auch)

J.P. ROMEU
(A.S. Montferrand)

G. NOVES	F. SANGALLI	R. BERTRANNE	D. BUSTAFFA
(Stade Toulousain)	(Narbonne)	(Bagneres)	(A.S. Carcassonne)

J.M. AGUIRRE
(Bagneres)

FRANCE

REFEREE: Mr C. Thomas (Wales)
ATTENDANCE: 33,751
CONDITIONS: Weather overcast and cold, ground firm.
HALFTIME: New Zealand 9, France 3.

SCORERS

NEW ZEALAND	**FRANCE**
Try: Wilson	Penalty goal: Romeu
Conversion: McKechnie	
Penalty goals: McKechnie, Seear	
Dropped goal: McKechnie	

367

Statistics

New Zealand International Rugby
1903-1977

NEW ZEALAND INTERNATIONAL PLAYERS

Legend. A Australia; AA All-America; AW Anglo-Welsh; BI British Isles; E England; F France; GB Great Britain; I Ireland; S Scotland; SA South Africa; W Wales; R signifies a replacement during a match.

Club and union affiliations are shown in brackets, preceded by date of birth and, where applicable, date of death. We have been unable to trace a few of these dates and these are indicated with a ?. War casualties are denoted with an asterisk.

ABBOTT, H.L. 1882-1971 (Star, Taranaki) F 1906.
AITKEN, G.G. 1898-1952. (University, Wellington). SA 1921 (2).
ALLEN, F.R. 1920- (Grammar O.B., Auckland). A 1946 (2) - 47 (2). SA 1949 (2).
ALLEY, G.T. 1903- (University, Canterbury). SA 1928 (3).
ARCHER, W.R. 1930- (Pirates, Otago and Gore Pioneers, Southland). A 1955 (2). SA 1956 (2).
ARGUS, W.G. 1921- (Linwood, Canterbury). A 1946 (2) - 47 (2).
ARNOLD, D.A. 1941- (Christchurch, Canterbury). I 1963. W 1963. E 1964. F 1964.
ARNOLD, K.D. 1920- (Hautapu, Waikato). A 1947 (2).
ASHBY, D.L. 1931- (Mataura, Southland). A 1958.
ASHER, A. 1879-1965. (City, Auckland). A 1903.
ATKINSON, H. 1888-? (Kohinoor, West Coast). A 1913.
AVERY, H.E. 1885-1961. (Wellington College O.B., Wellington). A 1910 (3).

BADELEY, C.E.O. 1896- (Grammar O.B., Auckland). SA 1921 (2).
BAIRD, J.A.S. 1893-1917* (Zingari-Richmond, Otago). A 1913.
BALL, N. 1908- (Hutt & Poneke, Wellington). A 1931-32 (3). W 1935. E 1936.
BARRETT, J. 1888-1971. (Marist O.B., Auckland). A 1913 (2).
BARRY, E.F. 1905- (Hutt, Wellington). A 1934.
BATTY, G.B. 1951- (Marist St. Pat's O.B., Wellington and Otumoetai Cadets, Bay of Plenty). W 1972. S 1972-75. E 1973 (2). I 1973-74. F 1973. A 1974 (2). SA 1976 (4). BI 1977.
BATTY, W. 1905- (Grammar O.B., Auckland). GB 1930 (3). A 1931.
BEATTY, G.E. 1926- (New Plymouth H.S.O.B., Taranaki). BI 1950.
BELL, R.H. 1925- (Pirates, Otago). A 1951-52 (2).
BELLISS, E.A. 1894-1974. (Moawhango Huia, Wanganui). SA 1921 (3).
BENNET, R. 1879-1962. (Alhambra, Otago). A 1905.
BERGHAN, T. 1914- (University, Otago). A 1938 (3).
BEVAN, V.D. 1921- (Athletic, Wellington). A 1949 (2). BI 1950 (4).
BIRTWISTLE, W.M. 1939- (Christchurch, Canterbury and St. Pat's O.B., Waikato). SA 1965 (4). E 1967. W 1967. S 1967.
BLACK, J.E. 1952- (University, Canterbury). F 1977
BLACK, N.W. 1925- (Ponsonby, Auckland). SA 1949.
BLACK, R.S. 1893-1916* (Pirates, Otago). A 1914.
BLAKE, A.W. 1922- (Carterton, Wairarapa). A 1949.
BOGGS, E.G. 1922- (Ponsonby, Auckland). A 1946. SA 1949.
BOND, J.G. 1920- (Albion, Canterbury). A 1949.
BOOTH, E.E. 1876-1935.(Kaikorai, Otago). F 1906. A 1907 (2).
BOWDEN, N.J.G. 1927- (New Plymouth H.S.O.B., Taranaki). A 1952.
BOWERS, R.G. 1932- (Athletic, Wellington). I 1954. F 1954.
BOWMAN, A.W. 1915- (Napier Technical O.B., Hawke's Bay). A 1938 (3).
BREMNER, S.G. 1930- (Grammar O.B., Auckland, and University, Canterbury). A 1952. SA 1956.
BRISCOE, K.C. 1936- (Tukapa, Taranaki). BI 1959. SA 1960 (4). I 1963. W 1963. E 1964. S 1964.
BROWN, C. 1887-1966. (Tukapa, Taranaki). A 1913 (2).
BROWN, R.H. 1934- (New Plymouth H.S.O.B., Taranaki). A 1955-57 (2)-58 (3)-62. SA 1956 (4). BI 1959 (2). F 1961 (3).
BROWNLIE, C.J. 1895-1954. (Hastings, Hawke's Bay). W 1924. E 1925. F 1925.
BROWNLIE, M.J. 1897-1957. (Hastings, Hawke's Bay). I 1924. W 1924. E 1925. F 1925. SA 1928 (4).
BRUCE, J.A. 1887-1970. (City, Auckland). A 1914 (2).
BRUCE, O.D. 1948- (Ohoka, Canterbury). SA 1976 (4). BI 1977 (3). F 1977 (2).
BRYERS, R.F. 1919- (Athletic, King Country). A 1949.
BUDD, T.A. 1922- (Bluff, Southland). A 1946-49.
BULLOCK-DOUGLAS, G.A.H. 1911-1958. (Wanganui & Old Boys, Wanganui). A 1932 (3)-34 (2).
BURGESS, G.F. 1883-1961. (Pirates, Southland). A 1905.
BURGESS, R.E. 1949- (University, Manawatu). BI 1971 (3). A 1972. W 1972. I 1973. F 1973.
BURKE, P.S. 1927- (Stratford, Taranaki). A 1955-57 (2).
BURNS, P.J. 1881-1943. (Albion, Canterbury). AW 1908. A 1910 (3)-13.
BUSH, R.G. 1909- (University, Otago). A 1931.
BUSH, W.K. 1949- (Belfast, Canterbury). A 1974 (2). S 1975. I 1976. SA 1976 (2). BI 1977 (3)R.
BUXTON, J.B. 1933- (Lincoln College, Canterbury). A 1955. SA 1956.

CAIN, M.J. 1885-1951. (Clifton Taranaki). AA 1913. A 1914 (3).
CALLESEN, J.A. 1951- (Palmerston North H.S.O.B., Manawatu). A 1974 (3). S 1975.
CAMERON, D. 1887-1947. (Stratford, Taranaki). AW 1908 (3).
CARLETON, S.R. 1904-1973. (Christchurch H.S.O.B., Canterbury). SA 1928 (3). A 1929 (3).
CARRINGTON, K.R. 1950- (Waitemata, Auckland). BI 1971 (3).
CASEY, S.T. 1882-1960. (Southern, Otago). S 1905. I 1905. W 1905. A 1907 (3). AW 1908.
CATLEY, E.H. 1915-1975. (United, Waikato). A 1946-47 (2). SA 1949 (4).
CAUGHEY, T.H.C. 1911- (University, Auckland). A 1932 (2)-34 (2)-36. S 1935. I 1935. E 1936. SA 1937.
CAULTON, R.W. 1937- (Poneke, Wellington). BI 1959 (4). SA 1960 (2). F 1961-64. E 1963 (2)-64. I 1963. W 1963. S 1964. A 1964 (3)
CHERRINGTON, N.P. 1924- (Horahora, North Auckland). BI 1950.
CHRISTIAN, D.L. 1923-1977. (Otahuhu, Auckland). SA 1949.
CLARK, D.W. 1940- (Cromwell, Otago). A 1964 (2).
CLARK, W.H. 1929- (University, Wellington). W 1953. I 1954. E 1954. S 1954. A 1955 (2). SA 1956 (3).
CLARKE, A.H. 1938- (Waitemata, Auckland). A 1958. BI 1959. SA 1960.

CLARKE, D.B. 1933- (Kereone, Waikato). SA 1956 (2)-60 (4). A 1957 (2)-58 (2)-62 (5)-64 (2). BI 1959 (4). F 1961 (3)-64. E 1963 (2)-64. I 1963. W 1963. S 1964.
CLARKE, I.J. 1931- (Kereone, Waikato). W 1953. A 1955 (3)-57 (2)-58 (2)-62 (3). SA 1956 (4)-60(2). BI 1959 (2). F 1961 (3). E 1963 (2).
CLARKE, R.L. 1909-1972. (Okaiawa, Taranaki). A 1932 (2).
COBDEN, D.G. 1914-1940.* (Christchurch H.S.O.B., Canterbury). SA 1937.
COCKERILL, M.S. 1928- (Athletic, Taranaki). A 1951 (3).
COCKROFT, E.A.P. 1890-1973. (Pirates, South Canterbury). A 1913-14 (2).
COLLINS, A.H. 1906- (Stratford & Clifton, Taranaki). A 1932 (2)-34.
COLLINS, J.L. 1939- (Marist O.B., Poverty Bay). A 1964. SA 1965 (2).
COLMAN, J.T.H. 1887-1965. (Hawera, Taranaki). A 1907 (2). AW 1908 (2).
CONNOR, D.M. 1935- (Marist O.B., Auckland). F 1961 (3). A 1962 (5)-64 (2). E 1963 (2).
CONWAY, R.J. 1935- (Zingari-Richmond, Otago and Whakatane United, Bay of Plenty). BI 1959 (3). SA 1960 (3)-65 (4).
COOKE, A.E. 1901-1977. (Grafton, Auckland and Hutt, Wellington). I 1924. W 1924. E 1925. F 1925. GB 1930 (3).
COOKE, R.J. 1880-1940. (Merivale, Canterbury). A 1903.
CORNER, M.M.N. 1908- (Grammar O.B., Auckland). GB 1930 (3). A 1931-34. E 1936.
COSSEY, R.R. 1935- (Pukekohe, Counties). A 1958.
COTTRELL, A.I. 1907- (Christchurch, Canterbury). A 1929 (3)-31-32 (3). GB 1930 (4).
COTTRELL, W.D. 1943- (Suburbs, Canterbury). A 1968 (2). F 1968 (2). SA 1970. BI 1971 (4).
COUCH, M.B.R. 1925- (Greytown & Gladstone, Wairarapa). A 1947-49 (2).
COUGHLAN, T.D. 1934- (Temuka, South Canterbury). A 1958.
CREIGHTON, J.N. 1937- (University, Canterbury). A 1962.
CROSS, T. 1876-? (Petone, Wellington). GB 1904. A 1905.
CROWLEY, P.J.B. 1923- (Marist O.B., Auckland). SA 1949 (2). BI 1950 (4).
CUMMINGS, W. 1889-1955. (Linwood, Canterbury). A 1913 (2).
CUNDY, R.T. 1901-1955. (Greytown, Wairarapa). A 1929 R.
CUNNINGHAM, W. 1874-1927. (Waitete & Ponsonby, Auckland). S 1905. I 1905. F 1906. A 1907 (3). AW 1908 (3).
CUPPLES, L.F. 1898-1972. (Tokaanu, Bay of Plenty). I 1924. W 1924.
CUTHILL, J.E. 1892-1970. (University, Otago). A 1913. AA 1913.

DALLEY, W.C. 1901- (Christchurch H.S.O.B., Canterbury). I 1924. SA 1928 (4).
DALTON A.G. 1951- (Bombay, Counties). F 1977
DALTON, D. 1913- (Technical O.B., Hawke's Bay). I 1935. W 1935. A 1936 (2)-38 (2). SA 1937 (3).
DALTON, R.A. 1919- (Wellington, Wellington). A 1947 (2).
DALZELL, G.N. 1921- (Culverden, Canterbury). W 1953. I 1954. E 1954. S 1954. F 1954.
DAVIES, W.A. 1939- (University, Auckland, and University, Otago). SA 1960. A 1962 (2).
DAVIS, K. 1930- (Marist O.B., Auckland). A 1952-55-58 (3). W 1953. I 1954. E 1954. S 1954. F 1954.
DAVIS, L.J. 1943- (Suburbs, Canterbury). I 1976. BI 1977 (2).
DAVIS, W.L. 1942- (Taradale, Hawke's Bay). A 1967-68 (2). E 1967. W 1967-69 (2). F 1967-68. S 1967. SA 1970.
DEANS, R.G. 1884-1908. (Christchurch H.S.O.B., Canterbury). S 1905. I 1905. E 1905. W 1905. AW 1908.
DELAMORE, G.W. 1920- (Hutt, Wellington). SA 1949.
DEWAR, H. 1883-1915* (Stratford, Taranaki). A 1913. AA 1913.
DIACK, E.S. 1932- (University, Otago) BI 1959.
DICK, J. 1912- (Grafton, Auckland). SA 1937 (2). A 1938.
DICK, M.J. 1941- (Ponsonby, Auckland). I 1963. W 1963-67-69 (3). E 1964-67. S 1964. F 1964-67. A 1965-70 (2). BI 1966. E 1967.
DIXON, M.J. 1929- (Sydenham, Canterbury). I 1954. E 1954. S 1954. F 1954. SA 1956 (4). A 1957 (2).
DOBSON, R.L. 1923- (Northcote, Auckland). A 1949.
DODD, E.H. 1880-1918*. (Wellington College O.B., Wellington). A 1905.
DONALD, J.G. 1898- (United, Wairarapa). SA 1921 (2).
DONALD, Q. 1900-1965. (Featherston, Wairarapa). I 1924. W 1924. E 1925. F 1925.
DONALDSON M.W. 1956- (High School O.B., Manawatu) F 1977 (2).
DOUGAN, J.P. 1946- (Petone, Wellington). A 1972. E 1973.
DOWNING, A.J. 1886-1915*. (Marist O.B., Auckland). A 1913-14 (2). AA 1913.
DUFF, R.H. 1925- (Christchurch, Canterbury). A 1951 (3)-52 (2)-55 (2). SA 1956 (4).
DUNCAN, J. 1869-1953. (Kaikorai, Otago). A 1903.
DUNCAN, M.G. 1947- (Hastings H.S.O.B., Hawke's Bay). BI 1971 (2) R.
DUNCAN, W.D. 1892-1961. (Kaikorai, Otago). SA 1921 (3).
DUNN, J.M. 1921- (Manukau Rovers, Auckland). A 1946.

EASTGATE, B.P. 1927- (Linwood, Canterbury). A 1952 (2). S 1954.
ELLIOTT, K.G. 1922- (Wellington College O.B., Wellington). A 1946 (2).
ELSOM, A.E.G. 1925- (Albion, Canterbury). A 1952 (2)-55 (2). W 1953.
ELVIDGE, R.R. 1923- (University & Union, Otago). A 1946 (2). SA 1949 (4). BI 1950 (3).
ERCEG, C.P. 1928- (Grafton, Auckland). A 1951 (3)-52.
EVANS, D.A. 1886-1940. (Napier H.S.O.B., Hawke's Bay). A 1910.
EVELEIGH, K.A. 1948- (Feilding, Manawatu). SA 1976 (2). BI 1977 (2).

FANNING, A.H.N. 1890-1963. (Linwood, Canterbury). A 1913.
FANNING, B.J. 1874-1946. (Linwood, Canterbury). A 1903. GB 1904.
FARRELL, C.P. 1956- (Suburbs, Auckland). BI 1977 (2).
FAWCETT, C.L. 1954- (University, Auckland). SA 1976 (2).
FEA, W.R. 1898- (University, Otago). SA 1921.
FINLAY, B.E.L. 1927- (Marist, Manawatu). BI 1959.
FINLAY, J. 1916- (Feilding H.S.O.B., Manawatu). A 1946.
FINLAYSON, I.H. 1899- (Kamo, North Auckland). SA 1928 (4). GB 1930 (2).
FITZGERALD, J.T. 1928- (University, Wellington). A 1952.
FITZPATRICK, B.B.J. 1931- (University, Wellington). W 1953. I 1954. F 1954.

FLETCHER, C.J.C. 1894-1973. (Waimauku, North Auckland). SA 1921.
FOGARTY, R. 1891- (Hawera, Taranaki). SA 1921 (2).
FORD, B.R. 1951- (Kaikoura, Marlborough). BI 1977 (2).
FRANCIS, A.R.H. 1882-1957. (Ponsonby, Auckland). A 1905-07 (3)-10 (3). AW 1908 (3).
FRANCIS, W.C. 1894- (Wellington, Wellington). A 1913 (2)-14 (3).
FRAZER, H.F. 1916- (Pirates, Hawke's Bay). A 1946 (2)-47 (2). SA 1949.
FRYER, F.C. 1886-1958. (Christchurch, Canterbury). A 1907 (3). AW 1908.
FULLER, W.B. 1883- (Merivale, Canterbury). A 1910 (2).
FURLONG, B.D.M. 1945- (Marist, Hawke's Bay). SA 1970.

GALLAHER, D. 1873-1917*. (Ponsonby, Auckland). A 1903. GB 1904. S 1905. E 1905. W 1905. F 1906.
GARD, P.C. 1949- (Kurow, North Otago). BI 1971.
GARDINER, A.J. 1948- (Tukapa, Taranaki). A 1974.
GEDDES, J.H. 1907- (Pirates, Southland). A 1929.
GEDDES, W. McK. 1893-1950. (University, Auckland). A 1913.
GEMMELL, B. McL. 1950- (Grammar O.B., Auckland). A 1974 (2).
GEORGE, V.L. 1908- (Invercargill, Southland). A 1938 (3).
GILBERT, G.D.M. 1911- (United, West Coast). S 1935. I 1935. W 1935. E 1936.
GILLESPIE, C.T. 1883-1964. (Oriental, Wellington). A 1913.
GILLESPIE, W.D. 1934- (Pirates, Otago). A 1958.
GILLETT, G.A. 1877-1956. (Merivale, Canterbury and Ponsonby, Auckland). S 1905. I 1905. W 1905. A 1907 (2). AW 1908 (2).
GILLIES, C.C. 1912- (University, Otago). A 1936.
GILRAY, C.M. 1885-1974. (University, Otago). A 1905.
GLASGOW, F.T. 1880-1936. (Eltham, Taranaki and Star, Southland). S 1905. I 1905. E 1905. W 1905. F 1906. AW 1908.
GLENN, W.S. 1877-1953. (Waimate, Taranaki). GB 1904. F 1906.
GODDARD, M.P. 1921-1974. (Zingari, South Canterbury). A 1946-47 (2). SA 1949 (2).
GOING, S.M. 1943- (Mid-Northern, North Auckland). A 1967-72 (3). F 1967-68-73. W 1969 (2)-72. SA 1970 (2)R-76 (4). BI 1971 (4)-77 (4). S 1972-75. E 1973 (2). I 1973-74-76R.
GRAHAM, D.J. 1935- (Christchurch H.S.O.B., Canterbury). A 1958 (2)-62 (5)-64 (3). SA 1960 (2). F 1961 (3)-64. E 1963 (2)-64. I 1963. W 1963. S 1964.
GRAHAM, J.B. 1884-1941. (Southern, Otago). AA 1913. A 1914 (2).
GRANT, L.A. 1923- (Temuka, South Canterbury). A 1947 (2). SA 1949 (2).
GRAY, G.D. 1880-1961. (Albion, Canterbury). AW 1908. A 1913. AA 1913.
GRAY, K.F. 1938- (Petone, Wellington). I 1963. W 1963-67-69 (2). E 1964. S 1964-67. F 1964-67-68 (2). A 1964-65-69 (3)-68. SA 1965 (4). BI 1966 (4).
GRAY, W.N. 1932- (Whakarewarewa, Bay of Plenty). A 1955 (2). SA 1956 (4).
GRENSIDE, B.A. 1899- (Hastings, Hawke's Bay). SA 1928 (4). A 1929 (2).
GRIFFITHS, J.L. 1912- (Poneke, Wellington). A 1934-36 (2)-38. S 1935. I 1935. W 1935.
GUY, R.A. 1941- (Waipu, North Auckland). BI 1971 (4).

HADEN, A.M. 1950- (Ponsonby, Auckland). BI 1977 (4). F 1977 (2).
HADLEY, S. 1904-1970. (Marist O.B., Auckland). SA 1928 (4).
HADLEY, W.E. 1910- (Marist O.B., Auckland). A 1934 (2)-36 (3). S 1935. I 1935. W 1935. E 1936.
HAIG, J.S. 1924- (Kaikorai, Otago). A 1946 (2).
HAIG, L.S. 1922- (Crescent, Otago). BI 1950 (3). A 1951 (3). W 1953. E 1954. S 1954.
HALES, D.A. 1947- (Lincoln College, Canterbury). A 1972 (3). W 1972.
HAMILTON, D.C. 1883-1925. (Pirates, Southland). AW 1908.
HAMMOND, I.A. 1924- (Blenheim Central, Marlborough). A 1952.
HARPER, E.T. 1877-1918*. (Christchurch, Canterbury). GB 1904. F 1906.
HARRIS, P.C. 1946- (Te Kawau, Manawatu). SA 1976.
HART, A.H. 1897-1965. (Tukapa, Taranaki). I 1924.
HART, G.F. 1909-1944*. (Christchurch, Canterbury). GB 1930 (4). A 1931-34-36 (2). S 1935. I 1935. W 1935.
HARVEY, I.H. 1903-1966. (Masterton, Wairarapa). SA 1928.
HARVEY, L.R. 1919- (Matakanui, Otago). SA 1949 (4). BI 1950 (4).
HARVEY, P. 1880-1949. (Christchurch, Canterbury.) GB 1904
HASELL, E.W. 1889-1966. (Merivale, Canterbury). A 1913 (2).
HAYWARD, H.O. 1883-1970. (Thames City, Auckland). AW 1908.
HAZLETT, E.J. 1939- (Drummond, Southland). BI 1966 (4). A 1967. E 1967.
HAZLETT, W.E. 1905- (Pirates, Southland). SA 1928 (4). GB 1930 (4).
HEEPS, T.R. 1938- (Athletic, Wellington). A 1962 (5).
HEKE, W.R. 1894- Played under the name of W. Rika. (Mangakahia, North Auckland). A 1929 (3).
HEMI, R.C. 1933- (Frankton, Waikato). W 1953. I 1954. E 1954. S 1954. F 1954. A 1955 (3)-57 (3). SA 1956 (3). BI 1959 (3).
HENDERSON, P. 1926- (Kaierau, Wanganui). SA 1949 (4). BI 1950 (3).
HEREWINI, M.A. 1938- (Otahuhu & Manukau Rovers, Auckland). A 1962-67. I 1963. S 1964. F 1964. SA 1965. BI 1966 (4).
HILL, S.F. 1927* (Army & Christchurch, Canterbury). A 1955-57 (2)-58. SA 1956 (3). BI 1959 (4.
HOLDER, E.C. 1908-1974. (Westport O.B., Buller). A 1934.
HOOK, L.S. 1905- (Ponsonby, Auckland). A 1929 (3).
HOOPER, J.A. 1913- (Sunnyside, Canterbury). SA 1937 (3).
HOPKINSON, A.E. 1941- (Cheviot, Canterbury). S 1967. A 1968. F 1968 (3). W 1969. SA 1970 (3).
HORE, J. 1907- (Southern, Otago). GB 1930 (3). A 1932 (3)-34 (2). S 1935. E 1936.
HORSLEY, R.H. 1932- (Wellington, Wellington). SA 1960 (3).
HOTOP, J. 1929- (Lincoln College & Christchurch, Canterbury). A 1952 (2)-55.
HUGHES, A.M. 1924- (Grammar O.B., Auckland). A 1949 (2). BI 1950 (4).
HUGHES, E. 1881-1928. (Britannia, Southland and Poneke, Wellington). A 1907 (3). AW 1908. SA 1921 (2).
HUNTER, B.A. 1950- (Pirates, Otago). BI 1971 (3).
HUNTER, J. 1879-1962. (Hawera, Taranaki). S 1905. I 1905. E 1905. W 1905. F 1906. A 1907 (3). AW 1908 (3).
HURST, I.A. 1951- (Lincoln College, Canterbury). I 1973. F 1973. E 1973. A 1974 (2).

IFWERSEN, K.D. 1893-1967. (Grammar O.B., Auckland). SA 1921.
INNES, G.D. 1910- (Christchurch H.S.O.B., Canterbury). A 1932.
IRVINE, I.B. 1929- (Whangarei H.S.O.B., North Auckland). A 1952.
IRVINE, J.G. 1888-1939. (Southern, Otago). A 1914 (3).

IRVINE, W.R. 1898-1952. (Waipukurau Rovers, Hawke's Bay and Carterton, Wairarapa). I 1924. W 1924. E 1925. F 1925. GB 1930.
IRWIN, M.W. 1935- (University, Otago). A 1955 (2)-58. SA 1956-60. BI 1959 (2).

JACKSON, E.S. 1914-1975. (Maori Agricultural College, Hawke's Bay). A 1936 (2)-38. SA 1937 (3).
JAFFRAY, J.L. 1950- (Green Island & Eastern, Otago). A 1972. S 1975. I 1976. SA 1976. BI 1977.
JARDEN, R.A. 1929-1977. (University, Wellington). A 1951 (2)-52 (2)-55 (3). W 1953. I 1954. E 1954. S 1954. F 1954. SA 1956 (4).
JESSEP, E.M. 1904- (Poneke, Wellington). A 1931-32.
JOHNSON, L.M. 1897- (Wellington, Wellington). SA 1928 (4).
JOHNSTON, W. 1881-1951. (Alhambra, Otago). A 1907 (3).
JOHNSTONE, B.R. 1950- (North Shore, Auckland). SA 1976. BI 1977 (2). F 1977 (2).
JOHNSTONE, P. 1922- (Taieri, Otago). SA 1949 (2). BI 1950 (4). A 1951 (3).
JONES, M.G. 1942-1975. (Omaha, North Auckland). E 1973.
JONES, P.F.H. 1932- (Awanui, North Auckland). E 1954. S 1954. A 1955 (2)-58 (3). SA 1956 (2)-60. BI 1959.
JOSEPH, H.T. 1949- (University, Canterbury). BI 1971 (2).

KARAM, J.F. 1951- (Marist St. Pat's O.B., Wellington and Paraparaumu, Horowhenua). W 1972. S 1972-75. E 1973. I 1973-74. F 1973. A 1974 (3).
KATENE, T. 1929- (Petone, Wellington). A 1955.
KEARNEY, J.C. 1920- (Ranfurly, Otago). A 1947. SA 1949 (3).
KELLY, J.W. 1926- (Training College, Auckland). A 1949 (2).
KEMBER, G.F. 1945- (University, Wellington). SA 1970.
KIERNAN, H.A.D. 1876-1947. (Grafton, Auckland). A 1903.
KILBY, F.D. 1906- (Wellington, Wellington). A 1932 (3)-34.
KILLEEN, B.A. 1911- (Grafton, Auckland). A 1936.
KING, R.R. 1909- (Excelsior, West Coast). A 1934-36 (2)-38 (3). S 1935. I 1935. W 1935. E 1936. SA 1937 (3).
KINGSTONE, C.N. 1895-1960. (Clifton, Taranaki). SA 1921 (3).
KIRKPATRICK, I.A. 1946- (Rangiora, Canterbury and Ngatapa, Poverty Bay). F 1967-68 (3)-73. A 1968 (2)R-72 (3)-74 (3). W 1969 (2)-73. SA 1970 (4)-76 (4). BI 1971 (4)-77 (4). S 1972-75. E 1973 (2). I 1973-74-76.
KIRTON, E.W. 1939- (University, Otago). E 1967. W 1967-69 (2). F 1967-68 (3). S 1967. A 1968 (2). SA 1970 (2).
KIVELL, A.L. 1897- (Stratford, Taranaki). A 1929 (2).
KNIGHT, A. 1906- (Grammar O.B., Auckland). A 1934.
KNIGHT, G.A. 1952- (Freyberg O.B., Manawatu) F 1977 (2).
KNIGHT, L.G. 1949- (Ngatapa, Poverty Bay). BI 1977 (4). F 1977 (2).
KREFT, A.J. 1945- (Ranfurly, Otago). A 1968.

LAIDLAW, C.R. 1943- (University, Otago and Shirley, Canterbury). F 1964-68 (2). A 1964-68 (2). SA 1965 (4)-70 (3). BI 1966 (4). E 1967. W 1967. S 1967.
LAIDLAW, K.F. 1935- (Nightcaps, Southland). SA 1960 (3).
LAMBERT, K.K. 1952- (University, Manawatu). S 1972 R. E 1973 (2). I 1973-74. F 1973. SA 1976 (3). BI 1977 (2).
LAMBOURN, A. 1911- (Petone, Wellington). A 1934 (2)-38. S 1935. I 1935. W 1935. E 1936. SA 1937 (3).
LE LIEVRE, J.M. 1934- (Culverden, Canterbury). A 1962.
LENDRUM, R.N. 1948- (Papakura, Counties). E 1973.
LESLIE, A.R. 1944- (Petone, Wellington). A 1974 (3). I 1974-76. S 1975. SA 1976 (4).
LEYS, E.T. 1907- (University, Wellington). A 1929.
LILBURNE, H.T. 1908-1976. (Albion, Canterbury and Hutt, Wellington). SA 1928 (2). A 1929 (3)-31-32-34. GB 1930 (2).
LINDSAY, D.F. 1906- (University, Otago). SA 1928 (3).
LINEEN, T.R. 1936- (Marist O.B., Auckland). A 1957 (2)-58 (3). BI 1959 (4). SA 1960 (3).
LISTER, T.N. 1943- (Timaru H.S.O.B., South Canterbury). A 1968 (2). F 1968. W 1969 (2). SA 1970 (2). BI 1971.
LITTLE, P.F. 1934- (Marist O.B., Auckland). F 1961 (2)-64. A 1962 (3). I 1963. W 1963. E 1964. S 1964.
LOADER, C.J. 1931- (Hutt, Wellington). I 1953. E 1954. S 1954. F 1954.
LOCHORE, B.J. 1940- (Masterton, Wairarapa). E 1964-67. S 1964-67. SA 1965 (4)-70 (4). BI 1966 (4)-71. A 1967-68. W 1967-69 (2). F 1967-68 (2).
LONG, A.J. ?-? (Newton, Auckland) A 1903.
LUCAS, F.W. 1902-1957. (Ponsonby, Auckland). I 1924. F 1925. SA 1928. GB 1930 (4).
LUNN, W.A. 1926- (Alexandra, Otago). A 1949 (2).
LYNCH, T.W. 1892-1950 (Timaru Celtic, South Canterbury). A 1913-14 (2).
LYNCH, T.W. 1927- (Marist, Canterbury). A 1951 (3).

McATAMNEY, F.S. 1934- (Strath-Taieri, Otago). SA 1956.
McCAW, W.A. 1927- (Marist, Southland). A 1951 (2). W 1953. F 1954.
McCORMICK, W.F. 1939- (Linwood, Canterbury). SA 1965-70 (3). E 1967. W 1967-69 (2). F 1967-68 (3). A 1968 (2). BI 1971.
McCULLOUGH, J.F. 1936- (Tukapa, Taranaki). BI 1959 (3).
McDONALD, A. 1883-1967. (Kaikorai, Otago). S 1905. I 1905. E 1905. W 1905. A 1907-13. AW 1908. AA 1913.
MACDONALD, H.H. 1947- (Oxford, Canterbury and Kaikohe, North Auckland). W 1972. S 1972-75. E 1973 (2). I 1973-74-76. F 1973. SA 1976 (3).
McELDOWNEY, J.T. 1948- (New Plymouth H.S.O.B., Taranaki). BI 1977 (2).
MacEWAN, I.N. 1934- (Athletic, Wellington). SA 1956-60 (4). A 1957 (2)-58 (3)-62 (4). BI 1959 (3). F 1961 (3).
McGREGOR, A.J. 1889-1963. (Ponsonby, Auckland). A 1913. AA 1913.
McGREGOR, D. 1881-1947. (Linwood, Canterbury and Petone, Wellington) A 1903. GB 1904. E 1905. W 1905.
McGREGOR, N.P. 1901-1973. (Christchurch, Canterbury). W 1924. E 1925.
McGREGOR, R.W. 1874-1925. (Grafton, Auckland). A 1903. GB 1904.
McHUGH, M.J. 1917- (Marist O.B., Auckland). A 1946 (2). SA 1949.
McINTOSH, D.N. 1931- (Petone, Wellington). SA 1956 (2). A 1957 (2).
McKAY, D.W. 1937- (North Shore, Auckland). F 1961 (2). E 1963 (2).
McKECHNIE, B.J. 1953- (Star, Southland) F 1977 (2).
McKELLAR, G.F. 1884-1960. (Wellington, Wellington) A 1910 (3)
McKENZIE, R.J. 1892-1968. (Petone, Wellington and Marist O.B., Auckland) A 1913-14 (2). AA 1913.

371

McKENZIE, R. McC. 1911- (Kiatoa, Manawatu). A 1934-36-38 (3). S 1935. SA 1937 (3).
MACKRELL, W.H.C. 1881-1917. (Newton, Auckland). F 1906.
MACKY, J.V. 1887-1951. (University, Auckland). A 1913.
McLACHLAN, J.S. 1950- (College Rifles, Auckland). A 1974.
McLAREN, H.C. 1926- (Matamata, Waikato). A 1952.
McLEAN, A.L. 1898-1964. (Whakatane, Bay of Plenty). SA 1921 (2).
McLEAN, H.F. 1907- (Wellington, Wellington and Grafton, Auckland). GB 1930 (2).
A 1932 (3)-34. I 1935. W 1935. E 1936.
McLEAN, J.K. 1923- (Taumarunui, King Country and Thames United, Auckland).
A 1947-49.
McLEOD, B.E. 1940- (Manurewa, Counties). A 1964 (3)-68 (2). SA 1965 (4)-70 (2).
BI 1966 (4). E 1967. W 1967-69 (2) F 1967-68 (3). S 1967.
McMINN, A.F. 1880-1919. (Carterton, Wairarapa and Institute, Manawatu). A 1903-05.
McMINN, F.A. 1874-1947. (College O.B., Manawatu). GB 1904.
McMULLEN, R.F. 1933- (Otahuhu, Auckland). A 1957 (2)-58 (3). BI 1959 (3). SA 1960 (3).
McNAB, J.R. 1924- (Owaka, Otago). SA 1949 (3). BI 1950 (3).
McNAUGHTON, A.M. 1947- (Kahukura, Bay of Plenty). BI 1971 (3).
McNEECE, J. 1885-1917*. (Waikiwi, Southland). A 1913 (2)-14 (3).
McPHAIL, B.E. 1937- (Christchurch, Canterbury). BI 1959 (2).
MacPHERSON D.G. 1882-1956. (University, Otago). A 1905.
MacRAE, I.R. 1943- (Marist O.B., Hawke's Bay). BI 1966 (4). A 1967. E 1967.
W 1967-69 (2). F 1967-68 (2). S 1967. SA 1970 (4).
McRAE, J.A. 1915- (Marist O.B., Southland). A 1946 (2)R.
McWILLIAMS, R.G. 1901- (Ponsonby, Auckland). SA 1928 (3). A 1929 (3). GB 1930 (4).

MAGUIRE, J.R. 1886-1966. (Grafton, Auckland). A 1910 (3).
MAHONEY, A. 1908- (Konini, Bush Districts). S 1935. I 1935. W 1935. E 1936.
MAINS, L.W. 1946- (Southern, Otago). BI 1971 (3). I 1976.
MAJOR, J. 1940- (Inglewood United, Taranaki). A 1967.
MANCHESTER, J.E. 1908- (Christchurch, Canterbury). A 1932 (3)-34 (2). S 1935. I 1935.
W 1935. E 1936.
MASON, D.F. 1923- (Wellington College O.B., Wellington). A 1947R.
MASTERS, R.R. 1900-1967. (Albion, Canterbury). I 1924. W 1924. E 1925. F 1925.
MATAIRA, H. 1910- (Nuhaka, Hawke's Bay). A 1934.
MATHESON, J.D. 1948- (Pirates, Otago). A 1972 (3). W 1972. S 1972.
MAX, D.S. 1907-1972. (Brightwater Pirate, Nelson). A 1931-34 (2).
MEADS, C.E. 1936- (Waitete, King Country). A 1957 (2)-58 (3)-62 (4)-64 (3)-67-68 (2).
BI 1959 (3)-66 (4)-71 (4). SA 1960 (4)-65 (4)-70 (2). F 1961 (3)-64-67-68 (3). E 1963
(2)-64-67. I 1963. W 1963-67-69 (2). S 1963-67.
MEADS, S.T. 1938- (Waitete, King Country). F 1961. A 1962 (2)-64 (3). I 1963. SA 1965 (4).
BI 1966 (4).
MEATES, K.F. 1930- (Marist O.B., Canterbury). A 1952 (2).
MEATES, W.A. 1923- (Ranfurly, Otago), SA 1949 (3). BI 1950 (4).
METCALFE, T.C. 1909-1969. (Pirates, Southland). A 1931-32.
MEXTED, G.G. 1927- (Tawa, Wellington). BI 1950.
MILL, J.J. 1899-1950. (Marist O.B., Hawke's Bay and Masterton O.B., Wairarapa). W 1924.
E 1925. F 1925. GB 1930.
MILLIKEN, H.M. 1914- (Sunnyside, Canterbury). A 1938 (3).
MILNER, H.P. 1946- (Waiouru Army, Wanganui). SA 1970.
MITCHELL, N.A. 1913- (Southland H.S.O.B., Southland and Alhambra, Otago). S 1935.
I 1935. W 1935. E 1936. A 1936-38 (2). SA 1937.
MITCHELL, T.W. 1950- (Linwood, Canterbury). SA 1976R.
MITCHELL, W.J. 1890-1959. (Merivale, Canterbury). A 1910 (2).
MITCHINSON, F.E. 1884- (Poneke, Wellington). A 1907 (3)-10 (3)-13 R. AW 1908 (3).
AA 1913.
MOFFITT, J.E. 1887-1964. (Oriental, Wellington). SA 1921 (3).
MOORE, G.J.T. 1923- (University, Otago). A 1949.
MORGAN, J.E. 1946- (Mid-Northern, North Auckland). A 1974. I 1974. SA 1976 (3).
MORETON, R.C. 1942- (University, Canterbury). A 1962 (2)-64 (3). SA 1965 (2).
MORRIS, T.J. 1942- (Motueka Huia, Nelson Bays). A 1972 (3).
MORRISON, T.C. 1913- (Timaru Star, South Canterbury). A 1938 (3).
MORRISON, T.G. 1951- (University, Otago). E 1973 R.
MORRISSEY, P.J. 1940- (Christchurch, Canterbury). A 1962 (3).
MOURIE, G.N.K. 1953- (Opunake, Taranaki). BI 1977 (2). F 1977 (2).
MULLER, B.L. 1942- (Eltham, Taranaki). A 1967-68. E 1967. W 1967-69. F 1967-68.
SA 1970 (2). BI 1971 (4).
MUMM, W.J. 1922- (Ngakawau, Buller). A 1949.
MURDOCH, K. 1943- (Zingari-Richmond, Otago). SA 1970. A 1972. W 1972.
MURDOCH, P.H. 1941- (Otahuhu, Auckland). A 1964 (2). SA 1965 (3).
MURRAY, H.V. 1888-1971. (Irwell & Springfield, Canterbury). A 1913-14 (2). AA 1913.
MURRAY, P.C. 1884-1968. (Wanganui College O.B., Wanganui). AW 1908.
MYNOTT, H.J. 1876-1924. (Tukapa, Taranaki). I 1905. W 1905. F 1906. A 1907 (3)-10 (2).

NATHAN, W.J. 1940- (Otahuhu, Auckland). A 1962 (5)-67. E 1963 (2). W 1963. F 1964.
BI 1966 (4).
NELSON, K.A. 1938- (University, Otago). A 1962 (2).
NEPIA, G. 1905- (Dannevirke Aotea, Hawke's Bay and Rangitukia Rangers, East Coast).
I 1924. W 1924. E 1925. F 1925. A 1929. GB 1930 (4).
NESBIT, S.R. 1936- (Marist O.B., Auckland). SA 1960 (2).
NEWTON, F. 1881-1955. (Linwood, Canterbury). E 1905. W 1905. F 1906.
NICHOLLS, H.E. 1900- (Petone, Wellington). SA 1921.
NICHOLLS, M.F. 1901-1972. (Petone, Wellington). SA 1921 (3)-28. I 1924. W 1924. E 1925.
F 1925. GB 1930 (2).
NICHOLSON, G.W. 1878-1968. (City & Ponsonby, Auckland). A 1903-07 (3). GB 1904.
NORTON, R.W. 1943- (Linwood, Canterbury). BI 1971 (4)-77 (4). A 1972 (3)-74 (3).
W 1972. S 1972-75. E 1973 (2). I 1973-74-76. F 1973. SA 1976 (4).

O'BRIEN, J.G. 1889-1958. (Marist O.B., Auckland). A 1914.
O'CALLAGHAN, M.W. 1946- (University, Manawatu). F 1968 (3).
O'CALLAGHAN, T.R. 1925- (Marist O.B., Wellington). A 1949.
O'DONNELL, D.H. 1921- (St. Pat's O.B., Wellington). A 1949.
O'LEARY, M.J. 1883-1963. (Ponsonby, Auckland). A 1910 (2)-13 (2).
OLIVER, C.J. 1905-1977. (Merivale, Canterbury). A 1929 (2)-34. S 1935. I 1935. W 1935.
E 1936.
OLIVER, D.J. 1907- (Wellington, Wellington). GB 1930 (2).

OLIVER, F.J. 1948- (Marist O.B., Southland). SA 1976. BI 1977 (4). F 1977 (2).
OLIVER, O.D. 1930- (University, Otago). I 1954. F 1954.
ORR, R.W. 1924- (Zingari-Richmond, Otago). A 1949.
OSBORNE, W.M. 1955- (Kaierau, Wanganui). S 1975. SA 1976 (2) 2R. BI 1977 (4).
F 1977 (2) R.
O'SULLIVAN, J.M. 1883-1960. (Okaiawa, Taranaki). S 1905. I 1905. E 1905. W 1905.
A 1907.
O'SULLIVAN, T.P.A. 1936- (Okato, Taranaki). SA 1960. F 1961. A 1962 (2).

PAGE, J.R. 1908- (Wellington, Wellington). A 1931-32 (3)-34 (2).
PALMER, B.P. 1901-1932. (Ponsonby & Otahuhu, Auckland). A 1929-32 (2).
PARKER, J.H. 1897- (Christchurch H.S.O.B., Canterbury). I 1924. W 1924. E 1925.
PARKHILL, A.A. 1912- (Pirates, Otago). SA 1937 (3). A 1938 (3).
PARKINSON, R.M. 1948- (Gisborne H.S.O.B., Poverty Bay). A 1972 (3). W 1972. S 1972.
E 1973 (2).
PATERSON, A.M. 1885-1933. (Zingari-Richmond, Otago). AW 1908 (2). A 1910 (3).
PATON, H. 1881-1964. (Dunedin, Otago). A 1910 (2).
PHILLIPS, W.J. 1914- (Mako Mako, King Country). SA 1937. A 1938 (2).
PICKERING, E.A.R. 1936- (Frankton, Waikato). A 1958. BI 1959 (2).
POLLOCK, H.R. 1909- (Petone, Wellington). A 1932 (3)-36 (2).
PORTER, C.G. 1899-1976. (Athletic, Wellington). F 1925. A 1929 (2). GB 1930 (4).
PROCTOR, A.C. 1906- (Zingari-Richmond, Otago). A 1932.
PURDUE, C.A. 1874-1941. (Britannia, Southland). A 1905.
PURDUE, E. 1876-1939. (Orepuki, Southland). A 1905.
PURDUE, G.B. 1909- (Star, Southland). A 1931-32 (3).
PURVIS, N.A. 1952- (Wanaka, Otago). I 1976.

QUAID, C.E. 1908- (Southern, Otago). A 1938 (2).

RANGI, R.E. 1941- (Ponsonby, Auckland). A 1964 (2). SA 1965 (4). BI 1966 (4).
RANKIN, J.G. 1914- (Christchurch H.S.O.B., Canterbury). A 1936 (2). SA 1937.
REEDY, W.J. 1881-1939. (Petone, Wellington). AW 1908 (2).
REID, A.R. 1929- (Frankton, Waikato). A 1952-57 (2). SA 1956 (2).
REID, K.H. 1904-1972. (Carterton, Wairarapa). A 1929 (2).
REID, S.T. 1912- (Maori Agricultural College, Hawke's Bay). S 1935. I 1935. W 1935.
E 1936. A 1936 (2). SA 1937 (3).
RESIDE, W.B. 1908- (Gladstone, Wairarapa). A 1929.
RHIND, P.K. 1915- (Christchurch, Canterbury). A 1946 (2).
RICHARDSON, J. 1899- (Alhambra, Otago and Pirates, Southland). SA 1921 (3). I 1924.
W 1924. E 1925. F 1925.
RIDLAND, A.J. 1882-1918*. (Star, Southland). A 1910 (3).
RIKA, W. See Heke, W.R.
ROBERTS, E.J. 1891-1972. (Athletic, Wellington). A 1914 (3). SA 1921 (2).
ROBERTS, F. 1881-1956. (Oriental, Wellington). S 1905. I 1905. E 1905. W 1905.
A 1907 (3)-10 (3). AW 1908 (2).
ROBERTS, R.W. 1889-1973. (Okaiwa, Taranaki). A 1913-14 (3). AA 1913.
ROBERTSON, B.J. 1952- (Ardmore College & Ardmore, Counties). A 1972 (2)-74 (3).
S 1972. E 1973. I 1973-74-76. F 1973-77 (2). SA 1976 (4). BI 1977 (3).
ROBERTSON, D.J. 1947- (Zingari-Richmond, Otago). A 1974 (3). I 1974-76. S 1975.
SA 1976 (2). BI 1977.
ROBILLIARD, A.C.C. 1903- (Christchurch, Canterbury). SA 1928 (4).
ROBINSON, C.E. 1927- (Bluff, Southland). A 1951 (3)-52 (2).
ROPER, R.A. 1923- (New Plymouth H.S.O.B., Taranaki). A 1949. BI 1950 (4).
ROWLEY, H.C.B. 1924-1956. (Hunterville, Wanganui). A 1949.
RYAN, J. 1887-1957. (Petone, Wellington). A 1910-14 (3).

SADLER, B.S. 1914- (Wellington College O.B., Wellington). S 1935. I 1935. W 1935.
A 1936 (2).
SAVAGE, L.T. 1928- (University, Canterbury). SA 1949 (3).
SAXTON, C.K. 1913- (Timaru H.S.O.B., South Canterbury). A 1938 (3).
SCOTT, R.W.H. 1921- (Ponsonby, Auckland). A 1946 (2)-47(2). SA 1949 (4). BI 1950 (4).
W 1953. I 1954. E 1954. S 1954. F 1954.
SCOWN, A.I. 1948- (Patea, Taranaki). A 1972 (3). W 1972 R. S 1972.
SCRIMSHAW, G. 1902-1971. (Christchurch, Canterbury). SA 1928.
SEEAR, G.A. 1952- (Southern, Otago) F 1977 (2).
SEELING, C.E. 1883-1956. (City, Auckland). GB 1904. S 1905. I 1905. E 1905. W 1905.
F 1906. A 1907 (2). AW 1908 (2).
SELLARS, G.M.V. 1886-1917*. (Ponsonby, Auckland). A 1913. AA 1913.
SIDDELLS, S.K. 1897- (University, Wellington). SA 1921.
SIMON, H.J. 1911- (Southern, Otago). SA 1937 (3).
SIMPSON, J.G. 1922- (Ponsonby, Auckland). A 1947 (2). SA 1949 (3). BI 1950 (3).
SIMS, G.S. 1952- (University, Otago). A 1972.
SKEEN, J.R. 1928- (Marist O.B., Auckland). A 1952.
SKINNER, K.L. 1927- (Pirates, Otago and Waiuku, Counties). SA 1949 (4)-56 (3).
BI 1950. A 1951 (3)-52 (2). W 1953. I 1954. E 1954. S 1954. F 1954.
SKUDDER, G.R. 1948- (University, Waikato). W 1969.
SMITH, A.E. 1942- (Stratford, Taranaki). W 1969 (2). SA 1970.
SMITH, G.W. 1874-1954. (City, Auckland). S 1905. I 1905.
SMITH, I.S.T. 1941- (Gimmerburn, Otago and Oamaru O.B., North Otago). A 1964 (3).
SA 1965 (3). BI 1966 (3).
SMITH, J.B. 1922-1974. (Kaikohe, North Auckland). A 1946-47-49 (2).
SMITH, R.M. 1929- (Christchurch, Canterbury). A 1955.
SMITH, W.E. 1881-1945. (Nelson, Nelson). A 1905.
SNOW, E.M. 1898-1974. (Nelson, Nelson). A 1929 (2).
SOLOMON, F. 1906- (Ponsonby, Auckland). A 1931-32 (2).
SONNTAG, W.T.C. 1894- (Kaikorai, Otago). A 1929 (3).
SPENCER, J.C. 1880-1936. (Melrose, Wellington). A 1905-07 R.
SPILLANE, A.P. 1888-1974. (Temuka, South Canterbury). A 1913 (2).
STEAD, J.W. 1877-1958. (Star, Southland). GB 1904. S 1905. I 1905. E 1905. F 1906.
AW 1908 (2).
STEEL, A.G. 1942- (Christchurch H.S.O.B., Canterbury). BI 1966 (4). A 1967-68 (2).
F 1967. S 1967.
STEEL, J. 1898-1941. (Star, West Coast). SA 1921 (3). W 1924. E 1925. F 1925.
STEELE, L.B. 1929- (Onslow, Wellington). A 1951 (3).
STEERE, E.R.G. 1908-1967. (Napier H.S.O.B., Hawke's Bay). GB 1930 (4). A 1931-32.

STEPHENS, O.G. 1947- (Athletic, Wellington). F 1968.

STEVENS, I.N. 1948- (Petone, Wellington). S 1972. E 1973. A 1974.

STEWART, A.J. 1940- (University, Canterbury and Timaru H.S.O.B., South Canterbury). E 1963 (2).-64. I 1963. W 1963. S 1964. F 1964. A 1964.

STEWART, J.D. 1890-1973. (City, Auckland). A 1913 (2).

STEWART, K.W. 1953- (Balfour, Southland). E 1973. A 1974 (3). I 1974-76. S 1975. SA 1976 (2).

STEWART, R.T. 1904- (Timaru H.S.O.B., South Canterbury and Christchurch, Canterbury). SA 1928 (4). GB 1930.

STOHR, L. 1889-1973. (Tukapa, Taranaki). A 1910 (3).

STOREY, P.W. 1897-1975. (Zingari, South Canterbury). SA 1921 (2).

STRAHAN, S.C. 1944- (Orua, Manawatu). A 1967-68 (2)-72-73. E 1967-73. W 1967. F 1967-68 (3). SA 1970 (2).

STRANG, W.A. 1907- (Timaru H.S.O.B. & Temuka, South Canterbury). SA 1928 (2). GB 1930 (2). A 1931.

STRINGFELLOW, J.C. 1905-1959. (Greytown, Wairarapa). A 1929 (2) R.

STUART, K.C. 1928- (Marist O.B., Canterbury). A 1949.

STUART, R.C. 1920- (University, Canterbury). A 1949 (2). W 1953. I 1954. E 1954. S 1954. F 1954.

STUART, R.L. 1948- (Waipukurau H.S.O.B., Hawke's Bay). F 1977 R.

SULLIVAN, J.L. 1915- (Tukapa, Taranaki). SA 1937 (3). A 1938 (3).

SUTHERLAND, A.R. 1944- (Opawa, Marlborough). SA 1970 (2). BI 1971. A 1972 (3). W 1972. E 1973. I 1973. F 1973.

SVENSON, K.S. 1898-1955. (Athletic, Wellington). I 1924. W 1924. E 1925. F 1925.

SWAIN, J.P. 1902-1960. (Technical O.B., Hawke's Bay). SA 1928 (4).

TANNER, K.J. 1945- (New Brighton, Canterbury). A 1974 (2). I 1974-76. S 1975. SA 1976.

TANNER, J.M. 1927- (University, Auckland). BI 1950. A 1951 (3). W 1953.

TAYLOR, H.M. 1889-1955. (Christchurch H.S.O.B., Canterbury). A 1913-14 (3). AA 1913.

TAYLOR, J.M. 1913- (Pirates, Otago). SA 1937 (3). A 1938 (3).

TAYLOR, N.M. 1950- (Ngongotaha, Bay of Plenty). BI 1977 (2) R. F 1977 (2).

TAYLOR, R. 1889-1917*. (Clifton, Taranaki). A 1913 (2).

TETZLAFF, P.L. 1920- (Ponsonby, Auckland). A 1947 (2).

THIMBLEBY, N.W. 1939- (Celtic, Hawke's Bay). SA 1970.

THOMAS, B.T. 1938- (Manukau Rovers, Auckland and Athletic, Wellington). A 1962 (2)-64 (3).

THOMSON, H.D. 1881-1939. (Oriental, Wellington). AW 1908.

THORNE, G.S. 1946- (University, Auckland). A 1968 (2). F 1968 (3). W 1969. SA 1970 (4).

THORNTON, N.H. 1918- (Grammar O.B., Auckland). A 1947 (2). SA 1949.

TILYARD, J.T. 1889-1966. (Poneke, Wellington). A 1913.

TINDILL, E.W.T. 1910- (Athletic, Wellington). E 1936.

TOWNSEND, L.J. 1934- (Southern, Otago). A 1955 (2).

TREMAIN, K.R. 1938- (Lincoln College, Canterbury and Napier H.S.O.B., Hawke's Bay). BI 1959 (3)-66 (4). SA 1960 (4)-65 (4). F 1961 (2)-64-68 (3). A 1962 (3)-64 (3)- 67-68. E 1963 (2) -64-67. I 1963. W 1963-67. S 1964-67.

TREVATHAN, D. 1912- (Southern, Otago). SA 1937 (3).

TUCK, J.M. 1907-1967. (Old Boys, Waikato). A 1929 (3).

TURTILL, H.S. 1880-1918*. (Albion, Canterbury). A 1905.

TYLER, G.A. 1879-1942. (City, Auckland). A 1903. GB 1904. S 1905. I 1905. E 1905. W 1905. F 1906.

UDY, D.K. 1874-1935. (Greytown, Wairarapa). A 1903.

URBAHN, R.J. 1934- (Eltham, Taranaki). BI 1959 (3).

URLICH, R.A. 1944- (Otahuhu, Auckland). SA 1970 (2).

UTTLEY, I.N. 1941- (University, Wellington). E 1963 (2).

VINCENT, P.B. 1926- (Christchurch H.S.O.B., Canterbury). SA 1956 (2).

VODANOVICH, I.M.H. 1930- (Marist O.B., Wellington). A 1955 (3).

WALLACE, W.J. 1878-1972. (Poneke, Wellington). A 1903-07 (3). GB 1904. S 1905. I 1905. E 1905. W 1905. F 1906. AW 1908.

WALSH, P.T. 1936- (Waiuku & Manurewa, Counties). A 1955 (3)-57 (2)-58 (3). SA 1956 (3). BI 1959. E 1963.

WARD, R.H. 1915- (Pirates, Southland). A 1936. SA 1937 (3).

WATERMAN, A.C. 1903- (City, North Auckland). A 1929 (2).

WATKINS, E.L. 1880-1949. (Wellington College O.B., Wellington). A 1905.

WATT, B.A. 1939- (Christchurch, Canterbury). A 1962. E 1963 (2)-64. W 1963. S 1964.

WATT, J.M. 1914- (University, Otago). A 1936 (2).

WATT, J.R. 1935- (Athletic, Wellington). A 1958-62 (2). SA 1960 (4). F 1961 (2).

WEBB, D.S. 1934- (Whangarei H.S.O.B., North Auckland). BI 1959.

WELLS, J. 1911- (Athletic, Wellington). A 1936 (2).

WEST, A.H. 1893-1934. (Hawera, Taranaki). SA 1921 (2).

WHINERAY, W.J. 1935- (Lincoln College, Canterbury; City, Waikato; Grammar O.B., Auckland). A 1957 (2)-58 (3)-62 (5). BI 1959 (4). SA 1960 (4)-65 (4). F 1961 (3)-64. E 1963 (2) -64. I 1963. W 1963. S 1964.

WHITE, A. 1894-1968. (Waikiwi, Southland). SA 1921. I 1924. E 1925. F 1925.

WHITE, H.L. 1929- (Northcote, Auckland). I 1953. E 1954. F 1954. A 1955.

WHITE, R.A. 1925- (Gisborne H.S.O.B., Poverty Bay). A 1949 (2)-51 (3) -52 (2) -55 (3). BI 1950 (4). W 1953. I 1954. E 1954. S 1954. F 1954. SA 1956 (4).

WHITE, R.M. 1917- (Petone, Wellington). A 1946 (2) - 47 (2).

WHITING, G.J. 1946- (Athletic, King Country). A 1972 (2). S 1972. E 1973. I 1973. F 1973.

WHITING, P.J. 1946- (Ponsonby, Auckland). BI 1971 (3). A 1972 (3) -74 (3). W 1972. S 1972. E 1973. I 1973-74-76. F 1973. SA 1976 (4).

WILLIAMS, B.G. 1950- (Ponsonby, Auckland). SA 1970 (4) - 76 (4). BI 1971 (3)-77 (4). A 1972 (3)-74 (3). W 1972. S 1972-75. E 1973 (2). I 1973-74-76. F 1973-77.

WILLIAMS, G.C. 1945- (Wellington, Wellington). E 1967. W 1967. F 1967. S 1967. A 1968.

WILLIAMS, P. 1884-1976. (Alhambra, Otago). A 1913.

WILLIMENT, M. 1940- (University, Wellington). A 1964-67. SA 1965. BI 1966 (4).

WILLOCKS, C. 1919- (Clutha, Otago). A 1946 (2). SA 1949 (3).

WILSON, A. 1886-1953. (Athletic, Wellington). AW 1908. A 1910 (3)-13 (2)-14 (3).

WILSON, B.W. 1956- (Matakanui, Otago). BI 1977 (2).

WILSON, D.D. 1931- (Christchurch H.S.O.B., Canterbury). E 1954. S 1954.

WILSON, H.W. 1924- (Ida Valley, Otago). A 1949-51 (3). BI 1950.

WILSON, N.L. 1922- (Zingari-Richmond, Otago). A 1951 (3).

WILSON, S.S. 1955- (Wellington College O.B., Wellington). F 1977 (2).

WOLFE, T.N. 1941- (University, Wellington and Star, Taranaki). F 1961 (3). A 1962 (2). E 1963.

WOOD, M.E. 1876-1956. (Christchurch, Canterbury and Ponsonby, Auckland). A 1903. GB 1904.

WRIGLEY, E. 1886-1958. (Masterton, Wairarapa). A 1905.

WYLIE, J.T. 1887-1956. (University, Auckland). A 1913. AA 1913.

WYLLIE, A.J. 1944- (Glenmark, Canterbury). SA 1970 (2). BI 1971 (3). W 1972. S 1972. E 1973.(2). I 1973. F 1973.

YATES, V.M. 1938- (Rarawa, North Auckland). F 1961 (3).

YOUNG, D. 1930- (Technical College O.B. & Shirley, Canterbury). SA 1956-60 (4). A 1958 (3)-62 (4). F 1961 (3)-64. E 1963 (2)-64. I 1963. W 1963. S 1964.

MOST INTERNATIONAL APPEARANCES FOR NEW ZEALAND

Meads C.E.	(1957-71)	55	Scott R.W.H.	(1946-54)	17
Kirkpatrick I.A.	(1967-77)	39*	MacRae I.R.	(1966-70)	17
Tremain K.R.	(1959-68)	38	Jarden R.A.	(1951-56)	16
Whineray W.J.	(1957-65)	32	Hemi R.C.	(1953-59)	16
Clarke D.B.	(1956-64)	31	Brown R.H.	(1955-62)	16
Williams B.G.	(1970-77)	31	Caulton R.W.	(1959-64)	16
Going S.M.	(1967-77)	29†	McCormick W.F.	(1965-71)	16
Norton R.W.	(1971-77)	27	Strahan S.C.	(1967-72)	16
Lochore B.J.	(1963-71)	25	Meads S.T.	(1961-66)	15
Gray K.F.	(1963-69)	24	Dick M.J.	(1963-70)	15
McLeod B.E.	(1964-70)	24	Batty G.B.	(1972-77)	15
Clarke I.J.	(1953-63)	24	Nathan W.J.	(1962-67)	14
White R.A.	(1949-56)	23	Muller B.L.	(1967-71)	14
Young D.	(1956-64)	22	King R.R.	(1934-38)	13
Graham D.J.	(1959-64)	22	Walsh P.T.	(1955-63)	13
Skinner K.L.	(1949-56)	20	Kirton E.W.	(1967-70)	13
MacEwan I.N.	(1956-62)	20	Roberts F.	(1905-10)	12
Laidlaw C.R.	(1964-70)	20	Lineen T.R.	(1957-60)	12
Whiting P.J.	(1971-76)	20	Connor D.M.	(1961-64)	12
Robertson B.J.	(1972-77)	20	Macdonald H.H.	(1972-76)	12

* includes 1 as a replacement   † includes 2 as a replacement

MOST SUCCESSIVE INTERNATIONALS FOR NEW ZEALAND

Kirkpatrick I.A.	(1968-77)	38	Jarden R.A.	(1952-56)	14
Meads C.E.	(1962-69)	31	Lochore B.J.	(1965-68)	14
Whineray W.J.	(1957-64)	28	McCormick W.F.	(1967-70)	14
Norton R.W.*	(1971-77)	27	Going S.M.	(1970-73)	14
Williams B.G.	(1971-77)	25	King R.R.*	(1934-38)	13
Clarke D.B.	(1958-64)	24	McLeod B.E.	(1967-70)	13
White R.A.*	(1949-56)	23	Scott R.W.H.	(1946-50)	12
Tremain K.R.	(1963-67)	21	Lineen T.R.*	(1957-60)	12
Skinner K.L.	(1949-54)	18			
Graham D.J.	(1961-64)	18	*Total number of appearances		
Gray K.F.	(1963-66)	16			

MOST APPEARANCES IN EACH POSITION FOR NEW ZEALAND IN INTERNATIONAL MATCHES

Full-back:	Clarke D.B.	(1956-64)	31
	Scott R.W.H.	(1946-54)	17
Wing three-quarter:	Williams B.G.	(1970-77)	29
	Jarden R.A.	(1951-56)	16
	Caulton R.W.	(1959-64)	16
Centre three-quarter:	Robertson B.J.	(1972-77)	20
	Davis W.L.	(1967-70)	11
Second five-eighth:	MacRae I.R.	(1966-70)	16
	Hunter J.	(1905-08)	11
First five-eighth:	Kirton E.W.	(1967-70)	13
	Haig L.S.	(1950-54)	9
	Herewini M.A.	(1962-67)	9
Half-back:	Going S.M.	(1967-77)	29
	Laidlaw C.R.	(1964-70)	20
Back row:	Lochore B.J.	(1963-70)	24
	Leslie A.R.	(1974-76)	10
Side row:	Kirkpatrick I.A.	(1967-77)	36
	Tremain K.R.	(1959-68)	26
Lock:	Meads C.E.	(1957-71)	47
	White R.A.	(1949-56)	23
Prop:	Whineray W.J.	(1957-65)	32
	Gray K.F.	(1963-69)	24
Hooker:	Norton R.W.	(1971-77)	27
	McLeod B.E.	(1964-70)	24

B.J. Lochore also made 1 appearance as a lock

I.A. Kirkpatrick also made 2 appearances as a back row forward

C.E. Meads also made 5 appearances as a side row forward and 2 in the back row

I.R. MacRae also made 1 appearance as a centre three-quarter

K.R. Tremain also made 2 appearances as a back row forward

B.G. Williams also made 2 appearances as a centre three-quarter

M.A. Herewini also made 1 appearance as a second five-eighth

NEW ZEALAND SCORERS IN INTERNATIONAL MATCHES

Note: † indicates tries, drop goals or goals from a mark worth four points. Otherwise these have a value of three points. Conversions have always earned two points.

	Tries	Convs	Pens	Drop Goals	Goals Mark	Total Points
CLARKE D.B.	2	33	38	5	2	207
McCORMICK W.F.	—	23	24	1	—	121
SCOTT R.W.H.	—	16	12	2	—	74
WILLIMENT M.	1	17	11	—	—	70
WILLIAMS B.G.	9(6†)	2	9	1	—	67
KARAM J.F.	1†	11	13	—	—	65
KIRKPATRICK I.A.	16(9†)	—	—	—	—	57
WALLACE W.J.	5	12	2	—	2†	53
NICHOLLS M.F.	—	11	5	2†	1	48
GOING S.M.	10(6†)	1	2	—	—	44
JARDEN R.A.	7	6	3	—·	—	42
MORRIS T.J.	—	9	4	1	—	33
MITCHINSON F.E.	10	1	—	—	—	32
ROBERTS R.W.	7	4	—	—	—	29
POLLOCK H.R.	—	9	1	2†	—	29
TREMAIN K.R.	9	—	—	—	—	27
TAYLOR J.M.	—	6	4	—	—	24
CAULTON R.W.	8	—	—	—	—	24
HART G.F.	7	—	—	—	—	21
MEADS C.E.	7	—	—	—	—	21
HEREWINI M.A.	1	—	1	5	—	21
STEEL A.G.	7	—	—	—	—	21
MAINS L.W.	1	3	4	—	—	21
GILBERT G.D.M.	—	5	2	1†	—	20
McGREGOR D.	6	—	—	—	—	18
SVENSON K.S.	6	—	—	—	—	18
FRANCIS A.R.H.	3	2	1	—	—	16
O'LEARY M.J.	—	6	—	1†	—	16
TREVATHAN D.	—	—	4	1†	—	16
BATTY G.B.	4†	—	—	—	—	16
McKENZIE R.J.	5	—	—	—	—	15
TAYLOR H.M.	5	—	—	—	—	15
BUSH R.G.	—	1	4	—	—	14
KEMBER G.F.	—	1	4	—	—	14
WILSON B.W.	—	1	4	—	—	14
ROBERTSON B.J.	2†	—	—	2	—	14
STRANG W.A.	1	3	—	1†	—	13
HUNTER J.	4	—	—	—	—	12
LYNCH T.W.	4	—	—	—	—	12
PORTER C.G.	4	—	—	—	—	12
BALL N.	4	—	—	—	—	12
MITCHELL N.A.	4	—	—	—	—	12
ARGUS W.G.	4	—	—	—	—	12
ELVIDGE R.R.	4	—	—	—	—	12
BROWN R.H.	3	—	—	1	—	12
McMULLEN R.F.	4	—	—	—	—	12
WALSH P.T.	4	—	—	—	—	12
NATHAN W.J.	4	—	—	—	—	12
GRAY K.F.	4	—	—	—	—	12
McLEOD B.E.	4	—	—	—	—	12
BIRTWISTLE W.M.	4	—	—	—	—	12
DICK M.J.	4	—	—	—	—	12
DAVIS W.L.	4	—	—	—	—	12
KIRTON E.W.	4	—	—	—	—	12
LAIDLAW C.R.	3	—	—	1	—	12
WHITING P.J.	3†	—	—	—	—	12
SUTHERLAND A.R.	3†	—	—	—	—	12
McDONALD A.	3	1	—	—	—	11
ROBERTS F.	2	1	1	—	—	11
COCKERILL M.S.	—	4	1	—	—	11
McKECHNIE B.J.	—	1	2	1	—	11
GRAHAM J.B.	—	5	—	—	—	10
DEANS R.G.	3	—	—	—	—	9
GLASGOW F.T.	3	—	—	—	—	9
GRAY G.D.	3	—	—	—	—	9
MURRAY H.V.	3	—	—	—	—	9
STEEL J.	3	—	—	—	—	9
IRVINE W.R.	3	—	—	—	—	9
COOKE A.E.	3	—	—	—	—	9
GRENSIDE B.A.	3	—	—	—	—	9
OLIVER C.J.	3	—	—	—	—	9
McLEAN H.F.	3	—	—	—	—	9
COLLINS A.H.	—	3	1	—	—	9
BULLOCK-DOUGLAS G.A.H.	3	—	—	—	—	9
HORE J.	3	—	—	—	—	9
CAUGHEY T.H.C.	3	—	—	—	—	9
SULLIVAN J.L.	3	—	—	—	—	9
SAXTON C.K.	3	—	—	—	—	9
KEARNEY J.C.	1	—	—	2	—	9
ROPER R.A.	3	—	—	—	—	9
LYNCH jnr. T.W.	2	—	—	1	—	9
WHITE R.A.	3	—	—	—	—	9
CLARK W.H.	3	—	—	—	—	9
WATT J.R.	3	—	—	—	—	9
MORETON R.C.	2	—	—	1	—	9
RANGI R.E.	3	—	—	—	—	9
MacRAE I.R.	3	—	—	—	—	9
ABBOTT H.L.	2	1	—	—	—	8

	Tries	Convs	Pens	Drop Goals	Goals Mark	Total Points
WYLLIE A.J.	2 †	—	—	—	—	8
HURST I.A.	2 †	—	—	—	—	8
ROBERTSON D.J.	2 †	—	—	—	—	8
GILLETT G.A.	1	2	—	—	—	7
McMINN A.F.	2	—	—	—	—	6
SMITH G.W.	2	—	—	—	—	6
HARPER E.T.	2	—	—	—	—	6
SEELING C.E.	2	—	—	—	—	6
WILSON A.	2	—	—	—	—	6
BURNS P.J.	2	—	—	—	—	6
STOHR L.	2	—	—	—	—	6
FRANCIS W.C.	2	—	—	—	—	6
BROWNLIE M.J.	2	—	—	—	—	6
HADLEY W.E.	2	—	—	—	—	6
WATT J.M.	2	—	—	—	—	6
REID S.T.	2	—	—	—	—	6
RANKIN J.G.	2	—	—	—	—	6
BOWMAN A.W.	2	—	—	—	—	6
SMITH J.B.	1	—	—	1	—	6
HENDERSON P.	2	—	—	—	—	6
BELL R.H.	1	—	1	—	—	6
HOTOP J.	1	—	—	—	—	6
DIXON M.J.	2	—	—	—	—	6
JONES P.F.H.	2	—	—	—	—	6
MacEWAN I.N.	2	—	—	—	—	6
WHINERAY W.J.	2	—	—	—	—	6
GRAHAM D.J.	2	—	—	—	—	6
McKAY D.W.	2	—	—	—	—	6
MORRISSEY P.J.	2	—	—	—	—	6
MURDOCH P.H.	2	—	—	—	—	6
SMITH I.S.T.	2	—	—	—	—	6
LOCHORE B.J.	2	—	—	—	—	6
LISTER T.N.	2	—	—	—	—	6
COTTRELL W.D.	1	—	—	1	—	6
BURGESS R.E.	2	—	—	—	—	6
BRUCE O.D.	—	—	—	2	—	6
TYLER G.A.	1	1	—	—	—	5
NEPIA G.	—	1	1	—	—	5
HAIG L.S.	1	1	—	—	—	5
ROBERTS E.J.	—	2	—	—	—	4
LILBURNE H.T.	—	2	—	—	—	4
MORRISON T.C.	—	—	—	1 †	—	4
DOUGAN J.P.	1 †	—	—	—	—	4
SCOWN A.I.	1 †	—	—	—	—	4
MURDOCH K.	1 †	—	—	—	—	4
LESLIE A.R.	1 †	—	—	—	—	4
STEVENS I.N.	1 †	—	—	—	—	4
MACDONALD H.H.	1 †	—	—	—	—	4
JAFFRAY J.L.	1 †	—	—	—	—	4
MORGAN J.E.	1 †	—	—	—	—	4
JOHNSTONE B.R.	1 †	—	—	—	—	4
WILSON S.S.	1 †	—	—	—	—	4
HADEN A.M.	1 †	—	—	—	—	4
KNIGHT L.G.	1 †	—	—	—	—	4
ASHER A.	1	—	—	—	—	3
McGREGOR R.W.	1	—	—	—	—	3
WRIGLEY G.	1	—	—	—	—	3
CROSS T.	1	—	—	—	—	3
CUNNINGHAM W.	1	—	—	—	—	3
NEWTON F.	1	—	—	—	—	3
HUGHES E.	1	—	—	—	—	3
CAMERON D.	1	—	—	—	—	3
THOMSON H.D.	1	—	—	—	—	3
HAYWARD H.O.	1	—	—	—	—	3
FULLER W.B.	1	—	—	—	—	3
MITCHELL W.J.	1	—	—	—	—	3
PATON H.	1	—	—	—	—	3
PATERSON A.M.	1	—	—	—	—	3
BROWN C.	1	—	—	—	—	3
HASELL E.W.	1	—	—	—	—	3
TAYLOR R.	1	—	—	—	—	3
CUMMINGS W.	1	—	—	—	—	3
FANNING A.H.N.	1	—	—	—	—	3
McGREGOR A.J.	1	—	—	—	—	3
WYLIE J.T.	1	—	—	—	—	3
McNEECE J.	1	—	—	—	—	3
BELLISS E.A.	1	—	—	—	—	3
STOREY P.W.	1	—	—	—	—	3
McLEAN A.L.	1	—	—	—	—	3
WHITE A.	1	—	—	—	—	3
RICHARDSON J.	1	—	—	—	—	3
LINDSAY D.F.	—	—	1	—	—	3
STEWART R.T.	1	—	—	—	—	3
SWAIN J.P.	1	—	—	—	—	3
CUNDY R.T.	—	—	1	—	—	3
McWILLIAMS R.G.	1	—	—	—	—	3
STRINGFELLOW J.C.	1	—	—	—	—	3
LUCAS F.W.	1	—	—	—	—	3
PURDUE G.B.	1	—	—	—	—	3

	Tries	Convs	Pens	Drop Goals	Goals Mark	Total Points
KILBY F.D.	1	—	—	—	—	3
PALMER B.P.	1	—	—	—	—	3
MANCHESTER J.E.	1	—	—	—	—	3
PAGE J.R.	1	—	—	—	—	3
SOLOMON F.	1	—	—	—	—	3
KNIGHT A.	1	—	—	—	—	3
MAX D.S.	1	—	—	—	—	3
DICK J.	1	—	—	—	—	3
PARKHILL A.A.	1	—	—	—	—	3
PHILLIPS W.J.	1	—	—	—	—	3
MILLIKEN H.M.	1	—	—	—	—	3
ELLIOTT K.G.	1	—	—	—	—	3
HAIG J.S.	1	—	—	—	—	3
FINLAY J.	1	—	—	—	—	3
WHITE R.M.	1	—	—	—	—	3
FRAZER H.F.	1	—	—	—	—	3
ARNOLD K.D.	1	—	—	—	—	3
MASON D.F.	1	—	—	—	—	3
THORNTON N.H.	—	—	—	1	—	3
GODDARD M.P.	1	—	—	—	—	3
JOHNSTONE P.	1	—	—	—	—	3
MOORE G.J.T.	1	—	—	—	—	3
KELLY J.W.	—	—	—	1	—	3
O'CALLAGHAN T.R.	—	—	—	1	—	3
CROWLEY P.J.B.	1	—	—	—	—	3
WILSON H.W.	1	—	—	—	—	3
SKINNER K.L.	1	—	—	—	—	3
WILSON N.L.	1	—	—	—	—	3
TANNER J.M.	1	—	—	—	—	3
FITZGERALD J.T.	1	—	—	—	—	3
ROBINSON C.E.	1	—	—	—	—	3
BOWDEN N.J.G.	—	—	—	1	—	3
STUART R.C.	1	—	—	—	—	3
DALZELL G.N.	1	—	—	—	—	3
VODANOVICH I.M.H.	1	—	—	—	—	3
ELSOM A.E.G.	—	—	—	1	—	3
HEMI R.C.	1	—	—	—	—	3
URBAHN R.J.	1	—	—	—	—	3
O'SULLIVAN T.P.A.	1	—	—	—	—	3
LITTLE P.F.	1	—	—	—	—	3
YATES V.M.	1	—	—	—	—	3
HEEPS T.R.	1	—	—	—	—	3
WATT B.A.	—	—	—	1	—	3
CONWAY R.J.	1	—	—	—	—	3
THORNE G.S.	1	—	—	—	—	3
SKUDDER G.R.	1	—	—	—	—	3
SEEAR G.A.	—	—	—	1	—	3
COLMAN J.T.H.	—	1	—	—	—	2
LENDRUM R.N.	—	1	—	—	—	2
Totals	**443**	**210**	**166**	**40**	**5**	**2445**
	391 x 3			9 x 4	2 x 4	
	52 x 4			31 x 3	3 x 3	

HIGHEST INDIVIDUAL POINTS SCORERS IN AN INTERNATIONAL MATCH FOR NEW ZEALAND

(14 Points or more)
† = 4 Points

	Tries	Convs	Pens	Drop Goals	Goals Mark	Total
McCormick W.F. v Wales, (14 June 1969 at Auckland)	—	3	5	1	—	24
Clarke D.B. v Brit. Isles, (18 July 1959 at Dunedin)	—	—	6	—	—	18
Clarke D.B. v France (10 August 1961 at Christchurch)	—	4	3	—	—	17
Scott R.W.H. v Australia, (28 June 1947 at Sydney)	—	3	3	—	—	15
Karam J.F. v Wales, (2 December 1972 at Cardiff)	—	—	5	—	—	15
Karam J.F. v Ireland, (23 November 1974 at Dublin)	1†	1	3	—	—	15
Bush R.G. v Australia, (12 September 1931 at Auckland)	—	1	4	—	—	14
Clarke D.B. v Australia, (20 September 1958 at Auckland)	—	1	4	—	—	14
Willment M. v Australia, (19 August 1967 at Wellington)	—	4	2	—	—	14
Kember G.F. v Sth. Africa, (12 September 1970 at Johannesburg)	—	1	4	—	—	14
Morris T.J. v Australia, (16 September 1972 at Auckland)	—	4	2	—	—	14

MOST POINTS BY AN INDIVIDUAL IN AN INTERNATIONAL SERIES

		Points	Tests
Clarke D.B.	v British Isles 1959	39	4
Williment M.	v British Isles 1966	37	4
Morris T.J.	v Australia 1972	33	3
McCormick W.F.	v Wales 1969	31	2

LEADING INDIVIDUAL TRY SCORERS FOR NEW ZEALAND IN INTERNATIONALS

(5 or more)

		Tries	Matches
Kirkpatrick I.A.	(1967-1977)	16	39
Mitchinson F.E.	(1907-1913)	10	11
Going S.M.	(1967-1977)	10	29
Tremain K.R.	(1959-1968)	9	38
Williams B.G.	(1970-1977)	9	31
Caulton R.W.	(1959-1964)	8	16
Jarden R.A.	(1951-1956)	7	16
Hart G.F.	(1930-1936)	7	11
Meads C.E.	(1957-1971)	7	55
Steel A.G.	(1966-1968)	7	9
McGregor D.	(1903-1905)	6	4
Svenson K.S.	(1924-1925)	6	4
McKenzie R.J.	(1913-1914)	5	4
Taylor H.M.	(1913-1914)	5	5

MOST TRIES IN AN INTERNATIONAL FOR NEW ZEALAND

McGregor D.	v England 1905	London	4
Wallace W.J.	v France 1906	Paris	3
Mitchinson F.E.	v Australia 1907	Sydney	3
Mitchinson F.E.	v Anglo Welsh 1908	Auckland	3
Lynch T.W.	v Australia 1913	Wellington	3
Roberts R.W.	v All-America 1913	Berkeley	3
Taylor H.M.	v Australia 1914	Brisbane	3
Caughey T.H.C.	v Scotland 1935	Edinburgh	3
Kirkpatrick I.A.	v Australia 1968	Sydney	3

MOST TRIES BY AN INDIVIDUAL IN AN INTERNATIONAL SERIES

		Tries	Tests
Mitchinson F.E.	v Anglo-Welsh 1908	5	3
Mitchinson F.E.	v Australia 1907	4	3
Taylor H.M.	v Australia 1914	4	3
Caulton R.W.	v British Isles 1959	4	4

TRIES FOR NEW ZEALAND FROM FULL-BACK IN AN INTERNATIONAL

Clarke D.B.	v British Isles at Wellington 1959
Clarke D.B.	v England at Auckland 1963
Williment M.	v British Isles at Dunedin 1966
Mains L.W.	v British Isles at Wellington 1971
Karam J.F.	v Ireland at Dublin 1974

MOST CONVERSIONS IN AN INTERNATIONAL FOR NEW ZEALAND

Scott R.W.H.	v Australia 1946	Dunedin	5
Wallace W.J.	v Australia 1907	Sydney	4
Graham J.B.	v All-America 1913	Berkeley	4
Pollock H.R.	v Australia 1936	Dunedin	4
Clarke D.B.	v France 1961	Christchurch	4
Williment M.	v Australia 1967	Wellington	4
McCormick W.F.	v England 1967	Twickenham	4
Morris T.J.	v Australia 1972	Auckland	4
Karam J.F.	v Scotland 1975	Auckland	4

MOST PENALTY GOALS IN AN INTERNATIONAL FOR NEW ZEALAND

Clarke D.B.	v British Isles 1959	Dunedin	6
McCormick W.F.	v Wales 1969	Auckland	5
Karam J.F.	v Wales 1972	Cardiff	5
Bush R.G.	v Australia 1931	Auckland	4
Clarke D.B.	v Australia 1958	Auckland	4
Kember G.F.	v South Africa 1970	Johannesburg	4

MOST DROPPED GOALS IN AN INTERNATIONAL FOR NEW ZEALAND

26 players in 40 separate matches have kicked one dropped goal

MOST GOALS FROM A MARK IN AN INTERNATIONAL FOR NEW ZEALAND

W.J. Wallace kicked two goals from marks against Australia at Sydney 1903

NEW ZEALAND'S INTERNATIONAL MATCHES

v. AUSTRALIA in AUSTRALIA

Year	Played	Won	Lost	Drawn	Tries	Convs	Pens	Drop Goals	Goals Mark	Total	Tries	Convs	Pens	Drop Goals	Goals Mark	Total
					POINTS FOR						POINTS AGAINST					
1903	1	1	—	—	3	1	1	—	2†	22	—	—	1	—	—	3
1907	3	2	—	1	11	6	—	—	—	45	2	2	1	—	1	16
1910	3	2	1	—	10	2	—	—	—	34	5	3	1	—	—	24
1914	3	3	—	—	12	4	—	—	—	44	1	—	—	1†	—	7
1929	3	—	3	—	6	3	2	—	—	30	6	1	7	—	—	41
1932	3	2	1	—	12	6	1	2†	—	59	8	4	2	—	—	38
1934	2	—	1	1	4	1	—	—	—	14	5	2	3	—	—	28
1938	3	3	—	—	10	6	4	1†	—	58	4	1	5	—	—	29
1947	2	2	—	—	6	5	4	—	—	40	2	2	3	—	—	19
1951	3	3	—	—	9	4	1	1	—	41	2	1	3	—	—	17
1957	2	2	—	—	8	4	3	1	1	47	2	1	4	—	—	20
1962	2	2	—	—	6	2	3	1	—	34	1	1	2	—	—	11
1968	2	2	—	—	9	5	3	—	—	46	2	1	7	—	—	29
1974	3	2	—	1	7	3	3	—	—	43	3	2	4	—	—	28
	35	26	6	3	113	52	25	6	3	557	43	21	43	1	1	310

v. AUSTRALIA in NEW ZEALAND

Year	Played	Won	Lost	Drawn	Tries	Convs	Pens	Drop Goals	Goals Mark	Total	Tries	Convs	Pens	Drop Goals	Goals Mark	Total
					POINTS FOR						POINTS AGAINST					
1905	1	1	—	—	4	1	—	—	—	14	1	—	—	—	—	3
1913	3	2	1	—	14	7	—	1†	—	60	8	5	—	—	—	34
1931	1	1	—	—	2	1	4	—	—	20	3	2	—	—	—	13
1936	2	2	—	—	12	5	1	—	—	49	3	2	2	—	—	19
1946	2	2	—	—	8	6	3	—	—	45	4	3	—	—	—	18
1949	2	—	2	—	2	—	2	1	—	15	6	3	1	—	—	27
1952	2	1	1	—	4	—	3	1	—	24	4	2	1	1	—	22
1955	3	2	1	—	5	3	1	1	—	27	3	2	1	—	—	16
1958	3	2	1	—	9	3	4	—	—	45	3	1	2	—	—	17
1962	3	2	—	1	4	2	3	1	—	28	1	1	4	—	—	17
1964	3	2	1	—	6	5	2	1	—	37	4	1	5	1	—	32
1967	1	1	—	—	4	4	2	1	—	29	2	—	—	1	—	9
1972	3	3	—	—	16	9	4	1	—	97	3	1	3	1	—	26
	29	21	7	1	90	46	29	8	—	490	45	23	20	3	—	253

Combined Total Home and Overseas against Australia
| | 64 | 47 | 13 | 4 | 203 | 98 | 54 | 14 | 3 | 1047 | 88 | 44 | 63 | 4 | 1 | 563 |

v. BRITISH TEAMS in NEW ZEALAND

Year	Played	Won	Lost	Drawn	Tries	Convs	Pens	Drop Goals	Goals Mark	Total	Tries	Convs	Pens	Drop Goals	Goals Mark	Total
					POINTS FOR						POINTS AGAINST					
1904	1	1	—	—	2	—	1	—	—	9	—	—	1	—	—	3
1908*	3	2	—	1	16	5	2	—	—	64	2	1	—	—	—	8
1930	4	3	1	—	12	5	—	1	1†	53	7	5	1	—	—	34
1950	4	3	—	1	7	2	2	1	—	34	3	1	3	—	—	20
1959	4	3	1	—	7	3	9	1	—	57	9	3	3	—	—	42
1966	4	4	—	—	13	8	6	2	—	79	4	1	5	1	—	32
1971	4	1	2	1	8	3	4	—	—	42	6	3	5	3	—	48
1977	4	3	1	—	6	3	7	1	—	54	3	1	9	—	—	41
	28	20	5	3	71	29	31	6	1	392	34	15	27	4	—	228

*Anglo-Welsh team

v. ENGLAND in ENGLAND

Year	Played	Won	Lost	Drawn	Tries	Convs	Pens	Drop Goals	Goals Mark	Total	Tries	Convs	Pens	Drop Goals	Goals Mark	Total
					POINTS FOR						POINTS AGAINST					
1905	1	1	—	—	5	—	—	—	—	15	—	—	—	—	—	0
1925	1	1	—	—	4	1	1	—	—	17	2	1	1	—	—	11
1936	1	—	1	—	—	—	—	—	—	0	3	—	—	1†	—	13
1954	1	1	—	—	1	1	—	—	—	5	—	—	—	—	—	0
1964	1	1	—	—	2	1	2	—	—	14	—	—	—	—	—	0
1967	1	1	—	—	5	4	—	—	—	23	2	1	1	—	—	11
1973	1	1	—	—	1	1	—	1	—	9	—	—	—	—	—	0
	7	6	1	—	18	8	3	1	—	83	7	2	2	1	—	35

v. ENGLAND in NEW ZEALAND

Year	Played	Won	Lost	Drawn	Tries	Convs	Pens	Drop Goals	Goals Mark	Total	Tries	Convs	Pens	Drop Goals	Goals Mark	Total
					POINTS FOR						POINTS AGAINST					
1963	2	2	—	—	5	3	1	1	1	30	2	1	3	—	—	17
1973	1	—	1	—	2	1	—	—	—	10	3	2	—	—	—	16
	3	2	1	—	7	4	1	1	1	40	5	3	3	—	—	33

Combined Total Home and Overseas against England
| | 10 | 8 | 2 | — | 25 | 12 | 4 | 2 | 1 | 123 | 12 | 5 | 5 | 1 | — | 68 |

v. WALES in WALES

Year	Played	Won	Lost	Drawn	Tries	Convs	Pens	Drop Goals	Goals Mark	Total	Tries	Convs	Pens	Drop Goals	Goals Mark	Total
					POINTS FOR						POINTS AGAINST					
1905	1	—	1	—	—	—	—	—	—	0	1	—	—	—	—	3
1924	1	1	—	—	4	2	1	—	—	19	—	—	—	—	—	0
1935	1	—	1	—	2	1	—	1	—	12	3	2	—	—	—	13
1953	1	—	1	—	1	1	1	—	—	8	2	2	1	—	—	13
1963	1	1	—	—	—	—	1	1	—	6	—	—	—	—	—	0
1967	1	1	—	—	2	2	1	—	—	13	—	—	1	1	—	6
1972	1	1	—	—	—	1	5	—	—	19	1	—	4	—	—	16
	7	4	3	—	10	6	9	2	—	77	7	4	6	1	—	51

v. WALES in NEW ZEALAND

Year	Played	Won	Lost	Drawn	Tries	Convs	Pens	Drop Goals	Goals Mark	Total	Tries	Convs	Pens	Drop Goals	Goals Mark	Total
					POINTS FOR						POINTS AGAINST					
1969	2	2	—	—	7	5	6	1	—	52	2	—	2	—	—	12

Combined Total Home and Overseas against Wales
| | 9 | 6 | 3 | — | 17 | 11 | 15 | 3 | — | 129 | 9 | 4 | 8 | 1 | — | 63 |

v. IRELAND in IRELAND

Year	Played	Won	Lost	Drawn	Tries	Convs	Pens	Drop Goals	Goals Mark	Total	Tries	Convs	Pens	Drop Goals	Goals Mark	Total
					POINTS FOR						POINTS AGAINST					
1905	1	1	—	—	3	3	—	—	—	15	—	—	—	—	—	0
1924	1	1	—	—	1	—	1	—	—	6	—	—	—	—	—	0
1935	1	1	—	—	3	1	2	—	—	17	1	—	2	—	—	9
1954	1	1	—	—	2	1	1	1	—	14	1	—	1	—	—	3
1963	1	1	—	—	1	—	1	—	—	6	1	1	—	—	—	5
1973	1	—	—	1	2	1	—	—	—	10	2	—	2	—	—	10
1974	1	1	—	—	1	1	3	—	—	15	—	—	2	—	—	6
	7	6	—	1	13	7	8	1	—	83	3	1	7	—	—	33

v. IRELAND in NEW ZEALAND

Year	Played	Won	Lost	Drawn	Tries	Convs	Pens	Drop Goals	Goals Mark	Total	Tries	Convs	Pens	Drop Goals	Goals Mark	Total
					POINTS FOR						POINTS AGAINST					
1976	1	1	—	—	2	—	1	—	—	11	—	—	1	—	—	3

Combined Total Home and Overseas against Ireland
| | 8 | 7 | — | 1 | 15 | 7 | 9 | 1 | — | 94 | 3 | 1 | 8 | — | — | 36 |

v. SCOTLAND in SCOTLAND

Year	Played	Won	Lost	Drawn	Tries	Convs	Pens	Drop Goals	Goals Mark	Total	Tries	Convs	Pens	Drop Goals	Goals Mark	Total
					POINTS FOR						POINTS AGAINST					
1905	1	1	—	—	4	—	—	—	—	12	1	—	—	1	—	7
1935	1	1	—	—	4	3	—	—	—	18	2	1	—	—	—	8
1954	1	1	—	—	—	—	1	—	—	3	—	—	—	—	—	0
1964	1	—	—	1	—	—	—	—	—	0	—	—	—	—	—	0
1967	1	1	—	—	2	1	2	—	—	14	—	—	—	1	—	3
1972	1	1	—	—	3	1	—	—	—	14	—	—	2	1	—	14
	6	5	—	1	13	5	3	—	—	61	3	1	2	3	—	27

v. SCOTLAND in NEW ZEALAND

Year	Played	Won	Lost	Drawn	Tries	Convs	Pens	Drop Goals	Goals Mark	Total	Tries	Convs	Pens	Drop Goals	Goals Mark	Total
					POINTS FOR						POINTS AGAINST					
1975	1	1	—	—	4	4	—	—	—	24	—	—	—	—	—	0

Combined Total Home and Overseas against Scotland
| | 7 | 6 | — | 1 | 17 | 9 | 3 | — | — | 85 | 3 | 1 | 2 | 3 | — | 27 |

v. ALL AMERICA in U.S.A.

Year	Played	Won	Lost	Drawn	Tries	Convs	Pens	Drop Goals	Goals Mark	Total	Tries	Convs	Pens	Drop Goals	Goals Mark	Total
					POINTS FOR						POINTS AGAINST					
1913	1	1	—	—	13	6	—	—	—	51	—	—	1	—	—	3

v. FRANCE in FRANCE

Year	Played	Won	Lost	Drawn	POINTS FOR Tries	Convs	Pens	Drop Goals	Goals Mark	Total	POINTS AGAINST Tries	Convs	Pens	Drop Goals	Goals Mark	Total
1906	1	1	—	—	10	4	—	—	—	38	2	1	—	—	—	8
1925	1	1	—	—	8	3	—	—	—	30	2	—	—	—	—	6
1954	1	—	1	—	—	—	—	—	—	0	1	—	—	—	—	3
1964	1	1	—	—	2	—	1	1	—	12	—	—	1	·	—	3
1967	1	1	—	—	4	3	1	—	—	21	1	—	3	1	—	15
1973	1	—	1	—	—	—	2	—	—	6	2	1	—	—	—	13
1977	2	1	1	—	2	1	4	2	—	28	1	1	4	1	—	21
	8	5	3	—	26	11	8	3	—	135	9	3	9	2	—	69

v. FRANCE in NEW ZEALAND

Year	Played	Won	Lost	Drawn	POINTS FOR Tries	Convs	Pens	Drop Goals	Goals Mark	Total	POINTS AGAINST Tries	Convs	Pens	Drop Goals	Goals Mark	Total
1961	3	3	—	—	8	7	3	1	—	50	2	—	—	2	—	12
1968	3	3	—	—	3	2	8	1	—	40	3	—	3	2	—	24
	6	6	—	—	11	9	11	2	—	90	5	—	3	4	—	36

Combined Totals Home and Overseas against France
	14	11	3	—	37	20	19	5	—	225	14	3	12	6	—	105

v. SOUTH AFRICA in SOUTH AFRICA

Year	Played	Won	Lost	Drawn	POINTS FOR Tries	Convs	Pens	Drop Goals	Goals Mark	Total	POINTS AGAINST Tries	Convs	Pens	Drop Goals	Goals Mark	Total
1928	4	2	2	—	3	—	3	2	—	26	5	2	3	2	1	39
1949	4	—	4	—	4	2	2	—	—	28	3	1	10	2	—	47
1960	4	1	2	1	2	2	4	1	—	25	5	4	4	--	—	35
1970	4	1	3	—	4	1	7	—	—	35	7	4	9	1	—	59
1976	4	1	3	—	5	1	6	2	—	46	4	3	8	3	—	55
	20	5	14	1	18	6	22	7	—	160	24	14	34	8	1	235

v. SOUTH AFRICA in NEW ZEALAND

Year	Played	Won	Lost	Drawn	POINTS FOR Tries	Convs	Pens	Drop Goals	Goals Mark	Total	POINTS AGAINST Tries	Convs	Pens	Drop Goals	Goals Mark	Total
1921	3	1	1	1	4	3	—	—	—	18	2	2	—	—	—	14
1937	3	1	2	—	3	—	4	1	—	25	8	3	1	1	—	37
1956	4	3	1	—	7	4	4	—	—	41	6	4	1	—	—	29
1965	4	3	1	—	13	5	1	1	—	58	4	2	2	1	—	25
	14	8	5	1	27	12	9	2	—	139	20	11	4	3	—	105

Combined Total Home and Overseas against South Africa
	34	13	19	2	45	18	31	9	—	299	44	25	38	11	1	340

SUMMARY

INTERNATIONALS PLAYED IN NEW ZEALAND

	Played	Won	Lost	Drawn	POINTS FOR Tries	Convs	Pens	Drop Goals	Goals Mark	Total	POINTS AGAINST Tries	Convs	Pens	Drop Goals	Goals Mark	Total
Australia	29	21	7	1	90	46	29	8	—	490	45	23	20	3	—	253
Britain	28	20	·5	3	71	29	31	6	—	392	34	15	27	4	—	228
England	3	2	1	—	7	4	1	1	1	40	5	3	3	—	—	33
France	8	6	—	—	11	9	11	2	—	90	5	—	3	4	—	36
Ireland	1	1	—	—	2	—	1	—	—	11	—	—	—	—	—	3
South Africa	14	8	5	1	27	12	9	2	—	139	20	11	4	3	—	105
Wales	2	2	—	—	7	5	6	1	—	52	2	—	2	—	—	12
Scotland	1	1	—	—	4	4	—	—	—	24	—	—	—	—	—	—
	84	61	18	5	219	109	88	20	2	1238	111	52	60	14		670

INTERNATIONALS PLAYED OVERSEAS

	Played	Won	Lost	Drawn	POINTS FOR Tries	Convs	Pens	Drop Goals	Goals Mark	Total	POINTS AGAINST Tries	Convs	Pens	Drop Goals	Goals Mark	Total
Australia	35	26	6	3	113	52	25	6	3	557	43	21	43	1	1	310
England	7	6	1	—	18	8	3	1	—	83	7	2	2	1	—	35
France	8	5	3	—	26	11	8	3	—	135	9	3	9	2	—	69
Ireland	7	6	—	1	13	7	8	1	—	83	3	1	7	—	—	33
South Africa	20	5	14	1	18	6	22	7	—	160	24	14	34	8	1	235
Wales	7	4	3	—	10	6	9	2	—	77	7	4	6	1	—	51
America	1	1	—	—	13	6	—	—	—	51	—	—	1	—	—	3
Scotland	6	5	—	1	13	5	3	—	—	61	3	1	2	3	—	27
	91	58	27	6	224	101	78	20	3	1207	96	46	104	16	2	763

Total	175	119	45	11	443	210	166	40	5	2445	207	98	164	30	2	1433

VENUES OF INTERNATIONALS

	No. of Matches
NEW ZEALAND	
Wellington (25)	
Athletic Park	25
Dunedin (17)	
Tahuna Park	1
Carisbrook	16
Christchurch (18)	
Lancaster Park Oval	18
Auckland (24)	
Potters Park	1
Eden Park	22
Epsom Showgrounds	1
Total in New Zealand	84
AUSTRALIA (35)	
Sydney Cricket Ground	22
Sydney Sports Ground	2
Brisbane Cricket Ground	2
Woolloongabba Ground	1
Exhibition Ground, Brisbane	6
Ballymore Oval, Brisbane	2
ENGLAND (7)	
Crystal Palace, London	1
Twickenham, London	6
WALES (7)	
Cardiff Arms Park	6
St. Helens Ground, Swansea	1
SCOTLAND (6)	
Inverleith Ground, Edinburgh	1
Murrayfield, Edinburgh	5
IRELAND (7)	
Lansdowne Road, Dublin	7
FRANCE (8)	
Parc des Princes, Paris	3
Colombes Stadium, Paris	3
Stade Ernest-Wallon, Toulouse	1
Stade et Toulouse	1
SOUTH AFRICA (20)	
Loftus Versfeld Stadium, Pretoria	1
Kingmead Ground, Durban	2
Ellis Park, Johannesburg	5
Crusader Ground, Port Elizabeth	2
Newlands, Cape Town	5
Free State Stadium, Bloemfontein	1
Boet Erasmus Stadium, Port Elizabeth	2
Kings Park, Durban	1
U.S.A. (1)	
California Field, Berkeley, California	1
Total Overseas	91
Total Internationals	175

MOST TRIES BY A NEW ZEALAND TEAM IN AN INTERNATIONAL

v All-America 1913	Berkeley	13
v France 1906	Paris	10
v Anglo-Welsh 1908	Auckland	9
v Australia 1936	Dunedin	9
v Australia 1910	Sydney	8
v Australia 1913	Wellington	8
v France 1925	Toulouse	8
v Anglo-Welsh 1908	Dunedin	7
v Australia 1946	Dunedin	7
v Australia 1958	Wellington	7

MOST TRIES BY NEW ZEALAND IN AN INTERNATIONAL SERIES

	Tests	Tries
v Anglo-Welsh 1908	3	16
v Australia 1972	3	16
v Australia 1913	3	14
v South Africa 1965	4	13
v British Isles 1966	4	13
v Australia 1914	3	12
v Great Britain 1930	4	12
v Australia 1932	3	12
v Australia 1936	2	12

Note: A Test series has been taken as two or more matches against the same opponent, played in the same country in the same year.

LONGEST INTERNATIONAL WINNING SEQUENCE BY NEW ZEALAND

Fourth Test v South Africa 1965 to second Test v Wales 1969 inclusive - 17 matches

LONGEST INTERNATIONAL LOSING SEQUENCE BY NEW ZEALAND

First Test v South Africa 1949 to second Test v Australia 1949 inclusive - 6 matches

LARGEST WINNING MARGINS IN INTERNATIONALS

		Score	Points Margin	Year	Venue
v AUSTRALIA	in Australia	26-6	20	1907	Sydney
	in New Zealand	38-3	35	1972	Auckland
v BRITISH TEAMS*	in New Zealand	29-0	29	1908	Auckland
v ENGLAND	in England	15-0	15	1905	London
	in New Zealand	21-11	10	1963	Auckland
v FRANCE	in France	38-8	30	1906	Paris
	in New Zealand	32-3	29	1961	Christchurch
v IRELAND	in Ireland	15-0	15	1905	Dublin
	in New Zealand	11-3	8	1976	Wellington
v SCOTLAND	in Scotland	14-3	11	1967	Edinburgh
	in New Zealand	24-0	24	1975	Auckland
v SOUTH AFRICA	in South Africa	13-5	8	1928	Cape Town
		11-3	8	1960	Cape Town
	in New Zealand	20-3	17	1965	Auckland
v WALES	in Wales	19-0	19	1924	Swansea
	in New Zealand	33-12	21	1969	Auckland
v ALL-AMERICA	in U.S.A.	51-3	48	1913	Berkeley

LARGEST LOSING MARGINS IN INTERNATIONALS

		Score	Points Margin	Year	Venue
v AUSTRALIA	in Australia	11-25	14	1934	Sydney
	in New Zealand	5-20	15	1964	Wellington
v BRITISH TEAMS*	in New Zealand	3-13	10	1971	Wellington
v ENGLAND	in England	0-13	13	1936	London
	in New Zealand	10-16	6	1973	Auckland
v FRANCE	in France	6-13	7	1973	Paris
	in New Zealand	—	—	—	—
v IRELAND	in Ireland	—	—	—	—
	in New Zealand	—	—	—	—
v SCOTLAND	in Scotland	—	—	—	—
	in New Zealand	—	—	—	—
v SOUTH AFRICA	in South Africa	0-17	17	1928	Durban
	in New Zealand	6-17	11	1937	Auckland
v WALES	in Wales	8-13	5	1953	Cardiff
	in New Zealand	—	—	—	—
v ALL-AMERICA	in U.S.A.	—	—	—	—

* includes 1908 Anglo-Welsh team

377

INTERNATIONALS IN WHICH NEW ZEALAND FAILED TO SCORE (8)

1905	v Wales at Cardiff	0-3
1910	v Australia at Sydney	0-11
1921	v South Africa at Wellington	0-0
1928	v South Africa at Durban	0-17
1936	v England at Twickenham	0-13
1954	v France at Paris	0-3
1960	v South Africa at Johannesburg	0-13
1964	v Scotland at Murrayfield	0-0

INTERNATIONALS IN WHICH OPPOSITION FAILED TO SCORE (22)

1905	v Ireland at Dublin	15-0
	v England at London	15-0
1908	v Anglo-Welsh at Auckland	29-0
1910	v Australia at Sydney	6-0
1914	v Australia at Sydney	5-0
	v Australia at Brisbane	17-0
1921	v South Africa at Wellington	0-0
1924	v Ireland at Dublin	6-0
	v Wales at Swansea	19-0
1950	v British Isles at Christchurch	8-0
1951	v Australia at Sydney	8-0
1954	v England at Twickenham	5-0
	v Scotland at Murrayfield	3-0
1955	v Australia at Dunedin	8-0
1962	v Australia at Dunedin	3-0
1963	v Wales at Cardiff	6-0
1964	v England at Twickenham	14-0
	v Scotland at Murrayfield	0-0
1965	v South Africa at Dunedin	13-0
1969	v Wales at Christchurch	19-0
1973	v England at Twickenham	9-0
1975	v Scotland at Auckland	24-0

MOST INTERNATIONAL APPEARANCES AGAINST NEW ZEALAND

Wood F. (Australia)	(1907-14)	12
Bonis E.T. (Australia)	(1929-38)	12
Thornett J.E. (Australia)	(1955-64)	12
Burke C.T. (Australia)	(1946-55)	11
Johnson P. (Australia)	(1962-68)	11
Shehadie N.M. (Australia)	(1947-57)	11
White J.P.L. (Australia)	(1958-64)	11
Windon C.J. (Australia)	(1946-52)	10
Miller A.R. (Australia)	(1952-67)	10
McBride W.J. (Ireland & British Isles)	(1963-74)	10
Gibson C.M.H. (Ireland & British Isles)	(1966-76)	10

MOST POINTS SCORED BY AN OPPOSITION PLAYER IN AN INTERNATIONAL AGAINST NEW ZEALAND

Geffin A. (SA)	at Durban, 1949	15
McGill A.N. (A)	at Brisbane, 1968	15
Osler B.L. (SA)	at Durban, 1928	14
McCallum I.D. (SA)	at Johannesburg, 1970	14
Ross A.W. (A)	at Sydney, 1934	13
Bennett P. (W)	at Cardiff, 1972	12

MOST POINTS SCORED BY AN OPPOSITION PLAYER IN INTERNATIONALS AGAINST NEW ZEALAND

		Matches	Points
McCallum I.D. (South Africa)	(1970)	4	35
John B. (Wales and British Isles)	(1967-71)	7	33
Bosch G.R. (South Africa)	(1976)	4	33
Geffin A. (South Africa)	1949)	4	32
Lawton T.S. (Australia)	(1929-32)	5	30
Bennett P. (Wales and British Isles)	(1972-77)	5	30

MOST TRIES SCORED BY AN OPPOSITION PLAYER IN INTERNATIONALS AGAINST NEW ZEALAND

		Matches	Tries
Towers C.H.T. (Australia)	(1929-34)	5	4
Gilbert H. (Australia)	(1910)	3	3
Suttor D.C. (Australia)	(1913)	3	3
Jones H.A. (Australia)	(1913)	3	3
Aarvold C.D. (British Isles)	(1930)	4	3
Cowper D.L. (Australia)	(1931-32)	4	3
Jones K.J. (British Isles/Wales)	(1950-53)	4	3
Davies T.G.R. (Wales/British Isles)	(1969-72)	7	3
Muller G.H. (South Africa)	(1970)	4	3

NEW ZEALAND INTERNATIONAL CAPTAINS

Whineray W.J.	(1958-65)	30
Lochore B.J.	(1966-70)	18
Leslie A.R.	(1974-76)	10
Kirkpatrick I.A.	(1972-73)	9
Porter C.G.	(1925-30)	7
Allen F.R.	(1946-49)	6
Elvidge R.R.	(1949-50)	5
Stuart R.C.	(1953-54)	5
Stead J.W.	(1904-08)	4
Hunter J.	(1907-08)	4
Gallaher D.	(1905-06)	4
Brownlie M.J.	(1928)	4
Kilby F.D.	(1932-34)	4
Manchester J.E.	(1935-36)	4
Johnstone P.	(1950-51)	4
Meads C.E.	(1971)	4
Norton R.W.	(1977)	4
Roberts F.	(1910)	3
Roberts R.W.	(1914)	3
Richardson J.	(1924)	3
King R.R.	(1937)	3
Clarke I.J.	(1955)	3
Graham D.J.	(1964)	3
McDonald A.	(1913)	2
O'Leary M.J.	(1913)	2
Aitken G.G.	(1921)	2
Griffiths J.L.	(1936)	2
Mitchell N.A.	(1938)	2
Smith J.B.	(1949)	2
Skinner K.L.	(1952)	2
Vincent P.B.	(1956)	2
Duff R.H.	(1956)	2
Reid A.R.	(1957)	2
Mourie G.N.K.	(1977)	2
Duncan J.	(1903)	1
Spencer J.C.	(1905)	1
Roberts E.J.	(1921)	1
Lilburne H.T.	(1929)	1
Strang W.A.	(1931)	1
Page J.R.	(1934)	1
McKenzie R.M.	(1938)	1
Laidlaw C.R.	(1968)	1
Tremain K.R.	(1968)	1

REPLACEMENTS IN NEW ZEALAND INTERNATIONAL TEAMS

Spencer J.C. replaced Booth E.E.
v Australia at Sydney 1907

Mitchinson F.E. replaced Taylor H.M.
v Australia at Wellington 1913

Stringfellow J.C. replaced Nepia G.
v Australia at Sydney 1929

Cundy R.T. replaced Oliver C.J.
v Australia at Brisbane 1929

McRae J.A. replaced Catley E.H.
v Australia at Dunedin 1946

Mason D.F. replaced Argus W.G.
v Australia at Sydney 1947

Kirkpatrick I.A. replaced Lochore B.J.
v Australia at Sydney 1968

Going S.M. replaced Laidlaw C.R.
v South Africa at Pretoria 1970

Duncan M.G. replaced Burgess R.E.
v British Isles at Wellington 1971

Scown A.I. replaced Wyllie A.J.
v Wales at Cardiff 1972

Lambert K.K. replaced Matheson J.D.
v Scotland at Edinburgh 1972

Morrison T.G. replaced Parkinson R.M.
v England at Auckland 1973

Going S.M. replaced Davis L.J.
v Ireland at Wellington 1976

Osborne W.M. replaced Batty G.B.
v South Africa at Bloemfontein 1976

Mitchell T.W. replaced Batty G.B.
v South Africa at Johannesburg 1976

Osborne W.M. replaced Morgan J.E.
v South Africa at Johannesburg 1976

Taylor N.M. replaced Ford B.R.
v British Isles at Auckland 1977

Bush W.K. replaced McEldowney J.T.
v British Isles at Auckland 1977

Stuart R.L. replaced Knight G.A.
v France at Toulouse 1977

Osborne W.M. replaced Williams B.G.
v France at Toulouse 1977

YOUNGEST NEW ZEALAND INTERNATIONAL CAPTAINS

Herbert Theodore Lilburne, born Burnham, 16 March 1908
v Australia 6 July 1929 21 years 112 days

George Gothard Aitken, born Westport, 2 July 1898
v South Africa 13 Aug. 1921 23 years 42 days

Wilson James Whineray, born Auckland, 10 July 1935,
v Australia 23 Aug. 1958 23 years 44 days

YOUNGEST NEW ZEALAND INTERNATIONAL PLAYERS
(under 20)

Edgar Wrigley, born Masterton 15 June 1886
v Australia 2 September 1905 19 years 79 days

Patrick Timothy Walsh, born Kaitaia, 6 May 1936
v Australia 20 August 1955 19 years 106 days

George Nepia, born Wairoa, 25 April 1905
v Ireland 1 November 1924 19 years 190 days

William James Mitchell, born St. Kilda, Victoria,
28 November 1890,
v Australia 27 June 1910 19 years 211 days

William Charles Francis, born New Plymouth,
4 February 1894,
v Australia 13 September 1913 19 years 221 days

Thomas Neil Wolfe, born New Plymouth,
20 November 1941,
v France 22 July 1961 19 years 244 days

James Alexander Steenson Baird, born Dunedin,
17 December 1893,
v Australia 13 September 1913 19 years 270 days

Bryan George Williams, born Auckland, 3 October 1950,
v South Africa 25 July 1970 19 years 295 days

OLDEST NEW ZEALAND INTERNATIONAL PLAYERS
(34 or over)

Edward Hughes, born Invercargill, 26 April 1881*
v South Africa 27 August 1921, 40 years 123 days.

Colin Earl Meads, born Cambridge, 3 June 1936
v British Isles 14 August 1971, 35 years 72 days

William Theodore Charles Sonntag, born Dunedin,
3 June 1894
v Australia 27 July 1929, 35 years 54 days

William Rika (Heke) born   3 September 1894
v Australia 27 July 1929, 34 years 327 days

Rangitane Will Norton, born Methven, 30 March 1943
v British Isles 13 August 1977, 34 years 136 days

James Edward Moffitt, born Waikaia, 3 June 1887
v South Africa 17 September 1921, 34 years 106 days

Harry Jonas Mynott, born New Plymouth 4 June 1876
v Australia 2 July 1910, 34 years 28 days

* Date of birth not apparently registered and this date taken from army records.

NEW ZEALAND INTERNATIONAL BROTHERS

Brownlie C.J. (1924-25) and Brownlie M.J. (1924-25-28)

Clarke D.B. (1956-57-58-59-60-61-62-63-64) and Clarke I.J. (1953-55-56-57-58-59-60-61-62-63)

Donald J.G. (1921) and Donald Q. (1924-25)

Fanning B.J. (1903-04) and Fanning A.H.N. (1913)

Hadley S. (1928) and Hadley W.E. (1934-35-36)

Haig J.S. (1946) and Haig L.S. (1950-51-53-54)

Meads C.E. (1957-58-59-60-61-62-63-64-65-66-67-68-69-70-71) and Meads S.T. (1961-62-63-64-65-66)

Meates K.F. (1952) and Meates W.A. (1949-50)

McMinn A.F. (1903-05) and McMinn F.A. (1904)

Nicholls H.E. (1921) and Nicholls M.F.(1921-24-25-28-30)

Purdue C.A. (1905) and Purdue E.(1905)

Stuart K.C. (1955) and Stuart R.C.(1949-53-54)

NEW ZEALAND INTERNATIONAL FATHER AND SONS

Dalton R.A. (1947) and Dalton A.G.(1977)

Dick J. (1937-38) and Dick M.J. (1963-64-65-66-67-68-69-70)

Irvine W.R. (1924-30) and Irvine I.B. (1952)

Lynch T.W. (1913-14) and Lynch T.W. (1951)

Purdue E. (1905) and Purdue G.B.(1931-32)

NEW ZEALAND INTERNATIONALS WHO HAVE APPEARED FOR OTHER COUNTRIES

Gilray C.M. (1905) represented Scotland 1908-09-12

MacPherson D.G. (1905) represented Scotland 1910

Wylie J.T. (1913) represented Australia 1912

Aitken G.G. (1921) represented Scotland 1924-25-29

Jessep E.M. (1931-32) represented Australia 1934

Connor D.M. (1961-62-63-64) represented Australia 1957-58-59

Stephens O.G. (1968) represented Australia 1973-74

NEW ZEALAND REFEREES OF INTERNATIONALS FEATURING NEW ZEALAND TEAMS

		Matches
Murphy J.P. (North Auckland)	1959-1969	13
Pring J.P.G. (Auckland)	1966-1972	8
Farquhar A.B. (Auckland)	1961-1964	6
Hollander S. (Canterbury)	1930-1931	4
Gillies C.R. (Waikato)	1958-1959	4
Millar D.H. (Otago)	1965-1977	4
Parkinson F.G.M. (Manawatu)	1955-1956	3
Tindill E.W.T. (Wellington)	1950-1955	3
McDavitt P.A. (Wellington)	1972-1977	3
Campbell A. (Auckland)	1908	2
Neilson A.E. (Wellington)	1921	2
King J.S. (Wellington)	1937	2
Fong A.S. (West Coast)	1946-1950	2
Fright W.H. (Canterbury)	1956	2
Taylor A.R. (Canterbury)	1965-1972	*2
Evans F.T. (Canterbury)	1904	1
Williams J. (Otago)	1905	1
Duncan J. (Otago)	1908	1
Simpson J.L. (Wellington)	1913	1
Downes A.D. (Otago)	1913	1
Nicholson G.W. (Auckland)	1913	1
McKenzie E. (Wairarapa)	1921	1
Sutherland F.E. (Auckland)	1930	1
Moffitt J. (Wellington)	1936	1
McKenzie H.J. (Wairarapa)	1936	1
Macassey L.E. (Otago)	1937	1
Matheson A.M. (Taranaki)	1946	1
Hill F.D. (Auckland)	1949	1
Walsh L. (Canterbury)	1949	1
Sullivan G. (Taranaki)	1950	1
Griffiths A.A. (Waikato)	1952	1
Frood J. (Otago)	1952	1
Wolstenholme B.H. (Poverty Bay)	1955	1
Forsyth R.A. (Taranaki)	1958	1
Fleury A.L. (Otago)	1959	1
McAuley C.J. (Otago)	1962	1
Robson C.F. (Waikato)	1963	1
McMullen R.F. (Auckland)	1973	1
Doocey T.F. (Canterbury)	1976	1
Duffy B.W. (Taranaki)	1977	1

* Includes one match as a replacement

NEW ZEALAND INTERNATIONALS WHO HAVE REFEREED INTERNATIONAL MATCHES

Duncan J. (1903) v Anglo-Welsh 1908

Nicholson G.W. (1903-04-07) v Australia 1913

Tindill E.W.T. (1936) v British Isles 1950 (2) Australia 1955

McMullen R.F. (1957-58-59-60) v England 1973

PROVINCIAL REPRESENTATION OF NEW ZEALAND INTERNATIONAL PLAYERS

AUCKLAND (92)

Allen F.R.	1946-47-49
Asher A.	1903
Badeley C.E.O.	1921
Barrett J.	1913
Batty W.	1930-31
Black N.W.	1949
Boggs E.G.	1946-49
Bremner S.G.	1952
Bruce J.A.	1914
Carrington K.R.	1971
Caughey T.H.C.	1932-34-35-36-37
Christian D.L.	1949
Clarke A.H.	1958-59-60
Connor D.M.	1961-62-63-64
Cooke A.E.	1924-25
Corner M.M.N.	1930-31-34-36
Crowley P.J.B.	1949-50
Cunningham W.	1905-06-07-08
Davies W.A.	1960
Davis K.	1952-53-54-55-58
Dick J.	1937-38
Dick M.J.	1963-64-65-66-67-69-70
Dobson R.L.	1949
Downing A.J.	1913-14
Dunn J.M.	1946
Erceg C.P.	1951-52
Farrell C.P.	1977
Fawcett C.L.	1976
Francis A.R.H.	1905-07-08-10
Gallaher D.	1903-04-05-06
Geddes W.McK.	1913
Gemmell B.McL.	1974
Gillett G.A.	1907-08
Haden A.M.	1977
Hadley S.	1928
Hadley W.E.	1934-35-36
Hayward H.O.	1908
Herewini M.A.	1962-63-64-65-66-67
Hook L.S.	1929
Hughes A.M.	1949-50
Ifwersen K.D.	1921
Johnstone B.R.	1976-77
Kelly J.W.	1949
Kiernan H.A.D.	1903
Killeen B.A.	1936
Knight A.	1934
Lineen T.R.	1957-58-59-60
Little P.F.	1961-62-63-64
Long A.J.	1903
Lucas F.W.	1924-25-28-30
McGregor A.J.	1913
McGregor R.W.	1903-04
McHugh M.J.	1946-49
McKay D.W.	1961-62-63
McKenzie R.J.	1914
Mackrell W.H.C.	1906
Macky J.V.	1913
McLachlan J.S.	1974
McLean H.F.	1934-35-36
McLean J.K.	1949
McMullen R.F.	1957-58-59-60
McWilliams R.G.	1928-29-30
Maguire J.R.	1910
Mill J.W.	1924-25-26
Nathan W.J.	1962-63-64-66-67
Nesbit S.R.	1960
Nicholson G.W.	1903-04-07
O'Brien J.G.	1914
O'Leary M.J.	1910-13
Palmer B.P.	1929-32
Rangi R.E.	1964-65-66
Scott R.W.H.	1946-47-49-50-53-54
Seeling C.E.	1904-05-06-07-08
Sellars G.M.V.	1913
Simpson J.G.	1947-49-50
Skeen J.R.	1952
Smith G.W.	1905
Solomon F.	1931-32
Stewart J.D.	1913
Tanner J.M.	1950-51-53
Tetzlaff P.L.	1947
Thomas B.T.	1962
Thorne G.S.	1968-69-70
Thornton N.H.	1947-49
Tyler G.A.	1903-04-05-06
Urlich R.A.	1970
Whineray W.J.	1959-60-61-62-63-64-65
White H.L.	1953-54-55
Whiting P.J.	1971-72-73-74-75-76
Williams B.G.	1970-71-72-73-74-75-76-77
Wood M.E.	1904
Wylie J.T.	1913

CANTERBURY (90)

Alley G.T.	1928
Argus W.G.	1946-47
Arnold D.A.	1963-64
Birtwistle W.M.	1965
Black J.E.	1977
Bond J.G.	1949
Bremner S.G.	1956
Bruce O.D.	1976-77
Burns P.J.	1908-10-13
Bush W.K.	1974-75-76-77
Buxton J.B.	1955-56
Carleton S.R.	1928-29
Cobden D.G.	1937
Cooke R.J.	1903
Cottrell W.D.	1968-70-71
Cottrell A.I.	1929-30-31-32
Creighton J.N.	1962
Cummings W.	1913
Dalley W.C.	1924-28
Dalzell G.N.	1953-54
Davis L.J.	1976-77
Deans R.G.	1905-08
Dixon M.J.	1954-56-57
Duff R.H.	1951-52-55-56
Eastgate B.P.	1952-54
Elsom A.E.G.	1952-53-55
Fanning A.H.N.	1913
Fanning B.J.	1903-04
Fryer F.C.	1907-08
Fuller W.B.	1910
Gillett G.A.	1905
Graham D.J.	1958-60-61-62-63-64
Gray G.D.	1908-13
Hales D.A.	1972
Harper E.T.	1904-06
Hart G.F.	1930-31-34-35-36
Harvey P.	1904
Hasell E.W.	1913
Hill S.F.	1955-56-57-58-59
Hooper J.A.	1937
Hopkinson A.E.	1967-68-69-70
Hotop J.	1952-55
Hurst I.A.	1973-74
Innes G.D.	1932
Joseph H.T.	1971
Kirkpatrick I.A.	1967-68-69
Laidlaw C.R.	1968
Le Lievre J.M.	1962
Lilburne H.T.	1928-29-30
Lynch T.W.	1951
McCormick W.F.	1965-67-68-69-70-71
Macdonald H.H.	1972-73-74
McGregor D.	1903
McGregor N.P.	1924-25
Mcl Ian D.L.	1955
Manchester J.E.	1932-34-35-36
Masters R.R.	1924-25
Meates K.F.	1952
Milliken H.M.	1938
Mitchell T.W.	1976
Mitchell W.J.	1910
Moreton R.C.	1962-64-65
Morrissey P.J.	1962
Murray H.V.	1913-14
Newton F.	1905-06
Norton R.W.	1971-72-73-74-75-76-77
Oliver C.J.	1929-34-35-36
Parker J.H.	1924-25
Rankin J.G.	1936-37
Rhind P.K.	1946
Robilliard A.C.C.	1928
Savage L.T.	1949
Scrimshaw G.	1928
Smith R.M.	1955
Steel A.G.	1966-67-68
Stewart A.J.	1963-64
Stewart R.T.	1930

WELLINGTON (82)

Stuart K.C.	1955
Stuart R.C.	1949-53-54
Tanner K.J.	1974-75-76
Taylor H.M.	1913-14
Tremain K.R.	1959-60-61
Turtill H.S.	1905
Vincent P.B.	1956
Watt B.A.	1962-63-64
Whineray W.J.	1957
Wilson D.D.	1954
Wood M.E.	1903
Wyllie A.J.	1970-71-72-73
Young D.	1956-58-60-61-62-63-64

Aitken G.G.	1921
Avery H.E.	1910
Ball N.	1931-32-35-36
Barry E.F.	1934
Batty G.B.	1972-73-74-75
Bevan V.D.	1949-50
Bowers R.G.	1954
Caulton R.W.	1959-60-61-63-64
Clark R.W.	1953-54-55-56
Cooke A.E.	1930
Cross T.	1904-05
Dalton R.A.	1947
Delamore G.W.	1949
Dodd E.H.	1905
Dougan J.G.	1972-73
Elliott K.G.	1946
Fitzgerald J.T.	1952
Fitzpatrick B.B.J.	1953-54
Francis W.C.	1913-14
Gillespie C.T.	1913
Gray K.F.	1963-64-65-66-67-68-69
Griffiths J.L.	1934-35-36-38
Heeps T.R.	1962
Horsley R.H.	1960
Hughes E.	1921
Jarden R.A.	1951-52-53-54-55-56
Jessep E.M.	1931-32
Johnson L.M.	1928
Karam J.F.	1972-73-74-75
Katene T.	1955
Kember G.F.	1970
Kilby F.D.	1932-34
Lambourn A.	1934-35-36-37-38
Leslie A.R.	1974-75-76
Leys E.T.	1929
Lilburne H.T.	1931-32-34
Loader C.J.	1953-54
MacEwan I.N.	1956-57-58-59-60-61-62
McGregor D.	1904-05
McIntosh D.N.	1956-57
McKellar G.F.	1910
McKenzie R.J.	1913
McLean H.F.	1930-32
Mason D.F.	1947
Mexted G.	1950
Mitchinson F.E.	1907-08-10-13
Moffitt J.E.	1921
Nicholls H.E.	1921
Nicholls M.F.	1921-24-25-28-30
O'Callaghan T.R.	1949
O'Donnell D.H.	1949
Oliver D.J.	1930
Page J.R.	1931-32-34
Pollock H.R.	1932-36
Porter C.G.	1925-29-30
Reedy W.J.	1908
Roberts E.J.	1914-21
Roberts F.	1905-07-08-10
Ryan J.	1910-14
Sadler B.S.	1935-36
Siddells S.K.	1921
Spencer J.C.	1905-07
Steele L.B.	1951
Stephens O.G.	1968
Stevens I.N.	1972-73-74
Svenson K.S.	1924-25
Thomas B.T.	1964
Thomson H.D.	1908
Tilyard J.T.	1913
Tindill E.W.T.	1936
Uttley I.N.	1963

Vodanovich I.M.H. 1955
Wallace W.J. 1903-04-05-06 07-08
Watkins E.L. 1905
Watt J.R. 1958-60-61-62
Wells J. 1936
White R.M. 1946-47
Williams G.C. 1967-68
Williment M. 1964-65-66-67
Wilson A. 1908-10-13-14
Wilson S.S. 1977
Wolfe T.N. 1961-62

OTAGO (75)

Archer W.R. 1955
Baird J.A.S. 1913
Bell R.H. 1951-52
Bennet R. 1905
Berghan T. 1938
Black R.S. 1914
Booth E.E. 1906-07
Bush R.G. 1931
Casey S.T. 1905-07-08
Clark D.W. 1964
Conway R.J. 1959-60
Cuthill J.E. 1913
Davies W.A. 1962
Diack E.S. 1959
Duncan J. 1903
Duncan W.D. 1921
Elvidge R.R. 1946-49-50
Fea W.R. 1921
Gillespie W.D. 1958
Gillies C.C. 1936
Gilray C.M. 1905
Graham J.B. 1913-14
Haig J.S. 1946
Haig L.S. 1950-51-53-54
Harvey L.R. 1949-50
Hore J. 1930-32-34-35-36
Hunter B.A. 1971
Irvine J.G. 1914
Irwin M.W. 1955-56-58-59-60
Jaffray J.L. 1972-75-76-77
Johnston W. 1907
Johnstone P. 1949-50-51
Kearney J.C. 1947-49
Kirton E.W. 1967-68-69-70
Kreft A.J. 1968
Laidlaw C.R. 1964-65-66-67-70
Lindsay D.F. 1928
Lunn W.A. 1949
McAtamney F.S. 1956
McDonald A. 1905-06-08-13
McNab J.R. 1949-50
MacPherson D.G. 1905
Mains L.W. 1971-76
Matheson J.D. 1972
Meates W.A. 1949-50
Mitchell N.A. 1938
Moore G.J.T. 1949
Morrison T.G. 1973
Murdoch K. 1970-72
Nelson K.A. 1962
Oliver O.D. 1954
Orr R.W 1949
Parkhill A.A. 1937-38
Paton H. 1910
Paterson A.M. 1908-10
Proctor A.C. 1932
Purvis N.A. 1976
Quaid C.E. 1938
Richardson J. 1921
Robertson D.J. 1974-75-76-77
Seear, G.A. 1977
Simon H.J. 1937
Sims G.S. 1972
Skinner K.L. 1949-50-51-52-53-54
Smith I.S.T. 1964
Sonntag W.T.C. 1929
Taylor J.M. 1937-38
Townsend L.J. 1955
Trevathan D. 1937
Watt J.M. 1936
Williams P. 1913
Willocks C. 1946-49
Wilson B.W. 1977
Wilson H.W. 1949-50-51
Wilson N.L. 1951

TARANAKI (40)

Abbott H.L. 1906
Beatty G.E. 1950
Bowden N.J.G. 1952
Briscoe K.C. 1959-60-63-64
Brown C. 1913
Brown R.H. 1955-56-57-58-59-61-62
Burke P.S. 1955-57
Cain M.J. 1913-14
Cameron D. 1908
Clarke R.L. 1932
Cockerill M.S. 1951
Collins A.H. 1932-34
Colman J.T.H. 1907-08
Dewar H. 1913
Fogarty R. 1921
Gardiner A.J. 1974
Glasgow F.T. 1905-06
Glenn W.S. 1904-06
Hart A.H. 1924
Hunter J. 1905-06-07-08
Kingstone C.N. 1921
Kivell A.L. 1929
McCullough J.F. 1959
McEldowney J.T. 1977
Major J. 1967
Mourie G.N.K. 1977
Muller B.L. 1967-68-69-70-71
Mynott H.J. 1905-06-07-10
O'Sullivan J.M. 1905-07
O'Sullivan T.P.A. 1960-61-62
Roberts R.W. 1913-14
Roper R.A. 1949-50
Scown A.I. 1972
Smith A.E. 1969-70
Stohr L. 1910
Sullivan J.L. 1937-38
Taylor R. 1913
Urbahn R.J. 1959
West A.H. 1921
Wolfe T.N. 1963

SOUTHLAND (29)

Archer W.R. 1956
Ashby D.L. 1958
Budd T.A. 1946-49
Burgess G.F. 1905
Geddes J.H. 1929
George V.L. 1938
Glasgow F.T. 1908
Hamilton D.C. 1908
Hazlett E.J. 1966-67
Hazlett W.E. 1928-30
Hughes E. 1907-08
Laidlaw K.F. 1960
McCaw W.A. 1951-53-54
McKechnie B.J. 1977
McNeece J. 1913-14
McRae J.A. 1946
Metcalfe T.C. 1931-32
Mitchell N.A. 1935-36-37
Oliver F.J. 1976-77
Purdue C.A. 1905
Purdue E. 1905
Purdue G.B. 1931-32
Richardson J. 1924-25
Ridland A.J. 1910
Robinson C.E. 1951-52
Stead J.W. 1904-05-06-08
Stewart K.W. 1973-74-75-76
Ward R.H. 1936-37
White A. 1921-24-25

HAWKE'S BAY (22)

Bowman A.W. 1938
Brownlie C.J. 1924-25
Brownlie M.J. 1924-25-28
Dalton D. 1935-36-37-38
Davis W.L. 1967-68-69-70
Duncan M.G. 1971
Evans D.A. 1910
Frazer H.F. 1946-47-49
Furlong B.D.M. 1970
Grenside B.A. 1928-29
Irvine W.R. 1924-25
Jackson E.S. 1936-37-38
MacRae I.R. 1966-67-68-69-70
Mataira H. 1934
Mill J.J. 1924-25
Nepia G. 1924-25
Reid S.T. 1935-36-37
Steere E.R.G. 1930-31-32
Stuart R.L. 1977
Swain J.P. 1928
Thimbleby N.W. 1970
Tremain K.R. 1962-63-64-65-66-67-68

NORTH AUCKLAND (15)

Cherrington N.P. 1950
Finlayson I.H. 1928-30
Fletcher C.J.C. 1921
Going S.M. 1967-68-69-70-71-72-73-74-75-76-77
Guy R.A. 1971
Heke (Rika) W.R. 1929
Irvine I.B. 1952
Jones M.G. 1973
Jones P.F.H. 1954-55-56-58-59-60
Macdonald H.H. 1975-76
Morgan J.E. 1974-76
Smith J.B. 1946-47-49
Waterman A.C. 1929
Webb D.S. 1959
Yates V.M. 1961

WAIRARAPA (15)

Blake A.W. 1949
Couch M.B.R. 1947-49
Cundy R.T. 1929
Donald J.G. 1921
Donald Q. 1924-25
Harvey I.H. 1928
Irvine W.R. 1930
Lochore B.J. 1964-65-66-67-68-69-70
McMinn A.F. 1903
Mill J.J. 1930
Reid K.H. 1929
Reside W.B. 1929
Stringfellow J.C. 1929
Udy D.K. 1903
Wrigley E. 1905

MANAWATU (14)

Burgess R.E. 1971-72-73
Callesen J.A. 1974-75
Donaldson M.W. 1977
Eveleigh K.A. 1976-77
Finlay B.E.L. 1959
Finlay J. 1946
Harris P.C. 1976
Knight G.A. 1977
Lambert K.K. 1972-73-74-76-77
McKenzie R.M. 1934-35-36-37-38
McMinn A.F. 1905
McMinn F.A. 1904
O'Callaghan M.W. 1968
Strahan S.C. 1967-68-70-72-73

SOUTH CANTERBURY (13)

Cockroft E.A.P. 1913-14
Coughlan T.D. 1958
Goddard M.P. 1946-47-49
Grant L.A. 1947-49
Lister T.N. 1968-69-70-71
Lynch T.W. 1913-14
Morrison T.C. 1938
Saxton C.K. 1938
Spillane A.P. 1913
Stewart A.J. 1964
Stewart R.T. 1928
Storey P.W. 1921
Strang W.A. 1928-30-31

WAIKATO (12)

Arnold K.D. 1947
Birtwistle W.M. 1967
Catley E.H. 1946-47-49
Clarke D.B. 1956-57-58-59-60-61-62-63-64
Clarke I.J. 1953-55-56-57-58-59-60-61-62-63
Hemi R.C. 1953-54-55-56-57-59
McLaren H.C. 1952
Pickering E.A.R. 1958-59
Reid A.R. 1952-56-57
Skudder G.R. 1969
Tuck J.M. 1929
Whineray W.J. 1958

BAY OF PLENTY (7)

Batty G.B. 1976-77
Conway R.J. 1965
Cupples L.F. 1924
Gray W.N. 1955-56
McLean A.L. 1921
McNaughton A.M. 1971
Taylor N.M. 1977

WANGANUI (7)

Belliss E.A. 1921
Bullock-Douglas G.A.H. 1932-34
Henderson P. 1949-50
Milner H.P. 1970
Murray P.C. 1908
Osborne W.M. 1975-76-77
Rowley H.C.B. 1949

COUNTIES (7)

Cossey R.R. 1958
Dalton A.G. 1977
Lendrum R.N. 1973
McLeod B.E. 1964-65-66-67-68-69-70
Robertson B.J. 1972-73-74-76-77
Skinner K.L. 1956
Walsh P.T. 1955-56-57-58-59-63

KING COUNTRY (6)

Bryers R.F. 1949
McLean J.K. 1947
Meads C.E. 1957-58-59-60-61-62-63-64-65-66-67-68-69-70-71
Meads S.T. 1961-62-63-64-65-66
Phillips W.J. 1937-38
Whiting G.J. 1972-73

POVERTY BAY (5)

Collins J.L. 1964-65
Kirkpatrick I.A. 1970-71-72-73-74-75-76-77
Knight L.G. 1977
Parkinson R.M. 1972-73
White R.A. 1949-50-51-52-53-54-55-56

WEST COAST (4)

Atkinson H. 1913
Gilbert G.D.M. 1935-36
King R.R. 1934-35-36-37-38
Steel J. 1921-24-25

MARLBOROUGH (3)

Ford B.R. 1977
Hammond I.A. 1952
Sutherland A.R. 1970-71-72-73

NELSON (3)

Max D.S. 1931-32
Smith W.E. 1905
Snow E.M. 1929

BULLER (2)

Holder E.C. 1934
Mumm W.J. 1949

NORTH OTAGO (2)

Gard P.C. 1971
Smith I.S.T. 1965-66

BUSH DISTRICTS (1)

Mahoney A. 1935-36

EAST COAST (1)

Nepia G. 1929-30

HOROWHENUA (1)

Karam J.F. 1975

NELSON BAYS (1)

Morris T.J. 1972

WAIRARAPA-BUSH (1)

Lochore B.J. 1971

CLUB REPRESENTATION OF NEW ZEALAND INTERNATIONAL PLAYERS

(Over Ten)

Ponsonby (24)
Black N.W. 1949
Boggs E.G. 1946-49
Cunningham W. 1907-08
Dick M.J. 1963-64-65-66-67-68-69-70
Francis A.R.H. 1905-07-08-10
Gallaher D. 1903-04-05-06
Gillett G.A. 1907-08
Haden A.M. 1977
Hook L.S. 1929
Lucas F.W. 1924-25-28-30
McGregor A.J. 1913
McWilliams R.G. 1928-29-30
Nicholson G.W. 1907
O'Leary M.J. 1910-13
Palmer B.P. 1929
Rangi R.E. 1964-65-66
Scott R.W.H. 1946-47-49-50-53-54
Sellars G.M.V. 1913
Simpson J.G. 1947-49-50
Solomon F. 1931-32
Tetzlaff P.L. 1947
Whiting P.J. 1971-72-73-74-75-76
Williams B.G. 1970-71-72-73-74-75-76-77
Wood M.E. 1904

Christchurch (20)
Arnold D.A. 1963-64
Birtwistle W.M. 1965
Cottrell A.I. 1929-30-31-32
Duff R.H. 1951-52-55-56
Fryer F.C. 1907-08
Harper E.T. 1904-06
Hart G.F. 1930-31-34-35-36
Harvey P. 1904
Hill S.F. 1955-56-57-58-59
Hotop J. 1955
Manchester J.E. 1932-34-35-36
McGregor N.P. 1924
McPhail B.E. 1959
Rhind P.K. 1946
Robilliard A.C.C. 1928
Scrimshaw G. 1928
Smith R.M. 1955
Stewart R.T. 1930
Watt B.A. 1962-63-64
Wood M.E. 1903

Otago University (20)
Berghan T. 1938
Bush R.G. 1931
Cuthill J.E. 1913
Davies W.A. 1962
Diack E.S. 1959
Elvidge R.R. 1946-49
Fea W.R. 1921
Gillies C.C. 1936
Gilray C.M. 1905
Irwin M.W. 1955-56-58-59-60
Kirton E.W. 1967-68-69-70
Laidlaw C.R. 1963-64-65-66-67-70
Lindsay D.F. 1928
MacPherson D.G. 1905
Moore G.J.T. 1949
Morrison T.G. 1973
Oliver C.J. 1929
Oliver D.O. 1953
Sims G.S. 1972
Watt J.M. 1936

Petone (16)
Cross T. 1904-05
Dougan J.P. 1972-73
Gray K.F. 1963-64-65-66-67-68-69
Katene T. 1955
Lambourn A. 1934-35-36-37-38
Leslie A.R. 1974-75-76
McGregor D. 1904-05
McIntosh D.N. 1956-57
McKenzie R.J. 1913
Nicholls H.E. 1921
Nicholls M.F. 1921-24-25-28-30
Pollock H.R. 1932-36
Reedy W.J. 1908
Ryan J. 1910-14
Stevens I.N. 1972
White R.M. 1946

Marist Brothers Old Boys, Auckland (14)
Barrett J. 1913
Connor D.M. 1961-62-63-64
Crowley P.J.B. 1949-50
Davis K. 1952-53-54-55-58
Downing A.J. 1913-14
Hadley S. 1928
Hadley W.E. 1934-35-36
Lineen T.R. 1957-58-59-60
Little P.F. 1961-62-63
McHugh M.J. 1946-49
McKenzie R.J. 1914
Nesbit S.R. 1960
O'Brien J.G. 1914
Skeen J.R. 1952

Athletic (13)
Bevan V.D. 1949-50
Bowers R.G. 1954
Heeps T.R. 1962
MacEwan I.N. 1956-57-58-59-60-61-62
Porter C.G. 1925-29-30
Roberts E.J. 1914-21
Stephens O.G. 1968
Svenson K.S. 1924-25
Thomas B.T. 1964
Tindill E.W.T. 1936
Watt J.R. 1958-60-61-62
Wells J. 1936
Wilson A. 1908-10-13-14

Christchurch High School Old Boys (13)
Carleton S.R. 1928-29
Cobden D.G. 1937
Dalley W.C. 1924-28
Deans R.G. 1905-08
Graham D.J. 1958-60-61-62-63-64
Innes G.D. 1932
Morrissey P.J. 1962
Parker J.H. 1924-25
Rankin J.G. 1936-37
Steel A.G. 1966-67-68
Taylor H.M. 1913-14
Vincent P.B. 1956
Wilson D.D. 1954

Grammar Schools' Old Boys (11)
Allen F.R. 1946-47-49
Badeley C.E.O. 1921
Batty W. 1930-31
Bremner S.G. 1952
Corner M.M.N. 1930-31-34-36
Gemmell B.M. 1974
Hughes A.M. 1949-50
Ifwersen K.D. 1921
Knight A. 1934
Thornton N.H. 1947-49
Whineray W.J. 1959-60-61-62-63-64-65

Victoria University College (11)
Aitken G.G. 1921
Blair W.H. 1980-81-82-83
Fitzgerald J.T. 1952
Fitzpatrick B.B.J. 1953
Jarden R.A. 1951-52-53-54-55-56
Kember G.F. 1970
Leys E.T. 1929
Siddells S.K. 1921
Uttley I.N. 1963
Williment M. 1964-65-66-67
Wolfe T.N. 1961-62

SECONDARY SCHOOL REPRESENTATION OF NEW ZEALAND INTERNATIONAL PLAYERS

(Seven or more)

Auckland Grammar School (22)
Badeley C.E.O.
Batty W.
Bowden N.J.G.
Bullock-Douglas G.A.H.
Corner M.M.N.
Dick J.
Dick M.J.
Francis A.R.H.
Geddes W.McK.
Gemmell B.M.
Ifwersen K.D.
Knight L.G.
McLaren H.C.
McLean A.L.
Macky J.V.
Nelson K.A.
Tanner J.M.
Thorne G.S.
Tremain K.R.
Waterman A.C.
Whineray W.J.
Whiting P.J.

Christchurch Boys' High School (22)
Alley G.T.
Carleton S.R.
Creighton J.N.
Cobden D.G.
Dalley W.C.
Deans R.G.
Duff R.H.
Elsom A.E.G.
Finlay J.
Harper E.T.
Innes G.D.
Joseph H.T.
McCormick W.F.
Morrissey P.J.
O'Callaghan M.W.
Parker J.H.
Rankin J.G.
Steel A.G.
Taylor H.M.
Thomson H.D.
Vincent P.B.
Wilson D.D.

Wellington College (21)
Avery H.E.
Caulton R.W.
Dodd E.H.
Donald J.G.
Donald Q.
Elliott K.G.
Glasgow F.T.
Gray K.F.
Griffiths J.L.
Killeen B.A.
Leys E.T.
Mason D.F.
Mexted G.G.
Nicholls H.E.
Nicholls M.F.
Porter C.G.
Sadler B.S.
Thomson H.D.
Uttley I.N.
Watkins E.L.
Watt J.M.

Nelson College (14)
Bowers R.G.
Callesen J.A.
Clark W.H.
Cundy R.T.
Holder E.C.
Hughes A.M.
Kember G.F.
MacEwan I.N.
Max D.S.
Mill J.J.
Morris T.J.
Pickering E.A.R.
Savage L.T.
Smith W.E.

Southland Boys' High School (13)
Cockroft E.A.P.
Geddes J.H.
Hamilton D.C.
Johnson L.M.
Kilby F.D.
McKechnie B.J.
Mitchell N.A.
Moreton R.C.
Page J.R.
Rowley H.C.B.
Stead J.W.
Strang W.A.
White A.

Waitaki Boys' High School (13)
Clark D.W.
Gillies C.C.
Hart G.F.
Hotop J.
Hunter B.A.
Hurst I.A.
Harvey L.R.
Hazlett W.E.
Lister T.N.
Matheson J.D.
Paton H.
Scrimshaw G.
Sims G.S.

New Plymouth Boys' High School (11)
Beatty G.E.
Briscoe K.C.
Donaldson M.W.
Gardiner A.J.
Graham D.J.
McEldowney J.T.
Mourie G.N.K.
Reid A.R.
Roper R.A.
Stohr L.
Wolfe T.N.

Sacred Heart College Auckland (10)
Brownlie C.J.
Brownlie M.J.
Davis K.
Erceg C.P.
Hart A.H.
Lineen T.R.
McHugh M.J.
Mahoney A.
Skeen J.R.
Walsh P.T.

Timaru Boys' High School (10)
Black J.E.
Clark D.W.
Goddard M.P.
Grant L.A.
Lindsay D.F.
Manchester J.E.
Smith R.M.
Stewart R.T.
Strang W.A.
Stringfellow J.C.

Otago Boys' High School (9)
Black R.S.
Cuthill J.E.
Fea W.R.
George V.L.
Gilray C.M.
Saxton C.K.
McKellar G.F.
Stewart K.W.
Watt J.R.

Wanganui Collegiate School (7)
Bullock-Douglas G.A.H.
Hunter J.
Irwin M.W.
Murray P.C.
Siddells S.K.
Tuck J.M.
Strahan S.C.

St. Patrick's College (Wgtn) (7)
Brownlie M.J.
Finlay B.E.L.
Harper E.T.
Kirton E.W.
Lynch T.W.
McKenzie R.J.
Mahoney A.

St. Kevin's College (7)
Coughlan T.D.
Kearney J.C.
Laidlaw K.F.
McAtamney F.S.
McCaw W.A.
Skinner K.L.
Stuart R.C.

Otahuhu College (7)
Boggs E.G.
Christian D.L.
Cossey R.R.
Herewini M.A.
Murdoch P.H.
Nathan W.J.
Thornton N.H.

King's College (7)
Brown R.H.
Catley E.H.
Caughey T.H.C.
Davies W.A.
Fletcher C.J.C.
Kirkpatrick I.A.
Macdonald H.H.

Appendix

During our research for this volume, we discovered details that differed from those included in previously published literature on Rugby. We have not listed below differences in playing positions from those hitherto accepted; the charts included in each match report we believe to have been as accurate as currently possible. Our checking included reference to photographs, books, newspapers, programmes and personal interviews.

Match 1

Robert Wylie McGregor is usually referred to as Robert "Dick" McGregor. Source: Registrar-General's Office (born Thames, 31 December 1874)

The information on the date of birth of David Gallaher at Ramelton, County Donegal was obtained from the records of the Oifig an Ard-Chlaraitheora, Dublin. It is interesting to note that the spelling of his surname in the register is Gallagher. No other reference to this spelling has been found in connection with research for this book. The commonly quoted date of birth is that found on Gallaher's marriage certificate a document sighted by N.A.C. McMillan which records his date of birth as 31 October 1875. When he was enrolled at Katikati school his date of birth was recorded as 30 November 1873

Sidney Austin Riley is usually referred to as S. Riley. Source: Nominal Rolls of the N.Z.E.F. 17th Reinforcements.

Match 2

The New Zealand scrum formation is taken from a description of the pack attributed to Bernard Fanning in *Players and Slayers* by Leo Fanning, page 86.

Edward Morgan is sometimes erroneously referred to as E.T. Morgan. Source: *British Medical Directory* and the Christ College, Brecon magazine *Breconian* April 1907 and obituary October 1949.

Willie Morris Llewellyn is sometimes referred to as W. Llewellyn. Source: Information supplied by Christ College, Brecon.

Match 3

Edward Purdue is usually referred to as E.G. Purdue. Source: Registrar-General's Office (died Invercargill, 16 July 1939)
Charles Alfred Purdue usually described as C. Purdue. Source: Registrar-General's Office (born Mataura, 10 June 1874)

Ernest Arthur "George" Anlezark is usually referred to as A.E. Anlezark. Source: Article in *The Green Line* (a Lancashire sporting newspaper) of 18 April 1925 titled Old Oldham Stalwarts No. 33.

The information on the death of H.S. "Jum" Turtill, who is not normally included in All Black war casualties, was supplied by his son Mr K.S. Turtill and confirmed in a letter from the Imperial War Museum, London to R.H. Chester dated 25 April 1972.

Match 4

George Smith's birth was registered in Auckland on 20 September 1874 as William George Smith. Source: The Registrar-General's Office, and a letter from his daughter (Mrs E. Stansfield) to R.H. Chester 30 April 1972.

Match 8

William Henry Clifton Mackrell is usually referred to as W.H. Mackrell. Source: His headstone at Waikaraka Cemetery and obituary *N.Z. Herald* 16 July 1917.

Match 9

John Thomas Henry Colman is usually referred to as J.D. Colman. Source: Registrar-General's Office (born Hawera, 19 July 1887) and obituary *Hawera Star* 29 September 1965.

Edward "Ned" Hughes is usually referred to as E.E. Hughes. Sources: Letter from Ministry of Defence to R.H. Chester 19 July 1974 (concerning details of his registration for active service 10th Reinforcements, N.Z. Rifle Brigade 1916) and Nominal Rolls of the N.Z.E.F. Also *Invercargill Pioneers* by F. George page 154.

Match 13

Alexander Marshall Paterson usually described and spelt A. Patterson. Source: Registrar-General's Office (born Dunedin, 31 October 1885, died Dunedin, 29 August 1933) also note signature page 47.

George Donaldson Gray is sometimes referred to as D. Gray. Source: Registrar-General's Office (died Christchurch, 16 April 1961)

Match 15

Leonard Stohr is sometimes referred to as L.B. "Jack" Stohr. Source: Registrar-General's Office (born New Plymouth, 13 November 1889) and *Rugby Almanack of New Zealand 1974* obituaries page 190.

Alexander James Ridland usually described as J. Ridland. Source: Registrar-General's Office (born Invercargill, 3 March 1882) N.Z.E.F. Roll of Honour (died of wounds, France 5 November 1918) *Invercargill Star R.F.C. 75th Jubilee* booklet 1886-1961. He is not usually included in All Black war casualties.

Match 18

The replacement of H.M. Taylor by F.E. Mitchinson is usually omitted from the published details of this match. However reports on this match that appeared in both *The New Zealand Herald* and *Auckland Star* of 8 September 1913 both refer to this replacement.

Match 19

James Alexander Steenson Baird is usually described as J. Baird. Source : Registrar-General's Office (born Dunedin, 17 December 1893) also *Rugby Football Internationals' Roll of Honour* by E.H.D. Sewell pages 24-25, Nominal Roll of N.Z.E.F., N.Z.E.F. Roll of Honour (he was killed in action in France 7 June 1917 not 12 October 1917 as is usually quoted), and *Otago Witness* circa July 1917.

William Charles Francis usually referred to as W. Francis. Source: Registrar-General's Office (born New Plymouth, 4 February 1894) and letter from Mr Francis to R.H. Chester 21 February 1972.

Match 20

Eric Arthur Percy Cockroft usually described as E.A. Cockroft. Source: Registrar-General's Office (born Clinton, 10 September 1890), *Southland Boys' High School Old Boys' Register 1881-1956* and *Rugby Almanack of New Zealand 1974* obituaries page 187.

Match 21

The details of the layout of the team, names and initials of the All America team were obtained from the archivists at the Stanford University Libraries, Bancroft Library, University of California and the University of Santa Clara. Other sources consulted were the scrapbook and diary of A.J. McGregor (courtesy of Mr J. Bourke, Ponsonby R.F.C.) and excerpts from *The Daily Californian*.

Match 23

R.J. McKenzie is usually described as being affiliated to the Wellington Union in 1914. A check with the Herald and Auckland Star reports of club matches during May and June 1914 confirms that he was playing with the Marist Bros. O. B. club in Auckland when selected for the 1914 tour, and included as an Auckland member of the side when the team was announced.

Match 25

Richard Fogarty is usually referred to as R.D. Fogarty. Source: Registrar-General's Office (born Matakanui, 12 December 1891) and interview between Mr Fogarty and R.H. Chester December 1976.

The New Zealand five-eighths are usually incorrectly listed with Nicholls at first and Badeley at second. Contemporary newspaper reports all confirm that Badeley was at first and Nicholls at second. Nicholls' book *With the All Blacks in Springbokland 1928* and conversation with Mr Badeley in November 1976 give confirmation of this fact.

Match 27

Charles John Compton Fletcher usually referred to as C.J. Fletcher. Source: *The Rugby Almanack of New Zealand 1974* obituary page 209.

Match 29

D.D. Hiddlestone is somtimes referred to as D. Hiddlestone. Source: *Rugby Recollections* by W.J.T. Collins page 86 and list of Welsh Internationals 1881-1966 contained in Wales v. New Zealand programme 1967 page 21.

Match 31

The details of the layout of the team, names and initials of the French team were obtained from information supplied by Jean-Pierre Bodis and from *La Depeche* of 18 January 1925.

Match 34

The name of the ground where this match was played is sometimes referred to as St. George's Park. The Crusader Ground formed part of a sporting complex called St. George's Park that included other sporting facilities in addition to the Rugby ground. Source: Letter from Mr T.T. Shnaps to R.H. Chester dated 21 November 1977.

Match 36

W.R. Heke played under his christian names William or Wiremu Rika. Discussion between Mr Heke and R.H. Chester September 1974, also *They Played for New Zealand* by A.C. Swan page 72.

Match 41

Howard Pool is usually referred to as N. Poole. Source: *Cardiff Rugby Club 1876-1975 History and Statistics, The Greatest* by D.E. Davies page 89.

Match 43

G.B. Purdue is usually described as the son of Charles Purdue whereas he is the son of Edward "Pat" Purdue and nephew of Charles. Source: Letter from G.B. Purdue to R.H. Chester dated 5 August 1973.

Match 45

Arthur Harold Collins is usually referred to as A.J. Collins. Source: Letter from Mr Collins to R.H. Chester 7 August 1975.

Match 63

Manuera Ben Riwai-Couch is usually referred to as M.B. Couch. Source: Article 'The Freshmen' *Auckland Star* 1 December 1975, and Electoral Roll, Wairarapa Electorate 1975. As the Riwai is not normally used we have incorporated this part of his surname as an additional initial.

Match 64

Nicholas Michael Shehadie is usually referred to as N. Shehadie. Source: *Who's Who in Australia 1974*.

Match 75

Charles Percy Erceg is usually referred to as P. Erceg. Source: Electoral Roll Hobson Electorate 1975.

Match 82

Peter Frederick Hilton-Jones is usually referred to as P.F. Jones. Source: *It's Me Tiger*. Although Mr Jones prefers the name P.F. Jones we have chosen to show the first part of his surname as an additional initial.

Match 83

Ernest Thomas Stutely Michie is usually referred to as E.J.S. Michie. Source: *The Lions on Trek* J.B.G. Thomas page 174.

Match 84

The venue of this match is named as Colombes Stadium although it is also correctly referred to as Yves du Manoir Stadium (*The Rise of French Rugby* by A. Potter & G. Duthen page 53 and mentioned in Match 31) and Au Stade Olympique de Colombes (official programme reproduced on page 187).

Match 101

Joseph George Michael Antelme is usually referred to as M.J.G. Antelme. Source: *Springboks in the Lions' Den* by M. Price page 34 and letter from T.T. Shnaps (Official Statistician to the South African Rugby Board) to R.H. Chester 28 May 1977.

Match 104

The name of the Boet Erasmus stadium is sometimes incorrectly called the J.C.K. Erasmus Stadium. Source: Letter from Mr T.T. Shnaps to R.H. Chester dated 21 November 1977.

Match 133

From 1967 the Welsh form of spelling Llanelly officially changed to Llanelli following pressure from Welsh nationalists.

Match 163

Michael Anthony Quinn is occasionally referred to as M.A.M. Quinn but we have been unable to authenticate his final initial. Source: Information supplied by Mr. T.W. Auty and from a pen-portrait in the official programme Ireland v. England 16 February 1974 page 15.

Variations in team layouts

Until the end of the 1931 season, New Zealand packed a 2-3-2 scrum with a wing-forward or rover. The two-fronted scrum was outlawed by the International Board and it became mandatory to have three players in the front row. From the start of the 1932 season New Zealand has used the 3-4-1 formation.

The wing-forward was really an extra back. He threw the ball into the line-out and put it into the scrum. On the opposition's throw or put in, he stood at the end of the line-out or at the side of the scrum in order to harass the opposing inside backs. A good wing-forward was a deadly tackler and a skilful ball handler as well as being a fast runner. According to overseas referees, he was frequently offside and the manager of the 1930 British team in New Zealand, Mr James Baxter, who was also a member of the International Board, was so incensed by Cliff Porter's activities in the Tests and the wing forward position in general that he instigated the move to have the New Zealand formation outlawed.

There is no law to say that a team cannot use a wing-forward. The only proviso on scrum formations is that there must be three players in the front row. This rule indirectly abolished the wing-forward however as it is very difficult for seven forwards to gain a fair share of possession against eight with a three-fronted scrum. The two-fronted scrum resulted in a very quick heel and the lack of the eighth forward was largely offset.

British teams had no set scrum formations before World War 1. They worked on the "first up first down" principle, normally packing 3-2-3. The South Africans were using the 3-4-1 scrum with set positions when the Springboks toured New Zealand in 1921, although they sometimes packed 3-3-2. Since World War II the 3-4-1 scrum has been almost universally adopted.

The two five-eighths system had been adopted by New Zealand before the first Test match was played against Australia in 1903. James Duncan, who captained New Zealand in 1901 and 1903, is credited with being the instigator of the system. The American team of 1913 also played with two five-eighths but New Zealand is now the only country using this formation.

Except for the names of the positions, however, the Australian and South African formations are similar to the New Zealand system. The British teams use the right and left centre positions in the three-quarter line, which means that the right centre always plays next to the right wing and the left centre next to the left wing. If a British back line is lined out on the right side of the field, the right centre marks the New Zealand centre three-quarter but if the backs are lined out on the left side, he marks the second five-eighth.

The table below shows the back positions under the various systems:

New Zealand	Australia	South Africa	Britain and France
Full-back	Full-back	Full-back	Full-back
Wing 3/4	Wing 3/4	Wing 3/4	Wing 3/4
Centre 3/4	Outside centre 3/4	Outside centre 3/4	Right or left centre 3/4
Second 5/8	Inside centre 3/4	Inside centre 3/4	Right or left centre 3/4
First 5/8	Five-eighth	Fly-half	Fly-half, out half or stand-off half
Half-back	Half-back	Scrum-half	Scrum-half

In our research we have discovered in many publications a number of inaccuracies with regard to team charts. These include the transposing of five-eighths, players on the wrong wings and incorrect setting out of scrum formations. We have corrected these errors in our layouts.

Jersey numbering

Since 1965 the International Board has decreed that teams shall be numbered from 1 (loose-head prop) to 15 (full-back). Prior to 1965, there was some variation in the numbering system. Early in the century, New Zealand sometimes numbered from forwards to full-back but until 1965 All Black teams were usually numbered from full-back to forwards. Letters instead of numbers were also used on occasions.

It was customary in early years for each member of a touring team to have a tour number, which he wore for all matches in which he took part but occasionally teams were numbered from 1 to 15 for the Test matches. The modern custom is for teams to be numbered from 1 to 15 for all games, with the reserves numbered from 16 to 21.

Replacements

Until 1968, replacements were not generally permitted in internationals. New Zealand and Australia however had a domestic arrangement whereby replacements were permitted in matches between those two countries but in 1949, after both countries had received seats on the International Board the previous year, they came into line with other countries. There were replacements also allowed in the New Zealand - All-America game of 1913.

Since 1968, a maximum of two replacements per team has been permitted in internationals, although four and later six reserves are usually named to cover all positions.

Kick into touch rule

Until 1969, kicking into touch on the full from any part of the field was permitted under international rules. Australia prohibited kicking into touch on the full except from within the kicker's own 25 in domestic matches and New Zealand experimented with this rule from time to time. In 1969 this rule became universal.

Club affiliations

In our list of New Zealand internationals, we have shown the club to which the player was affiliated at the time of selection. Four of these affiliations differ from the list in volume one of A.C. Swan's *History of New Zealand Rugby Football* in which the clubs of M.E. Wood, J.T. Wylie, R.J. McKenzie and C.N. Kingstone as Grafton, Auckland City, Petone and Tukapa respectively. Newspaper reports of 1904 show that Wood was playing for Ponsonby during that season and his name appears on the Ponsonby club's list of New Zealand representatives. Newspaper accounts of club matches and listings of Auckland representative teams of 1913 show that Wylie was playing for University during that year. McKenzie was playing for Petone when he won All Black honours in 1913 but he was a member of the Marist Old Boys' club in Auckland when he was selected for the Australian tour in 1914. A paragraph in the sports news in *The New Zealand Herald* of April 25, 1914, mentions McKenzie's transfer to Auckland and his joining the Marist club. Accounts of club matches confirm this, as does the Marist O.B.R.F.C.'s Souvenir Record. All newspaper listings of the 1914 New Zealand team show McKenzie's province as Auckland. Newspapers also show that Kingstone was a member of the Clifton club in 1921, which is confirmed by his obituary notice in the 1961 Rugby Almanack of New Zealand.

In the layout of British teams we have shown club and country affiliations, the club being the one to which the player belonged at the time of selection. Certain British players have been affiliated to a number of clubs and we cite examples to illustrate our point. C.D. Aarvold, of the 1930 team, played for four clubs — Cambridge University, West Hartlepool, Blackheath and Headingley. A letter from Sir Carl Aarvold to N.A.C. McMillan confirmed that he was a member of the Headingley club in 1930. Most published accounts of the British team's matches show Aarvold's club as Cambridge University but he "came down" in 1928. Another member of the 1930 British team, H.M. Bowcott, is also shown as a Cambridge player but he was playing for Cardiff by 1930. Similarly, D.D. Dobson of the 1904 British team had left Oxford and was playing for Newton Abbot when selected for the tour.

The haka

New Zealand teams perform the haka before overseas Test matches but seldom do so in New Zealand; one recent exception being against Scotland, at Eden Park in 1975.

International caps

Caps were awarded to New Zealand team members up to World War II. Each player received only one cap but the years in which he played for New Zealand were shown on it. Since the war, caps have not been awarded but the term "cap" is sometimes used to denote an international player.

Changes in points

A goal from a mark was reduced from 4 to 3 in 1905 and a dropped goal from 4 to 3 in 1947. A try was raised from 3 to 4 in 1972.

Change to metrics

The marking of fields in metres instead of in yards was universally adopted in 1976.

Crowd estimates

We have taken these from contemporary newspapers. In many cases the size of the crowd would be an educated guess and usually varied in each account of the match. In more recent years fairly accurate figures have been available, especially when all ground accommodation has been pre-sold.

In both Britain and South Africa, crowds in excess of 70,000 have watched the All Blacks while attendances of over 60,000 have witnessed Tests in New Zealand. The biggest crowd for an Australia versus New Zealand game in Australia is 50,000. The smallest attendance at an international involving New Zealand was the estimated 3,000 at Tahuna Park, Dunedin, in 1905.

Bibliography

Sources of reference consulted in the preparation of this book include the following:

DAILY NEWSPAPERS
The New Zealand Herald
The Auckland Star
The Dominion
The Evening Post
The Christchurch Press
The Christchurch Star
The Otago Daily Times
The Evening Star

PERIODICALS
The Weekly News
New Zealand Free Lance
The Weekly Press
The Otago Witness
New Zealand Observer
New Zealand Illustrated Sporting and Dramatic
   Review
Canterbury Times
New Zealand Graphic
New Zealand Sportsman
Sports Digest
Rugby News
Rugby World
S.A. Sportsman

ANNUAL PUBLICATIONS
Rugby Almanacks of New Zealand 1935-77
New Zealand Rugby Annuals 1920-32
D.B. Rugby Annuals 1971-77
S.A. Rugby Writers' Rugby Annuals 1971-75
Rothman's Rugby Yearbooks 1972-76
S.A. Rugby Annuals 1950-57
Rugby Annuals for Wales 1969-74
The Rugby Football Annuals 1924-26
Wisden's Rugby Football Almanacks 1924-26
Playfair Rugby Football Annuals 1962-63, 1968-69
Australian Rugby Union Almanacks 1947-72

BOOKS
International Histories
History of N.Z. Rugby Football Vl. 1 1870-1945
   A.C. Swan (Reeds 1948)
History of N.Z. Rugby Football Vol. 2 1946-57
   A.C. Swan (Whitcombe & Tombs 1958)
The N.Z. Rugby Football Union 1892-1967
   A.C. Swan (Reeds 1967)
The History of the Rugby Football Union
   O.L. Owen (Playfair 1955)
Centenary History of the Rugby Football Union
   U.A. Titley & R. McWhirter
   (Rugby Football Union, 1970)
History of Welsh International Rugby
   J. Billot (Ron Jones 1970)

The Story of Scottish Rugby
   R.J. Phillips (T.N. Foulis 1925)
One Hundred Years of Irish Rugby
   E. van Esbeck (Gill & McMillan 1974)
The Men in Green
   S. Diffley (Pelham Books, 1973)
Rugby in South Africa 1889-1964
   Johnstone & Neville (1964)
The Springboks 1891-1970
   A.C. Parker (Cassell, 1970)
New Zealand International Rugby 1884-1975
   A.H. Carman (Sporting Publications 1976)
History of South African Rugby Football
   (1875-1932) I.D. Difford (Specialty Press, 1933)

Tour Books
The Triumphant Tour of the N.Z. Footballers
   G.H. Dixon (Geddis & Blomfield, 1906)
Why the All Blacks Triumphed
   J.A. Buttery (Daily Mail, 1906)
With the British Rugby Team in Maoriland
   R.A. Barr (Otago Daily Times & Witness, 1908)
With the All Blacks in Great Britain, France,
   Canada & Australia 1924-25
   Read Masters (Christchurch Press, 1928)
The Triumphant Tour of the All Blacks in
   England, Ireland and Wales 1924-25
   L.T. Watkins (1925)
With the All Blacks in Springbokland 1928
   M.F. Nicholls (L.F. Watkins 1928)
With the British Team in New Zealand 1930
   G.T. Alley (Simpson & Williams, 1930)
The Tour of the Third All Blacks 1935
   C.J. Oliver & E.W. Tindill (Sporting Publications
   1936)
The All Blacks of Jubilee Year 1935
   (L.T. Watkins 1936)
South Africa's Greatest Springboks
   J.F. Sacks (Sporting Publications 1938)
The All Blacks on Trek Again
   W. McCarthy (Sporting Publications, 1950)
Round the World with the All Blacks 1953-54
   W. McCarthy (Sporting Publications, 1954)
Bob Stuart's All Blacks
   T.P. McLean (Reeds 1954)
The Fourth All Blacks 1953-54
   J. Hayhurst (Longmans, 1954)
Fifty Years of the All Blacks
   W. Wooller & D. Owen (Sportsman's Book Club,
   1955)
Springboks at Bay
   M. Price (Longmans 1956)

The Battle for the Rugby Crown
  T.P. McLean (Reeds, 1956)
The Kiwis Conquer
  R. Sweet (Howard Timmins, 1956)
Kings of Rugby
  T.P. McLean (Reeds, 1959)
Lions Courageous
  J.B.G. Thomas (Stanley Paul, 1960)
Lions Down Under
  V. Jenkins (Cassell, 1960)
Beaten by the Boks
  T.P. McLean (Reeds, 1960)
Trek out of Trouble
  N. Holmes (Whitcombe & Tombs, 1960)
Battle of the Giants
  C.O. Medworth (Reeds, 1960)
The All Blacks Juggernaut in South Africa
  A.C. Parker (Tafelberg-Uitgewers, 1960)
Springboks and Silver Fern
  R. Sweet (Reeds, 1960)
Cock of the Rugby Roost
  T.P. McLean (Reeds, 1961)
La Melee Fantasique
  D. Lalanne (Reeds, 1962)
Willie Away
  T.P. McLean (Reeds, 1964)
The Fifth All Blacks
  J.B.G. Thomas (Reeds, 1964)
Whineray's All Blacks
  R. Evans (Pelham Books, 1964)
All Blacks Tour 1963-64
  A.A.Mulligan (Whitcombe & Tombs, 1964)
The Bok Busters
  T.P. McLean (Reeds, 1965)
The Fourth Springbok Tour of N.Z.
  R.J. Urbahn & D.B. Clarke (Hicks, Smith, 1965)
Now is the Hour
  A.C. Parker (Whitcombe & Tombs, 1965)
The Lion Tamers
  T.P. McLean (Reeds, 1966)
Lions at Bay
  J.B.G. Thomas (Pelham Books, 1966)
All Black Magic
  T.P. McLean (Reeds, 1968)
The All Blacks 1967
  D. Frost (Whitcombe & Tombs, 1968)
The Unsmiling Giants
  W. Reyburn (Stanley Paul, 1968)
All Black Power
  T.P. McLean (Reeds, 1968)
Red Dragons of Rugby
  T.P. McLean (Reeds, 1969)
Rugby in Red and Black
  J.B.G. Thomas (Pelham Books, 1968)
Battling the Boks
  T.P. McLean (Reeds, 1970)
All Black-ed Out
  F. Labuschagne (Howard Timmins, 1970)

Rugby and be Damned
  G.R. David (Hicks, Smith & Sons, 1970)
Lions Rampant
  T.P. McLean (Reeds, 1971)
The Mighty Lions
  J. Reason (Eyre & Spottiswoode 1971)
The Roaring Lions
  J.B.G. Thomas (Pelham Books, 1971)
The Lions' Share
  G. David/D. Frost (Hicks, Smith 1971)
All Blacks in Wales
  J. Billot (Ron Jones, 1972)
They Missed the Bus
  T.P. McLean (Reeds, 1973)
The Winter Men
  W. Reyburn (Stanley Paul, 1973)
The Avenging All Blacks
  J.B.G. Thomas (Pelham Books, 1973)
All Blacks in the Lions Den
  T. Godwin (Philips Electrical, 1973)
All Blacks Come Home
  T.P. McLean (Reeds, 1975)
Goodbye to Glory
  T.P. McLean (Reeds, 1976)
One in the Eye
  B. Glasspool (Howard Timmins, 1976)
Lions '77
  K. Quinn (Methuen 1977)

General Rugby Books

The Complete Rugby Footballer
  D. Gallaher & J.W. Stead (Methuen, 1906)
Modern Rugby Footballer
  J.E. Raphael (Grafton & Co., 1918)
Rugby Recollections
  W.J.T. Collins (R.H. Johns, 1948)
Rugger the Man's Game
  E.H.D. Sewell (Hollis & Carter, 1947)
Report on Rugby
  W.J. Morgan & G. Nicholson (Heinemann, 1959)
They Played for New Zealand
  A.C. Swan (Sporting Publications, 1973)
Haka — The All Black Story
  W. McCarthy (Pelham Books, 1968)
Great Days in New Zealand Rugby
  T.P. McLean (Reeds, 1959)
I, George Nepia
  T.P. McLean (Reeds, 1963)
The Bob Scott Story
  R.W.H. Scott & T.P. McLean (Reeds, 1956)
Rugby on Attack
  R.A.Jarden (Whitcombe & Tombs, 1961)
"It's Me Tiger" — The Peter Jones Story
  N. Harris (Reeds, 1965)
Colin Meads All Black
  A. Veysey (Collins, 1974)

Fergie
  A. Veysey (Whitcoulls, 1976)
Grant Batty
  R.J. Howitt (Rugby Press, 1977)
The Boot — Don Clarke's Story
  D.B. Clarke & P. Booth (Reeds, 1966)
The Lions
  W. Reyburn (Reeds, 1967)
Encyclopaedia of Rugby Football
  J.R. Jones (Sportsmens Book Club, 1958)
All Blacks in Chains
  J.M. MacKenzie (Truth, 1960)
The Springboks Talk
  M. Price (Howard Timmins, 1955)
Legends in Their Lifetime
  W. Ingram (Reeds, 1962)
Champion Blokes
  M. Smith (Whitcombe & Tombs, 1964)
Game as You Like
  M. Smith (Whitcombe & Tombs, 1966)
Giants of South African Rugby
  A.C. Parker (Reeds, 1955)
Springboks Down The Years
  D.H. Craven (Reeds, 1956)
Goodbye Newlands Farewell Eden Park
  F. Labuschagne (Howard Timmins, 1974)
Tot Siens to Test Rugby
  H.S.V. Muller (Howard Timmins, 1953)
Nice Guys Come Second
  J.L. Gainsford (Don Nelson, 1974)
The Bennie Osler Story
  C. Greyvenstein (Howard Timmins, 1970)
Springbok Story 1949-53
  D.H. Craven (Reeds, 1954)
They Made Headlines
  C. Greyvenstein (Don Nelson, 1972)
On With The Game
  N. McKenzie (Reeds, 1960)
Black, Black, Black
  J.M. MacKenzie (Minerva, 1969)
Great Rugger Players
  J.B.G. Thomas (Stanley Paul, 1955)
On Tour J.B.G. Thomas (Stanley Paul, 1954)
Great Contemporary Players J.B.G. Thomas
  (Stanley Paul, 1963)
Rugger
  W.W. Wakefield & H.P. Marshall (Longmans,
    Green, 1930)
Rugby Football Up to Date
  E.H.D. Sewell (Hodder & Stoughton, 1921)
N.Z. Rugby Greats
  R.J. Howitt (MOA Publications, 1975)
The Game Goes On
  H.B.T. Wakelam (Sportsmans Book Club, 1954)
Rugger My Life   B. Williams (Stanley Paul, 1956)
Touch Down   (Rugby Football Union, 1971)
On the Ball   G. Slatter (Whitcombe & Tombs,
  1970)

Rugby Players That Made N.Z. Famous   R.A.
  Stone (Scott & Scott Ltd)
The Rugby Football Internationals Roll of
  Honour   E.H.D. Sewell (T.C. & E.C. Jack,
  1919)
The Book of Football   E.H.D. Sewell (J.M. Dent,
  1911)
Rugby Football Today   E.H.D. Sewell (John
  Murray, 1931)
Football The Rugby Union Game   F. Marshall &
  L.R. Tosswill (Cassell, 1925)
Giants Cast Long Shadows   R. Bruce-Lockhart
  (Putnam, 1960)
World of Rugby   W. Reyburn (Elek Books, 1967)
The Rise of French Rugby   A. Potter & G.
  Duthen (Reeds, 1961)
Springboks in the Lions Den   M. Price (Reeds,
  1961)
Football Is 15   G. Slatter (Whitcombe & Tombs,
  1972)
Heroes of the Silver Fern   (Simpson & Williams,
  1928)
Great Men of N.Z. Rugby   H. Tillman (Lancaster
  Press, 1957)
The Lions   W. Reyburn (Reeds, 1967)
Players & Slayers   L. Fanning (Gordon & Gorch
  1910)
The Reed Book of All Black Records
  1884-1971   R.F. Stokes (Reeds 1972)

Miscellaneous Histories

Rugby in Auckland 1883-1967   (Auckland Rugby
  Football Union, 1968)
Rugby in Auckland 1883-1933   A. Billington
  (Auckland R.F.U., 1933)
Wellington's Rugby History 1870-1950   A.C.
  Swan & G.F.W. Jackson (Reeds, 1951)
Rugby Football in Canterbury 1929-1954 J.K.
  Maloney   (Canterbury Rugby Football Union)
Canterbury Rugby Football Union Jubilee
  1879-1929   W.G. Garrard (Canterbury R.F.U.
  1929)
Canterbury Rugby Football Union 1971
  Handbook   (Canterbury R.F.U. 1971)
Otago Rugby Football Union Annual
  1956   (Otago Daily Times & Witness)
Waikato Rugby Union Golden Jubilee
  1921-1971   W. Hooper (Waikato R.F.U., 1971)
North Auckland Rugby Football Union Golden
  Jubilee 1920-1970   G. Frew (North Auckland
  R.F.U., 1970)
King Country Rugby Football Union 1922-1972
  (Jubilee Book Committee)
Rugby in Buller 1886-1967   A.C. Swan (Buller
  R.F.U. 1968)
Rugby in Poverty Bay 1878-1964   A.C. Swan
  (Poverty Bay R.F.U. 1965)

Rugby in Wairarapa 1876-1960   A.C. Swan
  (Wairarapa R.F.U. 1961)
Southland R.F.U. Jubilee Souvenir
  1887-1936 A.V. Keast (Southland R.F.U. ,1936)
Bay of Plenty R.F.U. 60 Grand Years of Rugby
  1911-1971   W. Inkster (B.O.P.R.F.U., 1972)
Centenary History of Oxford University R.F.C.
  1869-1969   R. McWhirter & Sir Andrew Noble.
  (Oxford University R.F.C., 1969)
Marlborough R.F.U. 75th Jubilee 1883-1963
  Programme of Celebrations
'Give 'Em the Axe'   R.T. Brittenden
  (Christchurch Football Club, 1963)
Ponsonby R.F.C. Centennial Album 1874-1974
Otago University R.F.C. 1886-1969   D. Hay
  (Light Blues Association, 1969)
Petone R.F.C. 1885-1959 Jubilee Souvenir
Poneke's 75 Years 1883-1958
Champagne Rugby — The Story of Secondary
  School Rugby in New Zealand P.B. Minogue
  (Reeds, 1961)
Unicorn Rugby Register   R.M. Thomson,
  (Coulls, Somerville Wilkie, 1947)
Star R.F.C. 1886-1961 Official Souvenir
Grammar Schools' O.B.R.F.C. Golden Jubilee
  Souvenir Booklet 1914-1964
75 Years of Rugby in Taranaki
  1885-1960   (Taranaki R.F.U. 1960)
Cardiff Rugby Club History & Statistics
  1876-1975   D.E. Davies (Cardiff Athletic Club)
Marist Bros. O.B.R.F.C. (Auckland) Souvenir
  Record (1949)
Easts Rugby Story 1900-1975   E. Kann (H.B.
  Chandler)

Tour Periodicals and Souvenirs
All Blacks in England, Ireland & Wales   Edited
  by R.A. Byers-Barr, 1924
The New Zealand Rugby Football Tour of Great
  Britain   Compiled by B.M. Turner, 1936
The 1956 Springboks in New Zealand   Edited by
  J. Fairburn (A.D. Organ, 1956)
The 1959 Lions in Australia & New Zealand
  F.W. Boshier (Evening Post, 1959)
All Blacks in South Africa   F.W. Boshier
  (Evening Post, 1960)
Whineray's Men   (New Zealand Newspapers,
  1964)
Springbok' 65   (New Zealand Newspapers, 1965)
Springbok Challenge — Books 1 & 2   J.W. Waters
  (Viscount Printing & Publishing, 1965)
Lions at Bay   J.W. Waters
The '66 Lions in New Zealand   (Viscount
  Printing & Publishing, 1966)
France in New Zealand   A. Veysey (Dominion &
  Sunday Times, 1968)
Wales in New Zealand   A. Veysey (Dominion &
  Sunday Times, 1969)

All Blacks in South Africa Vol. 1 & 2   A. Veysey
  (Dominion & Sunday Times, 1970)
All Blacks on Tour 1970   (Wilson & Horton,
  1970)
Lions Tour '71   (Wilson & Horton, 1971)
Britain's Finest Lions   L. Knight (Dominion &
  Sunday Times, 1971)
British Lions '71   R.C.C Thomas (Harry Darton,
  1971)
The Wallabies '72   L. Clark (A.B.D. Clark, 1972)
Kirky's All Blacks Vol 1. & 2   H. Mortlock & P.
  Bush (A.B.D. Clark, 1973)
Rugby News Irish Tour Special   R.J.
  Howitt   (Rugby Press, 1974)
Rugby News Blood, Sweat and Tears   R.J.
  Howitt   (Rugby Press, 1976)
All Blacks in South Africa   T. Hegh (Wilson &
  Horton, 1976)
'76 All Blacks in South Africa   A. Veysey & I.
  Mackley (Dominion & Sunday Times, 1976)
Lions '77 G. Douglas & R. Tucker (Wilson &
  Horton 1977)
Rugby '77   R. Charteris (Otago Daily Times,
  1977)

Non-Rugby Books
Nominal Rolls of the N.ZE.F. Vols 1-4
Nominal Rolls of the 2nd. N.Z.E.F.
N.Z. Expeditionary Force Roll of Honour   (Govt
  Printer, 1924)
Records of Officers and Others N.Z.E.F.   Lt-Col
  J. Studholme (1928)
Roll of the 2nd Division N.Z.E.F. Reserve Parts 1-4
Who's Who (various editions)
Who's Who in New Zealand (various editions)
Who's Who in Australia 1974   J.S. Legge (Herald
  & Weekly Times.)
Ad Augusta Auckland Grammar School
  1869-1969   K.A. Trembath (A.G.S. Old Boys
  Assn.)
Southland Boys' High School Old Boys Register
  1881-1956
St. Patrick's College 1885-1935   (St. Patrick's
  College Old Boys Assn. (Inc.))
King's College Register
A History of Waitaki Boys' High School
  1883-1958   K.C. McDonald (Whitcombe &
  Tombs, 1958)
Nelson College Old Boys' Register
  1856-1956   (Nelson College Old Boys Assn.
  (Inc))
Otago Boys' High School Centennial Register
  1863-1963   (Otago High School Old Boys
  Society (Inc)
Wanganui Collegiate School Register 1854-1963
  (Wanganui Collegiate School Old Boys' Assn.
  (Inc.))
Invercargill Pioneers   F. George (Southland
  Historical Committee, 1936.)